CW01175679

PUBLICATIONS

OF THE

NAVY RECORDS SOCIETY

Vol. 140

THE CUNNINGHAM PAPERS
VOLUME I: THE MEDITERRANEAN FLEET,
1939–1942

The NAVY RECORDS SOCIETY was established in 1893 for the purpose of printing unpublished manuscripts and rare works of naval interest. The Society is open to all who are interested in naval history, and any person wishing to become a member should apply to the Hon. Secretary, Department of War Studies, King's College London, Strand, London WC2R 2LS. The annual subscription is £30, which entitles the member to receive one free copy of each work issued by the Society in that year, and to buy earlier issues at much reduced prices.

SUBSCRIPTIONS and orders for back volumes should be sent to the Membership Secretary, 5 Goodwood Close, Midhurst, West Sussex GU29 9JG.

THE COUNCIL OF THE NAVY RECORDS SOCIETY wish it to be clearly understood that they are not answerable for any opinions and observations which may appear in the Society's publications. For these the editors of the several works are entirely responsible.

Errata

NAVY RECORDS SOCIETY
VOLUME 137; THE DEFEAT OF THE ENEMY ATTACK ON SHIPPING, 1939–1945, EDITED BY DR E.J. GROVE (1997)

Lt-Cdr D. W. Waters, R.N., joint author of the Admiralty Staff History on which the volume was based, has drawn our attention to certain errors and omissions. The Hon General Editor takes responsibility for these and apologises to Members and other readers. The corrections are as follows.

Introduction
p. xxiv, note 37: for '16', read '17'.
p. xxv, line 16: for '*Navy*', read '*Naval*'; also in n.46.
p. xxvii, note 51: for '35', read '36'.

Appendix A
p. xxx, para. 8, line 5: for 'over', read 'ever'.
p. xxxv, para. 35, line 6: for 'great at', read 'great as'.
p. xxxvii, line 5: for 'then', read 'them'.

Appendix B
p. xli, Law 14 reads: '$K \propto U$'
  Law 15 reads: '$K \propto E$'
  Law 18: insert a line _ beneath U.E.

Appendix 9 (iv)
pp. lix–lx: heading should read
  'Amendments to Appendix 9'.

Chapter 1
p. 4, Sec. 2, para. 2, line 8: for 'Table 2', read 'Table 1'.
p. 5, Sec. 4, line 3: for 'Table 2', read 'Table 1'.
p. 11, Sec. 9, line 4: for 'Plan 4', read 'Plan 5'.

Chapter 5
p. 32, Sec. 27, para. 3, line 1: for '1943', read '1944'.

Notes to Text
p. 233, Ch. 3, line 1: for 'Section 16', read 'Section 15'.

Acknowledgement
p. xlii: add: 'The late Lord Blackett, PRS, did much fundamental work on the elucidation of these Laws when Director of Naval Operational Research during the second world war. I was assisted in my researches by the late Cdr F. Barley, RNVR, and in formulating and expressing Laws (1–9), (17) and (19), and in qualifying Laws (11–13) by Dr W. E. Dawson of the Operational Research Department in the course of discussions and research in the Admiralty in the 1950s.'

Appendix Notes
p. xlii, add:

27. If $N_1=100$ and $U=10$, then $R \propto 100 \times 10$
$$\propto 1,000$$

28. If $S=100$, $N_C=1$, and $U=10$, then $R \propto \dfrac{1}{100} \times \dfrac{10}{1}$
$$\propto \dfrac{1}{10}$$

$R \propto \dfrac{1}{S}$ because in each war a U-boat sank on average only one ship in convoy per attack.

29. This age-old operational law was rediscovered and applied by Admiralty operational research scientists in early 1943. It was one of the keys to victory; the U-boats were defeated by 23 May 1943. In the next two years U-boats sank only 12 ships (all in the absence of an escort) from convoys in the Atlantic.

30. If $U=10$ and $E=10$, then $L=\dfrac{10}{10}=1$.

31. There are factors of proportionality applicable to these laws. Thus in 1941–42, the equations were approximately $5. \dfrac{U}{E}$ and $\dfrac{U.E.}{100}$.

32. In each war this exchange rate was 10 times as costly to the Allies as the convoy exchange rate. However, it was never evaluated by the Allies in either war, and nor was the convoy exchange rate (Law 17). The only exchange rate the Allies used, from time to time, was 'all ships sunk by submarines' per 'submarines sunk by all means', which was useless. It gave no measure of the relative efficiency of different anti-submarine and shipping defence operations. Thus it gave no measure – as Law (17) did to the U-boat Command in world war II – of the cost of sinking a ship in convoy in terms of submarines sunk in the process.

The 'convoy' and 'independent hunting' exchange rates when compared give of course a measure of the efficiency of convoy as opposed to hunting as an operation of war. In each war it was about 10 times as efficient as hunting.

33. This was another key to the victory in 1943. See also Law (10), and Figs. 8a and 8b. See also n.29, above.

34. Inter-ship spacing was increased in the spring of 1943 as a result of the elucidation of this Law, and this was another factor contributing to the victory of May 1943. It was adopted because the relationship between the area of a circle and its perimeter being understood, it was apparent that with a reduction in the number of convoys there would be a sufficiency of escorts, although the fewer convoys sailed were larger.

Key to relevant Appendix Notes and relevant Operational Laws
Appendix Note 27 applies to Law (3)
                  28   "   "   "   (9)
                  29   "   "   "   (10)
                  30   "   "   "   (13)
                  31   "   "   "   (16)
                  32   "   "   "   (19)
                  33   "   "   "   (20)
                  34   "   "   "   (21)

Admiral Sir Andrew Cunningham on board his flagship, HMS *Warspite*, in Alexandria Harbour, December 1940. HMS *Eagle* in background.

THE CUNNINGHAM PAPERS

Selections from the private and official correspondence of Admiral of the Fleet Viscount Cunningham of Hyndhope, O.M., K.T., G.C.B., D.S.O. and two bars

VOLUME I

THE MEDITERRANEAN FLEET, 1939–1942

edited by

MICHAEL SIMPSON, M.A., M.Litt., F.R.HIST.S.,
Reader in History, University of Wales, Swansea

PUBLISHED BY ASHGATE
FOR THE NAVY RECORDS SOCIETY
1999

© The Navy Records Society, 1999

Crown copyright material is reproduced by permission of the Controller of Her Majesty's Stationery Office

All rights reserved. No part of this publication may be reproduced, stored in a retrieval system, or transmitted in any form or by any means, electronic, mechanical, photocopying, recording, or otherwise without the prior permission of the publisher.

Published by
Ashgate Publishing Limited
Gower House
Croft Road
Aldershot
Hants GU11 3HR
England

Ashgate Publishing Company
Old Post Road
Brookfield
Vermont 05036–9704
USA

British Library Cataloguing-in-Publication Data
The Cunningham papers: selections from the private and official correspondence of Admiral of the Fleet Viscount Cunningham of Hyndhope.
Vol. 1: The Mediterranean fleet. – (Navy records series: vol. 140)
1. Cunningham, Andrew Browne Cunningham, Viscount, 1883–1963 – Correspondence 2. Great Britain. Royal Navy – History – 20th century
3. World War, 1939–1945 – Mediterranean Sea – Naval operations, British.
I. Simpson, Michael
940.5'45'941

Library of Congress Cataloging-in-Publication Data
  Cunningham, Andrew Browne Cunningham, 1st Viscount, 1883–1963.
    The Cunningham papers : selections from the private and official correspondence of Admiral of the Fleet Viscount Cunningham of Hyndhope / edited by Michael Simpson.
       (Publications of the Navy Records Society : vol. 140)
    Contents: v. 1. The Mediterranean fleet, 1939–1942
    1. Cunningham, Andrew Browne Cunningham, 1st Viscount, 1883–1963—Correspondence. 2. World War, 1939–1945—Campaigns—Participation, British. 3. Great Britain—History, Naval—20th century.
4. Admirals—Great Britain—Correspondence. I. Simpson, Michael (Michael A.) II. Navy Records Society (Great Britain) III. Title.
IV. Series.
DA70.A1 vol. 140   [DA89.1.C8]   98–6909
940.54'594'092—dc21   CIP

ISBN 1 84014 622 2

Typeset in Times by Saxon Graphics Ltd, Derby and printed in Great Britain on acid-free paper by MPG Books Ltd, Bodmin.

THE COUNCIL
OF THE NAVY RECORDS SOCIETY
1998

PATRON
H.R.H. THE PRINCE PHILIP, DUKE OF EDINBURGH,
K.G., O.M., F.R.S.

PRESIDENT
Admiral of the Fleet SIR BENJAMIN BATHURST, G.C.B., D.L.

VICE-PRESIDENTS
Professor D. M. LOADES, M. A., Ph.D., Litt.D., F.S.A., F.R.Hist.S.
A.N. RYAN, M.A., F.R.Hist.S.
Admiral SIR BRIAN BROWN, K.C.B., C.B.E.
Rear Admiral J. R. HILL

COUNCILLORS

J. COAD, M.A., F.S.A.
Professor J. B. HATTENDORF, D.Phil.
S. P. ROSE, M.A., Ph.D.
Professor G. E. AYLMER, M.A., D.Phil., F.B.A., F.R.Hist.S.
Lt. Commander L. PHILLIPS, R.D., R.N.R.
E. J. GROVE, M.A., Ph.D.
Lt. Commander A. GORDON, Ph.D.
N.A.M. RODGER, M.A., D.Phil., F.S.A., F.R.Hist.S.
A. P. MCGOWAN, M.A., Ph.D.
H. U. A. LAMBERT, M.A.
Lt. Cmdr. W. J. R. GARDNER, R.N., M.Phil.

Professor B. M. RANFT, M.A., D.Phil, F.R.Hist.S.
P. K. CRIMMIN, M.Phil, F.R.Hist.S., F.S.A.
J. D. DAVIES, M.A., B.Phil.
C. I. HAMILTON, M.A., Ph.D.
Captain P. G. HORE, R.N.
A. J. MCMILLAN, B.A., A.C.I.B.
M. DUFFY, M.A., D.Phil., F.R.Hist.S.
Captain C. H. H. OWEN, R.N.
M. BLACKWELL, M.A., Hon. D.Litt.
Capt. C. PARRY, R.N.
R. HARDING, Ph.D.
R. KNIGHT, M.A., Ph.D., F.R.Hist. S.
R. W. A. SUDDABY, M.A.

HON. SECRETARY
A. D. LAMBERT, M.A., Ph.D., F.R.Hist. S.

HON. GENERAL EDITOR
M. A. SIMPSON, M.A., M.Litt., F.R.Hist. S.

HON. TREASURER
J. V. TYLER, FCCA

MEMBERSHIP SECRETARY
Mrs A. GOULD

CONTENTS

	Page
List of Maps and Illustrations	viii
Introduction	ix
Acknowledgements	xiii
Glossary of Abbreviations	xv
Chronology of the Life and Career of Admiral of the Fleet Viscount Cunningham of Hyndhope	xxiii
A Brief Bibliography	xxviii
The Making of an Admiral, 1883–1939	1

The Mediterranean Fleet, 1939–1942
Part I:	The 'Phoney War' Period, June 1939 to June 1940	11
Part II:	The Anglo-Italian War, June to December 1940	53
Part III:	The Effects of German Intervention, January to May 1941	229
Part IV:	The Fight at Odds, June 1941 to March 1942	447

List of Documents and Sources	599
Index	609

MAPS AND ILLUSTRATIONS

Frontispiece: Admiral Sir Andrew Cunningham, on board his flagship, HMS *Warspite*, in Alexandria Harbour, December 1940. HMS *Eagle* in background. Courtesy of the Imperial War Museum.

MAPS

The Mediterranean Sea, 1939	12
The Action off Calabria, 9 July 1940	105
The Fleet Air Arm Attack on Taranto, 11 November 1940	182
The Battle of Cape Matapan, 28–29 March 1941	316
Greece and Crete, April–May 1941	372
The Eastern Mediterranean, 1941–42	448

INTRODUCTION

Admiral of the Fleet Viscount Cunningham of Hyndhope is widely regarded as the premier British naval figure of the Second World War. Beginning his officer training in the year of Queen Victoria's Golden Jubilee, 1897, he specialised not in a specific branch, such as gunnery or signals, but in the command of destroyers. He was associated just as closely with service in the Mediterranean, spending relatively little time in home waters or in shore appointments. His one spell at the Admiralty, as Deputy Chief of Naval Staff during 1938–39, was cut short by the necessity to relieve Admiral Sir Dudley Pound as Commander-in-Chief, Mediterranean in June 1939, when the latter returned home to succeed the ailing Admiral of the Fleet Sir Roger Backhouse as First Sea Lord. The triumphs of the Mediterranean Fleet during 1940–41, notably Taranto and Matapan, are indelibly associated with Cunningham's command of that fleet. Moreover, he was called upon to show even greater powers of leadership during the bitter fighting entailed by the evacuations from Greece and Crete in the spring of 1941, in which the fleet lost over 2,000 men and many valuable ships, a sacrifice matched by the merchant navies of Britain and her allies.

After almost three years in command of the Mediterranean station, in March 1942 Cunningham was appointed to head the British Admiralty Delegation in Washington, a task for which he felt ill-suited but in which he impressed the Americans in the summer and autumn of 1942. He was glad, however, to be appointed once more to an active command, again in the Mediterranean, when in November 1942 he became the Allied Naval Commander for the TORCH landings in North Africa, later (in January 1943) resuming his former post as Commander-in-Chief, Mediterranean. Following the retirement of the dying First Sea Lord, Admiral of the Fleet Sir Dudley Pound, in October 1943, Cunningham, now himself an Admiral of the Fleet, became First Sea Lord. He modestly proclaimed himself ill-equipped to serve in a desk job but he proved to be a resolute and loyal member of the Chiefs of Staff Committee and attended the crucial wartime conferences at Quebec, Tehran, Yalta and Potsdam, which included meetings of the Anglo-American Combined Chiefs of Staff. When peace finally came in August 1945, Cunningham was ready to retire. The strain of the war years coupled with the unpalatable task of 'downsizing' the Navy to a peacetime level, a reduction made more severe by Britain's dire economic crisis, left him with little heart to continue in the post. Persuaded by the new Prime Minister, Mr Attlee, to preside over the transition from war to peace, he remained until the spring of 1946. Following retirement, he continued to take a lively interest in naval and defence affairs, using his prestige to make the Navy's case in the press and, ennobled as a baron and ultimately as a viscount, in the House of Lords, remaining active until his death at the age of 80 in 1963.

Cunningham's prominence in British and Allied naval warfare and strategy during the Second World War and the wealth of documentation associated with his several major appointments merit the division of his papers into two volumes. The break falls naturally in the spring of 1942, when he relinquished command of the Mediterranean Fleet after almost three years of intensive and stirring activity. As few significant papers from Cunningham's naval career before 1939 survive, this volume is devoted to the period between June 1939, when he assumed command of the Mediterranean station, and March 1942, when he hauled down his flag. The second volume, now in the course of completion, deals primarily with Anglo-American maritime strategy between 1942 and Cunningham's retirement in 1946 and is therefore entitled appropriately *The Triumph of Allied Sea Power.*

Apart from chronicling the story of the Mediterranean Fleet through the eyes of Cunningham and his correspondents and subordinates, this selection of documents, supported by the introductory essays, seeks to elucidate Cunningham's strategic and tactical thought, his relations with Churchill, the Chiefs of Staff and the Admiralty, his approach to high command, and his attitude to cooperation with Britain's allies and with the Army and the RAF.

Inevitably, it becomes difficult to separate the leadership of the Admiral from the deeds of his forces and many documents speak of the actions of detached forces and units, such as submarines and minesweepers. However, it is essential to include operations of these forces to make clear the great geographical and functional range of the forces under Cunningham's command, thus demonstrating the extent and complexity of the problems that faced him in these difficult years. As the documents bear witness, he was ever mindful of the well-being of those who served with him, shared their burdens and suffering, and was proud to be associated with them. To the thousands of men and women of the Royal Navy, Royal Marines and Women's Royal Naval Service, the Merchant Navy, and the navies and merchant fleets of Britain's allies who served in the Mediterranean in those arduous days, especially to those whose last resting place lies in its waters or along its shores, this volume is dedicated.

For the most part the documents contained herein are drawn from Lord Cunningham's papers deposited in the Manuscripts Division of the British Library, the Churchill Archives Centre, Churchill College, Cambridge, and in the National Maritime Museum, supplemented by others of his papers found in the collections of his contemporaries, such as Admirals Blake, Cowan, Kelly, Somerville, Whitworth and Willis. Extensive use has been made also of the Admiralty records in the Public Record Office.

After a brief essay on Cunningham's development as a naval officer, his term in command of the Mediterranean Station is divided into four parts: the period before Italy entered the war, the following six months of Anglo-Italian warfare, then the results of German intervention in the first half of 1941 and, finally, the nine months of desperate defence from June 1941 to Cunningham's departure on 3 April 1942. As is usual with the Society's volumes, the documents have been edited as little as possible, only occasional punctuation marks being inserted to clarify passages. As many documents appear in abbreviated form, passages omitted are marked by an ellipsis (...). Many documents have numbered paragraphs and it will be noted that often there are gaps in the marginal numbers, indicating that paragraphs have been omitted. Missing words are indicated thus [-] or, if there is some doubt, thus [?-] Where a word is unintelligible, a possible interpretation is indicated by [?word]. Place names are contemporaneous. All Admiralty communications originated from London and most of Cunningham's from Alexandria but other places of origin, where known, are indicated at the heads of the documents. Where necessary, the time of origin as well as the date is included. Biographical details have been obtained from the *Navy List*, the *Dictionary of National Biography* and *Who Was Who*. Information on French, Greek and Italian officers has been provided by the historical branches of their respective navies. Details of ships and aircraft have been obtained from *Jane's Fighting Ships, Lloyd's Register of Shipping,* etc. Dates given are for completion in the case of ships and first flight for aircraft. The numerals in square brackets in the introduction to each part refer to the documents in the text.

ACKNOWLEDGEMENTS

I am grateful to my colleagues in the Navy Records Society who encouraged me to follow my volume of the papers of Admiral of the Fleet Sir James Somerville with volumes of the papers of his great friend and contemporary Admiral of the Fleet Viscount Cunningham of Hyndhope. In particular, I should like to thank my colleagues on the Society's Publications Committee for their warm support and co-operation, notably the Chairmen, first Captain A. B. Sainsbury and latterly Professor David Loades. I owe special thanks to Dr Evan Davies, Dr Eric Grove, Captain Hugh Owen, Mr Alan Pearsall, Mr Robin Brodhurst and my predecessor as Honorary General Editor, Mr Tony Ryan. I am grateful, too, to colleagues in the Society for Nautical Research for giving me the opportunity to air my views on Cunningham. Commander John Somerville, who served under Cunningham during 1939–42, has once again been an invaluable source of knowledge and sage advice. Captain E. H. Lee, who served as Cunningham's Flag Lieutenant during 1940–42, has kindly shared his recollections with me and has made numerous valuable comments on the draft. Lord Cunningham's niece, Mrs Hilda McKendrick, and nephew, Sir Hugh Byatt, have also kindly sent me their recollections of both Lord and Lady Cunningham. I am indebted also to Professor Philip Towle, Director of the Institute of Strategic Studies, University of Cambridge, for reading and commenting upon the typescript.

Works of this kind, drawing heavily on archival sources, depend greatly on the support given by archivists and I am pleased to record my thanks to the staff of the Western Manuscripts Division of the British Library, custodians of the bulk of Lord Cunningham's papers, for their cheerful and prompt assistance. I wish to acknowledge also the equally courteous, efficient and highly knowledgeable assistance of the staff of the Library of the National Maritime Museum; of Mr Correlli Barnett, formerly Keeper of the Churchill Archives Centre, Churchill College, Cambridge, and his successor, Dr Piers Brendon, and his staff; and of the staff of the Public Record Office at Kew. Crown Copyright material in the Public Record

Office is reproduced by permission of the Controller of Her Majesty's Stationery Office. Mr Roderick Suddaby, Keeper of the Archives at the Imperial War Museum, has again kindly drawn my attention to records in his care and made them available. Mr David Brown, Head of the Naval Historical Branch, kindly volunteered information about the French Squadron at Alexandria. I am indebted also to the Librarian of Christ Church College, Oxford, and his staff, for making available to me the papers of Marshal of the RAF Viscount Portal of Hungerford. Dr Vincent Orange, of the University of Canterbury, New Zealand, has generously shared with me the fruits of his researches on Marshal of the RAF Lord Tedder, and Dr Reynolds Salerno of Yale University has kindly sent me his thesis on the pre-war situation in the Mediterranean.

My Heads of Department, Professors Muriel Chamberlain and David Eastwood, have continued to encourage and facilitate my research. I have discussed a number of issues included herein with Professor Chamberlain and with Drs Eleanor Breuning and Julian Jackson; my thanks to them for a number of stimulating conversations. My research students Mr Martin Jones and Mr James Levy have contributed greatly to my understanding of the Royal Navy in the twentieth century. Mr Guy Lewis, lately Cartographer in the Department of Geography at the University of Wales Swansea, has interpreted my complicated cartographic requests with his usual cheerfulness, high skill and characteristic thoroughness. Dr John Morgan kindly translated from a Greek original.

I am indebted also to the British Academy for shouldering the principal costs of the research, and to the Scouloudi (formerly Twenty-Seven) Foundation and the Research Support Fund of the University of Wales Swansea for additional financial assistance.

I am grateful to my former college, Fitzwilliam, for providing hospitality during my research forays to Cambridge. Most of the research has been undertaken in London and I am especially grateful to John and Ann Charrington for their warm family hospitality and to Lynn and Kate for their welcome diversions from study. Neil and Alison Smith have latterly provided the London base and I have welcomed their good-humoured and tolerant hospitality. Once again my long-suffering wife Sue has provided invaluable support in many ways, not least her love.

Michael Simpson

GLOSSARY OF ABBREVIATIONS

AA	Anti-Aircraft
ABC	Andrew Browne Cunningham
a/c	aircraft
ACM	Air Chief Marshal
ACNAS	Admiral Commanding North Atlantic Station
ACNS	Assistant Chief of Naval Staff
	(H): Home
	(F): Foreign
	(U): Trade and U-boat Warfare
	(W): Weapons
Actg	Acting
ADC	Aide de Camp
ADGB	Air Defence of Great Britain
Adjt	Adjutant
Adm	Admiral
Admy	Admiralty
ADP	Assistant Director of Plans
ADPD	Assistant Director Plans Division
'A' Lighter	A type of landing craft
ALT	Air Launched Torpedo
AM	Air Marshal
Amb	Ambassador
AMC	Armed Merchant Cruiser
ANCXF	Allied Naval Commander Expeditionary Force
AOC	Air Officer Commanding
AOC-in-C	Air Officer Commanding-in-Chief
A of F	Admiral of the Fleet
A/S	Anti-Submarine
ASV	Air to Surface Vessel [radar]
ASW	Anti-Submarine Warfare
A/SWD	Anti-Submarine Warfare Division
A/T	Anti-Torpedo
Atl	Atlantic

AVM	Air Vice Marshal
BAD	British Admiralty Delegation [Washington, DC]
BCF	Battle Cruiser Force
BCS	Battle Cruiser Squadron
Bde	Brigade
BL	British Library
BM	British Museum
Bn	Battalion
BoT	Board of Trade
BPF	British Pacific Fleet
Brig	Brigadier
Brig-Gen	Brigadier-General
BS	Battle Squadron
B/S	Battleship
CEx	Chancellor of the Exchequer
Capt	Captain
	(D): Destroyers
	(S): Submarines
CAS	Chief of the Air Staff
CCS	Combined Chiefs of Staff [UK and US]
Cdr	Commander
Cdre	Commodore
Chllr	Chancellor
CID	Committee of Imperial Defence
CIGS	Chief of the Imperial General Staff
C-in-C	Commander-in-Chief,
	EI: East Indies
	HF: Home Fleet
	Med: Mediterranean
CM	Court Martial
Cmd	Command
Cmdt	Commandant
CNO	Chief of Naval Operations [US Navy]
CNSO	Chief Naval Staff Officer
Cntrlr	Controller
CO	Commanding Officer
COHQ	Combined Operations Head Quarters
COIS	Chief of the Intelligence Staff
Col	Colonel
Comb Ops	Combined Operations
COS	Chiefs of Staff Committee; Chief of Staff
CPO	Chief Petty Oficer

GLOSSARY OF ABBREVIATIONS

CS	Cruiser Squadron
CSO	Chief Staff Officer
DAAG	Director of Anti-Aircraft Gunnery
DASD	Director of Anti-Submarine Division
D/B	Dive Bomber
DCAS	Deputy Chief of Air Staff
DCNS	Deputy Chief of Naval Staff
DCO	Director of Combined Operations
DCOS	Deputy Chief of Staff
DCT	Depth Charge Thrower; Director Control Tower
DDMI	Deputy Director of Military Intelligence
DDPD	Deputy Director of Plans Division
DEMS	Defensively Equipped Merchant Ship
DF	Destroyer Flotilla
DFSL	Deputy First Sea Lord
D/F	Direction Finding
DGD	Director of Gunnery Division
DLDD	Director of Local Defence Division
DMI	Director of Military Intelligence
DNAD	Director of Naval Air Division
DNEqpt	Director of Naval Equipment
DNI	Director of Naval Intelligence
DNO	Director of Naval Ordnance
DOD	Director of Operations Division
DOIS	Director of Intelligence Section
DPD	Director of Plans Division
DPS	Director of Personal Services
DSD	Director of Signal Division
DTD	Director of Trade Division
DTSD	Director of Training and Staff Duties
DWI aircraft	Mine location aircraft
DY	Dock Yard
EF	Eastern Fleet
EO	Executive Officer
ERA	Engine Room Artificer
FAA	Fleet Air Arm
FEAF	Far East Air Force
FEO	Fleet Engineer Officer
FGO	Fleet Gunnery Officer
FM	Field Marshal
FMF	Force Maritime Français
FNO	Fleet Navigation Officer

FO	Foreign Office
FOAM	Flag Officer Attached Mediterranean
FOC	Flag Officer Commanding
FOCNA	Flag Officer Commanding North Atlantic
FOH	Flag Officer, Force H
FOIC	Flag Officer in Charge
For Sec	Foreign Secretary
FSL	First Sea Lord
FS & W/TO	Fleet or Flotilla Signal and Wireless Telegraphy Officer
FTO	Fleet or Flotilla Torpedo Officer
GCapt	Group Captain
Gen	General
GHQ	General Head Quarters
GO	Gunnery Officer
GOC	General Officer Commanding
GOC-in-C	General Officer Commanding-in-Chief
Gov-Gen	Governor-General
GR	General Reconnaissance
GS	General Staff
GSO	General Staff Officer
gt	gross tonnage
HA	High Angle anti-aircraft gun
HAA	Heavy Anti-Aircraft gun
HCmnr	High Commissioner
HDML	Harbour Defence Motor Launch
HE	High Explosive
HF	Home Fleet
HLB	High Level Bomber
HMG	His Majesty's Government
HMSO	Her Majesty's Stationery Office
HO	Home Office
HP pompoms	A type of short range AA gun
i/c	in command
IDC	Imperial Defence College
IE	Immediate Establishment [of aircraft]
Inf Bde	Infantry Brigade
Inspr-Gen	Inspector-General
Instr	Instructor
IR	Immediate reserve [of aircraft]
JPC	Joint Planning Committee
JPS	Joint Planning Staff

GLOSSARY OF ABBREVIATIONS

JSM	Joint Staff Mission [of UK armed services in Washington]
k	knots/killed
KAR	King's African Rifles
KOYLI	King's Own Yorkshire Light Infantry
KRRC	King's Royal Rifle Corps
L	[Destroyer Flotilla] Leader
LAA	Light Anti-Aircraft gun
LCA	Landing Craft, Assault
LCM	Landing Craft, Mechanized
LCS	Light Cruiser Squadron
LCT	Landing Craft, Tank
LDD	Local Defence Division
LL sweepers	Long Leg minesweepers
Lt	Lieutenant
Lt-Cdr	Lieutenant-Commander
Lt-Col	Lieutenant-Colonel
Lt-Gen	Lieutenant-General
L/R	Long Range
LV pompoms	A type of short range AA gun
Maj	Major
Maj-Gen	Major-General
ME	Middle East
Med	Mediterranean
MF	Mediterranean Fleet
mg	machine gun
Mid	Midshipman
Mil	Military
Minr	Minister
ML	Motor Launch
M/L	Mine Layer
MN	Merchant Navy
MNBDO	Mobile Naval Base Defence Organisation
MoS	Ministry of Shipping
M/R	Medium Range
M/S	Mine Sweeper
MT	Mechanical Transport ship
MTB	Motor Torpedo Boat
MV	Motor Vessel
MWT	Ministry of War Transport
NA	Naval Attaché
NAS	North Atlantic Station

Nav O	Navigating Officer
NAWI	North America and West Indies Station
NID	Naval Intelligence Division
NLO	Naval Liaison Officer
NMM	National Maritime Museum
NOIC	Naval Officer in Charge
NZ	New Zealand
OC	Officer Commanding
OD	Operations Division
PD	Plans Division
PM	Prime Minister
PO	Petty Officer
PoW	Prisoner of War
PRO	Public Record Office
PRU	Photographic Reconnaissance Unit
PSD	Personal Services Division
(R)	Repeat
RA	Rear Admiral: (A) Air; (D) Destroyers
RA	Royal Artillery
RAN	Royal Australian Navy
RCN	Royal Canadian Navy
RCO	Remote Control Office
RDF	Radio Direction Finding [radar]
RE	Royal Engineers
Res	Reserve
RFA	Royal Fleet Auxiliary
RFC	Royal Flying Corps
RIN	Royal Indian Navy
RM	Royal Marines
RME	Royal Marine Engineers
RNC	Royal Naval College
RNR	Royal Naval Reserve
RNSC	Royal Naval Staff College
RNVR	Royal Naval Volunteer Reserve
RNZN	Royal New Zealand Navy
R/T	Radio Telephony
R/V	Rendezvous
s	sunk
SAC	Supreme Allied Commander
SAP	Semi-Armour Piercing
SBNLO	Senior British Naval Liaison Officer
SBNO	Senior British Naval Officer

GLOSSARY OF ABBREVIATIONS

SBNOCA	Senior British Naval Officer [Suez] Canal Area
SD (Y)	Signal Division (Y) [intelligence gathering]
SEAC	South East Asia Command
SF	Submarine Flotilla
SGO	Squadron or Staff Gunnery Officer
Sig O	Signal Officer
S/M	Submarine
SNO	Senior Naval Officer
SNOIS	Senior Naval Officer, Inshore Squadron
SO	Staff Officer: (I) Intelligence; (O) Operations; (P) Plans
SOE	Special Operations Executive
Sqdn	Squadron
Sqdn Ldr	Squadron Leader
SS	Steam Ship
STO	Sea Transport Officer
t	tonnage [displacement]/torpedoed
TA	Territorial Army
T/B	Torpedo Bomber
TBGR	Torpedo Bomber/General Reconnaissance
Temp Paymr	Temporary Paymaster
TF	Task Force
TL	Their Lordships
TMD	Torpedo and Mining Division
TOO	Time of Origin
TS	Training Ship
TSD	Training and Staff Duties
TSDS	Twin Speed Destroyer Sweep [for mines]
TSMS	Twin Speed Mine Sweeper
TSR	Torpedo Spotter Reconnaissance
tt	torpedo tubes
USNLO	US Naval Liaison Officer
VA	Vice Admiral
VAA	Vice Admiral (Air)
VA(D)	Vice Admiral (Destroyers)
VACAC	Vice Admiral Commanding Aircraft Carriers
VALF	Vice Admiral Light Forces
VAM	Vice Admiral Malta
VA(S)	Vice Admiral (Submarines)
VC	Victoria Cross
VCIGS	Vice Chief of the Imperial General Staff
VCNS	Vice Chief of Naval Staff

VHF	Very High Frequency
V/S	Visual Signalling
W Apps	Western Approaches
WCdr	Wing Commander
WO	Warrant Officer, or War Office
WRNS	Women's Royal Naval Service
W/T	Wireless Telegraphy
WWI	World War I
Y reports	signals intelligence
1st Lt	First Lieutenant
1st Lord	First Lord of the Admiralty
1SL, 2SL, etc.	First, Second, etc., Sea Lords

CHRONOLOGY OF THE LIFE AND CAREER OF ADMIRAL OF THE FLEET VISCOUNT CUNNINGHAM OF HYNDHOPE

(From Admiral Cunningham's service record, ADM 196/8, Public Record Office, his autobiography, and other sources).

7 January 1883	Born in Dublin, second son of Professor Daniel J. Cunningham, M.D., F.R.S., T.C.D., and Elizabeth C. Browne Cunningham.
15 January 1897	Entered *Britannia* as a cadet.
15 June 1898	Became a Midshipman. Appointed to the cruiser *Fox*, Cape and East Africa.
May 1899	Appointed to cruiser *Doris*
February–September 1899	Served ashore in South Africa with Naval Brigade.
15 December 1900	Appointed to the battleship *Hannibal*, Channel Squadron.
15 July 1901	Appointed to the training brig *Martin*, Portsmouth.
1 November 1901	Appointed to the cruiser *Diadem*, Channel Squadron.
7 January 1902	Promoted Acting Sub-Lieutenant.
14 March 1903	Commissioned Sub-Lieutenant.
27 March 1903	Appointed to battleship *Implacable*, Mediterranean.
16 September 1903	Appointed to *Orion* additional for destroyer *Locust*, Mediterranean.
22 December 1903	Appointed to destroyer *Orwell*, Mediterranean.
31 March 1904	Promoted Lieutenant.
30 June 1904	Appointed to training ship *Northampton*, UK.

2 November 1904	Appointed to training cruiser *Hawke*, North America and West Indies Station.
June 1906	Appointed to cruiser *Scylla*, Channel.
3 July 1906	Appointed to cruiser *Suffolk*, Mediterranean.
13 May 1908	Appointed to *Hecla*, for Torpedo Boat No.14, in command, Reserve Fleet, Portsmouth.
24 January 1910	Appointed to *Topaze*, for destroyer *Vulture*, in command.
15 August 1910	Appointed to destroyer *Roebuck*, in command.
10 January 1911	Appointed to destroyer *Scorpion* in command, Home Fleet.
31 March 1912	Promoted Lieutenant Commander.
November 1913	*Scorpion* arrived in Mediterranean.
4 August 1914	War declared on Germany.
21 September 1914	War declared on Turkey.
19 February 1915	Opening of Dardanelles campaign.
30 June 1915	Promoted Commander.
14 March 1916	Appointed DSO for gallantry in operations off the Dardanelles.
4 August 1916	Appointed to destroyer *Rattlesnake* in command.
2 October 1916	Appointed to *Scorpion* in command.
11 February 1918	Appointed to destroyer *Ophelia* in command, Grand Fleet.
29 March 1918	Appointed to destroyer *Termagant* in command, Dover Patrol.
20 February 1919	Appointed to destroyer *Seafire* in command, for service in the Baltic, with Rear Admiral Walter Cowan.
31 December 1919	Promoted Captain. No appointment. Bar to DSO.
8 March 1920	Second bar to DSO.
29 September 1920	Appointed to Naval Inter-Allied Commission of Control: President of a Sub-Commission in charge of the destruction of defences of Heligoland.
22 April 1922	Appointed to *Victory* for Senior Officers' Technical Course.

2 May 1922	Appointed to flotilla leader *Shakespeare* as Captain (D), 6th Destroyer Flotilla, Port Edgar.
19 December 1922	Appointed to flotilla leader *Wallace* as Captain (D), 1st Destroyer Flotilla, Bosphorus.
March 1923	1st Flotilla joined Atlantic Fleet.
15 October 1924	Appointed as Captain-in-Command, *Columbine*, Port Edgar destroyer base.
1 April 1926	Appointed additionally as King's Harbour Master, Rosyth.
11 May 1926	Appointed to *Calcutta*, light cruiser, in command and as Flag Captain and Chief Staff Officer to Vice Admiral Sir Walter Cowan, C-in-C, North America and West Indies.
December 1928	*Calcutta* returned to Devonport for refit. Cunningham transferred to *Despatch* and returned to Bermuda.
1 October 1928	Appointed to *President* for Senior Officers' Course, Army School, Sheerness.
14 January 1929	Appointed to *President* for course at the Imperial Defence College.
15 December 1929	Appointed to *Rodney* in command, Atlantic Fleet.
22 December 1929	Married Miss Nona Christine Byatt.
6 July 1931	Promoted Commodore 2nd Class and appointed to *Pembroke* in command and Commodore RN Barracks Chatham.
24 September 1932	Promoted Rear Admiral.
8 May 1933	Appointed to *Victory* for Senior Officers' Technical Course, Portsmouth.
14 August 1933	Appointed to *Victory* for Senior Officers' Tactical Course, Portsmouth.
2 December 1933	Appointed in command of Mediterranean destroyer flotillas.

1 January 1934	Assumed command, flying his flag in the light cruiser *Coventry*. Appointed Companion of the Order of the Bath.
July 1935	Transferred flag to light cruiser *Despatch*.
October 1935	Transferred flag to new light cruiser *Galatea*.
8 April 1936	Struck flag on relief by Rear Admiral James Somerville.
22 July 1936	Promoted Vice Admiral.
11 January 1937	Appointed to *Victory* for Senior Officers' Technical Course.
3 July 1937	Appointed Vice Admiral Commanding, Battle Cruiser Squadron and Second-in-Command, Mediterranean Fleet, flying his flag in *Hood*, as temporary replacement following Vice Admiral Sir Geoffrey Blake's illness.
17 October 1938	Took up appointment as Deputy Chief of the Naval Staff.
2 January 1939	Appointed Knight Commander of the Order of the Bath.
1 June 1939	Promoted Acting Admiral and appointed Commander-in-Chief, Mediterranean Fleet.
7 June 1939	Assumed command of Mediterranean Fleet, flying his flag in *Warspite*.
3 September 1939	Britain and France declared war on Germany.
10 June 1940	Italy declared war on Britain and France.
22 June 1940	French armistice with Germany and Italy.
2–4 July 1940	Critical negotiations with French Vice Admiral Godfroy over the future of his squadron at Alexandria.
9 July 1940	Action with Italian Fleet off Calabria.
11 November 1940	Successful FAA attack on Italian Fleet at Taranto.

3 January 1941	Promoted Admiral.
10 January 1941	*Illustrious* crippled by German dive bombers off Malta.
4 March 1941	Beginning of movement of British forces to Greece.
	Appointed Knight Grand Cross of the Order of the Bath.
27–29 March 1941	Battle of Cape Matapan.
21 April 1941	Fleet bombardment of Tripoli.
24–30 April 1941	Evacuation from Greece.
15 May–1 June 1941	Battle for Crete.
7 June–10 July 1941	Battle for Syria and the Lebanon.
25 November 1941	*Barham* sunk by a German U-boat.
7 December 1941	Relief of Tobruk, supplied during 242-day siege by sea.
6–7 December 1941	Japanese attack on Pearl Harbor and other points in Far East. USA entered the war.
17 December 1941	First Battle of Sirte.
19 December 1941	*Queen Elizabeth* and *Valiant* severely damaged in Alexandria harbour by Italian human torpedoes.
January 1942	Second 'Great Siege' of Malta began with intensive Axis air attacks.
12–13 February 1942	Failure of convoy from Alexandria to reach Malta owing to air attack.
22 March 1942	Second Battle of Sirte.
3 April	Hauled down flag and flew home on being appointed Head of the British Admiralty Delegation in Washington.

The remainder of Cunningham's career will be listed in the second volume of his papers, forthcoming.

A BRIEF BIBLIOGRAPHY

C. Barnett, *Engage the Enemy More Closely: The Royal Navy in the Second World War* (London, 1991).
Admiral of the Fleet Viscount Cunningham of Hyndhope, *A Sailor's Odyssey* (London, 1951).
Vice Admiral Sir Peter Gretton, *Former Naval Person: Winston Churchill and the Royal Navy* (London, 1968).
R. L. Ollard, *Fisher and Cunningham: A Study of the Personalities of the Churchill Era* (London, 1991).
S. W. C. Pack, *Cunningham the Commander* (London, 1974).
S. W. Roskill, *The War at Sea*, 3 vols (London, 1954–61).
S. W. Roskill, *Churchill and the Admirals* (London, 1977).
M. Simpson, 'Admiral of the Fleet Viscount Cunningham of Hyndhope (1943–1946)', in M. H. Murfett (ed.), *The First Sea Lords: From Fisher to Mountbatten* (London, 1995), pp. 201–16.
O. Warner, *Cunningham of Hyndhope: Admiral of the Fleet* (London, 1967).
J. Winton, 'Admiral of the Fleet Viscount Cunningham', in S. Howarth (ed.), *Men of War: Great Naval Leaders of World War II* (London, 1992), pp. 207–26.
J. Winton, *Cunningham: the Greatest Admiral since Nelson* (London, 1998).

THE MAKING OF AN ADMIRAL,
1883–1939

Andrew Browne Cunningham was born in Dublin in 1883, the third of five children of a distinguished Scottish Professor of Anatomy at Trinity College, Daniel Cunningham and his wife Elizabeth (née Browne). His father was appointed to a chair at Edinburgh in 1903 and Andrew, though he spent little time in Scotland, always regarded himself as a Scot. In his autobiography,[1] Cunningham gave little explanation of his decision to seek a naval career. The initiative appears to have come from his father, who may have felt his boisterous son unsuited to an academic or civilian professional career; it was in any case common for sons of upper- and middle-class families to enter the armed forces. Andrew himself merely recorded that he had always been interested in ships and the sea, though the interest appears to have been somewhat vague and distant. However, he accepted his father's suggestion with enthusiasm and, aged ten, responded 'Yes. I should like to be an Admiral'.[2] There followed three years at a school devoted to preparing boys for the Navy and, having passed the entrance examination without difficulty, he joined the training ship *Britannia*[3] on 15 January 1897, barely a week after his fourteenth birthday. His term was a distinguished one; 11 of the 65 entrants reached flag rank, notably his lifelong friends Admiral of the Fleet Sir James Somerville and Admiral Sir Charles Little.[4] It was a good time to join the Navy, at last free of the

[1] *A Sailor's Odyssey* (London, 1951), p. 13.
[2] Ibid, p. 13.
[3] At that time a hulk moored in the Dart; the present college was built several years later. Captain J. Wells, *The Royal Navy: An Illustrated Social History, 1870–1982* (Stroud, 1994), pp. 40–41.
[4] A of F Sir James F. Somerville (1882–1949): ent RN 1897; Lt 1904; W/T splist; Cdr & DSO, Dardanelles 1915; Capt 1921; *Benbow* 1922; *Barham, Warspite* 1927–29; IDC 1929–31; Invergordon report 1931; Cdre, RN Barracks, Portsmouth 1932; RA 1933; DPS 1934; RA(D), Med F 1936–38; VA 1937; C-in-C, EI 1938–39; ret, medical grounds 1939; FO, Force H, June 1940–Jan 1942; Adm & C-in-C EF 1942–44; Head, BAD 1944–45; A of F 1945; ceased active service 1946. See M. Simpson (ed.), *The Papers of Admiral of the Fleet Sir James Somerville* (Aldershot: Scolar Press for Navy Records Society, 1995). D. Macintyre, *Fighting Admiral: The Life of Admiral of the Fleet Sir James Somerville* (London, 1961); J. D. Brown, 'Admiral of the Fleet Sir James Somerville', in S. Howarth (ed.), *Men of War: Great Naval Leaders of World War II* (London, 1992), pp. 455–73 (though I cannot accept many of the judgements).

Adm Sir Charles Little (1882–1973): ent RN 1897; Cdr, S/M Flotilla, Dover; Grand F S/Ms 1916; Capt 1917; *Cleopatra*, Baltic 1919; DTD 1920; Capt of F, Med F 1922; RN War Coll 1924; *Iron Duke* 1926; Dir, RN Staff Coll; RA 1929; 2nd BS, Home F 1930; RA(S) 1931; DCNS 1932; VA 1933; C-in-C, China 1936; Adm 1937; 2SL 1938–41; Head, BAD 1941–42; C-in-C, Portsmouth 1942; ret 1945.

sailing age, and under the stimulus of reformers such as Fisher and Scott developing the ships, equipment and tactics appropriate to the twentieth century. In particular the decade saw the emergence of the destroyer, shortly to become an all-purpose weapons platform calling for commanding officers of dash, initiative, stamina and determination; destroyers might have been introduced with Cunningham in mind.[5] The education the cadets received, though recently reformed, was narrowly focused on seamanship and other technical subjects. Cunningham, who seemed to settle readily anywhere and to almost any task, was a proficient cadet and passed out tenth in April 1898. Though of only medium height and build, he had a pugnacious streak, being involved frequently in fist fights.

Yearning for adventure, Midshipman Cunningham secured for himself an appointment to the cruiser *Fox*, then on the Cape Station.[6] Life as a midshipman was hard and generally dull but on the outbreak of the Boer War in 1899, Cunningham persuaded his seniors to allow him to join a Naval brigade, with which he saw occasional action in the field. Following the war and after service in a variety of big ships and several courses ashore, he seized an opportunity which was to exercise a profound influence on the rest of his career. In September 1903 he began a 30-year association with destroyers. He quickly adapted to 'hard lying' and identified himself with this new type of craft; whereas others specialised in gunnery, navigation or signals, Cunningham may be said to have specialised in destroyers – and service in the Mediterranean. Promoted to Lieutenant in 1904, he obtained his first command, *Torpedo Boat 14* in the Reserve Fleet, in 1908.[7] A number of distinguished officers were impressed by the young Cunningham – among them Wemyss, Tyrwhitt, Arbuthnot and Keyes, all of them using the term 'zeal' or 'zealous' and praising his judgement and ship-handling skills; they noted, too, his capacity for leadership.[8]

[5]The first destroyers appeared in 1893.
[6]*Fox*: 1893, 4,360t, 2×6in, 8×4in, 3×18in tt, 19.5k.
[7]*TB 14*: 1907, c.270t, 2×12pdr, 3×18in tt, 26k.
[8]A of F 1st Baron (Rosslyn) Wester Wemyss (1864–1933): Capt 1901; RA 1911; E Med 1914–15; C-in-C, EI 1916–17; 2SL, then DFSL 1917; FSL Dec. 1917–Nov. 1919.
A of F Sir Reginald Tyrwhitt (1870–1951): ent RN 1883; Capt 1908; Cdre, Harwich Force 1914–18; RA 1918; C-in-C, China 1927–29; Adm 1929; C-in-C Nore 1930–33; A of F 1934.
RA Sir Robert Arbuthnot (1864–1916): ent RN 1877; Lt 1885; Cdr 1897; Cdre 3DF 1910; RA 1913; 1CS, Grand F 1915; k at Jutland.
A of F Lord (Roger) Keyes (1872–1945): ent RN 1885; gallantry in Boxer campaign, China 1900; Insp Capt, S/M 1910–12; COS to de Robeck, Dardanelles 1915; RA, 4BS 1917; VA Dover 1918; DCNS 1921; C-in-C Med 1925–28; Adm 1926; C-in-C Portsmouth 1929–31; A of F 1930; Con MP Portsmouth 1934–43; Dir, Comb Ops 1940–41; baron 1943. See P. G. Halpern (ed.), *The Keyes Papers*, 3 vols (London: Allen & Unwin for Navy Records Society, 1972–81).

Appointed to the new destroyer *Scorpion* in 1911, he was in the Mediterranean when war broke out in 1914.[9] The Dardanelles campaign enabled him to demonstrate his courage, audacity, sense of initiative and gift for leadership, and he earned promotion to Commander and the DSO early in 1916 for his conduct under heavy fire; a fleet newspaper commented 'These operations reflected great credit on the vigilance and accurate shooting of HMS *Scorpion*'.[10] In particular, he gained a priceless knowledge of the Mediterranean – its moods, harbours and peoples. Sensing in 1917 that there was now more likelihood of action in the Harwich and Dover flotillas, he sought an appointment under the command of Tyrwhitt or Keyes and took command of *Termagant* of the Dover Patrol in the spring of 1918.[11] Though itching to 'engage the enemy more closely', he had little opportunity to do so, being confined largely to patrol and escort work and, frustratingly, missing the close encounters at Zeebrugge and Ostend. Nevertheless, his zest and efficiency earned him a bar to the DSO. In March 1919, in command of a division of destroyers led by himself in *Seafire*, he joined Rear Admiral Walter Cowan in the Baltic.[12] The situation was extremely confused but the Navy was there to uphold the independence of the new Baltic republics. Cunningham's bold and resolute actions in tense, dangerous and complicated situations brought him a second bar to the DSO and promotion to Captain at the early age of 37. In 1922 he became Captain (D) of the 6th Destroyer Flotilla, moving to the *Wallace* and the First Flotilla in December for further service in the Mediterranean.[13]

Cowan, appointed C-in-C, North America and West Indies Station in 1926, invited Cunningham to serve as his Flag Captain and Chief of Staff, in the light cruiser *Calcutta*, transferring in 1928 to the *Despatch*.[14] In 1929 he attended the Imperial Defence

---

[9]*Scorpion*: 1910, c.950t, 1×4in, 3×12pdr, 2×18in tt, 27.5k.
[10]*Peninsula Press*, 3 Jan. 1915, CNM 7, *Cunningham Papers*, National Maritime Museum (NMM).
[11]*Termagant*: 1915, 1,098t, 5×4in, 4×21in tt, 34k.
[12]*Seafire*: 1918, 1,075t, 3×4in, 4×21in tt, 36k.
Adm Sir Walter Cowan, Bt (1871–1956): ent RN 1884; Lt 1892; African expeditions; CO *Boxer*; Omdurman 1898; Boer War; Cdr 1901; destroyer splist; Capt 1906; *Gloucester* 1910; F Capt, *Princess Royal* 1915; Jutland; Cdre 1LCS 1917; RA 1918; Baltic 1919; BCS 1921; VA 1923; FO Scotland 1925; C-in-C, NAWI 1926–28; Adm 1927; ret 1931; enlisted as commando, W Desert, 1940; captd 1942; repat 1943; bt 1921.
[13]*Wallace*: 1919, 1,480t, 4×4in, 31k.
[14]*Calcutta*: 1919, 4,200t, 5×6in, 29k; conv to AA ship, 1937, 8×4in; s Ger a/c, E Med, 1 June 1941.
Despatch: 1922, 4,850t, 6×6in, 12tt, 29k.

College, intended for officers likely to progress to high command, though with typical self-depreciation he believed he was selected because he had no appointment at the time. Nevertheless, he found it a valuable year, studying foreign affairs and economics and coming to understand the points of view of the other services and of civil servants. To crown the year, he married Nona Byatt, whom he had known for some years, and was appointed to command the new battleship *Rodney*.[15] After serving as Commodore of Chatham barracks during the Invergordon Mutiny, a trauma which scarcely affected Chatham but which left Cunningham with much sympathy for the ratings who suffered substantial pay cuts, he was promoted Rear Admiral in September 1932. For much of the following year he attended technical and tactical courses at Portsmouth before achieving his heart's desire, appointment as Rear Admiral (D), Mediterranean Fleet.

The C-in-C, the formidable Admiral Sir William Fisher, 'Tall Agrippa', worked the fleet extremely hard. Cunningham found him 'a superb tactician and fleet handler . . . a great influence and inspiration'.[16] After Jutland much thought had been given to fleet actions at night, especially the role of destroyers, and Cunningham initiated a variety of exercises and training in all aspects of destroyer work. He soon added to his reputation for demanding the highest standards at all times, attention to every last detail, ship-handling of incredible skill and precision, and an incessant drive for efficiency. His eye, keener than anyone's, missed nothing and his captains, in awe of him, learned quickly that they could never relax when he was about. He handled his three flotillas adroitly, his orders always crisp, lucid and precise. He shared Fisher's vigorous response to the prospect of war with Italy over the Italian invasion of Abyssinia and the fleet exercised feverishly to reach wartime efficiency, while Fisher's intention of carrying the fight to the enemy was digested by Cunningham. Relieved in the spring of 1936 by his friend Rear Admiral James Somerville, Cunningham

---

[15]*Rodney*: 1927, 33,900t, 9×16in, 8×4.7in, 23k. Nona, Lady Cunningham (née Byatt): d.o.b. unknown; b Midhurst, Sussex, dtr of a Headmr; house manager & hostess for brother who was Col Sec, Gibraltar, 1912–14, Lt Govr, Malta, 1914–16, Govr of Tanganyika 1918–26 & Govr of Trinidad, 1928; d 1977.

[16]Cunningham, notes, pp. 30, 53, *Cunningham Papers*, BM Add Mss 52580B, British Library (BL); *A Sailor's Odyssey*, p. 178. Adm Sir William W. Fisher (1875–1937): ent RN 1880; Flag Cdr to C-in-C, HF 1909–11 and to C-in-C, Devonport, 1911–12; *St Vincent* 1916–17; DASD 1917; COS to C-in-C Med 1919; RA 1922; COS, AHF and 1BS 1922–24; 4BS 1924–25; DNI 1926; 4SL 1927; VA and DCNS 1928; 2nd-in-cmd MF and Adm 1930; C-in-C Med 1932–35; C-in-C, Portsmouth 1935–37.

returned home to a spell on half pay, though he was promoted Vice Admiral in July 1936.[17]

However, in the summer of 1937, Cunningham was rushed out to Malta to relieve the Second-in-Command of the Mediterranean Fleet, Vice Admiral Sir Geoffrey Blake, who had become ill. Admiral Sir Dudley Pound was now C-in-C.[18] Cunningham spent a further year in the Mediterranean and was then summoned by the new First Sea Lord, Admiral Sir Roger Backhouse, to become Deputy Chief of Naval Staff in October 1938.[19] Cunningham had largely avoided staff work and shore appointments; he was a deck sailor rather than a desk sailor and felt rather out of his depth in Whitehall. Lord Chatfield's great rearmament programme and the rising anxieties about war on three fronts were the Admiralty's central concerns.[20] Cunningham was engaged on planning for mobilisation not only of the fleet but also of the Merchant Navy and industry, as well as the defence of ports, the introduction of modern technology such as radar, and co-operation with the other services and civilian ministries. He also claimed paternity for the 'Hunt' class escort destroyers. In 1939, Backhouse worked himself into an early grave, followed by the brilliant Third Sea Lord, Admiral Henderson, who with Beatty, Chatfield and Fisher (who had died in 1937), was one of the ablest senior officers of the inter-war

[17]S. W. C. Pack, *Cunningham the Commander* (London, 1974), p. 57. Cunningham to Capt H. T. Baillie-Grohman, 8 May 1936, XGRO 1, *Baillie-Grohman Papers*, NMM. A. J. Marder, 'The Royal Navy and the Ethiopian Crisis, 1935–1936', in Marder (ed.), *From the Dardanelles to Oran* (London, 1974), pp. 64–101; G. A. D. Gordon, *British Sea Power and Procurement between the Wars: A Re-Appraisal of Re-Armament* (Annapolis, Md, 1988).

[18]Adm Sir Geoffrey Blake (1882–1968): ent RN 1897; Lt 1904; gunnery splist; Cdr 1914; Grand F 1914–18; Capt 1918; NA, Washington 1919–20; *Queen Elizabeth* 1921–23; N War Coll 1923–25; DD & Dir, N Staff Coll 1925–29; Cdre, NZ Sta 1929–32; RA 1931; 4SL 1932; VA 1935; BCS 1935–37; ret 1938; ACNS (F) 1940; FO Liaison US N Forces Europe 1942–45; apptd Black Rod 1944.

A of F Sir Dudley Pound (1877–1943): ent RN 1891; CO of a T/boat 1897; Cdr 1909; Capt 1914; *Colossus*, Jutland 1916; DOD (H) 1917; *Repulse* 1920–22; DPD 1922; COS, Med F 1925; RA 1926; ACNS 1927–29; BCS 1929; VA 1930; 2SL 1932; Adm 1935; C-in-C Med 1936–39; FSL 1939–43. See chapter by R. Brodhurst in M. H. Murfett (ed.), *The First Sea Lords: From Fisher to Mountbatten* (Westport, Conn. & London, 1995), pp. 185–200. Mr Brodhurst is now completing a full biography of Pound.

[19]A of F Sir Roger Backhouse (1878–1939): ent RN 1892; Lt 1899; gun splist; Harwich force 1914–16; FCapt *Lion* 1916–18; DNO 1920; *Malaya* 1923; IDC 1926; RA, 3BS, Atl F 1926; 3SL 1928–32; VA 1929; 1BS & 2nd-in-C, Med F; Adm 1934; C-in-C, Home F 1935–38; FSL 1938–39; A of F July 1939. See chapter by M. H. Murfett in Murfett (ed.), *First Sea Lords*, pp. 173–84.

[20]A of F Lord (Ernle) Chatfield (1873–1967): ent RN 1886 ; Flag Capt, *Lion*, Jutland 1916; RA & 4 SL 1919; C-in-C Atl & Med Fleets 1929–32; FSL 1933–38; Minr for Co-ord Defence 1939–40. See chapter by E. J. Grove in Murfett (ed.), *First Sea Lords*, pp. 157–71.

period.[21] These losses, together with the earlier resignation of Ramsay, who could not work with Backhouse, and the retirement on health grounds of Somerville, left the Royal Navy suddenly bereft of much of its flag officer talent.[22] Pound became First Sea Lord and Cunningham, who had acted for Backhouse during his terminal illness, was the obvious choice to succeed him as C-in-C, Mediterranean, in June 1939.

What, then, had made Cunningham such a clear choice for one of the three principal seagoing commands in the Royal Navy? He had certain natural gifts – self-confidence, enormous energy and determination, courage and belligerence, the capacity to grasp and resolve situations quickly and decisively, and the ability to lead men. He had revelled in the exercise of independent command conferred by his considerable time in destroyers, and in the Great War he had sought action and fought with verve, resolution and distinction. He was known throughout the service as a master of ship-handling and one of the most able exponents of the destroyerman's craft. The Baltic campaign further displayed all these attributes. His commander there, Rear Admiral Cowan, was always looking 'for officers who shine in emergencies and come well up to scratch under difficult circumstances'. Cunningham did not disappoint him and another senior officer noted that he was 'as good an officer as I can remember'.[23] There is no doubt that Cunningham had a high regard for senior officers of similar mettle – de Robeck, Keyes, Tyrwhitt and Cowan. He gained much – chiefly inspiration – from serving with them and acknowledged that Cowan 'taught the coming generation to think boldly and not

---

[21]Adm Sir Reginald Henderson (1881–1939): Lt 1902; gunnery splist; Cdr 1913; Jutland; A/S Div 1916; Capt 1917; F Capt *Hawkins,* China 1919; RN Coll 1923; *Furious* 1926; RA 1929; RA(A) 1931–33; VA 1933; 3SL 1934; Adm 1939.

A of F Earl (David) Beatty (1871–1936): ent RN 1884; DSO, Nile 1898, & Cdr; gallantry Boxer campaign 1900, & Capt; RA 1910; BCF 1913–16; Actg VA 1914; VA 1915; Adm & then A of F 1919; FSL 1919–27; earl 1919. See B. McL. Ranft (ed.), *The Beatty Papers,* 2 vols (Aldershot: Scolar Press for Navy Records Society, 1989 and 1993) and chapter by Ranft in Murfett (ed.), *First Sea Lords,* pp. 127–40.

[22]Adm Sir Bertram Ramsay (1883–1945): ent RN 1898; Somaliland War 1904 & Lt; signal splist; Grand F 1914–15; Cdr 1916; *Broke,* Dover Patrol 1917–18; Capt, *Weymouth* 1923; *Danae* 1925; *Kent,* China 1929; Imp IDC Coll 1931; *Royal Sovereign,* Med F 1933; RA & COS to Backhouse 1935; resigned Dec 1935; VA & FO, Dover 1939; Dep ANCXF, TORCH 1942; HUSKY 1943; ANCXF, NEPTUNE/OVERLORD 1943–45; k in air crash, 2 Jan. 1945. RA W. S. Chalmers, *Full Cycle: The Biography of Admiral Sir Bertram Home Ramsay* (London, 1959); W. J. R. Gardner, 'Admiral Sir Bertram Ramsay', in Howarth (ed.), *Men of War,* pp. 349–62, and forthcoming biography.

[23]Cowan to Cunningham, n.d., 1955, BM Add Mss 52562, *Cunningham Papers,* BL; Cowan to Captains, 1 Lt CS, June 1918, COW 6, *Cowan Papers,* NMM.

only think, to act boldly'.[24] In fact, Cunningham needed little instruction in that direction; he was drawn to these flag officers because he recognised kindred spirits. The admiral from whom he learned most of his 'fleetcraft' was clearly Sir William Fisher. Otherwise, Cunningham was not a student of warfare in the way that Wavell or Somerville were, nor does he appear to have associated with the 'Young Turks' of *The Naval Review* (though he was a Member). Much of what he needed for flag rank came naturally; much of the rest was derived from almost constant sea time and perpetual problem-solving. Cunningham was the epitome of the thoroughly practical professional seaman. Though he was not unreflective, he kept his thoughts to himself until compelled to expound them, which he did with economy and force.

[24]A of F Sir John de Robeck (1862–1928): ent RN 1875; Capt 1902; RA 1911; VA, 9CS 1914; 2nd-in-C, then C-in-C, Dardanelles 1915; 2BS, Grand F 1916–19; C-in-C Med 1919–22; Adm 1920; C-in-C Atl F 1922–24; A of F 1925. Cunningham to Cowan, c. 22 Mar. 1946, COW7, *Cowan Papers*.

PART I

THE 'PHONEY WAR' PERIOD
JUNE 1939 TO JUNE 1940

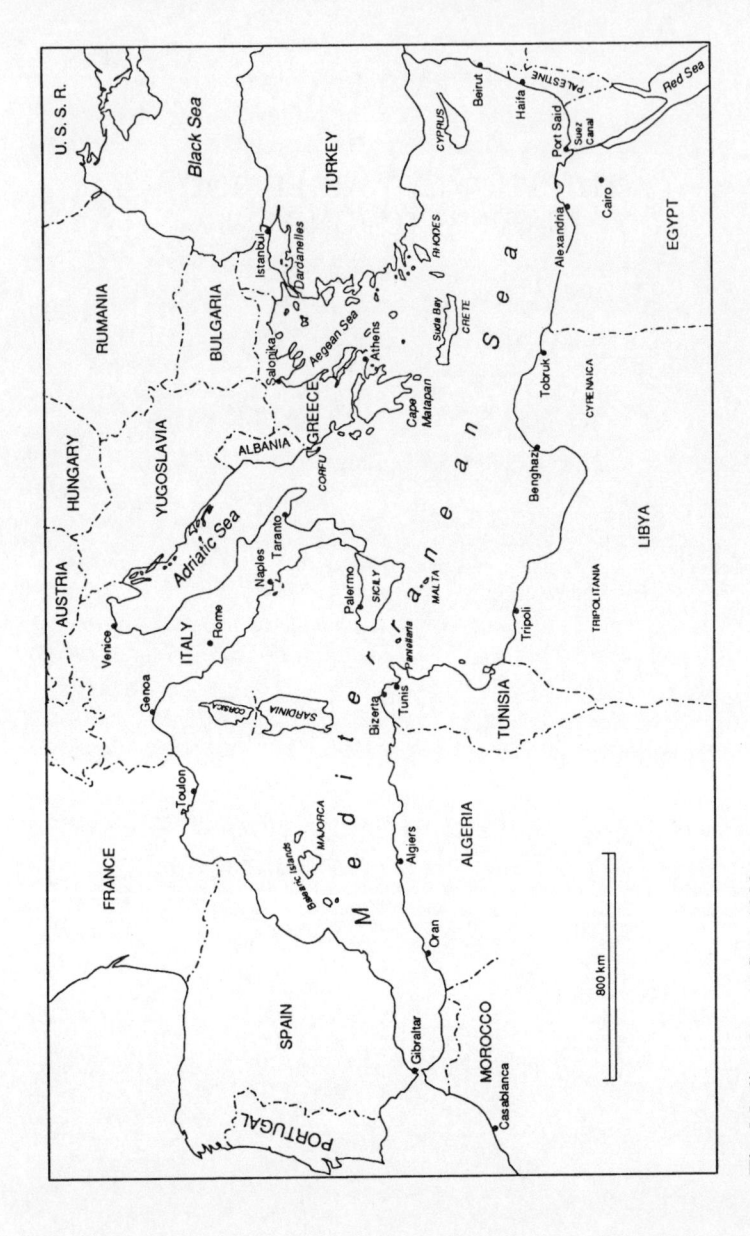

The Mediterranean Sea, 1939

Cunningham came to the Mediterranean Fleet with a formidable and awesome reputation, much of it forged in those very waters, as a firm disciplinarian, a hard man to please, a bold and fearless handler of flotillas and squadrons and a decisive leader. He was widely regarded as an uncompromising and demanding officer yet considerate of his men and able to command their confidence and devotion. He was not noted for patience and was at times irascible, though his fierceness seemed designed to determine whether or not subordinates would stand up to him; if they did so, he respected them and thus began long and ultimately enjoyable relationships. John Somerville recalled that 'he inspired affection as well as abundant respect from those who worked closely with him' and gained the trust and warm admiration of the lower deck.[1] Though at times he could appear stern and forbidding, he had a genuine and wide-ranging sense of humour. His niece Hilda remembered him as 'a very family minded man and a favourite uncle to us all! He was a great tease – always full of fun' and in time of trouble he was extremely sympathetic and understanding.[2] Unsparing of himself, he drove his fleet and his staff hard, though he possessed what Pound lacked, the art of delegation. He believed firmly in concise and precise orders, giving his subordinates the scope for initiative cultivated by Nelson. He was well served in his new command by an exceptionally able group of flag and staff officers.[3]

[1]Commander John Somerville to editor, 6 Oct. 1997.
[2]Cunningham's niece, now Mrs Hilda McKendrick, to editor, 2 Dec. 1997.
[3]Second-in-Cmd & VA, 1BS (Aug. 1939): VA (later Adm) Sir Geoffrey L. Layton (1884–1964): Lt 1905; Cdr 1916; Capt 1922; *Renown* 1933–34; Cdre, Portsmouth Barracks 1934–36; RA 1935; DPS 1936–38; VA & BCS 1938; VA, 18CS, HF, Nov. 1939; 2nd-in-C, HF 1939–40; C-in-C, China, July 1940; C-in-C, Eastern F, Dec. 1941–March 1942; C-in-C, Ceylon, March 1942–Aug 1944; C-in-C, Portsmouth, Aug. 1944–47.
  RA, 1CS: RA (later AoF Sir) John H. D. Cunningham (1885–1962): ent RN 1900: Lt 1905; navig splist; Med & Grand F 1914–18; Cdr 1917; Cdr, Navig Sch 1922–23; Master of F 1923; Capt 1924; staff cmds; N War Coll; DP; *Adventure, Resolution*; RA & ACNS 1936; ACNS (Air) & then 5SL 1937–39; VA & 1CS, HF 1939–40; N cdr, MENACE, Dakar 1940; 4SL 1941–43; C-in-C, Levant, & later Med, & Adm 1943; 1SL 1946–48; A of F 1948; Chm, Iraq Petroleum Co. 1948–58. See essay by M. H. Murfett, in Murfett (ed.), *The First Sea Lords: From Fisher to Mountbatten* (Westport, Conn. and London, 1995), pp. 217–28.
  RA, 3CS: RA (later Adm Sir) Henry R. Moore (1886–1978): ent RN 1902; Lt 1908; Grand F 1914–18; Cdr 1919; *Britannia* 1919–21; CID 1921–24; Capt 1926; IDC 1927; DDPD & DPD 1930–33; *Neptune* 1933–35; Cdre 1st Cl & COS to C-in-C, HF 1936–38; COS to C-in-C, Portsmouth 1938–39; RA 1938; ACNS(T) 1940–41; VA & VCNS 1941–42;

Though he inherited an efficient and confident fleet, Germany and Japan seemed more likely to commence hostilities than Italy and over the next few months its strength ebbed away. Italy adopted a policy of non-belligerency during the 'Phoney War' and, while Cunningham kept a wary eye on the situation, he was able to become thoroughly acquainted with his command, his Army and Air Force colleagues, his allies the French and neutrals such as Turkey, free from the pressure of hostilities. He assessed the strategic situation, noted his command's deficiencies and made his war plans.

In the Mediterranean, as elsewhere, Britain was over-extended. She was notionally the superpower of the day but in truth was unable to contemplate a war of any length with another major power; in manpower, finance, industry and technology, there were grave deficiencies which in wartime would be rapidly exposed. The far-flung empire, with its long lines of communication, was indefensible in the modern world and the British Isles were vulnerable to air attack and

2nd-in-C, HF 1943–44; Adm & C-in-C, HF 1944–45; Head of BAD Dec. 1945–Sept. 1948; C-in-C Nore 1948–50.

RA(D) (1938): RA (later A of F Lord) John C. Tovey (1885–1971): ent RN 1900; *Jackal* i/c 1915; *Onslow* 1916; distinguished service at Jutland; Cdr 1916; *Ursa* 1917; *Wolfhound*; RN Staff Coll 1919–20; OD 1920–22; Capt 1923; Capt (D) 1923–25; IDC 1927; N Asst to 2SL 1928–30; *Rodney* 1932–34; Cdre, RN Barracks, Chatham 1935; RA 1936; VA 1939; 2nd-in-Cmd, Med F 1940; Actg Adm & C-in-C, HF 1940–43; Adm 1942; C-in-C Nore 1943; A of F 1943.

COS (1939–March 1941): Cdre (later A of F Sir) Algernon U. Willis (1889–1976): ent RN 1903; Lt 1909; tpdo splist; Grand F 1916–18; Cdr 1922; Capt 1929; N War Coll 1930–32; *Kent*, China Sta 1933–34; *Nelson*, HF 1934–5; *Vernon* i/c 1935–38; *Barham*, Med F 1938; RA 1940; Actg VA & C-in-C S Atl Sept. 1941–Feb 1942; VA, 3BS & 2nd-in-Cmd, Eastern F March 1942; FOIC, Force H 1943; C-in-C, Levant 1943; 2SL 1944–46; Adm 1944; C-in-C Med 1946–48; C-in-C Portsmouth 1948–50; A of F 1949.

Sec to C-in-C (June 1939): Tempy Paymr Capt A. P. Shaw: Cdr June 1934; BAD 1942; *Hannibal* (Alexandria) 1943; Sec to Adm J. H. D. Cunningham, C-in-C Med 1943–44; Sec to FSL (ABC) & Capt June 1944–45.

Master of the Fleet (June 1939): Cdr T. M. Brownrigg: Cdr Dec. 1936; *President* 1942; Capt Dec. 1942; *Merganser* (Peterhead) 1944–45.

FGO (Dec. 1938): Cdr (later VA Sir) Geoffrey Barnard (1902–74): Cdr June 1935, *Daring*, China; *President* 1942; DCOS to C-in-C Med, 1943; *Aurora* Dec. 1943; *Victory* 1944–45; CSO to FO(Air) 1946–47; Dir, Tac Sch 1948; Indian N 1950–51; RA 1951; ACNS 1952–53; DCNS 1953–54; JSM, Washington 1954–56; Pres, RNC Greenwich 1956–58; ret 1959.

FTO (July 1939): Cdr W. P. Carne: Cdr June 1933; Capt June 1941; *Coventry*; BAD 1942–43; *Striker* 1944–45; Cdre 2nd Cl 1945.

SO(P) (May 1939): Cdr Royer M. Dick: Cdr June 1933; Capt June 1940; BAD 1942; Cdre 1Cl & COS to C-in-C Med 1943; *Belfast* 1944–45; RA Aug. 1949; Ret List 1953; later at NATO HQ.

SO(O) (Aug. 1939); Cdr (later VA Sir) Manley L. Power (1904–81): ent RN 1917; Lt 1926; Cdr June 1939; *Opportune* 1942; TORCH plans 1942; Actg Capt, *Hannibal* 1943; Capt Dec. 1943; *Saumarez* & Capt (D), 26DF, sank *Haguro*, 1945; RA 1953; VA 1956; DCNS & 5SL 1957–59; C-in-C Portsmouth 1959–61.

starvation. Though rearmament of all three services had made substantial progress since 1935, the programme's full effect would not be felt until 1942. The Government's strategic priorities were to defend the home base and its adjacent waters and to dispatch the main fleet to Singapore in the event of Japanese hostility. Until late in 1938 (when Cunningham helped to inspire a reconsideration of strategic priorities), the Mediterranean had hardly signified in British defence planning and this neglect, coupled with the acute shortage of forces, meant little had been done to reinforce the theatre, develop bases or devise plans. It is not surprising, therefore, that British policy towards Italy since 1935 had been one of appeasement, earnestly endorsed by the Chiefs of Staff. As late as September 1939 British leaders hoped, rather against hope, that Italy would remain on the sidelines or even detach herself from the Pact of Steel. British diplomacy endeavoured also to forge a Balkan coalition of Yugoslavia, Rumania, Greece and Turkey. However, these states, while fearing the evil designs of Italy, Germany and Russia, had little confidence in the will and ability of Britain and France to defend their independence. Cunningham quickly discovered both the limits of British power and the Byzantine complications of Balkan and Middle Eastern diplomacy when he visited Turkey in August 1939. He concluded that the Turks would maintain a strict neutrality while demanding British aid and advice, though after becoming Prime Minister, Churchill persisted in fruitless attempts to bring 'Johnny Turk' into the war [6, 8, 17, 18, 20–22, 30]. Moreover, Anglo-French control of their mandates and protectorates in the Middle East was precarious; below a thin crust of complaisant and collaborative monarchs and ministries lay a deep and increasingly volatile well of violent nationalism, some branches of which were openly pro-Axis. This was true especially of Egypt.[4]

[4] Winston L. S. Churchill (1874–1965): brief career as Subaltern, India & Sudan, 1890s; war correspondent Cuba & Boer War 1898–1900; MP, Con, Lib & Con again, most of 1900–65; Pres BoT, Home Sec & 1st Lord, 1906–15; Col, W Front 1915–16; M Muns 1917–19; S War & Air 1919–21; C Ex 1924–29; political wilderness 1931–39; 1st Lord Sept 1939-May 1940; PM & M Defence, May 1940–May 1945; Ldr of Oppn 1945–51; PM 1951–55.

See N. H. Gibbs, *Grand Strategy, I, Rearmament Policy* (London, 1976); A. Clayton, *The British Empire as a Superpower, 1919–1939* (Athens, Ga, 1986); L. R. Pratt, *East of Malta, West of Suez: Britain's Mediterranean Crisis, 1936–1939* (Cambridge, 1975); H. Cliadakis, 'Neutrality and War in Italian Policy 1939–40', *Journal of Contemporary History,* **9** (1974), pp. 171–90; J. Millman, 'Toward War with Russia: British Naval and Air Planning for Conflict in the Near East, 1939–40', *Journal of Contemporary History,* **29** (1994), pp. 261–83. See esp Cunningham, 'The Despatch of a Fleet to the Far East', 5 April 1939, CAB16/183A, and Chiefs of Staff, 'Mediterranean, Middle East and African Appreciation', 21 Feb. 1939, CAB16/182. CAB53, CAB79 & CAB80 have many such papers. The fullest account of Britain's Mediterranean policy and strategy is R. M. Salerno, *The Mediterranean Triangle: Britain, France, Italy and the Origins of the Second World War, 1935–1940,* unpublished Ph.D., Yale University, 1997.

The impending war in Europe and the ill will and opportunism of Mussolini concentrated the minds of British and French leaders on the practicalities of their uneasy and fumbling alliance. The French Navy, well equipped with modern vessels, most of which were in the Mediterranean, was buoyant in morale and aggressive in spirit. The British were especially careful to humour Admiral Darlan, head of the French Navy[5] and in discussions with the French, Cunningham was anxious to cultivate offensive sentiments, though he was sceptical of grandiose French military plans and historic rivalries were evident when Levantine issues were discussed. Talks in the spring of 1940 led to a rough strategic division of the Mediterranean, the French being responsible for the western basin and the British east of Malta, with the assistance of a powerful French squadron, based on Alexandria, under the able Vice Admiral Godfroy [2, 8, 15, 18, 22–3, 25–6].[6]

Talks with the French also brought Cunningham into close contact with the Army GOC-in-C, Middle East, General Sir Archibald Wavell, a taciturn, scholarly man noted for meticulous planning, broad strategic vision and subtle tactical skills.[7] The AOC-in-C, Middle East, Air Chief Marshal Sir William Mitchell, was soon succeeded by Air Chief Marshal Sir Arthur Longmore, formerly of the Royal Naval Air Service, which made him sympathetic to naval requests [134].[8] Cunningham, who was always sceptical of the value of a supreme commander, felt that the trio of Wavell, Longmore and himself operated

---

[5]Adm Jean-François Darlan (1881–1942): creator of modern French Navy; Adm & C-in-C 1939; M Marine June 1940; For M Feb. 1941; M Defence Aug. 1941; C-in-C Vichy armed forces; collaborated with Germans; in N. Africa at time of TORCH, Nov. 1942; collaborated with Allies; k by Royalist fanatic 24 Dec. 1942.
  On co-operation with the French, see 'Minutes of Strategic Appreciation Sub-Cttee', 17 April 1939, CAB16/183A; RA P. Auphan, 'The French Navy Enters World War II', *US N Inst Proceedings*, June 1956, pp. 592–601.
  [6]VA R. E. Godfroy (1885–1981): ent N 1901; Lt de V 1913; cruisers & gunboats, 1914–18; naval aviation 1920s; Capt de V 1931; cmded cruisers 1931–35; Contre-Amiral 1936; DCNS 1936–37; 4th C Div 1937; VA 19 June 1940; jnd Fr Fr N May 1943; removed from cmd but this injustice annulled 1955.
  [7]Gen (later FM Earl) Sir Archibald Wavell (1883–1950): ent Army 1900; Black Watch, Boer W; India; Staff Coll; Actg Maj, France 1914–16; Liaison O, Russia 1916–17; Brevet Col, Palestine 1917–18; WO 1921–26; Col & GSO I, 3rd Div 1926; Brig, 6 Inf Bde 1930–34; Maj-Gen, 2nd Div 1935–37; GOC, Palestine 1937–38; GOC, S Cmd 1938–39; GOC-in-C, ME 1939–41; C-in-C India 1941–43; Viceroy 1943–47; viscount 1943; earl 1947.
  [8]ACM Sir William Mitchell (1888–1944): b Australia; RFC 1914–18; W Cdr 1919; Dir Trng 1929–33; Cdt Cranwell 1933–34; AOC Iraq 1934–37; Air Mem Personnel 1937–39; ACM 1939 & AOC-in-C, ME; Inspr-Gen 1940–41.
  ACM Sir Arthur Longmore (1885–1970): b Australia; ent RN 1900; pilot 1910; CO, 1 Sq, RNAS, Dunkirk 1914; Lt-Cdr *Tiger* 1916, Jutland; i/c air ops, MF 1918; RAF 1918; G Capt, Iraq 1923; Cdt Cranwell; AM & Cdt IDC 1933; C-in-C, Training Cmd 1939; AOC-in-C, ME 1939–41; Inspr-Gen 1941–42; ret 1942. See his *From Sea to Sky* (London, 1946).

with harmony and efficiency, though he resisted his air and military colleagues' persistent requests that he should leave Alexandria and join them in Cairo [326]. He intended to be a seagoing C-in-C, particularly if there was the prospect of action with the Italian fleet. However, he made weekly visits to confer with his fellow Commanders-in-Chief and they constituted themselves a formal committee in September 1940 [7, 12, 13, 28–9, 39, 75, 78, 79, 84, 96, 326].

The two principal deficiencies with which Cunningham was faced were shortage of land-based air support and the lack of a satisfactory fleet base. The RAF in the Middle East, consisting of about 200 mostly obsolete aircraft, could provide little in the way of fighter cover for ports or units at sea and it had no anti-ship strike aircraft; most seriously, it could furnish only occasional and fragmentary reconnaissance of enemy bases and the eastern basin. The advent of air power and the likely hostility of Italy had persuaded the Government to write off Malta as virtually indefensible, certainly as a major fleet base, and to concentrate the fleet at Alexandria if hostilities threatened. Successive Naval Commanders-in-Chief had argued against this cautious policy and Cunningham redoubled the protests. He was in no doubt about Malta's vital significance; it not only possessed the only worthwhile dockyard but it was also the key to an offensive strategy in the central Mediterranean. He felt it could play a major role in the interdiction of Italian traffic to Libya and, if the AA and fighter defences were strong enough, he hoped to base the fleet there. The Navy's pressure led to a government decision to build up Malta's AA defences to 112 guns and four squadrons of fighters, though this would require a long time and much juggling of scarce resources [1, 3, 5, 26, 30].[9] In the mean time, Cunningham would have to make the best of Alexandria, a most unsatisfactory base in every respect. It lay far from the expected scenes of action in the Aegean and central Mediterranean. Like Malta, it was vulnerable to Italian air attacks and invasion from Libya. It was under the control of an unpredictable client state. It was shallow and had a difficult entrance. It lacked adequate docking facilities, even after the arrival from home of a large floating dock. Worst of all, it had practically no net defences, minesweeping and patrol forces, searchlights, AA guns, radar or fighters [1–3, 5, 8, 25, 27].

Following the German blitzkrieg in the west in the spring of 1940, Italy showed signs of joining the conflict and Pound began to reinforce the Mediterranean, albeit inadequately and with little more

---

[9]On Malta, see Chiefs of Staff, 9, 11, 15, & 23 July 1940, 9 Oct. 1940, CAB79/4; 'Air Defence of Malta', 22 Jan 1940, CAB80/6.

than a 'second eleven'. Cunningham and Pound had to consider urgently the strategy to be adopted. The Navy's chief tasks were to safeguard the homeland and its adjoining waters and the seaways, bases and territories of the empire. Historically, the Mediterranean was the principal artery to the empire east of Suez but since Italy lay astride this route and possessed not only a sizeable fleet but also a formidable air force, naval opinion was that, in the event of war, even warships would face an unacceptably hazardous passage through the middle sea. All communications with the Middle East would have to be via the Cape and the Canal, though this route would be subject to Italian naval and air attacks in the Red Sea. Within the Mediterranean itself the fleet's tasks were to sustain Malta, protect communications with Cyprus and the Levant, support the Army in the Western Desert and, with French assistance, attack Italian communications with Libya.

The major area of doubt concerned the central Mediterranean. Cunningham believed firmly that the consequences of war must be brought home to the Italian people by attacks on their coasts. As neither the Army nor the RAF were in a position to assume the offensive, the fleet must do so. However, he and Pound agreed that the Navy alone could not defeat Italy. Cunningham intended to exercise sea power in Nelsonian fashion – by seizing and maintaining the initiative and, by bringing the Italian fleet to battle, establishing a moral ascendancy over the enemy, being confident of British superiority in training, tactics and seamanship. He was in fact constitutionally incapable of any other strategy, though, mindful of his wide responsibilities and inadequate resources, like Nelson he was not reckless. However, despite Cunningham's known combativeness, Churchill condemned his plans as too defensive. He insisted that Commanders-in-Chief should be reminded of their duty to take the offensive. Churchill plainly did not know his man and as so often made a superficial judgement, dismissing the many problems with which Cunningham had to contend and of which he was not slow to remind the Prime Minister [1–3, 5, 7, 8, 22, 27–30].

The incident set a pattern for his relations with Churchill and, to some extent, with Pound. Cunningham had become familiar with Pound when the latter was in command of the Battle Cruiser Squadron at the time Cunningham commanded *Rodney*. Though he acknowledged that Pound brought fresh ideas, he found him prone to interfere with the operation of individual ships. Pound, he commented, was a driver rather than a leader. Andrew Gordon has observed that Pound's command of the Mediterranean Fleet 'appears to have been a retrogressive step as regards the fostering of initiative' and certainly Cunningham, upon assuming command, made short work of his predecessor's overelaborate orders.[10] Nevertheless, Cunningham was infallibly loyal to the new First Sea Lord and there was mutual trust and confidence. Pound had few friends and Cunningham was one of the select group; Vice Admiral Blake was possibly the only man closer to Pound. Cunningham and Pound carried on a frequent, frank, informal and intimate correspondence – there are over 60 examples in this selection. Pound gave Cunningham virtually unfettered freedom to run the Mediterranean Station. He supported him in the Chiefs of Staff Committee and against the Prime Minister, and endeavoured to maintain a flow of reinforcements to Cunningham's increasingly hard-pressed fleet. He asked Cunningham for uninhibited comments and for recommendations of flag officers for seagoing commands [5, 10]. Cunningham, in turn, tried to avoid burdening Pound with his own problems [26, 39, 160, 213]. Pound strove mightily and successfully to obtain a kind of Coastal Command for the Middle East, an improvement for which Cunningham had agitated following the Greek and Cretan campaigns [262–3]. For the most part, the two were in agreement on major issues and their differences tended to be over priorities and possibilities rather than strategies. In part these differences – notably over the proposed blocking of Tripoli – were the inevitable result of their differing perspectives. Pound at 'head office' was less aware of local problems than Cunningham, who in turn did not always comprehend the global scene [174–204]. Cunningham also protested vehemently against Pound's precipitate action in instituting a court of enquiry following Somerville's abortive encounter with the Italian fleet off Cape Spartivento [121, 125, 134].[11] However, their disagreements rarely became acerbic – perhaps surprising in view of the difference in their temperaments [158–60].

Cunningham, then, enjoyed a generally harmonious relationship with the First Sea Lord – but his relations with the Prime Minister, having started with a misunderstanding which created mutual distrust, never improved. Cunningham had been 'infuriated' by the Prime Minister's prodding message, relayed by Pound [27–8].

[10]G. A. D. Gordon, *The Rules of the Game: Jutland and the British Naval Command* (London, 1996), pp. 574–5. Mediterranean Station War Orders, 25 July 1939, ADM199/877, Public Record Office (PRO)

[11]M. Simpson (ed.), *The Somerville Papers* (Aldershot: Scolar Press for Navy Records Society, 1995), pp. 64–8; documents 103–20.

Encapsulating the difference between the way the two wartime First Sea Lords played the Prime Minister, Cunningham noted that Pound apologised for dispatching it but believed he should not have allowed it to be sent.[12] Pound's method of dealing with Churchill was to avoid confrontations, divert the Premier's attention and to let Churchill have his way on minor matters and to stand firm on major ones. On the whole, it was an amicable relationship, Pound finding 'Winston admirable to work with' [19] and acknowledging his incomparable gifts as the nation's leader [97]. Churchill, a prime example of Shakespeare's warning that a little learning is a dangerous thing, seemed to feel that Marlburian ancestry, the command of a battalion, the political headship of the three services and extensive reading conferred on him strategic genius. He was also the prisoner of his memories of the First World War and, obsessed with avoiding the stalemate, slaughter and sterility of that cataclysm, constantly exhorted his commanders to take the offensive boldly and relentlessly and he was displeased to hear recitals of reasons why this could not be done.[13] Cunningham found Churchill's remorseless pressure to take the offensive, his wild schemes and his ignorance of the manifold and manifest problems of the Mediterranean theatre intensely irksome – and made his views plain [92, 93, 98, 108–9, 122–6, 185–8, 193–6, 199, 202, 209, 271–3, 283–6, 301].

Despite the apparently formidable strength of their armed forces, the Italians were in scarcely better condition to fight a war than the British and French. They had enormous armies in Libya and East Africa and substantial reinforcements at home. However, the Army was poorly led and lacked modern equipment. The Air Force had a front-line strength of 2,350 aircraft but little in the way of reserves, while aircraft production was sluggish and inadequate; many of the aircraft were obsolete. The Navy had four battleships under construction, outclassing anything the British could spare for the Mediterranean, though only two had been completed by the outbreak of war. Four Great War battleships were undergoing extensive modernisation, emerging fast and well armed but lightly protected, though only two were in service in June 1940. There were seven heavy and 12 light cruisers and over 60 destroyers. Italian ships were speedy and well armed. Italy boasted the world's largest submarine fleet – over 100 boats – and

---

[12]Cunningham, notes, pp. 3–4, BM Add Mss 52581A, *Cunningham Papers* BL.

[13]On Churchill's relations with admirals, see S. W. Roskill, *Churchill and the Admirals* (London, 1977); V A Sir P. Gretton, *Former Naval Person: Winston Churchill and the Royal Navy* (London, 1968); A. J. Marder, 'Winston is Back: Churchill at the Admiralty, 1939–1940', in Marder (ed.), *From the Dardanelles to Oran* (London, 1974), pp. 110–78.

emphasised special forces – E-boats, midget submarines, human torpedoes, explosive motorboats and deep water mining. Though Mussolini had dismissed the need for a carrier, the Regia Aeronautica could quarter the Mediterranean regularly with reconnaissance flights, directing large forces of high-level bombers to attack Allied naval forces, while affording the Italian fleet strong fighter protection. Nevertheless, the Italian Navy did not enjoy good air co-operation. Furthermore, its ships lacked adequate protection, accurate rangefinders, radar, sonar and other modern equipment. The Navy was unschooled in night fighting, it was likely to suffer from the national shortage of fuel, and it could not easily replace losses. Its principal duty was to maintain communications with Libya, Albania and the Dodecanese; otherwise, it sensibly adopted a 'fleet in being' strategy.[14]

Thus, for several months, Cunningham was forced to wait on Mussolini's pleasure while the real war went on elsewhere, a frustrating situation for a man of action. Moreover, he was compelled to witness also the steady dwindling of his fleet and, even when it was built up again in the spring of 1940, in anticipation of Mussolini's entry into the gladiatorial ring, little could be done to strengthen its supporting elements – air reconnaissance, fighter cover and harbour defences. Between June 1939 and June 1940, Cunningham had a year of learning to make bricks without straw.

---

[14]On the Italian Navy in the war, see M. A. Bragadin, *The Italian Navy in World War II* (Annapolis, Md, 1957); J. J. Sadkovitch, 'The Italian Navy in World War II', in Sadkovitch (ed.), *Reevaluating the Major Naval Combatants of World War II* (Westport, Conn., 1990), pp. 129–46, and 'The Indispensable Navy: Italy as a Great Power, 1911–1943' in N. Rodger (ed.), *Naval Power in the Twentieth Century* (Basingstoke, 1996), pp. 66–76; VA G. Fioravanzo, 'Italian Strategy in the Mediterranean, 1940–1943', *US N Inst Proceedings*, Sept. 1958, pp. 65–72; Adm R. Bernotti, 'Italian Naval Policy Under Fascism', *US N Inst Proceedings*, July 1956, pp. 722–31.

New battleships: *Littorio* (1940; severely damaged Taranto 12 Nov. 1940), *Vittorio Veneto* (1940), *Impero* (incomplete 1943), *Roma* (1942; s Ger rocket bombs 9 Sept. 1943): 41–46,000t, 9×15in, 12×6in, 4×4.7in, 12×3.5in, 30k. Modernised 1933–40: *Conte di Cavour* (1915; total loss, Taranto, 12 Nov. 1940), *Giulio Cesare* (1914; severely damaged Taranto 12 Nov. 1940), *Andrea Doria* (1916), *Caio Duilio* (1915): 26–29,000t, 10×12.6in, 12×4.7in (*Doria, Duilio*: 12×5.3in, 10×3.5in), 26–28k.

Benito Mussolini (1883–1945): former teacher, journalist, socialist & WWI soldier; formed Fascist party 1919; PM 1922; dictator 1925; dismissed by king July 1943; seized by Germans Sept. 1943; puppet ruler N. Italy; captd & shot by partisans April 1945.

1. From Pound

The Admiralty
24 July 1939

... We have asked Darlan (French CNS) to come and stay with us in *Enchantress* during the Inspection of the Reserve Fleet.[15]

I am afraid we did not consult you as much as I should have liked about your going to Istanbul, but it had to be rushed. ...

If we did have to send a Fleet to the Far East it would, if we had time, probably be two *Nelsons* and five *Royal Sovereigns*, the three *Warspites* coming home. In that case I am not sure that the best thing would not be for you and Charles Forbes to change Commands *and staffs*. The situation would be very difficult in the Far East with Percy oble senior to you. I am definitely against the Admiral on shore at Singapore being senior to the C-in-C, Main Fleet. What are your reactions to that[?][16]

I will let you know as soon as possible if the situation is such that you can carry on with dockings and refits.

Attached Notes

A. There have been many indications of preparedness in Germany for the period after 15 August, and these were suspected of being in connection with a Danzig coup.

---

[15]*Enchantress*: Ady yacht/sloop; 1934, 1085t, 2×4.7in, 18.75k.
[16]*Nelson, Rodney*: 1927, 33,950t, 9×16in, 12×6in, 6×4.7in, 2×24.5in tt, 23k.
Royal Sovereign, Royal Oak (s Oct. 1939, Scapa, *U-47*), *Ramillies, Revenge, Resolution*: 1916–17, 29,150t, 8×15in, 12×6in, 8×4in, 21k.
Queen Elizabeth, Valiant: 1915–16, 32,700t, 8×15in, 20×4.5in, 24k, mod 1930s; *Warspite*, 1915, 30,600t, 8×15in, 8×6in, 8×4in, 24k, fully mod 1930s; *Barham* (s *U-331*, E Med, 25 Nov. 1941), *Malaya*: 1915–16, 31,100t, 8×15in, 12×6in, 8×4in, 2×21in tt, 24k; partly mod.
Adm (later A of F) Sir Charles Forbes (1880–1960): ent RN 1894; gunnery splist; Cdr 1912; Flag Cdr, *Iron Duke* 1915; Dardanelles, Jutland; Grand F staff; Capt *Galatea* 1917, then *Queen Elizabeth, Iron Duke;* DNO 1925–28; RA 1928; RA(D), Med F 1930–31; VA, 3SL 1934; 1BS, Med F 1934; Adm 1936; C-in-C, Home F April 1938–Oct. 1940; A of F 1940; C-in-C Plymouth 1941–43.
Adm Sir Percy Noble (1880–1955): ent RN 1894; *Ribble* i/c 1907–08; signal splist; Cdr 1913; Grand F 1914–18; Capt 1918; *Calliope, Calcutta* 1919; *Barham*, 1922; *Ganges* (TS), *St Vincent* 1925–27; DOD 1928–29; RA 1929; DNEqpt 1931; 2CS, Home F 1932; VA & 4SL 1935; C-in-C China 1937–40; Adm 1939; C-in-C W Apps 1941; BAD Oct. 1942–June 1944; ret 1945.

G. My policy is to get everything done which it is possible to do before hostilities commence and it was for that reason *Ramillies* was ordered home as it removed the necessity of an escort for her.

I. The situation as regards Allied War Plans is not at all satisfactory....

... Personally, I do not think that you would at the present time get sufficient out of a meeting of the Allied Commanders of the three Services to make it worth while collecting them from the opposite ends of the Mediterranean.

J. *'Knocking out' Italy at the beginning of a war*

I do not know who gave the politicians the idea that it could be done but it seems that they expect it and they are now undergoing the rather painful process of being undeceived. Italy can only be 'knocked out' by her armies being defeated, or by Italy being laid waste by air. We can't do either of these things at the beginning of the war and it is left to the Navy to do the 'knocking out'. I can only imagine that they thought the Fleet would steam slowly along the Italian coast and blow it to bits, which, even if it were possible, would not 'knock Italy out'.

Whilst on the topic of the Fleet 'knocking out Italy' there is one aspect which must be borne in mind. If there were no 'Far East' question the loss of a battleship or two in the so-called 'knocking out' of Italy would not matter much, but it would matter a great deal if Japan was wobbling as to whether she would come in or not.

The material damage we can do Italy by bombardment is not great, but it will affect their morale to a certain extent. My own idea is that the extent to which it will be affected will depend on what damage they do to us in the process. If for the damage (unknown), and which they will tell the world is nil, they can cause us the loss of a battleship (which we shall not be able to hide), then their morale is much more likely to be increased than lowered. Another fallacious idea is that by conquering Libya, which in turn would very likely lead to their losing Italian East Africa, we should 'knock out' Italy.

To my mind cutting off their supplies, interfering with their communications, bombarding their ports, killing their submarines and later on the capture of Libya and some of the Dodecanese Islands are all part of 'throttling' them, not knocking them out. If they are as gutless as we imagine them, in time the throttling may kill them without their being given a knock out blow.

L. *Air reinforcements*

... At the moment you are asking for fighters at both Malta and in Egypt and no doubt the locals at both places are very glad that you are boosting their show. As you no doubt realise as ADGB still holds the floor, there is, as during your time at the Admiralty, little coming out of the bag for other purposes.

What would help me would be to have your private opinion as to which you would like first.

M. *Increased air defence of Alexandria and Malta*

I have got Government to promise that one English battalion at Alexandria shall not be taken away. . . . Personally, I am more alarmed at the absence of AA defences on the seaward side of the harbour than on the weakness of those on the land side. . . .

As in the case of air reinforcements I should like your views by private letter as to priority. . . .

What we can't guarantee here is that any additional AA defence gear sent to Egypt will be allotted to Alexandria. When I know that any is going I will let you know and then you can tackle GOC and AOC about them – the latter, from what Newall said, may try to get them for his aerodromes.[17]

O. *Submarines*

I thought you would like to get some minelayers on the Station. I could not give you these in addition to the 'River' Class as I must have an Atlantic Flotilla to hunt the German submarines.[18] . . .

P. *New Fleet Air aerodrome at Alexandria*

Very glad to hear this is taking shape.

Q. *Berthing of a Far Eastern Fleet in Eastern Mediterranean*

I wonder if you considered using the Bitter Lakes instead of Haifa and Port Said. Ships at the two latter places would, I think, be easier to locate from the air than if they were in the Bitter Lakes.

R *Reserve Fleet cruisers*

I forget which four you get but anyway they are of low endurance. If you have no particular use for them I would propose offering C-in-C, East Indies, one or two, as he considered necessary, for steaming into Massawa and blowing it to bits.[19] I look upon these ships as expendable in a good cause. . . .

---

[17]ACM (later M of the RAF) Sir Cyril Newall (1886–1963): R Warks & Gurkhas; pilot 1911; RFC 1914–18; W Cdr 1918; Cdt Sch Tec Trng 1922–25; Air Staff (ops & intel) 1926–31; AOC, ME 1931–34; Air Mem for Supply & Org; CAS 1937–40; Gov-Gen NZ 1941–6; baron 1946.

[18]'River' class (*Thames,* s Norway, July 1940; *Clyde; Severn*): 1932–35, 1,850/2,710, 1×4in, 6×21in tt, 22.5/10k.

M/L S/M: 1937, 1,520/2,117t, 1×4in, 6×21in tt, 50 mines, 15.75/8.75k. *Rorqual* & *Grampus* (s It escort, June 1940) served in Med.

[19]Principal Italian port and base in E. Africa.

2. To Pound

26 July 1939

... The French Squadron arrive tomorrow morning. I hope in the midst of the junketings necessary to an official visit, I may be able to have a few hours to confer with Ollive.[20] I suppose the French thought the official visit was the best excuse but I rather hoped he would arrive quietly by air.

I hope our visit to Istanbul will do some good. ... I have been invited to go to Ankara to meet Marshal Fevzi [Chakmak] and propose to go ... .[21]

I am in full agreement with what you say about the command of the Far Eastern Fleet. I am quite sure that the SO should be afloat and am quite willing to change with Charles Forbes. However, I suppose that it must be quite an outside chance our sending a fleet of that size out there, as it would mean denuding the Mediterranean, which, unless, Italy were out of the war, would be unthinkable in view of all our Eastern Mediterranean commitments.

Now to comment on your notes serriatim:

I. The situation as regards Allied War Plans never has been satisfactory and I had hoped that a definite War Plan might emerge from the Anglo-French conversations. I thought that things were shaping between the French and ourselves to go for the weak end of the Axis. I am not sure the fault does not, to some extent, lie with ourselves. Have we got a definite plan agreed to by the Cabinet and all three Services that we can urge on our Allies?

I will discuss the question of the meeting of Allied Commanders with Wavell and Mitchell when I get back to Egypt. There is no doubt the Air and the Army have had useful meetings with their French opposite numbers and I hope to have the same tomorrow, but there has been no combined inter-service exchange of views. I can see there would be difficulties as the French Army notoriously does not share its plans with the other two services.

J. I know you would wish me to say quite frankly that my views are at variance with some of those expressed therein.

---

[20]Adm E. L. H. Ollive (1882–1950): ent N 1899; torpedo splist; Lt de V 1911; N arty batty W Front; CO *Fauconneau* 1918; *Téméraire* 1919; Capt de F 1922, *Algérien* & 2nd D Sqdn 1924; Capt de V 1927; N War Coll 1932; RA 1933; Inspr-Gen Northern N Forces; Cdt 1st D Sqdn 1935; 3rd Lt Sqdn 1936; VA 1937; C-in-C Med Sqdn 1937; Préfet Maritime Toulon 1938; C-in-C Med F 1939; then S Atl & Africa; C-in-C & Préfet Maritime, 4th Region, Algeria July 1940–Oct. 1942; Adm Nov. 1940; i/c Med convoys to Fr; ret 1943.
[21]Marshal Fevzi Chakmak: Turkish CGS.

I think the phrase 'knock Italy out of the war' was coined by the Politicians themselves. They were never given to understand that Italy could be knocked out in a week or so.

What they were given to understand was that if Libya was completely cut off and the Italians were kept fighting it was most likely that Libya followed by Abyssinia would be out of the war in about six months. Further that the surrender of the Italian Army in Libya coupled with attacks on the Italian Coast in places where material damage can be done would certainly have a great moral effect and might well cause the Italians to lose heart and think they had had enough of it.

Whether this is correct or not must remain a matter of conjecture but I have always held this view.

But whether this view is correct or not it appears to me to be the *only* plan before us which shows any sign of producing a success for us and our Allies in the early stages. I have never heard of any alternative and the extra forces required to make the operations against Libyan communications a certain success are not great. A trifling percentage of the aircraft now being provided for ADGB would suffice; sufficient to ensure 100% reconnaissance in the Central Mediterranean and some fighters and more guns to give Malta a measure of security.

I am not clear regarding note J whether you hold the view that we should preserve the battleships from damage in case a battlefleet may be required to go to the Far East. . . . If my reading of it is correct it appears that all plans for the bombardment of the Libyan and Sicilian coasts must be dropped. The fourth paragraph seems to favour these bombardments but half-heartedly. I think a policy of holding back the battlefleet would be a mistaken one. Wherever they go in the Mediterranean they are within range of air attack and liable to damage.

I feel that in spite of the submarine danger they are safer at sea than lying in such a poorly defended harbour as Alexandria and that they should be used to the full in attacks on the enemy coasts with a view to causing material and moral damage, and further these attacks may result in forcing the enemy fleet to sea.

To hold them back because they may be required later in the Far East might . . . be most damaging to our men's morale and might cause the same sort of outcry in Great Britain as was seen in the last war about the Grand Fleet. . . .

Later

We have now concluded our conference with the French C-in-C and I think it has been most useful to both of us. He produced a series of operations against Genoa, Savona and other places in the Gulf of Genoa and also suggested one against Palermo. In fact the French have decided on an identical policy I had hoped was ours, and at the discussions today we were in complete agreement that if these attacks were concerted to take place even to within a day or two of one another, they would be bound to force dispersion (Air as well as Naval) on the Italians, let alone the effect on their morale.

We noted that these operations were signed by the French DCNS and so apparently are sanctioned by the French Admiralty. The C-in-C also stated he would look to operate in the Gulf of Genoa in the first 24 hours of the war. . . .

P.S. . . . You know that we have no local defence forces for Alexandria and Port Said and have to use fleet destroyers for this purpose. I believe there are four 'S' class destroyers shortly going to Singapore or Hong Kong to be laid up in reserve.[22] In case of war it would take 10 weeks to get crews to them. Would they not be better employed at Port Said where their crews could be sent out with the other detachments for the Mediterranean, perhaps before the war started?

3. *To Pound*

Warspite at sea
1 August 1939

L. *Air reinforcements*
. . . I think more fighters for Egypt and a fighter squadron for Malta are both urgent but I consider that for Malta should have priority, because there are none at all there and Malta has no means of taking the offensive in the air, either (a) by intercepting enemy bombers, or (b) by attacking aircraft in Sicily on the ground.

Malta is of immense value to us and everything possible should be done to minimise the damage which Italian bombers may do to it.

M. *Increased air defence of Alexandria and Malta*
. . . I understand from Dundas that the latest proposal is:

(a) to send four 3.7" guns (out of the second allocation of 24 for Malta due to arrive about January) to Alexandria very soon and man them with Marines from the MNBDO.

---

[22]'S' class: 1917–24, 905t, 1–2×4in, 31k.

(b) to take four 3.7″ now mounted at Gibraltar with their Army crews and send them to Alexandria.[23]

I am much in favour of (a) because

(i) the weaknesses at Alexandria are the lack of modern guns and the lack of British crews.
(ii) we get four 3.7″ for the defence of vital naval targets soon instead of in January. At the same time I expect we shall lose the 3″ they replace.
(iii) by January, or soon after, the remaining 20 of Malta's second 24 should be coming along.

(b) is rather open to the objection that there are already only eight 3.7″ guns at Gibraltar and to take away 50% of them is a serious matter. But I suppose the COS have better information about the scale of air attack to be expected at Gibraltar than we have.

O. The minelaying submarines will be most welcome and much more suitable for this station than the 'River' Class.

R. *Reserve Fleet cruisers*

... I think we shall need the four for trade protection ... some local defence destroyers would quite likely enable us to release two cruisers.

From my study of Massawa operations I don't think they would be any good for that. ... Can we afford the men? ...

It appears to be more of an air operation than naval, but perhaps we could co-operate.

... I don't think I can give Marshal Fevzi Chakmak much comfort except to tell him that we shall have command of the Eastern Mediterranean and that if he keeps the Italian Air Force at Leros quiet, we shall have command of the Aegean too. ...

... I have three good exercises on tap to take place during the second week in August. One representing an attack on Libyan trade. The Italians have just completed an exactly similar exercise with the simulated British Fleet working from Rhodes. ... it was interesting to see that the whole Taranto squadron was operating off Cyrenaica, covered I should say, by heavy air reinforcements in Sicily and Libya. I only hope if it comes to war they will pursue the same strategy!!

... the one thing I have particularly noticed is the improvement in the AA shooting. I had the AOC-in-C, Middle East, out the other

---

[23]Capt J. G. L. Dundas: Capt June 1935; PD Sept. 1939; *Nigeria* June 1940; Cdre 1st Cl & COS to C-in-C Levant 1942–43; RA Jan. 1944; *President* 1945.

day and he was much impressed, especially with the actual guns' crews, who he said would break up any formation.[24]

4. *To Pound*

Warspite
5 August 1939

... Our reception [in Turkey] has been, as expected, most cordial ...
... I gave him [President Ismet] a short exposition on sea power in the Eastern Mediterranean and I hope he benefited by it.[25] ... I pointed out to him that it would be necessary to neutralise the Italian Air Force in the Dodecanese ...

I impressed on him the great importance of stopping all Italian supplies in neutral as well as Italian ships at the Bosphorus and the necessity for a Contraband Control organisation. He had heard about this and intimated that British naval advisers to help the Turks to get this organisation ready would be welcomed. I suggested a naval officer should be sent out forthwith to get this going in conjunction with Nicholls of the Foreign Office who is here now.[26]

The Marshal raised the importance to them of cutting the Italian line of communication to Albania and stated that if this were done, it might prevent an Italian advance into Greece. I pointed out that the passage from Italy to Albania was very short and well protected, that I hoped to carry out raids from time to time but of course could not guarantee to interfere seriously with these supplies. ...

To me, it seems desirable to hold further staff talks with the Turks, especially on naval matters. My opinion is that SOs would have to go, accompanied by junior staff officers and that the senior officers should get the Marshal to authorise his staff to deal quite openly with our staff officers without referring anything to him until general agreement is reached. ...

I think, also, a mixed French-British Mission party would be best. It would be most beneficial if any Admiral that went could speak French and German. The only one I know who can do this is Gerald Dickens.[27]...

[24] ACM Mitchell.
[25] Ismet Inönü: Pres of Turkey from 1938.
[26] Lt-Cdr O. E. Nicholls (ret): Asst NA, Ankara Dec. 1938.
[27] Adm Sir Gerald Dickens (1879–1962): ent RN 1894; Lt 1902; Cdr 1914; Dardanelles; ID; Capt 1919; DDPD 1920–22; *Carlisle* 1922–24; IDC 1926–29; *Repulse* 1929–31; RA 1932; DNI 1932–35; Res F 1935–37; VA 1936; ret 1938; NA The Hague 1940; SNLO, Allied Navies 1940; FO Tunisia 1943; FO Netherlands 1945.

5. *From Pound*

18 August 1939

As Regards Sending a Fleet to the Far East

I agree that this is unlikely whilst we have all our Eastern Mediterranean commitments, and as long as war in the West is more likely than in the East. There is always the possibility, however, that the situation may develop more quickly in the East than in the West.

There is the posibility also that we may send a weaker force of two battleships, etc., in which case Layton with *Barham* and *Malaya* would probably go, as I am sure you will agree that as long as we maintain a Fleet in the Eastern Mediterranean you should remain there. They would be relieved by *Ramillies* and *Royal Oak*.[28]

I am glad that you agree about changing round with Charles Forbes under certain conditions.

Increased AA Defences for Malta and Alexandria

You will, I know, be pleased at the scale which has been approved for Malta. The short term policy we are working on is that the operational base for the Fleet must have precedence as buildings can more easily be replaced than ships. Hence Gibraltar and Malta being *temporarily* robbed for the benefit of Alexandria. At the same time, as a long term policy we must get the Fleet back to Malta (as its operational base) as soon as possible; unless we do this, the situation will be an impossible one when the Italians have six capital ships, if the French have to provide a corresponding force at one end of the Mediterranean and we at the other. The next step, therefore, will be to get a priority laid down for the AA defences of Malta in relation to ADGB so that we shall have the AA defences complete by a given date. At the CID meeting at which we got the increased AA defences of Malta approved, I was asked whether, if Malta had the increased scale of defences (112 guns, etc.) I would be prepared to leave the Fleet there. My answer was 'Not at the present time, but I believe that the defence against air attack is progressing so rapidly that it will be possible before very long'. I should be interested to know whether you are in agreement with this policy and view. . . .

---

[28] VA Sir Geoffrey Layton.

[At the King's inspection of the Reserve Fleet] Darlan was charming and thoroughly enjoyed himself. His being asked over was much appreciated by the French Navy....

J. *Bombardments, etc.*

The interpretation you put on this was not altogether what I meant to express. I am not in favour of holding back the battlefleet altogether. I have always been in favour of a bombardment of Tobruk and other Libyan ports because it will try out the air menace, but I am of the opinion that the question of whether ports in Sicily and on the mainland of Italy should be tackled should depend on our experience on the Libyan Coast. The moral effect depends on relative damage. The damage caused by a bombardment and air attack of Augusta would not, I believe, be great, and would be given out to the world as nil. If, in the process, our Fleet were severely mauled (which it would not be possible to hide), then I believe it would raise the morale of the Italians ... When we attack Italy itself (in which I include Sicily), then I think there is a great deal to be said for making an attack by air on the Italian Fleet at Taranto. One reason for this is that I do not believe the *Glorious* will be able to remain in a serviceable condition in the Mediterranean for very long, what with air and submarine attack, and it might be a good thing to get the most one can out of her before she is placed *hors de combat*.[29]

I do hope you will not hesitate to remark quite frankly on anything I write – the more we discuss things the better and the easier for me to make any necessary decisions when the time comes.

6. *From Pound*

24 October 1939

I am very sorry to have had to skin the Mediterranean of destroyers to the extent that I have, but I am sure you will realise how hard put we are.

There has been some misunderstanding as regards the Australian destroyers, as Mr Bruce distinctly gave me to understand that they could go to the Mediterranean, but afterwards they said they did not want them to go further than Singapore. However, we are now

---

[29]*Glorious*: 1916/1930, 22,500t, 16×4.7in, 48 a/c, 30k; s Ger B/cs, off Norway June 1940.

offering them two 'C' or 'D' Class cruisers in lieu of the five destroyers, so I hope to be able to send them on to you.[30] ...

At the moment we are considering what help we could give to the Turks if they are threatened by the Russians, should the latter endeavour to browbeat the former. However, personally I do not think this is very likely.

I think events have proved that I was correct in thinking that it was necessary to try out the air menace on the African coast before getting involved with the main Italian metropolitan force! ...

I was really glad of the excuse to get the *Glorious* out of the Mediterranean, as I don't think her efficient life will be a very long one.

7. To Pound

Malta
31 October 1939

... Losing the *Warspite* is a blow but not unexpected. The real blow is having to go ashore at Malta when there is still a substantial fleet out here.

I feel it would have been better to have moved ashore at Alexandria. ... There is so much going on with regard to Middle Eastern affairs – I was constantly conferring with the GOC-in-C and the AOC-in-C. I fear I shall be rather remote at Malta. ...

It seems to be the general opinion out here, and the Turks also hold it, that the Germans and/or the Russians will come through the Balkans in the Spring.

I hope if anything of that sort happens you will let me get to sea again ...

I think the soldiers are liable to get a little dangerous over the Balkan and kindred questions if left to themselves. They have grandiose ideas of landing four or five divisions at Salonika or in Thrace but do not seem to have given much thought to how they are to get there or be maintained when there.

I have warned the GOC-in-C, Middle East, that before any plans can be considered, he must be quite certain that there is

---

[30] 'C' class: 1917–22, 4,120t, 5×6in, 2×3in, 8×21in tt, 29k.
'D' class: 1918–22, 4,850t, 5–6×6in, 3×4in, 12×21in tt, 29k.
Australian destroyers: *Stuart*: 1918, 1, 530t, 4×4.7in, 3×21in tt, 31k. *Vendetta, Waterhen, Vampire, Voyager*: 1918–20, 1,120t, 3×4in, 3×21in tt, 31k.
Stanley M. Bruce: (1883–1967), Australian PM, 1923–29; H Cmnr, London 1932–45; 1st Visct Bruce of Melbourne.

in existence sufficient Allied shipping to keep any force landed supplied. . . .

Weygand is, I think, rather a menace and seems to be determined to have a campaign in the Balkans.[31]

I feel we are not getting sufficient information of a technical nature out here. As an instance, although by questioning late arrivals from home we have ascertained that it appears certain that the Germans are using a magnetic torpedo pistol, we have had no information on the subject. There are many other matters on which we should like information and if someone at the Admiralty could be gingered up to give it to us it would be most helpful.

. . . We are all feeling a little flat out here through being so much out of things. . . .

8. *To Pound*

18 December 1939

. . . I am not surprised at what you say about the Air Force working over the sea. They have never taken navigation seriously and it is a great disappointment. . . .

I hope your view about battleships and aircraft is unduly pessimistic. As far as I know not a single hit has been made on a moving target and surely our battleships have been constructed and reconstructed to stand up to a bomb hit or two. . . .

The answer is a considerable improvement in the quality and quantity of the ships' AA fire.

. . . I am not at all sure that Generals Weygand and Wavell see entirely eye to eye over the Middle Eastern question nor, it would appear, are the Governments in entire accord. General Weygand is a convinced 'Middle Easterner' with an eye on a front in Salonika, or at least in Thrace; . . . He fears a move by Germany to the Balkans at any time and certainly in early spring . . . General Wavell, I gather, is rather lukewarm on some of these projects and has an eye on Russian movements towards Iran and India. . . . I have a feeling that the transport and naval aspect is apt to be taken rather lightly by General Weygand. . . . The Turks, however, have raised it

---

[31]Salonika was a great drain on shipping in WW1.

Gen Maxime Weygand (1867–1965): COS to Foch WW1; cmd Polish Army agst USSR 1920; ret pre-war; C-in-C Levant 1939; SAC 20 May 1940; Vichy Defence M June 1940; Deleg Gen, N Africa Sept. 1940–Nov. 1941; pris in Ger 1942–45; supported Pétain but foe of Germans.

very pertinently by demanding that the fact that they wished for a guarantee of control in the Mediterranean in all eventualities should be included in the memorandum in General Weygand's discussions. . . .

. . . French eyes turn more and more to the Middle East where will be concentrated large bodies of troops perhaps preponderantly French and they hope, under French command. It is only a step from this to the desire for French troops and escorts and doubtless bigger ships to move freely between the Western Mediterranean and Beirut. This, of course, they can already do, but it is being carried out increasingly without reference to us. . . . *Tourville* and *Colbert* have moved into the Eastern Mediterranean on a rather slender excuse of contraband control and showing the flag in Syria. *D'Iberville* has emerged from Beirut to carry out contraband control.[32] Finally, it has to be realised that French forces in the Mediterranean are considerably larger than ours. It may thus be found that we may be presented with a situation where the French say they have a preponderance of troops in the Middle East and a preponderance of naval forces and should they not therefore control the whole Station? It may be difficult to refute such an argument.

. . . The Turkish staff expected Baker-Cresswell to arrive in Ankara with full details of the C-in-C's plans in the Aegean and Black Sea . . . and also what force we were prepared to send there.[33]

Of course, until we know what the Government policy is with regard to Russian intervention in the Middle East, it is quite impossible to go any further with the Turks. . . .

Sir Percy Loraine spent last week end with me and was most interesting about Italy.[34] . . .

Later

I saw Wavell this morning on his way back to Egypt. He was not very informative but I gather that the War cabinet have not yet come to any decision on Balkan and Middle Eastern questions.

---

[32]*Tourville*: 1928, 10,000t, 8×8in, 8×3in, 33k.
Colbert: 1930, 10,000t, 8×8in, 8×3in, 6×21.7in tt, 31k.
D'Iberville: 1931, 1,969t, 3×5.5in, 15.5k.
[33]Cdr A. J. Baker-Cresswell: Cdr 1937; *Warspite* 1939; Asst NA, Ankara 1940; *Bulldog*, W Apps, Feb. 1941; NID 1941; Capt Dec. 1941; *Philante* (ASW Trng) 1943; Capt ASW, EF 1943; *Caradoc* April 1944, Capt Escorts, E Indies F; *Gorleston* 1945.
[34]Sir Percy Loraine, bt (1880–1961): Imp Yeo, Boer W; FO; Istanbul 1904; ME, China, S & W Eur; P Conf deleg 1918–19; Chargé, Warsaw 1919; Envoy, Tehran 1921; Athens 1926; HCmnr, Egypt & Sudan 1929; Amb, Turkey 1933; Amb Italy, May 1939; Chm, HO Advisory Cttee (Italy), Aug. 1940.

I hope something definite will be forthcoming soon as we have not too much time left for preparation if a move is to be expected in the Spring.

Although Malta is at the moment undoubtedly the best place for me to run the Station from, I feel that in the near future, when the decisions I have indicated above have been made, it will be necessary for me to pay fairly frequent visits to Egypt to consult with the heads of the other Services.

You know better than I do how difficult it would be to run the Station from Malta if the COS and I were absent for a few days in Egypt. It would therefore be most convenient if presently I could be spared a ship in which I could embark with my operational staff to go occasionally to Alexandria. There is also the question that the situation may suddenly deteriorate and we may be forced to move lock, stock and barrel to Alexandria in a hurry....

9. *To Pound*

30 December 1939

Now that the last of the 'D' class have left or are about to leave the Mediterranean Destroyer command, the position of the VA Destroyers has become very difficult. There is really nothing left for him to do and Tovey feels this very keenly.[35] ...

Of course, if the war should spread to the Mediterranean and it becomes necessary to send forces out here again Tovey would be invaluable and, if there is no way in which his unrivalled destroyer North Sea experience can be utilised at home, I should like to keep him here with that end in view....

I do not like these two AMCs, *Ranpura* and *Antenor*, which have just been allotted to us for Contraband Control duties. They are much too big for the job and unnecessarily expensive for it.[36] ...

---

[35]VA Sir John Tovey, then VALF & 2nd-in-C.
'D' class: 1933, 1,375t, 4×4.7in, 8×21in tt, 35.5k; Ldr: *Duncan* 1,400t.
[36]*Ranpura*: 1925, 16,688gt, 17k, P&O; later destroyer depot ship.
Antenor: 1925, 11,174gt, 16k, China Mutual SN.

10. *From Pound*

1 January 1940

... I should be very glad if you would send me your views as to which of the officers on the Vice Admirals' and Rear Admirals' lists will make the best fighting commanders of the future.

11. *From Pound*

7 January 1940

I do appreciate so much the way in which you have accepted one withdrawal after another from your Station. We have not, however, sufficient ships to go round and the only thing to do is to concentrate on the danger spots at the moment. ...

I will let you know as soon as I can about the Near East. I am sure you will realise that we have to move very cautiously in that area or we shall rub the Italians up the wrong way. ...

I note what you say about Tovey and am only keeping him where he is because I can't see where else to place him at the moment. ...

12. *To Air Chief Marshal Sir William Mitchell*

9 January 1940

Willis goes to Cairo tomorrow and I hope will be able to see you.

I was sorry you were unable to agree to our suggestion with regard to the training of bombing squadrons over the sea. ...

If we have to fight in Greece, Thrace or Anatolia or even if we only have to convoy troops to these places air reconnaissance, and maybe air attacks, may be necessary over the sea, and I don't suppose it would be practical politics to delay the movements until coastal reconnaissance and sea trained squadrons arrived from England. ...

If, as appears by no means unlikely, we have to fight in the Black Sea, extensive air operations over the sea will be essential.

I don't know if your information tallies with mine (mine comes from the highest authority) that though our reconnaissance in the North Sea finds the enemy all right they have not so far been able to bring the bombing squadrons on to the target due, I am told, to the faulty navigation of the latter. Of course it's an art and only acquired by practice and experience.

Perhaps you would like to discuss these points with Willis but I may say right away that I quite see the force of the views expressed in your letter.

13. *From Mitchell*

HQ, RAF, Middle East
Cairo
17 January 1940

... As regards training bomber squadrons over the sea, I am afraid the position is still the same as when my last letter was written. Moreover, if we have to go campaigning in Turkey, as now visualised, the number of squadrons at my disposal is entirely inadequate to carry out commitments over the land, i.e., the neutralisation of hostile air forces, plus the close co-operation with the Army.

If the war develops in the Balkans and Italy definitely keeps out, then I think it will be possible to bring up the GR squadron from Aden, since with Italy out of it, the major threat to Aden is removed. At the moment, however, I am afraid there is nothing I can do. The plain fact is, of course, that the air forces at my disposal in the Middle East are totally inadequate to carry out the various tasks they may be called upon to perform.

I think this is recognised at home, but up to the present, I have not received any indication that I am likely to receive any increases in the near future.

All I can say is that I am only too anxious to co-operate in every way that I can, and I will do all I possibly can when the time comes.

14. *From Captain B. A. Warburton-Lee*

HMS *Hardy*
Gibraltar
22 January 1940

I am sailing for home today with *Hostile, Hero* and *Hasty* following a week behind, so I hope to have seven of 2nd Destroyer Flotilla together shortly – what our fate is to be then I don't know but I suppose I may find myself in an office or alternatively on the dole.[37]

---

[37]'H' class: 1936, 1,340t, 4×4.7in, 8×21in tt, 36k; Ldr: *Hardy* 1,456t.
Capt B. A. Warburton-Lee: Capt 1936; Capt(D), 2DF, July 1939; led 2DF in 1st battle of Narvik, April 1940, & killed; post. VC.

I have hopes of Home Fleet and wonder whether the loss of *Grenville* may affect our destination.[38]

We have had a good run round the South Atlantic and 'also ran' after the *Von Spee*, but we never got further than Rio. Luckily we have been at sea nearly all our time, which was much preferable to Freetown.[39]

Our ships are wearing very well on the whole, and men at the top of their form at the prospect of England – I wonder whether they will like it so well when they get there.

I have just seen *Stuart*, who tells me things are very quiet in your command, but that you are confident there will be plenty of war for everyone out here before long![40] May the 2nd Destroyer Flotilla come back to you in time for the Black Sea, please.

15. *To Pound*

HMS *Birmingham*
en route to Malta
[from Alexandria]
11 February 1940

B. Admiral Esteva descended on us literally out of the clouds without warning.[41] ... The impression one gets is that the French, realising suddenly that problems affecting the maritime control in the Eastern Mediterranean would arise, dispatched Esteva to make it clear that their interest and share in arrangements to be made was a large one. ...

16. *To Pound*

Malta
2 March 1940

... These constant changes of programme [meetings with the French and the Turks] make the visits to Egypt difficult to arrange.

---

[38]*Grenville*: Ldr; 1936, 1,485t, 5×4.7in, 8×21in tt, 36k; mined, N Sea 19 Jan. 1940.

[39]*Admiral Graf von Spee*: German pkt b/s; 1934, *c.*12,000t, 6×11in, 8×5.9in, 6×4.1in, 8×21in tt, 26k; foll dmg in battle of R Plate, 17 Dec. 1939, scuttled 21 Dec.

[40]*Birmingham*: 1937, 9,100t, 12×6in, 8×4in, 6×21in tt, 32k.

[41]Adm J.-P. Esteva (1880–1951): Adm Sud; Vichy Res Gen, Tunisia; captd by Germans before he could aid Allied invasion but imprisoned after war for failure to prevent German seizure of colony.

One is usually wanting to be in Malta and Egypt at the same time and with one's staff divided between Malta, Egypt and Turkey (and Roumania at times) running the Station becomes rather a problem, especially as the communications are most inadequate and unreliable.

17. *To Pound*

26 March 1940

... The over-ruling ideas in the Turkish mind are:

First, that they wish to remain neutral if it is possible to do so.
Secondly, that they do not mean, under any circumstances, to be taken charge of or told what they have got to do.

They are supremely ignorant of naval affairs and in fact of modern warfare in general. ... it is suggested that there should be a Senior British Naval Officer attached to the Turkish General Staff who should be the link between it and the C-in-C. He would have to be conversant with all the plans, both naval and land, and have to be in a position to put the naval considerations plainly before the Marshal. But above all the British C-in-C must be the final authority as to naval operations. I feel there would be no difficulty in working with the Turkish Navy on a basis of co-operation under separate Cs-in-C. The French do not seem to be taking any naval interest in this question.

... Gerald Dickens is the man for the job ...

I think Willis handled his share of the conference [at Aleppo] most ably ...

Notes on Future Action in the Near East

3. The effective way to strike at Germany is through the Black Sea. If we have unrestricted access we can:

(i) If Germany attacks Roumania, implement our guarantee to her which is not in fact possible while the Straits are closed to us.
(ii) Control the Black Sea and thus the entry of supplies to Germany via the Danube or Bulgaria.
(iii) Be in a position to act against Roumanian oil supplies to Germany.
(iv) Protect Turkey.
(v) Cut off Russian supplies ex-Caucasia to Germany.

4. *Object.* The whole Allied policy should therefore be directed to obtaining free passage into the Black Sea for our warships *now*.
5. *Method.* This problem can be simplified by making use of the Southern interior of Turkey and Russia.

18. *From Admiral Esteva*

Commandant en Chef
de Force Maritimes
du Sud, Toulon
29 March 1940

... I see that you have a very busy life and that you are often at sea.

It is rather difficult to get an agreement with the Turks because they are very proud and are always fearing lest we try to dominate them. At the same time we must remember that in the Turkish Army there are still officers who remain pro-German and that Turkey generally speaking is friendly towards Russia. Nevertheless their interest is tied to ours.

The great trouble for the time being is the great shortage of small craft in the Mediterranean. I do not know what was decided by the Supreme Allied Council at London. I think that for the Balkans and the Black Sea, Asia Minor the policies are still: 'Wait and see!' But we must be prepared for the moment when an action is ordered to us.

I am to examine how French aircraft shall be able to cover convoys in the area you indicate to me. I am to arrange too the matter about the silhouettes....

19. *From Pound*

30 March 1940

... The struggle against the U-boats and mines and aircraft continues but I feel we are gradually getting the upper hand of them....

I do not know what Mussolini is up to but as we cannot afford to be caught napping, I am, as you know, gradually concentrating all the slow moving craft and some submarines from China in the Mediterranean so that if things look nasty all we shall have to do is to rush out the fighting fleet. It will be a very severe drain on the forces we require at home but if we have to send a fleet to the

Eastern Mediterranean there is no alternative. I am very glad to be able to send you back the *Warspite* even though it is on the conditions given in the telegram. . . .

By the time you get this there will be several changes in the Cabinet but I am glad to say it will not affect the Admiralty as I find Winston admirable to work with. . . .

What would I not give for another 100 destroyers.

20. To Pound

Malta
17 April 1940

B. I am sorry I was not able to agree about Sir Howard Kelly.[42] I do not think he would be the man to deal with the Turks where great patience and tact will be required. I must say I still hanker after Dickens. I suppose James Somerville is not available. I understand he has some job at home besides the broadcasting.
C. . . . The officers and men of these Australian destroyers out here are magnificent material and are quite wasted in these old ships. Tovey has suggested that they might be transferred lock, stock and barrel to five new ships and used at home. They certainly are the most lively and undefeated fellows I have ever had to do with.

21. From Pound

29 April 1940

I am sorry to have had to impose someone on you for the Turkish job whom you do not like, but opinion, except your own, is that he is ideal for the job, and I am quite certain that you will not have any trouble with him.

We are doing our best to scratch up a fleet for you in the Eastern Mediterranean, but it is not easy. The destroyers are, of course, the difficulty, and we cannot afford to send you any more until it is quite certain that it is necessary. . . .

Looking at all the various indications I do not think it is likely that Italy will declare war on us at the present time, though she may take

---

[42]Adm Sir W. A. Howard Kelly (1873–1952): Lt 1894; Somaliland 1902–04; Capt 1911; NA Paris; Capt *Gloucester* 1914; Cdre, LCS 1917; Cdre Adriatic 1918; N Mission Greece 1919–21; RA 1922; 1BS 1923; 2CS 1925; VA 1927; 1BS 1927–29; 2i/c MF 1929–30; Adm 1931 & C-in-C China; ret 1936; SBNLO, Turkey 1940–44.

the opportunity of staking out a claim in Yugoslavia. The question would then arise (and it is now under consideration) of what action we should take.

I do hope your additional AA guns for Alexandria will arrive in time.

Warspite is being sent to Gibraltar, but the question of whether she can get through to the Eastern Mediterranean depends on the situation.

We are hustling up *Ramillies* and taking her away from her convoy so that she can reach you earlier.

I know you will be glad to be getting a fleet of some kind again, even if it is rather a second-rate one as regards the age of the ships.

22. *To Pound*

Malta
2 May 1940

A. I'll say no more about Howard Kelly and, of course, will do my best to see that things go right but I can't say I am optimistic about him dealing with the Turks.

B. I am just back from Bizerta where I had a long and discursive talk with Esteva.

I don't think the French at the moment are very frightened of the Italians going to war, they certainly are not taking it very seriously....

D. The French have certain very definite ideas on the operations they mean to conduct should Italy enter the war against us.

Firstly, they mean to have their two battle cruisers, some small cruisers and some destroyers working from Mers-el-Kébir.[43]

Secondly, they will have a force of four 8in cruisers and some destroyers based on Toulon and keeping things lively in the Gulf of Genoa.

Rather unfortunately as I think they have given up the idea of a small force working from Bizerta to raid the Libyan communications.

E. Esteva's chief proposal was that the seven French submarines at Beirut should form one group with the British submarines at Alexandria and come under a British commander[?], similarly that the six British at Malta form one group with the French at Bizerta and come under their command, a dividing line

---

[43]*Dunkerque, Strasbourg.*

between operating zones being drawn roughly due south of Cape Matapan.

I consent to this in principle but it will require Admiralty concurrence. . . .

The destroyers situation seems pretty desperate. I see by the Pink List that no destroyers proper are being completed in 1940, only the little ones.[44]

The result of the craze for bigger and heavier armed destroyers which has been, in my opinion, such a mistake. Is it quite impossible to buy some as they stand from the USA?[45]

Again are those five 'S' class working from Hong Kong and Singapore pulling their weight? I should have thought it would have been well worth while having them with AS at Malta and employing them nearer home, not necessarily in the Mediterranean.

G. I hope to get away from Malta on Friday or Saturday. The office must go in *Resource* and will be out of action for about four days, then I trust to get the best part of it into *Malaya*.[46]

I trust that the sailing of the *Warspite* for Alexandria will not be left dependent on the three French battleships returning to the Western basin . . . but that she will be sent to Alexandria as soon as possible, so as to simplify the accommodation of the C-in-C's Staff and office which at the moment is very difficult.

23. *To Admiral Darlan*

7 May 1940

I was sorry to hear last night that some misunderstanding had arisen over the movements of *Warspite*. As you will recall *Warspite* was due to sail for the Mediterranean just before the occupation of Norway occurred. On arrival she was to report to her previous duty of Fleet flagship of the Mediterranean Fleet, for which she is specially equipped.

5. . . . it was decided to release *Malaya* and *Royal Sovereign* to proceed to Gibraltar. Further as soon as *Warspite* could be spared from Narvik where she had carried out the bombardment on 13 April and was still in that area, it was decided to order her to proceed to her original war station.[47]

---

[44]Pink List: Admy circular showing disposition of ships; 'little ones' are 'Hunts'.
[45]50 WW1 destroyers acquired from USA by 'Destroyers-for-Bases' deal of Sept. 1940.
[46]*Resource*: fleet repair ship; 1929, 12,300t, 4×4in, 15k.
[47]*Warspite* and 'Tribals' fought 2nd battle of Narvik, under VA Sir Jock Whitworth.

6. It was hoped that all three ships ... would be able to assemble at Gibraltar and proceed through the Mediterranean together. Unfortunately *Warspite* was delayed. The Italian situation having developed more unfavourably, a decision was therefore reached to send *Malaya* and *Royal Sovereign* through as soon as possible.

7. You were good enough to arrange for your three battleships to proceed in company with *Malaya* and *Royal Sovereign* with the intention that, if the situation did not appear critical, they should be detached at Bizerta to make good minor defects.

8. On 30 April, although the situation was unclear, the value of a strong force arriving at Alexandria was considered from a political point of view, to be of great importance. We were most grateful for the provision [?permission] which, in your answer to our request you then granted to your three battleships to continue their passage. The result of the arrival of five battleships at Alexandria has undoubtedly had a very beneficial effect on the Mediterranean situation as a whole.

9. At the time when the decision was taken to permit your three battleships to continue their passage to Alexandria without calling at Bizerta, it was agreed that *Warspite*, who was about to leave Home Waters, should remain temporarily at Gibraltar.

10. On 3 May as the situation *vis-à-vis* Italy was steady and no immediate change was anticipated, it was decided that the moment was opportune to pass *Warspite* through to Alexandria without delay.

11. This decision was communicated to Admiral Odend'hal to whom it was explained that on the arrival of *Warspite* at Alexandria you would probably desire to reconsider the future disposition of your battleships to meet your own wishes.[48] We felt that having persuaded you at much inconvenience to send your battleships beyond Bizerta, we should facilitate any further movements which you should desire as much as possible.

12. I feel I should have sought your concurrence before ordering *Warspite* beyond Gibraltar, and I regret that this was not done. However, the time was short and the moment opportune, apart from the fact that the escort destroyers had to receive the orders at once if they were to be available when required.

13. I most sincerely hope that after the most loyal and effective co-operation which you have arranged, you will appreciate that we had no intention of departing from the previous arrangement, and were acting for what we considered would be best for our mutual advantage.

---

[48] Adm Odend'hal: French NLO, London, 1939–40.

14. We shall be only too happy, should you decide to retain your battleships in the Eastern Mediterranean for the present, to put at your disposal all the facilities we have at Alexandria, such as they are. I very much hope that my suggestion as regards tactical exercises between our two battleships to test the new Tactical Code will meet with your approval.
15. In conclusion, I am quite sure that the close touch which has now been established between our Naval forces will lead to the most effective and cordial co-operation in the future.

24. *From Pound*

20 May 1940

... It looks as if your destroyers, sloops and AA cruiser might get through to you all right. I was very much afraid at one time that we had left it too late, but there was so much going on here that it was very difficult to send destroyers away from home waters until it seemed absolutely essential. However, there seems to be a general idea that Mussolini is not going to show his hand for another week. There is also the programme of the *Miraglia* which, if adhered to, means that she will be in the Canal on 25 May and will not arrive at Massawa until 27 May.[49]

I am afraid that you are terribly short of 'air' but there again I do not see what can be done because, as you will realise, every available aircraft is wanted in home waters. The one lesson we have learnt here is that it is essential to have fighter protection over the Fleet whenever they are within reach of the enemy bombers. You will be without such protection, which is a very serious matter, but I do not see any possible way of rectifying it.

I am glad to see that you have got rid of two French battleships. I can't understand why they did not send all three back again. I am sure you would find them more of a liability than an asset.

... I have sent out to you all the information I can about AA fire, and hope it may be of some value.

I do hope you have managed to hold on to the whole of the 24 HA guns we have just sent out, and that Cairo has not managed to pinch any.

... I would never have agreed to your being placed under French command because they have the wildest ideas in many respects and of imagining they are in the last war and not in this.

---

[49]*Giuseppe Miraglia*: seaplane carrier; 1923, 4,880t, 4×4in, 21k.

P.S. I have not envied you during the last eight months but I do now.

25. *From Vice Admiral Sir Geoffrey Blake*

The Admiralty
21 May 1940

... We know and feel how short you are of all we should like to give you. If we could clear out of Narvik it would be better, but even then it looks as if every destroyer will be required here to defend our shores....

I have been trying to get good contacts and relationship with Darlan and his staff, who seem inclined to play all right, but the politicians jump on to him now and then....

We have rather encouraged the Cretan project as it is limited in its scope. The marvellous French expedition all over the Aegean and up to Salonika might have been all right on paper but with no base equipment, particularly AA guns and fighters they were just hopeless. The Air is the devil in Combined Operations and Renouf will tell you all about it.[50]

I am sorry that you have not more base AA defence at Alexandria as it is not at all nice having to rely on AA guns [on warships]....

26. *To Pound*

Warspite
29 May 1940

I am afraid you are having an anxious time and I must be careful not to add any of mine to your load.

A. We are now all collected at Alexandria with the exception of *Liverpool*.[51] ...

The battleships are not in too good a condition. *Ramillies* is in the floating dock for about a fortnight I fear, to have the stem brushes relined. She also has a 15-in gun to check. I hope to have the spare at Port Said in two or three days, where the only lifting appliances are

---

[50]RA E. de F. Renouf: Capt 1928; *Sheffield* 1938; RA Jan. 1940; 3CS, Med F, *Gloucester* July 1940; spl & misc service, Admy May 1941; NSO, C-in-C, Home Forces March 1942; VA, ret & duty with ACNS (W) Apr. 1942; NA to DFSL 1945.

[51]*Liverpool*: 1938, 9,400t, 12×6in, 8×4in, 6×21in tt, 32k.

outside Malta. *Malaya*'s steering gear is on the point of collapse and when the big casting being made at Malta arrives she will have to go out of action for 10 days or so. *Warspite* is in good order but badly wants docking, and to put her in this dock means disembarking all the 15-in ammunition. However I feel we shall surmount all these difficulties if only Mussolini will give us a fortnight or so more time.

Mussolini is currently keeping us guessing, but he seems to be methodically preparing for war. I am a trifle anxious about Malta. A seaborne attack I don't worry about especially now *Terror*, moored in the shallow water in Lazaretto Creek, is incorporated in the defences, but I don't know how Malta would react to aerial bombardment coupled with parachute troops and other aerial visitors.[52]
B. The Crete operation is all organised. We can land a machine gun battalion (British) in about 20 hours. The French propose landing about 1,500 men at Suda and another 1,500 at Milo, but can't get there in under 60 hours, hence the British battalion landing first.

I do hope the Governments will make up their minds quickly and give the word 'go' at once as while we are waiting we can't do much else.

... The four French cruisers have gone to Beirut to be ready. Their lack of endurance is past belief, somewhere in the neighbourhood of 2,000 miles at 20 knots. ...

27. *From Pound*

6 June 1940

C. We are doing all we can to get some Hurricanes sent out for Alexandria, but have just heard from the Air Ministry that there are 50 tons of stores which must go out for them, whereas a fortnight ago we were told that they had everything necessary at Alexandria.
D. I do not think there is any chance of getting any Fighters out to Malta as the United Kingdom has got nothing like its appropriate quota.
F. You will be surprised, I think, to receive the telegram I sent to you, it having been suggested that the policy you outlined was defensive. I told the Prime Minister he need have no fears that you would act on the defensive, but he insisted that some telegrams should be sent to all Cs-in-C. I hope you find my telegram inoffensive [not reproduced].

[52]*Terror*: 1916, 7,200t, 2×15in, 12k; s a/c off Derna Feb. 1941.

G. It might be possible to send you the *Illustrious* later on if you feel she would *really* be of use to you. You might send me a personal telegram letting me know your views. As you will realise we can make full use of her at home.

H. We have just finished evacuation of the Allied forces from Dunkirk. The destroyers and small craft did splendidly, but it was a most trying ordeal for them and we can ill afford the eight destroyers we have lost in the process. However, it just had to be done. Geoffrey [Blake] showed me your letter. I certainly never imagined that you were going to remain in harbour at Alex.

I. There are so many things we should like to have kitted you up with before the crash comes – more destroyers, more submarines, more minesweepers, destroyer depot ship, and in particular more fighter aircraft, and if the situation changes at all [and] we can spare more from home, you may be sure they will be sent to you.

28. *To Pound*

9 June 1940

A. I must confess that I was rather taken aback by your signal about the defensive object, I hope my intention signal has cleared up all doubts. I feel that the only way in which we can hope to make the Italians think a bit, and perhaps catch them on the wrong foot, is to move a strong formation of the Fleet into the Central Mediterranean in the hours immediately preceding the outbreak of war, they may wonder what we are up to, and so delay their contemplated moves, if any.

D. I am sorry we did not keep you better informed about the Canal. Dealing with these Italian ships full of cement or munitions is tricky, and the SBNO, Suez Canal Area, has no real powers of delay, and has to put up fictitious reasons until the Home government make up their minds. It is hopeless to ask the Egyptian Government, as they will take no action which tends to annoy the Italians....

F. I have just returned from Cairo, seeing the C-in-C, Middle East, and the AOC-in-C, Middle East. They are nervous over an invasion of the Yemen, and also about Jibouti. I can't myself see how any large scale invasion of the former could be successful when our Red Sea Force is about.

G. They are both complaining strongly about having to deal with two Cs-in-C, one of them not 'get-at-able', so to speak, and were talking of raising the question with the Chiefs of Staff about the Red Sea coming under the C-in-C, Mediterranean. I declined to have any part in this suggestion.[53]

... Right away I must say I should hate to have to add the Red Sea to my responsibilities, but I have been brought to see that the Red Sea and Mediterranean should be under one supreme command in an Italian war. They are just bits of the same problem, and it would seem that it might result in an economy of force.

H. About *Illustrious*, may I reserve my answer until I see how *Eagle* comes out of the first clash? The force I propose initially in the Central Mediterranean will be *Warspite*, *Eagle* and *Malaya* only, so as to save destroyers and have a small compact easily manoeuvrable unit. There will also be *Gloucester*, *Liverpool* and *Sydney*. I am sure *Warspite* and *Malaya* are equal to anything the Italians will produce, and I must have *Eagle*'s torpedo aircraft to fix them if they emerge.

J. We are practising furiously, and also trying to get the battleships' defects completed. *Ramillies* is practically finished, but has still to change her 15-in gun. I can only hope *Malaya*'s steering gear will stand one more period at sea.

29. To Pound

7 June 1940

In the present situation in the Mediterranean it is not easy to pick out one clear object on which to base our operations. I would like it to be the control of sea communications in the central and eastern Mediterranean but for the reasons given in my 1231 of 23 May [not reproduced] as well as because of the other calls which will inevitably be made on the Fleet, I do not consider that this object is capable of attainment at the outset.

2. At the commencement of hostilities I prefer to adopt the more limited object of controlling the Aegean and Eastern Mediterranean which is not defensive, since, to achieve it the destruction of enemy naval forces in the Dodecanese, and of any reinforcements sent to their assistance, as well as the ultimate liquidation of these islands are necessary courses of action. In addition the policy of using our Naval power against Italian interests in the Aegean offers

---

[53]The other was C-in-C, E Indies.

prospects of drawing his Fleet to the Eastward. The selection of this object by no means excludes action in the Central Mediterranean and against the Italian Coast, which I hope will be possible.

3. You may be sure that all in the Fleet are imbued with a burning desire to get at the Italian Fleet but you will appreciate that a policy of seeking out and destroying his naval forces requires good and continuous air reconnaissance and a means of fixing the enemy when located. Indeed my chief fear is that we shall make contact with little or nothing except aircraft or submarines and I must get the measure of these before attempting sustained operations in the Central Mediterranean. It must not be forgotten that the fleet base and repair facilities are exposed to enemy air attack with very limited fighter protection and there is no alternative.

30. *To Pound*

7 June 1940

My intentions at the outset of hostilities are entirely governed by the necessity of being prepared at short notice to carry out the operation for the occupation of Crete. The actual occupation will be carried out by two cruisers carrying the troops supported by a division of destroyers followed a day later by four French cruisers now at Beirut ready to embark troops.

2. All the rest of the light forces less the 3CS together with a substantial part of the Battle Fleet will be required to cover the operation and will leave Alexandria for the area west of Crete as soon as it is ordered.

3. One of the 3CS is maintained on patrol in Kithera Channel, remainder at Port Said to ensure safety of Canal. The two river gunboats will also shortly be in the Canal Area to assist in defence.

4. The submarine patrol off Crete will be augmented by patrols off Augusta, Taranto, Straits of Otranto, Tobruk and Dodecanese. Minelaying at Augusta and off Cape Maria di Lenca.

5. It is strongly urged that the occupation of Crete should be proceeded with whatever the political situation, as it is desired to use Suda Bay as a fuelling base during operations in the Central Mediterranean and Aegean.

6. Should the Cretan operation not be ordered it seems that operations by the Fleet must unfortunately be governed by Italian action, but when war is imminent it is intended that a strong force

including battleships should proceed to the westwards ready to counter Italian action on Malta or in other directions. This move may be accompanied by sweeps of the Dodecanese and North African areas or by submarine hunts south of Crete or in the Kaso and Kithera Channels.

7. Should Malta be subject to seaborne attack it is intended to move with the whole Fleet to its relief. An attack on Port Augusta may be the best method of affording relief to Malta but is is hoped to test out the enemy's air and submarine strength before operating so close off his coasts.

8. If and when adequate reconnaissance has been established working from Tunisia or Malta it may be possible to keep a force of cruisers and destroyers in the central area almost permanently to prey on Libyan traffic. They would use Malta or a Greek island for fuelling at night.

9. Should Turkey enter the war on our side operations against the Dodecanese will probably be required and it is proposed at the outset to interrupt the Dodecanese communications with Italy.

10. With reference to paragraphs 2 and 6 above, after meeting other calls there are insufficient destroyers remaining to take the whole of the battlefleet to sea together.

31. *To the Admiralty*

10 June 1940

Intend to leave harbour at 0500/11 with *Warspite, Malaya, Eagle*, 7CS and available destroyers. Battleships will proceed NW and then along S coast of Crete to reach approximate position 80 miles S of Matapan 1200/12.

7CS will carry out sweep to westward until dark on 11 June then return to attack any patrols off Benghazi and Tobruk at daylight 12 June, subsequently joining me about 1200/12.

VA Force X has been instructed to proceed from Beirut as soon as possible with what force he thinks fit to sweep towards Dodecanese and Aegean N of Crete returning Alexandria p.m. 13th.[54]

---

[54]Force X: French ships under Godfroy.

PART II

THE ANGLO-ITALIAN WAR
JUNE TO DECEMBER 1940

With the Germans' swift demolition of France's defences in the spring of 1940, it became increasingly clear that Mussolini would bring Italy into the war and he did so on 10 June, by which time France was virtually prostrate and a week away from an armistice. In an effort to provoke the Italians into a fleet engagement following Mussolini's declaration of war, Cunningham took the fleet into the central Mediterranean, while light forces swept towards the Dodecanese. The Italian fleet did not appear, nor, more surprisingly, did the Regia Aeronautica. This initial operation indicated that the Italians would seek battle only on their own terms, that British air reconnaissance was grossly inadequate, and that Alexandria was too far distant for extended operations in the central basin. Cunningham hankered after a base at Suda Bay – denied to him by Greece's continuing neutrality [32–4].

Godfroy's French squadron was as eager to get at the Italians as Cunningham but, a week after Italy's entry, it was enveloped by the Armistice crisis. France's ensuing neutrality raised fundamental questions for Britain. Should she pursue an active campaign against Italy? Could she retain a substantial fleet in the Mediterranean? What policy would Vichy adopt on French North African colonies and the French fleet, the bulk of which lay at Mers-el-Kébir, Casablanca and Dakar? Moreover, Franco had declared non-belligerency and Fascist Spain might well enter the war, in which case Gibraltar would soon become untenable. Pound was forced to contemplate the unthinkable – virtual abandonment of the Mediterranean – but, after some consideration Cunningham responded that a relatively modest fleet could hold the eastern basin. Withdrawal of the fleet would entail the loss of Malta and the collapse of the entire British position in the Middle East, built up patiently over 150 years. Churchill, the old imperial lion, would have none of it; he committed the empire to a full-blown war in the Mediterranean.[1]

Once that was done, more and more forces were drawn in inexorably and it quickly became as important in Britain's war effort as the Battle of Britain and the Battle of the Atlantic. It represented a

---

[1] On the possibility of abandoning the Mediterranean, see Chiefs of Staff, 17 & 18 June 1940, CAB79/4, & 17 June 1940, CAB80/13. On fighting on alone, see Jt Planning Cttee, 'Future Strategy', 4 Sept. 1940, CAB80/17.

remarkable strategic transformation in just two years. If thought had been given to the Mediterranean before 1938, it was spasmodic and unsystematic. The underlying hope was that Italy could be kept on the sidelines and even if she was not, the French would assume the major responsibility for the theatre. Given that Italy had declared war and France had made peace, Britain would have to put up some sort of a fight in the Mediterranean but it could have been a basic defensive strategy. The Government and the Chiefs of Staff and certainly Cunningham, however, intended to take the offensive, seeing Italy as a weaker opponent which could be defeated by imperial forces unaided. A successful invasion of Italy could lead to the freeing of the rest of Europe. In any case, it was now the only theatre in which Britain could really get to grips with an enemy. By the time Cunningham left the scene in April 1942, the Empire's investment in the Mediterranean was enormous and the war there had a logic and momentum of its own. It was no surprise that the British sought to drag in the Americans. Cunningham, while acknowledging that Germany was the principal enemy and that she would have to be defeated on land in Europe, was nevertheless a convinced proponent of the Mediterranean strategy, feeling that it protected vital British interests and that it was necessary to forestall a German or perhaps a Russian descent on the region, which was likely to have repercussions on the eastern empire. The wisdom of that strategy has been questioned in recent years but in 1940, for a nation desperately seeking uplift, victories and battlefield experience for its army, there seemed little option but to fight Italy with might and main [1–2, 5–7, 8, 17, 35–7, 68, 87, 104, 124].[2]

The British had then to consider the future disposition of the French fleet, the second largest in Europe. Following the Armistice, French ships were to return to metropolitan ports, though Germany and Italy permitted those in colonial harbours to remain there for the time being. Darlan had assured Britain that none of the ships would pass into enemy hands but the British doubted his word. In part this was because he was known to be a 'politician' and believed to be an Anglophobe; this view seemed confirmed when he joined Pétain's government.[3] It was feared also that, under duress or out of

---

[2]See C. Barnett, *Engage the Enemy More Closely: The Royal Navy in the Second World War* (London, 1991); see also M. Howard, *The Mediterranean Strategy in the Second World War* (London, 1968); J. R. M. Butler, *Grand Strategy*, vol. II, *Sept 1939–June 1941* (London, 1957) and vol. III, *June 1941–Aug 1942* (London, 1964).

[3]Marshal Henri Philippe Pétain (1856–1951): hero of Verdun 1916; Marshal 1918; Vice Premier May 1940; Prime Minister 16 June 1940; Chief of State, Vichy, July 1940; condemned to death but commuted to imprisonment, July 1945.

conviction, Vichy would collaborate with the Axis powers or even join the war against Britain. Even if Vichy maintained strict neutrality, the predilection of Hitler and Mussolini for breaking their solemn words and their penchant for *coups de main* led the British to fear Axis seizure of French ships. In the desperate post-Dunkirk situation, the government determined to resolve the issue at once. French ships in British ports were to be seized and the uncompleted *Richelieu* and *Jean Bart,* at Dakar and Casablanca respectively, were to be put out of action. Efforts were made to persuade the fleet at Mers-el-Kébir, which included the modern battlecruisers *Dunkerque* and *Strasbourg*, to join the Royal Navy in continuing the war, to accept internment in a British port or in the French West Indies, or to sink their ships. After a day of tense and fruitless negotiations on 3 July, Force H, under Somerville, was compelled to open fire. Three of the four capital ships were sunk or damaged and 1300 French sailors died. Vichy adopted a hostile neutrality and two years of tit-for-tat reprisals followed.[4]

At Alexandria, Cunningham and Godfroy had established good personal relations. Cunningham, who enjoyed more freedom than Somerville, could police the behaviour of the French, who were confronted with *force majeure.* He believed Godfroy would accept demobilisation but the government's hard line and the events at Mers-el-Kébir prolonged and endangered the negotiations. Cunningham, who sought above all to avoid fighting, trusted in his own diplomatic skills and his sensitivity, patience and negotiating ability revealed an unsuspected aspect of his personality. Godfroy agreed to sink his ships but the news from Mers-el-Kébir scuppered that. Ignoring belligerent prodding from London, Cunningham then appealed over the head of the upright but obdurate Godfroy to his captains and ships's companies. The French Naval Liaison Officer with the Mediterranean Fleet, Captain Aboyneau, also played a prominent role. After several hours of high tension, with ships on both sides at action stations, Godfroy bowed to his cap-

---

[4]*Richelieu* (1943), *Jean Bart* (1948): 35,000t+, 8×15in, 9×6in, 12×3.9in, 30k.
Dunkerque (1937), *Strasbourg* (1938): 26,500t, 8×13in, 16×5.1in, 29.5k. Both scuttled, Toulon, Nov. 1942.

M. Simpson (ed.), *The Somerville Papers* (Aldershot: Scolar Press for Navy Records Society), pp. 37–47; documents 21–43; Capt C. Huan, 'The French Navy in World War II', in J. J. Sadkovitch (ed.), *Reevaluating the Major Naval Combatants of World War II* (Westport, Conn., 1990), pp. 79–90. See also Chiefs of Staff, 30 June 1940, CAB80/4.

Adolf Hitler (1889–1945): b Austria, failed artist, WW1 soldier; failed *putsch* 1923; formed National Socialist Party; author of *Mein Kampf;* Chancellor Jan. 1933; *Führer* 1935; d by own hand 30 April 1945.

tains' advice and accepted demilitarisation in Alexandria. Thereafter, the French caused no trouble and Godfroy was quick to congratulate Cunningham on his triumphs and to commiserate with him on his losses [115, 166, 244]. Thus a cool head, a Nelsonian eye to unhelpful signals from London and adroit exploitation of existing trust, respect and friendship with the French resulted in a peaceful solution, though at the last, Cunningham was also prepared to open fire [34–5, 38–9, 41–64].[5]

With the French squadron demilitarised, Cunningham was able to go to sea. The fleet left Alexandria after dark on 7 July to cover convoys and possibly bombard the Italian coast. On this occasion Cunningham was well served by air and submarine reconnaissance, which provided accurate reports of a sortie by the Italian fleet, covering a convoy to Libya. Further intelligence was provided by decrypts of Italian signals. On learning of the strength and position of the enemy, Cunningham moved to cut it off from its base at Taranto. *Eagle*'s Swordfish failed to slow down the enemy, though her small air component performed prodigies of reconnaissance and fighter defence [76].[6] The battleships and cruisers fired sporadically at the retreating Italians, *Warspite* scoring one hit on the *Giulio Cesare*.[7] As only two modernised battleships were then available to them, the Italians very sensibly made smoke, retired and tried to draw Cunningham on to their destroyers, E-boats, submarines and mines. He declined to continue the fruitless pursuit and returned to Alexandria, being bombed incessantly most of the way.

The British claimed a moral victory, though the Italians had taken the only sensible course and Cunningham had refused to take his heavy ships through a smokescreen. There were many disturbing

---

[5]C. W. Hines, 'The Fleet Between: Anglo-American Diplomacy and Force X, 1940–1943', in D. M. Masterson (ed.), *Naval History: The Sixth Symposium of the US Naval Academy* (Wilmington, Del. 1987), pp. 237–55.

[6]*Eagle*: 1923, 22,600t, 9×6in, 4×4in, 21 a/c, 24k, s *U-73*, Med, Aug. 1942.

P. C. Smith, *Action Imminent: Three Studies of the Naval War in the Mediterranean Theatre during 1940* (London, 1980), pp. 54–87.

On the FAA, see T. C. Hone and M. D. Mandeles, 'Inter-War Innovation in Three Navies', *Naval War College Review*, spring 1987, pp. 63–83; Naval Staff History, *The Development of British Naval Aviation, 1919–1945*, vol. 1 (1954), ADM234/383; J. D. Brown, *Carrier Operations in World War II*, vol. 1, *The Royal Navy* (Shepperton, 1968); VA Sir A. Hezlet, *Aircraft and Sea Power* (London, 1970); G. Till, *Air Power and the Royal Navy: An Historical Survey, 1914–1945* (London, 1979).

[7]Visct Cunningham, *A Sailor's Odyssey* (London, 1951), p. 262, gives the Italian Admiral as Riccardi but S. W. C. Pack, *Cunningham the Commander* (London, 1974), pp. 93, 96, 97 and O. Warner, *Cunningham of Hyndhope: Admiral of the Fleet* (London, 1967), p. 105, name him as Campioni.

features about the encounter. Cunningham's reconnaissance was extremely thin, his fighter cover negligible and his AA fire was unable to reach the high-level bombers. Rarely out of sight of Italian reconnaissance, the fleet was subjected to ceaseless heavy attacks, wearing and expensive in ammunition though more of a nuisance than a danger. The Italians, who would shortly possess a superior battle squadron, had a comfortable margin of speed, deep minefields, strong light forces and a coastal air umbrella. To counter the Italian advantages, Cunningham required at least another modernised battleship and a modern carrier with a fighter squadron and torpedo bombers well trained in hitting fast-moving targets. 'Our position in the Middle East depends almost entirely on the fleet,' he declared, 'and I want to keep it active and able to go anywhere with moderate security' [66–7, 69, 93].

At the beginning of the war, the Royal Navy was unsure about the aerial threat. Norway and Dunkirk emphatically underlined its seriousness and Pound, Somerville and Cunningham were understandably cautious about confronting the Regia Aeronautica [67, 69–70, 73–4, 79, 80–81, 84] . Though persistent and accurate enough to secure occasional hits, the Italians seemed less dangerous than German dive bombers. Radar warning and *Ark Royal*'s fighters proved the perfect antidote, destroying shadowers before they could report and forcing bombers to jettison their loads well away from the fleet; with practice and reflection, AA fire also improved.[8] In the light of these experiences, it was deemed possible to pass naval reinforcements through the Mediterranean, though the Navy continued to oppose Churchill's desire to send a fast mercantile convoy. Operation HATS, the passage of substantial reinforcements for the Mediterranean fleet, including *Valiant* and *Illustrious*, was accomplished successfully early in September 1940 [90–3, 98].

The successful negotiation of the first three months of war with Italy without serious loss, the arrival of substantial reinforcements and the new confidence in the fleet's ability to nullify the bombing threat led to a bolder strategy. Force H made numerous 'club runs' to fly fighters into Malta, whose other defences were built up by convoys from Alexandria covered by the fleet and from Gibraltar, shielded by Force H. There was a constant stream of local convoys to the Levant and Cyprus and when Greece was attacked by Italy on 28 October convoys

---

[8]*Ark Royal*: 1938, 22,000t, 16×4.5in, 60 a/c, 30.75k; s *U-81*, 13–14 Nov. 1941.

On AA and fighter defence at sea, see M. Simpson, 'Wings Over the Sea: The Interaction of Air and Sea Power in the Mediterranean, 1940–1942', in N. A. M. Rodger (ed.), *Naval Power in the Twentieth Century* (Basingstoke, 1996), pp. 134–50.

to Piraeus and Suda Bay in Crete were instituted. Fleet operations were dovetailed with these movements, to economise on wear and tear, to afford maximum protection to the convoys and to obscure attacks on Italian ports, shipping and airfields. Effective use was made of *Illustrious*'s and *Eagle*'s aircraft in these operations. Swordfish carried out deep reconnaissances and anti-submarine patrols while standing air patrols of Fulmars and Sea Gladiators dealt with enemy shadowers and broke up bombing attacks. To avoid fighters, Swordfish attacked Italian airfields at night. Though no Italian base suffered serious damage, enemy operations were disrupted. The fleet's ability to strike at widely separated points more or less simultaneously demonstrated the flexibility of sea power, now greatly enhanced by carriers. These complex operations depended on highly sophisticated planning, efficient co-operation by the several forces and convoys involved, and effective co-ordination by Cunningham himself [102–3, 105, 107, 110, 112, 113, 119–20, 127–8].

The most dramatic example of interlinked operations was the COAT-JUDGMENT series of 6–14 November. 'The operation became one of considerable complexity,' Cunningham observed, 'covering a large area with a wide succession of subsidiary movements' [113–19]. Reinforcements for the fleet were escorted to the Sicilian Narrows by Force H, convoys were run to and from Alexandria and Malta, Suda Bay and Piraeus and light forces raided Italian shipping in the Straits of Otranto but all these important operations were incidental to and cover for the strategically significant JUDGMENT – the Fleet Air Arm attack on Taranto.

The Italian fleet and squadrons of cruisers had been sighted by British submarines or long range reconnaissance on several occasions since Calabria but, frustratingly, Cunningham had never been able to bring the enemy to action [75, 90, 101, 104–5, 119]. In large part this was due to the comprehensive nature of Italian air reconnaissance, which enabled the enemy fleet to keep well clear of Cunningham, who was generally poorly served as the RAF lacked the resources to provide regular reconnaissance of enemy bases and home waters. However, two of his cruisers had distinguished themselves against detached enemy forces – *Sydney* and destroyers sinking *Bartolomeo Colleoni* and *Ajax* destroying two destroyers and damaging a third so severely that she was sunk on the next day [71–3, 105–7].[10]

[9]*Illustrious*: 1940, 23,000t, 16×4.5in, 36 (later 54) a/c, 31k.
[10]*Sydney*: 1936, 7,105t, 8×6in, 8×4in, 8×21in tt, 32.5k; s *Kormoran*, off W Australia, 19 Dec. 1941. VA Sir John Collins, *As Luck Would Have It* (Sydney, 1965), pp. 78, 84–8.
Ajax: 1935, 6,985t, 8×6in, 8×4in, 8×21in tt, 32.5k.
Bartolomeo Colleoni: 1932, 5,200t, 8×6in, 6×3.9in, 4×21in tt, 37k.

Cunningham was anxious to deal a crippling blow to the Italian fleet at an early date not only to sustain the moral superiority he felt he had won at Calabria but also because by November the enemy had six battleships in commission, including the two new *Littorios*. At best, Cunningham would have no more than three modernised *Queen Elizabeths,* though, in view of the Italians' lack of enterprise and his own possession of two carriers, his inferiority caused him no undue concern. It was sensible, however, to shorten the odds and singe the King of Italy's moustache. The Royal Navy had studied air attacks on fleets in harbour since 1916 and the idea was cultivated most assiduously in the Mediterranean fleet following the Abyssinian crisis. Certain prerequisites had to be satisfied. Constant and up-to-date reconnaissance of Taranto was necessary to establish whether capital ships were present, to locate their berths, and to ensure that they did not slip away unobserved. Other warship and dockyard targets had to be identified and the defences plotted. These tasks were accomplished magnificently by a flight of high-speed, long-range Maryland photo-reconnaissance aircraft, operating from Malta.[11] The strike squadrons had to be trained intensively in night flying and given operational experience against ports in the Dodecanese. Deception and surprise were vital, hence the diversionary operations and night attack. *Illustrious*'s fighters played a key role by destroying all shadowers before they could report the carrier task force. It was desirable also to attack in good weather, preferably by moonlight. Though the enemy lacked night fighters and radar, Taranto had forward observation posts, searchlights, barrage balloons and heavy shore and shipborne AA barrages.

The strike force was detached from the battle fleet, which remained in a covering position, at 1800 on 11 November. The Italians had been alerted to an impending air attack by the intensive reconnaissance but the task force was undetected. The raid was conducted in two waves as there were torpedo dropping positions for only six aircraft at a time. Twenty-one Swordfish were launched from *Illustrious*, including several planes from *Eagle*, unfortunately absent through defects caused by near-misses. While relatively minor damage was caused to installations and other warships, the Italian battlefleet was dealt a comprehensive blow. Three of the six battleships present were put out of action, one permanently and two for several months. Two Swordfish were lost, one crew being taken prisoner. The task force rejoined the main fleet at 0700 on 12 November.

[11] Martin Maryland: 1938, 278 mph.

The results were far reaching. It was the first major offensive success of British arms since September 1939 and the first significant Italian defeat. British morale and prestige soared. The naval consequences were felt far beyond the Mediterranean, for Cunningham was able to send home two battleships and reduce the strain on his destroyers. The Italian battlefleet was halved, the survivors fleeing at once to Naples; bombed there by the RAF, they retreated to Spezia and were thus unable to defend southern coasts and Libyan traffic or attack British convoys. Italian fear of British carriers was redoubled. Cunningham was now close to gaining control of the central Mediterranean. The raid remains the supreme triumph and final vindication of the Fleet Air Arm. It was achieved by an obsolescent weapons system and aircrew of high skill, immense courage and unquenchable enthusiasm. As Cunningham observed, 'As an example of "economy of force" it is probably unsurpassed'; indeed, even Pearl Harbor failed to match it in this respect [113–19].[12]

Taranto was the most spectacular demonstration of naval aviation thus far. Despite the small numbers of aircraft available and their obsolesence, the FAA formed an integral part of Cunningham's forces and he relied heavily on it for reconnaissance, protection and strikes against both ships and shore targets. His first carrier, *Eagle*, a first-generation ship, low in speed and endurance, poorly protected, with limited aviation fuel capacity and equipped with only 21 aircraft, was nevertheless a most efficient unit [32, 66, 76]. *Illustrious*, first of the armoured carriers, possessed high speed, a good radius of action, radar, modern flight-deck equipment and a powerful AA armament, though she carried only 36 aircraft. Moreover, her captain, Denis Boyd, was a committed exponent of air power and she brought with her Rear Admiral Lyster, a notable student of naval air power, who relieved Cunningham of the burden of supervising the FAA [90–1, 98, 101, 104–5, 110, 113–19, 127–8].[13] The torpedo-spotter-reconnaissance aircraft, the durable,

---

[12]At Pearl Harbor, 7 Dec. 1941, the Japanese employed over 350 a/c, sinking or seriously damaging 6 battleships and 6 other vessels.

[13]Capt (later Adm Sir) Denis Boyd: Capt 1931; Capt (D), 4DF Med F 1936; *Vernon* i/c 1938; *Illustrious* 1940; Actg RA (A), Med F April 1941; RA July 1941; RA(A), EF 1942; 5SL & Chief, N Air Eqpt 1943; VA June 1944; Adm (A) June 1945; C-in-C, BPF June 1946.

RA (later Adm Sir) Arthur Lyster (1888–1957): ent RN 1903; Instr *Excellent* 1912; GO *Glory* 1914; Dardanelles; *Cassandra* N Sea & Baltic 1917; GO *Renown* 1918; Capt 1928; *Danae, Despatch* 1931–32; 5DF 1933–35; *Excellent* 1935–36; DTSD; *Glorious* 1937–38; RA 1939; Norway 1940; RA(A), Med F, Sept. 1940-Feb. 1941; 5SL 1941–42; RA(A), Home F 1942; VA Oct. 1942; N African landings 1942; Ret List 1943; FO Corvette Trng & Adm-in-Cmd, Largs, 1943–44.

reliable Swordfish, was slow and poorly armed but highly adaptable with good endurance and a substantial payload. Swordfish were also employed from airfields against coastal targets in Cyrenaica [33, 38, 64, 65, 85, 97, 126–7]. The manouevrable but hastily adapted Sea Gladiator fighter continued to serve but the front-line fighter was the Fulmar, relatively slow and sluggish but with good all-round visibility and a powerful 8-gun armament. Despite its shortcomings and small numbers, the Fulmar ran up creditable scores of enemy aircraft destroyed, damaged or discouraged. A handful of fleet fighters proved the key to successful operations in the central Mediterranean, effectively nullifying the formidable strength of the Regia Aeronautica.[14]

Taranto was followed shortly by Army offensives in East Africa (led by Cunningham's younger brother Alan) and the Western Desert.[15] Wavell's attack in December was a considerable relief to Cunningham, who had been alarmed at the gradual but unopposed advance of the Italians from the Egyptian frontier, thus bringing Alexandria within reach of Italian bombers and denying the RAF forward airfields from which to reconnoitre and defend the convoy route to Malta [83, 84, 87, 88, 98]. Wavell's offensive pleased Churchill, too. The Prime Minister had pressed for it for several months, with good reason. He needed victories to offset the long catalogue of defeats and maintain morale. He was convinced also that if Britain did not take swift and decisive advantage of Italian weaknesses, she would find herself in a precarious position when Hitler's panzers, Luftwaffe and U-boats came to Mussolini's aid [92]. Wavell would not move until he was ready and the three Commanders-in-Chief presented a united front to the Prime Minister while smoothly co-ordinating their operations. Cunningham's fleet shelled Italian coastal positions and a newly-formed Inshore Squadron cleared captured harbours, swept mines, supplied the advance in the absence of land communications and bombarded the retreating Italians [38, 81, 98, 126–33]. Longmore worked wonders in mastering the much larger Italian Air Force and co-operated closely with Cunningham [64, 67, 80–1, 85, 91, 110, 129]. Wavell, O'Connor and Alan Cunningham implemented a bold

---

[14]Fairey Swordfish: 1934, 1×18in t or 1500lbs bombs, 2mg, 138mph, range 550mls.
Fairey Fulmar: 1940, 8mg, 280mph, range 800mls
Gloster Gladiator: 1934, 4mg, 253mph, range 410mls.
[15]Lt-Gen Sir Alan Cunningham (1887–1983): cmd forces in Kenya which took Italian E Africa, 1940–41; cmd 8th Army, Aug.-Nov. 1941; later GOC N Ireland; Gov-Gen Palestine.

mobile strategy which drove the Italians out of Eritrea, Abyssinia and Cyrenaica by early 1941.[16]

Cunningham and the Admiralty were fully alive to the urgency of disrupting Italian communications with Libya but the obvious base for striking forces, Malta, lacked adequate defences and offensive capability in this period. It was used only occasionally by a few submarines; most operated from Alexandria but British submarines achieved little at high cost to themselves in the first six months. In part this was because they were not permitted to wage unrestricted warfare in the early months and in any case were ordered to concentrate on warships and reconnaissance, while one or two minelaying submarines did good if limited service. Furthermore, Italian traffic to Libya offered few targets and there were too few boats for an effective patrol. Boats took time to gain war experience and ten were lost. The Italians, despite the lack of asdic, possessed good hydrophones and their thickly-laid inshore minefields caused the abandonment of coastal patrols. The clear waters of the Mediterranean facilitated location by aircraft and the old, noisy, oil-leaking, unreliable and unhandy 'O', 'P' and 'R' class boats were unsuited to Mediterranean conditions [33, 38–40, 67, 75–8, 102–3, 110, 120, 129].[17]

Despite the success of British arms by the end of 1940, Cunningham still suffered from inadequate air reconnaissance and ill-defended bases. Malta remained his principal concern. Despite a steady stream of Hurricanes and a few other types, flown in from the west, the island was still under constant air attack, it could furnish only spasmodic long-range reconnaissance and was able to undertake small-scale bombing and torpedo missions only from December.[18] It was still short of its full outfit of AA guns and its airfields and oil tanks lacked dispersal areas and protection. Cunningham felt unable to station light forces or submarines at Malta until the island was more secure. Nevertheless the situation was improving and he counselled the gradual development of Malta's offensive capability so as not to draw down upon the island a greater weight of attack than it could repel. Lamenting 'Was there

---

[16]Lt-Gen Sir Richard O'Connor (1889–1981): cmd W Desert Force, 1940–41; captd March 1941; escpd Sept 1943; cmd VIII Corps, Normandy 1944; India Dec. 1944; Gen 1945. O'Connor was a great admirer, friend and frequent guest of Cunningham; tribute written in captivity, n.d., BM Add Mss 52580A, *Cunningham Papers*, BL.

[17]See VA Sir Arthur Hezlet, *The Submarine and Sea Power* (London, 1967), pp. 118–23, 138–9.

[18]830 (Swordfish) Sqdn, FAA, & RAF Wellingtons: 1936, 6mg, 6,000lbs bombs, 255mph, range 1,325mls.

ever such folly as to allow our Mediterranean fortress to fall into such a state?' Cunningham declared that 'The rendering safe of Malta is the key to our Mediterranean strategy' and he hoped to re-establish it as a fleet base in the spring of 1941 [33, 36, 38–9, 64, 67–70, 73, 75, 82, 83, 86–7, 92, 95, 97–99, 103–5, 107, 110, 127–29].

Alexandria was under almost as much threat as Malta. It was threatened by bombing, mining and torpedo attacks which, delivered in half light, from a low height and at high speed, were difficult to counter. The RAF could spare few fighters and there were no night fighters. The AA batteries were totally inadequate. The fleet had often to provide its own air and AA defence, a wearying and wasteful situation. The Suez Canal was subject to aerial mining and was also virtually undefended, forcing Cunningham to station AA cruisers and fleet fighters there.[19] He was obliged also to send escort forces to the Red Sea (part of the East Indies Station) [33, 70, 73, 76, 80, 81, 83–4, 88, 118, 120, 129].

Other ports were in even worse state. Haifa, terminal of an oil pipeline and the fleet's fuel depot, had no defences and Cunningham's exhortations resulted in only the barest minimum being sent – at the expense of Alexandria [67, 74, 76, 95]. Cunningham had long cast covetous eyes on Suda Bay in Crete, a fine but undefended natural harbour which became available when Italy attacked Greece in October. Located half way between Malta and Alexandria, it was an admirable fuelling base and from there, the Navy could prey upon Italian traffic to Libya and the Dodecanese and secure its own convoy routes to Greece and Turkey. Nevertheless, Suda was almost defenceless, suffering from the general shortage of fighters, AA guns, radar sets, nets, booms and minesweepers. The cruiser *Glasgow* was torpedoed there [110–13, 118, 127, 129, 161].[20] Cyprus was in an even worse condition [94]. The Army's advance along the Libyan coast, though halting air attacks on the Canal and Alexandria, presented further difficulties as there were few fighters or guns to defend newly won ports such as Sollum [32, 126–9]. The lack of secure, well-resourced bases was a constant worry for Cunningham, as he could not dock vessels except in moonless periods, nor could ships' companies enjoy much rest.

Cunningham was responsible for over 25,000 men and had a genuine concern for their well-being, insisting that lower deck content-

---

[19]S. Morewood, 'Protecting the Jugular Vein of Empire: The Suez Canal in British Defence Strategy, 1919–1941', *War and Society*, vol. 10, no 1, May 1992, pp. 81–107.

[20]*Glasgow*: 1937, 9,100t, 12×6in, 8×4in, 6×21in tt, 32k.

ment bred high morale [40, 77]. He visited ships frequently and at his house in Alexandria, officers could enjoy short breaks for convalescence. He had a devoted staff though he drove it hard, Rear Admiral Willis working himself to exhaustion. Cunningham was much more interested in operations than administration of shore bases and was resolved to remain a deck rather than a desk sailor. He had implicit confidence in his principal subordinates, first Vice Admiral Tovey and later Vice Admiral Pridham-Wippell.[21] The station benefited immensely from the Commander-in-Chief's unrivalled knowledge of its farthest corners, its peoples and its diverse waters, islands, coastlines and harbours.

The 'second eleven' of largely ageing ships with which Cunningham began the war had been transformed into a powerful fleet of modern and modernised vessels by the year's end. Despite the pressing claims of other stations, Pound managed to send frequent reinforcements to the Mediterranean. The substantial re-armament programme began to bear fruit, notably in the shape of *Illustrious* and new cruisers and destroyers, some of them radar equipped and with improved (though still weak) AA batteries. New submarines of the 'T' and 'U' classes, better adapted to Mediterranean conditions, began to appear, together with corvettes, MTBs, minelayers, depot ships, landing ships and landing craft.[22] Nevertheless, Cunningham remained critically short of destroyers (always overworked) and escort vessels, he was often without an 8-in gun cruiser, and he bemoaned the lack of fast tankers and coasting craft. However, the fleet suffered few losses and had grown greatly in strength, cohesion and confidence by the end of 1940 [32, 34, 37, 64–70, 76–8, 80, 82–4, 96–8, 100, 103–5, 113–14, 119, 120, 126, 129].

The Italians, though rarely at sea in strength, nevertheless accomplished their main aims without much hindrance. Submarines and blockade runners kept the Dodecanese light forces and airfields operating and the Libyan convoys ran virtually undisturbed. The Italians mined extensively and to great depths, enjoying successes against British submarines and destroyers. Cunningham lacked sufficient minesweeping forces to cope fully with the mining of his harbours and coastal waters [34, 38–9, 77, 81]. Italian submarines,

---

[21]VA (later Adm Sir) Henry Pridham-Wippell (1885–1952): ent RN 1900; Lt 1907; Capt 1926; RA & DPS 1938; VA & 1BS, Med F, 1941; Actg C-in-C, Med April 1942; FOC, Dover, Aug. 1942–45; Adm June 1944; C-in-C Plymouth 1945–47; ret 1948.

[22]'T' class: 1939–45, 1,090/1,575t, 1×4in, 10–11×21in tt, 15.25/9k.

'U' class: 1938–43, 545/735t, 1×3in, 4×21in tt, 11/9k.

however, suffered severe losses (13 boats, plus four in the Red Sea) and sank few ships, displaying little initiative, though few targets presented themselves. The British broke the Italian submarine code and asdic, carrier air patrols and the propensity of the careless Italians to be caught on the surface contributed to these severe losses [32, 34, 38, 40, 77, 81, 89, 91, 101, 105, 127, 129].[23]

The Italian Air Force, which had seemed likely to deny the Mediterranean Fleet freedom of manoeuvre by virtue of its enveloping reconnaissance and hordes of bombers, ceased to be a serious threat at sea following the introduction of fleet fighters, radar and rudimentary fighter direction. Anti-aircraft fire, though never satisfactory in either accuracy or volume, improved greatly with practice, the boosting of short-range armaments, the use of radar and the development of suitable cruising orders and barrages. From the autumn of 1940, however, the Italians introduced low-flying torpedo attacks, made generally at dusk, severely damaging three cruisers. Defence against these attacks was difficult and the bombing and mining of Malta, other harbours and the Canal continued [32, 64–8, 70, 73, 75–6, 80–1, 83–4, 90–1, 101, 105, 107, 112–13, 127].

The Fleet War Diary for December noted 'that by the end of 1940 we were a fair way to achieving our first object, that is to say, control of the Mediterranean, and that the first fruits, namely an undisturbed advance into Italian territory by our troops, had fallen into our hands' [129]. The benefits were the relief from air attacks on Egyptian bases and air cover over the eastern basin. The neutralisation of the Italian fleet and bombers opened the trans-Mediterranean convoy route, enabling the swift reinforcement and supply of British forces in the Middle East. All three services recognised their interdependence and the three Commanders-in-Chief enjoyed personal compatibility, goodwill, mutual respect and a shared strategic vision. Cunningham and Somerville dominated the whole Mediterranean, thanks largely to carrier air power. Malta was the chief beneficiary of the co-operation of Force H and the Mediterranean Fleet. By November, though some strengthening was still required, the island was 'a formidable proposition', convoys were running regularly, the dockyard was working at full capacity and the defences were approaching full strength [120]. 830 FAA Squadron (Swordfish) and RAF Wellingtons were beginning to attack enemy shipping and bases and make Malta the mainspring of

---

[23]Hezlet, *Submarine and Sea Power*, pp. 137–8, 155–61.

the maritime offensive. Cunningham's resolute leadership, clear grasp of strategic essentials, bold tactics and optimum use of scarce resources had played a large part in attaining this happy position. Elsewhere, 1940 may have been an *annus horriblis* for Britain but in the Mediterranean it ended as an *annus mirabilis*.

32. *Mediterranean Fleet War Diary, 10–14 June 1940*

10 June

7. At 2230 *Decoy* reported sighting a submarine on the surface. She attacked, and later made three attacks on firm contacts; at dawn an oil track 2 miles long was seen.[24]

12 June

2. At 0200 *Calypso* was seen to drop back and subsequently reported that she had apparently been struck by a torpedo. *Caledon* and *Dainty* were detached to stand by her and rescued 24 officers and 394 ratings when she sank at 0330. One officer and 34 ratings are missing.[25]

[Cunningham's Summary]

2. This initial cruise had as its primary object the attack on any enemy forces at sea and it also provided a means of assessing the enemy's surface, submarine and air effort. Certain points have emerged.

(a) During the whole cruise only one enemy aircraft was sighted by any unit (*Gloucester*) though the main fleet spent over 12 hours within 100 miles of the North African coast, and cruiser forces attacked patrol craft off Tobruk and appeared twice off three different North African ports.

It is evidently early to form definite opinions on such small data but this experience is certainly encouraging as showing that Italian ideas on air reconnaissance at sea are not very developed, nor apparently is the co-operation of defence forces in Libya good if it allows our ships to appear off enemy ports without any retaliatory air action.

(b) As was to be expected and as Their Lordships are aware, the most serious obstacle in bringing the enemy to action is the

---

[24]*Decoy*: 1933 (RCN *Kootenay* 1943), 1,375t, 4×4.7in, 8×21in tt, 35.5k. S/M not sunk.
[25]*Calypso* (s S/M *Bagnolini*), *Caledon*: 1917, 4,120t, 5×6in, 2×3in, 8×21in tt, 29k. *Dainty*: 1933, 1375t, 4×4.7in, 8×21in tt, 35.5k; s a/c, Tobruk, Feb. 1941.

weakness of our air reconnaissance. HMS *Eagle* can supply my needs to a certain extent, but, if her air reconnaissance is used for the close reconnaissance and A/S protection of the Fleet – that is to say security – she cannot supply properly the distant offensive reconnaissance which will locate the enemy. Moreover, her comparatively small petrol stowage is presenting a problem. If the enemy is to be brought to action, extended air reconnaissance appears to provide the only sure way of doing so, the more so in view of the enemy's generally greater speed and probable reluctance to engage in close action.

While the Fleet was at sea at one time I had the *Garibaldi* in the middle of a triangle of our forces but I was unaware of the fact.[26] Three 8-in cruisers were at sea somewhere S and E of Augusta and my sweep up the Greek coast seems to have been 12 hours too late to meet enemy forces off Cephalonia. These statements are based on W/T interception results which at present provide good information too late to be of value. Any improvement possible in this respect is most desirable.

If our extended reconnaissance is to be effective, it seems that Malta or Bizerta must be used at least as refuelling bases for flying boats, and I am studying how best and most safely this can be done so that we may obtain the information so vital to us by means of a patrol between Malta and Greece.

(c) ... the third lesson of this operation was the need for a base in the Greek Islands, preferably Suda Bay. I am fully aware of the almost insuperable difficulties but I go so far as to say that we shall never effectively be able to control the Central Mediterranean till such a base is available. At this moment our Fleet is making for Alexandria; the enemy will no doubt shortly be aware of the fact. He has then a matter of up to three days during which he can act with impunity. With a reasonable base in the Greek Islands not only will he be under constant threat from our forces, but the problem of passing convoys through the Mediterranean – of which this week's experience gives me considerable hope – will be greatly simplified, linked up as it is with the question of fuelling our light forces. It would also greatly enhance the

---

[26]*Giuseppe Garibaldi*: 1937, 9,387t, 10×6in, 8×3.9in, 6×21in tt, 31k.

value of the French 8-in cruisers who with their endurance of only 2,500 miles at 20 knots are of little use to me in the Central Mediterranean for prolonged operations.

(d) I have not yet had time to study the submarine question beyond observing that our destroyers appear to have been able to give them a harassing time. The loss of *Calypso* is a piece of misfortune of the type one must expect in war, but the circumstances were such that I remain unconvinced that it was due to submarine action, and note that 48 hours later the Italians have made no claim.

3. To review these first operations, I feel that they are profoundly unsatisfactory in a vital respect, namely that the Fleet failed to make contact with the enemy nor am I really aware with any certainty if he was at sea in any force. The reasons for this situation are set out above. Apart from this statement, however, I feel that the operation was of considerable value in testing the enemy's strength and intentions to fight, in tuning up a fleet of very heterogenous elements who had little opportunity of working previously as a tactical unit, and in causing the enemy at least some inconvenience. The Italians were presumably aware that the British Fleet was absent for 3½ days from Alexandria and this fact and the appearances off their North African ports must have put them in some doubt about our intentions.

4. During the operations under report it will be observed that the attack on enemy coasts was not pressed home. This matter presents my most baffling problem. Experience has not shown that it is a profitable matter to engage targets well protected by shore defences with surface craft and doubly so in face of a very considerable air threat. Attacks on Italian and Sicilian ports, moreover, mean that a damaged ship may have to retire some 800 miles in order to dock. Such operations therefore cannot be undertaken lightly. On the other hand I am convinced that to knock Italy out of this war the practical application of it must be brought forcibly home to them. Furthermore, attack on enemy coasts seems the possible way to draw their Fleet to sea. It is therefore a question of whether these risks must not be accepted in view of the advantages of this policy despite its chances, and I am giving this matter careful study with a view to early action....

33. *War Diary, 14–30 June 1940*

2. *Orders to the Fleet*

The following instructions were promulgated by the C-in-C:
... My general intentions are:

(a) 2 battleships at 2 hours' notice, remainder at 6 hours.
(b) *Eagle* at 2 hours' notice, if all aircraft are embarked. At 6 hours' notice if aircraft are disembarked.
(c) 1 cruiser at 1 hour's notice; 1 cruiser at 2 hours' notice; remainder at 6 hours' notice for 24 knots, at 8 hours' notice for full speed, as arranged by VA (D) and Admiral, Force X.
(d) Destroyers: 1 Division on patrol; 1 Division at 2½ hours' notice. Remainder at 4 hours' notice for 24 knots, and 8 hours' notice for full speed.
(e) Submarines: at 24 hours' notice for 3 days after patrol, then at 6 hours.
(f) Depot and repair ships: 4 hours' notice for slow speed; 12 hours' notice for full speed.

In Alexandria harbour battleships, *Eagle* and cruisers, are to maintain the 4th degree of AA readiness by day and night. Destroyers are to man their close range weapons continuously. Air Defence stations are to be assumed during the following periods:

(a) From ¾ of an hour before sunset to half an hour after sunset.
(b) Half an hour before sunrise to ¾ an hour after sunrise.

RCOs are to be manned between these times ...
Local air and surface A/S patrols are to be maintained.

3. *Air raids on Malta*

An air raid on Malta was carried out this morning, *St Angelo* being struck by one heavy bomb.[27]

4. As a result of the frequent air raids on Malta, the Governor strongly urged that the 3 Hurricane fighters destined for Egypt should be diverted, temporarily at any rate, to Malta. While the morale of the population remained high, he feared that it might deteriorate unless active visible measures were taken for their protection.

5. This request was very strongly supported by C-in-C, Mediterranean, who proposed that the spares should be rushed from Gibraltar to Malta by destroyer, instead of being taken round to Egypt via the Cape.

---

[27]*St Angelo*: shore station, Malta.

15 June

2. *Aircraft*

C-in-C, Mediterranean, ordered a striking force of 3 aircraft, armed with torpedoes, to be at immediate notice at Dekheila between 2 hours before sunrise and 2 hours after sunrise daily.

3. A signal was received from the AOC-in-C Middle East, agreeing to the transfer to Malta of the 5 Hurricanes destined for Egypt.

4. *Air raids on Malta*

VA, Malta, informed C-in-C, that in view of incessant air raids he considered that the risk of loss made Malta unsuitable as a submarine base and proposed that the submarines based at Malta should proceed direct to Alexandria from patrol.

34. To Pound

15 June 1940

A. We are just back from our first tour in the Central Mediterranean. On the whole it was a most curious experience. I expected to spend most of the daylight hours beating off heavy bombing attacks on the Fleet. Actually the Battle Squadron never saw a plane although the best part of the day was spent 100 miles off the Libyan Coast. The five cruisers, although close off the African Coast (*Gloucester* and *Liverpool* were engaged by shore batteries), only saw one and were not attacked.

This is most encouraging at first sight, but perhaps we should not draw any hard and fast conclusions yet, but the outlook for Red Sea convoys appears distinctly hopeful.

B. The submarine situation is not so satisfactory. I am not convinced that *Calypso* was torpedoed; the Inquiry is sitting at the moment. If she was, it was a very fine piece of work on the Submarine Captain's part.

I don't think there is much doubt that they meant to mine the Fleet into Alexandria, and that our sweep to the west the day before upset that move. There appears little doubt that *Decoy* killed one that evening. The up-to-date bag is two for certain and two or three doubtful.[28] A feature is the depth of water they are laying mines in, i.e., up to 150 fathoms. We rather had to thread our way in yesterday. It is no use at the moment, I know, asking for more sweepers,

---

[28] No Italian S/M lost as yet, except *Macalle* (1937, 680/866t, 1×3.9in, 6×21in tt, 14/8k) by accident, Red Sea; 8 more s by end June.

but the fact remains that we have to leave these minefields unswept, if at all possible, for fear of losing one of our very small supply of sweepers.

C.   I am going to get after the submarines now for a bit, and get the Black Sea and our oiler traffic going, but I hope to get off to the west again as soon as possible. But first we have to try to get our reconnaissance working better. We must use Malta or Bizerta as a fuelling point for our flying boats. The Y reports also reached us too late to be of value. It is disappointing to know that on Wednesday morning *Garibaldi* was inside a triangle formed by two cruiser detachments and the battle fleet, and owing to no reconnaissance and low visibility, slipped through.

D.   *Eagle* has some pretty grim limitations. Small petrol stowage and small number of planes the most pressing. But her flying personnel are experts except in torpedo dropping and night landing on. I am working them up in this.

If later on you can spare *Illustrious* she would be very welcome, especially if she had some Skuas.[29]

E.   Malta at the moment is holding on well, but I am very concerned at the morale of the Maltese. It seems to me that if we do not take some more drastic steps to assist them, they may justly think that we have let them down badly, and compare our performances over defence of bases with those of Italy.

I contemplate giving Augusta a midnight knock, but the game must be worth the candle, at least three cruisers waiting to be torpedoed inside.

F.   ... The French Admiral here is full of fight; I have them all at Alexandria at the moment. He did a sweep of the Dodecanese and had the same experience – no enemy aircraft.

35.   *From Pound*

16 June 1940

A.   Every endeavour is being made to keep France in the war so that the French Fleet will continue to function in the Western Mediterranean even though it may in time only have the use of African ports.

B.   Should France however make a separate peace, every endeavour will be made to get hold of the French Fleet previously, or fail-

---

[29]Blackburn Skua: ftr/D/B; 1938, 4mg, 1×500lb bomb, 225mph.

ing that to have it sunk. Should this situation arise the protection of our Atlantic trade will become a very formidable problem unless we can hold western exit to Mediterranean which with our present resources could only be done by moving British Fleet from Eastern Mediterranean to Gibraltar.

C. In the event of Spain coming in against us the problem will be still more formidable and necessity for moving Fleet from Eastern Mediterranean will be greater still.

D. It is realised there are strong political and military objections to moving Fleet from Eastern Mediterranean but our Atlantic trade must be the first consideration.

E. The Government have not given a decision on above and until you have been informed that they have it is essential that possibility of withdrawal of Fleet from Eastern Mediterranean should not (R) not be conveyed to other services or to HM Ambassador Cairo.[30]

F. As, however, the move, if approved, might have to be made at short notice, I have thought it desirable to inform you of possibility in order that you may work out a plan for doing it.

G. As a result of our investigations here we consider it preferable that part of Fleet should proceed westward through Mediterranean rather than round the Cape, but I should like your view on this.

H. There is also question of whether submarines, depot ships and also possibly some other units should be retained in Eastern Mediterranean.

I. It is assumed that other depot ships and 'C' class cruisers and 'V and W' destroyers would have to take Red Sea route.[31]

J. I assume we should continue to defend Egypt with Army and that the latter would be supplied through Red Sea.

K. Should it appear at any time that Army was likely to lose control of Suez Canal we should be prepared to block it.

36. *To Pound*

17 June 1940

In the situation envisaged consider it would be practicable to move part of Fleet westward, i.e., *Warspite, Malaya,* the modern cruisers and all the destroyers in the Mediterranean less the

---

[30]Sir Miles Lampson (1880–1964): FO 1903; Tokyo, Sofia, Peking; Actg Br H Cmnr Siberia 1920; M to China 1926–33; H Cmnr Egypt & Sudan 1934–36; hugely influential Amb Egypt 1936–46; Spl Cmnr SE Asia 1946–48.

[31]'V' and 'W': Australian destroyers.

Australian Division. *Eagle* is a doubtful quantity and might be better employed in Red Sea. It is considered remainder of Fleet less in the first instance 'C' class, *Medway* and submarines and all auxiliaries should proceed through Red Sea, *Medway* and 'C' class cruisers to Port Said retiring through Canal when necessary.[32]

2. Consider it essential that the Red Sea Force should come under my orders for this operation and under the orders of Rear Admiral when I have sailed West.

3. The situation in Egypt if the Fleet has to leave the Eastern Mediterranean has already been considered by the C-in-C Middle East who is of the opinion that in these circumstances the country cannot be held for long.

4. If this move is to take place the question of Malta requires urgent consideration and decision. In my opinion if the Fleet has to leave the Mediterranean the morale of the Maltese will collapse and it is only a question of time before the island falls. If the decision [is made] to let Malta go and a start is made now it should be possible to evacuate some quantity of the valuable fleet stores now there and personnel not essential for the defence.

37. *To Pound*

18 June 1940

My 1905/17 [no. 36] may have sounded somewhat acquiescent and I should like to be allowed to add some further observations.

2. Although in my opinion it would be practicable to move the faster part of the Fleet westward from Alexandria and the rest through the Suez Canal I feel that the effects of this withdrawal would involve such a landslide in territory and prestige that I earnestly hope such a decision will never have to be taken.

3. As already pointed out the C-in-C Middle East considers Egypt would be untenable soon after the Fleet's departure, Malta, Cyprus and Palestine could no longer be held, the Moslems would regard it as surrender, prospects of Turkey's loyalty would be discounted and even the Italians would be stirred to activity.

4. I am well aware of the paramount importance of our Atlantic trade and of home defence but I feel that with our present forces we should be able to safeguard these as well as maintaining the Eastern Mediterranean.

---

[32]*Medway*: S/M depot ship; 1929, 14,600t, 6×4in, 16k; s *U-372*, E Med, June 1942.

5. The Italian Battlefleet has so far shown no signs of life and from all the signs available here it does not appear that the Italians are yet considering serious fighting. I consider the battleships now here are sufficient to contain the Italian heavy ships with something in hand and when required the route to Malta could be opened.

6. Though I suspect it is shortage of light craft which is causing you most concern I am prepared if it would be any help to release one 'R' class battleship round the Cape to join the Gibraltar force.

7. I feel even a comparatively small force at Gibraltar will suffice to prevent the Italians from interfering in the Atlantic particularly if its operations are co-ordinated with those in the Eastern Mediterranean.

Marginal Notes by Cunningham [not sent]

... Are the presence of *Warspite, Malaya*, 5 cruisers and two flotillas in the North Atlantic worth the complete abandonment of the Eastern Mediterranean and making a gift of it to Italy?

38. *War Diary, 14–30 June (cont.)*

14 June

2. *Future movements*

Information was received from the Admiralty that the 5 submarines remaining in China would be sailed immediately for the Mediterranean, and that *Jervis* would be sailed in the near future from the UK to become the leader of the 14DF.[33]

4. *Shipping*

C-in-C issued the following policy for shipping at the Eastern end of the Mediterranean:

> Coastal traffic to recommence, using inshore route and cover of darkness. Escorts will be provided for oilers and ASIS. Other merchant shipping may sail with them if of a similar speed. There will be no Aegean convoy for about 10 days. C-in-C proposed to the NA, Ankara, that ships for the Aegean convoy should sail unescorted until outside Turkish territorial waters and assemble at Cankale.[34]

---

[33]*Jervis*: Ldr; 1939, 1,760t, 6×4.7in, 10×21in tt, 36k.
[34]Capt G. E. M. O'Donnell: Capt June 1939; NA Ankara (inc Greece & Yugoslavia) Oct. 1939; *Enterprise* Feb. 1942; *Malaya* July 1943; *Valiant* Oct. 1943; Dir, Damage Control Sch, Apr. 1945.

17 June

6. *Attack on enemy shipping*

As a result of the sinking of the Norwegian tanker *Organkar* without warning, C-in-C ordered that Italian tankers should be sunk at sight without warning. This order, however, had to be rescinded as the Admiralty informed C-in-C that this would require a Cabinet decision.[35]

18 June

Allied Submarines

The disposition of Allied submarines in the Eastern Mediterranean is as follows:

British
Oswald on passage to Dardanelies
Pandora on passage to Doro Channel
Phoenix in Kithera Channel
Proteus relieving *Osiris* in Kithera Channel
Grampus off Augusta
Odin off Taranto
Rorqual in Straits of Otranto
Orpheus off Malta.

French
Phoque off Rhodes
Protée, Espadon off Leros
2 off Straits of Messina
1 off Tripoli
An unknown number round the coast of Galita Island to the Gulf of Gabes.[36]

2. *Grampus* has laid mines in the searched channel off Augusta, and *Rorqual* 9 miles E of Brindisi.

3. As a result of VA, Malta's report that Malta was unsuitable as a submarine base, the C-in-C proposed to Admiral Sud that these

---

[35]*Organkar (Orkanger):* 1928, 8,029gt, Westfal-Larsen, Norway.

[36]*Oswald* (s *U. Vivaldi,* Ionian Sea, 1 Aug. 1940), *Odin* (s It dest, off Taranto, 13 June 1940), *Orpheus* (s It dest, off Tobruk, 27 June 1940): 1928, 1,475/2,030t, 1×4in, 8×21in tt, 17.5/9k.

Pandora (s a/c, Malta March 1942), *Phoenix* (s It escort, 17 July 1940), *Proteus:* 1930, 1,475/2,040t, 1×4in, 8×21in tt, 17.5/9k.

Grampus: 1937, 1,520/2,117t, 1×4in, 6×21in tt, 50 mines, 15.75/8.75k; s It escorts, off Syracuse, 24 June 1940.

Protée: 1930, 1,379/2,060t, 1×3.9in, 11×21.7in tt, 17/10k.

Espadon, Phoque: 1926, 974/1,441t, 1×3.9in 10×21.7in tt, 16/10k.

submarines should be moved to Alexandria. ... and requested Admiral Sud to leave some of his submarines at Beirut.

Both these proposals Admiral Sud agreed to.

19 June

8. *Enemy submarines*
... *Galileo Galilei* – captured by *Moonstone* in Red Sea off Aden.[37]

20 June

Operations
An Allied force sailed today to carry out operation MD3, the object being to destroy military objectives at Bardia and to destroy enemy submarines.

2. One force under Captain (D), 2DF consisting of *Hyperion, Havock, Hero, Hereward* and *Hostile*, sailed at 0800 to carry out an A/S sweep along the North African coast as far as the longitude of Tobruk, reaching this position at 0400/21 and returning to Alexandria by 1830.[38]
3. A second force under VA (D), consisting of *Orion, Lorraine, Neptune, Sydney, Stuart* and *Decoy, Dainty, Hasty*, sailed at 1130 to make an offing to the northwestward and then to carry out a bombardment of Bardia at dawn on 21 June.[39] After this force had sailed, information was received from 202 Group that an early morning reconnaissance had shown that there were in Tobruk harbour, 3 cruisers, 3 destroyers, 2 submarines and 10 other ships over 400 feet long, and 11 smaller vessels.

It was therefore decided to send a further force to sea to provide support for Captain (D), 2DF, and engage any enemy forces which might put to sea.

4. This force, under Captain (D), 14DF, consisting of *Nubian, Ilex, Imperial, Suffren* and *Dougay Trouin*, left Alexandria at 1730 with orders to be in a position 40 miles N of Tobruk at 0600/21, and if no

---

[37]*Galileo Galilei*: 1934, 900/1,250t, 2×3.9in, 8×21in tt, 17/8.5k.
Moonstone: trawler; 1934, 615t, 1×4in, 12k.
[38]Cdr H. StL. Nicolson: *Hyperion* 1938; Capt Dec. 1940; *Griffin* Nov. 1941; CSO to FOC, Dover, Dec. 1942; *King George V* BPF, 1945
Destroyers: 'H' cl: 1936, 1,340t, 4×4.7in, 8×21in tt, 36k.
[39]*Lorraine:* Fr B/S; 1915, 22,200t, 8×13.4in, 14×5.5in, 21k; mod 1934–35.
Orion, Neptune (mined, off Libya, 19 Dec. 1941): 1934, 7,215t, 8×6in, 8×4in, 8×21in tt, 32.5k.

enemy forces were encountered to return to Alexandria by 2000 on 21 June.[40]

5. *Future operations*

The C-in-C made the following signal to the Admiralty:

> I intend to take the Fleet, less *Malaya* and *Lorraine*, to sea early a.m./23 to carry out a sweep into the Central Mediterranean and propose to include French cruisers, who are full of fight, in these operations.
>
> *Objects:*
> (1) To destroy enemy forces at sea.
> (2) FAA attack on cruisers at Port Augusta.
> (3) Bombardment of military objectives at Port Augusta.
> (4) Cruiser raid on Straits of Messina.
> (5) Cover movements of essential shipping to and from Malta.

21 June

5. *Policy*

The C-in-C was informed by the Admiralty that any offensive action taken in conjunction with the French forces would be all to the good at the present time.

22 June

10. At 2153 the following signal was received from the Admiralty:

> Most immediate. Your 1211/20 [item 5, 20 June]. Defer proposed operation. Acknowledge.

It transpired from subsequent Admiralty signals that this order was issued in view of the political situation. . . .

25 June

Submarines

2. The C-in-C has asked the Admiralty for authority to be given for submarines to have freedom to attack all vessels entering or leaving Libyan ports in order to prevent troop movements between Italy and Libya. He suggested that an Italian declaration broadcast

---

[40]Capt (later RA) Philip Mack: Capt 1934; Capt (D), 7DF, Home F, March 1939, *Jervis; Duke of York* May 1942; *King George V* Sept. 1942; RA Jan. 1943; k air crash April 1943.
Nubian: 'Tribal' cl; 1938, 1,870t, 8×4.7in, 4×21in tt, 36.5k.
Ilex, Imperial (s off Crete, May 1941): 1937, 1,370t, 4×4.7in, 8×21in tt, 35.5k.
Suffren: 1930, 10,000t, 8×8in, 8×3in, 6×21in tt, 31k.
Dougay Trouin: 1926, 7,250t, 8×6.1in, 4×3in, 33k.

THE ANGLO-ITALIAN WAR, 1940   81

from Rome on 12 June that all ships approaching within 30 miles of Allied coasts do so at their own risk, would be sufficient justification for this measure.

26 June

The C-in-C made the following signal to the Admiralty:

Operations of the Fleet are being severely cramped by uncertainty regarding the French Squadron. I am taking the opportunity of running a S bound convoy from the Dardanelles and Greek ports to Port Said. Escort force consisting of 3CS and 14DF, sail on 26th to a rendezvous with convoy off the Dardanelles. Air and submarine reconnaissance will be provided off the coast of Crete and a force kept at short notice at Alexandria.

In addition to the Aegean convoy it is now intended to run a convoy from Malta to Alexandria. Five destroyers leave a.m., tomorrow, Thursday, followed by 7CS as a covering force. Destroyers will proceed first to carry out a hunt for U-boats and thence to Malta to arrive at dusk on 29 June, fuel and sail with two convoys – one of 13 knots, the other 9 knots. The 2nd Division of 1BS and *Eagle* sail a.m./28 to cover the operation ... while 7CS operate on a line Cape Passero-Sapienza. Flying boat reconnaissance will be maintained to Northward of 7CS. ...

8. *Malta air raids*

VA, Malta, reported 5 air raids delivered by 35 to 40 aircraft, apparently coming from Libya as well as Sicily. Casualties were considerable but little military damage was done. It is suspected that magnetic mines were dropped.

27 June

5. *Shipping*

The C-in-C informed the Admiralty as follows:

It is intended to carry out the following shipping policy whilst the Naval situation remains as at present:

(a) South bound Aegean convoys (AS) and North bound Aegean convoys (AN) to be run periodically to connect with Red Sea convoys.

(b) Local convoys between Haifa, Port Said and Alexandria, for oilers, ASIS and transports, to be run approximately weekly.

(c) Remaining shipping for Cyprian, Syrian, Palestinian and Egyptian ports to sail independently.

(d) When occasion demands, a convoy will be run to Malta. . . .

13. *Aircraft*

The C-in-C has made the following signal to the Admiralty:

> I consented to the Swordfish of 767 Squadron being placed under the operational control of the AOC, Mediterranean in order that all aircraft at Malta should be under one authority, but I consider that they should be used for local reconnaissance, A/S patrols, as a torpedo striking force against surface forces which come within range, and also as a reserve for *Eagle*. I do not consider these slow aircraft should be expended against targets in Sicily. Could not the Air Ministry be persuaded even at this late hour to send some more offensive and defensive aircraft to Malta[?].

39. To Pound

Warspite
27 June 1940

I am afraid you are having a lot of worries and I must not add to them.

A. My signals will have told you pretty well all there is to know about the French Squadron here. At one time I thought the Admiral would stand firm, but he faded out. They all expressed resentment at their government being called unconstitutional. They one and all have great faith in Pétain and Weygand, and do not believe they would have acted as they did without good cause. Our bolstering up of General de Gaulle has done no good; no one has any opinion of him.[41]

Darlan appears to have let us down badly. I never trusted him. Too political.

I fear there is little to be saved from the wreck here. The younger officers and men are all for fighting on. In fact there is one complete destroyer's crew who want to go on as they are under the British flag.

---

[41]Brig-Gen Charles de Gaulle (1890–1970): inf WW1, captd 1916; writer on mil sci; CO 4 Armd Div March 1940; Brig-Gen 1 June; USec, Defence 6–16 June; escaped to London, raised Free French 18 June; recog by UK 28 June; ent Paris 26 Aug. 1944; recog as hd of govt Oct. 1944; Pres 1944–46 & 1958–69.

Godfroy is a very honest man and they cause me no anxiety, but there will be, I feel sure, an increasing demand for the sailors to go home to France.

I am not clear if it is Admiralty policy in no circumstances to use the ships, but if the men clear out, there are three fairly good destroyers I should like to make use of, and I could probably man an 8-in cruiser with a bit of an effort. These would prove a most welcome addition.

B. You will have seen the proposal put forward from the C-in-C, Middle East, that a sort of minor War Cabinet should be set up in Kenya to run the war in the East.

As the communications are so poor, and presumably we should attempt to draw on India, Australia and New Zealand for all our supplies, I agree in principle to this suggestion. I am not, however, clear about Naval representation on this body. I do not see how the operations of the Fleet in *all* theatres can be divorced from the control of the Admiralty.

But if some such body is set up, and I feel sure it would have its uses if only to co-ordinate strategy in this part of the world, there can only be one Naval representative on it, and that is the C-in-C of the principal Naval forces. Don't think I am hankering after the job; it sounds too much like going ashore.

There is also the possibility of the Admiralissimo with authority over all the Eastern Cs-in-C. I feel myself he would be the fifth wheel in the coach.

C. I was very sorry to have my operation against Port Augusta cancelled and the Frenchmen were much upset at being deprived of their opportunity of going to sea with us. I don't know now when it will be brought off. There are so many calls on us and so few destroyers, but in this respect everyone is in the same box. The loss of the *Khartoum* by such stupid means is most infuriating when we can ill spare one.[42]

D. I am very concerned about the losses of our submarines. With one exception every submarine operating off an Italian port has been lost, and we don't know how, which is the worst part of it. Myself, I think the Italians have the approaches to their ports smothered in defensive minefields laid very deep, and I think our submarines must have gone up on them. They are rather too gallant these young Commanding Officers, and I am putting a curb on them, except when in pursuit of the enemy.

---

[42]*Khartoum*: 1939, 1,760t, 6×4.7in, 10×21in tt, 36k; tot loss foll action with It S/M *Torricelli,* Red Sea 23 June 1940; S/M scut.

For the same reason one has had to be very careful about letting battleships or cruisers approach the coast, and there are few places one can get in gun range of without crossing the 100 fathom line. . . .
E. With the exception of destroyers and submarines, I don't believe an Italian ship has been out of harbour this last week, and the inactivity of their bombers is most surprising. When the cruisers and *Lorraine* bombarded Bardia a week ago, not an enemy aircraft was to be seen . . .
F. . . . I hope it will not be necessary to abandon the Eastern Mediterranean; the landslide would be frightful. If the Spaniards leave us alone I think quite a small force could hold that end, and if the efforts of the Eastern and Western Mediterranean are properly co-ordinated, I feel we can keep the Italians pretty well engaged.
G. Malta is doing very well I think, and the morale of the Maltese is surprisingly high. How long it will last like that I can't say. Six days ago they were down to the last one of the six Gladiator FAA spare aircraft I told them to use. Is it even now too late to get the Air Ministry to send out some fighters?

If we had 20 or 30 fighters at Malta ready to operate over the Fleet I think we could guarantee to make the Sicilians anyway very sorry that Italy had entered the war.

I am sure that the provision of aircraft for Malta would make all the difference to our operations both in the Eastern and Western Mediterranean.

H. . . . I think it is desirable that the VA(D) should command all the light forces, and I would recommend that Renouf goes to the 7th Cruiser Squadron as his second-in-command, hoisting his flag in *Liverpool* and administers the cruisers.

40. *War Diary, 14–30 June (cont.)*

28 June

Operations

2. As a result of flying boat reconnaissance the 7CS sighted 3 enemy destroyers about 75 miles WSW of Cape Matapan, steering to the Westward at high speed, at 1830. A long range action ensued during the course of which one destroyer was sunk.[43]

---

[43]*Espero*: 1928, 1,090t, 4×4.7in, 6×21in tt, 33k.

29 June

Operations

2. *Dainty* made the following signal:

Italian submarine *Liuzzi* sunk ... on 27 June. *Salpa* sunk ... *Uebi Scebeli* sunk ... Have secret orders for Italian submarines which order them to be in the following positions 0400 tomorrow 30 June
 Ondina 34° 16′N, 23° 24′E
 Anfitrite 34° 46′N, 23° 40′E ..., returning to Augusta 10 July.
Am sweeping towards Northern position.

5. *Diamond* also reported that *Voyager* has on board a large number of Italian secret documents.[44]

6. On receipt of these signals *Voyager* was ordered to Alexandria and *Stuart* and *Hostile* to sea to join the hunt for *Anfitrite* and *Ondina*.

8. The C-in-C requested the Admiralty that publication of these 'kills' should be deferred for the present.

15. *Own submarines*

It is regretted that both *Odin* and *Orpheus* must now be considered lost.

30 June

5. *Other movements*

Information has been received from the Admiralty that a special force H has been formed at Gibraltar under the command of [Vice] Admiral Sir James Somerville, ...

7. *Submarines*

The C-in-C has asked the Admiralty for permission for submarines to attack the bauxite traffic between Yugo Slavia and Trieste, and the tanker traffic from the Corinth Canal and Kithera Channel.

8. *Enemy Intelligence*

... Information was received from the COIS that important storeship and troopship movements were imminent between Italy and North Africa. ... In view of the above information C-in-C informed VA, Malta, that this appeared to be a chance of torpedo attack with Swordfish.

13. *Telegraphic facilities for the Fleet*

C-in-C has represented to the Admiralty that the morale and contentment of the men of the Fleet are to a large extent dependent on

---

[44]Not *Salpa* but *Argonauta*: 1932, 650/810t, 1×4in, 6×21in tt, 15/7.5k. *Liuzzi*: 1939, 1,166/1,484t, 1×3.9in, 8×21in tt, 18/8k. *Uebi Scebeli*: 1937, 680/866t, 1×3.9in, 6×21in tt, 14/8k. *Ondina, Anfitrite*: 1934, 680/860t, 1×3.9in, 6×21in tt, 14/8k; neither were found. *Rubino*: 1934, same cl, s by Sunderland, 29 June, Ionian Sea.

the knowledge that their people at home are well and cared for, and the present lack of postal facilities has had a deleterious effect. It is therefore recommended that telegraphic facilities should be arranged whereby relatives can communicate with officers and men and also that some arrangement should be made whereby officers and men can be given news of death or injury of relatives as a result of enemy action.

41. *To the Admiralty*

25 June 1940

Godfroy has received orders and officially requested that his squadron may be allowed to sail for Beirut today Tuesday. I have refused his request. Our relations exceptionally friendly and I rather feel he and many of his officers are very glad to have had to bow to *force majeure*. I anticipate no difficulty. I hope the intention with regard to these ships may be made known to me as soon as possible as Godfroy may have trouble with ships' companies.

42. *To the Admiralty*

27 June 1940

Admiral Godfroy has offered to discharge all oil fuel from his ships to save me embarrassment of having to keep a large force in harbour to look after them. He has also asked for an assurance that there is no intention of seizing his ships by force. My personal view is that he will not be able to keep his crews in their ships and that we shall in due course be faced with a demand to send all crews to France.

43. *From the Admiralty*

27 June 1940

Discharge of oil fuel will be welcomed. Assurance that ships will not be seized should not (R) not be given. If discharge of oil fuel is coupled with this assurance you should not press for it. We have no intention that French ships at Alexandria should pass out of our hands into those of the enemy. We should naturally prefer to use them with British crews but, if that is not possible, they must be sunk outside the harbour. Do you consider that Godfroy would sink his ships at their moorings if you demand that they should be handed over to us intact?

44. *From Pound*

28 June 1940

French liaison officer has just brought me a message from Darlan protesting against the retention of ships at Alexandria, Portsmouth and Plymouth. I replied that we had got to win the war not only for ourselves but for them, and all trivialities and sob stuff about friendship and feelings must be swept aside. He asked if the ships would be fired on if they attempted to leave Alexandria and I replied 'yes'; and now they know it the responsibility will be theirs.

45. *To the Admiralty*

28 June 1940

Admiral Godfroy has just given me his word and that of his captains that no attempt will be made to leave Alexandria. I therefore do not intend to ask for discharge of oil fuel unless it appears that the Admiral is losing control. There is no sign of this at present.

Godfroy is evidently hoping against hope that something will turn up to enable him to fight again on our side with his squadron, . . .

If Godfroy is told we intend to take over his ships consider he would take them to sea and sink them. If this were not permitted I would not be sure of his reaction if forcible steps were taken to seize them in harbour.

I would emphasise frank and cordial relations exist here and feel more can be done by friendly negotiations than by threatening forcible measures. In any case the ships will not go to sea.

46. *To the Admiralty*

29 June 1940

Admiral Godfroy has since made following points:

A. Darlan informed him that he had given way far too quickly and had made things far too easy for us. Godfroy very angry and has low opinion of Darlan.

B. Darlan stated further orders will be coming. If these order French to break out, Godfroy will first ask permission to withdraw his present parole not to leave harbour and then ask to sail with a British unit in company in order to scuttle all his ships outside.
C. If orders in B received in absence of British Fleet, Godfroy would await our return.
D. Godfroy maintains that until General de Gaulle's declaration French ships could have remained in Colonial ports, but thereafter Italian armistice terms insist on return of warships to France.
E. Gensoul still considering whether to return to France and is having trouble with reservists.[45] French morale here, however, good.
F. Godfroy states that whatever his orders nothing would induce him to fire a shot at the British Fleet.

The best solution might now be for us to offer to allow the ships to remain here with skeleton crews and to give undertaking that we would only use them if the Germans or Italians break the terms of the armistice. It is for consideration whether forcible attempts to seize with the likely result of a fight in Alexandria harbour and of ships sinking at their moorings counterbalances the advantages of having the use of the ships.

47. *From the Admiralty*

30 June 1940

A. It is under consideration to seize French ships at Alexandria – simultaneously with operation at Oran. Earliest date for this operation is a.m., 3 July.

Request your views as to best procedure to follow so as to achieve our purposes with minimum risk of bloodshed and hostilities on the part of the French.
B. It would also be desirable to deal with ships at Sfax in a similar manner to those at Oran immediately after operation at Alexandria has been completed.

As presumably you will require battleships at Alexandria for that operation it is not considered practicable to carry out Alexandria and Sfax operations simultaneously. It would be unsound to send a

---

[45] Adm Marcel-Bruno Gensoul (1880–1973): ent N 1898; Lt de V 1911; torpedo splist; Med 1914–18; staff work 1922; N War Coll 1926; Capt de V 1927 & CO *Bretagne; Provence* 1929; RA 1932; 3rd Lt Sqdn 1934; VA 1937; Préfet Maritime, Toulon; C-in-C, Atl Sqdn 1938; C-in-C Atl F 1939; Adm July 1940; Insp-Gen, Maritime Forces & Chief C Marine Works Service; Ret List Oct 1942. In cmd, Mers-el-Kébir, when Force H negotiated and then opened fire.

weak capital ship force to Sfax as they could be intercepted by Italian Fleet.

48. *To the Admiralty*

30 June 1940

I am most strongly opposed to proposal for forcible seizure of ships in Alexandria nor can I see what benefit is to be derived from it. Request urgent consideration of the following points.
2. Situation here is apparently quite different from that elsewhere in Mediterranean – see my 1825/29 [no. 46].
3. What is object of seizure? If it is to prevent ships falling into enemy hands that has already been achieved.
4. If it is desired to obtain ships for ourselves it is unlikely to be obtained by forcible seizure since I am convinced that the French would resist most vigorously and it would be more likely to result in ships scuttling themselves at their moorings before it could be prevented, unnecessary British and French casualties, and a harbour fouled with wrecks.
5. The effect in the Middle East moreover is likely to be disastrous particularly in the Suez Canal and Djibouti where French co-operation is vitally important and in Syria whose friendly attitude is very necessary.
6. On the other hand if matters are allowed to pursue their present course at Alexandria it may well be that under pressure of lack of pay and food ships drop into our hands – see my 1825/29.
7. The above does not however allow of the repercussions consequent on forcible action at Oran. I am very much against action there if it can possibly be avoided . . . the effect may be to alienate the whole of the French element friendly to us and in particular I would mention the effect in North America where friendly attitudes may make a great difference to Naval operations later on.
8. I have had no reports of French ships at Sfax and request information. I am unwilling to engage my cruisers in any action except against the enemy in view of critical ammunition situation.

49. *From the Admiralty*

2 July

A. We should like to obtain French ships at Alexandria for our own use, if this can be done without bloodshed. In this case, men who desired to remain would be accepted for service under Royal Navy conditions. The remainder would be repatriated.

B. If we can not (R) NOT obtain ships for our own use they must be dealt with in one of the following ways, which are in order of merit from our point of view.

(i) at Alexandria with skeleton crews but immediately put in a non-seagoing condition, on the understanding that we would only use them if the Germans or Italians broke the terms of the armistice. Responsibility for pay and maintenance of personnel and ships would be undertaken by HM Government. Should Admiral Godfroy insist that ships must be demilitarised before he leaves them you may accept this.

(ii) Sunk at sea.

C. As action at Oran will be taken early on Wednesday 3 July you should, unless you hear to the contrary, put 'A', and if this fails then the other alternatives in turn to Admiral Godfroy at 0700 on Wednesday 3 July.

50. *From the Admiralty*

3 July 1940

No time limit for acceptance of demands is contained in your instructions, but it is very important that operation should be completed during daylight hours today Wednesday.

51. *Account of an interview between the British Naval C-in-C, Mediterranean Station, and Admiral Godfroy, Commanding French Force X, held on board* Warspite

3 July 1940

Message from the British Government was read to Admiral Godfroy and he was given a copy. He appeared to accept the force of the argument and made no comment, except to say that he would like to have had this from his own government.

The C-in-C then explained that he had been instructed by the British Government to lay various proposals for the disposition of the French Squadron before Admiral Godfroy and that he must have definite acceptance of one or other of them today.

Alternative 'A' (AM 2100/1/7 [no. 49]) was then laid before him. Godfroy raised many objections to this alternative and said he could not possibly adopt it without consulting his Government and he said how could the ships fight except under the French flag and that officers and men would be deserters, and that if we used any of his ships for the war he felt sure the Germans and Italians would demand an equivalent number and class of French ships to be handed over for their use.

It was intimated to Godfroy that the terms were good and that the C-in-C could, if he wanted, communicate them to the French officers and men over the head of Godfroy, but that he naturally did not want to do so. Godfroy admitted that he was fully aware of this.

... It became evident that there were no prospects of Godfroy accepting this alternative.

Alternative B(1) was then laid before him. Godfroy brightened up when he read B(1) and he intimated he could accept this. He expressed the desire to have a little time to think it over, ... and 1130 was agreed to.

Godfroy was then shown alternative B(2), but this invoked no enthusiasm and on the C-in-C pointing out that this would in no way achieve Godfroy's object, he agreed to revert to consideration of B(1).

He demurred somewhat at idea of the majority of crews being removed from his ships and evidently had at the back of his mind strong hopes that the Italians would break the armistice and that he would be able to take his ships out to fight the enemy.

The interview concluded with the C-in-C impressing on Godfroy that he must make up his mind on his own and by the end of the forenoon, and he intimated most tactfully that it was a case of *force majeure* and that he could honourably accept one of the alternatives. The C-in-C added that if it could not be B(1) he hoped it would be B(2).

Terms Put to Vice-Admiral Godfroy

I

The British Government asks you to put at their disposition the Naval units under your command so that they can continue the struggle against the enemy side by side with the British Navy.

For those who wish to join us the conditions of service and pay will be the same as that of officers, petty officers and men of corresponding rank in the British Navy. Those who do not wish to continue the fight are entitled freely to return to France and arrangements will be made as soon as possible for them to do so.

You are asked to announce these proposals in such a way that they are known to all officers and ships' companies and to make it clear that they are free to make their choice without any constraint.

The British Government guarantees to return to France at the end of the war all ships which have thus taken part with us in the struggle against the enemy.

II

If you remain convinced that it is not possible to allow your forces to help the British Navy, the British Government asks you to put your ships in a condition in which they cannot go to sea, and leave on board only skeleton crews sufficient to keep the ships in good order.

In this case the British Government guarantees the pay and supplies for the officers and men left on board and that the ships will only be used if the enemy breaks the terms of the armistice . . .

III

If these proposals are neither of them acceptable, the British Government asks you as a third alternative to order your forces in Alexandria to sea in order to sink them outside the port in open waters.

52. *To the Admiralty*

3 July 1940

Admiral Godfroy has chosen the third alternative i.e. B(2) namely to sink his ships unless he can ask for instructions from his Admiralty in which case he will recommend alternative B(1) which is retention of ships at Alexandria in a non-seagoing condition. He further asks for 48 hours to make arrangements for carrying out alternative B(2) and this is in fact necessary as there are upwards of 4,000 men to be disposed of and accommodation is not immediately available.

2. There is no question of his attempting to put to sea without my consent and I wish at all costs to avoid sinking his ships in Alexandria harbour or Godfroy being ordered to do so by his Government.

3. I am formally accepting his decision and will hasten arrangements for putting it into effect as much as possible.

4. In meantime I am trying to persuade Godfroy to discharge the oil from his ships and to some extent disarm and leave the question of skeleton crews for further discussion.

5. I am sure Godfroy has at the back of his mind that the Italians will break the armistice terms and thus enable him to fight again.

53. *To the Admiralty*

3 July 1940

Although Godfroy will not accept alternative B(1) in its entirety, I have now induced him
(a) to discharge the oil from his ships
(b) to remove warheads

but he will not agree to skeleton crews without consent of his government. Urge most strongly that matters should be settled by negotiation between Admiralties if this is possible. Meanwhile Godfroy is making all preparations to execute alternative B(2) on Friday 5 July.

54. *From the Admiralty*

3 July 1940

Admiralty note that French ships discharging oil, but crews should commence being reduced at once by landing or transfer to merchant ships especially key ratings before dark tonight. Do not (R) NOT fail.

55. *From Godfroy*

Duquesne
3 July 1940

I have just learnt that an ultimatum has been addressed to our Atlantic Fleet by the British Admiralty.

For our part, my Admiralty has ordered me to sail; though I am pressing to be assured that the order is authentic.

I have replied that sailing is impossible, but the situation is wholly altered.

To save myself from the reproach of having diminished oil fuel *after* having received the order to sail, I have stopped the discharge of oil fuel while waiting events.

But that changes nothing. I give you my word about my intentions, which conform with those that I mentioned to you in writing this morning.[46]

56. *To the Admiralty*

0049, 4 July 1940

Admiralty telegram 1824/3/7/40 [no. 54] was received long after dark at 2015.
2. Godfroy having received a direct order from his Admiralty to proceed to sea using force if necessary and having heard of the engagement off Oran now flatly declines to continue discharging oil or to remove any of his men. He further refuses to proceed to sea voluntarily and sink his ships in deep water, in fact he asserts that if he is allowed out of the harbour he will run for it and fully realises this would lead to a battle.
3. No amount of persuasion and threats of force will move him though he is quite resigned to remaining here with his crews on board. He has stated emphatically that if faced with any demand backed by force he will sink his ships in harbour at the same time intimating that he will do so in a manner as convenient to us as possible.
4. I consider the courses of action open to me are:

A. To attempt to seize the French ships by boarding
B. To sink them by gun and torpedo fire at their moorings
C. To face Godfroy with a demand to intern or surrender his ships with the result that he will sink them.

5. I have given much consideration to A but have discarded it as being doubtful of success as the French ships are thoroughly on the alert as the result of the Oran action.
6. B will be resisted and will lead to useless bloodshed on both sides and result in the French ships being sunk in most inconvenient places and possibly damaging to our own ships.
7. Unless Their Lordships see fit to direct otherwise, I intend to put C into force a.m. Friday 5 July at which time I hope to have the necessary shipping to embark 4000 French sailors.
8. I fear that in the sense of your 1824/3/7/40 [no. 54] I have failed

---

[46]*Duquesne*: Godfroy's F/ship; 1928, 10,000t, 8×8in, 8×3in, 33k.

57. *From the Admiralty*

4 July 1940

Para. 4 (a) It does not seem at all certain that Godfroy in his present frame of mind will sink his ships unless you force him to do so by some threat. What threat do you propose to use?

(b) . . . could they be starved out?

(c) The undesirability of a battle in Alexandria harbour is fully realised but present situation could not be allowed to persist indefinitely. Have you considered less objectionable alternative of secretly raising steam and taking British ships to sea leaving the French inside? Your Fleet could then be suitably disposed for engaging the French ships and an ultimatum delivered. It is realised that damage would probably be done to shore establishments but any important damage to your ships should be avoided.

(d) You have no doubt taken steps to prevent ammunition ships being blown up.

58. *To the Admiralty*

0827, 4 July 1940

Godfroy now refuses to give any undertaking whatsoever. Am attempting to sow dissension among his ships' companies not presenting my ultimatum till transports for the crews arrive. Shall sink him if he moves. Have just had air raid in which at least one French ship fired vigorously.

59. *To the Admiralty*

1317, 4 July 1940

Situation very tense. Godfroy having withdrawn all previous undertakings course of action C in my 0049/4 [no. 56] no longer applies in full. Chance of a negotiated settlement seems remote, but efforts are being made by French Liaison Officer to persuade Godfroy through Captains to come to some arrangements on lines of alternative B(1). Honour and effect of Oran action stand in the way. Consider it would be unwise to force matters to a head just yet and prefer to give the various contacts on a lower plane which are being established chance to take effect. I feel that an action in this harbour ought to be avoided at almost any cost, but Godfroy in his present mood will not scuttle his ships, if faced with an ultimatum backed by force. He will certainly order his ships to open fire if I do.

I fully realise the vital necessity of an early solution if necessary by force....

60. *To the Admiralty*

1529, 4 July 1940

Following agreement just concluded with Godfroy:

(a) All oil fuel to be discharged from French ships forthwith.
(b) Ships to be placed immediately in a condition in which they cannot fight.
(c) Discharge of ships' companies to be a matter for further discussion.

2. I have hopes that reservists who include many key ratings will be discharged tomorrow Friday.

61. *To the Admiralty*

5 July 1940

Although most undesirable to have a battle in Alexandria harbour, the situation became such that the threat of sinking the French ships at their moorings had to be made.

2. During this forenoon signals to all ships and personal visits by the British Captains were made with the object of influencing the officers and ships' companies against useless resistance to overwhelming force.

3. These proved successful as at a post-prandial meeting the Captains of the French ships prevailed on Godfroy to accept the conditions set out in my 1529/4 [no. 60].

62. *To the Admiralty*

6 July 1940

2. I intend to use alternative B (i.e., offer of guarantee that the French ships will not be seized unless Italy or Germany break the Armistice terms) as a means of expediting the departure of crews and also to try and get an undertaking that the ships will not be

sunk at their moorings. There must inevitably be danger of this sooner or later, particularly if situation between us and French deteriorates.

63. *From Godfroy*

30 July 1940

I should be very sorry that you think my present reserve means a change in my feelings towards yourself.

You must believe that those feelings are always the same. I think of you and Admiral Willis with the same respect and sympathy as before and I have no reason to do otherwise.

But I feel obliged to take into account for some time the grief of officers and petty officers of my squadron who have lost sons or brothers at Oran and would perhaps be hurt if we behaved as if nothing had happened. . . .

64. *War Diary, July 1940*

1 July

Operations

4. As a result of the continued bombing of the Aegean convoy, C-in-C has represented to the Admiralty that he has no ships with sufficient AA armament suitable for convoy escort work and that he is forced to use 'Tribals' and 'J' Class destroyers for this duty, thus wasting ammunition and wearing out their guns. He therefore requests the provision of escort vessels in the Eastern Mediterranean.

5. *Malta*

. . . The C-in-C has pointed out to the Admiralty the vital necessity of Malta as a flying boat base when the Fleet is operating in the Central Mediterranean. The present continued air raids and lack of defences at Malta, however, make refuelling of the aircraft a hazardous operation, except in dark hours. He therefore requests that urgent consideration be given to the provision of fighters for Malta, and further that more Sunderland flying boats be allocated to the Eastern Mediterranean to replace casualties and assist in the valuable work already being done by the existing squadron.[47]

---

[47]Short Sunderland: 1937, 8–14mg, 2,000lbs bombs, 213mph, range 3,000mls.

7. *Shipping*

The C-in-C has instructed all British shipping in Syrian ports to sail for Haifa or Port Said forthwith.

5 July

Operations

813 Squadron, armed with torpedoes, moved from Dekheila to Sidi Barrani this afternoon and left there by sub-flights to attack Tobruk at dusk. Two sub-flights arrived Tobruk about 2020. Tobruk appeared to have been warned and they were met with a hot fire of 'flaming onions' and pom-pom and 0.5-in machine gun and red and green tracers. Seven aircraft fired their torpedoes inside the harbour, pilots selecting their individual targets. . . . An intercepted Italian report states that the motor vessel *Manzoni* and destroyer *Zeffiro* were sunk. The destroyer *Euro* was hit twice forward and all compartments flooded. The motor vessel *Liguria* damaged, but water being kept down.[48]

2. The success of this operation was largely due to excellent RAF co-operation in providing reconnaissance, diversionary attacks to draw the enemy fighters and aerodrome facilities.

4. All our aircraft returned safely.

French Situation

6. Instructions have been received from the Admiralty that as the attitude of the Bordeaux Government is uncertain and we may be at war with France shortly, ships are not to approach within 20 miles of French ports. British naval forces must be prepared for attack when meeting French forces but are not to fire the first shot.

Shipping

7. As three British ships are held up at Beirut, the C-in-C has stopped the sailing of British and French shipping to Syrian ports.

9. The oiler *British Union* has again caused anxiety to the Greek Government and the NA, Athens, suggested to the C-in-C that if she discharged 4,000 tons at Athens this will ease the situation. The C-in-C, however, would not agree to this, but informed the NA that the *British Union* would not be used for fuelling British destroyers in Greek waters except in exceptional circumstances.[49]

---

[48]*Zeffiro* (1928), *Euro* (1927) (s Ger a/c Oct. 1943): 1,090t, 4×4.7in, 6×21in tt, 33k. *Manzoni*: 1902, 3,955gt, Tirrenia.
Liguria: 1918, 15, 354gt, Lloyd Triestino.
[49]*British Union*: 1927, 6,987gt, 10k, Br Tkr Co.
RA C. E. Turle: NA Athens & SBNO, Greece, 1940–41; *Eaglet* (L'pl) Oct 1941; RA (Ret) *Nile* Sept. 1944.

65. *Report of an Action with the Italian Fleet off Calabria*

9 July 1940

2. It was during these operations that the Fleet first received serious attention from the Italian Air Force, and Calabria was the first time contact was made with Italian surface forces, other than destroyers.

3. It is still not clear what brought the enemy fleet to sea on this occasion, but it seems probable that it was engaged on an operation designed to cover the movement of a convoy to Libya. When our Fleet was reported S of Crete, it seems that the enemy retired close to his bases, fuelled his destroyers by relays, and then waited, hoping to draw us into an engagement in his own waters (under cover of his Air Force and possibly with a submarine concentration to the Southward of him) whence he could use his superior speed to withdraw at his own time.

4. If these were in fact the enemy's intentions, he was not altogether disappointed, but the submarines, if there were any in the vicinity of the action, did not materialise, and fortunately for us, his air attacks failed to synchronise with the gun action.

5. From an examination of enemy reports it appears that the enemy forces consisted of 2 battleships, 16 (possibly 17 or 18) cruisers, of which 6 (and possibly 7) were 8-in, and 25 to 30 destroyers.

6. It will be noted that the whole action took place at very long range and that *Warspite* was the only capital ship which got within range of the enemy battleships. *Malaya* fired a few salvoes which fell some 3,000 yards short. *Royal Sovereign,* owing to her lack of speed, never got into action at all.

7. *Warspite*'s hit on one of the enemy battleships at 26,000 yards range might perhaps be described as a lucky one. Its tactical effect was to induce the enemy to turn away and break off the action, which was unfortunate, but strategically it probably has had an important effect on the Italian mentality.

8. The torpedo attacks by the FAA were disappointing, one hit on a cruiser being all that can be claimed, but in fairness it must be recorded that the pilots had had very little practice, and none at high speed targets, *Eagle* having only recently joined the Fleet after having been employed on the Indian Ocean trade routes.[50]

---

[50] No hit obtained.

9. The enemy's gunnery seemed good at first and he straddled quickly, but accuracy soon fell off as his ships came under our fire.

10. Our cruisers – there were only 4 in action – were badly outnumbered and at times came under a very heavy fire. They were superbly handled by Vice Admiral J. C. Tovey, who by his skilful manoeuvring managed to maintain a position in the van and to hold the enemy cruiser squadrons, and at the same time avoid damage to his own force. *Warspite* was able to assist him with her own fire in the early stages of the action.

11. The enemy's smoke tactics were impressive and the smoke screens laid by his destroyers were very effective in completely covering his high speed retirement. With his excess speed of at least 5 knots there was little hope of catching him once he had decided to break off the action. An aircraft torpedo hit on one of his battleships was the only chance and this unfortunately did not occur.

12. The chase was continued under exceedingly heavy bombing attacks until the British Fleet was 25 miles from the Calabrian Coast, and was then reluctantly abandoned, the destroyers being very short of fuel and the enemy fleet well below the horizon.

13. I cannot conclude these remarks without a reference to HMS *Eagle*. This obsolescent aircraft carrier, with only 17 Swordfish embarked, found and kept touch with the enemy fleet, flew off two striking forces of 9 torpedo bombers within the space of 4 hours, both of which attacked, and all aircraft returned. Twenty-four hours later a torpedo striking force was launched on shipping in Augusta and throughout the five days' operations *Eagle* maintained constant A/S patrols in daylight and carried out several searches. Much of *Eagle*'s aircraft operating work was done in the fleeting intervals between, and even during, bombing attacks and I consider her performance reflects great credit on Captain A. R. M. Bridge, her Commanding Officer.[51] . . .

16. The meagre material results derived from this brief meeting with the Italian Fleet were naturally very disappointing to me and all under my command, but the action was not without value. It must have shown the Italians that their Air Force and submarines cannot stop our Fleet penetrating into the Central Mediterranean and that only their main fleet can seriously interfere with our operating there. It established, I think, a certain degree of moral ascen-

---

[51]Capt A. R. M. Bridge: Capt 1934; *Eagle* China June 1939; DNAD March 1942; CSO to FO Carrier Trng & Admin *Monck* May 1943; Cdre 1Cl *Merlin* (Donibristle); Cdre Carrier Trng & Admin & 2nd-in-C, NAS (N) June 1945.

dancy, since although superior in battleships, our Fleet was outnumbered in cruisers and destroyers, and the Italians had strong shore-based air forces within easy range, compared to our few carrier borne aircraft.

On our side the action has shown those without previous war experience how difficult it is to hit with the gun at long range, and therefore the necessity of closing in, when this can be done, in order to get decisive results. It showed that high level bombing, even on the heavy and accurate scale experienced during these operations, yields few hits and that it is more alarming than dangerous.

Finally, these operations and the action off Calabria produced throughout the Fleet a determination to overcome the air menace and not let it interfere with our freedom of manoeuvre and hence our control of the Mediterranean.

Narrative

The Mediterranean Fleet, less *Ramillies* and the 3rd CS, left Alexandria on 7 July to carry out Operation MA5, the object being the safe and timely arrival at Alexandria of two convoys from Malta with evacuees and Fleet stores.

2. It was intended that the Fleet should [detach] destroyers to Malta, which with *Jervis* and *Diamond*, who were already at Malta, would sail p.m. escorting the convoys. It was intended to carry out operations against the Sicilian Coast on the 9th.

3. The fast convoy, MF1, consisted of the Egyptian ship *El Nil*, the ex-Italian ship *Rodi* and the British ship *Knight of Malta*. The slow convoy, MS1, consisted of the British ships *Zeeland, Kirkland* and *Masirah* and the Norwegian ship *Novasli*.[52]

4. The Fleet sailed from Alexandria in three groups:

Force A – 7th CS and destroyer *Stuart*.
Force B – C-in-C in *Warspite,* with destroyers *Nubian, Mohawk, Hero, Hereward* and *Decoy*.

---

[52]*El Nil*: 1916, 7,769gt, Misr, Egypt.
Rodi: 1928, 3,320gt, Adriatica.
Knight of Malta: 1929, 1,553gt, Cassar, Malta.
Zeeland: 1936, 1,433gt, 10k, Currie Line.
Kirkland: 1934, 1,361gt, 10k, Currie Line.
Masirah: 1919, 6,578gt, 12.5k, Brocklebank.
Novasli: 1920, 3,204gt, Skibs A/S Novasli, Norway.

Force C – RA, 1st BS in *Royal Sovereign*, with *Malaya, Eagle* and destroyers *Hyperion, Hostile, Hasty, Ilex, Imperial, Dainty, Defender, Juno, Janus, Vampire* and *Voyager*.[53]

6. *Liverpool*, who was at Port Said, having just arrived there after transporting troops to Aden, sailed to rendezvous direct with VA (D).
8. At 2339/7 . . . *Hasty* sighted an Italian U-boat on passage on the surface at 1,000 yards' range. A full pattern depth charge attack was made and the U-boat was probably sunk. At 0100/8 when rejoining RA 1st BS, another attack was carried out on a confirmed contact. It is considered that this attack damaged a second U-boat.[54]
10. At 0807 a report was received from *Phoenix* of 2 enemy battleships and 4 destroyers . . . She attacked at extreme range but the attack was apparently unsuccessful.

As it was suspected from this report that the force might be covering an important convoy, VA, Malta, was ordered to arrange for a flying boat to locate and shadow this force. . . .

Two submarines were sighted by *Eagle's* A/S patrols, one of which was attacked with bombs.

11. In the mean time all forces were subjected to heavy bombing attacks by aircraft which appeared to come from the Dodecanese. Seven attacks were delivered on *Warspite* between 1205 and 1812, about 50 bombs being dropped. There were no hits.
12. Between 0951 and 1749 6 attacks were made on Force C, about 80 bombs being dropped. There were no hits.
13. Most ships experienced some very near misses but the only hit was on Force A, *Gloucester* being hit by one bomb on the compass platform causing the following casualties:

Officers, killed 7 (including Captain F. R. Garside), 3 wounded.[55] Ratings, 11 killed and 6 wounded.

The damage caused to the bridge structure, and DCT, necessitated gun control and steering from aft.
14. At 1510 flying boat L5803 reported 2 battleships, 6 cruisers and 7 destroyers . . . the enemy Fleet was resighted by another Sunderland from Malta early the next morning.

---

[53]*Mohawk* (s It dest *Tarigo*, C Med, April 1941): 1938, 1,870t, 8×4.7in, 4×21in tt, 36.5k. Others: 'D', 'H' & 'I' cls; *Juno* (s Ger a/c, Crete, May 1941), *Janus* (s Ger a/c, Anzio Jan 1944): 1939, 1,760t, 6×4.7in, 10×21in tt, 36k.
[54]None sunk.
[55]Capt F.R. Garside: Capt 1935; *Gloucester* Jan 1939 & COS to C-in-C, E Indies.

15. At the time it was suspected that these two battleships were in fact 8-in cruisers. The intensive bombing which had been experienced had already given the impression that the Italians had some special reason for wishing to keep us out of the Central Mediterranean.

This, in conjunction with these enemy reports, made it appear that the Italians might be covering the passage of some important convoy, probably to Benghazi, and it was decided temporarily to abandon the operations in hand and to move the fleet at best speed towards Taranto to get between the enemy and his base.

Force B maintained a mean line of advance of 310° at 20 knots during the night.

16. ... at 0440 *Eagle* flew off 3 aircraft to search to a depth of 60 miles between 180 and 300°.

The Approach Period, 9 July (0600–1430)

17. At 0600 the fleet was concentrated ... The 7th CS and *Stuart* were in the van 8 miles ahead of the C-in-C ... The RA 1st BS ... was 8 miles to the rear of *Warspite*. ...

18. At 0732 flying boat L5807 reported the main enemy fleet consisting of 2 battleships, 4 cruisers and 10 destroyers ... and at 0739 that 6 cruisers and 8 destroyers were stationed ... 20 miles from the main fleet.

At this time the main enemy fleet were about 145 miles 280° from our own fleet.

At 0810, as a result of these reports, the mean line of advance of the fleet was altered to 305° at 18 knots in order to work to the Northward of the enemy fleet and if possible get between him and his base.

At 0858 3 aircraft from *Eagle* were flown off to search a sector between 260 and 300° to maximum depth. ...

19. ... Reports up to this time [1105] indicated that the enemy force consisted of at least 2 battleships, 12 cruisers and 20 destroyers, and that during the forenoon they were dispersed over a wide area. ...

20. ... *Eagle*'s striking force was flown off at 1415 to attack the enemy fleet, which at this time was believed to be in position 295° 90 miles from *Warspite*, steaming North.

... owing to an insufficiency of aircraft in *Eagle*, touch was lost at 1135 and, in the event, the enemy battlefleet altered course to the Southward about this time and the striking force failed to find them.

23. At 1252 the striking force, having missed the battle fleet, sighted a large number of enemy ships steering to the Southward, and assuming that the battle fleet last reported steering North had altered to the Southward, worked round to the Westward of this force and attacked the rear ship of the enemy line at 1330. At the time this was presumed to be a battleship, but from the high speed and rapid turning which was observed it was almost certainly a cruiser. The 2 battleships were by this time considerably further to the Southward. No hits were observed. Heavy AA fire was encountered from the cruisers and attendant destroyers but the aircraft received only superficial damage. The striking force landed on at 1434.

25. ... It was now clear [1415] that after concentrating the enemy had turned Northward again and that our Fleet was rapidly closing the enemy.

At this time the impression was growing that the enemy intended to stand and fight, albeit on his own ground and with more than one road of escape left open to him.

Course was maintained to the North-westward to cut him off from Taranto until it became clear at 1400 that this object had been achieved, when course was altered to 270° to increase the rate of closing.

26. Speed of approach was limited by the maximum speed of *Royal Sovereign*, with *Warspite* acting as a battlecruiser to support the 7th CS who, being so few and lacking in 8-in ships, were very weak compared with the enemy's cruiser force.

Weather during the Approach

27. During the forenoon the wind veered from NW to N by W, force 5, but later back to NW again. The sea was slight, visibility 15 to 20 miles. The sky was clear up to 0800 but was 2/10ths clouded at noon.

The Fleet Action

28. At 1452 *Neptune* reported 2 enemy vessels in sight ...

29. At 1500 the 7th CS ... was 10 miles 260° from *Warspite* ... and steering 270° at 18 knots. ...

Eagle, screened by *Voyager* and *Vampire*, was proceeding to take up a position 10 miles to Eastward of *Warspite* and was shortly joined by *Gloucester* who ... was unfit to engage in serious action.

30. The cruisers were then rapidly closing the enemy forces which were distant 12 to 18 miles ... At 1508 *Neptune* sighted 2 enemy

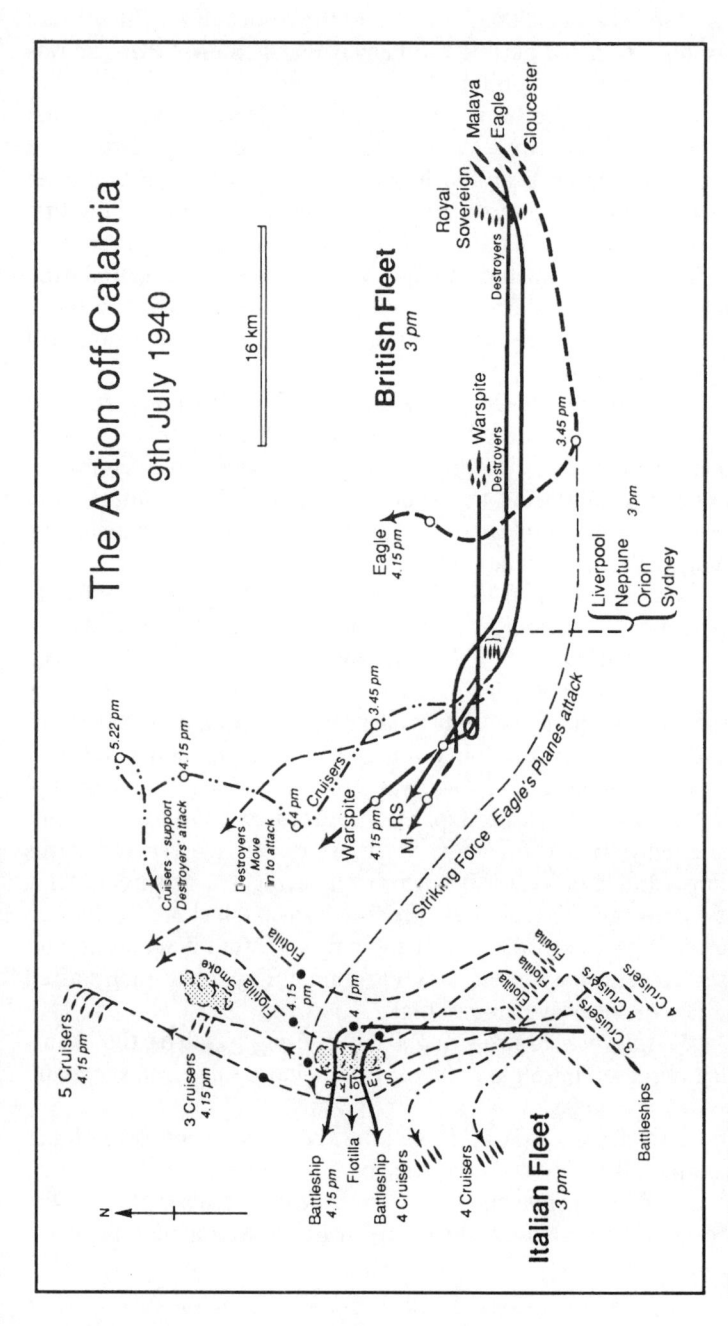

The Action off Calabria, 9 July 1940

battleships bearing 250° 15 miles, and the course of the 7th CS was altered ... to avoid getting too heavily engaged until *Warspite* was in a position to give support. ...

31. At 1512 the 7th CS was ordered by VA(D) to engage an equal number of enemy ships. *Neptune* and *Liverpool* opened fire at a range of 22,100 yards and *Sydney* opened fire at the fourth cruiser from the right, thought to be of the *Zara* class. *Orion* opened fire first on a destroyer then on the right hand cruiser, range 23,700 yards.

32. In the meantime the enemy advanced forces were sighted from *Warspite* who opened fire on an 8-in cruiser bearing 265° at a range of 26,400 yards. ... 10 salvos were fired and a hit possibly obtained with the last salvo. ...

33. At 1530 the enemy turned away making smoke and fire was checked. *Warspite* turned ... to enable *Malaya* who had been ordered by the C-in-C to press on at utmost speed to catch up. ... The enemy fire during this time was ineffective but our cruisers were straddled several times and at 1524 splinters from a near miss damaged *Neptune*'s catapult and aircraft. ...

34. Between 1533 and 1536 *Warspite* fired 4 salvos at each of two 6-in cruisers ... now steering to the Eastward apparently trying to work round to get at *Eagle*. At 1545 *Eagle* again flew off her striking force.

37. At 1553 *Warspite* opened fire on the right hand of the 2 enemy battleships of the *Cavour* class, bearing 287°, range 26,000 yards. *Warspite* was under fire from both enemy battleships and was shortly afterwards straddled. *Malaya* was now in station ... and fired 4 salvos at the enemy battleships at extreme range but these fell short. The enemy fired with moderate accuracy, the majority of salvos falling within 1,000 yards but nearly all having a large spread. Only one closely bunched salvo was observed which fell about 2 cables on *Warspite*'s port bow. At 1600 the enemy was straddled and one hit observed at the base of the foremost funnel. The enemy then started to alter course away making smoke ...

38. *Warspite* ceased firing at 1604 after firing 17 salvos, the enemy being obscured in smoke. *Malaya* fired 4 more salvos, all short and ceased fire at 1608.

At 1605 *Eagle*'s striking force attacked a cruiser of the *Bolzano* class and it is believed that at least one hit was obtained.[56] ...

39. At 1609 *Warspite* opened fire on an enemy cruiser ... Fire was checked after 6 salvos as the enemy turned away making smoke.

---

[56]*Bolzano*: 1933, 11,065t, 8×8in, 12×3.9in, 8×21in tt, 34k; s It-Br hum tpdos June 1944. Prob hit by 3×6in shells.

40. In the meantime the destroyers . . . had concentrated . . . Some of these destroyers were narrowly missed by heavy shells when passing to the Eastward of *Warspite* at 1554. At 1602 the 10th and 14th Flotillas came under heavy fire from enemy cruisers but were not hit. *Royal Sovereign* in the meantime was pressing on at the maximum speed her engines could give, but never got within range at all.

41. At 1605 enemy destroyers were observed from *Warspite* to be moving across to starboard from the van of the enemy fleet and at 1610 the tracks of 3 or more torpedoes were seen by the 14th Flotilla passing close to them. These were evidently fired at very long range.

42. Our destroyers were ordered at 1614 to counter attack enemy destroyers . . .

43. At 1619 the 10th Flotilla opened fire on the enemy destroyers at a range of 12,000 yards. *Stuart*'s first salvo appeared to hit. . . . The 7th CS were also engaging the enemy destroyers.

44. Between 1615 and 1630 a number of enemy destroyers, probably two flotillas, having worked across to starboard of their main fleet, delivered a half-hearted attack. As soon as they had (presumably) fired torpedoes they turned away Westward making smoke. . . . Sporadic firing was opened by all forces during the short intervals in which the enemy was in range and not obscured by smoke. No hits were observed by *Warspite*'s aircraft.

45. Between 1630 and 1640 enemy destroyers were dodging in and out of their smokescreens and spasmodic firing by our flotillas was opened. Two torpedoes were seen to cross *Nubian*'s stern at 1640. *Warspite* fired a few salvos of 6-in and *Malaya* one salvo, at enemy destroyers between 1639 and 1641 when they disappeared in smoke.

46. . . . P/L signals from the enemy were intercepted saying that he was 'constrained to retire', ordering his flotillas to make smoke, to attack with torpedoes, and also a warning that they were approaching the submarine line.

These signals, together with my own appreciation of the existing situation, made it appear unwise and playing the enemy's own game to plunge straight into the smokescreen.

Course was therefore altered to work round to the Northward and windward of the smokescreen, . . . Our destroyers were well clear of the smoke by 1700 but the enemy were out of sight, evidently having retired at high speed to the Westward and Southwestward.

47. Between 1640 and 1925 a series of heavy bombing attacks were made on our fleet . . . There were no hits and the fleet suffered no damage but there were numerous near misses and a few

minor casualties from splinters. *Malaya* claimed to have damaged 2 aircraft with AA fire but no enemy machines were definitely seen to crash.

48. ... By 1735 the fleet was within 25 miles of the coast of Calabria ... When, however, it became clear that the enemy had no intention of resuming the fight and could not be intercepted before making Messina, course was altered to 160° at 1830 to open the land ...

49. After the action, as subsequently reported by *Warspite*'s aircraft, the enemy fleet was left in considerable confusion, all units making off at high speed to the SW and Westwards towards the Straits of Messina and Port Augusta. It was not until 1800 that they sorted themselves out ...

They were attacked by their own bombers at 1705 and again at 1857. No hits were observed.

52. At 0800 the fleet was ... steering West, and remained cruising South of Malta throughout the day while destroyers were fuelled.

53. An air raid took place on Malta at 0855 but no destroyers were hit. Three or four enemy aircraft were shot down.

55. Flying boat reconnaissance of Augusta had located 3 cruisers and 8 destroyers in harbour and at 1850 *Eagle*'s striking force was flown off to carry out a dusk attack. Unfortunately these forces had left harbour before the striking force arrived. One flight, however, located a destroyer of the *Navigatori* class in a small bay to the Northward and sank it.[57] ...

Thursday, 11 July

59. At 0900 the C-in-C ... proceeded ahead at 19 knots to return to Alexandria. The RA, 1st BS, in *Royal Sovereign*, with *Eagle* and *Malaya* and remaining destroyers, proceeded ... at 12 knots to cover the passage of the convoys.

60. The fleet was again subject to heavy bombing attacks. Between 1248 and 1815 5 attacks were made on *Warspite* and attendant destroyers, 66 bombs being dropped. Between 1112 and 1804, 12 attacks were carried out on the forces in company with RA, 1st BS, about 120 bombs being dropped, and 4 bombing attacks were carried out on convoy MS1. There was no damage and no casualties. It was noted that the ship was shadowed by aircraft who transmitted 'longs' by W/T at intervals in order to direct attacking aircraft.

---

[57]*Leone Pancaldo*: 1929, 1,950t, 6×4.7in, 6×21in tt, 38k; raised, recomm, s a/c April 1943.

Friday, 12 July

63. There were no incidents during the night. Course was altered from time to time during the day to throw off shadowing and attacking aircraft. At 0700, VA(D) with the 7th CS rejoined the C-in-C and was then detached with *Orion* and *Neptune* to join convoy MF1 . . .

64. The following bombing attacks took place during the day:

> Between 0850 and 1150 17 attacks were made on *Warspite*, about 300 bombs being dropped.
> Between 1110 and 1804 3 attacks were made on the 1st BS and *Eagle*, 25 bombs being dropped.
> There were no hits but several near misses.

As a result of these attacks a course was set to close the Egyptian coast and No.252 Wing requested to send fighters. Fighters were sent later in the afternoon but no more attacks developed.

65. The RA, 3rd CS in *Capetown* and *Caledon*, sailed from Alexandria to rendezvous with convoy MS1 . . .[58]

Saturday, 13 July

66. The C-in-C in *Warspite*, with the 7th CS and escorting destroyers, arrived Alexandria at 0600 and convoy MF1 and escort at 0900. *Ramillies*, screened by *Havock, Imperial, Diamond* and *Vendetta*, was then sailed to escort convoy MS1,.

67. The force with RA, 1st BS, was subjected to bombing attacks between 1056 and 1623. During this time *Eagle*'s 3 Gladiators shot down a shadowing aircraft and 2 bombers and another was so severely damaged that it probably did not reach home. Blenheim fighters were sent out during the afternoon to provide protection.

68. Force C entered harbour at Alexandria at 0815 on 14 July, and the 3rd CS, convoy MS1 and escort, and *Ramillies*, at 0900 on the 15th.

66. To Pound

Warspite
Alexandria
13 July 1940

I am scribbling you a very hasty note on my arrival in harbour.

The brush with the Italian Fleet was most irritating and disappointing, but there is no doubt that it was a carefully set trap.

---

[58]*Capetown*: 1922, 4,200t, 5×6in, 2×3in, 8×21in tt, 29k.

We intercepted most of the Italian Admiral's signals as we had the decode on board from one of the sunk submarines, and most interesting they were.

I walked into the trap with my eyes open. Had the FAA been able to hit ships steaming at about 25 knots, we would have had him in his own snare, but as soon as *Warspite* hit him in the ribs at 26,000 yards he screamed for a smokescreen, ordered 25 knots and turned 90° away.

But there is one serious thing. The battleships and 8-in cruisers straddled us comfortably at 26,000 and more and I don't think any ship but *Warspite* crossed the target. Neither *Malaya* nor *Royal Sovereign* ever got into range, the latter's full speed being 18 knots! I must have one more ship that can shoot at a good range.

Tovey was also up against 6–7 8-in cruisers and about 4–5 6-in cruisers and of course could make no headway as they obscured themselves in smoke at about 22,000 yards. I know I said I could do without 8-in cruisers, but I would dearly like the *York* and *Exeter*.[59]

Naturally after the shooting was over and we were chasing towards the land, we took the bombs. I suppose not far short of 100 planes and some very heavy bombs. *Eagle* had a charmed life.

My heart was in my mouth lest *Royal Sovereign* should be hit as, if she had taken one of the nests of bombs that were dropping about, I think she'd have gone to the bottom or, at any rate, as we were only 25 miles from the Calabrian coast, we would have had to sink her. In fact I don't think it is a bit of good taking these unprotected old battleships up to the coast unless we are fully prepared to lose one.

Don't think I am discouraged. I am not a bit, but with our facilities at Alexandria, also within bombing range, the damaged ship is a nightmare especially one 900 miles from her base.

There is one thing on the bright side. I do not think we need expect anything very dashing from the Italian Fleet.

Perhaps the worst is yet to come. We left the vicinity of Malta on Thursday after the slow convoy, and all forces were continuously bombed that day up to about 220 miles from Sicily and nightfall. Next morning it started again off Cyrenaica on *Warspite* and cruisers at 9 a.m. and continued till 4 p.m., by which time the Dodecanese were also in action. The *Royal Sovereign, Eagle* and *Malaya* are at

---

[59]*York* (total loss foll It explosive MTB atk, Suda Bay, Mar. 1941), *Exeter* (s Jap sqdn, Java Sea Mar. 1942): 1930–31, 8,250–8,390t, 6×8in, 4×4in, 6×21in tt, 32k.

this moment being bombed continuously passing between Crete and Libya. Literally we have had to fight our way back to Alexandria against air attack.

I am sure that the reason is that the whole Italian Air Force is now in the South concentrated against the Fleet. I include Force H. We are well able to look after the Italian Fleet, but I doubt if we can tackle the Air Force as well.

Is anything being done to attack the North Italian towns? I hope so – if only to draw off some of these birds to the North.

You suggest that *Illustrious* might come here. We want some fighters badly. At the moment *Eagle* carries two Gladiators on her Upper Deck – FAA spares – and one of them brought down a bomber two days ago but died in doing it.

We also want an AA cruiser and a couple of convoy sloops. I don't believe *Carlisle* is needed in the Red Sea.[60] Our Air Force has been shaking the Italian East of Africa Air Force badly and I doubt if they are much menace to Red Sea Trade. . . .

Gloucester took a bomb on her Compass Platform. Such bad luck! Killed everyone on the bridge and some below it. She can steer from for'ard but has to control her fire from aft. The fore director circuits were just mashed up.

I apologise for all these demands, but our position in the Middle East depends almost entirely on the fleet and I want to keep it active and able to go anywhere with moderate security.

During the action our spotter sat over the Italian battleships and tells us there was the most dire confusion in the fleet.

I was glad to see Ford's KBE but wished it was a KCB, he has done splendidly at Malta since the Italians started.

67. *War Diary, July 1940 (cont.)*

13 July

Aircraft

7. The Admiralty have informed the C-in-C, the AOC-in-C, Middle East, and the AOC, Mediterranean, that 12 Hurricanes for Malta and 12 for Middle East, and various stores, will shortly be shipped in SS *Glenorchy* to Gibraltar and have requested C-in-C to report on the desirability of routeing this ship straight to

---

[60]*Carlisle*: 1918, 4,200t, 8×4in, 29k; rblt as AA ship 1930s; irrep dmgd Ger a/c Aegean Oct. 1943.

Malta.[61] The AOC, Mediterranean, is strongly of the opinion that this should be done, owing to the urgency of their requirement at Malta. The C-in-C and VA, Force H both consider this impracticable owing to the intense bombing experienced during the past week. VA, Force H, has proposed to the Admiralty that these aircraft should be transferred to a carrier at Gibraltar and transported to a position of 7° W whence they could be flown to Malta. . . .

14 July

3. *Shipping*

The Admiralty have authorised C-in-C to attack Italian shipping without warning when within 30 miles of the Libyan coast. The C-in-C has asked whether this may also be extended to the Italian coast.

15 July

4. *Italian air bombing*

(2) Attacks have all been high level bombing in daylight, average height 12,000 feet by formations varying from 9 to single aircraft but generally in sub-flights of three. Bombs have been dropped in sticks varying from 6 heavy bombs to 18 to 27 bombs per formation. Majority of bombs appear to be light case HE.

(3) Single aircraft have generally shied off when fired at, but formations have generally flown steadily on with surprising determination.

(4) Most unpleasant attack on *Warspite* at 1550 12 July resulted in 24 bombs along port side and 12 across starboard bow simultaneously, all within 1 cable but slightly out for line.

5. AA fire with exception of one or two ships has been below pre-war standard but is improving under stress. It has been disappointing that I have not seen any enemy aircraft directly hit and fall into the sea. I am however satisfied that any appreciable number of Italians have failed to return. . . .

---

[61]A Cdre (later AVM) F. H. Maynard (b 1893): RNAS 1914–18; F/Lt 1919; Staff Coll 1924–25; 12 Sq 1929; IDC 1931; U Ldn Air Sq 1935; A Cdre & AOC Med Jan 1940; AVM & AOC (Admin) Coastal Cmd 1941–44; AOC 19 Grp 1944–45; ret 1945. *Glenorchy*, 1939, 8,982gt, Glen Line.

6. Ammunition expenditure has been very heavy and Fleet has returned to harbour with less than half long range outfit remaining.
7. My summing up is:

(i) Intensive high level bombing is to be expected on each occasion of a Fleet operation in the Central Mediterranean.
(ii) The accuracy of Italian bombing entitled them to 1 per cent of hits and the Fleet were extremely lucky that this number was not obtained.
(iii) This probable percentage of hits rising to 2 per cent as the Italians get more practice must be carefully weighed in considering the employment of valuable ships in the Central Mediterranean.
(iv) That provided proper antidotes are supplied this scale of bombing attack can be accepted as a reasonable war risk like mines or submarines.
(v) Prolonged bombing is very wearing to personnel and system started by my predecessor of having at least two complete reliefs for whole AA armament in battleships and cruisers has been shown to be essential for prolonged operations.

17 July

3. *French situation*

The Admiralty have issued instructions that efforts are to be made to improve the relations between the French and British Navies as the present state of tension might lead to war between the two countries. Further attacks on French ships will therefore not be made except on ships proceeding to an enemy controlled port. As far as submarines are concerned the rules which were first generally accepted in the Nyon Convention will be followed.[62]

4. Pending further instructions British ships must be prepared for attack when meeting a French warship, but should not fire first if attacked.

5. *Aircraft*

Haifa was bombed by 10 Italian aircraft on 15 July. Damage was done to three oil tanks and 27,300 tons of crude oil is in danger of being lost. The C-in-C discussed the question of aerial defence of Haifa with the AOC-in-C, Middle East, and the latter states that he cannot provide fighters for Haifa nor take counter action against the Dodecanese.

---

[62]Nyon Convention: International agreement, Spanish Civil War, 1937, to halt S/M attacks on neutral ships.

Shipping

7. The C-in-C has requested the Admiralty to provide a fast ship of the Glen Line to perform the dual role of sea going oiler and to carry stores in and out of Malta, as the *Plumleaf* is too slow for this duty.[63]

18 July

Submarines

8. The Admiralty have given approval for Italian shipping to be sunk without warning within 30 miles of any Italian territory and for ships of any nationality to be sunk within 30 miles of Libyan territory.

68. To the Admiralty

16 July 1940

Naval Policy in the Mediterranean

2. Spain is assumed neutral. France semi-hostile. The vital [?strategical] importance of having the North African coast, at least, is evident.

Italian Policy

3. a) In Western Mediterranean the most direct harm to British interests lies in attacks on Gibraltar or a break out into Atlantic. Both seem unlikely while Spain remains neutral, and there is every reason to suppose that Italian Fleet will not go far from its bases.

b) In Eastern Mediterranean there is a concentration of Italian interests. Italians are used to the idea that their main danger lies in Eastern Mediterranean dominated by British Fleet.

c) The vulnerable points on Italian W coast are more easily covered by air protection than those in S, owing to relative position of Sicily and Sardinia. On the other hand [?manufacturing] area vital to industry lies in NW.

d) My conclusion from above is that while Italians will keep a certain portion of force to protect their Western coast, particularly with Force H working from Gibraltar, preponderant force will be based Messina, Taranto and Augusta.

---

[63]*Plumleaf*: oiler; 1917, 12,370t, 14k; s Malta Ger a/c April 1942.

British Tasks

4. a) *East*. Destruction of enemy naval forces; protection of Egypt, Palestine and Syria; interruption of Black Sea and Aegean trade, and of Libyan communications.

b) *West*. Interruption of all trade to Italy and possibly France; attacks on Western coasts; control of exit from Mediterranean.

British Dispositions

5. My opinion [is that] the more powerful force must be in the Eastern Mediterranean.

Reasons

Composition of forces

6. a) *Eastern Mediterranean*. *Warspite, Valiant, Malaya,* possibly *Barham, Illustrious, Eagle,* two 8-in cruisers, one AA cruiser and two convoy sloops, rest of fleet as at present.

b) *Comments on a)*

Essential there should be at least two capital ships whose guns can cross enemy line at 26,000 yards and who are fast enough to have some hope of catching up with enemy. It is also necessary to have at least two cruisers who can act similarly in van. On 9 July our cruisers were outnumbered, ougunned and outranged, and thus could not control area ahead of battlefleet. *York* and *Exeter* are particularly required owing to being small targets. I am of opinion we are over-insured against air in Red Sea and that *Carlisle* should come to Mediterranean with two convoy sloops to provide AA escort for convoys now being carried out by large cruisers.[64] .... First convoy (BD1) up the Red Sea was not attacked at all.

Illustrious and *Eagle* in combination will provide striking force without which faster Italian Fleet cannot be 'fixed', will double also [?large] measure of fighter support without which experience has shown unjustifiable hazards are incurred when operating in Central Mediterranean.

Intend to employ *Eagle* also in Red Sea against Massawa and shore objectives. Ample reserve of fighter and TSR should be provided so that proportion can be varied to provide very strong fighter support or a powerful striking force according to operation contemplated. *Valiant* would also provide RDF which no ship of present fleet has got. The 'R' class battleships can be released and sent via

---

[64]'County' cl 8-in cruisers had very high profile.

Cape to Gibraltar or elsewhere, since in face of present scale air attack they are simply a source of constant anxiety.

If *Barham* were available I would welcome her so as to provide a reserve of force, because unlike Western Mediterranean the passage of any reinforcements will be either a major fleet operation or else mean delay of at least six weeks, and if I was meanwhile reduced to two battleships, capital ship force would be on the weak side.

7. I consider that with forces proposed the Mediterranean can be dominated, and Eastern Mediterranean held indefinitely, provided the following matters also receive attention.

Malta
a) Proper fighter protection.
b) Adequate reserves and spares are essential for repairs.
c) Air co-operation. Replacements for flying boats are essential.

Passage of Reinforcements

8. By carrying out a concerted movement it should be possible to pass reinforcements through the Mediterranean, but it would probably be desirable to do it all in one operation.

69. *From Admiralty*

19 July 1940

B. As regards Capital Ship strength in the Eastern Mediterranean. Until the situation clears up as regards invasion it is not considered that *Barham* can be spared from Home Waters. It is proposed therefore that only *Valiant* [should be sent].

D. The only way of providing you with two 8-in cruisers without weakening the cruiser strength in Home Waters, which would be undesirable at the present time, is to take either *Ramillies* or *Royal Sovereign* for troop convoys in the Indian Ocean, thus releasing 8-in cruisers.

F. The question of how *Valiant* and *Illustrious* can join you is largely linked up with the question of reserve ammunition, ...

P. If the reinforcement takes place through the Mediterranean it would be desirable that in addition to the two ammunition carriers referred to above the following ships should be passed through at the same time.

a) One ship, 15 knots, containing: 12 Hurricanes for Malta, 12 Hurricanes for Middle East, 12 heavy and 10 light HA guns for Malta.
b) One ship, 16 knots with personnel for Hurricanes.

70. To the Admiralty

21 July 1940

1. I do not consider it would be prudent in present circumstances to risk this precious ammunition through the Mediterranean even in 16-knot ships.
2. 15-in ammunition situation can be accepted for a time . . .
3. I propose whole reserve of ammunition mentioned, less additional 4.5-in that can be packed into *Valiant* and *Illustrious*, should be sent in fastest ships possible (certainly of not less than 16 knots) round the Cape of Good Hope now or as soon as the ships can be loaded. I would arrange special escort through Red Sea. If these ships proceed with utmost dispatch they should arrive Alexandria in about five weeks.
4. Meantime suggest sending extra 4.5-in ammunition to Gibraltar for *Valiant* and sail her and *Illustrious* through the Mediterranean about 14 days after ammunition carrier leaves UK. They should then be here two or three days ahead of their meeting.
5. Further 12 Hurricanes for Malta to be flown off by *Argus* as already arranged for first 12. Maintenance personnel and as large a supply of stores as possible to be embarked in *Valiant*.[65]
6. AA guns for Malta would have to be sent in fast ammunition ship round Cape of Good Hope though perhaps light guns could go in *Valiant*.
7. With reference to para. 4 is it not possible to obtain some really fast ships of the order of 25 knots for this work, even if not primarily designed to take cargo?
8. As regards 8-in cruisers on escort work. I have not enough destroyers to take four battleships and *Eagle* to sea simultaneously in any case. Even one 8-in cruiser would be very welcome at the earliest moment.
9. Docking is a most difficult problem at Alexandria and it is highly desirable that any ship joining eastern [Mediterranean] fleet should have been recently docked.

---

[65]*Argus*: carrier; 1918, 14,450t, 6×4in, 20 a/c, 20k.

71. *To the Admiralty*

21 September 1940

HMAS Sydney – *Sinking of* Bartolomeo Colleoni

Forwarded for the information of Their Lordships. The credit for this successful and gallant action belongs mainly to Captain J. A. Collins, CB, RAN, who by his quick appreciation of the situation, offensive spirit and resolute handling of HMAS *Sydney*, achieved a victory over a superior force which has had important strategical effects.[66] It is significant that, so far as is known, no Italian surface forces have returned into or near the Aegean since this action was fought.

2. The destroyers were also ably handled and fought, except for the unfortunate mistake on the part of Cdr (D), 2DF, in delaying to pick up survivors instead of pressing on with the chase.
3. As a result of this incident I felt it necessary to issue to the Fleet a memorandum on the subject, . . . [No. 72]
4. *Sydney's* gunnery narrative is of great interest both technically and from the more general point of view. It shows the results obtainable by an efficient control team backed by good material, and it should be given the weight due to the experience of a ship which has had the unique opportunity of firing 2,200 main armament rounds in action in 6 weeks. . . .

Captain Collins' Account

20 July 1940

2. On that morning [19 July] I was, with HMS *Havock* in company, proceeding on a westerly course about 40 miles N of Crete in accordance with my instructions to afford support to D2 and destroyers engaged in a submarine hunt N of the island. My instructions included the second object of the destruction of enemy shipping in the Gulf of Athens. I decided however that it was my duty to remain in support of the destroyers until 0800 by which time they should have cleared the Anti-Kithera Strait, although this precluded the successful achievement of the second object.
3. At 0733 an enemy report was received from D2 and course was altered to southward to support him. D2 kept me well informed of

---

[66]Capt (later V-Adm Sir) John A. Collins, RAN: Capt 1939; DNI 1939; *Sydney* Nov. 1939; *Shropshire* 1943; Cdre 1Cl 1944; *Penguin* 1945; RA 1947; 1st N Member & VA 1950.

his and the enemies' movements. At 0826 on a southeasterly course to close D2, I sighted the enemy, two cruisers, type unknown, on an easterly course. At this time the enemy was steering 090° and my course was 120°. I withheld fire until a good plot was obtained and then opened fire on the leading ship at a range of 21,000 yards, the enemy were replying shortly afterwards in concentrated fire which fell mostly over though some straddles were obtained. I continued closing the enemy on a course to intercept D2 until 0835 during which time it appeared that our fire was effective on the leading ship, the minimum range being 19,200 yards. The enemy fire continued to be mostly over.

4. At 0835 I sighted D2 fine on the port bow on a southerly course, i.e. at right angles to enemy course. I directed him to attack with torpedoes and turned to the southward parallel and abreast of him at 0841.

5. By this time the enemy had turned 90° away and were retiring to the southward thus making it impracticable to carry out a torpedo attack. The gun action continued for some quarter of an hour at a range of about 18,000 yards when the left hand ship appeared to sheer off badly hit and reduce speed.

6. Firing was continued at the damaged ship until the range closed to 9,000 yards when it was seen that she was badly down by the bow and listing heavily. A signal was therefore made to D2 to torpedo her, followed by a signal to D2 to leave one destroyer to finish her off and to follow me up after the other cruiser. At 0921 the other cruiser got the range of *Sydney*. Several straddles were obtained, including one hit on the funnel. The chase continued with *Hero* and *Hasty*, D2, *Ilex* and *Havock* remaining with the sinking cruiser.

8. It was with great reluctance that I finally abandoned the chase of the second cruiser when the enemy was almost out of sight in the haze and outside gun range. Hits had been observed on the enemy cruiser but it was apparent that his speed was not reduced. Despite his many alterations of course to throw out my gunfire he continued to draw away until I had but little ammunition remaining. . . .

72. *Rescue of Survivors from Enemy Ships*

22 July 1940

While the instincts of the British race and the traditions of the sea produce in us all a powerful urge to rescue survivors of sinking ships, it must be remembered that there are other considerations to be weighed against this humane work.

2. We are waging a relentless war against odds, and here in the Mediterranean, not only are we competing against numerically superior naval forces, but we have also against us very considerable air forces which our own Air Force is not yet in a position to attack, except those in Eastern Libya.

3. It follows that no favourable opportunity must be lost of destroying enemy forces, and the rescue of survivors must never be allowed to interfere with the relentless pursuit of escaping enemy ships.

4. It must also be borne well in mind that practically the whole of our area of operations is subject to enemy bombing. Therefore ships cannot usually afford to hang about picking up survivors for, not only do they expose themselves to bombing attack under very disadvantageous conditions, but also subsequent operations are likely to be delayed. Moreover a destroyer with a large number of prisoners on board is bound to be considerably reduced in fighting efficiency.

5. Difficult and distasteful as it is to leave survivors to their fate, commanding officers must be prepared to harden their hearts, for after all the operations in hand and the security of their ships and ships' companies must take precedence in war.

73. *From Pound*

24 July 1940

... We have just received the signal about the *Sydney* sinking the *Bartolomeo [Colleoni]*. It must have been a fine piece of work but it looks as if, as usual, the ship had run for it, ...

The *Illustrious,* if and when she reaches you, will have the new Fulmar 8-gun fighters, and if these can only be got amongst the Italian bombers they ought to do good execution.

I am very glad you were able to square things up so successfully with the French ships at Alexandria. It must have been a very difficult business and required great patience and determination.

As regards the minor War Cabinet for the Middle East, you are quite right in thinking that the Admiralty could not divorce any part of their general control because, as you know, it is continually necessary to move ships from one Station to another to meet the various commitments, such as raiders, escorts of troop convoys, etc.

I can't understand why the Italians are only taking two capital ships to sea. There are rumours that at least one of the new ships has proved very unsatisfactory from a gunnery point of view; in fact, if I remember right, one report said that when the guns were fired one of the funnels went over the side!

I hope the fighters which are being flown from the *Argus* will get to Malta all right, there is always the chance that the *Argus* may get bombed before they are flown off. I am trying to arrange for a duplicate set to be sent round the Cape.

The situation here as regards aircraft is very much better, ...

P.S. ... we have had a meeting with the Air Ministry, and we raised the various points contained in your signal.

Flying boats – As regards these, apparently some of the spare engines and spare parts coming from Singapore have got mislaid, but everything is being done to chase them up.

Long-range fighters – I am afraid there is not much chance of getting any of these in the immediate future as there are practically none in existence, and the first ones that come out will be required for the Home Front.

As a matter of fact I believe there are some long-nosed Blenheims in Egypt, but I do not know whether you could persuade the AOC-in-C to allow them to be used for giving your ships protection, like they do in the North Sea. This may be possible, as the Middle East is to be gradually reinforced with machines of various kinds, including bombers, and when the bombers are sent out perhaps the Blenheims could be converted into fighters and used for protecting the Fleet.

Fighters for protection of the Fleet at Alexandria – The situation should be improved when you get the two Squadrons of Hurricanes which are being sent round the Cape, and which should arrive very early in September.

Fast ammunition carriers – Altogether we are sending out four ships with ammunition, fighters, Blenheims, Lysanders and AA guns, but I am afraid it is not possible to get ships of more than 16 knots.[67] However, you may be sure we will get the stuff out to you as soon as possible.

I think you were were quite right not to attempt to get either the ammunition ships, or merchant ships with fighters and AA guns, through the Central Mediterranean. ...

---

[67]Westland Lysander: Army co-op; 1936, 4mg, *c*.250lb bombs, 229mph, range 500mls.

74. *War Diary, July 1940 (concl.)*

25 July

Haifa

4. The C-in-C has informed the Admiralty that if the present situation at Haifa continues it will only be a matter of time before the refinery is put out of action and Haifa will cease to function as a source of supply of fuel to the Fleet. The real trouble is caused by aircraft from the Dodecanese being allowed to operate unhampered. These aircraft are also the most active against the Fleet. The C-in-C has proposed that long range bombers should be sent to Egypt forthwith for operations against the Dodecanese.

5. The VA(D) on his arrival at Haifa also made a similar report, pointing out that work on shipping and at the refinery was already suffering severely due to the lack of any up to date air raid warning system or means of defence.

26 July

Shipping

4. In reply to a request from the Governor of Cyprus that Egyptian ships should be allowed to sail from Cyprus to Syria with vital trade, the C-in-C has reaffirmed that no ships can be allowed to sail for Syrian ports as long as British ships are detained by the French authorities.

75. *War Diary, August 1940*

2 August

3. *Submarine* Oswald

At 1400 on 30 July *Oswald* on patrol off the Straits of Messina, sighted a troop convoy steering to the Southward, and at 1230 on 1 August she sighted a force of 5 cruisers and destroyers. . . .

4. Arising out of *Oswald's* first enemy report, the Admiralty asked VA, Malta, what action was taken.[68] The C-in-C replied to the Admiralty as follows:

By 2235 when *Oswald's* report was received it was too late for effective action. It was evident that the transports were making for Benghazi and that they would be beyond the range of the Malta Swordfish at daylight. I decided therefore that a dawn air

---

[68] *Oswald's* report gave away her position; she was sunk, all except 1 man saved.

search from Malta would be valueless particularly as it was not possible to get surface forces to the Central Mediterranean in time to intercept.

I fear that this situation will constantly arise as the enemy is immediately acquainted with our Fleet movements by his daily air reconnaissance over Alexandria and can thus seize his opportunity to pass fast convoys to Libya. If and when the defences of Malta are such as to allow it to be used as a base by our light forces our power to attack these convoys will be greatly improved.

3 August

Aircraft

6. The AOC, Mediterranean, has represented to the Air Ministry the urgent necessity for the provision of a striking force and general reconnaissance force at Malta when the present urgent fighter requirement is met. He has pointed out that he is not in a position to meet urgent calls for reconnaissance from Flag Officers operating in the Central Mediterranean. He considers that GR aircraft could undertake much of the sea reconnaissance now undertaken by Sunderlands which can operate away from Alexandria for brief periods only. FAA Swordfish are the only attacking aircraft at Malta, and offensive operations are necessarily limited. The AOC considers that one complete TBGR Squadron of 15 aircraft would produce results out of all proportion to the numbers of aircraft involved.

Malta

7. The following report on supplies for Malta has been made by VA, Malta:

> ... certain army and civil stocks are much below figure of 6 months' consumption.... Recommend also that convoy be run at least every 2 months [and] immediate shipments of supplies to bring reserves to 8 months' stock ...

76. *To Pound*

3 August 1940

A. I am very much concerned about our S/M losses. The *Oswald* yesterday. There is no doubt that the Italians have very efficient D/F arrangements and also their hydrophones must be first class.

As soon as one sends a S/M off an Italian port, it seems only a matter of time before she is discovered and put under. At the moment it is not a question of sending them where they will be useful, but where they will be safe.

I think these 'O's', 'P's' and 'R's' are too big, too old and their auxiliary machinery too noisy for work out here. Also I have the feeling at the back of my mind that the conditions of clear water and constant surveillance from the air have not been firmly grasped by the China officers.

B. Our principal trouble is that we can't move without our movements being known. There is no doubt that the Italians have now got a very efficient reconnaissance going. They send planes over Alexandria every day and no force in the last three weeks has been at sea without being discovered and bombed, in some cases very heavily.

We had a big stroke of luck with the *Liverpool*. The bomb came from ahead through the superstructure clear under the compass platform and failed to explode, otherwise we would have had another *Gloucester*. I can't think why these big cruisers are the ones to get [hit], but it may be because they are slow on the turn.

I shall be very glad when the reinforcements arrive so as to strengthen our AA, as there is no doubt that the sailors, specially those in the destroyers, look a bit askance at going to sea knowing they will be bombed for two or three days running. At the same time they are all in very good heart and cheerful.

C. I am using this moonless period to get the bigger ships docked. I don't like it but *Malaya* goes in tomorrow and *Warspite* follows. . . .

E. . . . *Eagle*'s work has been above all praise. The greatest credit naturally goes to Bridge . . . Quiet, imperturbable and thorough, he has carried out his flying programmes to the minute whether bombs were falling thick about him or not.

To me *Eagle*'s survival unhit is nothing short of a miracle as she has been a special object of attack.

Keighly Peach is in charge of the flying, but when we got a brace of Sea Gladiators, he volunteered to go up himself, and although shot through the leg the first day, brought down two Italian planes the second.[69] . . .

---

[69]Cdr C.L. Keighly-Peach: Cdr 1938; *Daedalus* Sept. 1939; Cdr (F), *Eagle* 1940; ofc of NA, 2SL 1942; Capt 1943; CO *Heron* (Yeovilton) 1944–45. Awarded DSO; Cunningham also recommended several other officers, feeling that early decorations would have a good effect on morale.

F. I don't wish to appear pessimistic, but I hope you are aware of the Army and Air position out here. If we have to withdraw from Egypt, it will not be for naval reasons but because the Army and Air Force have not been given sufficient reinforcements.

It seems to me that if we can hold on for the next three months and the other two Services are properly reinforced in the interim we shall pull through all right, but we all have an anxious three months ahead of us. . . .

G. Haifa is causing me anxiety. I understand an RDF (from Alexandria of course) and four Hurricanes are going there shortly. I have asked if an RDF can be sent out in *Valiant*.

77. War Diary, August 1940 (cont.)

4 August

RAC, 7CS, in *Liverpool*, with *Gloucester, Jervis* and *Mohawk*, sailed p.m. today to maintain pressure in the Aegean and cover the movements of shipping in the Eastern Mediterranean, and the movement of the convoy of Danube barges from Athens to Alexandria.

2. *Hero, Hereward* and *Imperial* sailed today to carry out A/S sweeps. . . .

6 August

Minesweepers

6. The C-in-C has reported to the Admiralty that the conversion of *Moy* and *Ouse* as LL sweepers would seriously deplete his already inadequate sweeping force against contact mines which are the primary menace in the Mediterranean.[70] . . .

8 August

Turkish Boom Defences

4. . . . The Turks have laid moorings for their heavy net in the Bosphorus and Dardanelles. . . . the C-in-C considers that the provision of sufficient material to render the Bosphorus and the Dardanelles submarine proof at short notice is of great importance and proposes that the material for the A/S booms should be supplied as early as possible and that boom working vessels should be loaned to the Turks while the booms are being laid.

[70]*Moy, Ouse* (mined, N Af Feb. 1941): trawlers; 1917, 551t, 2×3in, 11k.

12 August

Submarines

7. Owing to heavy submarine losses incurred in inshore patrols it has been decided to establish a movable patrol line N of 36°N adjusted to cover routes from Taranto to Benghazi. *Pandora*, now on patrol off Benghazi, has been given freedom of movement within 40 miles of Benghazi outside the 200 fathom line.

Mails

10. ... no mails have been received by the Fleet since the dispatch from London of 3 June. The early and regular arrival of mails directly concerns the contentment of personnel. The C-in-C has requested that this matter may be taken up urgently ...

78. *From Pound*

14 August 1940

... I think he [Wavell] has had a pretty stiff argument with the PM who wished to impose some amateur strategy on him, and at the moment I am not quite certain how the argument ended. I had a great fight over the ships carrying the tanks. I was always against their being included in HATS, but everyone was so keen on getting them out at the earliest possible moment that I agreed to look into the question and hence my telegram to you. Your reply that all of them might be sunk was exactly what I expected, and I came to the conclusion that it was unsound to include any merchant ships in the operation, firstly because it would be quite clear where they were going and the Italians would have two days in which to concentrate everything they could in the Sicily area, also the loss of speed was serious. It is no good sending you reinforcements and having them arrive in a damaged condition if it can possibly be avoided. I only got my way by promising to hustle them [the tanks] round the Cape as soon as possible, and I could only do this by sending *York* as an escort.

(c) I hope to be able to send you the submarines I spoke of before very long, as I know how badly you will want them in trying to stop stuff getting into Libya. We have none too many submarines at home at the moment, and I don't like letting them go whilst the weather is still favourable for invasion, ...

(d) There are many other things I would like to send you, such as more capital ships with long range guns, more 8-in cruisers and a great many more destroyers, but I don't see how it is possible at the present time. As regards capital ships it appears to be pretty certain that *Cavour* and *Cesare* are both under repair and if this is correct it will relieve a great strain on you for some time. We must, however, realise that in two or three months you may have six capital ships of high speed with long range guns against you, and if at any time you feel that you want further reinforcements, I do hope you will ask for them, however impossible it may seem to comply with your request. I do not think the Italian capital ships will do much damage once we started hitting them, but a ship which is unfired at might, from what you have said, put up a good shoot.

(i) Everyone is very appreciative of all you are doing, and have every confidence that you will give our friends a good knock whenever they give you a chance.

79. *From Pound*

14 August 1940

We have had a great battle today with the PM about the question of sending the MT ships through the Mediterranean or round the Cape. He was all for sending them through the Mediterranean, as he considers that the Italian advance may develop very rapidly, and that it is essential to get the MT ships to Egypt as soon as possible. Wavell has given it as his considered opinion that he would prefer that the MT ships arrived in safety at a later date, rather than risk losing a lot of MT during the passage, even if some arrived at an earlier date. As far as I can calculate, the MT ships should arrive at Alexandria on 3 September if they go through the Mediterranean, or on 22 September at Suez if they went via the Cape.

The arrangement which has been firmly arrived at, and which I think is a correct one, is that if by the time the MT ships are in the latitude of Gibraltar the situation appears sufficiently suitable to allow them to go via the Cape, they will then do so. On the other hand, if the Italian advance develops in such a way as to threaten Egypt seriously and drastic measures are necessary, then the MT ships will be diverted through the Mediterranean. . . .

. . . it will therefore be necessary for you to keep in touch with Wavell so that you may together be able to send a reply should you be asked which procedure should be carried out. . . .

I see that the *Neptune* has come in handy to rush a battalion down to Somaliland. I am sure that you do not wish to have to bring the MT through the Mediterranean, so the more you can do in harassing the Italian advance by bombardment, the less chance will there be of your having to do so. I am not too happy about the four destroyers making a passage from Malta to Gibraltar by themselves, but do not see any way out of it. I imagine Ford will be able to provide some air reconnaissance to prevent them falling into a trap. I am doing all I can to have some really long-range photographic reconnaissance machines sent out to the Mediterranean immediately. Both from your point of view and Wavell's it appears essential that you should know what is going on.

80. *To Pound*

19 August 1940

C.   It now seems absolutely certain that the low flying aircraft over Alexandria harbour were each carrying two 18-in torpedoes. . . . We must get some type of balloon or kite barrage on the breakwater, that seems the only sure deterrent.

D.   I am so glad Lyster is coming out. He will be most useful in getting the shore establishments going and also operationally at sea. Happily our relations with the Air Force out here are most cordial and we seem to get closer and closer to them. I find Longmore excellent to deal with and he does wonders with his rather small forces.

E.   I am not very concerned about the Italian capital ships. It is quite true there may be six in the spring, but with *Warspite, Valiant, Malaya* and perhaps *Barham* later on I see no reason to doubt our ability to deal faithfully with them especially with the FAA Striking Forces of two carriers. I fear *Ramilllies* is too slow ever to get into action.

F.   We are having great difficulty in maintaining secrecy about our operations. We intercepted an Italian message to Addis Ababa to bomb *Royal Sovereign* as she passed down the Red Sea, made just after she had left Port Said.

There are so many Italians uninterned due to our being so kind to the Egyptian Government. I go to Cairo on Wednesday to see Wavell and I will see the Ambassador as well and try to get something done.

G.   I am so much in agreement with you over operation HATS. I hope we shall not have to do BONNET but it might turn out all right. The trouble is that one can't tell until one tries.[71]

---

[71]HATS ('Hands Across The Sea') was voyage of *Valiant, Illustrious* & other warships through Med; BONNET would have been same + merchantmen.

I also didn't care much about the destroyers going alone to Gibraltar, but they will be a good strong party two 'Tribals' and two 'H' class. VA, Malta, will reconnoitre the Cape Bon narrows the evening before they pass through and I am sending a flying boat ahead of them during the daylight hours they have to spend going along the Algerian coast so I have little doubt of their safe arrival.

Returning from Malta it is my intention to pass the whole force, convoy as well, if we are doing BONNET, North of Crete and hit Rhodes a crack with the aircraft from the two aircraft carriers.

The Rhodes aircraft have been very annoying to us and I propose to give them another dose as well and probably a bombardment very soon after our return.

H. ... Our destroyers out here are showing signs of wear and tear and many defects are cropping up.

We got *Malaya, Warspite* and all the cruisers docked this last three weeks, which has been a great relief.

81. *Narrative of Attack on Bardia, 15–17 August 1940*

(10 December 1940)

As a preliminary precaution Cdr D2 in *Hyperion*, accompanied by *Ilex, Juno* and *Hero,* sailed at 1200 on 15 August to carry out an A/S sweep along the coast ... This was followed by a sweep with TSDS in Sollum Bay during the dark hours and the force was ordered to rendezvous with the C-in-C at 1400 on 16 August ...

2. ... Cdr D2 reported at 0925 that he was being bombed ..., and was instructed by the C-in-C to keep inshore in order to obtain shore based fighter support which in fact reached him at 1045 and covered him until 1315. The force was, however, bombed again at 1205 and 1400 but there was no damage or casualties. The fighters failed to intercept.

3. The forces for MB2 left Alexandria at 1030/16. It was necessary to exercise particular caution as the previous night the first low flying attack on Alexandria took place and either torpedoes or magnetic mines were dropped just inside the breakwater. Magnetic sweeps and DWI aircraft were employed but no explosions resulted.

6. At 0030/17 *Ilex* obtained a confirmed submarine contact and the Fleet turned away to avoid it. *Ilex* dropped a pattern of charges but lost the contact in the ships' wakes.

7. ... The six destroyers fitted with TSDS streamed them and the fleet split into two forces and catapulted aircraft at 0600.

9. Fire was opened by *Malaya* at 0658, followed shortly afterwards by *Warspite*.

10. Reports from spotting aircraft showed that *Warspite* had well covered the area round Fort Capuzzo, one shell falling in the fort and one in the native troop compound.... *Warspite*'s secondary armament meanwhile fired on Fort Ramla.

Kent meanwhile engaged the gun positions W and NW of Marsa-el-Ramla.[72]

Malaya and *Ramillies* attacked their targets at Bardia itself, *Malaya* reporting hits on target 8 and in the vicinity of target 9, also that the town had been damaged. *Ramillies* landed 4 salvos on her target and 3 secondary armament broadsides in the vicinity of Bardia W/T station, as well as some salvos in the town.

11. At 0720 the whole force withdrew...

12. The Fleet continued along the coast under fighter protection, having taken up loose formation in expectation of air attack. There was a considerable amount of cloud and in consequence the first attack by five aircraft at 1050 came without being sighted. Thereafter a number of attacks took place until about 1130. The bombing was inaccurate, mostly falling round the screens. In some cases it appeared that bombs were jettisoned in consequence of fighter attack, and at 1100 two enemy aircraft crashed in flames, shot down by the fighters over the fleet....

Cunningham's Observations

2. This operation was undertaken when considerable Italian concentrations had appeared near the Western Desert frontier and an advance into Egypt seemed imminent.

3. My object was to cause material damage and disturbance to the enemy's forward areas. The operation also provided a useful test of arrangements made for co-operation with the Army and RAF.

4. The choice of zero time for the operation is of some interest, as it required the balancing of two factors:

(a) Time after first light to be sufficient for fixing and for the usual morning mist to clear.

(b) Time not to be so late that the superior numbers of enemy fighters would be up to oppose our spotting aircraft.

---

[72]*Kent*: 1928, 10,570t, 8×8in, 8×4in, 8×21in tt, 31.5k.

THE ANGLO-ITALIAN WAR, 1940   131

In the event, the time chosen proved somewhat early and all spotting aircraft had difficulty in spotting the initial salvos due to mist.
5. *Warspite*'s 15-in firing was accurate and satisfactory. *Ramillies* made mistakes which should not have occurred.
6. A very satisfactory feature of the operation was the RAF fighter co-operation assisted by FAA Gladiators. This resulted in the destruction of 11 certain and 1 probable enemy aircraft.
7. The Italians have shown themselves skilful in dispersing MT and stores over wide areas in the desert, and the targets offered do not justify a repetition of this type of operation with heavy ships so long as warfare in the Western Desert remains static.

82. *From Vice Admiral Sir Geoffrey Blake*

The Admiralty
17 August 1940

... The position in Greece looks at the moment pretty unpleasant, and I am afraid, as you are aware, that the question of occupying Crete has now faded into the background. The necessity for troops in the Middle East is so immediate that I don't think it would be possible to sponsor [? any] for such an operation. It is a great pity, because I think we all realise, as you do, the importance of Crete, and if it gets into Italian hands it will be a first class nuisance to you....

We are trying to get a flotilla of MTBs out to you as soon as possible. Whether they would be more valuable at Malta than Alexandria, I don't know... They would be within more reasonable distance of the line of Libyan sea communications and might be able to strike at it more effectively. Unfortunately they are all boats with a rather limited endurance and have only a top speed of 34 knots.... In fact aircraft everywhere have the highest priority, and it holds up other activities very considerably. However, if we get these MTBs out to you I think they may be very useful, and in addition, as you know, VA(S) has arranged to reinforce your submarines. I also managed to get *Woolwich* at last.[73]

---

[73]*Woolwich*: dest depot ship; 1935, 8750t, 4×4in, 15k.
VA(S): V Adm (later Adm) Sir Max Horton (1883–1951): ent RN 1898; Lt 1905; S/M 1905–21; Cdr 1914; distinguished exploits, Baltic, in *E9*, 1914–16; Capt 1920; *Conquest* 1922; *Dolphin* 1924; RA 1932; 2BS 1933; 1CS, MF 1935; VA 1936; Res F 1937–39; N Pat 1939; FO S/M Jan 1940; Adm Jan. 1941; C-in-C W Apps Nov. 1942–Aug. 1945; Ret List Oct. 1945.

83. *To Blake*

29 August 1940

2. We are just waiting to sail for HATS and I hope it will come off all right and that James [Somerville] will not expend too many of *Illustrious*'s aircraft before I get hold of her. I am very glad BONNET is off. While we might have got everything through unscathed, on the other hand we might have lost the lot.

3. I am rather at a loss about the signal from the PM this morning. ... The fact, however, remains that if the enemy get 20 miles from Alexandria, we shall probably have to clear out of the Mediterranean for want of a base.

4. Bad luck losing the *Hostile* especially when we are so short of destroyers out here. I suppose you can't rake us up half-a-dozen or so more[?] Actually the five Australians are rapidly dying on us; and they won't last much longer without protracted refits. The four 'D's' are not much better. I very much grudge my three 'K's' in the Red Sea where the scale of attack is insignificant and there are only 1.5 enemy submarines remaining. I am quite serious. I must get some more destroyers or our operations will come to a standstill. A few convoy sloops would ease the position, as at present I have to use destroyers with 8-knot convoys.

5. So glad *Woolwich* is coming out at last. She will make a great difference. I won't say what I thought and said when she did not come in the first instance.

I wonder if it is realised at home what the repair facilities of this place are. The whole thing is a lash up. We can't get the Maltese workmen and the Egyptians have their limitations, the principal one being that they won't work on the day of an air raid or the day after. We have to pass out the work to Suez and Port Said who are only capable of dealing with small ships. The only docks are a small one here and at Suez and the Admiralty Floating Dock, which may go out of action any moonlit night – I hope without a ship in it. What is to happen when a battleship or cruiser must refit doesn't bear reflecting upon. Actually when we take *Malaya* to sea we never know whether she will stay the course owing to Condenseritis. They tell me, although I can't believe it, that in her 25 years' life the condensers have never been retubed!!!

6. The Italian Battle Fleet don't cause me any sleepless nights although it is true we may see (or hear of) six of them [i.e., battleships] by January, but at any moment I may be left with *Warspite*

only as *Ramillies*'s boilers are also dying on us. You will have observed that *Royal Sovereign*'s did ... So you had better consider sending out the *Barham* very soon. The cruisers are better except *Kent* who has chronic condenser trouble, but they will all want a refit soon. A dreary picture and I am sure it can be matched at home. Have you any spare cruisers? I so much want to keep a permanent party in the Aegean. With eight I could do it but of course not as regards destroyers.

7. Another of our wants is reconnaissance aircraft. We can't move out of harbour without the whole Italian Navy and Air Force knowing it within the hour and we never know what they are doing except in certain areas which our limited number of flying boats cover on occasions. We should be able to quarter this end of the Mediterranean and not a thing should move without our knowing it. Malta is the crux of the situation. A good GR squadron working from there would keep us well informed and we should be able to keep light forces in the Central Mediterranean. At the same time, until Malta is properly defended and the airfields reasonably secure, I don't think one could work a whole GR squadron from there. Was there ever such folly as to allow our Mediterranean fortress to fall into such a state?

8. I hope I haven't painted too gloomy a picture. Really we are pretty cheerful and planning a few knocks for the 'Iteys' when HATS is successfully achieved.

9. You will have seen that we had our first T/B attack at sea. A feeble affair but it caught our cruisers unprepared and they never opened fire until after the mouldy was dropped. Fancy the plane approaching from 3 miles at a height of *200* feet. Of course it should never have got away.

The one on the harbour was equally unsuccessful though it gave us a turn as we thought it was magnetic mines being dropped. Now every ship in the harbour is flying a kite or kites and every now and again there is a devastating report in the air as locally made bombs attached to the kites are touched off. All bluff of course but the news travels so fast here (through the Jap consul) that they may think they are lethal kites.

10. So glad the MTBs are to come out. I don't think they should in the first instance go to Malta. Malta until properly defended should do nothing to invite retaliation. I make an exception in favour of attacking sea targets and reconnaissance.

Alexandria is the best place for MTBs at the moment and I will work them from Mersa Matruh. Later when I can get at the

Dodecanese, I will capture Kastellorizo and use that as an MTB base. They will be very useful in spite of their regrettably low speed.

11. ... The difficulty I find with the soldiers is that they don't [?know] that we can help them and are only too ready to do so. I almost had to force the bombardment of Capuzzo on them the other day. You would have thought that, with an enemy with one flank on the sea, naval assistance would be essential, but I have never been asked to help. I wish we had an ex-Gallipoli soldier out here; he would know the value (and also the weakness at times) of naval guns. The truth is that they are all constipated with the motor transport. In a few years' time they'll be so motorised that they won't be able to move at all.

12. ... You know, I expect, that we have a JPC out here at Cairo. The naval representation at the moment is left to a young Commander, who has done very well, but the thing is getting beyond him. ...

I want a Captain who has been through the IDC. This latter qualification I think highly important, and with a Commander in addition he should be able to hold the job down. ... The above two could also represent the C-in-C, East Indies. ...

84. *War Diary, August 1940 (cont.)*

14 August

AA Armament

5. The C-in-C has reported to the Admiralty that in view of the heavy scale of air attack to be expected and the expected arrival of dive bombers that conversion of LV pom-poms of the Mediterranean Fleet to HP firing self-destroying shell should proceed as quickly as possible. He also requests the shipment of modern light AA guns and AA devices, such as, Oerlikon guns and case shot for 12-pdrs and UP projectors. At present the Mediterranean Fleet and auxilliary vessels have only Lewis guns to reinforce ships' standard equipment.

18 August

Alexandria – Air raid precautions

3. The following order has been issued by the C-in-C:

The Fleet is now menaced by low flying aircraft attack in harbour and energetic measures are required to combat it. It is not yet established whether torpedoes or magnetic mines were dropped during attack on Thursday night, but we must be prepared for both. The following preliminary action is to be taken:

(a) *Medway* in collaboration with RA Alexandria [RAL], is to produce kites for flying from outer breakwater whenever wind permits.[74]

(b) All ships including destroyers are to make a kite capable of being flown at sea or in harbour when wind permits.

(c) RAL is requested to investigate the possibility of small balloons locally for the same purpose as (a). It is presumed that coal gas is available and that small winches can be made up locally.

(d) RAL is requested to arrange for an A/T baffle to be laid in a position which will be discussed verbally, to guard the capital ship anchorage from T/B attack.

(e) The 2 Battle Practice targets are to be secured in tandem with a span between L1 buoy to act as an obstruction to low flying aircraft. Targets should be rigged with masts at each end.

(f) Berths for 2 cruisers or 'Tribal' destroyers are to be arranged inside and parallel to Kamaria breakwater.

(g) All ships are to overhaul their organisation for dealing with low flying attacks. We must shoot these aircraft down.

19 August

Movements

2. Information from secret sources indicates that the following movements of French transports are taking place:

Providence sailed from Beirut for Toulon on 16 August.
Athos II sailed from Beirut for Bizerta on 19 August.[75]
(Both ships routed via the Straits of Messina).
Italian forces have been ordered not to molest these ships.

3. As the C-in-C was given no official information of these movements he has asked Vice Admiral Godfroy to inform the Admiral Commanding, Division Navale du Levant, of the dangers of sailing French ships without first informing him of their movements, pointing out that though our naval forces do not sink vessels at sight, as

---

[74]RA F. Elliott: Capt 1925; RA 1936; ret April 1939 & RA, *Nile* (Alexandria); Cdre i/c, Ceylon & Cdre (A), NAS, E Indies, *Lanka* (Colombo), Jan. 1942; Cdre 2C1, NAS, E Africa, *Kipanga* (Kilindini); *President* 1944; DSVP 1945.
[75]*Providence*: 1914, 11,996gt, 15.5k; *Athos II*: 1925, 15,275gt, 16.5k, both Messageries Maritimes.

do the Italians, there is a danger of transports being mistaken for enemy ships and in any case it is the duty of naval forces to order in for examination any neutral ship which has not been given a clearance by British Naval authorities. . . .

21 August

Infringements of Greek neutrality

10. In a note to the British Minister at Athens dated 12 August, the Greek Government have drawn attention to the presence of British destroyers close to Hydra on 27 July and the bombing of them by Italian aircraft. In order to avoid such incidents they desire that Greek territorial waters should be respected. The C-in-C has made the following signal to the British Minister, Athens:

> No British destroyers were patrolling off Hydra within close distance of the shore on 27 July or at any other time. Presume it is clear to the Greek Government that British warships are fully within their rights in making the passage through territorial waters. It appears important to ensure that the Greek Government appreciates that there can be no question of abrogating our rights under International Law in this respect. In point of fact, however, HM Ships have orders to remain outside territorial waters until in pursuit of the enemy or to pass through such waters only if navigational considerations make it desirable. There is thus no question of carrying out patrols within Greek territorial waters.

11. The only infringements of Greek neutrality which have in fact occurred, have been committed by Italian forces. The most flagrant case was the sinking of the Greek cruiser *Helle* off Tinos harbour on 15 August by an Italian submarine, and the bombing of Greek warships on the following day by Italian aircraft.[76]

24 August

AA Defence of the Fleet

7. The C-in-C has drawn the attention of all concerned to the necessity of improving the AA fire of the Fleet. This has not been good, and the fact that not a single enemy aircraft has been seen to

---

[76]*Helle*: 1913, 2,115t, 3×6in, 2×3in, 2×18in tt, 20.5k; s without warning while dressed overall for holiday. The Greeks, anxious to avoid war, turned a blind eye to Italian infringements of neutrality.

fall as a result of the AA fire of the Fleet, is not a matter to be regarded with complacency.

85. *Aircraft Torpedo Attack on Shipping off El Gazala, 22 August 1940*

(13 September 1940)

Cunningham's Observations

2. This attack, which achieved the phenomenal result of the destruction of, or serious damage to, four enemy ships with three torpedoes, was brilliantly conceived and most gallantly executed. The dash, initiative and co-operation displayed by this sub-flight is typical of the spirit which animates the FAA Squadrons of HMS *Eagle*, under the inspiring leadership of her Commanding Officer, Captain A. R. M. Bridge, RN, and Cdr (F), Cdr C. L. Keighly Peach, DSO, RN.
3. The success of the operation was in no small degree due to the excellent co-operation of No.202 Group, RAF, who carried out the preliminary reconnaissance and provided fighter protection for the Swordfish aircraft.
4. The basing of a sub-flight with the RAF at Maarten Bagush ready to act on reconnaissance reports of 202 Group will be continued when the carriers are in harbour, and it is hoped later when sufficient crews are available to make this permanent. . . .

Copy of Report of Aircraft E5B

Pilot: Lt (A) J.W.G. Wellham, RN
Observer: P/O Airman Marsh[77]

The target was approached in open vic formation from the NW at a height of 30 feet.

The first ship to come within range was a submarine which appeared to be charging her batteries on the surface, about 4 miles from the shore.

I observed Captain Patch preparing to attack this ship, so broke away from the formation and passed the Submarine on my starboard side.[78] She was firing with twin machine guns, one forward and one aft, on the conning tower. They appeared, from the size of the bullets, to be 0.5s.

[77]Wellham flew at Taranto; see note 114.
[78]Patch flew at Taranto: see note 114.

PO Marsh opened fire with his Lewis Gun. A few seconds later the submarine blew up, leaving only a small fraction of the stern above the surface.

We were now under fire of 4-in HA from the depot ship which was lying about 3 miles inshore of the submarine. As we closed this ship it became apparent that there was a destroyer lying alongside her on her port side and a submarine lying alongside the destroyer. The destroyer opened fire with pom-poms, multi-machine guns and 0.5-ins. The fire was accurate and at 3,000 yards range my aircraft was struck by an 0.5-in bullet which entered the bottom of the aircraft and struck the forward main spar, the petrol tank and did a certain amount of minor damage.

At a range of about 500 yards I dropped my torpedo on a bearing of green 45° from the depot ship. I observed Lt Cheeseman's torpedo strike the submarine and explode.[79] Three seconds later my torpedo exploded on the depot ship just forward of amidships. The ship was left blazing furiously.

Four minutes later there was a further large explosion which caused smoke to rise to a height of 300 feet. All three ships were then blazing.

86. *To the Admiralty*

22 August 1940

1. There appears to be a need for defining more definitely the policy concerning Malta.
2. In my view that policy should be to bring base defences at the earliest possible moment to such a state that we can operate offensive[ly] from island with all three services, secure in the knowledge that defences are efficient to [repulse?] any scale of retaliatory action which enemy may produce.
3. At present various deficiencies, notably lack of civilian air raid shelters, inadequate anti-aircraft defences, and lack of underground protection for certain vital services are such that if we provoke a really large scale retaliation the civilian morale would fall rapidly to a point when the population would become a grave menace instead of an assistance to the garrison in resisting attack. Moroever, until there is greater protection Malta is of little use to us as a base, and its invaluable docking and repair services are lost to us.

---

[79]Lt(A) N. A. F. Cheeseman: Lt July 1938; *Eagle* 1940; Instr, 736 Sqdn, *Jackdaw* Nov. 1941; k 30 Dec. 1941.
Iride: 1936, 700/860t, 1×3.9in, 6×21in tt, 14/7.5k.

4. That the Service policy on this subject is not co-ordinated is evident from the fact that whilst the NOIC, Malta, holds views expressed above, the War Office are at the moment considering sending a force to be based at Malta for offensive raids into enemy territory, whilst the RAF are about to send bomber squadron to work from Malta against Italian targets.

5. NOIC, Malta, informs me that deficiency referred to in para. 3 can be remedied and all work completed by spring 1941, if HMG will decide *now* to supply materials and if energetic and co-ordinated action is taken to see that requirements are shipped with minimum of delay.

6. The rendering safe of Malta is key to our Mediterranean strategy and provides the first step in developing our offensive policy. As our grip on Italy and the Mediterranean increase so will our need of Malta.

7. Details of requirements will be the subject of separate signal but for the moment I submit that our policy should be as follows:

a) Offensive action from Malta should be restricted to attacks on sea targets and to reconnaissance.
b) We should aim to to be ready to make full use of Malta offensively by April 1941.
c) That by that date:

1. A force of cruisers and destroyers can be permanently based at island.
2. It will be reasonably safe to carry out dockings, refits and repairs to HM Ships.
3. A submarine flotilla can be based at island.
4. Sufficient protection and aerodromes available to work bomber and reconnaissance squadrons and four squadrons of fighters.
5. Raiding forces of troops can operate based at Malta.

9. Are COS fully satisfied that Malta with its present defences can stand up to a determined effort to capture fortress backed up by the immense scale air attack that can be brought to bear?

Personally my doubts on this point cause me considerable concern.

87. *From the Admiralty*

25 August 1940

The following general directive for Cs-in-C, Middle East, has been drawn up by the Minister of Defence [Churchill] in consultation with the Chiefs of Staff on which your observations are requested:

1. A major invasion of Egypt from Libya must be expected at any time now. . . .

17. The campaign for the Defence of Egypt may, therefore, as a last resort, resolve itself into: strong defence with the left arm from Alexandria inland, and a reaching out with the right hand, using sea power upon his communications. At a later date it is hoped that the reinforcement of the AA defence of Malta and its reoccupation by the Fleet will hamper the sending of further reinforcements – Italian or German – from Europe into Africa, and that an air offensive may ultimately be developed from Malta against Italy. . . .

88. *To the Admiralty*

26 August 1940

. . . The defensive positions to be adopted by Alexandria are intimately connected with protection of Bases from which the Navy is to work. I do not consider Fleet will be able to use Alexandria at all in face of the probable scale of air attack if Army is forced back to line of Delta which is within 20 miles of Alexandria, . . . It must be evident that Fleet cannot operate without a secure base and if Alexandria had to be abandoned as such it will be possible to operate for a few weeks only before being forced out of Mediterranean for lack of a base unless Malta has by that time been made properly secure. Even with the enemy in Mersa Matruh he will have advanced his Air Bases over 150 miles and to within 120 miles of Alexandria which will make its use as a base very precarious.

I feel it necessary to press most strongly that Mersa Matruh line be held at all costs otherwise it may come to pass that Alexandria will be deprived of assistance of Fleet just when it is most needed.

89. *War Diary, August 1940 (concl.)*

29 August

Submarine attacks

6. The Admiralty have directed that on all occasions of a U-boat being attacked one ship should wherever practicable remain in the vicinity for at least 24 hours.

5 September

Aircraft

9. The C-in-C has represented to the Admiralty the urgent necessity for the immediate provision of IR Fulmars for 805 and 806 Squadrons. Since the fighter effort of the fleet cannot be maintained without adequate reserve aircraft and crews, and it is essential too to maintain the present moral superiority over the Italians, the C-in-C is prepared to accept Gladiators or Skuas if the Fulmar IR requirement cannot be met.

United States Observer

14. Lt Cdr Opie of the US Navy has arrived and is accommodated in *Valiant*.[80]

90. *Operation HATS, 29 August–5 September 1940*

(14 January 1941)

Cunningham's Observations

2. This operation, which was the first attempt at passing forces on a large scale between Cape Bon and Sicily, passed off smoothly and with remarkably little incident.
3. The seamanlike performance of the Master of the SS *Cornwall*, Captain F. C. Pretty, after his ship was bombed in convoy MF2, materially assisted the operation by reducing the delay to a minimum.[81]
4. The use of RDF and the Fulmar fighters of *Illustrious* placed an entirely different complexion on the air bombing menace, ...
5. The good work put in by all departments at Malta in fuelling ships and unloading stores was of the greatest assistance.
6. ... It appears that satisfactory results were obtained against a portion of the Italian Air Force which has caused much annoyance to the Fleet ...

Narrative of the C-in-C

D1 day for this operation was finally decided upon as 30 August. Accordingly, Convoy MF2, consisting of *Cornwall, Plumleaf* and

---

[80]Lt-Cdr Opie, USN: one of several serving with the RN.
[81]Capt F. C. Pretty: awarded OBE.
Cornwall: 1920, 10,605gt, 14k, Fed SN.

Volo, sailed after dark on 29 August escorted by *Jervis, Juno, Dainty* and *Diamond*.[82] . . . On 30 August, just before light, the C-in-C in *Warspite*, with *Eagle, Malaya, Orion, Sydney, Kent, Gloucester, Liverpool* and 12 destroyers, left Alexandria. The Flag Officer, Force H, also passed Gibraltar in the forenoon.

2. . . . The RA, 3CS, with the 3CS and 3 destroyers, was detached to pass through the Kaso Strait N of Crete so as to give the impression of a raid into the Aegean.

5. The convoy had also been sighted by enemy aircraft, and one of the A/S patrols which had been sent to sight the former, reported that it had been bombed and SS *Cornwall* hit. A fire was started but quickly got under [control]; the steering gear was damaged but the ship continued at 9½ knots, steering by main engines.

6. At 1430 the Fleet was sighted and shadowed and 2 Gladiators were flown off. The shadower, a Cant Z510, was shortly afterwards shot down.[83] A further shadower, however, was heard between 1650 and 1800.

7. The C-in-C decided to detach the 3CS until dusk to give better AA protection to the convoy. At 1600 the mean line of advance was altered to 180° with the object of giving the impression that the Fleet had merely been covering an Aegean convoy, and was now returning to Alexandria after making a cast South.

8. At 1813, *Eagle*'s duty C reported sighting the enemy battle fleet, consisting of 2 battleships, 7 cruisers and some destroyers, distant 120 miles . . . from *Warspite*. . . .

The situation presented was one of some difficulty. The immediate and natural reaction was to turn towards the enemy to seek action. On further consideration, however, it appeared that it was far from certain that contact could be gained in the dark and that the enemy, with his superior speed and numerous light forces, would be well able to evade action with the Fleet while striking with his light forces at the convoy, whose safe arrival was so essential at Malta.

The C-in-C therefore decided that he must return to protect the convoy during the night, ready to engage the enemy if he came on and hoping that daylight would bring a chance of action.

10. The 3CS had been sent back to locate the convoy but had not succeeded and it was necessary to break W/T silence to obtain its position from *Jervis*. . . .

---

[82]*Volo*: 1938, 1,587gt, 13.5k, Ellerman's Wilson Line.
[83]Cant Z510: flying boat

11. At 2209, *Rainbow* reported sighting three cruisers and some destroyers, at 0855, and *Parthian* reported 4 cruisers and 5 destroyers... *Parthian* estimated 2 hits on the enemy.[84]...

12. All ships were kept at the first degree of readiness, as if both forces continued their courses, contact might have occurred at about 0200. However, nothing was sighted, and at 0630 on 1 September a search to a depth of 100 miles between bearings 310 and 140° was carried out by 9 Swordfish. This also revealed nothing. Course was altered to 210° to close the convoy, cruisers being spread to the NW. One aircraft returning from the first search was lost.

13. A second air search to a depth of 50 miles was then flown off between bearings 235 and 315°, but sighted nothing. At 1600, reports were received from flying boats that the enemy battle fleet was steering between 330 and 000° and was about 100 miles from Taranto. It was thus evident that he had turned back on the previous night and was now on the way back to his base.

14. During 1 September no aircraft were seen at all. This was possibly attributable to attacks carried out by the RAF on Libyan air bases and the successful destruction of shadowers on the previous day. There were no incidents during the night of 1/2 September, except that the convoy was sent on under general cover of the 3CS. It arrived at Malta about 0900, *Cornwall* reaching harbour three hours later.

15. ... on 2 September ... contact was made with Force F at 0900.

16. During the day the Fleet cruised about 35 miles S and W of Malta, while carrying out the fuelling programme and disembarkation of stores. In view of the fact that the expected air attack did not develop early, the C-in-C decided to send *Valiant* into Malta by day....

17. Shortly after, the RA, 3CS, broke W/T silence to say that he was being shadowed and asking for fighters. He also stated his intention of steering away from the main forces to throw off shadowers. Unfortunately he sighted our Fleet before turning and the shadower reported the presence of large naval forces. This shadower, a Cant 501, was shortly afterwards shot down by Fulmars.[85]

18. At 1450, Fulmars shot down one S79 and damaged 3 others, chasing the latter almost to Sicily. These Fulmars nearly ran out of petrol and forced landed on *Eagle*.[86]

---

[84]*Rainbow*: 1932, 1475/2015t, 1×4in, 8×21in tt, 17.5/9k; s off Calabria Oct. 1940. *Parthian*: 1930, 1,475/2,040t, 1×4in, 8×21in tt, 17.5/9k; s off Sicily Aug. 1943.

[85]Cant 501: F/boat: 171mph; obsolete.
Cunningham had requested *Illustrious* carry 19 Fulmars & 18 Swordfish, with 4 Fulmars in IR.

[86]Savoia Marchetti S79: 1934, 4mg, 2,750lb bombs/2t, 270mph, range 1,250mls.

19. A series of bombing attacks were made on the Fleet during the afternoon and evening. At 1500, *Janus* and *Imperial* were unsuccessfully attacked by 3 Ju87B dive bombers when entering Malta, and at 1600 a surprise attack by a small formation was made on *Eagle*, 8 bombs being dropped.[87] Between 1900 and 1910, two air attacks were made on the Fleet.

Bombing was inaccurate and many bombs were jettisoned a long way from the Fleet when the enemy were pursued by fighters. Two S79s were shot down by gunfire and one shot down and one damaged by fighters. The total score for the day was 5 enemy aircraft shot down and 4 damaged. The only casualty was a Fulmar which forced landed at Hal Far.

20. Three floating mines were encountered during the day.

91. *War Diary, August-September 1940 (cont.)*

3 September

Operation HATS [cont.]

At 0130 *Valiant* took station astern of the line ... At 0640, A/S patrols were flown off, two aircraft searching to a depth of 60 miles.

3. At noon, Force I was ... steering for the Kithera Channel, and Force A ... steering for the S of Crete. The 3CS, *Nubian* and *Mohawk*, had been detached by RA, 1BS, at dawn and were proceeding direct to rendezvous with convoy AS3 ... at 1800.

6. ... At 2230, ... the 7CS, *Ilex* and *Decoy*, [were] detached for a dawn bombardment of Scarpanto.

4 September

2. At 0345, ... 8 Swordfish were flown off from *Illustrious* to attack Callato Aerodrome. Owing to a crash on deck it was not possible to fly off 12 as originally intended. Twelve TSRs were also flown off from *Eagle* to attack Maritza Aerodrome (Operation MB3).

3. At 0400, *Calcutta* parted company to join convoy AS3.

4. ... *Sydney* proceeding to bombard Makriyalo aerodrome and *Orion* to bombard Pegadia Bay.

6. RA, 1BS in *Malaya*, with *Eagle*, was sighted at 0730. The striking forces were landed on between 0730 and 0740.[88]

Illustrious reported that 2 Swordfish attacked barracks and ammunition dumps SE of Callato at 0555. Explosions and a large

---

[87]Junkers Ju87B: 1936, 4mg, 3,960lb bombs, 255mph, range 620mls; these were It AF.
[88]Pridham-Wippell.

fire were seen. Six Swordfish attacked Callato aerodrome and a number of aircraft parked on the N edge were probably destroyed. Explosions and fires started on buildings at the S end. . . .

7. *Eagle* reported two main hangars hit, a petrol dump, barrack blocks and workshops set on fire. The aircraft encountered fighters and 4 Swordfish failed to return, one of which probably forced landed at Kaso.

8. . . . At 0820 large volumes of smoke were seen in the direction of Rhodes.

9. At 1055, VALF in *Orion*, with *Sydney, Ilex* and *Decoy*, rejoined. VALF reported that no military targets could be identified at Pegadia . . . *Sydney* reported that the Eastern part of the landing ground at Makriyalo was plastered. . . . Two E-boats which came out were engaged by *Ilex* and sunk. *Sydney*'s aircraft reported that 3 others were present, 2 of which retired and the third damaged.

10. At 1030 a sub-flight of Fulmars attacked 4 S79s damaging one, and at 1130 attacked 3 S79s, shooting down one and damaging another.

11. Three bombing attacks were made on the fleet between 1110 and 1158. Three aircraft dropped 6 bombs four cables astern of *Warspite*, one aircraft dropped 6 bombs in the vicinity of the screen and one aircraft dropped a stick of bombs near *Ilex*.

12. At 1145 an A/S patrol dropped a bomb on a suspected submarine 2 miles from *Warspite*. *Imperial* obtained a faint contact and attacked without result.

13. At 1345, two S79s were engaged by two Fulmars; one S79 was damaged . . . Although small enemy formations were detected from time to time during the day, no more approached the fleet.

16. The force with RA, 1BS, arrived Alexandria at 2100.

5 September

At 0610 *Hereward* investigated a contact and the fleet made an emergency turn. The swept channel was reached at 0700 and the fleet entered Alexandria harbour without further incident.

2. The 3CS was ordered to remain with convoy AS3 until dark. *Imperial* and *Hereward* were sailed p.m. to rendezvous with the convoy . . . to relieve *Nubian* and *Mohawk*.

3. During Operation HATS, particularly on 31 August and 4 September, 202 Group, RAF, carried out offensive operations against the Libyan aerodromes. These were very successful and certainly reduced the enemy's air effort against the fleet.

4. RA, 1BS, reported that Force E was attacked by 4 dive bombers at 1840 on 2 September . . . and *Janus* reported that on the same day when off Malta she was attacked by 3 Ju87B dive bombers.

5. Captain (D), 13DF, reported that between 1125 and 1430 on 4 September, Force P (*Gallant, Griffin, Greyhound, Hotspur, Garland*) were attacked by high level bombers without result. *Garland,* having two leaks in two boilers, was towed by *Griffin* from 1715 until 1845 and then proceeded on one boiler. Force P was . . . expected to arrive at Gibraltar at 2230/5.[89]

92. *From Churchill*

9 September 1940

I congratulate you on the success of recent operation in Eastern and Central Mediterranean, and upon accession to your Fleet of two of our finest units with other valuable vessels. I am sorry however that armoured Brigade which is so necessary to the defence of Egypt and Alexandria is still . . . more than three weeks from [point of arrival]. I hope you will find it possible to review naval situation in light of experience gained during HATS, and arrival of *Illustrious* and *Valiant.* Not only paper strength of Italian Navy, but also degree of resistance which they may be inclined to offer should be measured. It is of high importance to strike at Italians this autumn, because as the time passes Germans will be more likely to lay strong hands on Italian war machine, and then the picture will be very different. We intend to strengthen AA defences of Malta by every possible means, and some novel weapons of which I have high hopes will shortly be sent there for experiment.[90] I trust that Malta may become safe for temporary visits of the Fleet at an earlier date than April 1941. If in the meanwhile you had any proposals for offensive action to make, they should be transmitted to the Admiralty. I shall be glad if you will concert with Army and Air Force, plans for an operation against Italian communications in Libya. I consider at right time it could be used to hamper any large scale offensive against Egypt. The advantages gained by the initiative are obviously very great. I hope Fulmars have made a good impression. The battle here for air mastery continues to be severe, but firm confidence is felt in its eventual outcome.

---

[89]Capt G. F. Stevens-Guille: Capt Dec. 1939; Capt(D) Mar. 1940; *Victory* 1941; *Cardiff* 1942; *Durban* 1943; Capt of F, MF Dec. 1943.

'G' cl: 1936, 1345t, 4×4.7in, 8×21in tt, 35.5k. *Garland* Polish N.

[90]UP rockets: 'unrotating (or 'useless') projectiles'.

93. To Pound

10 September 1940

Please thank the Minister of Defence for his telegram. I hope that it has been made clear to him that the prerequisite of successful operations in the Central Mediterranean is constant and complete air reconnaissance in that area in which respect we still fall far short, and that operations of the Fleet are drastically limited by the number of destroyers available.

94. War Diary, September 1940

9 September

Cyprus Defences

4. Cyprus is at present without fixed defences of any sort. The increasing importance of Famagusta harbour as a port of embarkation for copper pyrites and other commodities make it necessary to provide coast defences adequate to deal with sporadic raids by light craft or bombardment by submarines. It is therefore considered that a proper establishment of coast defences should be laid down and the matter taken up with the War Office accordingly. In the interim, two 4-in guns and equipment can be provided as a temporary measure from items at Alexandria intended for the Turks. The C-in-C has requested the C-in-C, Middle East, to undertake to erect the guns and provide personnel who might well be recruited locally. (C-in-C 1845/9 to Admiralty.)

95. Minutes of Meeting of Commanders-in-Chief, Middle East

11 September 1940

1. It was agreed that the Cs-in-C should meet periodically to consider the various JPS papers prior to submission to the COS.
3. The C-in-C, Mediterranean, stated that the Navy would, in the near future, be represented on the JPS by a Captain, who would have a Cdr as his assistant.
4. *Alternative fleet bases*
It was agreed that Brig[adier] AA should examine, in conjunction with the Naval and Air Staff, the provision of additional AA defences for Port Said and Haifa in *certain eventualities*.
5. *Naval co-operation in the defence of Egypt*
The note by C-in-C Middle East was discussed and the following points arose:

(a) Naval activities would not draw off any appreciable scale of air attack from Egypt, as sea bomber squadrons were used against the fleet.
(b) Land targets for naval bombardment should be within about 6 miles from the coast.

A Naval surveyor was selecting places where the Navy could bombard the coast road and was arranging for the necessary marks to be put in position. The Navy required information of other likely places.

In the event of Italian attack the RAF would be fully employed and could not be relied on to provide fighter protection for the fleet.
(c) It was decided that the JPS should study the question of combined raids with small bodies of troops.

6. *Air defence of Malta*

Until good reconnaissance of [?from] Malta could be guaranteed and light naval forces could be based on Malta, communications between Italy and Libya could not be interrupted entirely.

It was considered that when the Malta defences had been brought up to the scale recommended by the COS, Malta could be used by the fleet.

The scale was 112 AA guns and four squadrons of fighter aircraft.

The AOC-in-C explained the present position and stated that his reinforcements were limited and at present he did not consider that he could increase the fighter strength at Malta. He would keep the matter under review.

7. *Malta reconnaissance*

It was agreed that daily reconnaissances over the northern portion of the Ionian Sea would give the information of convoy movements required by the Navy and the Army.

12. *Combined Operations school*

It was agreed that a small school should be formed at Haifa and that a committee should consider the question and submit recommendations.

13. *Fighter protection for Red Sea convoys*

AOC-in-C asked whether C-in-C Mediterranean would send an aircraft carrier to protect important Red Sea convoys, as owing to the distance involved RAF protection was necessarily limited.

C-in-C Mediterranean stated that if Gladiator aircraft could be provided he would send *Eagle* but C-in-C East Indies was not in favour of an aircraft carrier owing to the difficulty of providing destroyer escort.

THE ANGLO-ITALIAN WAR, 1940   149

The RAF cannot supply the Sea Type Gladiators and it was agreed that for the present the risks of air attack must be accepted.

96.   *War Diary, September 1940 (cont.)*

13 September

State of Mediterranean Destroyer Command

6. The C-in-C has reported the present state of the Destroyer Command today to the Admiralty.

2nd Flotilla – 7 ships
Havock making good bomb damage at Suez.
Ilex in dock repairing torn rudder.
Imperial in dock repairing leaky fuel tanks.
14th Flotilla – 6 ships
Wryneck rearming.[91]
Nubian in service but 'A' bracket bushes worn.
Mohawk in service but rudder requires lifting.
10th Flotilla – 9 ships
Stuart out of action. Urgently requiring extensive refit.
Voyager refitting at Malta.
Vampire docking at Port Said to repair 'A' bracket bushes.
Defender making good essential machinery defects.
Dainty and *Diamond* sailing for Red Sea convoys.

7. This leaves only 12 destroyers for operations, of which 2, *Nubian* and *Mohawk*, have urgent defects. (C-in-C, 2009/15.)

19 September

A/S and Torpedo Striking Forces

6. An A/S striking force of 3 aircraft is being kept at short notice by day and on moonlight nights at Aboukir. This force is also available for any search required. A torpedo striking force of 3 aircraft is being kept at similar notice at Dekheila.

21 September

Report on Enemy T/B Attacks

8. *Kent* was attacked by bombing aircraft about 2355 on 17 September in bright moonlight, and immediately afterwards by 2

---

[91]*Wryneck*: 1918, 1,100t, 4×4in, 24.5k; s Ger a/c, Greece April 1941.

torpedo aircraft from positions on the starboard quarter; 2 torpedoes dropped, 1 hit.

97. *From Pound*

20 September 1940

... I think you should be pretty well off for aircraft before long with the various reinforcements that are being sent to you. ...

I have pretty difficult times with WSC [Churchill] occasionally as he is quite impervious to arguments and sweeps them aside as if they did not exist. For instance, he either cannot (which I do not believe) or refuses to acknowledge that there was any difference between HATS and BONNETS, and is always saying that the Admiralty are exaggerating risks. I have told him that we do not mind putting anything through the Mediterranean as long as the possibility of its loss is recognised, but in the case of the content of AP1 and AP2 I felt that it was so vital that these tanks should reach the Middle East that I held out against their going through the Mediterranean. If they only make a safe passage through the Red Sea and arrive on the 24th we shall be justified, but I do not suppose we shall get the credit for it. However, WSC is so magnificent in many ways and the ideal leader of the Nation in these times that I must put up with his idiosyncrasies.

I think it is possible about 18 October that we shall ask you to pass an MT ship with guns, etc., for Malta through the Mediterranean, and I hope that at the same time *Barham* will be able to join you as I feel you must have three efficient ships, taking into account that *Malaya* will be returning. You must not bank on this too much, but I hope that at the same time we may be able to send you a reinforcement of four destroyers. In one of your telegrams the other day you stated that at the moment you only had 12 destroyers available for the Fleet, but I can assure you that this is in excess of what C-in-C, Home Fleet, has had for a very long time. However, I do realise how short you are.

I have had a hard job to pull *Woolwich* away from C-in-C, Home Fleet, but he really did want her at Scapa. However, I also realised how necessary she is to you.

P.S.   ... The dive bomber is easy meat to the fighters – so much so that the Huns have given up sending them over here but they are the greatest menace which ships have to stand up against.

98. *To Pound*

22 September 1940

A. I have been feeling rather harassed lately as it does not appear that our difficulties out here are realised at home. As an example I would point to the signal made by the Minister of Defence on 9 September in which he certainly implies that now *Illustrious* and *Valiant* have joined we should be up and doing more. These two ships are certainly a most welcome reinforcement and have already put a much more favourable aspect on the air situation, but all my operations are drastically limited by the number of destroyers available. At the moment about one-third are continually out of action and the remainder are quite insufficient for the numerous commitments and for fleet operations.

Among these are the numerous slow convoys to Haifa, Port Said and Cyprus on which it is sheer waste to use destroyers. I have asked several times for some slow escort vessels, but so far have had no reply to my signals.

I acknowledge how difficult it must be to supply these needs from home and how hard up you are for these craft and I would have no objection to having my requests turned down, provided it is clearly understood by those in authority what drastic limitations this imposes on the fleet.

At the moment, to carry out any fleet operations I have to hold up all local work and wait until I can scrape sufficient destroyers together.

B. I don't know if the situation as regards supplying Malta has been brought to your notice. By 1 April 1941, Malta has to be supplied with just under 400,000 tons of supplies. Something like two convoys a month and each one involving a complete fleet operation without counting bringing back the empties. Of course these convoy trips will provide excellent opportunities for operations against the enemy but naturally the fleet will be at reduced strength owing to convoy escorts and to fight hampered with a convoy is not the most acceptable moment.

C. Another of our difficulties which I feel is not fully realised is the repair situation. Until Malta is secure it can only be used to repair odd submarines and destroyers and the facilities at Alexandria are just a lash up. . . .

On top of it all is the constant anxiety as to what is to be done with a damaged capital ship and this makes me very reluctant to risk them in minable waters without some very good reason.

D. ... What I am doing is to keep the *Ladybird* at Mersa Matruh pretty constantly and she works in close co-operation with the GOC, Western Desert.[92] She has had plenty of adventures with mines and torpedo attack, but she keeps going and is doing stout work. Every few nights I am also sending a destroyer division to beat up Sidi Barrani and the escarpments near the coast road, though it only acts as an irritant....

The Army outlook on the Italian advance is rather different from the Air Force['s] and ours. They rather want the Italians to butt into the Mersa Matruh defences so that they can hit him hard on the front and flank. The Air view and ours of course is that we don't like the Italians any closer than is necessary to our bases....

E. Our organisation for retiring to Port Said and Haifa is well in hand but I don't mean to be driven out of Alexandria unless we have to go. Your signal re German dive bombers has just arrived and I have answered as above.

G. I see the interrogation of some prisoners of war from a Cant flying boat shot down by a Sunderland three days ago, tends to show that all six Italian battleships are in commission. Certainly the two *Venetos* were out on 1 September and one other. It looks rather as though I shall not be able to go to sea less than three battleships strong. The *Ramillies* only hampers us with her slow speed and she has to fuel at Malta if she does more than two days out in the Central Mediterranean.

I don't believe the two damaged ships are back from Trieste yet, but having to take the three to sea brings more strain on the destroyers.

I intend, if the destroyer situation allows it, always to take the two carriers so as to bring the greatest possible weight of torpedo attack on the Italian battle fleet. If we can damage two we may get the lot.

The working of two carriers of such different characteristics as *Illustrious* and *Eagle* presents various new problems.

I would not have believed it possible that such an advance as appears in *Illustrious* would have been possible in the time. Her Swordfish fly on in line ahead about 100 yards apart.

Incidentally, we are most dreadfully short of reserve aircraft and personnel for the next two months. Literally we have to live on what is out here now, which is what the carriers have on board. This is another reason why I hesitate to go in for any big operation until the situation as regards reserves improves....

---

[92]*Ladybird*: gunboat; 1916, 625t, 2×6in, 1×3in, 14k; s It a/c off Tobruk May 1941.

99. *War Diary, September 1940 (cont.)*

25 September

Deep reconnaissance in the Mediterranean

6. With the arrival of Glenn Martin aircraft at Malta, the question of reconnaissance requirements in the Mediterranean has been under review by the C-in-C, Mediterranean, AOC-in-C, Middle East, and AOC, Mediterranean.[93] The C-in-C's reconnaissance requirements are, in order of priority:

(a) A watertight reconnaissance of the Ionian Sea.
(b) Occasional reconnaissance of Taranto, Bari, Brindisi, Messina, Augusta and Tripoli.
(c) Reconnaissance to enable torpedo attacks to be delivered on enemy ships between Malta and Tunisia.

7. It has been decided to meet these requirements as follows:

(a) By Glenn Martins and 3 Sunderlands from 228 Sqdn.
(b) As practicable and as required.
(c) Reconnaissance to cover the general area between Malta and Kerkenah Island by Swordfish fitted with extra fuel tanks to give a range of about 900 miles.

The AOC, Mediterranean, will deal direct with the C-in-C, Mediterranean, to co-ordinate these requirements.

100. *From Blake*

25 September 1940

4. We hope to get *Barham* and four destroyers out to you as soon as possible, and at the same time, pass one MT ship through, but as you will know this will not occur until Force H is reconstituted.
5. We were very sorry to hear about *Kent*. ... However, you are obtaining *York* and *Ajax*, although I have no doubt they will be a little out of breath by the time they reach you.
6. It is difficult at the moment to see when we shall get some MTBs out to you. Personally, I think we should send those which we obtain from America, and which have a much better performance than the boats which we are producing at home. ... the top speed of

---
[93]Glenn Martin: Marylands.

the American boats with the Packard engine should be in the neighbourhood of 42 knots with a full load. They should also have an endurance of about 1,200 miles at 10 knots.

7. We have just made you a signal regarding corvettes, minesweepers and A/S craft generally. As you can imagine, we are having a pretty heavy task here to keep even with all the attacks on our trade, and also minelaying, and have had fairly heavy casualties in the process. Your need is quite realised but it is purely a question, as it is with the Army, of producing the equipment.

9. As you know, Norman should shortly be with you, and I can't think of a better Captain to be the Naval Member of the JPC. He knows the Mediterranean well and is a very good fellow who gets on with everybody.[94]

10. ... It is a pretty hard and strenuous life for him [Pound], but he seems to be bearing up remarkably well and never shows any desire to turn in before 2 a.m. I don't think his Staff stand the strain as well as he does....

101. *Operation MB5, 28 September–3 October 1940*

(24 January 1941)

Cunningham's Observations

2. The sudden discovery on 30 September of a numerically superior battlefleet within 100 miles of our Fleet, in spite of the shore-based reconnaissance from Malta, was disquieting. This sighting was the first intimation that as many as five Italian battleships were in effective commission.

3. Subsequent investigation showed that this force was in fact sighted by a shore-based aircraft at 0920, but owing to an error caused by inexperience this report was not made until the aircraft returned to base at Malta. It was also found subsequently that the photographic reconnaissance of Taranto on the 28th actually revealed the presence of 5 battleships, 3 of which had been mistaken for cruisers. These matters were taken up energetically by the VA, Malta, and the AOC, Mediterranean, in concert and the situation in this respect is now satisfactory.

---

[94]Capt H. G. Norman: Capt 1938; IDC 1939; *President* 1940; Cdre & Addnl COS, Med F 1940; *Queen Elizabeth* 1943 & EF 1944; RA. 'His work as NLO to COS Cttee in Cairo was absolutely invaluable and greatly admired by ABC' (Captain Hugh Lee).

4. The good work of the two aircraft from *Illustrious* which sighted and shadowed the Italian Fleet, provided a very clear picture of the situation on the Admiral's plot. . . .
5. The disembarkation of troops from *Gloucester* and *Liverpool* at Malta was carried out expeditiously and reflects credit on the organisation of the VA, Malta, the RA, 3CS, and of the ships concerned.
6. The good fortune of *Stuart* on 29 September and of *Havock* and *Hasty* on 2 October in encountering U-boats was ably exploited by these ships.
7. The bombardment of Stampalia on the night of 2/3 October by *Orion* and *Sydney* was less satisfactory. The selected approach course led to fire being opened at very long range so that the trajectory could clear the hills, and the bombardment was of too short duration to be effective and partook rather of the nature of an indiscriminate bombardment.

Narrative of the C-in-C's Proceedings

The object of this operation was to pass about 1,200 military and RAF drafts, and stores, to Malta, and to engage the enemy fleet if a favourable opportunity offered. . . .

2. The Fleet, consisting of *Warspite, Valiant, Illustrious, Orion, Sydney, York, Hyperion, Hereward, Hero, Ilex, Imperial, Jervis, Juno, Janus, Nubian, Mohawk* and *Stuart,* sailed from Alexandria p.m. on 28 September . . .
3. *Liverpool* and *Gloucester* embarked personnel and stores during the night and joined the C-in-C before daylight.
4. It had been intended that the battle fleet should carry out practice firings during the forenoon but these were cancelled owing to the detection of a shadowing aircraft at 1030. Three Fulmars were flown off at 1037 and shot down this aircraft, a Cant S507. One Fulmar forced landed after the combat and the crew were rescued by *Stuart.* A second Cant 507 was also shot down at 1420.
6. During the afternoon the Fleet was attacked three times by enemy aircraft. At 1453 a formation of three S79s dropped about 30 bombs near *York.* Fire was opened by *Warspite, Illustrious, Valiant* and *Gloucester* and one aircraft was shot down. . . .

At 1510 an attack was made by a formation of five S79s. A stick of 20–30 bombs straddled *Warspite,* splinters causing slight damage to gun shields and 3 minor casualties.

At 1641, four T/B aircraft approaching at a low height carried out an unsuccessful torpedo attack on *Illustrious.* They were not engaged by the Fleet as they were mistaken for Fulmar aircraft returning to the Fleet.

7. Two Fulmar aircraft failed to return to *Illustrious* late in the evening, and the Consul at Candia reported that they had forced landed near Sitia, the crews being safe.

8. ... At 2215/29, *Stuart*, who had been detached to return to Alexandria with a burst steam pipe, made contact with a submarine ... *Stuart* carried out a series of attacks during the night, forcing the submarine to the surface in the morning, when she was also bombed by a flying boat. She sank at 0925/30, 47 of her crew of 49 being rescued. This submarine was later identified as the *Gondar*.[95]

9. At 0700/30 and 1030, aircraft were flown off to search a sector 270–330°, the first search going to 80 miles and the second to 120 miles. Nothing was sighted by the first search, but during the second search Duty F reported three 8-in cruisers, four 6-in cruisers and 7 destroyers, steering to the NW ... At this time they bore 340° 80 miles from the C-in-C.

10. At 1225, ... the course of the Fleet was altered to close the enemy and the striking force was ranged in *Illustrious*.

11. At 1230, Duty D sighted the enemy battlefleet and a large number of destroyers, and reported at 1245 that these forces consisted of 2 *Cavour* class and 2 *Littorio* class, with 10 destroyers, steering 325° at 22 knots. Amplifying reports by Duty F, who was also in contact, revealed the presence of 5 battleships. They were then 116 miles from the C-in-C.

12. In view of the small size of the striking force (7–9 aircraft) due to reconnaissance requirements, the heavy odds against a successful attack in broad daylight against so strong a force, the impossibility of supporting the attack due to the distance away of the enemy, and finally that it would be impossible to come up with the enemy before dark, the C-in-C decided not to launch the striking force. If the enemy turned towards our fleet it was intended to launch an attack at dusk. At this time the enemy appeared to be making for Taranto.

15. At about 1630 a section of the enemy fleet, consisting of 5 cruisers and some destroyers, altered to the SW, ... steering for Messina.

16. *Gloucester* and *Liverpool* were detached to Malta at 1450 and *York* and *Mohawk* stationed to the NW of the Fleet to assist the return of the shadowing aircraft. *Mohawk* was subsequently detached to Malta for repairs.

---

[95]*Gondar*: 1938, 680/866t, 1×3.9in, 6×21in tt, 14/8k; fitted to take hum tpdos.

20. During the afternoon [of 1 October] *Voyager* and *Calcutta*, who with *Havock* and *Hasty*, had been escorting convoy AN4, joined the C-in-C, the latter two ships proceeding independently to Alexandria.
21. *Liverpool* and *Gloucester* joined at 1745 and at sunset *Orion* and *Sydney* were detached to carry out a sweep of the Gulf of Athens, the Doro Channel and towards Tenedos, and if conditions were favourable to carry out a night bombardment of the Port Maltezana area in Stampalia.
22. The Fleet proceeded during the night without incident, until at 0500 a report was received from *Havock* that she was in contact with an enemy submarine ... She was surprised on the surface, attacked by gunfire and later depth charged, surfacing, surrendering and scuttling at 0715. 45 survivors were rescued and *Havock* and *Hasty* joined the C-in-C at noon ....[96]
23. A formation of S79s were sighted and chased by Fulmars during the forenoon but escaped.

The Fleet proceeded to Alexandria without further incident, gunnery practices and a runner T/B attack being carried out before entering harbour at 2000.
24. *Orion* and *Sydney* arrived Alexandria a.m. 3 October on completion of their sweep through the Aegean. A bombardment of Stampalia was carried out at 2350/2. No opposition of any kind was encountered ...

102. *War Diary, October 1940*

3 October

2. RA, 1BS, in *Malaya*, with *Eagle, Ramillies, Ajax* and *Coventry, Voyager, Vendetta, Vampire, Waterhen, Dainty, Decoy, Diamond* and *Defender*, sailed ... to exert a threat to enemy Libyan convoys and to cover Crete and to exercise *Eagle* working in conjunction with *Ajax* and *Coventry*.[97]
3. *Submarine Movements*

On patrol	Bari-Durazzo	*Rainbow, Regent*
	Straits of Messina	*Proteus, Rover*
	Off Benghazi	*Rorqual*
	Off Spezia	*Triton, Tetrarch*

---

[96]*Berillo*: 1936, 696/860t, 1×3.9in, 6×21in tt, 14/8k.
[97]*Coventry*: 1918, 4,200t, 10×4in, 29k; s a/c off Tobruk Sept. 1942.

Triad and *Truant* arrived Malta on 2 and 3 October respectively. *Osiris* and *Pandora* arrived Alexandria on 1 and 2 October respectively.[98]

Osiris reported having sunk a small transport by gunfire in the Straits of Otranto on 15 August and one destroyer on 22 September. She also reported having sighted a large number of ships during her patrols in the Straits of Otranto.

Pandora reported having sunk a supply ship of about 4,000 tons off Ras Amer on 28 September.

4 October

AA defence of the Fleet at sea
2. The C-in-C has issued the following instructions:

> During operations at sea, ships fitted with RDF are to be prepared to indicate the approach of enemy aircraft to the fleet and to the fighter patrols in the following manner:
>
> If a detected formation of aircraft is suspected as hostile and closes to a range of 12,000 yards without being sighted a 'blind' barrage of up to 3 rounds per gun should at once be fired on a bearing as indicated by RDF at an angle of sight about 30° and at a height between 9,000 and 11,000 feet. To avoid fleet aircraft being endangered, fighters on patrol must be at 14,000 feet or above, except when in pursuit of the enemy. Aircraft carriers should hoist the signal to indicate the approach of friendly aircraft in the appropriate sector when own friendly aircraft are expected to return from search or patrol. Friendly aircraft must approach the fleet at a height between 800 and 1,000 feet . . .

103. *From the Admiralty*

2 October 1940

A. The intensification of the attack on Egypt possibly with the assistance of Germany must depend to a large extent on sea-borne supplies reaching Libya.

---

[98]*Regent* (1930) (s Med April 1943), *Rover* (1931): 1,475/2,015t, 1×4in, 8×21in tt, 17.5/9k.
Triton (s It escorts, Str of Otranto, Dec 1940), *Tetrarch* (s W Med Nov. 1941), *Triad* (mined, Taranto, Oct. 1940), *Truant*: 1939–40, 1,090/1,575t, 1×4in, 10×21in tt, 15.25/9k.

B. It is realised with the Fleet based at Alexandria and with the present strength of your Fleet and degree of air reconnaissance it is impossible to maintain an adequate force in the Central Mediterranean to cut permanently the Italy–Libya lines of communication.

C. The additional submarines now reaching you together with those we hope to send you in the future may cause interrruption but cannot stop them altogether.

D. It would be possible to cut these lines of communication if you had the following:

1. Sufficient light forces at Malta . . .

    This requires not only adequate air reconnaissance to prevent these light forces being surprised but also sufficient AA and fighter aircraft to make Malta tenable as a base for the light forces.
2. Adequate air reconnaissance to prevent light forces from being surprised when operating from Alexandria with the object of cutting Italian communications to the Eastern part of Libya.

E. You will realise that with our many commitments at the present time it is impossible to provide sufficient reinforcements of surface craft, aircraft or AA guns to deal with the above.

F. It would be a great help, however, if you could give an indication of the minimum (R) minimum, reinforcements that would be required under the following categories:

1. Cruisers.
2. Destroyers.
3. Reconnaissance aircraft at Malta.
4. Reconnaissance aircraft at Alexandria.
5. Fighter aircraft at Malta.
6. AA guns at Malta.

G. It is realised that the final answer is to base the Battle Fleet at Malta, but this would require the full scale defences of 112 HA guns. . . .

104. *To the Admiralty*

5 October 1940

There are two opposing aspects of Central Mediterranean problems:

a) The cutting of Libyan communications
b) The security of Malta.

2. As regards a), to do the work effectively three things are needed:

(i) Efficient air reconnaissance;
(ii) Suitable light striking forces, surface and submarine;
(iii) Suitable air striking force.

... if we are to take the risks to Malta ... it is essential that the forces at Malta should be of such effectiveness that risk is justified.

3. *Effective air reconnaissance.* ... our present shore-based reconnaissance failed to locate the enemy on 29 September, though he was at sea with his entire fleet, and it was left to Fleet reconnaissance to do so. Moreover it has to be admitted that our Central Mediterranean reconnaissance has so far been a failure. We have only succeeded in spotting a single convoy on its way across to Libya. We suspect they may be going in driblets via Pantelleria Channel, Tripoli and then coasting to Benghazi but this is still supposition. No convoys have been found going straight across from Eastern Italy.

4. From the above it will be seen that what is really needed is all round reconnaissance from Malta. At present the attempt is being made to do the Western, Cape Bon–Sicily area by Swordfish but they have not suitable range or speed.

5. A further necessity is periodical inspection of Italian bases. This can adequately be done by Glenn Martins.

6. ... The problem for covering force operating from Alexandria is fortunately not the same [as] for those operating from Malta, as Italian forces based outside Italy and Sicily are negligible.

7. I consider to carry out duties in paras 4–6 we need Glenn Martins now at Malta (for duties in para. 5) and a force of 10 IE and 6 IR aircraft of good speed and long range. Not more than half these aircraft should be flying boats owing to their vulnerability; ships are to be at the base. It would appear that Beauforts or aircraft of equal performance are suitable.

8. *Suitable light forces.* Our raiding forces must be prepared to deal with an enemy escorting force of four 8-in cruisers and accompanying destroyers. It must therefore have good speed, gunpower and protection, and for this I consider that four *Gloucesters* and four 'Tribal' or similar class are desirable. The submarines being provided should be adequate though obviously the more that can be put on patrol at a given time the better.

9. *Suitable air striking force.* I attach the very greatest importance to this as it provides the only sure way of hitting at enemy heavy ships when our own are out of range or on way back to or at Alexandria. Moreover the effect will be to force convoys and Italian Fleet further away from Malta and thus increase time on passage and opportunities for us to get at them. For this duty a squadron of Beauforts is suggested.

10. *Security of Malta.* As no doubt is realised the main difficulty in answering questions on defence [?problems] is that the intensity for [?of] attack depends not so much on types and numbers of ships sent to the island as on degree of success they attain against enemy. As stated in my 2015/22/8 [no. 86] if we are to avoid a serious threat to Malta itself it appears necessary that in any given period the scale of attack drawn down should not be disproportionate to the state of the defences it has been possible to install. It is only logical therefore to expect the full weight of Italian attack if our light forces work effectively. I cannot therefore well suggest an interim figure to aim at for defences. I feel that [corrupt group] as soon as war appears about to develop successful attack on Libyan communications is becoming essential and hence the need for full scale defences to be built up as quickly as resources will permit, and conditions of accommodation will allow. All we can do meanwhile is to accept what disparity may exist between scale of attack and means of defence. The risk in fact must be accepted and it will at least be reduced by presence of surface forces. I am in fact prepared now to operate the light forces and submarines on scale of [corrupt group] from Malta but surface ships would at present enter harbour at night only.

11. *Summary*

(i) Four *Gloucesters* and one 8-in cruiser (*Note:* This force is necessary so long as I can only use Malta by night so as to have a similar force at Alexandria and work relief).
(ii) Four 'Tribals'.
(iii) Two [squadrons], of flying boats and Beauforts
(iv) Four IE and two IR flying boats.
(v) & (vi) The maximum number of fighters and AA guns that can possibly be spared, up to the 4 squadrons of fighters and [?further] of establishment guns.

Requirements (i) and (ii) are exclusive of present forces in Mediterranean; and rest are inclusive.

12. Another and perhaps more obvious method of stopping the enemy's supplies is ... making port entries in Libya unusable for shipping by continuous bombing.

This has to some extent been achieved at Tobruk, Derna and Benghazi by the Canal Air Force and FAA, but a much greater scale of air attack is necessary which can only be produced by a large increase in the number of long range bombers in the Middle East. Backed by heavy attacks from UK on embarkation ports in Italy this would be most effective. Tripoli is as yet untouched but I hope to start the process shortly.

Finally I submit that there is much evidence that war is swinging this way. The cardinal factor is time. If we can on this occasion succeed in carrying our disposition ahead of the enemy moves the gain may be immeasurable. It is evident that he will move quickly and the specified [?air attack] when enhanced by German aircraft is likely to result in serious [?attacks] against Malta and might well bring whole of our policy of using island to naught unless we act quickly.

105. *Report on Operation MB6, 9–15 October 1940*

2. It was the intention to run Convoy MF3 (4 ships) from Alexandria to Malta, and Convoy MF4 (3 ships) from Malta to Alexandria, and to make every effort to engage the enemy if at sea.

3. The Fleet, consisting of *Warspite, Illustrious, Valiant, Malaya, Eagle, Ramillies, Gloucester, York, Ajax, Orion, Sydney, Liverpool, Hyperion, Ilex, Havock, Hasty, Hereward, Imperial, Vampire, Vendetta, Dainty, Decoy, Defender, Jervis, Juno, Janus* and *Nubian*, sailed p.m. and carried out gunnery practices after leaving harbour partly as cover for departures. ...

4. At 2000 convoy MF3, consisting of *Memnon, Lanarkshire, Clan Macaulay, Clan Ferguson,* escorted by *Calcutta, Coventry, Voyager, Stuart, Waterhen* and *Wryneck*, sailed from Alexandria.[99]

5. At 0524/9 a contact was obtained by *Nubian*. *Hyperion* reported that a torpedo was approaching *Malaya*. ...

6. Three more contacts were obtained during the day.

8. Air reconnaissance on 9 October had revealed that there were no *Littorio* class battleships in harbour at Taranto, and it was therefore decided to provide close cover for the convoys during the day in

---

[99]*Memnon*: 1931, 7,506gt, 16k, China Mutual SN.
Lanarkshire: 1940, 9,816gt, 17k, Scottish Shire Line.
Clan Macaulay: 1936, 10,492gt, 17.5k, Clan Line.
Clan Ferguson: 1938, 7,347gt, 17k, Clan Line.

view of the possibility of enemy forces being at sea in the Central Mediterranean.

9. ... Air searches were flown off ... to search a sector 270 to 340° to maximum depth, and during the last two searches one aircraft also maintained a warning patrol to the S of the convoy.

10. The first air search located a submarine on the surface ... The submarine was attacked with depth charges but both charges failed.

12. At 1432 aircraft duty C reported an enemy submarine submerging 20 miles ahead of the fleet and later that she had straddled it with 4 bombs. Three destroyers were sent ahead to investigate but without result. At 1600, however, *Vampire*, the port wing ship of the screen, obtained a contact and made 4 attacks with a reasonable chance of success. A further contact was obtained by *Defender* at 1825. There appears to have been a submarine concentration ...

13. At 1645 the 3CS was detached to join the convoy and at 1715 *Ramillies, Nubian, Hero* and *Hereward*, and at 1800 *Hyperion, Hasty* and *Ilex* were detached to Malta to complete with fuel....

14. During 11 October, destroyers were sent in to Malta to refuel as necessary. *Imperial* on her way in struck a mine ... She entered harbour in tow of *Decoy* at 1600. This incident caused delay and dislocation of the destroyer fuelling programme, which was later exacerbated by the late arrival of convoy MF3.... it was evident that there was an enemy minefield in this area. This was reported to the Admiralty ... stressing the importance of the necessity for more minesweepers at Malta.

16. *Ramillies*'s departure from Malta was delayed by the hang up in the fuelling programme. In the low visibility prevailing *Sydney* was sent to the end of the searched channel to meet *Ramillies* and tell her the fleet's position and night intentions. This was unfortunate as it led in the end to *Sydney* being absent from the cruiser search when *Ajax*'s action took place later.

17. Convoy MF4 consisting of *Aphis, Plumleaf* and *Volo*, escorted by *Calcutta, Coventry, Wryneck* and *Waterhen*, sailed from Malta at 2230.[100]

18. The course of the fleet was worked round to the S and E ..., the 7CS being detached to carry out a diverging search ... It had been intended to carry out a bombing attack on Tripoli during the night but owing to the weather conditions and the dislocation of the destroyer fuelling programme this had to be cancelled.

19. At 0230/12 a report was received from *Ajax* that she was engaging three enemy destroyers ... and that she had sunk two. *Ajax*

---

[100]*Aphis*: 1916, 625t, 2×6in, 1×3in, 14k.

then reported two cruisers . . . at 0306, and that she had lost touch at 0333. . . .

20. At 0400 the C-in-C's position was . . . approximately 50 miles SW of *Ajax*. As it was thought that the enemy might be present in force, 7CS was ordered to close the C-in-C and the 3CS sent to their support. *Orion* reported that one ship was still burning .. at 0510, and at 0710 a flying boat from Malta reported one destroyer on fire being towed by another in the same position. . . .

21. On receipt of these reports a striking force of 4 aircraft was flown off and the course of the fleet was altered to 010 to close. At 0715, CS3 reported smoke on the horizon. He had, however, obviously been sighted by the towing destroyer who made off at high speed and successfully evaded the attack delivered by T/B aircraft and the long range fire of the 3CS.

22. In the mean time CS3 had been ordered to sink the crippled destroyer. Observing that the position was within 90 miles of the SE coast of Italy and in submarine waters the C-in-C did not consider it justifiable to stop or delay to pick up survivors, particularly in view of bomb damage received by *Havock* after picking up the *Bartolomeo Colleoni*'s survivors. Carley rafts were therefore thrown over from *York* and when abandoned the destroyer was sunk by gun and torpedo fire. A W/T signal on commercial wave was then broadcast in Italian giving the position of the survivors. . . . This destroyer was the *Artigliere,* the other two sunk by *Ajax* being the *Airone* and one other of the same class.[101]

Ajax casualties were 2 officers killed and one seriously wounded; 10 ratings killed and 20 minor casualties.

24. At 1150 a flying boat from Malta reported three *Fiume* class cruisers and three destroyers . . . steering to the south-eastward. This flying boat did not shadow and no further reports of this force were received. CS3 with *Liverpool, Orion, Sydney* and *York*, were therefore detached to return to convoy MF4 . . . , 55 miles to the southward of the enemy cruisers. VA, Malta, sent 830 Squadron to attack the enemy but they were not located.

25. In the mean time the fleet had been located by enemy aircraft and one Cant 501 was shot down by Fulmars at 1145. The fleet was attacked by a formation of 11 aircraft at 1232 and by 5 aircraft at 1345. During this time Fulmars intercepted 6 S79s and dispersed

---

[101]*Artigliere*: 1938, *c.*1,750t, 4×4.7in, 6×21in tt, 39k.
Airone, Ariel: 1938, *c.*800t, 3×3.9in, 4×17.7in tt, 34k.
All probably on mining operation.

them before bomb release, damaging one aircraft, and made another formation jettison their bombs 9 miles from the fleet, shooting down 2. The total destroyed for the day was – *Illustrious*'s Fulmars: 1 Cant 501, 2 S79s and one S79 possible. *Eagle*'s Gladiators one probable S79. This aircraft was last seen with one engine stopped and a damaged wing, flying low. The crew of an S79 were later rescued by a flying boat from Malta.

26. The fleet remained in close cover of the convoy during the afternoon . . . . The weather had deteriorated rapidly during the day . . . A search had been maintained in a sector 330–070° throughout the day. Reconnaissance from Malta in the afternoon revealed that the Italian battlefleet was in its bases.

27. . . . On the morning of the 13th, *Ajax, Coventry, Jervis* and *Janus* were detached to rendezvous with convoy AS4, which sailed from the Gulf of Athens at 0700. . . . As *Volo* was capable of 12 knots, *Wryneck* was ordered to proceed ahead with her. RA(A) in *Illustrious*, with *Gloucester, Liverpool, Nubian, Hero, Havock* and *Hereward*, were detached to proceed N of Crete to carry out a night attack on Leros.

28. . . . at 0840 RA(A)'s forces rejoined . . . RA(A) reported that a very successful attack on Porto Lago had been delivered. Complete surprise had been achieved. 15 aircraft took part and dropped 92 250lb bombs. Hangars at Lepida Cove were set on fire, workshops and probably a fuel tank hit at San Giorgio. Ineffective short range AA fire was experienced and all our aircraft returned. . . .

29. At 0900 *York* and *Defender*, who were short of fuel, were detached to Alexandria. The morning air search located convoys MF4 and AS4 together W of Gavdo Island . . .

30. The fleet had been sighted by aircraft during the forenoon and at 1435 a bombing attack was made by 5 aircraft. They were engaged by gunfire and dropped their bombs outside the screen. A second raid by 3 aircraft took place at 1442, 4 bombs falling between *Warspite* and *Illustrious*.

31. . . . The RA, 1BS, with the 2nd Div., *Nubian, Juno, Vampire, Vendetta* and *Waterhen*, was detached to proceed independently at 1830, and the 3rd and 7th Cruiser Squadrons were detached to spread astern of the fleet.

32. At 1845 (dusk), *Illustrious*, who was RDF guard, reported the approach of a small formation, and at 1857 *Illustrious* and *Valiant* fired a blind barrage and it appeared certain that at least one enemy T/B aircraft had been shot down. The fleet was turned away when the blind barrage commenced.

At 1911 a report was received from *Liverpool* that she had been struck by a torpedo . . . at 1855, and that she was heavily on fire and required assistance. . . .

33. The 3rd and 7th Cruiser Squadrons closed *Liverpool* and the C-in-C detached *Hereward* and *Decoy* to her assistance. *Ajax* was ordered to join the RA, 1BS and instruct him to proceed to Alexandria at best speed, fuel and sail the destroyers to *Liverpool*'s assistance. The RA Alexandria, sailed *St Issey* at midnight.[102]

35. CS3 reported at 0100/15 that *Liverpool* was in tow of *Orion* . . ., making good 9 knots. The fire was under control but the ship's side opened out from the stem to the chains.

36. . . . at this time [noon] *Orion*'s tow had parted after towing *Liverpool* 100 miles. *Liverpool*'s back was broken abreast 'A' turret, and the stem head level with the water, the fore part acting as a drogue and rudder. Fortunately the damaged structure broke off and sank at 1430 and, when the tow was repassed, she towed more easily. The C-in-C remained in close company until dusk. . . .

37. The C-in-C arrived at Alexandria at 0100/16. An air raid was taking place while the fleet was in the Great Pass, but no bombs were dropped near. Barrage fire as a precaution against T/B attack was put up by *Warspite, Valiant* and *Illustrious*.

38. The 3rd and 7th Cruiser Squadrons and destroyers escorting *Liverpool* arrived off the harbour early a.m. and *Liverpool* was brought into harbour at midday.

Convoy MF4 arrived at Alexandria a.m., and convoy AS4 at Port Said p.m. 16 October.

106. *Cunningham's observations on Action of HMS* Ajax *with Italian Destroyers, 12 October 1940*

(7 April 1941)

2. This well fought action resulted in the destruction of two enemy destroyers and the disablement of a third so that she became an easy prey for other units of the Fleet at daylight . . .

3. Great credit is due to Captain McCarthy and his ship's company in this satisfactory achievement so shortly after commissioning.[103] This engagement, the first night full calibre firing and night torpedo

---

[102]*St Issey*: 1918, 820t, 12k; s off Benghazi Dec. 1942.
[103]Capt E. D. B. McCarthy: Capt 1935; *Ajax* 1940; *King George V* & Capt of F, Home F, March 1942; *Anson* June 1943; RA Aug. 1944 & ACNS(H).

firing of the commission, was admirably conducted and produced very satisfactory results.

4. The damage to RDF at the very start of the action was unfortunate, because the moonlight conditions would have provided an ideal opportunity to exploit gun control by RDF against surface targets.

5. The need for a flashless propellant at night, particularly for cruisers and destroyers in a melée, is so important that, if we cannot produce a flashless charge with acceptable ballistic properties for use by day, a special 'night charge' should be produced.

6. The paucity of enemy reports from *Ajax* and the resulting obscurity of the general situation in the C-in-C's plot led to the cruisers being ordered to retire on the battlefleet, in the belief that the enemy's whole fleet might be in the vicinity, and thus the chance of inflicting further losses on the enemy may have been missed. The situation in *Ajax*, with Remote Control Office and plot out of action, was admittedly difficult; but this only serves to accentuate the need for sound emergency organisation.

107. *To Pound*

16 October 1940

A. We are just in from eight days at sea. Most successful until the last evening. The convoy of big ships got into Malta without seeing an aeroplane the whole trip and we brought a small one away and also one from the Aegean, all without loss. I fear we can't expect this good luck to be always with us.

Imperial being mined was very bad luck; on the 180 fathom westerly extension of the Hurd Bank. But we were really lucky as the convoy went right over it and *Coventry* cut a mine with her paravanes. We had a very quiet day off Malta. Heavy thunderstorms kept the aeroplanes quiet and we never saw one.

Ajax's night actions were most spirited affairs. Actually I don't think there were any enemy cruisers – only large destroyers. McCarthy doesn't know how many he really saw, but considering he had not done a night shoot this commission it must be considered as a very satisfactory working up practice. *Ajax* has six holes in her and very considerable damage to her bridge and RDF wiring caused chiefly by a fire in a store room.

Liverpool being torpedoed was a nasty blow just when everything was turning out well. Actually the torpedo damage was not too extensive and she could have got along nicely with a hole in her bows. But, according to those on board, a few minutes after being hit the petrol store exploded and that did all the damage. Personally I incline to the opinion that the foremost magazine went up, too, or part of it, as the roof of 'A' turret was blown right off, but we shall not know until we examine her. *Orion* towed her in stern first and we had an anxious day or rather moonlit night for fear that the Italians should come and try to finish her off and perhaps bag the *Orion* too.

These moonlight torpedo attacks are rather a menace – very difficult to meet. A ship with RDF provided she opens up her barrage fire before she sees anything is I think all right. That is what we did in the battle squadron and I think we brought down our attacker, but without RDF, they can't be seen until it is too late. That night we broadcast the presence of low flying aircraft some time before the attack, but the bearing isn't much good to a ship 20 miles away.

B.   I am so glad Tovey has been selected for the HF though I shall badly miss his sane and optimistic outlook out here. I am quite sure he will justify your selection of him.

Pridham-Wippell is doing very well and will be glad to get back to something a little faster than *Malaya*. Ion Tower I shall welcome.[104]

C.   I am giving serious thought to re-tubing *Malaya* at Suez so as to save the long trip to Durban and back. In any case I wish to retain *Ramillies* until she is completed. *Malaya* is an anxiety every time we go to sea so the sooner she is done the better.

D.   I had the Turkish delegation to lunch. They make no secret they are out to probe our strength and report on what they see....

108.   *From the First Lord, A. V. Alexander*

16 October 1940

The Prime Minister is also very pleased with operation just completed, but asks me to say that in view of feeling of public here suffering under intensive and ruthless attacks, it might be well to exclude from future communiques reference to gallantry of enemy or to compromising our fleet's position for benefit of enemy.[105]

---

[104]Capt I. B. B. Tower: Capt 1929; *Malaya* Sept. 1939; RA June 1940; IDC Sept. 1940; d 14 Oct. 1940.

[105]Rt Hon A. V. (later Earl, of Hillsborough) Alexander (1885–1965): local govt officer; NALGO; Capt, Artists' Rifles, WW1; lay preacher; prominent in co-op movt; Lab MP, Hillsborough, Sheffield 1922–31 & 1935–50; Parl Sec BoT 1924; 1st Lord 1929–31 & May 1940–Dec. 1946; M Defence 1946; Chllr Duchy of Lancaster & Visct 1950; Lab Ldr, H Lords 1955; Earl 1963.

Churchill offered Tovey command of Home Fleet.

109. *From Vice Admiral Tovey*

17 October 1940

... My next meeting with the PM was at dinner the next night (1st Lord, Harwood and self being the only ones there), it was a fascinating experience.... you know the PM much better than I do and you will understand how I loved him at first sight, but he made such astounding statements about naval warfare both at home and abroad I still don't know if he was wanting to find out if I was prepared to applaud everything he said or whether he really believes half of what he says.[106] ... The PM was quite charming and, I believe, really enjoyed every minute of it and all he said was that he didn't mind my being absolutely outspoken, in fact that he liked it but that one must keep one's mind open to honest conviction – a very fair remark.... He actually stated that he considered you were too pussy-footed in your dealings with Godfroy at the time of Oran. I remarked that I was afraid he could not be in full possession of the facts and presumably did not know that at any moment in the discussions you only had to make a two-letter signal and the French fleet was sunk. I asked him which he felt was preferable, to have valuable harbour space cluttered up with wrecks of French ships and to accept the appalling effect throughout the Near East of a battle in Alexandria or to leave the French ships afloat but demilitarised and still a potential resource and even a possible ally – he had the grace to admit there could be no argument.

The expression 'pussy foot' had got me rather on the raw and I found I had a great deal more to tell him of you and your doings ...

110. *War Diary, October 1940 (concl.)*

25 October

Aphis, working in collaboration with the RAF, who dropped flares, carried out a successful 40 minute bombardment of an enemy concentration 15 miles E of Sidi Barrani early on 25 October. Shells

---

[106]R Adm (later Adm) Sir Henry H. Harwood (1888–1950): ent RN 1903; t splist; GF 1914–18; S Am 1919–21; Cdr 1921; staff posts; IDC; FTO, MF; Capt 1928; *Exeter* 1936; Cdre S American Div 1936–39; RA & kthd immed after battle of R Plate Dec. 1939; ACNS(F) Dec. 1940 & VA; C-in-C Med 1942; undermined by unsubstantiated charges of lethargy by Montgomery; C-in-C Levant 1943; invalided home March 1943; FOIC Orkney & Shetland April 1944; Adm on Ret List Aug. 1945.

landed among the motor transport causing much damage and ignited what appeared to be a petrol dump. *Aphis* was engaged by field gun fire but sustained no hits or casualties.

Operation MAQ2

2. *Calcutta* sailed p.m. 24 October, and convoy AN5, escorted by *Havock* and *Hero,* sailed from Port Said p.m. 24th, all to rendezvous . . . , thence proceeding through the Kaso Strait and the Doro Channel.
3. RA, 1BS in *Malaya,* with *Eagle, Coventry, Vampire, Hyperion, Mohawk, Janus, Voyager* and *Wryneck,* sailed a.m. today to support the convoy from a position SE of Crete until p.m. 27 October. *Orion, Sydney, Jervis* and *Juno* sailed at 0600 today to pass through the Kaso Strait at 2300 tonight and Doro Channel at 1400 tomorrow.
4. It is intended that *Eagle*'s aircraft shall carry out an attack on Maltezana, at Stampalia, at dawn on 26 October.

Submarine policy

7. It is now intended to employ our submarines in the interruption of Italian traffic to Libya to the exclusion of other operations.

26 October

Submarines

2. *Rainbow* and *Triad* having been overdue since 19 and 20 October respectively, must now be presumed lost.
3. It is intended to base the 'T' class submarines, and the 'U' class on their arrival on the Station, on Malta.

27 October

Air reconnaissance – Central Mediterranean

7. The AOC, Mediterranean, informed the C-in-C that he was not certain whether the C-in-C's reconnaissance requirements were being met to the best advantage, and requested further information on the following points:

   (i) The object of the daily Ionian Sea reconnaissance. As organised at present it would not catch an enemy fleet leaving Taranto in the evening at 20 knots, nor would it catch 15-knot convoys leaving Sicilian ports overnight for Benghazi.

(ii) Whether recasting of this patrol could be accepted to enable more Westward patrols to be completed. This Western patrol has already sighted enemy shipping near the Tunisian coast.

8. The C-in-C has replied as follows:

The objects of the daily Ionian Sea reconnaissance are:

(a) To discover the nature and extent of enemy movements in this area.
(b) To provide security from surprise for units operating in the Aegean or along the Libyan coast.
(c) To gain early information of enemy movements towards the Dodecanese or Crete.
(d) To watch for traffic from the Straits of Taranto to North Africa.

While it is recognised that this reconnaissance is not watertight it appears to offer a good chance of sighting enemy fleet which leaves Taranto at times other than between 1400 and 1800, and any 12-knot convoys from the Straits of Messina. It is therefore desired to continue this reconnaissance.

It is recognised that any long patrols without sighting may be disheartening and appear to achieve nothing, but these patrols are of great value to me and it must be remembered that negative reports are informative in themselves.

28 October

Italian Ultimatum to Greece

Information was received from the British Minister at Athens that an Italian ultimatum was delivered at 0300 this morning demanding Greek consent to the occupation of certain strategic points by 0600 this morning. The President of the Council has refused and has told the Italian Minister that he considers this as a declaration of war.[107] He asks for immediate help by sea to defend Corfu and for air assistance to defend Athens, also financial assistance.

2. Consequent on the receipt of this information, the following action was taken:

CS3 in *Gloucester*, with *York* and *Decoy*, who had sailed early a.m. for an operation (CHURCH), were recalled to Alexandria. *Ilex* was recalled from convoy escort duty to Alexandria. *Fiona* and *Defender* were sailed from Port Said to Alexandria.[108]

---
[107]General Ioannis Metaxas (1871–1941): dictator of Greece.
[108]*Fiona*: 1933, 2,198 gt, Colonial Sugar Refining Co, Australia.

RA, Alexandria, was ordered to carry out Operation BN (the establishment of a fuelling base at Suda Bay).

The AOC, Mediterranean, was requested to institute the maximum scale of air reconnaissance in the Ionian Sea N of 37°N and including examination of Taranto, Corfu, Argostoli and the Western Greek ports. Air reconnaissance off Crete was instituted by 201 Group.

The Fleet was brought to 2½ hours' notice for steam.

Operation MAQ2

3. RA, 1BS, . . . reported that *Eagle*'s aircraft had carried out a successful attack at Maltezana at dawn on 27 October. Hangars were hit and set on fire; one hit was obtained on the seaplane slipway; about 20 250-lb bombs were dropped on barracks and ammunition dump area, one explosion occurring in the approximate position of the dump. . . . Eight aircraft took part and all returned. There was no enemy air activity.

4. The convoy AN5 arrived safely at their destination without having been bombed. Five Greek ships were intercepted and examined by the escorting forces.

29 October

The C-in-C in *Warspite*; RA(A) in *Illustrious*; *Valiant*, RA1 in *Malaya, Eagle, Ramillies;* CS3 in *Gloucester, York;* VALF in *Orion, Sydney,* 2DF, 14DF and 20th Destroyer Division, sailed from Alexandria and were clear of the harbour by 0130. It is the C-in-C's intention to be off the W coast of Crete at dawn on 31st, ready for eventualities and to cover the passage of ships to Suda Bay.

Establishment of advanced fuelling base at Suda Bay

5. A convoy consisting of the RFAs *Olna, Brambleleaf,* and HM Ships *Fiona* and *Chakla*, escorted by *Coventry, Calcutta, Protector,* 19th Destroyer Division, *Wryneck* and *Fareham*, left Alexandria at 1400 today. A reconnaissance party consisting of all three Services was previously flown to Suda Bay by flying boat.[109]

---

[109]*Olna*: oiler; 1921, 15,000t, 11k; s a/c Suda Bay May 1941.
Brambleleaf: oiler; 1917, 12,370t, 14k; t E Med, tot loss, June 1942.
Chakla: 1914, 3,081gt, 14k, Br India SN; armed bdg ves, 2×4in; s a/c Tobruk 29 Apr 1941.
Protector: net layer; 1936, 2,900t, 1×4in, 20k.
Fareham: M/S; 1918, 800t, 1×4in, 1×3in, 16k.

111. *To Naval Attaché, Athens*

31 October 1940

I cannot use Suda to berth big ships until adequate A/T baffles are available against torpedo aircraft so I am obliged to return to Alexandria. Consequently I cannot guarantee to intercept a seaborne attack on Western Greece after 1 November for a few days after which fleet will again be in Central Mediterranean. Meanwhile S/M are operating in the vicinity.

112. *War Diary, November 1940*

1 November

Suda Bay

8. The following work has been completed by this evening:
Military personnel disembarked from *Ajax*. One net laid by *Protector* and damage caused by *Defender* made good. (*Defender*'s propellors freed by divers). *Chakla* and *Fiona* alongside and discharging stores. Battery site and dump established near Suda Point.
10. There was a heavy air raid at 1400. 25 aircraft approached along the Crete coast and dropped bombs on the mainland and harbour entrance. Further bombers made a determined attack on the pier, bombs falling close to *Ajax* who was alongside. Canea was attacked by bombers and fighters. . . . At least two aircraft were shot down by *Calcutta* and *Coventry*, and others probably damaged.

3 November

Suda Bay – Boom defence requirements

2. A/S net at entrance. A/T baffle at Western end of anchorage for protection against torpedoes dropped in the harbour.

A line of B1 nets has been laid by *Protector* and it is intended to use a table cloth net, provided for the Canal Area, and to lay the four A/T baffles being supplied . . .

RAF attacks on Italian ports

5. VA, Malta, and the AOC, Mediterranean, have asked the C-in-C for a priority of targets from naval point of view. They have been requested at present to concentrate on Naples, Brindisi and Bari, omitting Sicilian ports for the present owing to the increased possi-

bility of Italian retaliatory action against Malta. Taranto should not be included at present until bombing attacks can be combined with FAA torpedo bomber attack, which is being planned for an early date.

4 November

Operation MB8

Convoy AN6, escorted by *Kingston Chrystal* and *Kingston Cyanite*, and consisting of *Adinda, British Sergeant* and other ships with coal and essential stores for Greece, and *Pass of Balmaha* with aviation spirit for Suda Bay, sailed today.[110] . . .

Ajax and *Sydney* left Alexandria to embark troops at Port Said for Crete.

5 November

Convoy MW3, escorted by *Coventry, Calcutta, Vampire, Voyager, Waterhen, Diamond, Abingdon,* and consisting of *Waiwera, Devis, Plumleaf, Volo, Rodi,* for Malta, and *Brisbane Star, Brambleleaf* and HM Ships *Chakla, Fiona* and *Protector* for Suda Bay, sailed today.[111]

6 November

VALF, in *Orion,* left Alexandria for Piraeus to consult with the Greek authorities. Certain RAF personnel were embarked for passage.

113. *Report on Operation MB8, 6–14 November 1940*

(3 March 1941)

Cunningham's Observations

2. The operation was originally initiated on the instructions of the Admiralty for the passage of *Barham, Berwick* and *Glasgow* to reinforce the Mediterranean Fleet (operation COAT). The period of

---

[110]*Kingston Chrystal, Kingston Cyanite*: A/S trawlers, 1936, 433t.
Adinda: 1939, 3,359gt, Nederlandsch Indisch Tank Stoom.
British Sergeant: 1922, 5,868gt, 10k, Br Tkr Co.
Pass of Balmaha: 820gt, Bulk Oil SS Co; s W of Alexandria, Oct. 1941, Ger U-boat.
[111]*Waiwera*: 1934, 12,435gt, 17k, Shaw Savill & Albion.
Devis: 1938, 6,054gt, 15k, Lamport & Holt Line.
Brisbane Star: 1937, 11,076gt, Union Cold Storage/Blue Star Line.

the moon was also favourable for the execution of the oft-postponed Operation JUDGMENT (the attack on Taranto).[112]

3. Coming as it did after the entry of Greece into the war there were also outstanding commitments in the way of passing supplies to Greece and the establishment of naval and military base forces and equipment at Suda Bay. These were in addition to the passage of convoys to and from Malta, which have always to be made when operations in the Central Mediterranean provide suitable cover.

4. In addition it was necessary to get *Terror* away from Malta, to provide temporary defence at Suda Bay while the coast defence guns were installed, and with a view to her ultimate employment on the flank of the army in Libya.

5. Finally it was decided to carry out a raid into the Straits of Otranto while the opportunity offered, with the object of enheartening the Greeks and of dealing an additional blow to the enemy in his own waters.

6. It can therefore be seen that the operation became one of considerable complexity, covering a large area with a wide succession of subsidiary movements. Apart from the excellent results obtained in offensive action, perhaps the most surprising feature of the operation was the almost clockwork regularity with which convoys ran, ships unloaded guns and material, and with which the rendezvous of widely dispersed units were reached at the appointed time.

7. These results were only rendered possible by the good co-operation of the Naval, Army and Air Force authorities concerned at Suda Bay in the establishment of the base, whereby ships were released punctually to their duties; and not least by the good performance of merchant ships in convoys whose punctual arrivals contributed much to the success of the operation,

The work of Malta in the rapid unloading of stores and troops and in the refuelling of destroyers was excellent.

9. The raid into the Straits of Otranto by the 7CS, *Nubian* and *Mohawk*, under the VALF, ... was a boldly executed operation into narrow waters where the enemy might well have been expected to be encountered in force. It succeeded in doing considerable damage to the enemy and undoubtedly had considerable moral effect.

10. The entry of HM Ships *Barham, Berwick* and *Glasgow* into the Grand Harbour with troops fallen in and bands playing, was reported by the VA, Malta, to have had a most excellent effect on the Maltese.

---

[112]*Berwick*: 1928, 10,900t, 8×8in, 8×4in, 31.5k.

Narrative

... The C-in-C, in *Warspite*, left Alexandria at noon 6 November with the 1st Division of *Illustrious* and *Valiant* and the 2nd Division of *Malaya* and *Ramillies*, under RA, 1BS, in company. The 1st Division was screened by the 2DF, *Decoy* and *Defender*, and the 2nd Division by the 14DF. The 3CS was also in company ... Course was set for a mean line of advance of 310° at 18 knots with the 2nd Division stationed ahead.

2. *Eagle* was unable to accompany the Fleet on account of defective petrol tanks.

3. ... [At] daylight 7 November *Gloucester* and *York* were detached to join RA, 1BS 6 miles ahead of the C-in-C.

4. Fighter and TSR patrols were maintained throughout the day ... *Sydney* joined the C-in-C at 1700 and reported that all ships for Suda Bay had arrived and been unloaded by dark on 6 November.

5. ... At 0900/8 course was altered to the Southward to close the convoy MW3 which was sighted at noon 10 miles to the South-westward. ... At this time the convoy was reported by an enemy reconnaissance machine which was attacked by Gladiators but escaped.

6. Air searches were made to the westward during the day but no enemy were sighted. At 1400 an aircraft was dispatched to Malta with signals for transmission.

7. The Fleet was reported by enemy reconnaissance at 1520 and at 1610 a formation of 7 S79s was detected approaching the Fleet and attacked by the fighter patrol of 3 Fulmars. Two of the enemy planes were shot down and the remainder made off after jettisoning their bombs.

8. At 1700 *Ajax* joined the Fleet from Suda Bay and the C-in-C remained in a covering position N of the convoy throughout the rest of the day and the night.

9. At 0920/9, *Ramillies, Ilex, Hyperion* and *Havock* were detached to escort the convoy into Malta. The Fleet remained to the South-eastward of the Medina Bank throughout the day, the 3rd and 7th Cruiser Squadrons being detached to sweep to the Northward. The weather was overcast and squally and no air search was flown off. ...

10. The Fleet was shadowed by enemy aircraft during the day but was not attacked. One Cant 506B was shot down by a Fulmar at 1640. At 2100 course was set for the rendezvous with Force F.

11. At 0010/10 ... two heavy explosions were felt which may have been from torpedoes. The Italian broadcast subsequently claimed that a submarine had sunk a battleship at about this time.

THE ANGLO-ITALIAN WAR, 1940   177

13. The 3rd and 7th Cruiser Squadrons rejoined the C-in-C at 0715 and shortly afterwards the escort force of 6 destroyers rejoined from Malta. Remaining destroyers were detached as convenient during the course of the day as requisite to fulfil the fuelling programme.

14. At 1015, two hours later than expected, the rendezvous was made with Force F, which consisted of *Barham, Berwick, Glasgow, Faulknor* and 5 destroyers. *Fortune* and *Fury* joined the screen and the remaining ships were ordered to Malta to disembark troops and stores.[113]

15. ... at 1330 the battlefleet was attacked by 8 aircraft, bombs being dropped at random. One Cant 501 was shot down by Fulmars and one S79 damaged.

16. Convoy ME3 from Malta, escorted by *Ramillies, Coventry, Decoy* and *Defender*, was sighted to the Eastward at 1500... *Mohawk* rejoined at 1535 and *Hero* was despatched to Malta with correspondence. At 1915 *Terror* and *Vendetta* from Malta were sighted on passage to Suda Bay, ... At this time the 3rd and 7th Cruiser Squadrons were detached to search to the North-eastward and rejoin at daylight 11 November.

17. ... [At noon/11] VALF in *Orion* joined the C-in-C from Piraeus. ...

18. At 1800, RAA in *Illustrious* was detached with 3CS, Captain D2 and 3 destroyers for Operation JUDGMENT, the attack on Taranto. The C-in-C remained in a covering position for these operations during the night.

20. At 0700/12, RAA and VALF were sighted rejoining with their respective forces. RAA reported that the atack on Taranto had been a success and strongly urged the attack to be repeated before the AA defences could be made still heavier. Torpedo hits were obtained on one *Littorio* and two *Cavour* class battleships, besides other damage from bombs. Two Swordfish were lost.

21. VALF reported sighting a convoy of 4 merchant ships off Valona. The two destroyer escorts made off at high speed and escaped, though one was hit. One merchant ship was sunk, 2 set on fire and the fourth escaped into Valona damaged.

22. ... the C-in-C ... remained in this area during the day in order to repeat Operation JUDGMENT. The Fleet was not reported by air reconnaissance, three Cants being shot down by Fulmars before making their reports.

---

[113]*Faulknor*: Ldr; 1935, 1,475t, 5×4.7in, 8×21in tt, 36k.
    Fury (mine, Normandy, June 1944, tot loss), *Fortune* (RCN *Saskatchewan*, 1943): 1935, 1,405t, 4×4.7in, 8×21in tt, 35.5k.

23. Unfortunately the weather deteriorated in the Gulf of Taranto and the C-in-C, after consulting RA(A) by signal, decided to cancel the repetition of Operation JUDGMENT. Accordingly at 1800 a course of 140° was set for Alexandria. At 1830, RA, 1BS, with the 2nd Division, *Ajax* and 5 destroyers, were detached to Suda Bay to refuel, and *York* and *Berwick* were detached to Alexandria.

24. *Ramillies* and Convoy ME3 reached Alexandria a.m. 13 November.

25. ... During the afternoon shadowing aircraft located the Fleet and course was therefore altered to 050° at 1600 and to 090° at 1800. One Cant was reported to have been shot down while shadowing. An enemy aircraft formation was detected by RDF but the Fleet was not again located and continued to Alexandria without incident, arriving there at 0700 on 14 November.

114. *Fleet Air Arm Operations against Taranto on 11 November 1940*

(16 January 1941)

Cunningham's observations

2. An attack on the Italian fleet at Taranto by the FAA with torpedoes had been under consideration for many months and long before the outbreak of war with Italy. The bridge between planning and execution was, however, a wide one, since several requirements had to be met before the operation could be undertaken with a reasonable prospect of success.

3. The most important of these requirements was good and timely photographic reconnaissance, since to plan the attack it was necessary to know not only that the battleships were in harbour but also their position and berthing with some accuracy. It was not until the Glenn Martins arrived at Malta that such reconnaissance was possible, war experience having shown that flying boats are too vulnerable and slow to approach defended ports with impunity.

4. In the event the success of the FAA attack was due in no small degree to the excellent reconnaissances carried out by the RAF Glenn Martin Flight (No.431) from Malta, under very difficult conditions and often in the face of fighter opposition.

5. An undetected approach to the selected flying off position was also most important, and to achieve this the use of long range tanks in the Swordfish aircraft was very desirable. They were not available until *Illustrious* arrived on the station early in September.

6. A considerable amount of night flying training was also necessary before the pilots and observers could be regarded as fully competent to undertake the long flight required for this hazardous enterprise and it was not until mid-October that the necessary state of training was reached.

7. The attack was first planned to take place on the night of 21 October, but owing to a fire in *Illustrious*'s hangar a few days before, which destroyed and damaged a number of aircraft, the operation had to be deferred. It was considered again for the night of 30/31 October, when the fleet was operating off the West coast of Greece, but it was decided not to attempt it as there was then no moon and the attack would have had to be carried out with flares, in the use of which the aircraft crews had had little practice.

8. In the mean time further photographs had been taken of the outer anchorage at Taranto by the Glenn Martins, and close examination revealed the presence of balloons and of nets surrounding the battleships. This discovery was most fortunate as these defences naturally affected the attack very considerably.

9. It had always been intended that both *Illustrious* and *Eagle* should take part in this attack. Two days before the fleet sailed for the operation *Eagle* developed serious defects to her petrol system, caused undoubtedly by the many near bomb misses she had experienced in the early days of the Italian war, and she therefore had to be left behind. Six of her TSR aircraft and crews, however, were embarked in *Illustrious*, so that the *Eagle*, whose squadrons had reached a high standard of efficiency, was to some extent represented in the attack.

10. ... It was admirably planned and the determined and gallant manner in which it was carried out reflects the highest credit on all concerned.

11. The results achieved, as disclosed by subsequent photographic reconnaissance, appear to have been:

One *Cavour* class battleship beached and apparently abandoned.
One *Cavour* class battleship heavily damaged and beached.
One *Littorio* class battleship damaged and subsequently docked in the Taranto graving dock.

There is no definite evidence of damage to cruisers and small craft as a result of the bombing attacks but it seems probable that two cruisers may have been hit.

12. This was the first occasion on which Duplex pistols were used in the Mediterranean. It is considered that the results achieved have proved the value of this weapon and that the many years of

research and experiment devoted to its development have been well repaid.

13. There can be little doubt that the crippling of half the Italian battlefleet is having, and will continue to have, a marked effect on the course of the war. Without indulging in speculation as to political repercussions, it is already evident that this successful attack has greatly increased our freedom of movement in the Mediterranean and has thus strengthened our control over the central area of this sea. It has enabled two battleships to be released for operations elsewhere, while the effect on the morale of the Italians must be considerable. As an example of 'economy of force' it is probably unsurpassed.

Captain Denis Boyd's report

13 November 1940

2. The proposed plan was as follows:

(i) *Illustrious* and escort to be in position 270° Kabbo Point (Cephalonia) 40 miles at 2000 on 11 November and fly off the first range of 12 aircraft at that time. The second range of 12 aircraft to be flown off in about the same position at 2100.

(ii) The first attack to be made at about 2245 and the second at about 2345 and aircraft to be landed on in position 270° Kabbo Point 20 miles.

(iii) Both attacks to be carried out in the following form:

The squadron of 12 aircraft to pass up the centre of the Gulf of Taranto and approach the harbour from the SW. The primary attack to be by six torpedo aircraft against the battleships in the Mar Grande. This attack to be preceded by two aircraft dropping flares (and bombs) along the eastern side of the Mar Grande in order to illuminate the targets and distract attention from the torpedo aircraft, and by four aircraft making a dive bomb attack on the attractive target presented by the line of cruisers and destroyers in the Mar Piccolo. It was expected that this attack would also distract attention from the torpedo attack.

Narrative: Preliminary Movements

3. *Illustrious* had left Alexandria on 6 November with the Mediterranean Fleet in order to carry out operation COAT.

4. Before sailing from Alexandria, in order to provide the maximum number of aircraft that could be flown off in two ranges with no surface wind, and as *Eagle*, to their great disappointment, was unable to take part in the operation due to defective petrol tanks, eight pilots and eight observers were embarked in *Illustrious* from *Eagle*, all being experienced in night flying. Five of *Eagle's* Swordfish were also embarked.

5. All Swordfish aircraft embarked were fitted with 60-gallon internal auxiliary petrol tanks.

7. While at Malta the opportunity was taken to discuss with AOC, Mediterranean, the reconnaissance and meteorological forecasts required, and on the morning of 11 November one aircraft was flown to Malta to collect some extremely good photographs of Taranto taken by the RAF on the previous day. Further reports were received from the AOC, Mediterranean and RAF reconnaissance aircraft during the day confirming that no important movements had taken place, and an RAF aircraft carried out a patrol of Taranto until 2230 to ensure that the Italian Fleet did not leave harbour unobserved.

Flying Off Aircraft

8. At 1800 on the 11th ... *Illustrious* and escort comprising 3CS, *Gloucester* (CS3), *Berwick*, *Glasgow*, *York*, *Hyperion* (D2), *Ilex*, *Hasty* and *Havock* were detached by C-in-C and steered as requisite for the flying off position.

9. At 2035 the first range commenced to fly off, course 060° speed 28 knots and all 12 aircraft of the first striking force were off by 2040. The surface wind at this time was light and variable, the upper winds westerly and about 10 knots and 8/10 thin cloud at 8,000 feet. The moon was three-quarters full.

10. The second range of 9 aircraft commenced flying off at 2128 and 8 aircraft were off by 2134. The ninth aircraft (Clifford/Going) was accidentally damaged and had to be struck down to the hangars for repairs to the fabric. It was at first considered that this aircraft could not be flown off in time for the attack but in view of the confidence of the crew that they could catch up and their keenness to take part in the attack, it was flown off at 2158.

Narrative of first attack

11. The first striking force having taken off formed up ... and at 2057 set course for Taranto then distant 170 miles.

12. At 2115 when at a height of 4,500 feet the squadron entered the base of a cumulus cloud and some aircraft became separated

with the result that the whole squadron did not arrive at Taranto simultaneously.

13. The squadron commander continued with 8 aircraft (5 torpedo, 2 flare droppers and one bomber). They sighted flashes of HE at 2252. At 2256 the flare droppers were detached to lay their flares along the eastern side of the harbour. The other four aircraft having lost their leader, all made their attacks independently.

Individual narratives

1. *Williamson/Scarlett*
Task: Torpedo attack on the battle fleet.
Did not return. Last seen by Sparke at 4,000 feet over San Pietro Island.
2. *Sparke/Neale*
Task: Torpedo attack on battleship.
Came in at 4,000 feet over San Pietro Island with Williamson (4A) ... The original intention had been to strike at the more

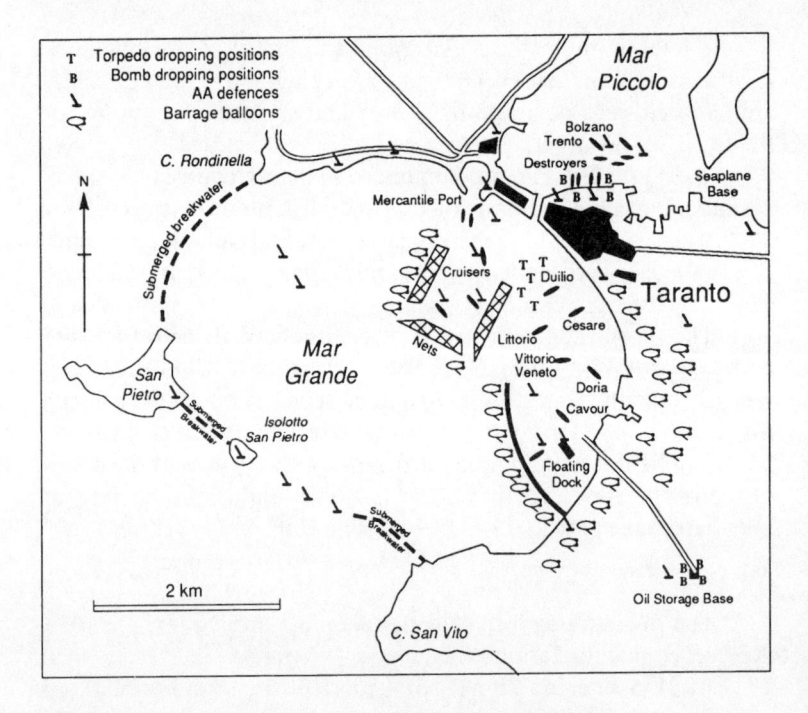

The Fleet Air Arm Attack on Taranto, 11 November 1940

southerly *Littorio* (B in Plan) but the pilot was unable to identify it. He saw, however, the most easterly *Cavour* (E in Plan) directly ahead and he dropped his torpedo at a range of approximately 700 yards. An explosion, probably that of the torpedo, was observed at the ship about a minute later. 'Get away' was made by a sharp 180° turn to port over the Taranto shoal breakwater. Intense AA fire was experienced from the batteries at the entrance to the harbour along the approach and the 'get away'. The aircraft landed on at 0120.

3. *Macdonald/Wray*

Task: Torpedo attack on battleship.

This aircraft was part of the Sub-Flight led by Williamson and its narrative follows closely that of Sparke/Neale, the most easterly *Cavour* (E in Plan) being the target in this case also. The torpedo was dropped at approximately 600 yards range. While making a 'get away' balloons were seen by the observer in a line outside the Taranto shoal breakwater at 1,000 feet. AA fire was experienced from the batteries on the eastern side of the harbour and from the southern batteries during the 'get away'. The aircraft returned without incident and landed on at 0125.

4. *Kemp/Bailey*

Task: Torpedo attack on the battleships.

... AA fire was met from Rondinella point on the mainland and from Lo Scanno on San Pietro Island. Fire was continued from batteries along the shore as the aircraft dived down to a position midway between Taranto Island and the most northerly cruiser, where the pilot flattened out on a line for the more northerly battleship of the *Littorio* class (A in Plan). Prior to reaching the water level intense AA fire was met from the cruisers and from small merchant vessels lying inshore off Taranto Island. Projectiles from the cruisers were observed to hit the merchant vessels and the fire only ceased when the aircraft passed between the merchant ships. The torpedo was dropped at 2318 in a position estimated at 1,000 yards from the *Littorio* and the pilot was satisfied that the aim was accurate. The observer saw the torpedo running correctly. Immediately after the drop fire was reopened from the cruisers. ... A fire was observed in the direction of the seaplane hangars. The aircraft then returned to the ship without incident.

5. *Swayne/Buscall*

Task: Torpedo attack on battleships.

Having got detached from the leader this aircraft waited off the harbour for 15 minutes for the arrival of the other aircraft. The first flare was seen and the pilot came in at 1,000 feet over the westerly breakwater, encountering severe AA fire from the ships and batteries at the entrance.... he made a sharp turn to port so as to approach the more northerly *Littorio* (A in Plan) from the east. The torpedo was dropped at about 2215 at a range of approximately 400 yards and the aircraft continued passing directly over the *Littorio*. A column of smoke was observed to arise from directly abaft the funnels of the *Littorio*. The 'get away' was made past the cruisers who fired at the aircraft and over San Pietro Island when severe AA fire was encountered. Three balloons round the harbour were observed to catch fire, probably as a result of the enemy's own AA fire. *Illustrious* was sighted at 0140 and the aircraft landed on 10 minutes later.

6. *Maund/Bull*

Task: Torpedo attack on battleships.

Came in over land N of Rondinella Point encountering AA fire from the end of the point, followed by fire from the cruisers and from the entrance to the canal... When the aircraft reached the water the fire was passing overhead and the pilot was able to flatten out and make an accurate drop at the more southerly *Littorio* (B in Plan) at a range of approximately 1,300 yards.... The aircraft then returned to the ship without incident.

7. *Kiggell/Janvrin*

Task: To drop flares along the eastern shore and SAP bombs on any convenient target.

... Over Cape San Vito and the promontory HE AA fire was encountered. Commencing at 2302 a line of 8 flares was dropped at half-mile intervals set to burn at 4,500 feet. After the flares had been dropped and appeared to be providing satisfactory illumination, the pilot... then made a dive bombing attack on the most southerly oil storage depot from which a pipeline leads to the new jetty. No results were observed.... the aircraft landed on at 0120.

8. *Lamb/Grieve*

Task: Stand by flare dropper.

... as the first flares appeared satisfactory no flares were dropped.... the same oil storage depot was the target for a dive bombing attack but no results were observed.

9. *Patch/Goodwin*

Task: Dive bombing attack on the line of cruisers and destroyers moored stem on against the quay side on the south of the Mar Piccolo.

... a dive bombing attack was made from 1,500 feet obliquely across two cruisers from NW to SE at 2315. Pom-pom fire from a number of points along the quay side, and from the cruisers in the Mar Piccolo was encountered.... Further AA fire was met from a point near the village of San Giorgio but this was avoided by diving behind the neighbouring range of hills. *Illustrious* was sighted at 0135 and landed on at 0155.

10. *Sarra/Bowker*

Task: Dive bombing attack on cruisers and destroyers in the Mar Piccolo.

... the pilot was unable to identify the target. He accordingly continued along the southern shore of the Mar Piccolo and delivered an attack on the seaplane base from a height of 500 feet. A direct hit on one hangar and further hits on the slipways were observed and a large explosion occurred in the hangar. Much pom-pom and machine gun fire was met, it being particularly intense just after the attack. The aircraft... returned to the ship without incident.

11. *Forde/Mardel-Ferreira*

Task: Dive bombing attack on cruisers and destroyers in the Mar Piccolo.

This aircraft was separated from the leader and arrived as the first flare was dropped and came in E of Cape San Vito, a large fire being observed on the oil storage depot... The pilot... delivered his attack on the target from NE to SW releasing at 1,500 feet. The first bomb hit the water short of two cruisers but the remainder should have hit the cruiser although no immediate results were observed. Intense AA fire from the cruisers moored in the Mar Piccolo was met throughout the dive....

12. *Murray/Paine*

Task: Dive bombing attack on cruisers and destroyers in the Mar Piccolo.

This aircraft arrived when the attack was in progress... The attack was delivered from 3,000 feet, the bombs dropping in a line running from E to W commencing by the most eastern jetty and extending across four of the destroyers to the most westerly cruiser in the line....

Section II

Narrative of second attack

15. The second striking force formed up... at a distance of 175 miles from Taranto and took departure at 2145...

16. Morford/Green were in an aircraft which was fitted with an external overload petrol tank. At 2205 the tank fell off ... the pilot was therefore forced to return to the carrier.

Individual narratives (second force)

1. *Hale/Carline*
Task: Torpedo attack.
Considerable fire was experienced from San Pietro Island during the last stages of the approach ... The pilot then steered directly for the more northerly battleship of the *Littorio* class (A in Plan), the torpedo being dropped at a range of 700 yards. ... AA fire was met intermittently throughout the attack – particularly from destroyers on leaving. *Illustrious* was sighted at 0155 and aircraft landed on at 0200.

2. *Bayly/Slaughter*
Task: Torpedo attack.
This aircraft is missing. It was last seen following the Sqdn Cdr over Rondinella Point.

3. *Lea/Jones*
Task: Torpedo attack.
... The torpedo was dropped at the most northerly *Cavour* (C in Plan) at a range of approximately 800 yards. ... Severe AA fire was received from batteries on each side of the southern end of the Canal, and from cruisers and destroyers in the Mar Grande. When leaving a fire and petrol smoke were observed near the power station on the mainland behind Rondinella Point. Aircraft landed on at 0230.

4. *Torrens-Spence/Sutton*
Task: Torpedo attack.
... AA fire was experienced from positions on Taranto Island [and] from the cruisers and the largest battleship.... The torpedo was dropped at the more northerly *Littorio* (A in Plan) at a range of approximately 700 yards. Pom-pom and machine gun fire was met from San Paolo, San Pietro and from small gate vessels in the gap on the way out. The aircraft landed on at 0215.

5. *Wellham/Humphreys*
Task: Torpedo attack.
... Encountering a balloon which was avoided, the pilot then dived down to attack, during which period the aircraft received hits from machine gun bullets, one of which hit the outer aileron rod, putting the aircraft temporarily out of control. Control was

however regained and the torpedo was dropped at a range estimated at 500 yards on the port quarter of one of the *Littorios* (B in Plan). . . .

Intense AA fire was directed towards the aircraft during the 'get away' and a hit was received on the port wing, probably from a 40mm explosive projectile.

Aircraft landed on at about 0205.

6. *Hamilton/Weekes*

Task: Dropping flares.

Came in over Cape San Vito at 7,500 feet, and dived to 5,000 feet, dropping a line of flares at intervals of 15 seconds to the eastward of the harbour. Pom-pom fire was experienced when coming over Cape San Vito and HE while releasing the flares.

After dropping all flares successfully, this aircraft delivered a dive bombing attack from a height of 2,500 [feet] on the oil storage depot. A small fire was caused. The aircraft made a 'get away' well to the eastward and landed on at 0230.

7. *Skelton/Perkins*

Task: Dropping flares.

. . . the flares were dropped SE of the harbour. Eight flares were dropped at between 6,500 and 5,000 feet, set to burn 3,000 feet lower. Bombs were dropped near the oil storage depot, but it is not considered that hits had been secured. AA fire similar to that of Hamilton/Weekes was experienced, some of the bursts during the dive bomb attack being particularly close.

The aircraft landed on at 0200.

8. *Clifford/Going*

Task: Bombing cruisers and destroyers in Mar Piccolo.

This aircraft started half an hour late. . . . and arrived off Taranto when the second attack was already in progress. The aircraft . . . steered straight over the dockyard to the far side of the Mar Piccolo.

Turning to port a dive bombing attack was made from 2,500 feet along the line of cruisers and destroyers from W to E. A stick of 250 -lb bombs was dropped across the cruisers. . . .

A large fire in one of the battleships was seen to be raging for over 5 minutes.

AA fire was experienced the whole time the aircraft was over the land, the pom-pom fire being particularly intense during the bombing attack.

Aircraft landed on at 0250.

19. All aircraft, except the two missing, were landed on by 0250, and the Force rejoined the C-in-C at 0730.

20. It is noteworthy that the enemy did not use the searchlights at all during either of the attacks.

Results of the attacks

21. The only information so far available of the results of the attacks are in VA Malta's 2031/12 and 2345/12, as follows:

[2031/12] Have examined Taranto photographs carefully and until enlarged I do not wish unduly to raise your hopes but definitely appears that:

(a) One *Littorio* class is down by the bows with forecastle awash and a heavy list to starboard. Numerous auxiliaries alongside.
(b) One *Cavour* class beached opposite entrance to graving dock under construction. Stern including 'Y' turret is under water. Ship is heavily listed to starboard.
(c) Inner harbour: 2 cruisers are listed to starboard and are surrounded by oil fuel.
(d) Two auxiliaries off commercial basin appear to have sterns under water. . . .

[2345/12] My 2031/12. The stem only of northern *Cavour* class battleship shows on photograph but by fix from entrance of Passagio Piccolo which also just shows the bows is in about 4 fathoms. There is oil round the stern and it seems certain the ship has been beached. The remaining one *Littorio* and two *Cavour* class battleships appear undamaged.

RAF co-operation

22. The excellent photographic reconnaissance promoted by the RAF was a most important factor in the success of this operation. The accurate meteorological forecast from Malta was also most useful.

Repetition

23. It was proposed to repeat the operation on the following night and a Striking Force of 15 aircraft comprising 6 torpedo aircraft, 7 dive bombers and 2 flare droppers was prepared, but the operation was cancelled owing to the unfavourable weather report.

General remarks

Duplex Pistol

24. There was considerable debate as to the wisdom of using Duplex pistols in such constricted waters. It was decided to run off 100 yards of the safety range and the battery resistance was removed

to ensure that the torpedoes would remain dangerous on completion of their run.

The decision to use them was indeed fortunate as the results could not have been obtained by any other weapon.

To those whose faith in this weapon has remained unshaken the greatest honour is due and their faith has been amply justified by 3 battleships having been either sunk or crippled by 9 – or possibly 11 × 18-in torpedoes.

Spirit in which the attack was carried out

25. This attack was carried out under somewhat difficult conditions. Owing to the heavy Fleet programme no rehearsals had been possible. Aircraft from *Eagle* were embarked the day before leaving harbour and had had no previous experience of landing on *Illustrious's* deck or of our controlled landing and the use of the barrier. A third obstacle was presented by the discovery that our petrol was contaminated, three Swordfish being lost on the preceding days from this cause. In spite of this the zeal and enthusiasm of everyone to carry out this great enterprise was unabated and it is impossible to praise too highly those who in these comparatively slow machines made studied and accurate attacks in the midst of intense AA fire.

The Fleet Air Arm

26. Although the proper function of the FAA may perhaps be the operation of aircraft against an enemy in the open sea it has been demonstrated before, and repeated in no uncertain fashion by this attack [that] the ability to strike unexpectedly is conferred by the FAA.

It is often felt that this arm which has had a long struggle with adverse opinions and its unspectacular aircraft is underestimated in its power. It is hoped that this victory will be considered a suitable reward to those whose work and faith in the FAA has made it possible.[114]

---

[114] Aircrew taking part in Taranto operation:
815 Sqdn, *Illustrious*
Lt-Cdr K. Williamson: CO, 815 Sqdn, July 1940; shot down, PoW.
Lt(O) N. J. Scarlett PoW.
Sub-Lt(A) P. D. J. Sparke: d 11 May 1941.
Sub-Lt(A) J. W. Neale: *Jackdaw* 1941; Lt & *Daedalus* Sept. 1942; Actg Lt-Cdr, *President* Nov. 1943; *Shrike* (Derry) 1944; *Nairana* 1945.
Sub-Lt(A) J. M. Macdonald.
Sub-Lt(A) A. L. O. Wray: k *Illustrious* 10 Jan. 1941.
Lt N. McI. Kemp: k *Illustrious* 10 Jan. 1941.
Sub-Lt J. S. Bailey: *Indomitable* EF Jan. 1942; Actg Lt-Cdr(A) Feb. 1942.
Lt(A) H. I. A. Swayne: Lt Aug 1940; *Condor* 1941; *Illustrious* 1942; *Saker* (BAD) 1943; 1820 Sqdn 1944; Actg Lt-Cdr(A), *President* 1945.
Tempy Sub-Lt J. Buscall, RNVR: Sub-Lt May 1941; *Grebe* Jan. 1942.

(*Footnote 114 is continued over the page*)

115. *From Godfroy*

Duquesne
Alexandria
15 November 1940

Would you accept my warmest congratulations for your great success at Taranto.

116. *To Pound*

21 November 1940

A. *Barham* is by no means an efficient unit. She went to Suda four days ago, got her feed water contaminated somehow and just managed to crawl through the Great Pass and then anchor until tugs brought her into harbour ... her machinery is in a poor way and she is out of action for eight days. ...

Berwick is also in a bad way and can just do 28 knots. Her turbines are very groggy and we can do nothing to them out here. ...

B. Suda has already proved its value. We can operate without danger of running short of fuel. It is fast getting consolidated but I can't yet leave heavy ships there at night owing to indifferent net defence.

Lt(A) L. J. Kiggell: Lt 1937; *Grebe* 1941; *Daedalus* 1942; *Vulture* (St Merryn) 1943; *Daedalus* 1944; Actg Lt-Cdr *Bherunda* 1945.

Lt H. R. B. Janvrin: Lt 1937; *Condor* 1942; Actg Lt-Cdr PD 1943–45; Actg Cdr 1944.

Lt(A) C. B. Lamb: Lt 1938; *Grebe* 1941; Malta 1942; PoW, Vichy, N Africa 1942; *Daedalus* 1943; Lt-Cdr(A) *Implacable* 1944–45. See his *War in a Stringbag* (London, 1977).

Lt K. C. Grieve: Lt 1935; *Condor* 1941; *Grebe* 1942; Lt-Cdr 1943; *St Angelo* 1943; Carrier Trng & Admin, *Monck* 1944.

Sub-Lt(A) W. C. Sarra: Lt Feb. 1942.

Actg Sub-Lt(A) J. A. Bowker: Sub-Lt(A) 1942; Lt(A) 1943.

819 Sqdn, *Illustrious*

Lt-Cdr J. W. Hale: CO 819 Sqdn Feb. 1940; Cdr Dec. 1940; *Phoenix* May 1941; *Garuda* 1942; *Jackdaw* 1943; *Phoebe* 1944–45.

Lt G. A. Carline: Lt 1937; *Audacity* Aug. 1941; Lt-Cdr Nov. 1941.

Actg Sub-Lt(A) A. J. B. Forde: *Buzzard* 1941; Lt(A) June 1942; *Illustrious* Nov. 1942; Actg Lt-Cdr & CO 810 Sqdn 1943–44; *Urley* 1945.

Probny Sub-Lt(A) A. F. X. Mardel-Ferreira RNVR: k *Illustrious* 10 Jan. 1941.

Lt C. S. E. Lea: Lt 1939; *Grebe* 1941; *Nightjar* (Preston) 1943; Actg Lt-Cdr *Implacable* 1945.

Sub-Lt(A) P. D. Jones: *Jackdaw* 1941; Lt(A) *Landrail* 1942; Actg Lt-Cdr *Begum* 1943; *Bambara* 1945.

Lt F. M. A. Torrens-Spence: Lt 1936; *Grebe* 1941; Lt-Cdr *Daedalus* 1942; Actg Cdr 1944; *Illustrious* 1945.

Lt(O) A.W. F. Sutton: Lt 1935; *Condor* 1941; Lt-Cdr 1943; Actg Cdr *Implacable* 1944–45.

Lt R. W. V. Hamilton: k 26 Nov. 1940.

Mid(A) J. R. B. Weekes: k 26 Nov. 1940.

Lt(A) R. G. Skelton: d *Illustrious* 11 Jan. 1941.

Tempy Sub-Lt(A) E. A. Perkins: k *Illustrious* 10 Jan. 1941.

(*Footnote 114 is continued opposite*)

The first air raid was a bad one, but since then the raids have been on a small scale and have done little damage. The Greeks have returned from the mountains and labour is again plentiful.

C. It is looking very much as though the Dodecanese are becoming ripe for plucking. There are signs of petrol and food shortage and unrest among the Greeks. That is the reason why I signalled asking if there was a Marine Brigade wanting a job. I know there is one at Freetown but don't know if it's free. If I had it I should start biting off the lesser isles starting with those near Crete.

MTBs would also be most handy both among the islands and in the Strait of Otranto...

The C-in-C, Middle East, has got a party of 400 thugs that we are planting in Crete to make a start and I can collect our very good Danube party together again.

D. I have been shaking up the military about the defences of Alexandria. The Italians are making a dead set at it very naturally. It is all right when the fleet is in as they won't face the fleet barrage but on our return from the last trip I found they had been doing pretty well as they liked, flying low over the harbour. *Decoy* got a bomb in her wardroom which fortunately did very little serious damage but – much worse – round the floating dock were a number of time bombs

---

Lt E. W. Clifford: k *Illustrious* 10 Jan. 1941.

Lt G. R. M. Going: Lt 1935; *President* 1941; *Activity* 1942; Actg Lt-Cdr *Illustrious* 1943; Cdr 1944; Actg Cdr, *Goldcrest* 1945.

Lt(A) W. D. Morford: Lt 1938; *Jackdaw* 1941; *Daedalus* 1943; *President* 1944–45.

Sub-Lt(A) R. A. Green: *Buzzard* 1941; Lt Dec. 1941; *Illustrious* 1942; *Daedalus* 1943; Actg Lt-Cdr *Bherunda* 1945.

813 Sqdn, *Eagle*

Lt G. W. L. A. Bayly: (824 Sqdn); k Taranto 11 Nov. 1940.

Lt H. J. Slaughter: (813 Sqdn): k Taranto 11 Nov. 1940.

Lt M. R. Maund; Lt Nov. 1938; *Jackdaw* 1941; *St Angelo* (Malta) 1942; d 11 Jan. 1943.

Sub-Lt(A) W. A. Bull: Lt(A) May 1941; *Victorious* 1942; Airfield & Carrier Reqrmts Dept 1943; N Air Org Div 1944–45.

824 Sqdn, *Eagle*

Capt O. Patch RM: Lt 1935; Capt 1939; *Eagle* 1938; *Jackdaw* 1941; *Heron* 1943; Tempy Major *Thane* Sept. 1944; Commandos 1945.

Lt P. G. Goodwin: Lt 1938.

Lt(A) J. B. Murray: Lt April 1939; *Jackdaw* 1941; *Unicorn* 1942; M A/C Prodn 1943; Actg Lt-Cdr(A) 1944.

Actg Sub-Lt S. M. Paine: Lt(A) Jan. 1941; *President* 1941; *Illustrious* 1942–43; Actg Lt-Cdr(A) *Saker* 1944–45.

Lt(A) J. W. G. Wellham: Lt(A) Aug. 1939; 767 Sqdn *Condor* (Arbroath) 1941; *Grebe* 1942; Actg Lt-Cdr(A) *Biter* 1943; *Empress* 1944–5.

Lt P. N. Humphries GC: Lt 1936; *Condor* 1941; *Merlin* 1942; Actg Lt-Cdr *Daedalus* 1943.

Capt Patch and Lt Wellham took part in the attack on shipping at El Gazala, 23 Aug. 1940, described in Doc. No. 86. Eight aircrews, all experienced in night flying, and 5 a/c, were embarked from *Eagle*.

which went off three days later. We might easily have, and nearly did, lose the dock as these are quite big missiles of about 800 lbs in weight.

The whole AA organisation is so bad. Egyptian manned guns and British manned guns, Egyptian and British manned searchlights, each under a different command. However, I hope things will now improve.

E. I hope to get busy on the Otranto Strait again presently, but first we have to locate the sound members of the Italian Fleet. One *Cavour* is definitely in the Western Mediterranean. I don't think James Somerville need worry very much about her as she'll run from a Swordfish aircraft. I have a notion that the remaining two are in the Adriatic probably to protect the Albanian convoys, but we can't definitely locate them.

Malta is very low in reconnaissance aircraft and we are little better this end. That was why your signal about two Sunderlands for Freetown was so unwelcome but we must make the best of it.

117. *To Rear Admiral Hugh England*

23 November 1940

... The Taranto show has freed our hands considerably & I hope now to shake these damned Itiys up a bit[115] I don't think their remaining three battleships will face us and if they do I'm quite prepared to take them on with only two. But I expect it will be some time before they face the FAA. ...

At one time out here I began to think that the airmen who said the day of the ships was gone were right. We were bombed in every corner of the sea and just couldn't get away or bring down the enemy planes.

Now our carrierborne fighters have the mastery and Italian planes approaching within 25 miles of the fleet take a big risk. I saw three come down in flames in under an hour the morning after Taranto.

The bombers also unload on the horizon when our fighters get busy. It's an amusing game to watch and we also shoot one out of the sky now and then.

---

[115]R Adm Hugh England (Ret): Capt 1923; RA 1935; Cdre & Prin STO Egypt Dec. 1941; STD, *Eaglet* (L'pl) March 1942; Cdre 2Cl, RNR, *Eaglet II* 1943–44.

118. War Diary, November 1940 (cont.)

14 November

Operation BARBARITY

3. A fast convoy is being arranged to sail for Piraeus with RAF, Army, AA and maintenance units. *Waterhen* sailed from Port Said today, escorting *Johann De Witt* to rendezvous with the remainder of the convoy....[116]

15 November

2. A fast convoy, consisting of *Clan MacArthur, Imperial Star* and *Nieuw-Zeeland*, sailed a.m. today escorted by *Coventry, Vampire, Nubian* and *Mohawk*, routed through the Kaso Strait.[117]

3. The 3CS (*Berwick, York, Gloucester, Glasgow*) and *Sydney*, sailed for Piraeus after embarking troops and stores at 1500 today. VALF, in *Orion*, with *Ajax*, sailed to take general control of this operation and to visit Suda, Piraeus and Candia as necessary.

16 November

RA, 1BS in *Barham*, with *Valiant, Eagle, Hyperion, Vendetta, Dainty, Diamond, Jervis, Greyhound, Gallant* and *Griffin*, sailed early a.m. today for Suda Bay to cover these movements. *Eagle* has nine Gladiators. This force will also provide cover for movements of Greek convoys in the Aegean.

Greek Movements

4. One submarine proceeding for Bari-Durazzo patrol. One submarine in Gulf of Corinth bound for Adriatic. Convoy of three ships, with escort of two destroyers, off Phalconera bound for Suda.

Air Reconnaissance

5. Flying boat reconnaissance is being provided by 201 Group from 16 to 19 November between Crete and Cape Spartivento for the security of the above movements.

18 November

Defence of Alexandria

6. The C-in-C has made the following signal to the C-in-C, Middle East:

---

[116]*Johan De Witt*: 1920, 10,474gt, 15k, Nederland NV Stoomvaart.
[117]*Clan MacArthur*: 1936, 10,528gt, 17.5k, Clan Line.
Nieuw-Zeeland: 1928, 11,069gt, 15k, Koninklijke Paketvaart.

I am much concerned at the impunity with which enemy aircraft are now attacking Alexandria. While the Fleet was at sea recently a number of bombs were dropped in the harbour damaging a destroyer and other craft. Some of these were delay action which detonated on Saturday, 16th, causing some damage to the floating dock.

On Sunday, 17th at about 1715 mines or torpedoes were dropped close to the Great Pass. These aircraft were not apparently detected by RDF and little fire was directed at them by the shore batteries. Recently when the Fleet has been in harbour, the blind barrage now developed has kept attacking aircraft from dropping bombs inside the harbour, but they are never illuminated by the searchlights and the fighters never get contact. No aircraft attacking Alexandria has yet been shot down.

Thus at the present time Alexandria harbour is largely being defended by the Fleet, but the wear on personnel who have long hours of standing to at sea will become serious unless the shore defences can be made to perform their proper function of defending the Fleet at its base.

Request all possible measures may be taken forthwith to remedy this state of affairs. I do not consider the political considerations can be allowed to prejudice this important matter.

19 November

Gun Defences for Suda Bay

12.   The following gun defences have been provided from naval sources:

Four 4-in; five pom-poms; two 0.5-in and four 3-pdrs and the 6-in coast defence battery of four Mark VII guns originally intended for Turkey. All personnel have been provided from *Liverpool.*

23 November

Greek Movements

8.   A convoy of nine ships, with six destroyers, will leave Candia at dawn tomorrow for Piraeus.

9.   Greek slow ships from the Canal Area will be sailed independently under cover of Fleet movements.

Malta – Air Raid

10.   There were two air raids today. The first by 10 bombers and 16 fighters, the second by 5 bombers and 12 fighters. Damage was negligible and two enemy aircraft were probably shot down.

119. *Report on Operation COLLAR, 23–30 November 1940*

(20 July 1941)

Cunningham's Observations

2. The object of the operation was the safe passage of Convoy COLLAR consisting of three fast MT ships from Gibraltar to Malta and Alexandria, accompanied by HM Ships *Manchester* and *Southampton* carrying troops to Alexandria.[118]

3. Opportunity was taken to send *Ramillies, Berwick* and *Newcastle* to Gibraltar ... , to pass four corvettes (*Peony, Gloxinia, Hyacinth* and *Salvia*) from Gibraltar to reinforce the Mediterranean Fleet, to run inward and outward Malta convoys and to cover the passage of various minor units and Aegean convoys.[119]

4. As there was a considerable number of rather slow movements to be covered in the Central Mediterranean, the Mediterranenan Fleet was worked in two halves, each consisting of a battleship division, a carrier, cruisers and destroyers. This allowed the presence of an adequate covering force in the Central Mediterranean for four days, and also enabled simultaneous FAA offensive operations to be carried out at points as widely separated as Port Laki, Leros and Tripoli (Africa).

5. It was also hoped that the multiplicity of forces would confuse the enemy; but in the event it proved that his eyes were turned the other way and the Mediterranean Fleet had the somewhat mortifying experience of 'listening in' to Force H in action on the other side of Sicily with the enemy who were inclined to be regarded as our own exclusive property.

6. As far as the Mediterranean Fleet itself was concerned, the operation, which was long and complicated, passed off with remarkable smoothness and lack of incident.

7. The FAA attacks from *Illustrious* and *Eagle* were delivered with customary gallantry and efficiency. Damage was inflicted on the enemy at the cost of the loss of one aircraft only, that at Port Laki.

8. It is of interest to note that at this period our control of the Mediterranean was close on being re-established, a number of lengthy and complicated movements of warships and merchant vessels having been successfully carried out in face of the enemy's full air and sea opposition. It is a reasonable assumption that such

---

[118]*Manchester*: 1938, 9,400t, 12×6in, 8×4in, 8×21in tt, 32k; s It E-boats, off Tunisia Aug. 1942.

[119]*Peony, Gloxinia, Hyacinth, Salvia* (s *U-568*, E Med Dec. 1941): 'Flower' cl corvettes; 1940, 925t, 1×4in, 16k.

movements would have been increasingly practicable had not strong and skilful German air reinforcements started to operate from Italy in December.

Narrative

Force C (7CS, *Malaya, Ramillies, Eagle* and 8 destroyers), under VALF, sailed from Alexandria at 0600, 23 November and proceeded by the Kaso Strait and arrived Suda Bay 0800/24 to fuel.

2. Convoy MW4 escorted by Force D (*Coventry, Calcutta* and 4 destroyers) sailed from Alexandria at 0800/23, proceeding through the Kaso Strait in the wake of Force C and thence by the Kithera Channel to Malta.

3. *Berwick* sailed independently from Alexandria p.m./23 to join Force C off Suda Bay a.m./24.

4. Force C sailed from Suda Bay at 1215/24 and passed through the Kithera Strait giving close cover to Convoy MW4. MW4 was attacked by 3 T/B at 1200/24 without damage to either side. *Malaya* had developed flooding through cracked plates into the Tiller Flat which reduced her safe speed to 15 knots; but continued with the operation.

5. Force A (*Warspite* (Flag of C-in-C), *Valiant, Illustrious* and 9 destroyers) left Alexandria at 0300/25 and proceeded by the Kaso Strait to arrive Suda Bay at 0700/26. 3CS sailed after Force A, carried out exercises and joined the C-in-C at 1600/25. *Ulster Prince* from Port Said with Army details for Piraeus joined the C-in-C at 1200/25 and followed the fleet at best speed through the Kaso Strait.[120]

6. At 0230/26 ... the RA, Mediterranean Aircraft Carriers, was detached from Force A with *Illustrious, Gloucester, Glasgow* and four destroyers to fly off aircraft. 15 Swordfish were flown off at 0300 to attack Port Laki.

Aircraft were flown on by *Illustrious* at 0600 off Suda Bay, and fighters were flown off to work from Heraklion for the protection of the Fleet at Suda Bay.

7. *York* was detached from Force A at 0500 to proceed ahead to Suda, fuel and join 3CS at 1530 in position 250° Cape Matapan 12 miles.

8. Force A with the exception of *Gloucester* and *Glasgow* entered Suda Bay between 0700 and 0830/26. Destroyers were fuelled and 50 ME Commando, who had taken passage in the battleships, were

---

[120]*Ulster Prince*: 1930, 3,791gt, 18k; s a/c Greece April 1941.

disembarked. Force A sailed at 1030 and passed the Kithera Channel at 1600, when course was shaped for Malta.
9. The 3CS, after making a feint towards the Straits of Otranto, carried out a sweep of the Calabrian coast and had orders to rejoin Force A at 1100/27.
10. *Malaya, Ramillies,* Force D and four other destroyers and Convoy MW4 had arrived at Malta at 0815/26. Temporary repairs were made to *Malaya* and she with *Ramillies, Coventry, Newcastle* and 5 destroyers sailed at noon to join the VALF who, with 7CS, *Berwick, Eagle* and four destroyers had carried out a FAA attack on Tripoli at 0520. *Dainty* was delayed at Malta by engine defects and sailed at midnight to join Force C.
11. Convoy ME4, 5 ships escorted by *Calcutta* and three destroyers, left Malta for Alexandria at 1630/26 and the drifters *Fellowship* and *Lanner* sailed from Malta for Suda Bay at 0800.[121]
12. In the mean time Force H had left Gibraltar on the 25th with the COLLAR Convoy of 3 MT ships and 4 corvettes and Force F (*Manchester* (CS18) and *Southampton*) and was approaching S of Sardinia on the evening of 26th.
13. Force C, after leaving Malta, proceeded eastward covering Convoy ME4. Force D, which now consisted of *Ramillies, Berwick, Newcastle, Coventry* and 5 destroyers proceeded westward through the Narrows to join the FO, Force H, on the morning of the 27th.
14. ... 3CS rejoined from their sweep at 1100/27.
15. From 1005/27 onwards enemy reports started to be received from *Ark Royal*'s aircraft and it became evident that Forces H, F and D were about to gain contact with enemy forces consisting of two battleships and a number of cruisers and destroyers.

3CS was detached to support the FO, Force H, if required and to cover the passage of the COLLAR Convoy. The 3CS was ordered to reach position 36° 32′N, 12°00′E, at 0400/28, the convoy being due at this point at 0500.
16. The course of the subsequent action S of Sardinia could be followed to some extent from intercepted signals. It had become clear by 1500 that the enemy had retired, and the FO, Force H, informed the C-in-C ... that Force H and COLLAR convoy would be two hours early at the rendezvous. The 3CS was accordingly ordered to keep clear to eastward and join Force F at daylight.
17. *Ramillies* and *Berwick* joined the FO, Force H, the remainder of Force D joined Force F to escort COLLAR Convoy through the

---

[121]*Fellowship*: drifter, 1914, 99t, M/s; to Greek N Oct. 1941.
Lanner: drifter, 1912, 103t, M/S.

Narrows. The four corvettes proceeded independently through the Narrows, keeping clear of the convoy.

18. Force A in the meantime had remained in a covering position N of ME4 convoy during the day. At 1830 . . . course was set 270° to meet Force F in the morning. . . .

20. At 0800/28 3CS was sighted and at 0900 rendezvous was made with Force F and COLLAR Convoy . . .

21. CS18 reported two large explosions had taken place at 0138 . . . At 0321 a message was intercepted from an Italian unit saying two torpedoes had been fired at an enemy unit.[122] A similar incident and interception had occurred during the passage of Force D the previous night.

22. At 0930/28 *Clan Fraser* and *Clan Forbes* were detached to Malta escorted by *Decoy* and *Hotspur* both of whom were to stay at Malta for repairs. *New Zealand Star* proceeded eastwards S of Medina Bank, escorted by *Defender* and *Hereward* and covered by *Manchester* and *Southampton*.[123]

23. . . . At 1230 [Force A's] course was altered to westward to sight the corvettes who were about 12 miles astern of the convoy. At 1250 *Glasgow*, who had been detached to close the corvettes, was attacked by 6 Ju87s, one of which she shot down without damage to herself. At 1246 two sections of Fulmars were directed on to a formation which proved to be 6 CR42s of which they shot down one and damaged two.

24. The corvette *Gloxinia* had developed a hot bearing and was sent into Malta for repair. The remaining three proceeded direct to Suda Bay.

25. . . . 3CS was detached at 1600 . . . to sweep to northward of Hurd Bank and cover the passage of the corvettes. At 1700 *Griffin* developed engine defects and was sent into Malta for repair.

26. The night passed without incident with Force A proceeding eastward supporting the various groups of small ships and Force C, with Convoy ME4 nearing Alexandria, where they arrived a.m./29.

27. . . . 3CS joined the C-in-C at 1330 and were then detached to Suda Bay. At 1450 CS18 joined, with *Manchester* and *Southampton*, and were detached at 1720 to proceed independently to Alexandria.

28. Force A reached Alexandria at 1800/30. 3CS, corvettes, *Lanner* and *Fellowship* arrived Suda Bay a.m./30. *Manchester* and *Southampton* arrived Alexandria a.m./30.

[122]CS18: VA L. E. Holland: Capt 1926; RA Jan. 1938; RA, 2BS 1939; VA & jt head, Ady-Air M staff cttee Dec. 1939; VA 18CS April 1940; cmded BC Force May 1941; lost in *Hood*.
[123]*New Zealand Star*: 1935, 10,740gt, Blue Star Line.
Clan Forbes (1938), *Clan Fraser* (1939; blew up after air attack, Piraeus, April 1941): 7,529 gt, 17k, Clan Line.

120. War Diary, November 1940 (concl.)

25 November

Operation MB9 (COLLAR)

9. Force B under FOC, Force H, consisting of *Renown, Ark Royal, Sheffield, Despatch, Manchester, Southampton* and 9 destroyers, sailed from Gibraltar to provide cover for these movements.[124]

Greek Movements

7. A convoy of 7 merchant ships and 4 destroyers left Suda Bay for Piraeus at 1700.

Haifa

8. The NOIC, Haifa, reported that the SS *Patria* was sabotaged at 1140, capsized and sank.[125]

26 November

Force A

... At 0230, ... RA(A) in *Illustrious*, with *Gloucester, Glasgow, Janus, Juno, Nubian* and *Mohawk*, were detached for an air attack on Port Laki. ... RA(A) reported that 15 aircraft took part. Targets were difficult to distinguish but fires were started in the dockyard and other areas. Two aircraft attacked a ship, believed to be a cruiser, but results were unobserved. One aircraft failed to return.

6. The drifters *Fellowship* and *Lanner* were sailed for Suda Bay at 0800, and at 1630 convoy ME4, consisting of *Waiwera, Cornwall, Rodi, Volo* and *Devis*, sailed for Alexandria escorted by *Calcutta, Vampire, Vendetta* and *Voyager*. ...

Operation TRIPE

8. Operating under cover of Force C, a bombing attack on Tripoli was carried out by 8 aircraft from *Eagle* at 0520 this morning. One large ship was set on fire and a major fire started on Spanish Quay which was visible 80 miles away. All aircraft returned.

---

[124]*Renown*: 1916, 32,000t, 6×15in, 20×4.5in, 8×21in tt, 29k; mod 1930s; Force H F/ship. *Sheffield*: 1937, 9,100t, 12×6in, 8×4in, 8×21in tt, 32k.
[125]Actg Capt G. O. Lyddeker: NOIC Palestine Ports June 1940–Sept. 1944; ret Mar. 1942.
Patria: 1913, 11,885gt, 15.5k, Messageries Maritimes.

Suda Bay

9. *Protector, Chakla, Fiona,* arrived at 1700 and *Waterhen, Ulster Prince* and *Bantria* sailed for Piraeus.[126]

29 November

4. Force C and convoy ME4 arrived Alexandria today, *Volo, Rodi* and *Cornwall* escorted by 2 destroyers proceeding to Port Said.
5. Force B arrived at Gibraltar today.

30 November

Suda Bay

3. The 3CS and corvettes arrived at Suda Bay a.m. *Terror* sailed p.m. for Alexandria. *Fellowship* and *Lanner* arrived Suda Bay a.m.
4. *Ulster Prince, Diamond, Waterhen* and *Vendetta* arrived at Port Said and *Waterhen* and *Vendetta* sailed again escorting *Woolwich* to Alexandria.

Summary and Appreciation of Events for months of September, October and November 1940

Strategical

The period under review has seen a very definite improvement in the general strategical situation in the Mediterranean.

At sea. We have intensified our hold over the Eastern Mediterranean and the Aegean, which now amounts to practically complete command, a large measure of control over the Central Mediterranean East of Malta has been obtained whilst a beginning has been made in re-establishing the through Mediterranean route. The principal contributing factors have been – the arrival of important reinforcements, including RDF ships and a modern aircraft carrier which have enabled the air menace to be largely overcome; the use of Suda Bay as an advanced fuelling base; *Ajax*'s very successful action with Italian destroyers East of Malta; and last but by no means least the crippling of the Italian battlefleet by the FAA attack on Taranto.

On land. The Army in the Middle East has been building up its resources, and a steady stream of men and equipment has arrived from Home via the Cape under the nose of not inconsiderable naval

---

[126]*Bantria*: 1928, 2,402gt, 10k, Cunard SS Co.

and air forces in Italian East Africa. The much advertised advance by the Italians into Egypt from Libya commenced in September but halted in the vicinity of Sidi Barrani, since when the enemy has done no more than consolidate his positions. The Army and RAF, assisted by the FAA and the light forces of the Fleet, have continued to harass his lines of communication and supply ports.

Air. The RAF in the Western Desert, with a handful of aircraft, have done wonderful work against greatly superior numbers, and the moral ascendancy they have established over the Italian Air Force has materially assisted the operations of the Fleet. The attack by Italy on the Greeks, combined with the arrival of long range bombers in Egypt, have enabled the RAF to extend its operations to Adriatic ports, to Benghazi, and by using Malta, to ports in Italy and Sicily. The attacks, coupled with those undertaken by the FAA on Tripoli and the Dodecanese, have materially contributed to the general improvement in the strategical situation.

Bases

5. *Alexandria.* The growing menace of torpedo attack has made it necessary to take a number of measures; in particular A/T baffles have been laid; berthing of ships, targets, etc., as obstructions; fitting of physical obstructions on breakwaters; routine flying of kites from ships and shore, have all been instituted. Personnel and material for a kite balloon barrage have arrived and are being placed.

Bombing has been on the scale shown. The increase of AA fire and the use of RDF by the Fleet has reduced enemy activity in this respect:

Month	No. of attacks	No. of bombs dropped
September	2	7
October	2	36
November	6	61

. . .

In the harbour area little damage has been done. Two ships, *Decoy* and *Zamzan*, were hit on 13 November when the greater part of the Fleet was at sea.[127] During this raid four delay action bombs were dropped which exploded on 16 November. One of these caused slight damage to the floating dock.

The Fortress HQ at Ras-el-Tin was hit on 12 November and the Ports and Lights building on 17 November.

[127] *Zamzan*: 1909, 8,299gt, Misr, Egypt.

7. *Malta*. After a period of severe bombing whilst AA defences were comparatively inadequate, Malta was gradually built up with AA guns and fighters and is now a formidable proposition. The air attacks have not recently been heavy and in face of really intensive bombing the present scale of defence is still not sufficiently adequate as to justify use of the island as a Fleet base.

Air

8. *Enemy activities*. These three months have seen an interesting change in the situation. During the first months of the war the Fleet was always sighted, reported and usually bombed. With the arrival of RDF and the development of the technique of controlling fighters over the Fleet from the carrier, a great change has taken place. Shadowers have been detected and shot down with such frequency as to make that duty exceedingly hazardous, and the fighters have also been directed onto enemy formations of bombers in time to break up their attacks on the Fleet. In consequence, relative immunity from bombing attacks has lately been obtained and on a number of occasions Fleet movements have apparently remained unreported.

On the other hand, the torpedo menace has developed. The attacks, occurring chiefly in dusk or moonlight, are exceedingly difficult to combat and the toll of two cruisers hit with the loss of only one aircraft is an unsatisfactory result. The attacks by day have not so far been pressed home and have in consequence been less successful. The problem is receiving earnest attention, for if the enemy increase their scale of attack by this method the danger to convoys as well as to warships will become serious.

9. *Own activities*. The value of aircraft carriers has been amply demonstrated, particularly when the high speed of *Illustrious* made it possible to attack distant targets. The most striking success has of course been at Taranto, but the attacks on Tobruk, Benghazi, Tripoli, and Dodecanese targets, have all assisted to keep up the pressure on the enemy. A great need to reinforce the attack has been for shore-based long range torpedo bombers. The Italians have demonstrated to us the value of this form of attack and there is no doubt that such [air]craft based on Malta would be a very serious menace to Libyan communications.

10. *Reconnaissance*. Our Fleet reconnaissance has, of course, been performed by carrier borne aircraft, but strategical reconnaissance has been carried out most efficiently by Sunderlands, and lately Glenn Martins, based on Alexandria and Malta. The aircraft available have, however, been woefully inadequate, and the strengthen-

ing of shore-based reconnaissance remains one of the greatest needs in the Mediterranean.

Submarines

11. The Mediterranean, as expected, has proved an extremely dangerous place for submarine operations. Both sides have experienced heavy losses and the results achieved have been small. Our submarines were first concentrated on the duties of intercepting the Italian fleet and on trying to interrupt Libyan communications. One effective attack only was brought off against the enemy fleet, resulting, it is believed, in the damage or sinking of a cruiser. As regards Libyan traffic, inadequate air reconnaissance has prevented us from finding the Italian routes with any certainty; and submarines off the ports and on the coast, though they have achieved some successes, have not been able to obtain really good results. Since the entry of Greece into the war, submarines in the Adriatic have obtained a certain measure of success.

Political

12. *Egypt.* The help or otherwise of the Egyptians has been chiefly dependent on their estimate of the likelihood of our success. Their failure to enter the war has been of some inconvenience in regard to shipping matters and the like, but on the whole, considering that the Court has been steadily pro-Italian, matters have run better than might have been expected and have lately improved.

13. *France.* The French Squadron (except the Admiral, who is personally well disposed) have maintained a state of sullen correctness. There have been moments of crisis when it seemed that France might declare war on us, and it was necessary to prepare plans to rush the ships. The French on their side were evidently fully prepared to scuttle.

The administration in Syria has been hostile and in consequence the colony is really in a state of blockade.

There have been desertions from the French Squadron but they do not amount to more than about 200 men.

14. *Greece and Turkey.* Both countries have sent delegations to study our methods and a fairly close contact has been maintained. Officers to advise on A/S work and on defences have been sent to both countries. A naval mission was established in Greece on the outbreak of war, and Admiral Sir Howard Kelly has been in Turkey watching the situation and ready to take over as head of the Naval Delegation should that country declare war.

121. *From Pound*

1 December 1940

G. You will have seen that an enquiry is to be held into the conduct of the operation to the South of Sardinia. I felt like a pricked ball when I read FOH's signal saying he had given up the chase and was going to the convoy. However, there may be some reason we do not know of.[128] ...

H. The PM is very difficult these days, not that he has not always been. One has, however, to take a broad view because one has to deal with a man who is proving a magnificent leader and one just has to put up with his childishness as long as it isn't vital or dangerous. Also with a man like that it is not good policy to present him with a brick wall unless it is a thing which is really vital.

J. ... Keyes intrigued himself into the position of Director of Combined Operations in spite of the protests of the Chiefs of Staff...

N. I am trying to send you some destroyers and will do so immediately it is possible....

122. *From Admiral of the Fleet Sir Roger Keyes*

Director of Combined Operations
War Cabinet Office Annexe
Richmond Terrace, London SW1
3 December 1940

Very many congratulations on your success in the Mediterranean. That was a grand performance of the FAA. If we had only been free to develop the latter during the past 20 years, how much further ahead we would be now.

I daresay you do not know much about my appointment here. I have had it for four months but owing to the lack of landing craft, vessels to carry them, aeroplanes to drop parachutists and the objections raised by certain brass bound soldiers in the War Office, who hate the very thought of my irregular troops, I find it exceedingly hard to make any progress....

... it does give me definite command of raiding operations carried out by the 5,000 irregular troops we have raised and trained.

---

[128]See M. Simpson, *The Papers of Admiral of the Fleet Sir James Somerville* (Aldershot: Scolar Press for Navy Records Society, 1995), pp. 64–8 and documents nos 100–20.

It seems to me that the only raiding operations – on a scale within our present means – to affect seriously the course of the war, must be in the Mediterranean.

For a long time I have been urging that a strong force of my troops should be sent out to you for raiding operations as soon as landing craft and transports to carry them are ready. The delays and hesitations have been exasperating.

You will have heard about ... WORKSHOP. I hope you approve. I have been striving to be allowed to do that for ages. Every sort of difficulty was raised until, at last, the PM took a hand. He told me that he wished me to take command – so I said I would take off two or three stripes in order to do so. However, I understand I am to retain my rank but that my directive will not in any way interfere with the naval command afloat and will only include the light craft when they are actually taking part in the attack.

If you and Wavell want them, I would urge that the two Dutchmen and two of the Belgians and another 1,500 men be sent out to you as soon as possible.[129] With such a force it would be difficult to put a limit to what they might be able to do in the way of harrying the Italians.

We are also training a number of volunteers for raiding operations in the submarine punts.

If you have no objection I would stay for a bit and organise this force – before going home – either from Crete or Malta or the WORKSHOP.

123. *From Churchill*

11 December 1940

... We have considered whole matter exhaustively. DCO Sir Roger Keyes will execute it with full control of all forces employed and final plans are now being prepared by him. His appointment will not be Naval but limited to these Combined Operations. If necessary he will waive his Naval rank. Can't feel air counter-attack will be serious having regard to size of Islands, broken character, many mountains and detached fort[?] in which comparatively small attacking force will be intermingled with defenders. Enemy aircraft will not know who hold what till all is over and even then Italian Flag may be displayed on soft spot.

---

[129] 6 Belgian and 2 Dutch cross-Channel steamers, 18–25k, taken up by Keyes.

2. Capture of WORKSHOP no doubt a hazard, It may be surprisingly easy. It may be a heavy proposition. But Zeebrugge would never have got past scrutiny bestowed on this. Besides we are dealing with Italian sedentary troops not Germans. Commandos very highly trained. Carefully trained volunteers for this kind of work. Weather and fixed date of convoy or detection of attackers in approach stages would of course prevent attempt in which [?-] whole outfit will go to Malta or Suda Bay for other enterprises. If position is favourable nothing will be stinted.

3. Apprehensions that you have that AA guns, etc., will be diverted from Eastern Mediterranean and new commitments created may be mitigated by capture of enemy AA which are numerous. Enemy unlikely to attempt recapture [so] even the garrison will be small. Commandos will come away after handing over to regular troops and be available for further operations. Our reports indicate bulk of civilian population has already been evacuated. One hopes for increasing air command of Mediterranean making maintenance easier.

4. Comparing WORKSHOP with other operations you mention in future MANDIBLES kindly weigh follow[ing] considerations. MANDIBLES require 10 or 12,000 men and is far [?-] off if two bigger ones are to be taken. Little ones you mention would stir up all this area without any important reward unless process continued. Secondly captures in MANDIBLES area would excite keen rivalry of Greek and Turk [?-] which above all we do not want now. Thirdly our reports show MANDIBLES slowly starving and perhaps we shall get them cheaper later. Apart from above trying WORKSHOP does not rule out MANDIBLES afterwards unless ships and landing craft are lost which they may be. I am quite willing to start MANDIBLES with you and work upon it has already begun here. Also perhaps operations on enemy's land communications along North African shores may present opportunities.[130]

5. On strategic grounds WORKSHOP gives good air command of most used lines of enemy communications with Libyan army and also increased measure of air protection for our convoys and transports passing so-called Narrows. Undoubtedly blow to Italy at this time [would] create consternation besides [?-] this need to show ourselves capable of vehement offensive [?-] action.

6. Outfit leaves 18th and zero might be 10 days later. Before then we shall take stock of the whole situation including results obtained

---

[130] MANDIBLES was the plan to capture certain Dodecanese islands.

[in] Libyan battle. Whilst I am anxious to have everything ready it may well be better alternatives will present themselves.

124. *To Churchill*

12 December 1940

I fully appreciate your view about the advantages to be gained from WORKSHOP and as stated in my 1233/10 every effort will be directed to ensure the success of the operation. I have never questioned the feasibility of WORKSHOP given thorough planning but my concern has always lain in its subsequent maintenance.

2. The hard fact is that my resources are strained beyond their limit already and the extra burden means that something else will have to suffer in consequence. The real point of difference is that in my view the advantages to be gained are outweighed by the disadvantages resulting from having to withdraw ships and light craft from other and more important work. The calls on my forces increase almost daily, for instance today I am arranging for the supply of the Army in the Western Desert and for the removal by sea of some 20,000 prisoners. All these calls reduce by so much the Fleet forces available for offensive action at sea.

3. As regards air counter-attack on WORKSHOP I agree that it will not greatly affect the capture but when it comes to landing supplies, disembarkation of casualties and change round of garrisons the work will have to be carried out without any AA defences unless we have been able to seize AA guns and ammunition.

4. The organisation for command appears likely to lead to awkward and unsatisfactory situations.

5. As regards the MANDIBLES perhaps the strategic implications seem to loom larger to us out here than at home. In Spring, 1941, if not before, it seems that we may well be faced with a drive South East by Germany and I suggest that the importance is incalculable of ensuring that our line of communication to Greece, Turkey and the Dardanelles is not menaced by enemy ports and aerodromes on its flank.

6. The MANDIBLES are already alert to the fact that now we are in Crete they may be attacked at any time and in consequence the capture of the outlying islands will not affect that aspect. What such capture will do is to accelerate the starving process, scare the enemy, and give us better jumping off grounds for the eventual attack on the two big objectives.

125. *From Pound*

12 December 1940

... The WORKSHOP plan started the wrong end, as RK[eyes] put up the suggestion without having made any investigation of it whatsoever. The next step was that a half-baked plan was put before the Chiefs of Staff, and of course when we criticised it, it was insinuated that we were trying to kill it and wanted to do nothing!

As you will realise as soon as you have anything to do with him RK is not capable of making out a plan, and you would certainly be very unwise to allow him to do so. I am very sorry he is going out as I am afraid he will be a great worry to you. However, as I have said, I did all I could to stop him, and can't do more, as of course the PM is in a strong position being a self-appointed Minister of Defence.

I am very much aware of the difficulties of maintenance of WORKSHOP if it comes off, which it probably will not, as it is very unlikely that the weather will be suitable when they arrive on the spot. If it does not come off you will find RK straining at the leash and saying that he has 2,500 roughnecks who are trained to the minute and must be employed somehow.

I am going to try to arrange that he goes out as a Commodore....

We have raked up four destroyers to send out with WORKSHOP and they must remain at Malta as long as is necessary, though you can recognise that we can ill spare them from Home Waters. There will not be much of the destroyers left after WORKSHOP if RK misuses them....

I do not know whether you will be surprised or not at there having been a board of enquiry on the conduct of the operation on 27 November. Troubridge's failure to bring the *Goeben* to action set a very low standard in the conduct of naval operations.[131] Harwood's conduct of affairs at the Plate and your conduct of operations in the Mediterranean put it back on a high plane again, and I can't afford that anything should again lower it....

---

[131]RA E. C. T. Troubridge, RA 1911; RA 1CS (4 armd cruisers), Med F, Aug. 1914, at time of escape of *Goeben* and *Breslau* to Turkey. He forbore to intercept. CM but acquitted; later head Br mission to Serbia. See P. G. Halpern, *The Naval War in the Mediterranean, 1914–1918* (Annapolis, Md, 1987), pp. 12–14, or his *A Naval History of World War I* (London, 1994), pp. 56–7. See also G. A. D. Gordon, *The Rules of the Game: Jutland and the British Naval Command* (London, 1996) for a general discussion of WW1 naval attitudes and conduct.

126. *From Pound*

15 December 1940

a. Since operations EXCESS and WORKSHOP were contemplated the general situation has changed in following respects:

(i) Our success in Western Desert must have wide repercussions in both Italy and Germany and latter instead of waiting for spring before embarking on any major move may now consider it necessary to take some action to bolster up Italy or to restore the prestige of Axis. . . .

b. Taking above factors into consideration it appears undesirable that we should at present time be committed to operations which will lock-up all available shipping suitable for transporting MT and personnel apart from considerable Naval escorting forces.

c. It has been decided therefore that operations EXCESS and WORKSHOP shall be postponed until moonless period in January.

d. This decision will have the following advantages:

(i) Mediterranean Fleet will be free to concentrate on any operations which are necessary to assist the army in exploiting magnificent success they have achieved.

(ii) *Malaya* need not be sent to join Force H if such an operation would be inconvenient to you.

(iii) It will not be necessary to station *Barham* at Malta.

127. *War Diary, December 1940*

3 December

HMS Glasgow

4. At 1540 today, *Glasgow* received one hit forward and one hit aft from torpedoes dropped by two S79K aircraft. *Glasgow* was at anchor in Suda Bay inside the A/T nets. One officer and one rating were killed and three ratings seriously wounded. The full extent of the damage is not yet known, but at 2300 RA, 3CS, reported that he was proceeding in *Gloucester* with *Glasgow* in company and making good 16 knots. *Glasgow* had outer shafts and steering compartment working. CS3 is expected to pass through the Kaso Strait during dark hours.

Employment of Greek Destroyers

6. The C-in-C has informed the Naval Attaché, Athens, that it would be of assistance if Greek destroyers could be employed on the

protection of trade N of the Doro Channel. The escort of AN and AS convoys between Suda Bay and Piraeus, and the lightly escorted AN and AS convoys through the Kaso Strait.

9 December

Libya

The British offensive in the Western Desert started today....

During the night 8/9th, *Terror, Aphis* and *Ladybird* (Force A), bombarded Maktila Camp and the HQ camp at Sidi Barrani. The RAF and FAA co-operated with bombing and dropping of flares.

10 December

4. The RA, 1BS, in *Barham, Valiant, Coventry, Gallant, Vampire, Vendetta, Voyager, Wryneck, Dainty* and *Juno* (Force C) sailed today so as to be able to bombard Sollum and the escarpment roads should the Army require.

5. RAA in *Illustrious*, CS3 in *Gloucester, York, Ilex, Hero,* and *Hasty,* [Force D] sailed today ... to fly off aircraft at 2300 to attack El Adem aerodrome (Tobruk). Forces C and D will rendezvous tomorrow.

6. *Hereward* sailed to join Captain (D), 14DF (*Jervis, Nubian, Janus* and *Hereward* form Force B).

11 December

Libya

2. Forces A and B have been bombarding the neighbourhood of Sollum, harassing the enemy during the day, and *Terror* is now returning to Alexandria with all ammunition expended. The gunboats are remaining to continue harassing fire tonight. Force B is returning to Alexandria, leaving one destroyer to fuel gunboats at Mersa Matruh.

Submarines

4. It has been decided to base the 'O', 'P', 'R' and 'T' class and *Rorqual*, on Alexandria, and the 'U' class on Malta.

14 December

HMS Coventry

4. *Coventry* reported having been torpedoed by a submarine.... The fore portion of the stem is missing below 16 foot waterline.... There were no casualties.

THE ANGLO-ITALIAN WAR, 1940

6. At 1850, Captain (D), 2DF, reported having sunk the Italian submarine *Naiade* and that he had picked up 3 officers and 32 ratings.[132]

Air Attack on Tripoli

13. Eight aircraft of 830 Squadron operating from Malta, attacked Tripoli on the night of 13/14th. Four tons of bombs were dropped and three direct hits on ships alongside were observed, as well as explosions and damage to two warehouses. Other ships in the harbour were also bombed.

Malta

6. *Naples air raid.* Four Wellingtons attacked naval units and docks. Three sticks were dropped on the quays near the battleships, and 5 hits were obtained on a concentration of cruisers and destroyers. Five Wellingtons attacked the aerodrome and railway. All aircraft returned.

16 December

Operation MC2

The C-in-C in *Warspite, Illustrious, Valiant, Gloucester, York, Jervis, Janus, Juno, Mohawk, Greyhound, Dainty, Hyperion, Ilex, Hero, Hasty* and *Hereward*, sailed today ...

3. *Convoys.* AN10 proceeding, escorted by Greek destroyers, *Gallant* returning to Suda Bay.

MW5B. The Alexandria section, consisting of *Devis, Hoegh Hood* and the submarine *Parthian*, sailed a.m.[133]

MW5A, consisting of *Waiwera* and *Lanarkshire*, escorted by *Malaya, Dainty, Defender, Diamond*, sailed p.m. ...

Libya

5. RA, 1BS, has assumed operational control of the naval forces operating off Libya.
6. *Terror* bombarded MT concentrations and the Bardia area most of the day and night. She was fired at by coast defence batteries at a range of 1,900 yards but was not hit. At 1737 she was unsuccessfully attacked by 4 torpedo aircraft.
7. *Military Situation.* Sollum and Capuzzo were captured today.

---

[132]Capt Nicolson, *Hyperion*, with *Hereward*.
Naiade: 1933, 679/860t, 1×3.9in, 6×21in tt, 14/8k.
[133]*Hoegh Hood*: 1936, 9,351gt, A/S Atlantica, Norway.

128. *Report on Operations MC2 and MC3, 16–24 December 1940*

(February 1941)

Cunningham's Observations

2. The flying off of aircraft for the attack on the Dodecanese on 17 December was carried out with *Illustrious* operating in the line. This was the second occasion that this has been done by night in this fleet, and was entirely satisfactory. . . . the manoeuvres [were] performed entirely without signal, battleships and destroyers conforming to *Illustrious*'s movements.

In the existing weather conditions it is considered creditable that so many aircraft found their targets.

3. The very variable weather conditions and local storms in the mouth of the Adriatic caused an excellent opportunity of seriously damaging the enemy at Valona to be missed. At the time the battlefleet were off Valona conditions were ideal for a combined air striking force attack with torpedoes and a heavy bombardment with air spotting, which might well have had far reaching results.

4. The successful search and attack on an Italian convoy by *Illustrious*'s aircraft on 21 December was undertaken on the initiative of the RA, Mediterranean Aircraft Carriers, acting on air reports received from RAF shore-based reconnaissance working to the NW of Sicily.

This action is a useful example of the results which may be expected when adequate air reconnaissance and striking forces have been established at Malta.

The attack was well executed but would have been more satisfactory had some torpedoes been reserved for use against the escorting destroyers.

5. The satisfactory results obtained in the FAA attack against Tripoli on the morning of 22 December conformed to the previous high standard of performance by FAA aircraft of *Illustrious*.

6. With reference to para. 6 of *Malaya*'s report of Convoy MG1, *Malaya*'s signal was insufficiently informative. The fact that *Ilex* had been detached to stand by *Hyperion* would, if known to the C-in-C, have had a considerable influence on the problem whether an attempt should be made to extricate *Hyperion* or sink her.

Further, both Captain (D), 14DF, and *Ilex* were left in doubt as to further intentions for *Ilex*. If *Malaya* intended *Ilex* to join him if possible she should have been told so. The CO, *Malaya*, has since been informed to this effect.[134] ...

C-in-C Mediterranean's Report and Narrative

Operation MC2 was originally planned in concert with FOC, Force H, to pass *Malaya* through the Narrows to join Force H, accompanied by two empty MT ships *Clan Forbes* and *Clan Fraser* from Malta which had arrived there in Operation COLLAR.

Five destroyers of the 2DF were to accompany *Malaya* in readiness for Operation EXCESS.

5. The Fleet ... left Alexandria at 0100/16. Passage was made to Suda Bay via the Kaso Strait without incident. At 0745/16 the 3CS was detached with two destroyers to proceed ahead to Suda Bay and fuel.

6. Between 0330 and 0430/17 *Illustrious* flew off two air striking forces of 6 and 5 Swordfish to attack Rhodes and Stampalia respectively. Weather conditions were bad to the Eastward. Results of the attack on Stampalia could not be observed owing to cloud, but some fires were started. Only one aircraft found the target in Rhodes. One bombed Scarpanto, the remainder did not attack.

7. At 0900/17 the Fleet arrived at Suda Bay; *Orion* and the 3CS were already present fuelling and sailed shortly afterwards to sweep to the NW from Kithera, covering the convoys.

8. At 0730, AT 0217/17 was received, requiring *Malaya* to be sent to Gibraltar to join Force H after all, but the passage of the Narrows was to be one day later than originally intended. ...

9. ... *Warspite* sailed at 1800/17, proceeding independently, and was joined by the Battlefleet and 3rd and 7th Cruiser Squadrons during the early forenoon ...

10. It had been intended to send off an air search at 1200 but the weather became too bad for operating aircraft. Shore based reconnaissance of Taranto, Brindisi, Naples and Messina, showed the main portion of the enemy fleet to be absent from these ports. The position of the enemy fleet was thus unknown to the C-in-C at 1800/19, though it appeared possible that they had merely withdrawn to Spezia and Genoa after the severe RAF attack on Naples on the night of 16/17 December.

---

[134]D14: Capt Mack.
Capt *Malaya*: Capt (later Adm Sir) Arthur F. E. Palliser: *Excellent* (Whale I) 1938; Capt *Malaya* May 1940; Force H Feb. 1941; RA Aug. 1941; COS, EF Dec. 1941; Dep N Cdr, ABDA Jan 1942; RIN June 1943; HF cruisers 1943–44; VA Feb. 1944; 4SL Mar. 1944; C-in-C EI Sept. 1945.

11. Meanwhile the Fleet had been working Northward in very unpleasant weather to carry out the subsidiary operation MC3. It was apparent from weather forecasts that flying operations were unlikely to be possible. It also appeared likely that the 7CS and attendant destroyers might be unable to make the necessary speed to maintain the programme.

12. It was, however, decided to proceed with the operation. VALF accordingly parted company at 1600, having been informed by the C-in-C that the bombardment of Valona was unlikely, but that *Warspite* and *Valiant* would come up the centre of the Straits of Otranto in support as far as the line Brindisi–Valona.

13. *Illustrious* and the 3CS, with four destroyers, were detached at 1800/18. In accordance with the C-in-C's orders, RA, Mediterranean Aircraft Carriers made his final decision at that time that spotting aircraft would be unable to co-operate in existing and forecast weather conditions; but he expressed a hope that the weather might later allow torpedo bomber attack on the ships reported by air reconnaissance in Valona.

14. The operations in the Adriatic proceeded according to plan. Weather improved rapidly as ships proceeded Northward, and in the vicinity of Valona it was almost calm and visibilty was excellent with a bright moon.

VALF's forces found neither warships nor merchant vessels and were obliged to withdraw empty handed.

15. In the excellent visibility off Valona it was found possible to fix the battle fleet with accuracy. The C-in-C therefore decided to carry out the bombardment in spite of the absence of spotting aircraft.

The Fleet was accordingly turned to close the coast. . . . fire was opened at 0115/19. The bombardment was carried out as an indirect 'area' bombardment . . . The attack appears to have been a complete surprise. Ninety-six rounds of 15-in shell were fired, to which the enemy made no reply other than a few misdirected starshell fired from Saseno Island after the withdrawal had begun. The results of the bombardment cannot be assessed, but Captain (D), 14DF, reported that fires were still burning in Valona harbour when destroyers passed the harbour entrance about 2 hours later.

16. All forces made a rendezvous at 0900 . . ., after which course was shaped for Malta. The day passed without incident except that enemy air reports of both convoys were heard during the day.

17. At 1200, VALF was detached with the 3rd and 7th Cruiser Squadrons and 5 destroyers to cover the convoys. The destroyers were to fuel at Malta during the night and joined Force A at 0800/20.

18. Convoy MW5A arrived at Malta at 0230, six hours late. *Malaya* fuelled and sailed from Malta at 1250 to join Force A which was now close off the searched channel. Convoy MW5B arrived three hours late, having been delayed by *Hoegh Hood* who could not keep up. The latter eventually arrived 24 hours late, escorted by *Havock*.

19. Meanwhile destroyers were being detached from Force A in groups to fuel and rejoin. At noon *Warspite* parted company with Force A and proceeded into Malta, passing *Malaya* outward bound in the searched channel, and arrived at the breakwater at 1430/20. An enthusiastic reception was given to the C-in-C by the Maltese as the ship entered harbour. . . .

20. The sailing of convoy ME5A was delayed by the late arrival of MW5B, as the escort had to fuel. This convoy left Marsa Xlokk at 1530, escorted by *Calcutta* and the 3 corvettes.

21. Force A proceeded to the Eastward during the night 20/21, covering ME5A, returning to rendezvous with Convoy MG1 S of Malta at 1500/21 prior to *Malaya* and MG1's passage of the Narrows.

The 3rd and 7th Cruiser Squadrons continued to cover ME5A's passage to the Eastward.

22. During the forenoon of 21 December an air search was flown off by *Illustrious* to the Westward to look for an Italian Southbound convoy whose presence was suspected from reports by shore based aircraft. This convoy was located and successfully attacked during the afternoon by 9 T/B aircraft, two ships being sunk. One reconnaissance aircraft failed to return.

23. *Malaya* with Convoy MG1 and 5 destroyers of the 2DF parted company with Force A at 1930 and proceeded through the Narrows to rendezvous with Force H.

In the meantime, Force D (Captain (D), 14DF, in *Jervis*, with *Janus* and *Juno*), had left Malta and gone ahead to carry out a sweep in the Narrows to clear *Malaya*'s passage.

24. Force A turned back to the SE to carry out an FAA attack on Tripoli. Fifteen aircraft were flown off in two ranges at 0330 and 0430/22. The raid was successfully carried out by dive bombing and all aircraft returned safely by 0745/22.

25. At 0240 *Malaya* reported that *Hyperion* had been mined . . . , and ordered Captain (D), 14DF to stand by her. *Ilex* was also detached to stand by *Hyperion*, while *Malaya* proceeded with the 3 remaining destroyers.

26. The fact that *Ilex* had been left with *Hyperion* was not reported to the C-in-C. Appreciating that Force D was by then well to the S of *Hyperion* on his way back to Malta and that, unless *Hyperion*

could still steam, daylight would find the force dangerously close to Pantelleria if towing were attempted, the C-in-C ordered Captain (D), 14DF to sink *Hyperion* if she could not steam.

27. In the event *Ilex* had taken *Hyperion* in tow at 0345. When Captain (D), 14DF arrived at 0435, the tow had parted once and had just been resecured. D14 ordered the tow to be cast off, remaining crew was removed and *Hyperion* was sunk by a torpedo from *Janus*. The four destroyers then returned to Force A.

28. During this time the C-in-C ordered RA, Mediterranean Aircraft Carriers to detach two destroyers from Force A to Malta to screen *Warspite*. *Dainty* and *Greyhound* were sent and *Warspite* sailed at 0700 screened by these two and *Havock*.

29. At 1110 a rendezvous was made with Force A . . . , and at 1122 Captain (D), 14 DF was seen approaching with Force D and *Ilex*.

30. *Ilex* was sent into Malta to land the wounded, and *Dainty* and *Greyhound* were sent in to fuel and ordered to divide *Hyperion*'s crew among the three destroyers for passage to Alexandria.

31. Course was then set to the Eastward and an air search flown off to search a sector between the E coast of Sicily and 070°. Nothing was sighted except an Italian hospital ship.

32. *Dainty*, *Greyhound* and *Ilex* left Malta at 1700/22 to rendezvous with the C-in-C . . . at 0900/23. They were delayed by defective steering gear in *Greyhound* and the fleet turned back to the Westward to meet them.

33. These destroyers rejoined at 1315 and the fleet again turned to the Eastward to return to Alexandria. Air searches during the 23rd disclosed nothing and no incidents occurred.

34. VALF in *Orion*, with *Ajax* and convoy ME5 arrived at Alexandria. *Sydney* had been detached at 0845/21 to complete with fuel at Suda Bay, and collect her damaged aircraft. She then proceeded to Malta, passing S of Force A, and arrived there on 23 December for repairs to her rudder.

35. RA, 3CS, in *Gloucester*, with *York*, arrived at Piraeus on the 23rd, having fuelled at Suda Bay after covering Convoy ME5.

36. Force A continued Eastward without further incident, . . .

The C-in-C entered harbour in *Warspite* at 1500.

129. *War Diary, December 1940 (concl.)*

17 December

Libya

8. Egypt is now clear of enemy forces. An advance supply base for the Army is being established at Sollum.
9. *Aphis* bombarded the Bardia area at 1630 and reported having sunk three ships. *Terror* commenced bombardment at 2130. RA, 1BS, intends to develop the harbour facilities and W/T communication at Sollum and Bardia. He has asked for the early provision of fixed AA defences. Destroyers will continue A/S work and give store ships protection against E-boats and T/B attack.
10. Movements of Force F were as follows:

Vampire, Voyager, Waterhen, patrolling Mersa Matruh to Raz Azzaz.
Vendetta sails with *Protector* for Sollum p.m., *Protector* carrying provisions and petrol.
Aphis establishing base at Sollum.
Ladybird towing 'X' lighter to Sollum.
Terror proceeding Alexandria for ammunitioning.
Huntley and *Moy* are carrying out sweeping operations off Sollum.[135]
Myriel, Chakla, Atid, St Issey and pontoon lighters and 2 water lighters proceeding to Sollum with necessary stores and equipment.[136]

Captain (D), 10DF, is providing cover for these movements.
11. Ferrying of prisoners of war is continuing in *Fawzia, Knight of Malta, Farouk* and *Fiona*.[137]

HMS Truant - *Summarised report*

12. Night of 13/14th – Sank 1 and possibly 2 merchant ships off Cape Spartivento.
Night of 15/16th – Sank 1 large tanker off Cape Colonne.

21 December

Air Reconnaissance

6. Two battleships (*Vittorio Veneto* and *Giulio Cesare*) were relocated at Naples today. As a result the C-in-C has requested the

---

[135]*Huntley*: M/S; 1919, 800t, 1×4in, 1×3in, 16k; s a/c E Med Jan. 1941.
[136]*Myriel*: 3,560gt, Euxine Shipping Co.
Atid: 1921, 509gt, Atid Nav, Palestine.
[137]*Fawzia, Farouk*: unidentified.

AOC, Mediterranean, to repeat his bombing attacks with Wellington aircraft.

23 December

Libya

7. The GOC, Western Desert Forces, has reported that *Terror* and gunboats will not be required for bombardment purposes.[138] An unsuccessful T/B attack was made on *Chakla* at 1720.

Malta

8. Wellington aircraft attacked Castel Benito and Tripoli today. Explosions were caused on hangars at Castel Benito and at Tripoli the Custom House and jetty were hit and fires started. . . .

24 December

Libya

4. Sollum was bombed twice today, a jetty and one lighter being hit. There were about 50 casualties. . . .
5. . . . It is essential that adequate AA defences are provided if supplies are to be maintained at Sollum.

25 December

Libyan Situation

Terror and other ships off Sollum were attacked by bombers and torpedo bombers. The attacks were unsuccessful. Bombs fell all around *Chakla* but there was no damage or casualties.

2. The OC, 202 Group, is providing the maximum fighter protection during daylight hours.

26 December

AA defence of Alexandria

4. The C-in-C has agreed with the AOC-in-C, Middle East, that the fighter protection of Alexandria will be taken over by *Eagle*'s Gladiators to release RAF fighters for the Western Desert.

29 December

Captain (D), 14DF in *Jervis,* with *Nubian, Mohawk, Juno, Greyhound* and *Griffin*, sailed a.m. today to carry out an A/S sweep. . . .

---

[138] GOC, W Des Forces: Lt-Gen O'Connor.

2. *Perth* and *Coventry* support the destroyers. After nightfall tonight the destroyers sweep to the Longitude of Tobruk, inshore, keeping clear of Tobruk minefield and supported by *Perth* to seaward.[139]

Greek Operations

6. Greek destroyers are carrying out a sweep into the Adriatic on the night 29/30th.

30 December

Malta – Air Reconnaissance

5. Air reconnaissance yesterday showed one *Littorio*, one *Cavour*, three 8-in cruisers, and two 6-in cruisers in Naples.
6. Seven Wellingtons carried out a bombing raid on the battleships, using SAP bombs, and reported 5 bombs in the target area.

31 December

Malta

5. Wellington bombers attacked the battleship in dock at Taranto, and 5 aircraft dropped bombs in the target area.

General Appreciation

Survey

The month of December has been the most interesting and productive since Italy entered the war. During this period the events in the Mediterranean in the preceding five months have borne fruit.... The result of this situation was that we found ourselves with a great degree of control in the Central Mediterranean and it was possible to exercise this during the month by completing the passage of valuable convoys direct through the Mediterranean in both directions and by passing warships through both Eastward and Westward....

The second activity, which was a corollary of our command of the sea, was the spectacular advance of the Army ... These operations occupied a good deal of the Fleet activities and presented many problems, but the contribution of the Fleet both in supporting the attack and in dealing with subsequent supply was undoubtedly a factor of great importance in the successful results obtained.... Our

---

[139]*Perth*, RAN: 1936, 7,105t, 8×6in, 8×4in, 8×21in tt, 32.5k; s Java Sea, Feb. 1942.

control of the sea had moreover much to do with enemy shortage of supplies and inability to rush up help.

Subsequent events, due to German intervention, have renewed our problems, but it is correct to say that by the end of 1940 we were a fair way to achieving our first object, that is to say, the control of the Mediterranean, and that the first fruits, namely an undisturbed advance into Italian territory by our troops, had fallen into our hands.

Air Operations

4. ... During December the receipt of certain Glenn Martin aircraft in Malta, coupled with the flying boats, resulted in stronger reconnaissance resources and allowed of approaching nearer to the proper reconnaissance needs of the Fleet.

Western Desert

5. ... Two factors hindered naval support; one was the need for secrecy which prevented moving forward supplies and suitable shallow draft craft until the very last moment; the second factor was the weather, which besides holding up small craft movements caused a severe sandstorm, making it necessary to cancel a battleship bombardment of Bardia which the RA, 1BS went to sea to undertake. At one time the supply situation was serious, particularly as regards water, but the matter was rectified just in time. Another serious problem was the evacuation of the large number of prisoners, but by means of using the supply ships and warships on a ferry service on their return trips this difficulty was also overcome. The crying need for small coasting merchant ships early became evident.

Enemy Forces

6. The immediate effect of Taranto was that the undamaged portion of the Italian battle fleet moved to Naples. This fortunately coincided with the arrival of the Wellington Squadron in Malta and a series of attacks were made on Naples with good results against battleships and cruisers. It seems probable that at least one of the former was damaged by a bomb on the stern and one or more cruisers were hit.

Bases

7. *Alexandria.* The Western Desert advance relieved the threat to Alexandria and removed an anxiety which had been worrying at

times. For the moment too it stopped air attacks and dangers of dislocation due to those attacks.

Malta. . . . the island had definitely got the measure of the Italian air force and was relatively immune from damage in air raids. The damage in the early attacks was being repaired and the base was really as effective as when the war broke out, besides being far better defended against air attack or invasion. The AA defences were, however, not up to establishment nor was there an adequate fighter defence to meet an increased scale of attack.

Suda Bay. Was increasingly used as a fuelling base and advanced base for warships. Defences were well advanced but the usual shortage of AA guns and fighters had resulted in a state of air defence not really adequate to the scale of attack. Moreover, owing to the lack of the necessary equipment there was no proper anti-torpedo defence and this fact was to result in serious damage to *Glasgow.*

Greek Assistance

8. The Greek Naval Authorities were exceedingly anxious to cooperate with us and as a first step Greek destroyers started work as convoy escorts between Crete and the Piraeus. Their standard of efficiency was satisfactory.

Casualties

9. . . .

Submarines

Regulus. Lost, possibly by enemy air action, in the Adriatic. Official date 6 December.[140]

Triton. Lost, possibly by mine, in lower Adriatic. Official date 18 December.

Free French submarine *Narval* – Failed to return from Tunisian coast patrol, 16 December. Not known whether sunk or deserted.[141]

130. *Operations in Support of the Army off the Western Desert, 7 December 1940–31 May 1941*

(1 January 1942)

Cunningham's Observations

3. I agree with the opinion of Rear Admiral Rawlings that in peace time our preparations and study of combined services operations

---

[140]*Regulus*: 1930, 1,475/2,015t, 1×4in, 8×21in tt, 17.5/9k
[141]*Narval*: 1925, 974/1,441t, 1×3.9in, 10×21.7in tt, 16/10k.

lacked thoroughness. Only the problem of assault from the sea was normally studied or practised whereas it is the problem of supply and transportation by sea which has been the main combined operational problem of the Mediterranean.

4. This campaign brought into prominence problems and requirements which had to be met largely with last minute improvisation, which though good training for the seaman, is not always particularly efficient. There was, and still is, a lack of suitable ships for running supplies, transporting heavy lifts, such as tanks and lighters, or for the carriage of petrol. No naval or army organisation existed in the Middle East for the taking over and running of a port as opposed to its defence. There is a gap between the naval and army organisations at a port which should be filled in theory by the Sea Transport Department; but at operational ports such as Tobruk, Sollum and Benghazi, where no local or civilian labour is available, in actual fact all port services – pilots, tugs' crews, lightermen, crane drivers, stevedores, boat and ship repairs and salvage, etc. – have to be met by army and naval personnel. For this reason the naval party at Tobruk eventually reached 400 men found from the Fleet.

5. The combined service organisation for the defence of newly acquired ports against air attack was very sketchy and was particularly unsatisfactory at Benghazi. On the other hand the arrangements and organisation for sea bombardments proved adequate owing to the close contacts and preliminary study by the naval and army staffs.

6. The gallantry, devotion to duty, and resource of the officers and men of the Inshore Squadron in this campaign is worthy of the highest praise....

131. *War Diary, January 1941*

2 January

Other Operations

9. Bombardment of [Bardia] was also carried out by *Terror, Aphis* and *Ladybird* from first light until the fleet bombardment and was resumed after the fleet bombardment. Three bombing attacks were made on *Terror* during the afternoon....

Strength of FAA Squadrons

13. Experience has shown that it is desirable to increase the strength of operational squadrons over their IE complement of fly-

ing personnel and aircraft in order to maintain each squadron at maximum operational strength, allowing for sickness, casualties, etc.

By the use of reserve aircraft and personnel it has been possible to bring 815 Squadron up to 10 aircraft, 819 up to 12, and to form *Eagle*'s fighter flight of 6, and it is considered that the maximum efficiency will be achieved if the squadrons are maintained at the following IE figures:

805 Squadron		12 aircraft	
806	"	12	"
813	"	10	"
815	"	12	"
819	"	12	"
824	"	10	"

Additional TSR Squadron: 12 aircraft
Eagle's fighter flight: 9 aircraft. . . .

132. *Operation MC5: Bombardment of Bardia, 3 January 1941*

(6 March 1941)

Narrative of the C-in-C

Forces A and B left Alexandria on 2 January and proceeded . . . without incident.

2. From 0530 onwards gun flashes were constantly observed from the direction of Bardia as the bombardment by field artillery and aircraft commenced.
3. At 0718 *Warspite* and *Valiant* catapulted spotting aircraft. . . . arrangements had been made for a Swordfish operating from shore to spot for *Barham*.
4. By 0730 the coast at Bardia was clearly visible and artillery fire could be seen over a wide arc round the defended perimeter. *Terror* and the gunboats were bombarding the Northern sector and had raised a thin layer of dust and cloud over that area.
7. Fire was opened at 0810 and 15-in armaments engaged targets selected by their spotting aircraft. *Warspite*'s secondary armament at first found an excellent target in an encampment and MT on the cliff top near Habs-el-Harram, but otherwise once 15-in fire had started the dense dust pall hanging over the area and blowing to seaward was so thick that secondary armament and destroyer gunfire

had to be confined to counter battery fire and blind ladders up the Wadi Raheb.

8. The coast defence battery on Bardia South cliff (two twin 120 mm) opened fire at 0818 with fair accuracy and was engaged by secondary armaments until temporarily silenced in a cloud of dust.

9. At 0830 the course of the fleet was reversed, ...

11. At 0830 the bombarding force had steadied on course 150°, and fire was opened on the former 15-in target areas. The Bardia battery was resolutely fought and fired at intervals whenever the dust round it cleared away. Finally, at 0900 after the bombardment had ceased and the fleet turned away on a course of 100°, the battery continued to fire with 2 guns at 19,000 yards, and from being merely a nuisance became uncomfortably accurate, both *Warspite* and *Barham* being hit by splinters. *Warspite* and *Valiant* therefore fired a few salvos with their after turrets.

12. Forces A and B then returned to Alexandria without incident. Fighter patrols were provided by *Illustrious*.

C-in-C's Remarks on Points of Interest

Effect of the Bombardment

6. There is no doubt whatever of the paralysing moral effect of a heavy bombardment of this nature. ... The GOC, 13th Corps, in a personal letter, states that 'it produced the greatest confusion and was most effective in every way'.

7. The effect was that the enemy went to ground and took no further military action on that day.

15-in Targets

9. It is known from observers' reports at the time that *Warspite* had hit an MT column with 3 consecutive salvos and set many on fire, and that salvos from *Barham* and *Valiant* had fallen consistently among groups of dispersed MT.

10. NLO, W Desert, reports the 2 most effective rounds as follows:

> One 15-in shell had landed in a large pile of stores in the middle of the MT section. Twelve lorries had been destroyed by fragments of metal or pieces of rock. Another shell had landed in the middle of an enemy AA battery with the guns arranged in the form of a diamond. All guns were put out of action and the control gear wrecked.

11. The MT targets in areas B and C were generally well dispersed and no shot got more than 2 lorries. *Valiant* damaged an aircraft in which it is reported that a General was proposing to escape.

Wadi Raheb

12. Coast defence, searchlight and defensive positions near the mouth of the wadi were damaged and some MT near the head and upper slopes of the wadi, but in general the main effect of the secondary and destroyers' bombardment was to drive all personnel underground, where in many cases they remained until captured next day.

133. *War Diary, January 1941 (cont.)*

5 January

Western Desert

Owing to the new commitments of transport and supply for the Army and Air Force in the Western Desert, as well as active operations along the coast, an Inshore Squadron was formed. Captain H. Hickling, of *Glasgow*, was appointed SNO, Inshore Squadron....[142]

3. Owing to our heavy commitments, Greek destroyers were asked for to escort Convoy AS10 from Piraeus to Alexandria and Port Said, leaving on 8 January.

134. *To Pound*

5 January 1941

A. *Hyperion* was definitely a mine, moored I think, and we have now issued orders that all ships are to steer a steady course passing through the Narrows.[143]

Unfortunately *Malaya* never informed me that she had left *Ilex* with *Hyperion* and, thinking that it would be just on daylight before any help reached her, I ordered her to be sunk if she couldn't steam. Had I known there was some 4 to 5 hours' darkness I possibly would have ordered her to be towed.

---

[142]Capt (later RA) H. Hickling: Capt 1935; *Glasgow* 1940; SNO, Inshore Sqdn Jan. 1941; duty with Controller, July 1942; Misc Weapon Dev Dept Sept. 1943; Trng Est, *Raleigh*, Torpoint Sept. 1944; RA Jan. 1945; *Lanka* (Colombo) 1945.

[143]*Hyperion* t by It s/m *Serpente*.

Actually it made no difference. *Ilex* took her in tow but the tow parted. Not surprising as her stern was alive from the engine room aft and, I expect, made the towing very heavy.

B.   The Army continue to do well in the Western Desert. Today they have practically all Bardia and some 20,000 prisoners. I had the three battleships on the coast bombarding on Friday with *Illustrious*'s fighters over us. Our job was to prevent the big accumulation of enemy forces, tanks, etc., in the northern third of the area taking the Australians in the flank while they were attacking. It looks rather as though the timing was perfect as both our spotters and the RAF prevented them massing and moving off in that direction.... We never saw an enemy aircraft the whole time – they are very frightened of the Fulmars – but when we had left *Terror* was very heavily bombed.

Terror and the two small gunboats have done splendid work, the latter close inshore using everything they have got. The former has had goodness knows how many torpedoes fired at her by torpedo-bombers but so far without result. Her guns are worn nearly to the limit of safety, but she can still bowl lobs.

The Army intend when they have mopped up Bardia to move on Tobruk, which they do not think should be so hard a nut to crack. It will take them about three weeks to accumulate stores, ammunition, etc. It has all got to be done by sea. In fact it has, up to date, been done practically altogether by sea, so you can imagine it is no small commitment.

It is at the moment a full time job for one division of destroyers to guard the line of supply and when they get to Tobruk I shall have to augment this force.

C.   I am sorry to keep on harping about the shortage of destroyers. I know well that every one possible is needed at home but what I am trying to convey is that we can't have it both ways. I am being asked to run convoys through the Sicilian Narrows east and to pass back the empty MT ships. I also want to help the Greeks and try to get a grip on the Italian communications with Tripoli and Benghazi. Convoys to Malta and Greece are always with us, also local escorts for troop ships and oilers. It simply can't be done with the present number of destroyers – and provide a screen for the heavy ships. The position is of course accentuated by having six out of action and about the same number waiting to take their places in the dockyard when they rejoin.

D.   You ask me if I was surprised at the Board of Inquiry on Force H's action south of Sardinia.

You will wish me to speak outright quite frankly and say that I was very sorry for that decision and did not agree with it, more especially as the Board was set up even before Force H had returned to harbour.

The action was an unsatisfactory one. When one is burdened with a convoy one's hands are always tied to a certain extent. Of course the FAA got no hits . . . and it is obvious that all the enemy ships had the legs of Force H.[144]

It is one of our disappointments about the FAA that the torpedo-bombers can't hit a fast-moving target. . . .

E. I see that the Coastal Command have now been put under the Admiralty . . . We have already to a great extent the operational control of all reconnaissance aircraft and (I hope you won't tell the CAS this) we also have lately secured what amounts to the operational control of the Wellington bombers working from Malta. Of course the AOC-in-C, Middle East, can override us, but I find him fairly easy to deal with and I doubt that there is much to be gained by making a change. . . .

---

[144]See M.A. Simpson, *The Papers of Admiral of the Fleet Sir James Somerville* (Scolar Press for Navy Records Society, Aldershot: 1955), pp. 64–8, 189–218.

PART III

THE EFFECTS OF GERMAN INTERVENTION, JANUARY TO MAY 1941

It is a commonplace that German intervention was the result of Italian failure; certainly Italy's lacklustre performance exasperated the German high command but, even if Mussolini had turned out to be a second Caesar, the Germans would have intervened. They, too, had ambitions in the Balkans and would not have countenanced a rampant Italy. Mussolini's well-grounded fear of German hegemony may have prompted his ill-judged attack on Greece in October 1940, a campaign too far for the creaking Italian war machine, which virtually condemned his African adventures to rapid failure. Whatever the reasons, Rommel's Afrika Korps began to deploy in the Western Desert in February 1941 and, taking advantage of the diversion of British strength to Greece, together with Rommel's own bold and novel tactics, it swept the British back to Egypt in double-quick time. Only the besieged port of Tobruk was left in 8th Army hands; it may have been a thorn in Rommel's side but it was a spear in that of Cunningham as he haemorrhaged ships in keeping it supplied.

Cunningham experienced the advent of the Germans in dramatic form – the crippling of *Illustrious* by the dive bombers of Fliegerkorps X, an air group with successful anti-shipping experience in Norway. British intelligence noted its deployment in Italy in the late autumn of 1940 and by the end of the year it had grown to 150 dive bombers and 25 long-range fighters. Its mission was to deny the fleet its newly won freedom of action. Not surprisingly, *Illustrious* was its primary target and it practised attacks against a dummy. On 10 January, as the fleet was covering the EXCESS convoy west of Malta, two wave-skimming Italian torpedo bombers drew the patrolling Fulmars down to sea level, thus affording over 40 Stukas an unhindered dive on the carrier. Despite a formidable barrage, these expert airmen pressed home a precision attack, scoring seven hits and four near misses.[1] *Illustrious*, though out of action, was saved by the determination of her captain and ship's company

---

[1] Cdr C. Lamb, in *War in a Stringbag* (London, 1977), pp. 121–2, states that Lyster and Boyd, knowing *Illustrious* would be attacked by Stukas on 10 Jan., signalled to Cunningham saying there was no need for her to be in range, especially as only 6 fighters were serviceable. Cunningham replied that morale of fleet was always high when *Illustrious* was in sight and could not answer for consequences when she was not. Confirmed in VAdm Sir ML Power, *Autobiography*, pp. 23–4, Power Papers, Churchill Archives Centre, Cambridge.

and by her robust construction (not, it seems, by her armoured deck). Following a nightmare voyage to Malta and further attacks en route and in harbour, she was able to dash to Alexandria at the end of the month and thence to the United States for year-long repairs. *Warspite,* turning to avoid a torpedo, was narrowly missed by a bomb which hit the water abreast the bridge but failed to explode. Further evidence of the awesome power of the Luftwaffe was provided on the following day when *Gloucester* and *Southampton*, proceeding in company but beyond fleet support, were heavily attacked, *Gloucester* suffering damage and *Southampton* having to be sunk.[2] Surprised out of the sun by another well-executed attack, they were probably victims of weariness and loss of concentration; more crucially, they lacked radar. The incident demonstrated the vulnerability to dive bombing of detached units. Cunningham had no doubt as to what the arrival of the Luftwaffe presaged: 'it is a potent new factor in Mediterranean war and will undoubtedly deny us that free access to the waters immediately surrounding Malta and Sicily which we have previously enjoyed, until our own air forces have been built up to a scale adequate to meet it' [135]. He explored variations on the AA barrage, enhanced armament and fitted more ships with radar but the only effective defence was fighters and he was fortunate to receive *Formidable* before the next major fleet operation [135–8, 140–45, 147].[3]

The Luftwaffe quickly made itself felt throughout the central and eastern Mediterranean. Malta came in for crippling attacks and the little ships on the Tobruk run suffered severe losses, while mines were sown in the Canal and Libyan harbours under British occupation. No activity or resource of British sea power escaped serious damage and Cunningham was gravely concerned as to whether Malta could survive, the Canal be reopened, the support of the Army in Libya maintained, and fleet operations conducted before *Formidable* joined the fleet. He must have been thankful that he did not have to deal also with a clutch of German U-boats (they arrived only in the autumn) [136, 138, 140, 142–4, 146, 148, 150–57, 160–61].

Formidable's arrival was delayed until March. In the interval, *Eagle*, plagued by defects, badly in need of a refit and beset by unfavourable weather for flying, strove to take *Illustrious*'s place. However, disembarked FAA TSR squadrons proved to be

---

[2]*Gloucester*: 1939, (s Ger a/c, off Crete, 22 May 1941), *Southampton* :1937, (s Ger a/c off Malta, 11 Jan 1941), 9,100–9,400t, 12×6in, 8×4in, 6×21in tt, 32k.
[3]*Formidable*: 1940, 23,000t, 16×4.5in, 36 (later 54) a/c, 31k.

extremely accurate night bombers in the Western Desert, supported later by a fleet fighter wing, while 830 Squadron, operating from Malta, achieved many successes against Italian convoys and Tripoli [168, 172–3, 197–8, 204]. Cunningham recognised that future operations in face of the Luftwaffe would depend even more heavily on RAF support but Longmore's forces were already stretched to the point that, faced with requests from the Navy for air cover for convoys and from the Army for ground attack support, he was compelled to give the land advance priority. The withdrawal of squadrons in March for the campaign in Greece further reduced the skimpy protection for the Inshore Squadron. Attrition was high – 200 aircraft being lost in Greece alone. There were still major difficulties in meeting Cunningham's long-range reconnaissance requirements due to shortages of suitable aircraft and the insecurity of their bases. Cunningham, anxious to defend his bases and the Canal from the increasing weight of air attacks, and to protect the Inshore Squadron, called incessantly for more fighters, reacting sharply to any hint that the ferrying of Hurricanes to Takoradi or, via Force H, to Malta was about to be terminated, telling Pound that 'If HMG decide they must ensure we hold the Mediterranean then adequate air forces must be sent'. His repeated demands led to sharp clashes with Pound and Churchill, who claimed that 'extreme exertions' were being made [145, 150–1, 153–5, 157–60]. The almost total lack of air cover during the Greek and Cretan operations, in which half the fleet was lost or crippled, coupled with the relief of the sympathetic Longmore, led Cunningham to demand a Middle Eastern version of Coastal Command. This would involve the total dedication of reconnaissance, fighter and anti-shipping squadrons to maritime duties, all under Cunningham's operational control. Longmore's successor, Tedder, whose relationship with Cunningham was somewhat cool and distant, while striving to meet naval requests, refused to commit scarce resources inflexibly to maritime operations [196–7, 217, 226–7, 237–51],[4]

Air defence was the most important aspect of base security but the situation, while improving, was still unsatisfactory everywhere.

---

[4]Air Marshal (later Marshal of the RAF Lord) Arthur Tedder (1890–1967): Col Service 1914; RFC, France; cmd 70 Sq 1917–18; S/Ldr 1919; training splist; IDC; Staff Coll 1929–31; G/Capt 1931; Cdt, Air Armt Sch; Dir Training 1934–36; AOC, Far E 1936–38; AVM 1937; Dir-Gen, R & D 1938; Dep AOC-in-C, ME 1940; AOC-in-C June 1941; AM 1941; ACM & VCAS 1942; C-in-C, Med Air Cmd 1943; Dep Sup Cdr, OVERLORD; Marshal of RAF 1945; CAS & baron 1946; ret 1949. See his *With Prejudice* (London, 1966). See biography (forthcoming) by V. Orange.

For Cunningham as for Nelson, Malta was always on his mind. The steady increase in fighter and AA defences, largely at his instigation, led to a falling off in Italian air attacks and enabled Malta to take the offensive against Italian bases and convoys. Heavy bombers, torpedo planes, ASV and flare dropping aircraft were sent to the island, along with a steady stream of fighters. The 10th Submarine Flotilla, composed of the new small 'U' class, ideal for restricted waters, returned and, after initial defects had been corrected and they had gained experience, they and the air forces, assisted by Ultra decrypts revealing convoy details, began to take a steady if not yet crippling toll of Libyan convoys.[5] Success, however, invoked retaliation and the Luftwaffe joined the Italians in subjecting Malta to a redoubled onslaught. The dockyard sustained severe damage and absenteeism was rife. The harbour was mined so regularly that on occasion sweepers were unable to keep it clear. As Cunningham was prevented by other commitments and the lack of a carrier from running in convoys and extracting trapped merchantmen, fuel and other vital stocks fell to danger point. Submarines from Alexandria had to be used to carry essential supplies. The enemy then focused on airfields, destroying many aircraft. There were several raids daily and the defences were frequently overwhelmed; fighter strength dropped to less than a squadron. By early March Cunningham was telling Pound 'I am really seriously concerned about Malta', realising that, if it was incapable of defending itself, it could neither undertake vital reconnaissance nor protect convoys or shipping in harbour. However, fighter reinforcements, dispersal of aircraft, shelters and the excavation of caves for offices and workshops countered enemy attacks, while the dockyard manifested miraculous powers of recovery. By April, the island's improved security and the vital need to disrupt Rommel's supply line persuaded Cunningham to form a high-speed striking force of four powerful destroyers. They achieved a notable early success, destroying a whole convoy in a spirited night action but again retaliation was swift and the harbour was increasingly bombed and mined. Though its great offensive potential was recognised by both sides, Malta still absorbed considerable British resources and the enemy was always able to deploy at once superior strength to nullify any increase in its forces [136–8, 142, 145–6, 148, 152–3, 156–60, 174–5, 188–9, 191–3, 196–202, 205, 210, 213–14, 236–7].

---

[5]J. Wingate, *The Fighting Tenth: The Tenth Submarine Flotilla and the Siege of Malta* (London, 1991).

At Alexandria there had been improvements in fighter and balloon defences [144]. A greater worry was Suda Bay, its inadequate defences, exposed by the torpedoing of *Glasgow,* underlined by the disabling of *York* at the time of Matapan [142, 152, 161, 163, 204, 214].[6] The newly acquired Libyan ports – Sollum, Benghazi and Tobruk – lacked AA and fighter defences and required continuous minesweeping [144, 152, 194]. Mining was a major problem everywhere. The Italians tried to close the Sicilian Narrows with a mine barrier across to the African shore and mined Valetta and Alexandria, leaving the Canal to the Luftwaffe. Contact, acoustic and magnetic mines were laid at widely varying depths. Ships were either trapped in harbours or in the Canal or left waiting to enter. Countermeasures were stretched to breaking point. Minesweepers and specialised equipment were in desperately short supply and Cunningham was forced to switch sweepers from one port to another and improvise additional sweepers from destroyers and corvettes. Sweepers, the most precious vessels on the station, were themselves victims of mining and bombing. The Canal was virtually indefensible and was closed more than it was open. Mining took place at night and, though Cunningham exhorted the other services to greater efforts, AA guns and fighters were scarce. Specialised diving and sweeping gear was also in short supply. In the early part of 1941 nothing harassed him more than mining, which seriously handicapped the movements of his forces [135–7, 142, 144, 146–8, 150–4, 156, 212–14, 217].[7]

British minelaying was feeble by comparison, though the fast minelayer *Abdiel* and the submarine *Rorqual* laid several small fields, which enjoyed modest success.[8] The submarine effort in the first half of 1941 was encouraging. The accent was now on mercantile targets and 38 ships of 130,000 tons were sunk for the loss of three boats and the rapid decline in tanker tonnage alarmed the enemy. However, 500,000 tons of supplies reached Libya, together with 82,000 men.[9] Nevertheless, one-third of the Italian merchant fleet was sunk in the first year of the war and Cunningham believed that the enemy could not long withstand this rate of loss. Apart from the 'U' class boats at Malta, there was a flotilla of 'T' boats at

---

[6]*Glasgow* was torpedoed in Dec. 1940; *York* over 3 months later; clearly net defences had not been improved.
[7]Cunningham to Adm Sir Howard Kelly, Istanbul, 5 March 1941, KEL 43, *Kelly Papers*, NMM.
[8]*Abdiel*: 1940, 4,000t, 6×4.7in, 160 mines, 40k; mined Taranto, 9 Sept. 1943.
[9]VA Sir A. Hezlet, *The Submarine and Sea Power* (London, 1967), pp. 139–41.

Alexandria and a handful of older ones. 'Aces' began to appear – Linton in *Turbulent,* Miers in *Torbay* and Wanklyn in *Upholder*; all became VCs.[10] Cunningham, always keen to deploy more submarines, was particularly appreciative of his submariners and was sensitive to the pressures and dangers to which they were subject [136, 142, 144, 152, 168, 174–5, 204, 212, 219, 236–7, 239].

Convoy requirements became more demanding in this period, as British troops were sent to Greece and Crete, Malta's needs grew and the military base in the Nile delta was built up. Cunningham had either to mount fleet operations to cover important convoys or keep his capital ships in harbour because his destroyer screen was escorting Aegean convoys. Following EXCESS in January, during which the Luftwaffe introduced itself, the next major trans-Mediterranean convoy was TIGER in May. Fortunately, heavy cloud and stupendous efforts by carrier fighters limited enemy attacks. As usual, Cunningham directed several subordinate operations while TIGER was in progress – minelaying off Lampedusa, two bombardments of Benghazi and convoys to Malta and Suda Bay [210, 212–14, 217].

The convoys to Piraeus and Suda Bay had run virtually undisturbed for several months, much to the Germans' chagrin. Believing that Cunningham had only *Valiant* available and probably unaware that *Formidable* had now joined the fleet, they persuaded the Italians to mount an attack on these convoys with their fleet, confident the British would be unable effectively to defend them. The Italian fleet would not have ventured so far east otherwise and would have been unwilling to expend scarce fuel on anything other than a 'racing certainty'. The Italian and German air forces promised, somewhat vaguely, effective reconnaissance and fighter cover.

Unfortunately for the enemy, Cunningham was privy to the Italian plan, thanks to Ultra decrypts. Suspecting that the LUSTRE convoys were the enemy's target, craftily he held out the bait for as long as he dared and then, on the eve of the Italian operation, made a series of rapid, concise signals, for the most part precise but giving scope for independent action. As his Flag Lieutenant at the time,

---

[10]Cdr J. W. Linton: Lt-Cdr 1936; *Pandora* 1940; *Turbulent* 1941; Cdr Dec. 1941; lost in Med March 1943; posthumous VC.

Cdr (later VA) A. C. C. Miers: Lt-Cdr 1938; SO2 (O), Home F 1939; *Torbay*, Med, Nov. 1940; Cdr Nov. 1941; VC Mar. 1942; BAD Nov. 1942; Australia 1943; *Maidstone* 1944. See P. Chapman, *Submarine Torbay* (London, 1989).

Lt-Cdr M. D. Wanklyn: Lt 1933; 1st Lt *Otway* 1939; *H31* i/c May 1940; *Upholder* Aug. 1940; Lt-Cdr Jan. 1941; VC May 1941; lost off Tripoli Apr 1942.

Captain Hugh Lee, has observed, Cunningham possessed a first-rate operational mind.[11] Convoys were suspended or turned back and submarines and aircraft deployed to report the approach of the Italian fleet. A flying boat was ordered to reveal itself to the Italians so as to protect the true source of Cunningham's information.

The fleet left Alexandria after dark on 27 March, following an elaborate charade in which enemy agents were duped into thinking that it would remain in harbour.[12] Pridham-Wippell's cruisers were already at sea and Cunningham intended to rendezvous with them south of Crete on the morning of 28 March and thus cross the enemy's line of advance. Cunningham's brilliant Staff Officer Operations, Commander Manley Power, proposed the movements and arranged the timing with great skill. For once, Axis reconnaissance failed to detect the fleet's movements, though RAF reconnaissance reported the enemy fleet, a report scoffed at initially by Cunningham, who thought it was a mis-identification of his own forces. However, at about 0830 Pridham-Wippell, almost 100 miles ahead of the fleet, encountered three Italian heavy cruisers and retired on the battle squadron, hoping to draw the enemy after him. This decision has been criticised on the grounds that the British cruisers were more numerous and had more guns, better protection and fire control. Moreover, by turning away from the enemy, it has been argued that Pridham-Wippell might have shaken morale and could well have advertised the battle fleet's presence. On the other hand, he knew that the enemy outranged him and could outrun him. Following an inconclusive long-range engagement, the Italians turned away to the west; after a time Pridham-Wippell followed them. Any quibble about his caution quickly became academic when shortly before 1100, his squadron came under accurate long-range fire from the *Vittorio Veneto*. About to be sandwiched between two enemy forces, with a third cruiser squadron bearing down from the north, Pridham-Wippell was in an uncomfortable position. Making smoke, he turned once again towards Cunningham. The C-in-C was now faced with a difficult decision. He had intended to launch *Formidable*'s torpedo bombers at close range, so that the battleships could administer the *coup de grace* to a crippled enemy. Since Pridham-Wippell was now 'in serious danger', he was compelled to order an immediate torpedo strike. The wind having veered to the

[11] Capt Hugh Lee, conversation with editor, 29 Nov. 1996.
[12] This consisted of the C-in-C going ashore with a suitcase, conversing on golf course within earshot of Japanese consul, hidden in bushes, and setting up a non-existent dinner party.

north west, *Formidable* was able to operate her aircraft virtually from her position in the line, thus maintaining the fleet's speed of advance; this, remarked Captain Lee, 'was almost a miracle'.[13] While scoring no hits, it forced the Italians to turn away. Cunningham realised that he was now unlikely to bring the Italian fleet to action. Nevertheless, had *Formidable*'s striking force been held back, it might have been the Italians who went home with the scalps of several cruisers.

Further air searches and attacks by the FAA and RAF were launched, the last at dusk. The second strike scored a hit on the *Vittorio Veneto*, reducing her speed drastically, while the third air attack immobilised the heavy cruiser *Pola*.[14] The battleship was still 30 miles ahead of Cunningham and his only hope was that a destroyer flotilla could slow her down sufficiently for the battle squadron to complete her destruction. Any such actions would take place in the dark, with all the dangers of confusion, firing at one's own ships, and hostile torpedo attacks. Confident that his fleet could perform successfully at night and unwilling to let the enemy off the hook, Cunningham resolved to accept the risks of a night action. If he delayed till daylight, the enemy would be under fighter cover and the Stukas would be waiting for the British fleet.

In the event, it proved impossible to bring the *Vittorio Veneto* to action, in part due to imprecise signals and unfortunate decisions in the British forces. Nevertheless, Cunningham's bold pursuit, the fleet's night fighting skills, aided by radar and the Fleet Air Arm's gift of a crippled enemy, coupled with Italian innocence abroad in the dark, brought him a handsome reward. The Italian C-in-C, Admiral Iachino, on learning of the disablement of *Pola*, ordered two of her sisters, accompanied by four destroyers, to close her and decide whether to save her or sink her.[15] Iachino, 'badly let down by his air reconnaissance', was still unaware of the presence of the British fleet. The story of how the British heavy ships came upon the *Zara* and *Fiume*, guns trained fore and aft, and blew them out of the water, and of the later sinking by the destroyers of the helpless *Pola*, together with two Italian destroyers, is a familiar one.

---

[13]M. A. Bragadin, *The Italian Navy in World War II* (Annapolis, Md, 1957), pp. 88–100; R. Seth, *Two Fleets Surprised: The Story of the Battle of Cape Matapan* (London, 1960); Adm A. Iachino, 'Gaudo and Matapan' (1946), trans. from Italian, in BM Add Mss 52584, *Cunningham Papers*, BL; S. W. C. Pack, *The Battle of Matapan* (London, 1961); M. Stephen (ed. E. J. Grove), *Sea Battles in Close Up: World War II* (Shepperton, 1988), pp. 50–67.

[14]*Pola* (1932), *Zara, Fiume* (1931): 11,500t+, 8×8in, 12×3.9in, 32k+.

[15]*Zara* and *Fiume*. *Alfieri, Carducci* also sunk: 1937, 1700t, 4×4.7in, 6×21in tt, 39k.

THE EFFECTS OF GERMAN INTERVENTION, 1941   239

Cunningham himself described it as 'more like murder than anything else'.[16]

Matapan ended happily after all but there were disquieting features for the British and it could have finished in disaster. Though British reconnaissance was more thorough and successful than that of the Axis, it was often inaccurate and confusing and its shortcomings helped to lead the cruisers into a trap. The torpedo hit on the *Vittorio Veneto* was the first on a major warship at speed but it was achieved only by a sacrificial point-blank attack. The inevitable confusion of night engagements, together with an unusually loosely worded signal from the C-in-C and a recovery of speed by the Italian battleship, allowed her to escape. The most interesting comment came from DNAD, who observed that 'the chief lesson . . . is that one aircraft carrier is insufficient for a main fleet operation.'[17] Had the carrier strike force numbered 20 or 30 planes, the *Vittorio Veneto* might not have escaped. Once she had been hit, the Italians had no option but to retire. Iachino, however, should have been more alert to the possible proximity of British battleships, especially as he knew *Formidable* was within striking distance. He should have appreciated that she would not be at sea without battlefleet support. Matapan confirmed the moral superiority of Cunningham's fleet and ensured that there would be no surface interference with operations off Greece and Crete [165].

British successes against Axis convoys to Libya, though increasing in 1941, were still far short of causing serious losses, the Italians often evading British reconnaissance and striking forces by evasive routing and night passages. The arrival of Rommel made more urgent the need to halt this traffic, especially after his whirlwind advance in the spring. By early April panic was beginning to seize London. Since almost all enemy shipping went to Tripoli, it was suggested that the harbour be rendered unusable and various proposals were put to Cunningham. Recognising the imperative need to stop Rommel far from the Egyptian frontier, he was prepared to consider some of them. He felt a fleet bombardment was too risky in the face of the Stukas and, in any case, believed the best means of closing the harbour was by long-range heavy bombing raids [174–82]. By the middle of April, Churchill and the Admiralty were becoming desperate and determined on the sacrifice of *Barham* and an old

---

[16]Cunningham, in Seth, *Two Fleets Surprised*, p. xxi; Cunningham, address at Foyle's literary luncheon, 28 March 1951, BM Add Mss 52582, *Cunningham Papers*, BL.
[17]DNAD (Capt A. R. M. Bridge, formerly of *Eagle*), 10 March 1942, ADM 199/781.

cruiser in a death-or-glory blocking operation. Cunningham expressed 'amazement at the ill-advised and reckless irresponsibility of those who ordered the bombardment or its alternative' but replied in more measured terms.[18] He considered the operation impracticable but even if it were successful, it could not close the port completely and it would sacrifice needlessly not only a valuable capital ship but also the lives of perhaps 1,000 officers and men. In the face of Cunningham's reasoned (and reasonable) objections and his description of the fleet's many other urgent commitments, Pound agreed to a compromise, a fleet bombardment of Tripoli. Though less objectionable than the blocking proposal, it was still distasteful to Cunningham [184–91]. Before it took place, there arrived a bizarre example of Churchillian long-distance strategy; Cunningham referred to it as the Prime Minister's 'hot air directive'. It was insulting, childish and wildly unrealistic in its demands and expectations [193].[19]

The bombardment of Tripoli took place on 21 April and, mercifully, no casualties were incurred by the fleet, owing to the occupation elsewhere of the Luftwaffe and poor visibility which shielded the British force. The damage caused to the harbour was modest and not commensurate with the risks run by the fleet [203]. Cunningham ascribed the fleet's untroubled passage to 'good luck and the favour of Providence only' though Churchill, characteristically, was scornful of what he clearly regarded as faintheartedness on Cunningham's part [199].[20] The two continued to cross swords over air power in the Mediterranean. Cunningham expressed bluntly home truths about the vital need for an immediate and substantial increase in RAF strength in the Mediterranean. His experiences had led him to a truly interdependent strategy in which the success of one arm rested on the effective support of the others. In the first six months of 1941, the relative weakness of the RAF, despite the careful husbanding of their meagre forces by Longmore and Tedder and the gallantry of their men, was to cost the Navy dear [196, 198, 202].

Cunningham had persuaded the Army of the Navy's ability to assist it on the seaward flank and, once the British counter-attack began in December 1940, the lack of land communications placed

[18]Cunningham to Capt G. R. G. Allen, 7 Oct. 1949, BM Add Mss 52575, *Cunningham Papers*, BL.

[19]Cunningham, note, n.d., p. 92, BM Add Mss 52581A, *Cunningham Papers*, BL.

[20] Cunningham to Capt G. R. G. Allen, 7 Oct. 1949, BM Add Mss 52575, *Cunningham Papers*, BL.

the burden of supply on the Navy. This function and that of bombardment was formalised at the beginning of 1941 with the formation of the Inshore Squadron, while the FAA also provided invaluable air support [134, 136–8]. The Army's success was something of a mixed blessing for Cunningham for, while it made Alexandria more secure and provided the RAF with forward airstrips, it also extended the Navy's commitments in distance and scale [142]. Harbours required to be cleared, managed and swept under constant air attack and with scant AA or fighter protection, yet miracles were achieved in making them quickly available [138–9, 142–4, 146–8]. Coasting craft were scarce and destroyers and other light craft were overworked but sustained the Army's advance [137–9]. Cunningham, an early visitor to Tobruk, congratulated the Inshore Squadron and shore parties on their superhuman efforts [146]. Nevertheless, as he confessed to Pound, 'We have been stretched to the limit and past it in keeping them supplied ... our long line of supply was very open to attack all the time' [147].

The situation worsened rapidly early in 1941. British troops and aircraft were withdrawn for service in Greece. Rommel and the Afrika Korps, recently arrived, went on to the offensive, supported by the Luftwaffe, and the whole of Cyrenaica was lost. Only Tobruk remained in British hands, Churchill ordering it to be held so as to absorb enemy forces in a wearing siege. Cunningham, in what he came to feel was a rash decision, committed the Navy to supplying Tobruk, though he felt that the commitment was likely to be no more than one of a month or two; it lasted until November, seven months. It was a heroic tale, the voyages, known as the 'beef and spud run', being finely judged to afford maximum air or night cover.[21] Loading and unloading were accomplished within an hour, at night in a harbour without lights, littered with wrecks and subjected to regular mining but irregular minesweeping. Nevertheless, despite these precautions and skilful seamanship, 27 naval vessels were lost and 27 damaged, in addition to numerous mercantile casualties. Cunningham, disturbed at these losses, continued to praise and encourage his overstretched ships' companies. Though the cost to the Royal and Merchant Navies and their allies was high in life and limb, strain and matériel, Tobruk was maintained, to become the fulcrum of the next British advance in November 1941 [148, 150, 152, 154, 156, 168–9, 171–3, 204–5, 212–14, 236, 238, 242].

---

[21]Cdr H. Hodgkinson, *Before the Tide Turned: The Mediterranean Experiences of a British Destroyer Officer in 1941* (London, 1944), pp. 176–96.

The use of sea power for one of its traditional functions, amphibious operations, was often considered but carried out on only a small scale and generally with indifferent results. The first proposal was a typical example of Churchill's simplistic approach to strategy and his ignorance of the complexities of modern warfare. The instigator of the scheme was one of the Prime Minister's Great War heroes, Admiral of the Fleet Sir Roger Keyes, whom Churchill had made Director of Combined Operations. Operation WORKSHOP was designed to capture the Italian island of Pantelleria, lying west of Malta and close to the North African coast. Though it possessed a good airfield equipped with underground hangars, it was of little military significance. It might have been taken cheaply but, as Cunningham pointed out, the problem lay in supplying it across hundreds of miles of hostile sea, for which forces, already overstretched in supporting Malta, Greece and the advance into Libya, could not be found. Much to Cunningham's relief, events elsewhere forced the abandonment of WORKSHOP [121–6]. Cunningham suggested that the commandos would be employed far better on operation MANDIBLES, a plan for the seizure of some of the Italian Dodecanese islands. MANDIBLES was on the verge of being executed on a number of occasions but again other events, such as the campaigns in Greece and Crete, prevented it. The taking of Dodecanese islands would have led to British domination of the Aegean, secured communications to the Black Sea and eliminated much of the aerial threat to the fleet, its bases and the Canal [137, 143, 152]. It would have been impossible to take and hold all of the scattered islands, especially Rhodes, but an attempt was made to seize Kastelorizo, a tiny island close to Turkey but well placed for air attacks on Rhodes, Leros and other larger islands. It was occupied by commandos in February but lost almost immediately because of inept leadership, insufficient planning, ineffective inter-service co-operation, lack of air cover, inadequate armament, and an unexpectedly vigorous counter-attack by the Italians. As Cunningham told Pound, 'The taking and abandonment of Kastelorizo was a rotten business and reflected little credit on anyone' [152, 156].[22]

The decision to send an expeditionary force to mainland Greece, together with several RAF squadrons and one of FAA Swordfish, to meet an anticipated German invasion had been taken in London early in February. Following a flying visit to Athens and Cairo by the Foreign Secretary, Anthony Eden, and the CIGS, Field

---

[22]P. C. Smith and E. Walker, *War in the Aegean* (London, 1974), pp. 17–36.

Marshal Sir John Dill, the Middle East Commanders-in-Chief agreed [149].[23] Cunningham and Longmore did so with reluctance but as the expedition was chiefly a military one, they followed Wavell's lead. After much cogitation, Wavell had concluded that it was necessary to send an army to Greece. In conjunction with the Greeks, who had fought magnificently and successfully against the Italians, the force might just hold the Germans on a defensible line, thus preserving an Allied presence in mainland Europe and encouraging the Yugoslavs and Turks also to resist German pressure and arms. Britain was bound also by a 1939 treaty to go to the aid of Greece and the demands of prestige and her global interests required that she should fulfil her pledges. Her response would be monitored closely in the United States, where the Lend-Lease bill was about to be debated in a potentially hostile Senate. It was (and remains) a controversial decision, an uneasy combination of strategic and diplomatic considerations. It seems now incredible that experienced military leaders believed it possible to stop the panzer and Luftwaffe juggernaut and that to do so they were prepared to abandon the Western Desert Force's triumphal march across Cyrenaica.[24]

Cunningham never felt comfortable about the decision. The numerous convoys would pass close to enemy bases and could be given little or no air cover [154–5]. He expressed his concern to Pound: 'I hope it will turn out that our policy of helping Greece is the right one. To me it is absolutely right but I much doubt if our resources, particularly naval and air, are equal to the strain' [156]. In fact the operation was highly successful; between 4 March and 24 April, 58,000 troops, thousands of vehicles and other supplies were transported safely to Greece. Though ships were lost, there were no troop casualties [155–6, 167–8, 170, 172]. Within two weeks of the beginning of the German offensive on 6 April, however, operation DEMON, the withdrawal of Allied forces, began. The Germans

---

[23]R. A. Eden (later Earl of Avon) (1897–1977): Oxford 1st, Oriental Langs; Brig Maj, WW1; Con MP, Warwick & Leamington, 1923–57; M for League Affairs, then For Sec, 1935–38; SSt Doms 1939; Sec War May 1940; For Sec Dec 1940–45, 1951–55; PM 1955–57.

FM Sir John Dill (1881–1944): Brig Gen, 1918; I Corps, BEF, 1939–40; VCIGS, April 1940; CIGS May 1940–Dec. 1941; Head, British Jt Staff Mission, Washington, Dec. 1941–Nov. 1944; member CCS.

[24]H. E. Raugh, Jr, in *Wavell in the Middle East, 1939–1941: A Study in Generalship* (London and New York, 1993) argues (pp. 132–67) that Wavell convinced himself of the military feasibility of the Greek campaign. See also M. van Creveld, 'Prelude to Disaster: The British Decision to Aid Greece, 1940–41', *Journal of Contemporary History*, **9** (1974), pp. 65–92.

began by wrecking the only major port, Piraeus, and continuous bombing and mining claimed ships every day; on 24 April it was reported that 23 had been sunk in two days. Nevertheless, the evacuation, undertaken on moonless nights between 24 April and 1 May over a wide area of the Peloponnese, from shallow, rock-bound harbours and perilous beaches, was unmolested, though communications were poor and loading desperately slow. Early types of landing craft were an invaluable resource. The troops, confident that the Navy would be there, maintained a high standard of discipline. Ships' companies, exhausted and bombed in daylight on passage, struggled determinedly to evacuate the Army, though minus its transport, armour and artillery. The operation ashore was conducted superbly by Rear Admiral Baillie-Grohman, a trusted flag officer retained by Cunningham as a 'trouble shooter' and by the calm and adaptable Pridham-Wippell at sea.[25] The one failure was at Kalamata, where the enemy were in the town and where British organisation and decision-making broke down, much to Cunningham's fury.[26] Nevertheless, the evacuation of 47,000 of the 58,000 troops who had gone to Greece was a proud feat for the Royal Navy, Allied merchantmen and the Greeks [190–1, 193, 195–6, 202, 204, 206, 207–10, 213, 241, 245].

The Greek odyssey was but a prologue to the Navy's greatest trial and tragedy in the Mediterranean, the battle for Crete, which took place three weeks after the final evacuation from Greece. If the Greek expedition was an unavoidable moral and diplomatic commitment, the decision to hold Crete was essentially a military one. The island, situated within a hundred miles of the mainland, lay athwart enemy communications with Greece and the Dodecanese and the British passage to Malta. Suda Bay was a fine harbour and refuelling base. In Allied hands, Crete could provide essential reconnaissance and fighter cover and, in time, air striking forces. In Axis hands, it would endanger not only the convoy route to Malta but also Alexandria and the Canal. However, though the British had

---

[25]RA (later VA) H. T. Baillie-Grohman (1888–1978): ent RN 1903; Lt 1909; Med & China; N Sea & Channel, 1914–18; Persian G & Red Sea 1922–23; Cdr & SO, 1 M/S F 1923–26; Capt 1930; SO, Br N Mission to China 1931–33; Capt (D), 1DF, Med F 1934; *Ramillies* 1939; RA Jan. 1941; FOAM March 1941; Comb Ops, Sept. 1943; FO Harwich; VA Nov. 1943; ret 1946. See unpublished memoirs, 'Flashlights on the Past', 2 vols, GRO 33, *Baillie-Grohman Papers*, NMM.

[26]Cunningham to Kelly, 18 May 1941, KEL 43, *Kelly Papers*, NMM; Cunningham, note, n.d., p. 100, BM Add Mss 52581A, *Cunningham Papers*, BL; Cunningham to Baillie-Grohman, 4 May 1961, 3 & 10 June 1962, XGRO 2, *Baillie-Grohman Papers*, NMM. D. A. Thomas, *Crete 1941: The Battle at Sea* (London, 1972), pp. 92, 102–7.

moved into Crete promptly following the Italian attack on Greece in October 1940, they lacked the forces and equipment to develop the primitive landing fields, establish adequate air defences and secure Suda Bay. The troops were mostly exhausted, ill-equipped evacuees from Greece. An enemy assault probably could be beaten off but it was doubtful whether the island could long be sustained thereafter, given the enemy's overwhelming air superiority and the 400-mile voyage from Alexandria, almost certainly devoid of air cover. Not unnaturally, the Government took some time to decide to fight for Crete but the three Middle Eastern Commanders-in-Chief supported the decision, essentially to deny the island to the enemy [205, 209, 215–17, 245].

The Army commander, General Freyberg, was in possession of the enemy's general plan through Ultra decrypts.[27] He organised the island's defence capably and knew the first attacks would be by airborne and parachute troops but was nervous of a seaborne landing; as a result, he failed to devote sufficient forces to holding Maleme airfield. No British aircraft remained on the island. The ability of the Germans to fly in reinforcements unhindered once they had captured the landing ground enabled them to win a narrow victory.

The Navy's task was to prevent a seaborne landing. Cunningham, directing operations from Alexandria, organised the fleet into a number of small forces to sweep north of the island at night to destroy invasion convoys, but retreating southwards before dawn in order to be outside bombing range in daylight [234]. It was unlikely, however, that the fleet could avoid serious losses. Almost no British air cover was available; *Formidable,* reduced to a handful of fighters after the TIGER convoy, was wisely kept at Alexandria. Fliegerkorps VIII had available 430 bombers and 180 fighters and heavy air attacks on naval forces began shortly after the airborne assault was launched on 20 May. Cunningham knew well the added strain this would place on his already weary ships' companies, issuing one of his most famous signals, exhorting the Navy not to let the Army down and concluding: 'STICK IT OUT' [219]. One enemy convoy, caught at night, suffered considerable damage though many caiques and men escaped (less than 400 were lost). The escorting Italian torpedo boat *Lupo* bravely engaged the British cruisers, suf-

---

[27]Maj-Gen Sir Bernard Freyberg, VC (1889–1963): VC, WW1, Naval Div & Actg Brig-Gen; Brig-Gen 1934; ret 1937; Maj-Gen, NZ Div 1939; Lt-Gen 1942; Gov-Gen, NZ 1946–52. C. MacDonald, *The Lost Battle: Crete 1941* (London, 1993); A. Beevor, *Crete: The Battle and the Resistance* (London, 1991), pp. 156–8; R. Lewin, *Ultra Goes to War: The Secret Story* (London, 1978), p. 158; J. Winton, *Ultra at Sea* (London, 1988), *passim,* on Ultra in Mediterranean.

fering heavy damage and casualties.[28] Another convoy, encountered in daylight, had already turned back. The British ships did not pursue it, a decision which displeased Cunningham [241]. He continued to believe after the war 'that the failure to destroy this convoy was one of the principal factors which led to the loss of Crete', arguing that had German troops ashore learned of its destruction, they might have abandoned the struggle. It is unlikely that the airborne troops would have been aware of early seaborne reinforcements, nor was the morale of élite German units likely to collapse. Cunningham, erroneously believing that 4,000 Germans had drowned in the night action, thought a similar number might have been dispatched. Once again the Italian escort, *Sagittario*, gallantly and ably shepherded the convoy to safety, though an Italian historian claimed that 'It should have been only a few minutes' work for' the British force 'to destroy the whole convoy'.[29] Rear Admiral King, however, considered that to linger in the area would be to invite heavy losses from air attack. He was limited to a speed of 20 knots, his AA ammunition was alarmingly low and his ships scattered. Since the convoy had turned back, he decided to hasten south to reduce the scale of air attacks. This was undoubtedly wise but Cunningham thought he would have been safer in the middle of the convoy, arguing that the Germans would not have risked bombing their own men; that is a matter of debate. The decision was a difficult one but King's assessment was probably correct.[30]

The last eleven days of May became a bitter, relentless contest between the Mediterranean Fleet and the Luftwaffe. Ships were lost or severely damaged every day at the cost of a handful of German aircraft. Substantial numbers of planes were employed on a 'shuttle service' basis and this scale of attack was impossible to counter [227]. British AA armaments were still weak and fire control lacked accuracy. Ammunition was fired away at an alarming rate. Crews were compelled to stand to action stations for long spells. Captains, particularly in the destroyers, rarely left their bridges, calculating precisely when to order sharp alterations of course. Expert manoeuvring saved

---

[28]*Lupo*: 1938, 790t, 3×3.9in, 4×17.7in tt, 34k; s by RN ships, 2 Dec. 1942. Bragadin, *The Italian Navy*, p. 109; MacDonald, *The Lost Battle*, pp. 237–42; Thomas, *Crete 1941*, pp. 138–41.

[29]*Sagittario*: 1936, 790t, 3×3.9in, 4×17.7in tt, 34k. Bragadin, *The Italian Navy*, p. 110. Cunningham to Sec of Admiralty, 22 Jan. 1946, BM Add Mss 52573, *Cunningham Papers*, BL.

[30]Thomas, *Crete 1941*, pp. 145–9; MacDonald, pp. 242–4; S. W. C. Pack, *The Battle for Crete* (Shepperton, 1973), p. 35; E. J. Grove (ed.), *Sea Battles in Close Up: World War II*, vol 2 (Shepperton, 1993), p. 44; Beevor, p. 167; Cunningham to Baillie-Grohman, 4 May 1961, XGRO 2, *Baillie-Grohman Papers*, NMM.

THE EFFECTS OF GERMAN INTERVENTION, 1941   247

many ships but the weight of attack was such that many bombs struck home. It took an average of four bombs to sink a cruiser and two for a destroyer. Some ships sank 'like a stone' – *Juno* and *Kashmir* in two minutes [234].[31] Survivors were machine-gunned in the water (German survivors alleged that troops in the caique convoy were also shot up in the water).[32] Some losses were probably avoidable, notably those of detached ships which, rapidly running out of AA ammunition, were overwhelmed by air attack [227]. The doctrine of concentration under air attack was 'rather vaguely considered to be a good thing' but it does not seem to have been written in fleet battle orders.[33] Shortcomings in communications, understandable in the hectic circumstances with forces widely separated, played a part, too [234]. Cunningham had remained at Alexandria in order to control his scattered forces but it is arguable (as he admitted later) whether he should have been in command at sea, where his experience, speed and sureness of decision, and fortitude might have produced more order, maintained better concentrations and saved several ships [241].

Within three days of the opening of the battle, Cunningham told Pound that 'in coastal area we have to admit defeat'; the threat posed by an unchallenged Luftwaffe was 'too great odds' [220]. At this point, the Government and the Chiefs of Staff seemed prepared to commit the fleet recklessly in a last desperate bid to save Crete. Cunningham reminded them tartly that Crete, important as it was, could never justify the crippling of British sea power in the eastern Mediterranean, which would expose the whole Imperial position in the Middle East [221–5].

By 27 May, yet another evacuation was under way, again at night, mostly from open beaches and this time entirely by cruisers and destroyers [235]. Ships were attacked on passage in daylight and serious casualties, losses and damage were suffered. The ordeal of Rear Admiral Rawlings's Force B on 29 May, en route for Alexandria with 4,000 soldiers, was probably the worst of any force in the Greek and Cretan sagas.[34] Almost all of Rawlings's nine ships were hit or near-

---

[31]*Juno, Kashmir:* 1939, 1.760t, 6×4.7in, 10×21in tt, 36k; s 21 & 23 May resp. Hodgkinson, pp. 142–3.

[32]McCallum, pp. 240–1. RA R. L. Fisher, *Salt Horse: A Naval Life* (privately published, 1989), quoting RA Glennie, p. 139.

[33]Cunningham, note, p. 110, BM Add Mss 52581A; Capt M.L. Power, comments on Crete dispatch, Oct. 1946, BM Add Mss 52573, *Cunningham Papers*, BL .

[34]Grove, *Sea Battles*, vol. 2, pp. 50–51.

RA (later Adm Sir) Bernard Rawlings (1889–1962): ent RN 1904; Mil Mission to Poland 1918–21; Capt 1930; *Active, Curacoa, Delhi;* NA Tokyo 1936–39; *Valiant* 1939; RA & 1BS, Jan. 1941; 7CS 1941; ACNS(F), 1942; Actg VA & FOC, W Africa 1943; VA Nov. 1943; FO, E Med, Dec. 1943; VA, 1BS & 2nd-in-C, BPF, Dec. 1944. Adm & ret 1946.

missed, two of the destroyers being sunk and *Orion* and *Dido* suffering horrific damage and casualties.[35] Rawlings's calm decisiveness in the face of confusion and destruction was noted by Cunningham, who, as First Sea Lord, rewarded him with the major sea-going appointment in the British Pacific Fleet in 1945 [245]. Once again, Cunningham was determined not to leave the Army in the lurch, making a further celebrated statement: 'It takes the Navy three years to build a ship. It would take three hundred to build a reputation. The evacuation will continue'.[36] Ultimately over 17,000 men were brought off but 5,000 had to surrender. The evacuation was terminated on 1 June. It has been argued that Cunningham 'succumbed to despair and cast aside resolve', failing to make a further attempt to rescue troops on the following night. This is not so. The situation in Crete was confused, the men were running short of supplies, many were not in organised bodies and further naval losses were to be expected; moreover, few ships remained fit to sail.[37] Cunningham had also persisted with the evacuation a day longer than the Army expected [228–32, 234].

The losses and damage suffered in the Cretan struggle were severe. As the Fleet War Diary expressed it, 'the tale of the Navy is one of disaster after disaster' [233]. Over 2,000 sailors and about 1,000 soldiers became casualties. Two cruisers, one AA cruiser and six destroyers were sunk. One carrier, two battleships, two cruisers and two destroyers would have to be repaired away from the station. Two cruisers, an AA cruiser and six destroyers would require substantial repairs at Alexandria or Malta. Of the ships fit for service, a battleship, a cruiser and an AA cruiser were suffering from defects; the rest – a battleship, a cruiser and 17 destroyers – were mostly in need of refits or just plain rest [237]. Many ships' companies had suffered high casualties, their physical strength had just about given out and, as Cunningham was aware, they were at the point of nervous exhaustion [245]. He visited ships and sought to encourage their crews, with more success in some ships than in others [217]. He talked quietly to captains uncertain whether their ships could return to the killing grounds.[38] He grieved at his men's suffering, his anguish underlined by the fact that he was tied to Alexandria. To

---

[35]*Dido*: 1940, 5,450t, 10×5.25in, 6×21in tt, 33k.

[36]S. W. C. Pack, *Cunningham the Commander* (London, 1974), p. 184; O. Warner, *Cunningham of Hyndhope: Admiral of the Fleet* (London, 1967), p. 152.

[37]Thomas, *Crete 1941*, p. 205; Pack, *Cunningham the Commander*, p. 185.

[38]Cunningham, speech at Foyle's literary luncheon, 28 March 1951, BM Add Mss 52582, *Cunningham Papers,* BL; Pack, *Cunningham the Commander,* p. 187.

one victim of the Stukas, Captain Lord Louis Mountbatten, he confessed that he felt like going out in a destroyer into the thick of the fighting and getting killed.[39] More soberly but equally morosely, he offered to relinquish command, feeling that confidence in his leadership might have collapsed in view of the intense suffering imposed on the fleet by his do-or-die orders. Pound quickly disabused him of the notion that confidence in his leadership had been sapped by the gruelling, gruesome, grinding series of operations, shared by the Allied merchant navies [227, 239–40, 243]. Nevertheless, at the end of the campaign, Cunningham declared 'I have never felt prouder of the Mediterranean Fleet than at the close of these particular operations' [235].

The casualties, damage and losses suffered around Crete reduced the fleet by a half but by far the most serious incidence of loss or damage so great as to require prolonged dockyard work away from the station was that suffered by *Formidable*. On 26 May, Pridham-Wippell led a force including the carrier into the Aegean to attack Scarpanto aerodrome on Rhodes. This base, which had been bombed and bombarded on several occasions, was perhaps the most dangerous enemy airfield. It lay beyond the range of shore-based aircraft, so *Formidable*, which now had a dozen Fulmars (most of them of dubious airworthiness) and a handful of Albacores, was sent. In the event, only two Fulmars and six Albacores were able to attack Scarpanto, modest damage being inflicted. On the return voyage, the force was attacked by 20–25 Ju88s, escorted by Me110s. Despite determined defence by the four airworthy Fulmars, two hits and a damaging near miss were scored. *Formidable* shortly made passage to an American yard and did not return to service until February 1942 [219].

The decision to employ the carrier on this mission when it was known that both her striking force and, more particularly, her fighter squadron were so weak is beyond comprehension. *Formidable*, sensibly, had been kept away from Crete because of the low state of her fighter complement. Scarpanto was never likely to suffer substantial damage, even if a full hand of aircraft had been deployed. The return, both actual and possible, was too meagre to justify exposing *Formidable* to the high risk of air or submarine attack.[40] The operation betrays a lack of understanding of the true

---

[39] O. Warner, *Admiral of the Fleet: The Life of Sir Charles Lambe* (London, 1969), p. 101.
[40] Pack, *Cunningham the Commander*, p. 175, and *The Battle for Crete*, p. 54; Grove, *Sea Battles*, vol. 2, pp. 48–9; Hodgkinson, *Before the Tide Turned*, p. 131.

role, capability and vulnerability of carrier air power. It is doubtful whether Somerville would have exposed *Ark Royal* in that way. Cunningham might have allowed his irritation at the freedom of action of the Scarpanto bombers to influence his judgement, or he might have been distracted by the battle for Crete. He might have been misled by his FAA advisers or he might have failed to understand the equation between the size, determination and precision of German attacks and the considerable scale of air defence required to defeat them – though *Illustrious*'s experience in January should have forewarned him [147]. The dire state of *Formidable*'s air group is a devastating commentary on the total absence of reserve carrier planes in the Mediterranean, to which Cunningham had drawn attention [68, 89, 98, 131, 209, 217, 220, 234, 241].

It is a matter of wonder also that Cunningham failed to realise that such damage to *Formidable* would deprive him of fleet air power for many months. He must have been aware that, as Pound pointed out, the cupboard was virtually bare. One senses a note of reproach in Pound's comment that to send him another carrier 'would be a sheer waste' [243]. The absence of a carrier enabled the Italians to regain control of the central Mediterranean, made trans-Mediterranean and Alexandria-Malta convoys extremely hazardous and tied Cunningham to the eastern basin, within shore-based fighter cover. Carrier-borne A/S patrols might well have saved *Barham* in November 1941 and the TSRs might also have handled the Italian fleet roughly in the two battles of Sirte late in 1941 and early in 1942.

The fleet thus ended this phase in considerably less heart and strength than it did the previous one. *Warspite* had suffered damage so severe as to require repairs in an American yard. Three carriers had come and gone [135–6, 219, 243]. Two heavy cruisers had left the station – one damaged, one defective – and one had been effectively lost [163, 204]. Five 12-gun cruisers had been sunk or severely damaged and by the end of the Cretan episode, Cunningham had shown a clear preference for the small but handy *Dido*s, up-to-date AA cruisers [135, 137, 227].[41] Destroyers and light craft were sunk or badly damaged regularly, though submarine losses were much lighter [137, 152, 156, 173, 192, 206, 212–13, 219, 227, 228, 236–7, 239, 245]. Reinforcements tailed off from the spring of 1941, as losses and severe damage mounted, commitments increased and

---

[41]On the *Dido*s, see N. Friedman, 'AA Cruisers: The Life of a Class', *US Naval Inst Proceedings*, **91**, no. 1, Jan. (1965), pp. 83–99.

new construction was delayed, often by bombing. Cunningham reminded the Admiralty constantly that he had inadequate resources to meet his expanding responsibilities [154, 164, 196, 200–202, 204, 225–8, 233, 235–7, 244–5]. Fortunately, Matapan, fuel shortages and the increasing demand for convoy escorts prevented sorties by the Italian fleet. Italian submarines enjoyed little reward though convoy escorts fought bravely, often at night, when surprised and against superior forces [135, 142, 157, 165–8, 192, 234].

The triumph of Matapan sealed Cunningham's reputation as a fleet handler of the highest order but the first few months of 1941 were a much sterner test of his general qualities as a commander-in-chief. He remained exacting, determined, tireless, brusque and quick to roar. Despite the rigours and pressures of wartime, he continued to insist on peace time standards of smartness in ships, officers and men. However, the trials, disasters, costs and suffering of this period brought out an underlying paternalism, a deeply caring nature, genuine anguish at his men's torments and, as Captain Lee noted, a soft heart.[42] The demands of Tobruk, Greece and Crete kept the light forces constantly at sea, frequently at action stations, often under attack, coping with damage, casualties, rescues and evacuations. Men and machinery were driven beyond normal limits of endurance yet Cunningham had to extract further efforts from them. Many ships' companies and some captains came close to cracking. Some men had to be relieved. Cunningham, while doing what he could to cheer up ships' companies, encourage them to fight on, and listen to their worries, was constantly anxious about the fleet's morale [136, 137, 146, 147, 156, 213, 217, 219, 224–5, 227, 240]. It is not surprising that Crete brought even Cunningham to the verge of despair.

The period from 1 January to 31 May was, then, one of very mixed fortunes for Cunningham's command. Malta had become stronger and was taking the offensive, buoyed by regular convoys. The enemy was beginning to become disturbed at the rising curve of losses on the Libyan run. Tobruk had been kept going by good organisation, high courage and sheer determination. The Army had been supported, landed and re-embarked under conditions akin to those of Norway and Dunkirk and at great cost to the fleet in lives, ships and

---

[42]Conversation with Capt Lee, 29 Nov. 1996. Cunningham shed tears on visiting Malta in Dec. 1940 and was extremely concerned about safety of his niece, widow of his former Flag Lt, Walter Starkie, killed in *Juno*, on her voyage to the UK. Pack, *Cunningham the Commander*, pp. 128–9, 188–9, 203; R. L. Ollard, *Fisher and Cunningham: A Study of the Personalities of the Churchill Era* (London, 1991), pp. 63, 111–14, 119.

exhaustion. Italian forces in the Red Sea had been destroyed or driven away. The Italian fleet had been soundly defeated. The German Air Force, however, was triumphant. Its flying skills and determination had brought it great triumphs at trifling cost. Without adequate fighter cover, ships had no effective counter to the Luftwaffe's overwhelming strength and its subtle tactics. As spring turned into summer, as well as assuming a new commitment in Syria and the Lebanon, Cunningham had to restore energy, self-confidence and purpose in his battered command. The loss of ships and bases, and in particular the blows to shore-based and seaborne air power, forced upon him a new strategy.

135. Report on Operation EXCESS

(19 March 1941)

Cunningham's Observations

2. These operations marked the advent of the German Air Force in strength in the Mediterranean, and included the damaging of *Illustrious* on 10 January and the loss of *Southampton* on 11 January.

6. The dive bombing attacks by German aircraft were most efficiently performed and came as an unpleasant surprise. The results of short range AA fire were disappointing, though it has been subsequently learned that this fire was in fact more effective than it appeared, and the Germans suffered considerable loss.

Nevertheless, it is a potent new factor in Mediterranean war and will undoubtedly deny us that free access to the waters immediately surrounding Malta and Sicily which we have previously enjoyed, until our own air forces have been built up to a scale adequate to meet it.

7. The dive bombing attacks on the 3CS on the afternoon of 11 January – resulting in the loss of *Southampton* – were a complete surprise, delivered at a time when the ships concerned believed themselves to have drawn clear of the threat of air attack, and when officers and men were doubtless relaxing their vigilance to some extent after a very strenuous four days.

This damaging attack served to emphasise the importance of including an RDF ship in detached units whenever possible.

8. The remarks of the CO, *Jaguar*, are of considerable interest, in particular his practice of firing 4.7-in barrage over the stern of a ship attacked by dive bombers. The idea is now under development in the Mediterranean Fleet with a view to the destroyer screen putting an 'umbrella barrage' over the fleet.[43]

9. Force X had originally put to sea to take part in the offensive operations intended in Operation MC6, which had to be abandoned. It was most unfortunate that persistent bad weather prevented the RA, 1BS, from delivering any of the attacks which he

---

[43]*Jaguar*: 1939, 1,760t, 6×4.7in, 10×21in tt, 36k; s U-boat, off Libya, Mar. 1942.
Lt-Cdr J. F. W. Hine: Lt-Cdr Feb. 1937; CO *Jaguar* Aug. 1939; k 1 Dec. 1941.

intended, and which would have been a most useful counter to the undoubted set back which the fleet as a whole had received.

10. It is satisfactory to record that Convoy EXCESS whose safe passage had been the main object of the operation, reached its destination safely.

Operations MC4 and MC6
Narrative

Operation MC4 was devised in co-operation with the FOC, Force H, to cover the passage of the much-delayed Convoy EXCESS. It was intended to continue at sea in the Central Mediterranean after the passage of the convoy and to conduct a further operation (MC6), which was to have consisted of operations against shipping on the Italian coasts.

7 January

3. Force H, consisting of *Renown, Malaya, Ark Royal, Sheffield, Bonaventure* and destroyers, left Gibraltar, convoy EXCESS, consisting of *Essex* for Malta, and *Clan Cumming, Clan MacDonald* and *Empire Song* for Piraeus, having sailed the previous evening.[44]

4. Force A, consisting of *Warspite, Valiant, Illustrious, Jervis, Nubian, Mohawk, Dainty, Greyhound, Gallant* and *Griffin*, sailed at 0500.

5. ... There were no incidents until 1640 when an enemy aircraft was located by RDF, ... [at] 32 miles. The aircraft itself was sighted, and *Illustrious*'s fighters which were standing by on deck were flown off but were too late, and Force A was reported. The aircraft then sighted *Brambleleaf* and the corvettes. In view of this sighting the C-in-C sent an aircraft to *Peony* to order her to make a drastic alteration of course so as to throw off torpedo bombers. Two groups of aircraft approached the fleet during the afternoon but retired on sighting the Fulmars. The second group sighted and reported the fleet at 1720.

7. Force B, consisting of *Gloucester, Southampton, Ilex* and *Janus*, left the Aegean for Malta.

9. Convoy MW5½, consisting of *Breconshire, Clan Macaulay* escorted by *Calcutta, Diamond* and *Defender*, sailed from Alexandria for Malta at 1400.

---

[44]*Bonaventure*: 1940, 5,450t, 8×5.25in, 6×21in tt, 33k; s It s/m *Dagabur*, E. Med. Mar. 1941. *Essex*: 1936, 11,063gt, 17k, Federal SN Co. *Clan Cumming*: 1938, 7,264gt, 17k, Clan Line. *Clan MacDonald*: 1939, 7.980gt, 17.5k, Clan Line. *Empire Song*: 1940, 9,228 gt; mined off Malta May 1941.

10. Force D, *Orion* and *York*, left Alexandria at 0300 to cover the passage of *Brambleleaf* through the Kaso Strait. *Ajax* and *Perth* left Piraeus to rendezvous with VA, Light Forces, at Suda Bay at 0800/8.
11. Five floating mines were sighted during the day. There were no further incidents and course was set to pass S of the Medina Bank at 2200...

8 January

12. ... Force D and the corvettes were met leaving Suda Bay, which was entered at 1230. After fuelling destroyers Force A sailed again at 1400, passing through the Anti-Kithera Channel at 1800....
13. Force B arrived at Malta a.m., fuelled, and sailed again p.m. to rendezvous with Force H, *Janus* remaining at Malta to dock. *Sydney* and *Stuart* sailed from Malta p.m. to join Force A, ...
14. Force C. *Brambleleaf* arrived Suda a.m., the corvettes fuelling and proceeding to Malta independently.
15. Force D. *Ajax* and *Perth* joined VA, Light Forces at Suda Bay at 0800, and the force then sailed to cover the passage of the corvettes.
16. *Air reconnaissance*

    Taranto – 1 *Cavour*, 4 cruisers and 2 destroyers.
                 (The dry dock was not visible.)
    Naples – 1 *Littorio* and 2 *Cavours* (indicating that the enemy again have 3 battleships in commission).
    Messina – 3 cruisers and 3 destroyers.
    Cagliari – 2 destroyers.
    Trapani – 4 destroyers.

17. At 1537 a flying boat of 201 Group located a convoy of 4 merchant ships and 1 hospital ship... These were unfortunately out of range of *Illustrious*'s striking force.

9 January

19. At 1030, VALF, with Force D, and *Sydney* and *Stuart* from Malta, joined the C-in-C. At about this time a reconnaissance aircraft was detected by RDF and also sighted from the fleet. The Fulmars unfortunately failed to intercept owing to low cloud, and at 1140 the aircraft made a sighting report.
20. On the return of the first air search [sent off at 0730], which sighted nothing, an armed reconnaissance consisting of 6 Swordfish was flown off at 1130 to search the Tripoli–Benghazi route... *Sydney* and *Stuart* were detached to Alexandria at 1240 and VALF

with Force D at 1330 to cover the convoys and to provide AA support for Convoy ME6 on 10 January.

10 January

21. At 0430, ... course was altered to 290° to rendezvous with Convoy EXCESS. At 0741 a report was received from *Bonaventure* ... that she had sighted 2 enemy destroyers ... at 0756 the RA, 3CS reported that *Southampton, Bonaventure, Jaguar* and *Hereward* were engaging.
23. At 0810 one enemy destroyer blew up, having been torpedoed by *Hereward*, the second having escaped to the NW at high speed. The destroyer sunk is believed to have been the *Vega*.[45]
24. In the meantime a rendezvous had been made with Convoy EXCESS ... A fighter patrol of 6 and an air search ... was flown off at 0815 ...
25. At 0834 ... *Gallant* was torpedoed or mined, her bows being blown off. She was taken in tow by *Mohawk,* and *Bonaventure* and *Griffin* were detached to stand by her, *Hereward* and *Jaguar* joining the fleet screen. *Gloucester* and *Southampton* were also detached to stand by *Gallant* at 1000, the fleet remaining close to the convoy for the remainder of the forenoon.[46]
26. One of the A/S patrol aircraft sighted a *Spica* class destroyer about 5 miles from Pantelleria and attacked with bombs, reporting a near miss.[47] Two enemy aircraft attacked *Bonaventure* with torpedoes.
27. The movements of the Malta convoys were as follows:

MW5 arrived at Malta at 0800.
ME6 escorted by *Peony, Salvia* and *Hyacinth*, sailed at 0700.
ME5½ escorted by *Diamond* sailed at 1130 to join Convoy EXCESS.

Janus left Malta at 1200 and joined the fleet screen, and *Calcutta* joined ME6.

28. In the meantime the fleet had been located by enemy aircraft at 0930 and reported at 1015, and at 1127 a shadower was shot down over Linosa Island by Fulmars. At 1223, two S79s dropped two torpedoes which missed astern of *Valiant*. These aircraft were engaged in good time by the close range weapons of the battlefleet, without effect.

---

[45]*Vega*: 1936, 790t, 3×3.9in, 4×17.7in tt, 34k.
[46]*Gallant*: 1936, 1,335t, 4×4.7in, 8×21in tt, 35.5k, mined; bombed, Malta, Apr. 1942; total loss.
[47]*Spica* cl: 1935–38, 790t, 3×3.9in, 4×17.7in tt, 34k.

29. At 1235 large formations of aircraft were sighted approaching from the north. These were identified as Ju87 and 88 aircraft with German markings.[48]

A very heavy, determined and skilful dive bombing attack developed on the fleet, mainly directed on *Illustrious*, and lasting for some 10 minutes.

Illustrious was hit by six heavy bombs, and hauled out of line heavily on fire and with her steering gear out of action, but with her armament still in lively action.

Warspite sustained slight damage . . .

At least two enemy aircraft were seen to be shot down by gunfire.

30. *Illustrious* reported that she was 'badly hit' and making for Malta; but it was not until 1530 that she was got under control and steering steadily for Malta at 17 knots. In the meantime she was turning circles while the battlefleet was manoeuvred to maintain supporting distance from her. *Hasty* and *Janus* were detached to screen her.

31. *Illustrious*'s aircraft in the air (8 Swordfish and 5 Fulmars) had in the meantime been ordered to Malta and all arrived with the exception of one Swordfish and one Fulmar, the crew of the Swordfish and the pilot of the Fulmar being picked up. The air gunner of the Fulmar was killed.

32. Between 1600 and 1700, a second attack developed on *Illustrious* and the battlefleet by about 20 aircraft. *Illustrious*'s Fulmars, who had been refuelled at Malta, were able to intervene and shot down 6 or 7 Ju87s, damaging others. The attack on the battlefleet was mostly concentrated on *Valiant* who had one killed and two wounded from splinters.

34. *Illustrious* was met in the swept channel by a tug and arrived safely at 2145.

35. In the meantime, *Gallant* and escorting forces were making good 6½ knots . . . The convoy movements proceeding according to plan, and *Essex* escorted by *Hero* arrived safely at Malta at 2045. Owing to the delays to the battlefleet, VALF was ordered to remain to the northward of Convoy EXCESS . . . . Convoy ME6 was at this time making good 9½ knots.

36. The C-in-C with Force A then proceeded to the eastward without further incident, . . .

11 January

38. The fleet remained close to EXCESS for the remainder of the day, . . .

---

[48] Junkers Ju88: 1936, 2–3 cannon, 4mg, 3,960lbs bombs, 273mph, range 1,550mls

39. At 1500, CS3, who had left *Gallant* off Malta at 0500, reported that *Southampton* and *Gloucester* had been attacked ... by 12 dive bombers who achieved a surprise attack down sun, and both ships had been hit. *Southampton* was making good ... 22 knots.

At 1605, CS3 reported that *Southampton* was stopped ...

40. Course was therefore altered to 210° to close CS3, and at 1645 *Orion, Perth, Jervis* and *Janus* were detached to his assistance. Owing to lack of fuel, *Juno* and *Nubian* were detached to join the convoy and *Hereward* joined the fleet screen. *Mohawk* and *Griffin*, who had seen *Gallant* safely into Malta, were sailed by VA, Malta, at 1700, to close CS3 at high speed.

41. At 1819, however, CS3 reported that *Southampton* saw little prospect of getting the fires over the engine room and 'X' magazine under control, and at 1906 that he was forced to abandon ship and would sink her. The C-in-C approved this action ...

42. At about 1800, ... Convoy ME5½ parted from Convoy EXCESS to pass south of Crete, EXCESS proceeding through the Elaphonisos Channel.

43. CS3 later reported the first attack was carried out by 12 or more dive bombers and was a complete surprise from the sun in a clear blue sky. The speed of advance of the squadron at the time was 24 knots. The attack was well pressed home in spite of gunfire from both ships. High level bombing attacks continued intermittently until about 1630 and the squadron was shadowed until sunset.

Gloucester's forward 6-in director was damaged by an unexploded bomb through the roof of the director tower. One aircraft was unserviceable from machine gun bullets; the other was in the air at the time and force-landed near *Diamond*. *Gloucester*'s casualties were 1 officer and 8 ratings killed and 1 officer and 13 ratings wounded.

Southampton survivors were embarked in *Gloucester* and *Diamond* after abandoning ship, *Gloucester* taking 33 officers and 678 ratings, of whom 4 officers and 58 ratings were wounded, and *Diamond* taking 16 wounded ratings.

12 January

44. ... at 0800 all forces, including Force X, made a rendezvous ...

45. The C-in-C in *Warspite,* with *Valiant, Gloucester, Jervis, Janus, Greyhound, Diamond, Voyager, Hero* and *Defender,* proceeded to Alexandria.

46. VALF, 7CS, *York, Mohawk, Griffin* and Force X then all proceeded to Suda Bay to fuel.

Convoy EXCESS arrived at Piraeus at 1200.

13 January

47. At 0230 *Orion* and *Perth* arrived at Piraeus and embarked passengers from Convoy EXCESS, sailing again for Malta at 0600. VALF informed the VA, Malta that their route would be through the Kithera Channel, N of the Medina Bank, ... and requested fighter protection.

48. *Air reconnaissance*

Naples – 2 cruisers, 3 destroyers.

Two convoys [at sea] ... No. 830 Sqdn was not dispatched from Malta to attack owing to adverse weather report.

14 January

49. *Orion* and *Perth* arrived at Malta a.m. Owing to machinery defects *Perth* remained at Malta and *Orion* sailed with *Bonaventure* and *Jaguar*. The latter two ships were brought to Alexandria to reduce the concentration of ships subject to air attack in Malta.

15 January

50. RA, 1BS, with Force X, made a rendezvous with VALF in *Orion*, with *Bonaventure* and *Jaguar* and proceeded to Suda Bay.

136. *War Diary, January 1941 (cont.)*

15 January

Submarines

2. It was reported that *Pandora* sank 2 merchant ships on 9 January off the E coast of Sardinia while on passage Alexandria to Gibraltar, and that *Regent* had also sunk one merchant ship, the *Citta di Messina* of 2,500 tons, off Misurata on 15 January.[49] On 7 January, *Rover* heard three explosions when attacking 2 merchant vessels off Tobruk and one ship is thought to have been sunk.

16 January

Air activity

8. Malta dockyard was raided heavily just before dark and Malta W/T was put out of action for 1½ hours. *Illustrious* was again hit but

---

[49]*Citta di Messina*: 1930, 2,472gt, Tirrenia.

was not seriously damaged. MT ship *Essex* was severely damaged. *Perth* was damaged below water aft by a near miss and was sailed by VA, Malta for Alexandria at 2200. She is capable of 24 knots. Her boiler repairs were not due to be completed until p.m. 17th.

HMS Glasgow

11. *Glasgow* can be made fit for service by 31 January, with 3 turrets and a maximum speed of 23 knots. It is proposed to accept this reduced efficiency and forgo complete repairs, which would extend over a long period.

RAN

13. A signal of appreciation was sent by the C-in-C to the Australian Navy Board for the work of *Voyager, Vampire, Waterhen* and *Vendetta*, under Captain H. M. L. Waller, RAN.[50]

Intelligence

14. *Rover* reports that schooners are working as decoys for enemy E-boats along the Cyrenaican coast.

15. The AOC-in-C, Middle East, visited the C-in-C on board *Warspite*. Questions of general policy in connection with the change in the air situation were discussed.

17 January

Air activity

9. Further details are now available of the air raid on Malta at about 1800/16. About 70 Ju87 and 88s attacked in two waves. MT *Essex* was hit in the engine-room, which was wrecked, and had casualties of 15 killed and 23 wounded. Her cargo, which included some 4,000 tons of ammunition, was not damaged.

Illustrious was hit on the quarterdeck but suffered no more casualties nor any serious damage. Considerable destruction was caused in the dockyard, and No.2 dock is out of action. The W/T station was hit twice and there were many civilian casualties, especially in Senglea. Ten enemy planes were certainly destroyed, 1 other probably and 3 possibly.

10. Enemy aircraft raided the Canal Area during the night of 17/18 ... Bombs were dropped on the canal itself only, the aircraft

---

[50]Capt H. M. L. Waller, RAN: Cdr 1934; N Office, Melbourne; Act Capt, *Stuart* & 10DF, Sept. 1939; Capt June 1940; *Perth* Oct. 1941; lost with ship, Battle of Java Sea, March 1942.

flying very low ... No damage and no casualties were caused but the canal traffic was held up for 24 hours, while unexploded bombs were dealt with.

Intelligence

12. The C-in-C, Middle East, General Wavell, visited the C-in-C on board *Warspite* on return from his visit to Athens. ...

18 January

Illustrious's *aircraft*

10. The remaining Swordfish aircraft from *Illustrious* were reorganised into:

   (a) One flight in Crete operating from Maleme or Heraklion to patrol the Kithera channels and maintain pressure on the Dodecanese.
   (b) One flight in the Western Desert as a torpedo and A/S striking force operating with 202 Group under the SNO, Inshore Squadron.

19 January

Operations

A report of the general situation was sent by the C-in-C to the Admiralty as follows:

> Situation out here which is rather difficult is as follows:
> A. Malta being heavily raided and urgently necessary to get *Illustrious* and large MVs away but weather has precluded sending destroyer escorts up to present. These will proceed as soon as possible and available cruisers are assembling Suda prior to providing cover in Central Mediterranean.
> B. Convoy EXCESS left Piraeus early today, *Clan Cumming* submarined off San Giorgio Island but I hope has now reached Piraeus.
> C. Convoy of important military stores for Greece due to leave Alexandria p.m. tomorrow 20th.
> D. Attack on Tobruk delayed by weather. Inshore Squadron standing by to bombard. Cruiser and destroyer cover withdrawn for more urgent operation.
> E. *Eagle* out of action due to trouble with stern glands but *Glasgow* not out of dock till 22 January. *Gloucester* at Port Said having damaged DCT removed. *Perth* at Alexandria with minor damage from near miss requires docking.

F. Barely enough destroyers can be raised to send two battleships to sea to support operation of getting *Illustrious* and MVs away from Malta.
G. Most urgent requirement is more fighters for Malta and am pursuing this with AOC-in-C, Middle East.

Malta

6. A further heavy air attack on Malta during the forenoon again caused serious damage to *Illustrious* by near misses below water and the operation to move her had to be postponed.

VA, Malta's proposal to sail two valuable cargo ships, *Breconshire* and *Clan Macaulay*, from Malta was not approved since no escort could be provided in the prevailing weather.

137. To Pound

18 January 1941

A. Well, we have had a setback, but we have been in the same position before and I have no doubt we shall overcome our present difficulties. We may want some heavy air reinforcements for Malta. In fact after Thursday's raid I am quite sure they will require another Hurricane squadron. In the interim I am bringing the Fulmars there up to 12 and leaving them there as much for distant cover of convoys approaching and leaving as anything else.

The AOC-in-C is very sympathetic and will, I know, do all he can. We must face the fact that it will be an air war between Malta and Sicily and, if Malta is given the necessary means, I am sure they will win it.

B. *Illustrious* is a fine advertisement for British shipbuilding. The brunt of the first attack was borne by her and she stood up to it marvellously. It was a heartening sight to see in the second attack all guns except one pom-pom going all out.

C. On the other hand *Southampton* is a sad loss. Twenty-seven officers and about 25 CPOs and ERAs killed in the first moment of attack. They had no RDF and were completely surprised out of the sun. Inadequate direction of the damage control consequently and she was ablaze fore and aft in a short time.

I can assure you they did not abandon her too soon. Brooke came off the bridge over the fore side, the after part was in flames.[51]

---

[51]Capt B. C. B. Brooke: Capt June 1938; *Curlew* Aug. 1939; *Southampton* June 1940; COS to RA, Alexandria, Feb. 1941; Cdre 2Cl, MNBDO(1), Sept. 1943; *Renown* Nov. 1943–June 1945.

THE EFFECTS OF GERMAN INTERVENTION, 1941   263

It does not seem to me much good sending cruisers out here unless they have RDF. I don't like these *Southampton* class. They are fine ships but that great hangar structure seems to provide a good point of aim; they are always being hit there.

If you are thinking of sending *Exeter* here in due course, I hope it will be realised that she must have RDF and a much better close range AA armament than *York*.[52]

This is the second time Renouf has had his bridge hit with a dud bomb. He is most unfortunate with his ships, but personally extraordinarily lucky.

I do not know what you are thinking about him. This is the fourth ship of his squadron to be put out of action, but he brought through EXCESS very well and also showed much determination in bringing the damaged *Gallant* back to harbour. He undoubtedly has too much imagination, but he has brains and his nerve has not suffered.[53]

D. Our commitments in support of the army in the Western Desert grow daily and with the fall of Tobruk expected in a day or two, they will reach, I hope, a peak. Everything is going by sea including, since a few days ago, practically all the personnel. The strain on our destroyers and small auxiliary craft is tremendous and also it is very difficult to find the right type of shipping for the job. Small coastal carriers are what is required but there just aren't any.

E. I see by a signal just arrived that the Chiefs of Staff have ordered us to abandon our raid on Kaso. I hope they realised what we were after. We meant to capture the island and hold it so as to command both sides of the Kaso Strait where there is constant submarine and E-boat activity. Further we intended to mount a gun or two to command the Scarpanto aerodromes, which is where the Dodecanese aircraft refuel to attack our aerodromes in Crete.

I suppose the reason for cancellation is the dispute between the Turks and the Greeks over the final possession of the island, but I feel it is a great mistake to allow our operational necessities to be hampered by political factors of a minor sort.

F. I was indeed thankful that WORKSHOP was not being carried out. I don't think there is much doubt we should have lost the 'Glen'ships and anything else lying off the island.[54]

---

[52]*York* and *Exeter* had the weakest AA armament of all front-line Br cruisers.

[53]Renouf returned home in May 1941 and ret as a VA in 1942 but served in Admy throughout war.

[54]*Glen* ships in Med: *Glenearn*: 1938, 8,986gt, 18k; *Glengyle*: 1939, 9,919gt, 18k; *Glenroy*: 1938, 8,997gt, 18k, Glen Line; LSI & fast cargo ships.

I don't know what to think about that passage through the Sicilian Narrows. It cost us two valuable destroyers quite unavoidably and *Gloucester* and *Southampton* both cut mines when they hauled over the 200 fathom line to get out of sight of Pantelleria.

The place is heavily mined, I think, pretty well everywhere inside the 200 fathom line ... I don't know what *Gallant* hit. I think a mine as there were two destroyers on the battleship screen outside her, which should preclude a torpedo.

... I had a most cordial meeting with Donovan and as he volunteered to send his cable I was certainly not for putting him off. I only hope it produces some fighters. He appears to be pressing for many more destroyers – he mentioned 103, to be released to us and I gathered he thought the USA would be in the war about June. He visualised a US fleet in the Western Mediterranean. He has been ordered to see Weygand, I gathered.[55]

138. *War Diary, January 1941 (cont.)*

19 January

Western Desert

8. A report was forwarded to the Admiralty outlining the extensive work carried out by the Inshore Squadron in support of the Army during the past 10 days. This included chiefly the ferrying of 35,000 prisoners to Alexandria, the supplying of stores to Sollum and Bardia at the rate of some 500 tons daily, and the clearing of these two harbours. Rather more difficulty was anticipated in clearing and establishing Tobruk harbour.

Intelligence

13. This [use of Italian submarines to carry supplies to Rhodes], together with the reported move of 2 German Heinkel 111 aircraft from Sicily to Rhodes, is thought to be preliminary to the establishment of German air units in Rhodes. The present strength of the German air force in Sicily is assessed as 100 Divebombers, 150 Long

---

[55]Col W. J. (Bill) Donovan: US Army: Republican poln but confidant of Roosevelt, who sent him on several information-gathering missions in Eur and ME; reported on Br defences, July 1940; to ME via London, Dec. 1940; later Chief of Office of Strategic Services, a foreunner of CIA and equivalent of SOE. Accompanied here by Col (later Brig) Vivian Dykes, Br liaison officer, later a Secy of CCS.

THE EFFECTS OF GERMAN INTERVENTION, 1941

range bombers, and 50 reconnaissance planes, about 50% of which could possibly be spared for the Dodecanese.[56] ...

20 January

10. *Operation MBD2* to extract *Illustrious* from Malta is planned as follows:

  (a) *D1.* Force A of 4 destroyers from VALF's force to Malta, making the passage of the Central Mediterranean in dark hours.
  (b) RA, 1BS's force (Force C) to sail D1 p.m. from Alexandria to support VALF to the SW of Crete from p.m. D2.
  (c) *Illustrious* to leave with destroyers after dark D2 and rendezvous at dawn D3 with VALF and Force B, MT ships remaining at Malta.
  (d) If *Illustrious* is not ready to leave, two destroyers sail with ME7, consisting of MT ships *Breconshire* and *Clan Macaulay*.
  (e) If *Illustrious* is unlikely to be ready for a long time all 4 destroyers sail with MT ships.
  (f) VA, Malta, to signal the date for *Illustrious* leaving.
  (g) RAF to maintain maximum effort against Benghazi and Derna on D3.

Malta – Air Raid

12. Another heavy air attack in the evening of 19th was reported from Malta. Further below water damage was done to *Illustrious* by near misses, but at 1927/20 VA Malta reported that *Illustrious* would be ready to sail p.m. 23rd at about 20 knots.

Destroyer Armament

16. It was decided that destroyers joining the Mediterranean Fleet should in future be fitted with one 4-in HA gun in lieu of one set of torpedo tubes.

22 January

Conference of Cs-in-C

... The following subjects were included in the agenda for discussion:

1. The employment of 'Commandos'.
2. Future operations and possible raids.

[56] Heinkel He111: 1936, 1 cannon, 6mg, 5,510lbs bombs, 258mph, range 1,740mls.

3. CRME/2265 of December 1940 – Secrecy of moves of formations.
4. The supply of forces in Cyrenaica.
5. Support to Greece.
6. The policy of operations in the Sudan.
7. Current JPS papers.

Air Activity

12. During the night 22/23 Malta aircraft carried out an attack on Catania in order to reduce the chance of further damage to *Illustrious* during the next 24 hours.

13. Re-distribution of Middle East aircraft have included 12 Gladiators to Athens, 5 Fulmars and 6 Hurricanes to Malta, and 3 FAA Swordfish to Sollum.

139. *Mediterranean Chiefs of Staff*

22 January 1941

83. *Supply to Cyrenaica*

It was decided that supply to Cyrenaica should be primarily by sea to Tobruk when captured, and that the use of Sollum should be discontinued. . . . The shortage of small supply ships and lighters for use in small harbours was stressed and it was stated that endeavours were being made to procure shallow draft vessels from Cyprus. The C-in-C Mediterranean stated that, with our present resources, Tobruk was the limit of maintenance by sea. . . .

140. *War Diary, January 1941 (cont.)*

23 January

VALF and RA, 1BS, with their respective forces B and C, proceeded in accordance with with the plan for D3 of MBD2.

2. *Illustrious* left Malta at 1930 escorted by Force A. No further attacks on her were reported before sailing.

24 January

Illustrious made better speed than anticipated (about 24 knots) during the night 23/24. Visibility was poor and Force B under VALF did not make contact with her. Air reconnaissance also failed to locate her but she was sighted and joined by RA, 1BS's force during the forenoon.

2. Enemy aircraft sighted and reported our ships at 1010 and again at 1230, but no attack was made on *Illustrious*. The cruisers (Force B) were heavily attacked later in the day. T/B and high level and shallow dive bombing attacks were carried out. *Hero* became detached due to a breakdown in steering gear and was singled out for specially heavy attack. Although there were many near misses no ships were hit; at least one aircraft was thought to have been brought down by AA fire.

25 January

Illustrious, with her escort of destroyers, entered Alexandria harbour safely at noon. She was cheered by *Warspite* and other ships as she passed.

3. All cruisers from Force B were about 50% short of AA ammunition and had various minor defects. Accordingly *Perth* only was detached from Force C for duty in the Aegean, to be joined by another cruiser as soon as possible. *Perth* proceeded to Suda Bay to arrive a.m. 26th.

141. *Passage of HMS* Illustrious *from Malta to Alexandria*

(19 March 1941)

3. On 10 January when she arrived at Malta *Illustrious*'s steering gear was out of action, she was slightly holed below water in several places and there was much water in the ship. . . .
6. . . . *Eagle* was unfortunately defective, so no fighter support or carrierborne reconnaissance was available for the operation.
7. . . . the VALF, in view of uncertain weather conditions, decided in the end to sail the destroyers to arrive in Malta on 22 January, . . . accepting the risk of the extra day in Malta. This decision proved to be a wise one.
11. Great credit is due to the VALF, and to all concerned, in the successful conduct of this difficult operation.

142. *War Diary, January 1941 (concl.)*

25 January

Canal Area

13. All shipping in the Canal is now stopped at night when enemy raids may be expected. The SBNO, Canal Area, has again stressed

the danger of the canal being blocked by a sunken ship, especially in view of the weak AA defences in the Canal Area.[57]

26 January

Western Desert

4. The SNO, Inshore Squadron, reported from Tobruk that out of 5 piers two could be used now for ships of 15 feet draft and one in 3 days' time. Buoys were already available for merchant ships up to 300 feet in length and draft 18 feet. Further berths for larger ships would be available later . . .

5. All coast defence guns and *matériel*, however, had been destroyed by the enemy before capture, and a full equipment will have to be transported.

Air

8. The RAF reported that heavy and successful air attacks on the main enemy aerodromes were carried out on the 23rd and 25th. These contributed largely to the safe passage Eastwards of *Illustrious*.

Malta

11. Labour troubles now constitute the main difficulty in Malta dockyard. There are signs of this improving but there is still a high proportion of absentees and little work gets done if there seems any likelihood of a raid.

12. The underground engineering workshop is not yet complete, and lack of electric power has held up work everywhere. But within 2 or 3 weeks the general working conditions should be back to 80 or 90% of the normal. Emergency workshops are being equipped underground. The docks are not damaged as seriously as was feared and can be made serviceable shortly.

There is a serious shortage of steel plates, etc., for completing repairs.

27 January

A reconnaissance aircraft reported 3 enemy merchant vessels in line ahead, escorted by auxiliaries, steering S about noon off the Tunisian coast.

---

[57]VA Sir James M. Pipon: Capt 1920; RA 1932; RAIC & Adm Supt, Gibraltar, 1935–37; Ret List 1936; SBNO, S Australia, 1940–41; SBNO, Canal Zone 1941–42; FOIC Southampton 1942–44.

2. At 1550 these were attacked by a striking force of 6 Swordfish from Malta. The leading ship of 4,000 tons was dive bombed and a near miss scored. The second ship of 6,000 tons was thought to have been hit by a torpedo and was last seen down by the stern, in smoke, and with the crew in boats. The last ship of 4,000 tons was torpedoed amidships and sank in 15 minutes.
3. There were no aircraft casualties nor much AA opposition.

Western Desert

8. The following report was included in a signal to the Admiralty:

Tobruk is now open to sea traffic and army are proceeding with installation of AA and coast defences. *Terror* is acting as Guardship pending establishment of coast defences. *San Giorgio* completely gutted. Boom defence 80% efficient and good depot. A good number of small craft and lighters available, plenty of coal and water. Considerable damage to quays and cranes and a number of sunken vessels in harbour. Internal communications efficient. Cucumbers swept but did not explode. Evacuation of prisoners and provision of supplies to Tobruk proceeding.[58]

11. Arrangements have been made to fit the RDF equipment from *Illustrious* into *Gloucester* and to equip *York* with RDF type 286 (ASV).

28 January

Intelligence

8. From certain Italian signals intercepted it appears that certain of our messages have been decyphered. Syko is suspected. Accordingly the use of Syko for operational signals is suspended. . . .

29 January

The C-in-C, accompanied by the Chief of Staff, went to Libya by air, returning in the afternoon. He visited Tobruk and inspected the harbour, shore defences . . . He also met the AOC, Western Desert at Sollum aerodrome.[59]

Convoys and Merchant Shipping

8. A reorganisation of Middle East shipping administration was proposed in the C-in-C's message 0927/27 to develop the resources

---

[58]*San Giorgio*: 1910; reblt 1937–38; 11,700t, 4×10in, 8×7.5in, 10×3.9in, 16k. Harbour defence. Scuttled 22 Jan. 1941.
Cucumbers: magnetic mines.
[59]AOC W Desert: A/Cdre Collishaw.

of the Egyptian ports on account of the greatly increased requirements of supplies to Greece and Turkey.

Mediterranean Destroyer Strength

11. The C-in-C's 1327/26 to Admiralty proposed the retention of *Jaguar* in the Mediterranean. The C-in-C regretted having to make this proposal when the need for destroyers elsewhere might be equally great, but he stressed the risk of passing ships without bow protection [against mines] through the Narrows W of Sicily, particularly when adequate support could not be provided. Three destroyers had already been lost in this way.

30 January

Cruiser Aircraft

9. The C-in-C proposed to Admiralty ... to remove aircraft and equipment from ships of the 7CS and to replace them with two 4-barrel pom-poms ... It was considered that the aircraft do not justify the topweight, space, and risk from their petrol arrangements, when the AA armament is so badly needed.

31 January

Aegean

3. At 1800 the British tanker *Desmoulea* was torpedoed by a destroyer or E-boat ... She was on passage to Suda Bay with a cargo of petrol and white oils and had been detached from the Alexandria section of AN14 after passing Kaso Strait. *Dainty* at once proceeded to her assistance and took her in tow at 2000, although she had previously been abandoned.

4. Meanwhile *Levernbank* was without escort, and *Perth* was proceeding to *Desmoulea* in order to take her in tow. The C-in-C at 2221 then placed *Ajax* in command of all forces escorting AN and AS convoys with orders:

(i) To get *Desmoulea* into harbour if possible.
(ii) To get *Levernbank* and *Ethiopi*a to Piraeus.
(iii) To cover AN14.
(iv) To comply with orders for Operation MC7.

Perth was ordered not to take *Desmoulea* in tow and the tug was sent out from Suda Bay.[60]

[60]*Desmoulea*: 1939, 8,120gt, Anglo-Saxon Petm.
Levernbank: 1925, 5,150gt, 11k, A Weir.
Ethiopia: 1922, 5,574gt, 16k, Br India SN.

War Diary for January
Part II – General Summary

Strategical

... the disablement of *Illustrious*, the loss of *Southampton*, and the heavy air attacks on Malta, quickly made it clear that until adequate fighter protection was available, not only must the through Mediterranean convoys be suspended, but the fleet itself would operate by day within range of the dive bombers only at considerable risk. In the absence of a modern aircraft carrier it therefore became necessary to abandon any idea of offensive operations against the enemy's coasts.

2. It seemed however that the acquisition of aerodromes in Libya would enable the RAF to provide a high degree of immunity to shipping all along the Libyan coast. This would simplify the running of convoys to Malta and the Aegean, and enable light forces to operate from these advanced bases. But in spite of the rapid advance of the Army to beyond Derna by the end of the month, there was still little security gained to compensate for the enormously increased supply requirements.

Previously a fair proportion of supplies could reach the advanced units of the Army and Air Force by road and rail, but now, owing to the rapidly lengthening lines of communication, everything had to be transported by sea. The Air Force was fully extended in meeting pressure on the retreating enemy and had no fighters to spare for the protection of shipping.

3. In these circumstances it was to be expected that the enemy light forces known to be based at Brindisi and Taranto, would attempt to interfere with our extended lines of communication in the Aegean and along the Libyan coast, but apparently the German influence had not yet reached the Italian Navy, for no attacks developed.

4. *Army.* The Army's great advance into Libya continued rapidly. Bardia fell on 5 January, Tobruk on 22nd and Derna on 30th, and an embarrassing number of prisoners and worn out material fell into our hands. By the end of the month the capture of the whole of Cyrenaica was in sight.

5. *Air Force.* The Air Force was mainly occupied in supporting the Libyan campaign, but additional fighter strength was sent to Malta, and a flying boat base was put into operation at Scaramanga near Athens as Suda Bay was found to be unsuitable.

Western Desert

9. ... Unloading facilities were always poor and shipping scarce; but fortunately the clearance of Tobruk harbour was effected without great difficulty within 5 days from the first entry into the port, and its possession greatly eased the supply problem. A supply of fresh water, together with a complete distilling plant, was found there ready for use, and by 27 January fairly large ships could be berthed in the harbour. An unloading rate of 1,000 tons per day was reached before long. A total of some 50,000 prisoners of war were transported back to Alexandria.

There were many air raids on the captured ports and on the force operating along the coast, but comparatively little damage was done. On 30 January the Egyptian ship *Sollum* was beached following air attack, and on 31 January *Huntley* was sunk by torpedo bombing and dive bombing attacks.[61]

Greece

10. There was decided slowing up in the rate of advance of the Greek Army.... The Greek supply problems were eased by the arrival at Piraeus of the three remaining ships of the EXCESS convoy; but the most important of all, *Northern Prince*, with ammunition and essential supplies for the Greek powder factories, had been left at Gibraltar having grounded there.[62]

11. Supplies to Greece from Port Said and Alexandria were maintained... A patrol of the Elaphonisos and Kithera Channels was established by corvettes and trawlers, supported by destroyers when available and by one or more cruisers.

12. Greek destroyers escorted one convoy from Port Said to Piraeus and many other small convoys between Suda Bay, Piraeus and other Aegean ports. Greek submarines operated with considerable success against the Italian lines of communication in the Adriatic.

Bases

13. *Alexandria.* The opportunity was taken to refit and rest as many destroyers and other ships as possible, since it was not intended to undertake any major fleet operation without a modern aircraft carrier. There were no air raids on Alexandria during the month.

---

[61]*Sollum*: unidentified.
[62]*Northern Prince*: 1929, 10,917gt, 16.5k, Prince Line.

15. *Malta.* During the month there were 58 raids in all on 21 different days. Considerable damage was done to the aerodromes and aircraft and to the dockyard, but casualties were on the whole few and damage slight in comparison to the very heavy scale of attacks. Besides *Illustrious, Perth* and *Decoy* were slightly damaged below water by near misses. MT *Essex* was hit in the engine room and damaged beyond repair but her cargo of ammunition was untouched. The most serious damage in the dockyard was to the engine fitting shop whose output was reduced to 10% for 10 days and thereafter to between 50 and 75%. Caissons of Nos. 2 and 3 docks were severely damaged but makeshift arrangements allowed continued use of the docks. The most serious casualties were in the crowded area of Senglea which was ultimately evacuated. The three main raids were on the 16th, 18th and 19th, when 39 enemy aircraft were shot down for certain, 5 others probably, and 9 damaged.

16. In spite of these raids repairs to ships were continued and completed without serious delay and the air effort was maintained.

17. *Suda Bay.* The A/T baffle was still not in place and the base could only be used for cruisers while fuelling and for destroyers and light craft to operate from. There were occasional air raids but the scale of attack was small. The FAA established an aerodrome at Maleme and commenced operations from it.

Fleet Air Arm

20. Little air offensive was possible after the damage to *Illustrious*, and both *Eagle*'s intended attacks on Rhodes and Benghazi had to be cancelled owing to bad weather. *Eagle,* however, was able to provide the necessary fighters and A/S patrols for the battle fleet at sea.

21. Offensive day and night patrols by T/B aircraft from Malta were started against the Tripoli trade route on 25 January and quickly resulted in the success of 27 January. Reconnaissance flights and bombing operations from Malta and Crete were continued in spite of enemy attacks. . . .

Enemy Air Attack

22. The heavy divebombing attacks on the fleet at sea and on Malta were the first of their kind in the Mediterranean and were delivered with great determination and skill. Some 400 or 500 German bombers were probably diverted to Catania and North African aerodromes, of which perhaps 100 were destroyed in action, or on the ground in our counter bombing raids from Malta.

23. On 30 January 7 or 8 mines were laid in the Suez Canal by aircraft, probably German, from Rhodes [*Admiralty marginal query*: from Benina, nr Benghazi?]. This was the first of a series of similar raids which were to prove a very serious threat to the whole war effort in the Middle East. It demonstrated sadly the weakness of the Canal defences and the lack of preparedness against such an eventuality.

Anti-Aircraft

24. The AA fire of the fleet proved ineffective against the big scale dive bombing attacks, due chiefly to lack of experience and practice. It was felt, as demonstrated by *Illustrious*, that given the necessary practice severe casualties would be inflicted on the enemy sufficient to deter him from close range attacks. Accordingly every opportunity was taken both at sea and in harbour for the fleet fighters to carry out dummy dive bombing attacks to exercise the control of close range weapons.

Submarines

25. Patrols were maintained off the Calabrian coast, in the Gulf of Sidra and off Cape Bon. *Rorqual* laid mines in the Adriatic. The result of the patrols was disappointing, only two merchant ships being sunk, . . . No submarines were lost.

143. *From Pound*

27 January 1941

First of all let me congratulate you on the way you have supported the Army in the Western Desert. One doesn't like to say so to the Soldiers, but I am quite certain that they could never have advanced at anything like the speed they have unless the Navy had provided them with supplies at Sollum, Bardia, etc.

The advent of the German Air Force in the Mediterranean has altered the picture very considerably, and will make your task a much more difficult one.

I do feel very much that it is essential for us to get Benghazi and the Dodecanese, so that your position at Alexandria is safeguarded, and also that your lines of communication from Egypt to either Greece or Turkey are cleared.

The Chiefs of Staff have been trying to get the 'Glen' ships with their Commandos out to you for some time, but certain people became obsessed with WORKSHOP. . . .

If it is possible for you to relieve the *Eagle* when you get the *Formidable* it would be a great help to us as we simply must do something to try and run these raiders down.[63] . . .

144. War Diary, February 1941

1 February

Operation MC7

5. [Fleet sweep to Rhodes and Suda Bay] During the afternoon Fulmar and Gladiator fighters carried out dummy dive bombing attacks on the fleet to exercise the control of close range weapons. Destroyers on the screen were also exercised in firing an 'umbrella' barrage to burst at about 3,500 feet directly over the capital ships. This had the appearance of proving a useful defence against dive bombing attacks.

Aegean

7. *Desmoulea*, towed by *Dainty*, reached Suda Bay safely at 0800 and was beached with her cargo undamaged. . . .

Western Desert

9. The minesweeper *Huntley* was reported p.m. as having sunk at 1000/31 January, 30 miles W of Mersa Matruh. She was on her way to Tobruk to take the clearance party to Derna. It appears that she was sunk by aircraft torpedoes, after having been bombed and machine-gunned as well. The officers and ship's company fought the limited armament of the ship coolly and well but unluckily and without known success. Survivors were landed in the ship's boats and on rafts.

10. The hospital ship *Dorsetshire* was bombed at 1850/31 and again at 0630/1 in the Gulf of Sollum. She was not hit but received some damage from a near miss.

11. The town and harbour of Sollum was bombed from 0545 to 0630, a number of magnetic mines being laid. Traffic to and from the harbour was stopped and the LL minesweepers *Arthur Cavanagh* and *Milford Countess* were asked for from Tobruk.[64]

12. Consequent on this increased scale of enemy air attack along the coast, RA, Alexandria, stated his intention of sailing transport

---

[63]German raiders at sea were just reaching their maximum strength: *Scharnhorst, Gneisenau, Scheer* and *Hipper*, with several auxiliary cruisers, were at large.

[64]*Dorsetshire*: 1920, 9,645gt, 13k; ex-trooper, mgd by Bibby Line.
Arthur Cavanagh: trlr, 1918, 277gt.
Milford Countess: 274gt, Milford Steam Trawling Co.
Capt A. L. Poland succ Capt Hickling as SNOIS: Capt *Black Swan* 1939; *Nile* & SNOIS Feb. 1941; *St George* (IoMan) Feb. 1943; Cdre (D), EF, *Woolwich*, Apr. 1944.

and supply ships to keep between the 25th and 28th meridians during day and close along the coast. He asked for fighter protection in this area but was told that none could possibly be given owing to the requirements of the front line and new commitments W of Derna.[65]

2 February

9. The clearance of Derna harbour was commenced and a channel swept by *Moy* . . .

10. The magnetic minesweepers *Arthur Cavanagh* and *Milford Countess* had to return to Alexandria from Sollum on account of damage to their sweeps. Sollum harbour remained closed to shipping on account of mines.

Submarines

14. *Upholder* reported sinking an 8,000 ton ship on 28 January and a 5,000 ton ship on 30 January. Both ships were laden and in convoy off the E coast of Tunisia. . . .

Tetrarch and *Rover* were sailed from Alexandria and Malta respectively to reinforce the patrols off Tripoli.[66]

3 February

Canal Area

9. The canal was reopened to shipping on 2 February after intensive sweeping, no more mines having been dropped since 30 January. A number of mines had been exploded by DWI sweeps and by skids and one counter-mined. At 1505 SS *Derwenthall* was mined . . . She suffered no casualties but her rudder was blown off and she grounded across the channel. She was later hauled into the bank to clear the channel for shipping.[67]

4 February

Operation MC7

2. On arrival in harbour the C-in-C made a general signal, explaining the general Mediterranean situation to the ships' companies.

---

[65]Capt G. H. Cresswell succ RA Elliott as RA Alexandria: Capt 1931; 4DF, MF, Dec. 1937; *Afridi* 1939; COS to RA June 1940; Actg RA Sept. 1941; ret Feb. 1942.

[66]*Upholder*: 1940, 540/730t, 1×3in, 6×21in tt, 11/9k; most famous Br s/m & CO of war: L-Cdr M. D. Wanklyn, VC; lost with crew, It a/s vessel, 14 Apr. 1942.

[67]*Derwenthall*: 1940, 4,950gt, 12k, W Hartlepool SN.

3. The following signal was made to *Eagle* from the C-in-C: 'It has been a pleasure to have *Eagle* in company again and to watch her efficient handling of awkward and unaccustomed aircraft.'

Western Desert

4. There was an air raid on Tobruk from 0510 to 0600 in which bombs and a number of parachute mines were dropped. There was no serious damage but the harbour was closed to traffic; unloading continued.

6. There being no magnetic minesweepers at present available for Tobruk, the corvettes *Peony, Gloxinia, Salvia* and *Hyacinth* were recalled to Alexandria from the Kithera patrol and from convoying AS14, in order to be ranged and prepared for LL sweeping.

7. The advance of the Army continued very fast towards Benghazi, which town is apparently being evacuated. No.830 Sqdn (Malta) was ordered to bring maximum effort to bear on the Tripoli route and to plant cucumbers off Tripoli.

Submarines

8. Captain (S), 1SF, assumed operational control of all submarines and ordered dispositions to intercept enemy traffic:

Rover to patrol off the Calabrian coast.
Unique to join *Usk, Utmost* and *Upright* on patrols along the Tunisian coast between Tripoli and Misurata.
Truant and *Tetrarch* from Alexandria to patrol off Tripoli.
Triumph and *Ursula* to remain at Malta for the present.[68]

9. *Rorqual* left the Adriatic during the night 3/4 having laid two minefields, one off Ancona and one off Sansego Island in Gulf of Quarnero. She also sank by gunfire a tug towing a floating battery. She was forced to dive, however, when the latter opened heavy fire at close range.

Canal Area

10. A second ship was mined in the Canal and all traffic was again stopped, the channel being obstructed. This was the Greek 3,800 ton steamer *Aghios Georgios*, who was the 13th ship in the convoy to

---

[68]*Unique* (lost, Atl, Nov. 1942), *Usk* (lost off C Bon, May 1941), *Utmost* (s It a/s vessel, Nov. 1942), *Upright, Ursula*: 1938–40, 540/730t, 1×3in, 6×21in tt, 11/9k.
Triumph (s Aegean Jan. 1942): 1938, 1,090/1,575t, 1×4in, 10×21in tt, 15.25/9k.
Capt (S), 1SF: Capt S. M. Raw: Cdr 1933; Capt June 1940, *Medway* & 1SF; *Dolphin* (s/m base, Gosport) 1942; *Phoebe* 1943.

pass over the mine.[69] LL hoppers sent from Alexandria and DWI aircraft had swept thoroughly ahead of the convoy. . . . .

5 February

3. In view of the urgency of Army requirements for stores, and particularly petrol, Tobruk was kept open, the risk from mines being accepted. No sweepers could be got there for several days. The daily unloading average of 1,000 tons of stores was maintained, and a further 150 tons of petrol were unloaded at Derna.

4. The shortage of all forms of minesweepers was shown by the fact that the sending of a relief TSMS for *Huntley* left only one available at Alexandria.

Canal Area

3. HT *Ranee* of 8,500 tons was mined in the centre of the channel in a section of the canal which had been swept daily since the mining occurred on 30 January and through which 23 ships had already passed safely. All traffic was stopped S of Ismailia.[70]

6. Arrangements were made to reinforce the Canal AA defences against further attacks, a balloon barrage previously destined for Malta being sent there. Troops were being asked for to act as watchers posted every half mile along the Canal.

8. The possibilities of transhipping cargoes of ships from Suez to Port Said by lighter was being investigated. The additional labour required seemed likely to prove a big difficulty.

Alexandria

10. Dawn and dusk fighter patrols are being instituted to seaward of the harbour to counter possible enemy minelaying activities. A balloon barrage is also being established in the Great Pass.

AA protection for Merchant Ships

11. The supply of AA guns to merchant ships operating in the Eastern Mediterranean is causing concern. This has now become an urgent necessity and some valuable supply ships are operating on the Libyan coast armed only with captured Italian machine guns. It is impracticable to work a shuttle service of AA machine guns for merchant ships on account of their exposure to air attack in ports as well as on passage. The local supply of Breda guns is not

---

[69] *Aghios Georgios*: 1912, 3,283gt, A. G. Vassopulos.
[70] *Ranee*: 1928, 5,060gt, 12k, Asiatic SN.

nearly sufficient, and 60 Hotchkiss guns have been demanded urgently from the UK.

6 February

Western Desert

5. The general policy regarding Libyan ports was explained in C-in-C's 1201/6:

i) Tobruk will continue to be the army's main supply base at present.
ii) Benghazi: Clearance party and small permanent party will be sent to port as soon after capture as possible. Supply to Benghazi can be by occasional convoy only.
iii) Derna: Port is only to be used for merchant ships which can berth inside breakwater.
iv) Sollum: Port is to be kept open if possible as subsidiary in case Tobruk is temporarily closed.
v) Bardia: Harbour may be used as refuge for small ships and for coasting schooners to wait favourable conditions for onward passage.

7 February

2. Captain (D), 14DF in *Jervis*, with *Janus*, *Jaguar* and *Mohawk*, sailed from Alexandria at 0100 to operate in the Aegean from Suda Bay. In conjunction with *York*, 815 Sqdn, and NOIC, Suda, the following operations were to be carried out:

(a) Patrol Kithera Strait at intervals.
(b) Night sweeps into the Dodecanese and round Rhodes.
(c) Cover convoys in the Aegean.
(d) Act as an A/S striking force.

6. Orders were issued for the clearance of Benghazi harbour and the establishment of a base there. Heavy gales and sandstorms held up the transport and supply work at Tobruk and other forward bases. Another mine exploded in Tobruk harbour damaging the petrol carrier *Rodi* and the petrol carrier *Adinda* was struck by 2 mines which exploded forward and set her on fire. It is hoped to save the deck cargo and after holds. The ship has Diesel engines and it is thought possible that the mines might have been acoustic.

Canal Area

8. All movement in the Canal was suspended until the sweepers could again be got into action.

9. A number of signals were dispatched to the Admiralty stressing the seriousness of the mining in the Suez Canal and requesting urgently for additional personnel to deal with sweeping and with degaussing, and for all kinds of equipment to deal with magnetic and acoustic mines, the latter to be sent out by special cruiser if possible. Balloons, short range AA weapons, DWI aircraft, cable and material for making LL sweeps and non-magnetic diving suits were amongst the requirements stated.

8 February

York reported the intended operations to be carried out in the Aegean. On the night 8/9, destroyers were to patrol the Kithera and Antikithera Channels. On the night 9/10, destroyers with cruisers in support, were to sweep through the Kaso Straits and round Rhodes, retiring to the Eastward during daylight 10th. On the night 10/11 a similar sweep was to be executed through the Scarpanto Strait and round Stampalia, returning afterwards to Suda Bay.

145.   From Pound

8 February 1941

... We will do all we can to keep Malta well stocked with fighters, and the poor old *Furious*, after she has had her boilers put right, will do another trip to Takoradi. I hate her being used for this transport business but cannot under the circumstances resist it very strongly. I want to get the *Furious* refitted and then put her with Force H so that I can employ the *Ark* on the trade routes. I will go into the question of the RDF and short-range armament of the *York*....[71]

I am sorry the dive bombers are giving you trouble, but I am sure you will give them a good reception if they worry you again. The difficulty is to give ships practice in dealing with this form of attack and the only real answer is fighters. At the moment the situation is most involved in many directions as we do not know what Hitler's intentions are as regards Spain, Vichy and the Balkans, and in addition the situation in the Far East does not look too stable.

In one of your signals you suggest that you might require a reinforcement of capital ships, and I have been wondering whether it would be a good thing, if we can manage it, to send *Queen Elizabeth*

---

[71]*Furious:* 1917, lt b/c; reblt as carrier, 1918 & 1925; 22,450t, 12×4in, 33 a/c, 31k.

to the East Indies Station to help hunt down raiders until such time as you might require her in the Mediterranean.

146. *War Diary, February 1941 (cont.)*

9 February

Western Desert

6. The following signal was made by the C-in-C to the SNO, Inshore Squadron:

> The feat of the Army in clearing Egypt and occupying Cyrenaica in a period of 8 weeks is an outstanding achievement to which the Inshore Squadron and the shore parties along the coast have contributed in no small measure. I am fully alive to the fact that this result has been made possible by an unbreakable determination to allow no obstacle to stand in the way of meeting all requirements. All officers and men who took part in these operations may well feel proud as I do of their contribution to this victory.

7. The transport of troops and supplies to the Western Desert was brought back into full swing with the re-opening of Tobruk. *Rosaura* and *Chakla* sailed from Alexandria a.m., escorted by *Voyager*, and *Ulster Prince* with 1,300 troops sailed p.m. escorted by *Stuart*.[72]

10. Communications are very difficult. The use of Syko and Nyko having been stopped, there are not the facilities, books or personnel sufficient to compete with the traffic. The one W/T line is badly congested, and communication by air is continually being stopped by dust storms.

Air Activity

14. Tripoli was attacked by 10 Swordfish during the evening 8/9. The seaplane station was attacked heavily and 'cucumbers' were planted in the channel. One Swordfish was lost.

15. About 40 Ju88 raided Malta throughout the night 8/9, attacking singly from various heights. Some damage was done to the aerodromes but none to the dockyard. There were a few military casualties only. Two of the enemy were shot down and one damaged.

---

[72]*Rosaura:* 1937, 3,173gt, 10k, Anglo-Saxon Petroleum.

10 February

Canal Area

7. The C-in-C, accompanied by the COS, flew to Ismailia for a conference with the SBNO, Canal Area, and to inspect the progress of the anti-mining arrangements in the Canal Area.

147. *To Pound*

10 February 1941

A. I am afraid we are in a damn mess here over this magnetic mining. . . . They have had three ships mined and two hoppers, one an LL sweeper. Unfortunately two of the ships are across the channel to some extent and they are hard at it dredging round them. . . .

. . . Myself I think the place is so vital that I feel we should put a light net over the whole thing. . . .

At Tobruk we are by no means certain that we are not dealing with acoustic mines as all the ships that have touched them off have been diesel engined. There has only been one loss, but our repair resources will be badly strained trying to patch up the damaged ones. The port *is* open but a bit chancey.

B. *Formidable* can't transit the canal until 24 February at the earliest and then will have only six feet to spare past one of the wrecks. *Illustrious* will go the same way at much the same date. This delay is a nuisance as I want to pass in a Malta convoy and don't like to expose *Eagle* to dive bomber attacks.

We are trying some new methods against them. One which looks very promising is to make the destroyer screen put up an umbrella barrage over a particular ship probably the carrier. I am also going to have 12 fighters in the air over the fleet when we encounter these gentlemen again. I haven't much doubt of the result. Pridham-Wippell's four cruisers kept them at arm's length and inflicted casualties when the *Illustrious* was on passage.

D. The capture of Benghazi is a magnificent piece of work on the Army's part. . . . We have been stretched to the limit and past it in keeping them supplied. It's a mercy the Italians showed so little initiative for our long line of supply was very open to attack all the time. The Heinkels went for several ships and got the *Huntley*, one of our precious minesweepers.

There has been, I think, a lot of nonsense talked about the advantage of Benghazi to the Navy. The only advantage I can see is that we have 200 miles less of enemy coast. Actually it's a commitment and it seems to be forgotten that it's 200 miles nearer the Italian bases than ours.

The Army haven't got a coast defence gun to fit the place out with nearer than England. . . . It can also be mined by enemy aircraft at night and we just haven't sweepers for any type of mine to deal with it. . . .

I don't think we'll be able to get at MANDIBLES before the first week in April. It's an absolute necessity to take the important islands. Nothing will better secure the canal against this mining.

E. I am very sorry to lose Lyster; he has done great work out here and is quite unshaken by his experiences in *Illustrious*. I am sure he will make a very good 5th Sea Lord. Boyd should do well as his relief. He *was* a bit shaken – he had all the Malta attacks to put up with which Lyster did not have, but he has bobbed up again splendidly and is much gratified at having been thought of for RA(A). . . .

148. *War Diary, February 1941 (cont.)*

13 February

Operation SHELFORD

SNOIS and the Inshore Squadron arrived at Benghazi . . . Enemy aircraft laid 12 magnetic mines in Benghazi harbour . . .

2. SNOIS reported his intention of taking all ships to sea for the night on account of the heavy night raids, but since no particularly heavy raids had been reported and since cruiser cover could not be provided indefinitely, the C-in-C instructed SNOIS to obtain from the Army at once the maximum AA protection possible and rely for the safety of his ships on good dispersion in the harbour. Orders were also issued for Convoy AC1, the first convoy from Alexandria to Benghazi, to sail on 14 February.

3. 202 Group reported that since only 2 Swordfish aircraft are now available, an A/S patrol could not be maintained at both Tobruk and Benghazi.

Tanker Desmoulea

9. Arrangements for the lifting of *Desmoulea*'s cargo have still not been completed and the following signal was sent by the C-in-C to the authorities concerned:

It is important that immediate action be taken to lift *Desmoulea*'s cargo. While the matter is discussed between various authorities the Greeks grow daily shorter of petrol and the chances of saving the cargo and ship decrease. Action not argument is required.

Air Activity

9. A force of 3 Swordfish from Malta attacked a convoy on the Tripoli coast with torpedoes during the night 13/14 and sank one out of 4 merchant ships. Another may have been hit. A second striking force of 4 Swordfish failed to find the convoy.[73]

15 February

Western Desert

4. General Wilson, GOC, Cyrenaica Force, again raised the question of making Benghazi the main supply base instead of Tobruk, since adequate AA protection could not be provided for both. The C-in-C refused to accept this proposal but added that occasional convoys would be run to Benghazi provided there was sufficient AA protection.[74]

16 February

5. Benghazi harbour was reported to be in a considerably worse position than was at first thought. Our own bombing had breached the breakwater, admitting usually a heavy swell, and has destroyed most of the buildings and equipment on the foreshore. The inner harbour is blocked by several big sunken ships which will require extensive salvage operations to clear, and which were probably also sunk by our bombing. There are only 2 or 3 berths available for good sized ships inside the harbour and it seems unlikely that more than 500 tons could be unloaded daily. It is reported, however, that the road and rail transport from Tobruk is easier than was expected.

7. There were heavy air raids on Benghazi and the neighbouring air and military positions during both nights 14/15 and 15/16.... Two mines were laid in the harbour...

---

[73]*Juventus*: 1920, 4,920gt, SA Commerciale di Nav.

[74]Gen (later FM) Sir Henry Maitland Wilson (1881–1964): Lt-Gen, Br Troops in Egypt, Sept. 1939; Mil Govr, Cyrenaica, 1940–41; GOC, Greece, 1941; GOC Palestine & Transjordan, May 1941; Syria, June–Aug 1941; Gen Dec. 1941; 9th Army, Levant; Persia–Iraq Cmd Aug. 1942; C-in-C, ME Jan. 1943; SAC, Med, Jan. 1944; Head, Jt Staff Mission, Washington, Dec. 1944–47; FM, Jan. 1945.

THE EFFECTS OF GERMAN INTERVENTION, 1941

Air Activity

11. Four Swordfish from Malta on offensive patrol along the Tunisian coast during the night 15/16 attacked an Italian merchant ship which was hit with one torpedo and stopped. A second sub-flight of 4 Swordfish found the target and sank it with one more torpedo. Three Wellingtons attacked Catania and Comiso.

13. HQ, RAF Middle East, raised the question of removing the flying boat squadron from Malta on account of increasing enemy air activity there, but it was considered in Malta that dispersion and constant changes of anchorages rendered the flying boats reasonably safe and it was still most important to maintain their central operating position.

17 February

Greece

9. The NA, Athens, reported that the progress of the Greek Army had been considerably slowed up and that the possibility must be faced of a failure to capture the key point of Teppeleni. It was suggested that naval interference with Italian sea routes might be decisive both in its direct and psychological effects on the Greek and Italian armies. The possibility of using blockships at Durazzo was also raised and the NA asked if a captured Italian submarine could be made available.

20 February

Aircraft

6. It was suggested by the RAF that FAA aircraft from Maleme should relieve the Sunderland flying boats on a reconnaissance patrol (WAA) to the Eastward from Suda Bay, in order to make better use of the Sunderlands. The C-in-C would not agree to this and pointed out that the 6 Swordfish at Maleme were already fully occupied in maintaining:

(a) The Kithera patrol.
(b) Dodecanese reconnaissance.
(c) A/S patrol towards Gavdo Island.

The Sunderland patrol, however uneconomical, must be continued since it was essential to the security of Suda Bay and to the maintenance of Aegean and Greek lines of communication.

Canal Area

7. There was little progress with the sweeping of the Canal and it was felt that the watching organisation had not proved adequate.

The C-in-C asked the C-in-C, Middle East, for further military assistance in providing observation posts.

149. *Eden to Churchill*

20 February 1941

2. CIGS and I have today had full discussions with three Cs-in-C.
4. We are agreed we should do everything in our power to bring the fullest measure of help to the Greeks at the earliest possible moment. If help we can offer is accepted by the Greeks we believe that there is a fair chance of halting a German advance and preventing Greece from being overrun. Limitation of our resources, however, especially in the air, will not allow of help being given to Turkey at the same time if Greece is to be supported on an effective scale.
5. ... C-in-C, Mediterranean, considers that he can supply necessary protection at sea to enable Salonika to be used as base but emphasises that to do this he will need air protection which we fear will prove an insurpassable difficulty....
6. ... Further complication reported by C-in-C, Mediterranean, is that troops at Benghazi cannot at present be maintained by sea owing to destruction of port. In addition heavy air attack and mining have further reduced usefulness of Benghazi....
8. Timings cannot yet be given as these depend on discussion with Greeks and shipping. It is estimated that to move above forces at least 53 ships will be required. These can of course only be obtained by holding ships of convoys arriving in Middle East with all that implies. Additional present anxiety is menace of mines to Suez Canal. Energetic measures are being taken to deal with this, but until they are fully organised and material arrives there is always a risk that Canal may be closed from 5 to 7 days.
9. My own conclusion, which CIGS and Cs-in-C share, is that in the immediate future assistance to the Greeks who are fighting and are threatened must have first call on our resources....

THE EFFECTS OF GERMAN INTERVENTION, 1941   287

150. *Operations in Support of the Army off the Western Desert,*
7 December 1940–31 May 1941 (cont.)

Narrative

February 1941

149. When ships of Convoy AC1 were sailed from Benghazi to Tobruk on 19 February, *Terror, Fareham* and *Salvia* remained to assist the clearance party in getting the port facilities working and to give protection. Enemy air attacks were intensified and it was clear that they were out to pay off old scores on the *Terror*. The shore AA defences did not materialise on anything like the required scale whilst fighter protection was almost non-existent. The attacks reached their maximum on 22 February when, in a dawn raid, extensive damage was done to *Terror* by a near miss which started slow flooding into several compartments including the 15-in magazine.

150. It had been expected that the advanced air striking force and fighter squadrons in Cyrenaica would be reduced shortly for refitting and for work elsewhere, but the decision which had now been made to withdraw them without warning at a time when the Army was requiring urgent supplies at Benghazi had not been anticipated and came as an unpleasant shock.

Terror, summing up the situation, reported to the C-in-C on 22 February – 'With no (R) no dawn fighter protection as at present, I consider it only a matter of time before the ship receives a direct hit.'

She, with *Salvia* and *Fareham*, was ordered to sail at dusk for Tobruk, leaving the clearance party to do the best they could, and the C-in-C signalled to the Military and Air Cs-in-C, Middle East, 'In view of scale of air attacks, inadequate defences and damage to HMS *Terror*, I have withdrawn HM Ships from Benghazi.'

151. There remains the story of *Terror*'s last voyage. Dive-bombed when leaving Benghazi, she herself was undamaged although *Fareham* received a severe shaking from a near miss. In the swept channel, however, two mines exploded within 200 yards of *Terror* causing flooding but without putting the ship in danger.

152. There were no incidents of note the next day until about 1830 when the final attack by dive bombers was delivered and near misses which put all dynamos out of action broke the ship's back between the turret and the bridge. The boiler room flooded rapidly and all steam was lost. *Fareham* endeavoured to tow her towards Tobruk but little headway was made by 2230, by which time the ship was

slowly settling. Just before midnight, with the quarterdeck awash and four feet of freeboard forward, *Terror* abandoned ship.

To allow *Fareham* and *Salvia* to get as far as possible to the eastward by daylight, the ship was depth charged and early on 27 February, heeling slowly over to starboard, she capsized and sank. Thus, through lack of adequate AA defences and particularly fighter protection, at a critical period, we lost a ship which had done more than any other naval unit to start the western advance and keep it going.

153. Her loss stood for more than the end of a notable old veteran and for more than the little ships which had been, and were to be, sunk, from just the same cause, whilst on the business of supplying the Army and the Air. It pointed to the fact that it was an enemy of a very different calibre whom we now had to face; an enemy who was not to be bluffed by AA defences that were 'on the way' or who would be turned from his purpose as the Italians had been turned. And the inability of the Navy to use Benghazi was, in the not distant future, to mark more than the giving up of our most advanced supply base, for with it we were sure to lose not only the control of Cyrenaica, but the possibility of opening the Mediterranean route in the spring of 1941. It suggested also the need to limit the employment of makeshift in combined operations today.

It may well be that the historian when he sets out the credits and debits of this campaign will note three things in particular.

First, that Fascism had done little to change that military ineptitude which the Italians have shown throughout this century.

Next, that for an Empire which plans in peacetime for the command of sea in war, we tend to fall curiously short in our interservice preparations to use that command to the full.

And the third is that a gift for improvisation will not always carry us through in the face of new fangled devices.

He may perhaps add that there is always an answer to the new device, if only we will contrive to agree on it in time, and that new devices or not the sea roads, in this as in all our campaigns, still remain the most flexible, essential and effective carriers of that which the other forces must have. But the roads themselves impose today an additional and vital duty on the other two services.[75]

---

[75] The peroration seems likely to have been written by Cunningham's new COS, Cdre J. H. Edelsten, who succeeded Willis in March 1941: Adm Sir John Edelsten (1891–1966): Lt 1913; Cdr 1926; Capt 1933; DPD 1938; SNO, Somaliland, 1940; COS, MF 1941; RA 1942 & ACNS (UT); RA(D); BPF 1945; VA, 1BS, 1945; 4CS 1946; VCNS 1947; Adm & C-in-C Med 1950; C-in-C, Portsmouth 1952–54; ret 1954.

151. Operation MC8

(16 July 1941)

2. The operation [in February] was undertaken with the object of transporting reinforcement troops to Malta in cruisers, and at the same time, of allowing the passage to Alexandria of *Breconshire* and *Clan Macaulay*, escorted by *Havock* and *Hotspur* on completion of their damage repairs at Malta. Opportunity was also taken to pass *Diamond* into Malta for refit.

3. The operation passed off without incident except for bombing attacks on *Coventry*, *Clan Macaulay* and *Hotspur* in company on the evening of 21 February, and on *Hero* the same evening after she had been detached from Force A.

4. The attack on *Clan Macaulay* was of interest, being a synchronised high level bombing and dive bombing attack. One bomb passed through *Clan Macaulay*'s funnel without exploding. Fulmars from *Eagle* intervened and shot down one of these aircraft certain and one probable.

152. War Diary, February 1941 (cont.)

23 February

Operation MAR2 (ABSTENTION)

2. The object of this operation, which was to be executed under the orders of the RAC, 3CS, was the capture of the island of Kastelorizo (ABSTENTION), the most easterly of the Dodecanese Islands. *Parthian* had been carrying out a reconnaissance during the past two nights and would be used as a navigational beacon if necessary. *Hereward* and *Decoy*, supported by *Gloucester*, were to land a 'commando' from Crete during the night of D1, and *Ladybird* would land a further 24 Marines to give support if required at daylight D2. *Rosaura* was to transport the main garrison from Cyprus to arrive at Kastelorizo at daylight D3.

24 February

Loss of Dainty

6. *Dainty* sank after being hit at dusk in a dive bombing attack off Tobruk while proceeding for patrol.

25 February

Operation ABSTENTION

The island of Kastelorizo was attacked during the night of 24/25. The Commando was landed before dawn in ships' boats from *Hereward* and *Decoy* and the opposition seems to have been slight. ... *Ladybird* arrived in the harbour at daylight and landed her party of 24 Royal Marines in the town after silencing some persistent rifle fire with her 6-in and pom-pom guns. *Ladybird* then reported heavy air raids between 0800 and 0930 in which she received one hit while in harbour. Three of her crew were severely injured. The OC, Commando, ordered the Royal Marines to re-embark as he did not require them, and *Ladybird* withdrew, reporting her intention of proceeding to Cyprus. This was approved by the C-in-C. She was likely to be seriously short of fuel since she had not obtained any from *Rosaura* as intended, and there might not be any at Famagusta.

2. It had been intended for the Commando to be relieved by the garrison at daylight, 26th, and *Rosaura* sailed from Famagusta accordingly. But in view of the heavy air attacks the C-in-C suggested to CS3 that the relief should take place at night. CS3 reported that *Rosaura*'s slow speed would make the operation hazardous in face of night surface attack as well as day air attack and proposed to effect the relief from destroyers. This could not be done during the night of 26/27 as the destroyers were short of fuel, having been taken on a roundabout passage from Suda Bay at 27 knots. Presumably it was also too late to effect the transfer of the garrison and land it during the night of 25/26, for at 0230/26 CS3 ordered all forces engaged (less *Ladybird*) to return to Alexandria, intending to fuel destroyers and transfer the garrison there.

3. There was no means of communicating with the Commando since it had been decided not to land a W/T set other than the Commando's short range set, as *Ladybird* would form a W/T link until the arrival of the garrison. But at midnight 25/26 *Hereward* reported that 2 enemy [torpedo boats] were attacking Kastelorizo from Northward of the main harbour; *Hereward* however was continuing Southward to rejoin CS3.[76]

---

[76]*Lince* (s *Ultor*, Aug. 1943), *Lupo* (s Br force, Dec. 1942): 1938, 790t, 3×3.9in, 4×17.7in tt, 34k.

26 February

2. Since it was not clear what forces were being left in the vicinity, *Perth* was ordered by the C-in-C to raise steam in order to proceed from Alexandria to cover the island against any counter-attack during the night 26/27. But a signal was received from CS3 that his staff officer was being flown to Alexandria and it was decided to wait his arrival before sailing *Perth*. He did not arrive however until 1530, when it was learnt that no ships were being left in the vicinity of Kastelorizo; but it was then too late to sail *Perth*.

3. *Gloucester, Bonaventure* and *Decoy* reached Alexandria at 2000, and *Rosaura* and *Hereward* at 0400/27. The garrison was transferred to *Hero* and *Decoy* on the arrival of *Rosaura*. *Ladybird* was ordered to remain at Famagusta.

Malta

12. There was a heavy air raid on Malta by 30 Ju87, 12 Ju88, 10 Do215 and 10 He111, escorted by 20 or 30 fighters.[77] Luqa aerodrome was the main target and aircraft losses were as follows:

Own losses
Burnt out or destroyed   6 Wellingtons, 1 Glenn Martin
Badly damaged   3   "   3   "   "
Lost in action   3 Hurricanes

Enemy losses
Confirmed shot down by fighters   2 Ju87
    "   "   "   " AA fire   6 Ju87
Probably   "   "   " fighters   7 Ju87
    "   "   "   " AA fire   4 Ju87

There was much damage to the aerodrome but few casualties. A Red Cross plane accompanied by 20 fighters later searched the vicinity, giving the impression that the enemy losses may have been still more severe.

13. It had been under discussion whether to withdraw Fulmars from Malta on account of the superior performance of enemy fighters. VA, Malta, agreed to their withdrawal ultimately but asked that they be retained until more Hurricanes were available, since they were useful against Ju87s when covered by some Hurricanes.

14. VA, Malta's views on the running of convoys MW6 and 7 were given in his 1025/26. It was considered preferable to run the ships in

---

[77]Dornier Do215: 1934, 6 mg, 2,200lbs bombs, 263mph, range 1,860mls.

convoys of 4 rather than in ones and twos. The heavy scale of air activity made it most unlikely that even single ships could arrive unobserved.

27 February

Operation ABSTENTION

On arrival in harbour p.m., 25th, CS3 was reported sick and *Bonaventure* was placed in charge of the remainder of the operation, sailing from Alexandria with *Perth* during the forenoon. *Decoy* with half the garrison and *Hasty* sailed at 0700, and *Hero* with the other half and *Jaguar* sailed with *Bonaventure*.

Decoy and *Hero* were to land the garrison at Kastelorizo and embark the Commando while covered by *Jaguar, Hasty* and the two cruisers.

2. [The force] found the Commando in a demoralised state. They had been heavily bombed during both days 26th and 27th and also bombarded by enemy destroyers. It was decided to withdraw the garrison and as many of the Commando as possible. The men were badly spread out and about 40 were left behind, there having already been 15 to 20 casualties. At 0212/28 *Decoy* made the following signal to the C-in-C reporting the situation:

> Commando hemmed in at Niphti Point. Heavy air and sea bombardment daily experienced. Island untenable without artillery and air support. Commando and OC garrison agree withdrawal is essential which is being carried out. About 250 Italian troops have been landed.

3. Meanwhile *Jaguar* had seen an unknown ship inside the harbour and fired 5 torpedoes into the entrance. Shortly afterwards *Jaguar* only just avoided 2 torpedoes which passed close astern fired from an enemy destroyer. *Jaguar* engaged and reported securing two hits before his searchlight jambed on causing some delay until starshell could be fired. The enemy had then got clear and *Jaguar* could not regain contact. . . .

4. The whole force then proceeded to Suda Bay. . . .

28 February

2. *Ajax* was instructed by the C-in-C (0945/28) to arrange for *Nubian, Hasty* and *Jaguar* to carry out a sweep after dark 28th between Kastelorizo and Rhodes with the object of intercepting probable Italian reinforcements and supplies being sent to

Castelorizo. *Ajax* and *Perth* were ordered to cover the passage of convoys AN16 and ANF16 through the Kaso Straits during the night of 28/1 March. . . .
3. *Decoy* and *Hero* were ordered to land the Commando at Suda Bay and then to sail for Alexandria with the OC Commando and the intended garrison for ABSTENTION. . . .
4. An Italian warship was reported by RDF between Rhodes and Kastelorizo and there was heavy Aegean W/T traffic, but nothing was sighted. The destroyers completed their sweep without incident and returned to Alexandria.

Part II – General Appreciation

Strategical

. . . The Libyan offensive was abandoned with great regret by the Commanders in the Mediterranean as there is little doubt that by pressing on we might have made ourselves masters of the North African coast as far as Tunisia; had this been possible we should have been saved much subsequent difficulty.
2. The extended army lines of communication made supply necessary by sea and the problem was greatly complicated by the strength of the German air force. They were able to roam at will along the North coast attacking our coasting ships, minelaying and bombing. We had considerable casualties and it soon became evident that it was useless to try and use Benghazi as a port of supply. In consequence it was decided to build up Tobruk and gradually dump forward. . . .
5. Towards the end of the month anxiety began to arise over German activities and troop concentrations in Italy. It became evident that the Germans were possibly coming to the support of Italy with armoured units, and the question of Libyan convoys became a matter of urgent importance.

Unfortunately at this time new 'U' class submarines had just arrived and were inexperienced. In consequence, in the early stages a high proportion of our submarine attacks were unsuccessful and this allowed the enemy to put important units into Tripoli comparatively unchallenged. We were at this juncture still so critically short of light craft that there were none to spare to work from Malta, where they might have interfered with this traffic.

Western Desert

12. The month has been one of continuous endeavour to cater with the immediate needs of the Army (including the evacuation of

prisoners and wounded) and to build up supplies for them. This should have been simple in view of our command of the sea, but it has in fact been made most difficult owing to enemy air superiority. Not only has a heavy scale of minelaying been experienced but our coastal traffic has been the subject of constant attack. In addition all harbours have been frequently raided.

As regards defences the extreme weakness of our AA defence, coupled with very small fighter protection owing to withdrawal and exhaustion of our air forces, has given the enemy a fairly free run. In consequence it has proved impossible to use Benghazi as a forward base, and Tobruk also has not been able to work to capacity. Owing to lack of air protection casualties to ships have been heavy. Benghazi was effectively blocked on evacuation by the Italians and will take some time to make serviceable for more than 500 tons a day. Steps were taken to clear each harbour as sweeping resources allowed; Derna was operating by 2nd, Sollum and Bardia by 6th, and Benghazi by 19th. Tobruk was open, with intervals, all the time and was made the main Army supply base. In order to assist supply four captured Italian schooners were taken over for this work, their wooden hulls making them particularly suitable. . . .

Bases

15. *Canal area.* Intensive minesweeping has been carried out in order to get the rate of clearance in the Canal ahead of the rate at which mining took place. . . . The result has been to some extent successful and the Canal re-opened to traffic except for very large ships. . . . Machine gun positions, fighters and balloons are now being used to strengthen the AA defences. . . .

The Canal was mined afresh on 19 and 22 February . . . At the end of the month the Canal was still closed and there was a serious congestion of 110 ships at Suez. . . . it was hoped to re-open in the first week of March. . . .

17. *Malta.* . . . The intensity of attack was less than in January but there were several big scale raids, probably provoked by attacks by Wellingtons on Tripoli. Enemy aircraft were shot down in some number, but the cumulative effect is serious. Steps are being taken to reinforce fighter strength. A new feature has been the start of minelaying attack, to meet which Malta resources are not adequate. The problem of keeping Malta supplied remains serious as it involves a full scale operation at least once a month to pass ships in and it is increasingly important to remove empty ships as quickly as possible.

18. *Suda Bay.* The development of Suda Bay continues slowly, and the first portion of the A/T baffle was laid by 6 February. Suda Bay cannot, however, be made into a properly defended Fleet base until the arrival of the MNBDO in April, since there is no suitable equipment on the Station to allow of anything more than improvised arrangements. . . . The scale of air attack was not heavy . . .

Submarines

19. The policy has been to concentrate submarines on the Sicily–Tripoli route and this has resulted in some successes and 6 ships were sunk. . . .

153 *War Diary, March 1941*

4 March

Canal Area

7. In spite of many requests from the C-in-C and SBNOCA there was still no adequate motor transport to move the mine destruction, sweeping and diving parties along the canal quickly. The following signal was accordingly made by the C-in-C to GHQ, Middle East:

> Probably the most urgent commitment in the Middle East at the moment is the adequate minesweeping of the Canal Area, yet after four days no reply has been received to this urgent request for three lorries to avoid delay to this vital work. It would greatly ease my mind if instructions could be issued that highest priority is to be given by all departments to any matters affecting the Canal Area.

7 March

Malta

12. Heavy raids were reported on 5 and 6 March. That on the 5th was by 70 bombers and 50 fighters, mainly on Hal Far. There were no casualties but the aerodrome and buildings were badly damaged. One Gladiator was destroyed on the ground and one Hurricane in action. The 11 available Hurricanes were all in action and a total of 16 enemy aircraft were shot down as well as 6 damaged and one probably destroyed. The raid prevented the execution of a minelaying attack on Tripoli.

8 March

9. VA Malta had been asked to clear a greater portion of the mined area off Malta in order to reduce the convoy route. He reported that he was unable to do this, partly on account of danger to minesweepers from the air without fighter protection and partly because of the necessity to conserve coal. The shortage of coal was proving the weakest part of the island's defences.

10. Due to enemy action there was only one flying boat in four serviceable and that was waiting to convey the Foreign Secretary to the UK. The reconnaissance patrol to cover Kithera convoys could not therefore be repeated.

154. *To the Admiralty*

4 March 1941

The move of the Army and RAF to Greece is about to start. This will involve continual personnel, MT and stores convoy for next two months. Escort and cover for these movements will absorb the whole activity of Fleet and Destroyers in particular will have to be very heavily worked. It is intended, however, to run a convoy to Malta as soon as possible after *Formidable* is available, but this can only be done at expense of some delay to aviation movements. It appears inevitable that combined operation against Mandibles [Dodecanese] and other offensive operations will have to be deferred.

2. I feel I must make it quite clear that [?movement] of this large force to Greece involves considerable risk. If Germans start an air offensive from Bulgaria against convoys and ports of disembarkation loss must be expected as scale of AA and fighter defence available will be very weak for some time to come. Surface action against convoys by Italian Fleet cannot be excluded and battleship cover is to be provided[?] effective from Suda Bay though this means weakening convoy destroyer escort and leaving Cyrenaican supply line practically unprotected.

3. Although I am confident that problems can and will be solved in time, the susceptibility of Canal to magnetic and acoustic mines gives cause for much anxiety just now when these big movements of troops and MT are starting.

4. Malta too is having a difficult time and I realise strain on personnel, particularly fighter pilots, is considerable.

5. I am very conscious that this next two months is going to [be] an equally critical period in home waters and I represent the situation out here not in order to press my need but rather so that Their Lordships can strike a just balance with the knowledge of available resources. It would be useless hiding the fact mine are taxed to the limit and that by normal security standards my commitments exceed available resources.

6. I have, however, considerable hope that all these difficulties can be overcome. We are, I am convinced, pursuing right policy and risk must be faced up to.

155. *Cunningham's report on operation LUSTRE*

(11 December 1941)

Be pleased to lay before Their Lordships the following report concerning operation LUSTRE – the move to Greece of some 58,000 troops with their mechanical transport, full equipment and stores. The operation commenced on 4 March and ceased on 24 April when the evacuation from Greece commenced.

3. The passage from Egyptian ports to the Piraeus, virtually the only port of the country, led past the enemy bases in the Dodecanese from which his air and sea forces were in a good position to operate against our lines of communication. Cover had also to be provided against interference from enemy surface forces from Italy. In consequence it was desirable to move as many personnel as possible in warships whose high speed would take them quickly through the danger zone. In the event the movement of personnel in HM Ships became a necessity owing to the mining of the Suez Canal which prevented sufficient troopships being available.

This policy proved successful and during the whole period of this complicated operation no men or equipment were lost at sea except for a few casualties from bomb splinters in one merchant ship. The losses sustained were either in ships proceeding in the convoys but not connected with LUSTRE or in ships returning empty.

4. During the greater part of the move a proportion of the Battle Fleet was kept at sea to the westward of Crete to provide heavy cover for our forces. In addition, Operation MC9, running a Malta convoy, was carried out between 19 and 24 March whilst LUSTRE still proceeded.

5. The whole operation was smoothly carried out owing to the hard work and willing spirit shown in the ships concerned. It threw

a considerable strain on the port of Alexandria where nearly all commercial shipping movements had to be stopped. The difficulties were, however, overcome, including some trouble with Asiatic crews of merchant ships, by a firm insistence that, whatever the numbers of men or vehicles the Army had ready to move, the demand must be met and men and stores reach Greece without delay.

Appendix
Casualties Caused to Shipping at Sea during LUSTRE

21 March

Danish oiler *Marie Maersk*, in Convoy AN21, hit and set on fire. Crew taken off by *Waterhen* who towed the ship to Suda Bay.

22 March

Convoy AS21 attacked by He111s SE of Gavdo. Greek *Nicholas Embiricos* and *Solheim* both badly damaged. *Nicholas Embiricos* sank later and *Solheim* abandoned.

31 March

Bonaventure, escorting Convoy GA8, was hit amidships by two torpedoes at 0830 and sank almost immediately.

2 April

Convoy AS23 attacked by 6 Ju88 D/B. *Koulandis Xenos* and *Homefield* hit and abandoned. SS *Teti,* who had apparently been near missed, reported that she was leaking badly and proceeded to an anchorage near Lissmoss.[78]

Convoy ANF24 attacked by HLB. SS *Devis* hit in No.6 hold and fire started, 7 men being killed and 14 injured.

3 April

Convoy ANF24 attacked by D/B. *Northern Prince* (carrying important stores for Greece from UK) was hit and set on fire – later blew up and sank.

---

[78]*Marie Maersk*: 1928, 8,271gt, tkr, Svendborg/Moller, Copenhagen.
Solheim: 1934, 8,070gt, Hvalfangereslk Norge.
Nicholas Embiricos: 1919, 5,295gt, Coulouthros & Embiricos.
Koulandis [Coulouras] Xenos: 1915, 4,914gt, Ath. Coulouras, Hydra.
Homefield: 1919, 5,324gt, 10k, Br India SN.
Teti: 1903, 2,747gt, Mme K. G. Sigalas, Greece.

17 April

Convoy AN27 attacked by HLB and T/B. Oiler *British Science* torpedoed and speed reduced to 6 knots. Proceeded independently for Suda Bay. Torpedoed again at 1530/18 and caught fire. Ship abandoned and later sank.

21 April

Convoy AS26 attacked by D/B. *British Lord* hit and later taken in tow by *Auckland*.[79]

156. To Pound

11 March 1941

A. We are having rather an anxious time out here. We are losing so many small ships on the Cyrenaican coast.

I hope it will turn out that our policy of helping Greece is the right one. To me it is absolutely right but I much doubt if our resources, particularly naval and air, are equal to the strain.

... Having driven us out of Benghazi the Germans are now trying the same at Tobruk and bagged the *Dainty* going on patrol at dusk. Hit in the larger after oil tank she caught fire and the torpedo air vessels exploded, rather blowing her to bits.

It is unbelievable but there are only 16 heavy AA guns between Alexandria and Benghazi and they are all now at Tobruk. All the rest have been withdrawn to go to Greece.

B. The taking and abandonment of Kastelorizo was a rotten business and reflected little credit on anyone.

I put Renouf in charge and he, poor man, cracked in the middle of it. To this must be ascribed some of the consequences but I feel I should have stepped in myself and straightened things out. The Italians were unbelievably enterprising and not only bombed the island heavily but bombarded it and landed reinforcements from destroyers.

For some reason the Army W/T set did not work and so we had little information of what was going on.

These commandos we have out here are on a tommy gun and knuckle duster basis and apparently can't defend themselves if seriously attacked. I had 25 picked marines bristling with machine guns in the *Ladybird* but some fool ordered them to re-embark.

---

[79]*British Lord*: 1922, 6,098gt, 10k, Br Tkr Co.
British Science: 1931, 7,138gt, 10k, Br Tkr Co.

All we can say is that we have learnt a lot from it and won't repeat the mistakes.[80]

We had a meeting in Cairo this morning with Dill and Eden and hope to get on with the main MANDIBLE operation during the third week in April provided forces can be spared from the rush to Greece which isn't due to ease up till the middle of May.[81]

D. Malta is in a very bad state. I have just seen the Air Vice Marshal who is here to report. He tells me the Germans are right on top of them. He has only eight serviceable Hurricanes left and the German fighters are coming over in droves and machine gunning people in the streets of St Paul's Bay and other outlying villages.

He is being sent six from the shortage here but that is no good, he ought to have two full squadrons and at once. I am really seriously concerned about Malta. I am running a convoy there in about 10 days' time but with their defences in the present state I am quite expecting some of the ships to be damaged. The Grand Harbour and the creeks are also being mined whenever the enemy cares to come.

This is a gloomy picture but someone is misinforming the Chiefs of Staff about the real state of affairs out here. We must have large numbers of fighters rushed out to us if we are to make headway and indeed they are needed to save what may be a serious setback.

E. I am more optimistic about the Canal although it was mined again last night. The last lot took only 5 days to clear and we had the traffic going for over 48 hours and cleared away a lot of the congestion. I also got *Formidable*. I tried to push *Eagle* through but they must dredge before they can manage a ship of her beam. *Illustrious* just missed the bus and must now wait until the Canal is clear again. So I fear it will go on until the Canal is adequately defended. Shortage of fighters and AA guns again.

F. The 'Glen' ships have arrived and Walter Cowan. He tackled me about Roger Keyes coming out here but I stood firm and wrote to Sir Roger pointing out how awkward it would be as there was a young Rear Admiral already in command.[82] . . . I have no objection to Walter Cowan; he is a very old and dear friend.

---

[80] An enquiry was held by RA Baillie-Grohman & Maj-Gen J. F. Evetts: b 1891; 2Lt 1911, Cameron Hldrs; Capt Oct 1915; France 1916–19; Iraq 1925–28; Lt-Col 1931; WO, 1932–34; Col 1934; Palestine 1935–36; Act Brig 1939; Actg Maj-Gen July 1940; Cdr, W (Indpdt) Dist, India, Apr 1941.

[81] FM J. C. Smuts (1870–1950), S African PM; Boer War 1899–1902; lawyer & poln; M Defence, Un S Af, 1910–19; as field cdr, evicted Ger forces from SW Af, 1914–17; Imp War Cab 1917–19; PM 1929–29, 1939–48. His CGS, Gen Pierre van Ryneveld, and Lt-Gen Sir Alan Cunningham, Andrew's younger brother, were also present.

[82] Baillie-Grohman.

G. I am grateful to you for letting me have Edelsten. Both Roger Backhouse and I thought him the the pick of the Plans party when we were at the Admiralty. I like and admire Mountbatten but he is very junior still and I doubt if he is as sound as Edelsten.

I am terribly sorry to lose Willis but he is mentally tired out. He has never spared himself and has done splendid work. After a month or two he will bob up again and I am sure you will be able to use his great abilities.[83]

Renouf just cracked up through anxiety but he also has some stomach trouble. I am sure Glennie will be excellent.

I. The move to Greece is in full swing. A large convoy every three days. We're taking great risks with thin escorts but time is the essence of this move being a success.

The Italians are bombing most convoys as they go by, but the AA cruisers are keeping them high and so far they have been unscathed.

One AA cruiser, *Coventry,* is running with very little bow below water and *Carlisle* is running on one shaft only, the other being drawn for repair. But they must just run while this move is on.

It was a most timely performance *Greyhound* bagging the submarine in the Kaso Strait. The prisoners said there are six to eight in Leros who are refusing to go to sea.[84]

157. *War Diary, March 1941 (cont.)*

11 March

Malta

12. One Sunderland was burnt out and another damaged in enemy fighter raids on Malta on 10th. One fighter was shot down and 2 others damaged by AA fire. There were a number of other raids during the day and a heavy raid on the dockyard and aerodromes during the night 10/11 by 20 aircraft. The Dockyard generating station was reported as now altogether out of action, with only one machine working in the new underground station. Three enemy aircraft were shot down and 2 others damaged.

13. There were not sufficient Swordfish aircraft available at Malta for an effective minelaying raid on Tripoli before the expiration of the life of the mines at Malta. It was therefore decided to employ the 4 available aircraft at once in anti-convoy patrols.

---

[83]Willis became Act VA and C-in-C S Atl Sept. 1941.
[84]*Anfitrite*: documents captured before she sank.

12 March

DEMS

8. The Admiralty was asked to give full support to the requirements of the DEMS organisation now being established in the Mediterranean. Merchant ships were deplorably ill equipped, compared with those in Home Waters, to meet the increasing threat of air attack. Operation LUSTRE had increased the difficulties in this direction.

16 March

Intelligence

7. A report from the US Naval Attaché at Rome indicated that the Italian cruiser *Bande Nere* had been damaged recently by mine and was at Naples, and that more ships were sunk in the Adriatic than we believed. The Navy and Air Force were reported to have 'lost their nerve' and the recently appointed Admiral Iachino to have proved a disappointment.[85]

158. *To Pound*

0830, 16 March 1941

Am informed by Secretary of State that delivery of Hurricanes to Malta by carrier has been abandoned on account of risk to carrier.[86] It is hoped to run a convoy into Malta on 23 March which will involve considerable risk to *Formidable*, and even more to convoy both when approaching Malta and when unloading there which will be much accentuated if Malta cannot be reinforced with Hurricanes by then. Hope therefore that decision can be reconsidered.

159. *From Pound*

1715, 16 March 1941

A. At no time has the delivery of Hurricanes by carrier been abandoned, but the earliest date Hurricanes could reach Malta by this route would be 28 March.

---

[85]*Giovanni delle Bande Nere*: 1930, 5,200t, 8×6in, 6×3.9in, 37k; s *Urge* 1 Apr 1942.
Adm Angelo Iachino: apptd C-in-C, Italian F, foll Taranto.
[86]Eden, Foreign Sec, then in Egypt.

B. The risk to the carrier is certainly one of the factors which must be taken into account but by no means the only one.

I am sure you are in no doubt as to what the fate of *Ark Royal* would have been had she been in *Illustrious*'s place.

C. 1. I am not sure that you entirely appreciate what is going on outside the Mediterranean.

2. At the moment we are engaged in the battle of the Atlantic which transcends all things as we cannot afford to lose it.

3. We are stretched to the limit as not only have we the U-boat, mine and aircraft menace round our coasts to deal with but also the U-boat menace in the Freetown area and there is good indication that U-boats may even now be operating in the Newfoundland area.

4. In addition to the above there are at the moment two enemy battlecruisers in the North Atlantic, and 8-in cruiser of *Hipper* class at Brest and one pocket battleship at large.[87]

The only answer to this is battleship escort and at the moment the whole of the capital ships of both Home Fleet and Force H with the sole exception of *Nelson* are employed on convoy escort duty.

D. From the above I am sure you will appreciate that whilst the present situation lasts it will be necessary for Force H to be looking to the Westward much more than to the Eastward.

E. From various telegrams I have seen I can't help feeling that Longmore hopes that the reinforcement of Malta with Hurricanes will be a routine matter. I hope you will disabuse him of any such hopes.

I have been only too glad that carriers should have been used as aircraft transports to meet a grave emergency but it is quite wrong that they should be used for this purpose when by looking ahead sufficiently I feel that this can be avoided.

160. *To Pound*

0929, 17 March 1941

I fully recognise the great difficulty confronting you in the Atlantic and believe me I do not wish to add to your anxiety but I feel I should be failing in my duties if I did not point out our difficulties here and suggest means of meeting them.

(ii) I am seriously alarmed about Malta. The enemy air forces are operating just as they please over the island and most drastic and early measures are required to restore the situation.

---

[87]*Hipper* at Brest & in N Atl; *Scheer en route* N-about to Kiel.

(iii) Para (e) of your message, I am not aware that Longmore has expressed any opinion about the reinforcement of Malta by aircraft from carriers but I feel you are not being kept well informed about fighter situation in Middle East. Large reinforcements of this type of aircraft are urgently necessary if we are not to find ourselves on all points in serious difficulties. Are you aware that in February only one Hurricane (R) one Hurricane was received in Middle East and that in March none have yet arrived?

Secretary of State Foreign Affairs and CIGS have lately fully represented this situation in their messages.

(iv) I agree that by looking ahead it would be quite possible to supply fighter necessity of Malta without use of carriers but as you will realise there has been a definite failure to do this which has placed us in present rather grim situation.

161. *War Diary, March 1941 (cont.)*

19 March

Establishment of the Naval Base at Suda Bay

2. The outstanding feature of this operation was the fact that although the need for an advanced base in the Eastern Mediterranean had been appreciated for many years and was fully provided for in 1935, in 1940 owing to more urgent requirements in home waters it had not been possible to allocate any personnel or special material to the Mediterranean. When the possibility of using Suda Bay was considered in May 1940, Middle East resources allowed only one machine gun battalion for the defence of the island.

3. It was, therefore, a fortunate coincidence that when it became necessary to establish a fuelling base at Suda Bay, the disablement of *Liverpool* and the fact that guns were being prepared at Alexandria for other services, enabled the necessary personnel and equipment to be improvised from station resources at 24 hours' notice. Military coast defence personnel were not available until February 1941.

4. It was appreciated that ships at Suda Bay would be exposed to aircraft torpedo attacks, but no A/T nets were available to defend the anchorage. To overcome this deficiency an improvised defence was constructed at Alexandria consisting of four layers of B2 net stopped together to make a light net and the remainder of the anchorage covered by a line of buoys. Little or no reliance was

placed in this defence but it was hoped that enemy reconnaissance machines would report that the anchorage was defended by nets and would be discouraged from attacking it with torpedo aircraft. Unfortunately this hope was not realised and *Glasgow* was torpedoed by aircraft notwithstanding.

162. Report on Malta Convoy MC9, 20–24 March 1941

30 April 1941

Cunningham's Observations

2. The operation passed almost without incident as far as the Battlefleet was concerned, the most surprising feature being the complete absence of air action in the Central Mediterranean on the 22nd, during which the Fleet and convoy were in close company steering for Malta.

3. It can only be assumed that the feint made to the Northward on the evening of the 21st, as though entering the Aegean, had the desired effect of making the enemy believe that this operation was a part of the covering operations for LUSTRE convoys carrying troops to Greece.

4. The simple form of bow protection gear fitted to *Havock* and *Hotspur* at Malta made it possible to route this convoy direct to Malta instead of passing round the mined area S of Hurd Bank, thus saving some four hours' steaming and enabling the convoy to keep outside the range of Ju87 bombers at sea in daylight.

7. The operation was negative and passive in its nature, but the object was achieved.

Narrative

Force A left Alexandria at 0700 on 20 March.[88]

2. During the forenoon of 20th, practices were carried out, including 15-in and 6-in throw off shoots, sleeve target firings and dummy dive bombing attacks. . . .

---

[88]*Warspite, Barham, Valiant, Formidable,* 14th & 2nd DFs, *City of Lincoln, City of Manchester, Clan Ferguson, Perthshire* & escorts. *City of Lincoln*: 1938, 8,039gt, 16k, Ellerman & Bucknall. *City of Manchester*: 1935, 8,916gt, 15k, Hall Line. *Perthshire*: 1936, 10,496gt, 17k, Scottish Shire Line.

4. ... At 1036 *Bonaventure* was heard asking for fighter support. She was at that time to the Northward of Gavdo Island with convoy MW6 ... shortly afterwards the convoy came in sight and at 1220 *Bonaventure* was seen to be firing ... At 1225 a Ju88 ... passed about 4,000 yards to the N of the battleships and was heavily engaged and crashed 2 miles astern.... a Fulmar fighter section flown off on receipt of *Bonaventure*'s call for fighters had attacked and damaged a Ju88. It seems likely that this was the one that came over the fleet.

At 1600, VALF, the 3rd and 7th Cruiser Squadrons, *Stuart, Hereward* and *Hasty*, joined the fleet ... and *Havock* was detached to join Force C at 1630. Considerable enemy W/T air activity persisted throughout the afternoon, and evidently AN21 was attacked, the enemy claiming to have destroyed a large tanker, presumably the *Marie Maersk*. There were also a number of RDF reports in the fleet but nothing was sighted.

5. At 1700 a cast was made to the Northward by the convoy and battlefleet to convey the impression that ships would pass through the Kithera Straits during the night. At 1900 the convoy turned to 240° and the battlefleet to the same course after opening some 25 miles to the Northward. During the night VALF and the cruisers were a further 20 miles to the NW of the battlefleet.

6. At 0800/22 all forces were in sight of each other ... and course was altered to the Westward until 1600 when the convoy steered for Malta at its best speed and using smallest safe zigzag. Air searches were cancelled in order not to betray the positions of ships. During the forenoon one Fulmar force landed in the sea, the crew being saved. A/S and fighter patrols were kept going all day. Malta and Suda Bay reconnaissance aircraft made 'Nil' reports from the Ionian Sea area.... Both Fleet and convoy appear to have remained undetected during the day. At dark VALF and cruisers and two 'Tribals' were detached to the NW to cover the convoy during the early part of the night. VALF reported his intention to turn to the Eastward at midnight so as to rejoin the battle fleet at 0800/23....

7. At 0900/23 VALF rejoined ... followed by *Defender* at 0930. At 0915 RDF reports started to come in, and two aircraft obviously sighted the fleet at about 0920. Fighters intercepted and one aircraft was damaged at 0945.... At 1900, VALF, 3rd and 7th Cruiser Squadrons and two destroyers were detached to duty in the Aegean and to cover and meet Force C. The general trend was – speed of advance 17 knots ... *Stuart* attacked two contacts.

8. ... At 0915[/24] the fleet was sighted and reported, ... The Fleet entered Alexandria harbour at 2330 without further incident.

163. *War Diary, March 1941 (cont.)*

26 March

HMS York

An attack was made on Suda Bay at 0515 by six Italian one man 'human torpedoes'. *York* was severely damaged below water amidships, both engine rooms and boiler rooms being flooded. She grounded in 4½ fathoms, and being unable to raise steam had no power for pumping, lighting or for working turrets.

2. The oiler *Pericles* was also holed amidships and was beached, though most of her cargo was reported undamaged.[89]
3. Six prisoners were picked up on rafts and it appeared that the attack was carried out by fast planing dinghies with explosive charges. They were apparently released from a parent ship or submarine and were abandoned by the crew before reaching the target. They were set to explode on impact or possibly having sunk alongside. One boat was recovered intact.

Ilex and *Hasty* hunted the submarine off Suda without success.

31 March

3. The C-in-C made a general signal stressing the need for alertness in ships in harbour. The success of the recent attack on Suda Bay, together with the defeat of the enemy fleet at sea, were likely to provoke further attempts by submarines, special craft or torpedo aircraft against our defended harbours.

164. *From Pound*

28 March 1941

... It was yesterday that we heard of the revolution in Yugoslavia and we only hope it will turn out well.

... *Exeter* has left Plymouth ... and is now at Scapa working up. I will get her out to you as soon as possible.

---

[89]*Pericles*: 1938, 3,167gt, 13.4k, R Neth SS Co; broke in two and sank in heavy seas while on passage to Alexandria under own power, 13 Apr. 1941.

As you know I am longing to send you reinforcements, but we have so many commitments that it is almost impossible. . . .

165. *Cunningham's Dispatch on the Battle of Matapan*

(11 November 1941)

The C-in-C's Observations

Be pleased to lay before Their Lordships the attached reports of the Battle of Matapan, 27–30 March 1941. Five ships of the enemy fleet were sunk, burned or destroyed. Except for the loss of one aircraft in action, our fleet suffered no damage or casualties.

2. . . . Long and anxious consideration had been given to the disposition of available forces, important factors being the necessity to maintain the flow of LUSTRE convoys to Greece, and the difficulty of finding sufficient destroyers for a fleet operation when demands for convoy escorts were so heavy. . . .

3. The disposition described in para. 3 of the C-in-C's narrative was adopted with the intention of countering a possible cruiser raid into the Aegean. It was designed to give flexibility and allowed for a quick change of plan if more intelligence came to hand to clarify the situation.

I was concerned to avoid any movement which might alarm the enemy and cause him to defer any operation he might have in mind. To allow a state of suspense to continue, with Operation LUSTRE in full swing, would have imposed an increased strain on the light forces of the fleet.

4. The disposition originally ordered left the cruisers without support. The battlefleet could if necessary have put to sea, but very inadequately screened. Further consideration led to the retention of sufficient destroyers to screen the battlefleet. The moment was a lucky one when more destroyers than usual were at Alexandria having just returned from or just awaiting escort duty.

5. It had already been decided to take the battlefleet to sea under cover of night on the evening of the 27th, when air reconnaissance from Malta reported enemy cruisers steaming eastward p.m./27th. The battlefleet accordingly proceeded with all possible secrecy. It was well that it did so, for the forenoon of the 28th found the enemy S of Gavdo and the VALF with Force B in an awkward situation which might have been serious had the support of the battlefleet been lacking.

6. The situation at 0812 when surface contact was first made did not appear unsatisfactory although in fact at this time Force B was very uncomfortably placed with a second and powerful enemy cruiser squadron out of sight to the NE and well placed to cut Force B off from the battlefleet. The squadron had actually been sighted and reported by *Gloucester*'s spotting aircraft but fortunately for everybody's peace of mind this report did not get beyond *Gloucester*'s TS.

7. Aircraft from *Formidable* had sighted and reported a further force to the northward of the cruisers and in one case had reported battleships, but the situation was not very clear.... The situation did not, therefore, appear unduly alarming, but the air striking force was made ready and *Valiant* ordered ahead to join VALF.[90]

8. The sighting by Force B of a battleship at 1058 put a very different complexion on affairs. The enemy was known to be fast and *Gloucester* had been reported only capable of 24 knots. Force B looked like being sandwiched between the *Vittorio Veneto* and the 8-in cruisers they had already engaged. It was with great relief that it was realised that Force B was able to make 30 knots and that the range was not closing.

VALF handled the squadron with great skill, holding the range open and taking every advantage of his smoke screen as he worked round to SE to close the battlefleet; but there were some unpleasant minutes with 15-in salvos straddling the cruisers before the intervention of the T/B striking force which gained a hit on the *Vittorio* had caused her to turn away.[91]

9. It had always previously been my intention, if contact were made with the enemy's fleet, to hold back the torpedo air striking force until the battlefleets had closed within about 50 miles of each other, or until the enemy had definitely turned away. On this occasion owing to the exposed position of the cruisers it was necessary to launch the striking force unduly early. Few things could have been more timely than their intervention but it had the effect I had always feared, that the damaged enemy turned for home with a lead that could not be closed to gun range in daylight.

10. Meanwhile the battlefleet was pressing on fast to close the enemy. VALF's signal timed 1210 reporting he had lost touch actu-

---

[90] Captain Lee, then Cunningham's Flag Lieut, recalls that the C-in-C was in his bath when told of VALF's sighting of the Italian Fleet and stood up 'in a state of nature' to dictate precise orders to increase to maximum speed and prepare a torpedo striking force.
Captain Lee to editor, 20 Oct. 1997.
[91] No hits by 1st striking force but struck aft by 2nd air attack in afternoon.

ally reached me as Force B hove in sight at 1230. It might be argued that Force B should have followed and maintained touch when the enemy turned westward, but with the considerable chance which then existed of being cut off by superior force, and adequate air reconnaissance being available, it is considered that VALF was correct in his decision to gain visual contact with the battlefleet and check respective positions before resuming the chase. His force had been outranged and outgunned by all enemy vessels with which he had so far made contact.

11. The attacks carried out by RAF Blenheim bombers from Greece were most welcome as giving the enemy a taste of his own medicine, this being the first time that our bombing aircraft had cooperated with the fleet at sea. In actual fact it is not thought that any hits were scored, certainly no appreciable damage was done, but the attacks must have worried the enemy and made him even more chary of approaching our coasts. The work of 230 F/B squadron was, as ever, invaluable.

12. It cannot be said for certain how many, if any, further hits were obtained on *Vittorio* by the successive FAA attacks during the afternoon and evening. All that is certain is that the *Pola* was hit and stopped in a dusk attack, but whatever the result, the gallantry and perseverance of the aircraft crews and the smooth efficiency of deck and ground crews in *Formidable* and at Maleme are deserving of high praise.

An example of the spirit of these young officers is the case of Lt F. M. A. Torrens Spence, who, rather than be left out, flew with the only available aircraft and torpedo from Eleusis to Maleme and, in spite of reconnaissance difficulties and bad communications, arranged his own reconnaissance and finally took off with a second aircraft in company and took part in the dusk attack.[92]

13. In spite of continual air sighting reports the situation towards the end of the afternoon had become rather confused. This was due to the presence of both shipborne and shore-based aircraft, a considerable change of wind, the presence of several separate enemy squadrons and finally the ever present difficulty of distinguishing the silhouettes of enemy warships. It was difficult to decide the tactics for the night.

The situation was however rapidly cleared up by about 1800. VALF's cruisers were just gaining touch ahead and two aircraft, Duty V of *Formidable* and Duty Q from *Warspite* had made contact.

[92] Torrens Spence was a Taranto veteran.

Mention must be made here of the excellent work of *Warspite*'s catapult aircraft (Lt-Cdr A. S. Bolt, DSC, Observer).[93] This aircraft had, by a fortunate mistake, returned to the ship instead of going to Suda Bay as ordered. It was recovered, refuelled and catapulted as Duty Q at 1745. Within an hour and a half this experienced observer had presented me with an accurate picture of the situation which was of the utmost value at this time.

14. The last report, however, showed that a difficult problem was before us. The enemy had concentrated in a mass which presented a most formidable obstacle to attack by cruisers and destroyers. By morning he would be drawing under cover of dive bombing aircraft from Sicily. The question was whether to send the destroyers in now to attack this difficult target or to wait until morning in the hope of engaging at dawn, but with the certainty of exposing the fleet to a heavy scale of air attack. Decision was taken to attack with destroyers and to follow up with the battlefleet.

15. Meanwhile VALF was also faced with difficult decisions. As dusk fell he was drawing up on the enemy with his cruisers spread, to maintain contact. In the last of the afterglow it appeared that an enemy squadron was turning back towards him which obliged him to concentrate his force. This was undoubtedly a right decision, but from then onward every time he wished to spread his cruisers to resume the search he was foiled by some circumstance not least of which was the decision of Captain (D), 14DF to lead the destroyer flotillas round the northern flank of the enemy before attacking. This decision of Captain D14 was most unfortunate, as it cramped the cruiser squadron and left the southern flank of the enemy open for escape. It is thought that the enemy did in fact 'jink' to the S at about this time and thus get away.

16. The battleship night action presented no novel aspect, apart from the employment of Radar and the outstanding success of the illumination provided by *Greyhound* . . .

17. On conclusion of the battlefleet action, the signal was made 'All forces not engaging the enemy retire NE'. The order was intended to ensure withdrawal on parallel tracks clear of the destroyer melée, and was made under the impression that cruisers and striking force were in contact with the enemy. Heavy fighting had been observed to the south-westward which supported this

---

[93]Lt-Cdr A. S. Bolt: Lt-Cdr 1937; *Warspite* Aug. 1940; Cdr Dec. 1941; *Grebe* (NA Sta, Egypt) March 1942; N Air Warfare & Flying Trng Div, Apr. 1942; Airfield & Carrier Rqrmts Dept Sept. 1944; Act Capt, N Air Radio Div, June 1945.

belief. Unfortunately the cruisers were not in fact engaged and the VALF accordingly withdrew to the NE. He had sighted a red pyrotechnic signal some distance to the NW some 40 minutes earlier and was at this time about to spread to investigate. This red light signal was sighted simultaneously by Captain D14 bearing 010°, who seeing it in the direction of 7CS and knowing from their GAB signal they had seen it, forbore to investigate.

There seems little doubt, from subsequent analysis, that this must have been the remainder of the Italian Fleet withdrawing to the NW.

I am of the opinion that the course I selected for withdrawal led the fleet too far to the eastward, and that a more northerly course should have been steered.

18. I hoped when ordering the eight destroyers of the striking force to attack that the cruisers would regain touch to assist Captain D to launch his attack. The bearing and distance of the enemy given to the striking force when detached (286° 35 miles from *Warspite*) was based on the plot and was in fact approximately correct but the enemy's course appears to have been 45° further to the north-westward than that estimated. In spite, therefore, of Captain D14's intention to pass to the northward of the enemy, the striking force apparently passed under the stern of the enemy to his southern flank whilst the cruisers were steering on an approximately parallel course on the enemy's northern flank. The red pyrotechnic was shown between these two British forces.

19. The mistake made by *Havock* in reporting the *Pola* as a *Littorio* class did not actually bring any ill effect, since the flotillas had by then missed the *Vittorio* and did useful work in polishing off the damaged cruisers. The movements and the results achieved by *Stuart*'s division during the night remain most obscure. *Havock* certainly sank a destroyer.

They had an exciting time and did considerable execution. . . .

20. It seems that the enemy must have been able to increase speed again during the night, since although extensive reconnaissance was flown the next morning, he remained unsighted and must by then have been nearing the Italian coast. The search for survivors was interrupted by the appearance of German aircraft and it was decided to withdraw the fleet before the expected heavy air attacks developed . . .

The fleet was in fact subjected to a fairly severe dive bombing attack by Ju88s at 1530, when *Formidable* was narrowly missed by several bombs.

21. The mistake which prevented the Greek destroyer flotilla taking part in the action was perhaps not unfortunate. These destroyers had been sent through the Corinth Canal to Argostoli with admirable promptitude to a position where they were well placed to intercept the retreating enemy fleet, a task which they would have certainly undertaken with characteristic gallantry. Nevertheless the presence of yet another detached force in the area, and that force one with which I could not readily communicate, would have seriously added to the complexity of the situation. It was, however, disappointing for the Greeks.

22. The results of the action cannot be viewed with entire satisfaction, since the damaged *Vittorio Veneto* was allowed to escape. The failure of the cruisers and destroyers to make contact with her during the night was unlucky and is much to be regretted. Nevertheless substantial results were achieved in the destruction of the three *Zara* class cruisers. These fast well armed and armoured ships had always been a source of anxiety as a threat to our own less well armed cruisers and I was well content to see them disposed of in this summary fashion. There is little doubt that the rough handling given the enemy on this occasion served us in good stead during the subsequent evacuations of Greece and Crete. Much of these later operations may be said to have been conducted under the cover of the Battle of Matapan.

Narrative of the C-in-C

Preliminary Intelligence

From 25 March onwards various indications were noticed of increasing activity on the part of German and Italian forces. Features of the activity noticed were an increasingly active sea reconnaissance by aircraft to the S and W of Greece and Crete and daily attempts to reconnoitre Alexandria harbour.

2. These activities together with the obvious imminence of the German attack on Greece and Yugoslavia led to belief that some important step by the enemy was impending. The unusual keenness with which the enemy was watching the movements of the Mediterranean Fleet made it appear possible that an operation by enemy surface forces was intended.

The most probable actions by enemy surface forces appeared to be:

(a) An attack on our convoy routes in the Aegean.
(b) The escorting of a convoy to the Dodecanese.

(c) A diversion to cover a landing either in Cyrenaica or in Greece.
(d) The possibility of an attack on Malta could not be excluded.

3. The C-in-C was therefore faced with the problem of meeting a threat which he knew to exist, but whose nature he could not foretell. Our most vulnerable point at this time lay undoubtedly in the convoys carrying troops and material to Greece. They were moving, at the time, comparatively lightly escorted, under the rather inadequate cover of 7CS in the Aegean.

It was important to avoid interruption on the passage of these convoys if possible.

4. The obvious course to prevent enemy surface action against the convoys would have been to move the battlefleet into the area W of Crete. It was, however, almost certain that, had this been done, the fleet would have been sighted on its way, in which case the enemy would only have deferred his operation until the fleet was obliged to return to harbour to refuel.

5. ... It was accordingly decided that the best course would be to clear the threatened area of convoys and merchant shipping so that the enemy's blow would be struck in a vacuum, at the same time making such disposition of available forces as would enable us to engage enemy surface forces should they appear.

6. At the same time it was important to maintain an appearance of normality in the area concerned, lest the enemy should 'smell a rat'. It was lucky that only one convoy was actually at sea, AG9 bound for Piraeus with troops, which was then S of Crete. The convoy was ordered to maintain its course until nightfall 27th and then turn back in its tracks. A southbound convoy from Piraeus was ordered not to sail.

In the meantime authorities in the Aegean were warned at the last possible moment to clear the area of shipping.

Dispositions

7. The following dispositions were then ordered:

(a) Force B, consisting of VALF with four cruisers and four destroyers to be SW of Gavdo Island at daylight 28 March.
(b) Force C, consisting of five destroyers, to join him at that time.
(c) TSR Squadrons in Crete and Cyrenaica to be reinforced.
(d) RAF requested to exert maximum effort of reconnaissance and bomber aircraft in Aegean and to W of Crete on 28 March.

THE EFFECTS OF GERMAN INTERVENTION, 1941   315

(e) Submarines *Rover* and *Triumph* ordered to patrol off Suda Bay and Milo respectively.
(f) Force D, consisting of *Juno, Jaguar* and *Defender,* who were at Piraeus, to be at short notice.
(g) *Carlisle* ordered to Suda Bay to augment AA defences.
(h) Greek Naval forces warned to be at short notice.

Air Reconnaissance Report

8. This plan was adhered to in the main but at noon 27th three enemy cruisers and one destroyer were sighted by air reconnaissance ... Visibility was bad and the flying boat could not shadow. The C-in-C decided to take the battlefleet to sea, cancelled the move to Cyrenaica of the TSR aircraft, and made the following redispositions:

> Force B, consisting of the VALF in *Orion, Ajax, Perth, Gloucester,* Captain (D), 2DF, in *Ilex, Hasty, Hereward* and *Vendetta* (all from operations in the Aegean) were to rendezvous ... *Gloucester*'s speed was reported down to 24 knots due to trouble with a plummer block.
> Force C was to remain with the battlefleet.
> RAF reconnaissance was arranged for 28th over the southern Ionian Sea, the SW Aegean, and S of Crete.

Fleet Sailing from Alexandria

9. Enemy reconnaissance planes were over the fleet at Alexandria at noon and again p.m., 27th. At dusk, 1900/27, the C-in-C sailed the Fleet from Alexandria. *Warspite, Barham, Valiant* and *Formidable* were in company, the RA, 1BS, being in *Barham*, and the RA, Mediterranean Aircraft Carriers, in *Formidable*. The fleet was screened by Captain (D), 14 DF, in *Jervis, Janus, Nubian, Mohawk,* the Captain (D), 10DF in *Stuart, Greyhound, Griffin, Hotspur* and *Havock*.[94]

28 March: First Sight and Contact with the Enemy – Forenoon Action

10. A dawn air search was flown off from *Formidable* and at 0739 an aircraft reported four cruisers and six destroyers (to be known as Force X) about 30 miles S of Gavdo Island ... This was at first thought to be an inaccurate report of Force B which was known to be in that area, but at 0827 the VALF's first sighting report of three

[94] Capt D14: P. J. Mack; Capt D10: H. M. L. Waller.

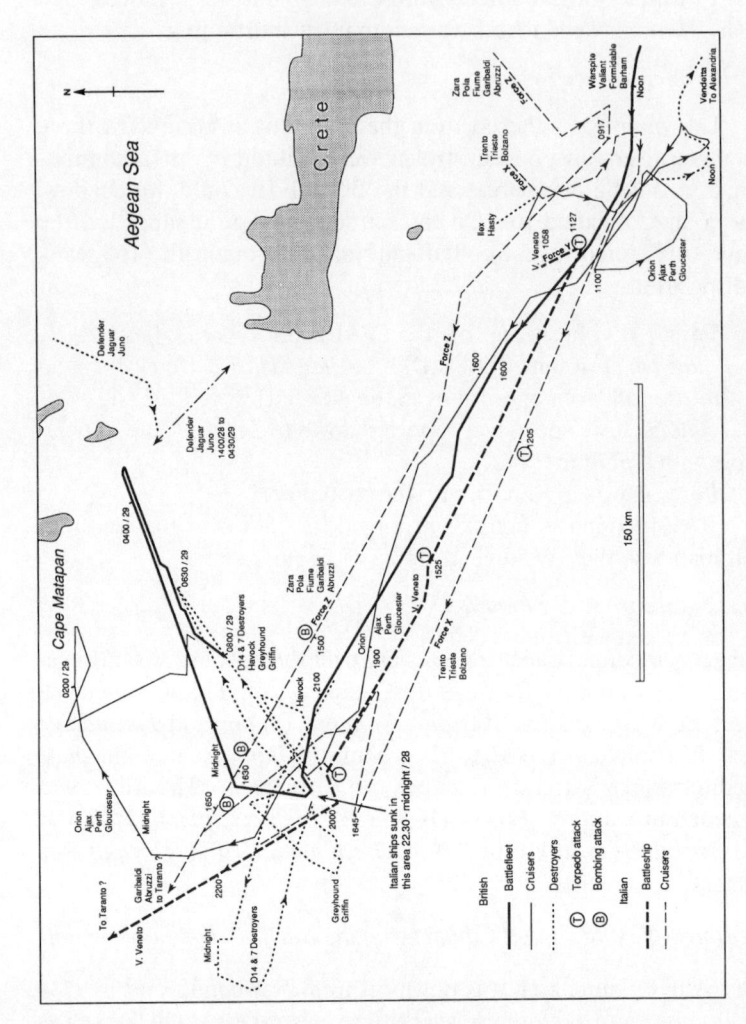

The Battle of Cape Matapan, 28–29 March 1941

cruisers and destroyers was received. The C-in-C increased speed to 22 knots . . . The VALF was estimated to bear 267° 90 miles from the battlefleet and the enemy were reported 009° 18 miles from him . . . At 0900 the enemy were reported turning back to 300° with the VALF also turning to the north-westward. The C-in-C detached *Valiant* to proceed ahead at maximum speed with *Nubian* and *Mohawk*; *Warspite* (who was having slight condenser trouble) and *Barham* remained in company with *Formidable*.

11. . . . An enemy force was being reported to the northward of the cruisers, but it was not clear to the C-in-C whether this was another force or either of those already in contact. The term 'battleships' was used on one occasion. On balance it seemed probable that there was another enemy force containing battleships, on which the cruisers were retiring; the C-in-C, therefore, decided to keep the air striking force back until the doubt about this had been cleared up. The aircraft, however, lost touch with the enemy and at 0939 the C-in-C ordered the air striking force to attack the cruisers in contact with the VALF; if another squadron was sighted first it was to be attacked instead.

12. At this time Force X was estimated to be 75 miles from the C-in-C, being reported 16 miles from the VALF. In order to increase the speed of the fleet, *Barham* was ordered to follow in the wake of the screen independently of flying operations. *Vendetta* was sighted ahead having been detached by VALF to join the battlefleet on account of engine trouble. The C-in-C ordered her to proceed independently to Alexandria.

13. By 1030 there was still no further news of the enemy to the northward and it seemed possible that Force X in contact with the VALF was after all the only enemy squadron in the vicinity; but at 1058 the VALF reported two battleships . . . 16 miles from him . . . The VALF turned away to the south-eastward making smoke, but was evidently placed in a most uncomfortable position with the cruisers on his starboard quarter and the battleships (to be known as Force Y) to port. The C-in-C ordered *Formidable* to put the air striking force on to the battleships and decided to close the VALF as quickly as possible rather than work round between the battleships and their base. The doubt as to whether *Gloucester* would be able to maintain the VALF'S reported speed of 30 knots weighed in favour of this decision, but the VALF's 1123 showed that he was still keeping the battleships at a range of 16 miles.

14. The VALF was estimated to bear 280° 65 miles from the C-in-C at 1135 . . . but there was some doubt as to the accuracy of this

owing to possible difference in reference positions. In order, therefore, to be certain of making contact with the VALF as early as possible, the C-in-C altered course to 290° at 1135 and to 270° at 1200. *Formidable* was detached with two destroyers to operate aircraft independently, *Valiant* was still in company and *Barham* had been keeping up well.

Surface Contact Lost – First Air Attack

15. At 1200 Force Y, which was now reported to consist of only one *Littorio* class battleship with destroyers, was estimated to bear 200° 45 miles from the C-in-C; the destroyer screen was detached ahead to join the Captain (D), but at 1210 the VALF reported having lost touch with the enemy battlefleet and five minutes later the air striking force returned with the news that the battleship had last been seen at 1145, . . . with cruisers 20 miles to the SE. The striking force reported one probable hit on the battleship. A Ju88 had been shot down by a Fulmar.

Second Heavy Enemy Force Reported

16. A new force (to be known as Force Z) was now sighted to the northward by Flying Boat Duty V. It was reported to consist of two *Cavour* class battleships, one *Pola* and two *Zara* cruisers and five destroyers . . . 35 miles W of Gavdo Island . . . 25 knots.

Contact Made with the VALF

17. At 1230 the VALF was sighted bearing 220° 12 miles with all his force undamaged. The C-in-C . . . ordered the second air striking force to attack the *Littorio* battleship. The VALF's signal timed 1245 was the first intimation to the C-in-C that the enemy had turned northward, but this was later assumed to be a signal error and the enemy to have turned westward as reported by the striking force.

By 1250 it was evident that Forces X and Y had turned back and there was no prospect of overtaking them unless the speed of the *Littorio* was reduced by air attack. The destroyers were, therefore, ordered to reform a battlefleet screen, the Captain (D), 2DF and two destroyers being sent to the assistance of *Formidable* who was now a long way astern and was seen to be engaging two T/B aircraft. Speed was reduced . . . at 1325 to 21 knots to allow *Formidable* and *Barham* to keep up. Force B was now . . . 6 miles from the battlefleet.

The Chase

18. At 1350 course was altered to 310° as it was thought probable that Forces X and Y were trying to make contact with each other.

An air search was also ordered to the north-westward since no further reports had been received for Forces X and Y.... 201 Group were instructed to concentrate all flying boats in the area S and W of Crete to maintain touch with the enemy. *Juno* and Force D were ordered to patrol the Kithera Straits.

19. During the afternoon [?forenoon] a strong breeze from the NE had made flying operations delay the fleet, but in the afternoon the wind dropped altogether and the heavy cloud dispersed....

20. Force Y was sighted again at 1515 when *Formidable*'s aircraft 4NN reported one battleship and four destroyers... 65 miles from the C-in-C. The second air striking force which had been in the air since 1235 attacked the battleship with torpedoes; they reported three hits and that her speed was reduced to 8 knots.[95]...

21. Shortly afterwards aircraft 4NN reported Force X consisting of three cruisers and four destroyers stationed 25 miles... from the *Littorio* battleship which was steering 280° about 10 knots. Duty V also reported three 6-in cruisers and two destroyers... [making] 30 knots.

22. At this time Maleme FAA reported that three Swordfish had attacked the cruisers of Force X with torpedoes at 1205 scoring one possible hit and that another striking force was being dispatched.[96] *York* was instructed to arrange with Maleme for a dusk attack to be carried out in conjunction with the flying boat reports.

23. At 1600 the two *Cavour* battleships with Force Z were estimated to bear 305° 120 miles from the C-in-C still steering north-westward at 30 knots. The damaged *Littorio* with Force X was estimated at 60 miles... from the C-in-C; it soon became apparent that she must be making good 12 to 15 knots and would not be overhauled by the battlefleet before dark. So at 1644 the VALF was ordered to press on and gain contact. *Nubian* and *Mohawk* were also sent ahead to form a V/S link with the VALF. Soon afterwards a third air striking force was flown off to attack the *Littorio* at dusk.

Night Intentions

24. Duty V's admirable reports of Force Z still showed it to be in two groups, each making 30 knots, the battleships steering 310° and the cruisers about 60 miles to the SE of them, ... It was always possible, however, that this second force of cruisers was in reality Force X which at 1727 was seen to turn back and take station 5 miles S of

---
[95] One hit only.
[96] No hits.

the *Littorio*. The situation was still, therefore, somewhat confused when at 1810 the C-in-C signalled his night intentions; if the cruisers gained touch with the damaged battleship the destroyers would be sent in to attack, followed if necessary by the battlefleet; if the cruisers failed to make contact then the C-in-C intended to work round to the N and W and regain touch in the morning.

Situation at Dusk

25. At 1745 *Warspite*'s aircraft was catapulted for the second time and at 1831 made the first of a series of reports which rapidly cleared up the position. By 1915 it was clear that the damaged battleship was about 45 miles from the C-in-C, steering 290° at 15 knots. Another cruiser force had joined it from the north-westward and the enemy fleet was now in five columns. The *Littorio* was in the centre with four destroyers screening ahead and two astern; to port of her were three 6-in cruisers in the inner column and three *Navigatori* class destroyers in the outer column, to starboard there were three 8-in cruisers in the inner column and two 6-in cruisers (later found to have been large destroyers) in the outer column. In addition Force Z was still to the north-westward and apparently consisted of two *Cavour*s, the three *Zara*s and five destroyers. The second force reported by Duty V of two *Savoia*s, one *Diaz* and two destroyers, was probably that which had just joined the *Littorio*.[97]

26. At 1925 the VALF reported two unknown ships and concentrated his cruisers. Almost immediately afterwards he reported enemy ships 9 miles to the NW of him and engaging aircraft and making smoke. Duty 4NN reported that the enemy's centre bore 310° 14 miles from four destroyers in the van (probably VALF's four cruisers). At the same time *Warspite*'s aircraft reported the enemy altering course to 230° 15 knots, but no indication was given that this was a compass turn of the whole fleet.

Decision to Engage at Night

27. At 1935 the air striking force reported 'probable hits' but no definite information of damage, and the C-in-C wondered whether he would be justified in taking the fleet at night through a screening force of at least 6 cruisers and 11 destroyers, with another force of at least two battleships, three cruisers and five destroyers in the vicin-

---

[97]No *Cavour*s present. *Navigatori* cl: 1929–31, *c.*2,000t, 6×4.7in, 4–6×21in tt, 38k. *Savoia* cl: 1935–36, 8,662t, 8×6in, 6×3.9in, 6×21in tt, 36.5k. *Diaz* cl: 1933, 5,400t, 8×6in, 6×3.9in, 4×21in tt, 37k.

ity. On the other hand if the enemy were able to continue at 14 or 15 knots during the night they would be well under cover of the Ju87 dive bombers at daylight being already 320 miles from their base; if they were intercepted at dawn, our forces would almost certainly be subjected to a very heavy scale of air attack throughout the day. The C-in-C decided to accept a night action and at 2040 ordered the destroyers to attack.

28. The attacking force was formed of 8 destroyers under Captain D14, organised into two divisions (the second under Captain D2).[98] while the remaining four destroyers under Captain D10 formed the battlefleet screen. The enemy fleet was estimated to bear 286° 33 miles from the C-in-C, steering 295° at 13 knots. Captain D14 decided to pass to the northward and attack from the van . . .

29. At 2111 a Radar report was received from the VALF of an unknown ship stopped about 5 miles to port of him; the C-in-C at once altered course to pass nearer to the position. The VALF continued to the north-westward without investigating this report and at 2215 reported that he was steering 340° with his cruisers concentrated and would keep clear to the northward of the destroyers. The VALF did not again make contact with the enemy . . .

Night Action

30. At 2210 what was apparently the same ship was detected by *Valiant*'s Radar 6 miles on the port bow. The C-in-C decided to investigate and at 2213 the battlefleet altered course together to 240°, the destroyer screen being ordered over to the starboard side.

31. At 2225 two large cruisers were unexpectedly sighted on the starboard bow, with a smaller vessel, thought at first to be a 6-in cruiser, ahead of them. The battlefleet were turned back to 280° into line ahead, and at 2228 when the enemy were on the port bow at a range of about 4,000 yards, *Greyhound* illuminated one of the enemy cruisers with her searchlight, and *Warspite* opened fire. *Formidable* hauled out of line to starboard and the battlefleet engaged. The enemy were seen to be two cruisers of the *Zara* class on an opposite course; they were apparently completely taken by surprise and their turrets were fore and aft. *Warspite*'s first 15-in broadside hit the rear cruiser with devastating effect, five out of six shells hitting. Both cruisers were thereafter repeatedly hit, set severely on fire and put out of action. A destroyer was seen passing behind the burning cruisers; this was probably the smaller vessel originally sighted ahead of them.

[98]Capt D2: Capt H. StL. Nicolson.

32. Except for flashing signals seen on the port quarter, nothing further was seen of the original damaged ship ... (*Barham* was unable to carry out searchlight sweeping procedure on the port quarter owing to damage to her searchlights by blast).

33. At 2230 three enemy destroyers were sighted on the port bow closing from a position astern of their cruisers and were engaged. At 2232 they were seen to turn away making smoke and one at least fired torpedoes.

The battle fleet was turned 90° to starboard together by Fixed Light Manoeuvring Signal to avoid torpedoes and at 2233 steadied on course 010°. At this time *Formidable* was acting independently on the starboard bow.

34. During the engagement with enemy destroyers, the leading destroyers had been hit by 6-in fire from *Warspite,* and some confusion was caused by *Havock* being closely engaged with the enemy destroyers and failing to burn fighting lights. As a result *Warspite* fired two salvos at her. *Havock* was not damaged although it was thought at the time that she had possibly been hit.

35. The battle fleet ceased fire at 2235 and was re-formed into line ahead on a course 010°; *Formidable* was ordered to rejoin the line at 2310. The four screening destroyers (*Stuart, Havock, Greyhound* and *Griffin*) were released at 2238 and ordered to finish off the two cruisers seen to be on fire ...

36. At 2245, when the burning cruisers were still seen right astern (190°), starshell and heavy firing with tracer ammunition could be seen bearing 230°, and this continued for 10 minutes or a quarter of an hour. Since none of our ships were on that bearing it was thought possible that the Italians were engaging their own forces. Firing was seen to continue in the vicinity of the damaged cruisers for some time and at 2300 a heavy explosion was seen and thought to be the torpedoing of one of them.

Withdrawal – Light Forces Engagement

37. The C-in-C then decided to withdraw to the north-eastward in order to avoid the possibility of our own forces engaging each other and to return to the battle area in the morning. He, therefore, ordered all forces not engaging the enemy to withdraw to the north-eastward, and at 2330 altered course to 070°, speed 18 knots. The Captain (D), 14DF, was told not to withdraw until after the striking force had attacked. Firing and occasional heavy flashes were still seen intermittently until about 0100 ...

38. At 0020 *Havock* reported contact with a *Littorio* battleship in the position of the damaged cruisers. The Captain (D), 14DF, with the striking force, reported that he was joining *Havock*, as did *Greyhound* and *Griffin*, but at 0110 *Havock* altered the report to that of an 8-in cruiser. At 0036, the Captain (D), 10DF, had reported leaving three cruisers stopped and on fire and two other cruisers in the vicinity, as well as two damaged destroyers. At 0314 *Havock* reported being alongside *Pola* and asked whether 'to board or blow her stern off with depth charges'; the Captain (D), 14DF, then reported having sunk *Zara* and being about to sink *Pola*.[99]

29 March

39. At 0006 the C-in-C had ordered the fleet to rendezvous at 0700 . . ., and requested air reconnaissance the following morning. *Juno*, *Jaguar* and *Defender* were ordered to join the C-in-C, and also *Bonaventure*, who had left Alexandria the previous afternoon. A Greek flotilla of 7 destroyers had been sent through the Corinth Canal to await orders on the first reports of the engagement, but owing to a cyphering error they were not ordered to join the C-in-C until 0350. The NA, Athens, reported that 23 Blenheims had attacked the northern force of enemy ships between 1445 and 1655/28 and had stopped one cruiser with two direct hits and a destroyer with one direct hit. Maleme also reported at least one torpedo hit on the *Littorio* battleship at 1940/28.[100]

Fleet Re-formed

40. At 0430 the C-in-C altered course to 250° and informed the fleet that he was keeping W/T silence. At daylight an air search was flown off from *Formidable* and between 0600 and 0700 all units of the fleet rejoined the C-in-C. It was thought that at least one of our destroyers had been seriously damaged in all the firing subsequent to the main action, but no ship reported either damage or casualties. One Swordfish was later reported missing.

41. At 0800 the C-in-C was in position . . . to sweep the area of the action. Between 0950 and 1100 many boats and rafts with Italian survivors were seen and a large number of survivors were picked up by destroyers, but at 1100 enemy aircraft were sighted and as there was no report of enemy surface ships in the vicinity, course was set . . . for

---

[99] A of F Lord Chatfield to Cunningham, 31 March 1941: he and Adm Sir W. W. Fisher used to practise night fighting 'in that very spot': *Cunningham Papers,* BM Add Mss 52569.
[100] Blenheims scored no hits.

Alexandria. A signal was broadcast to the Chief of the Italian Naval Staff giving the position of the remaining survivors. The Greek flotilla was ordered to return to Athens.

42. The fleet was shadowed during the forenoon and at 1530 a dive bombing attack was made by about 12 Ju88s, the main attack being directed on *Formidable*. There was no damage, however, the fleet 'umbrella barrage' proving effective. One Ju88 was shot down and one Fulmar crashed in the sea just before landing on. There were shadowers during the rest of the day but no further attack developed. *Stuart, Griffin* and *Hereward* were detached at 0920 to Piraeus, as escort for Convoy GA8, and *Ajax, Perth, Defender* and *Hasty* at 1930 to Suda Bay in order to cover Aegean convoys. *Bonaventure* was also detached at this time to join convoy GA8 at daylight 30 March.[101]

Damage Inflicted on the Enemy

43. It was not at all clear to the C-in-C what ships had been sunk, and the fate of the *Littorio* battleship was in doubt. But it seemed certain from the 900 survivors on board ships of the fleet that *Pola* was the damaged cruiser that had been detected stopped and that she had been sunk; that the two 8-in cruisers engaged by the battle fleet were *Zara* and *Fiume* and that they were both sunk; that *Havock* had sunk one destroyer and the battle fleet possibly another; in addition there might be further losses due to the RAF bombing attacks. It was also a possibility that the enemy had suffered damage in an encounter between their own forces.

30 March – Fleet Return to Alexandria

44. The fleet continued to Alexandria and arrived there at 1730. An S79 shadower was shot down by fleet fighters at 0834. A submarine was reported just as the fleet entered the Great Pass and the destroyer screen were ordered to clear the area ahead of the fleet with depth charges. This operation had no result apart from creating a marked impression on the Italian survivors.

Vice-Admiral Pridham-Wippell's report

10 April 1941

1. *Orion, Ajax, Perth, Gloucester, Vendetta* and *Hereward,* having fuelled, left Piraeus at 1300/27.

---

[101]*Bonaventure* s by It s/m *Dagabur* with 2 torpedoes, while with convoy; 148 men lost.

3. *Ilex* and *Hasty* were ordered to leave Suda Bay so as to join the cruisers 30 miles S of Gavdo Island . . . at 0630/28.

Phase I (0630–1230)

7. As soon as the enemy aircraft shadowing was identified, at 0633, as a type that is sometimes carried in catapult ships, it was realised that enemy surface forces might be in the vicinity. But when the first enemy report from one of *Formidable*'s aircraft reported four cruisers and four destroyers . . . some 35 miles to the NE of my own position, steering a course similar to my own, I was in some doubt whether it was not, in fact, my own force that was being reported. Enemy warships were sighted astern before any further aircraft reports had been received and decoded.

8. The enemy sighted were at once suspected of being *Zara* class, since cruisers of this class had been reported at sea on the previous day by flying boats. This suspicion soon proved correct. Knowing that vessels of that class could outrange my squadron and that, having superior speed, they could choose the range I decided to try to draw them towards our own battlefleet and carrier.

9. The enemy followed and opened fire at 25,500 yards at 0812. At the same time one of the enemy cruisers was seen to catapult one aircraft. The fire was accurate to begin with and the enemy appeared to be concentrating on *Gloucester*. She snaked the line to avoid hits.

10. At 0829, when the range had closed to 23,500 yards, *Gloucester* opened fire with three salvos, but they all fell short. The enemy made an alteration away of some 35° after the first salvo and put himself outside our gun range. After this time, although the enemy resumed a course similar to my own and continued to fire until 0855, all his salvos fell short.

13. At 0855 the enemy turned away to port and ceased fire. He eventually steadied on a course of about 300°. I decided to follow and endeavour to keep touch. *Vendetta* . . . was ordered to join the battlefleet.

14. At 0854 a signal from aircraft 5F had been received, reporting 3 enemy battleships at 0805 in a position which was 7 miles from my own position at 0805. Though this report was manifestly incorrect as regards position, it prepared me for a meeting with enemy battleships at any moment.

16. A battleship was sighted to the northward at 1058. Half a minute later she opened an accurate fire from about 32,000 yards

and no time was lost in altering to the southward, increasing to full speed and making smoke. *Orion* was the target for the first 10 minutes and the first salvos fell over. *Orion* was straddled and suffered minor damage from a near miss.

17. When the smoke began to take effect, *Gloucester*, being to windward, was the only ship in view to the enemy battleship and she became the target. She was repeatedly straddled. The destroyers could hardly keep up at the speed of about 31 knots which the cruiser was maintaining. Only one destroyer, *Hasty*, succeeded eventually in reaching a position from which her smoke was of any benefit to *Gloucester*.

18. At 1127 our own aircraft attacked the enemy with torpedoes and she turned away and ceased fire . . .

20. When certain that the enemy had ceased fire, I ordered ships to stop making smoke. . . . when the horizon could be seen (at 1148) there was nothing in sight. The enemy cruisers evidently proceeded to join the battleship.

21. Course was steered to make contact with our own battlefleet.

166. *From Godfroy*

Duquesne
Alexandria
31 March 1941

. . . I suppose the night-battle has been very interesting. In any case it has been extraordinarily successful and your country is to be more and more proud of you.

My contentment is unhappily darkened by the news that a French convoy has been attacked in our Algerian waters, near Oran, by some British naval units. It is really painful to feel that a hostile feeling is still lasting in some spheres between France and Great Britain. It would be so easy to come to an understanding if both sides were more reasonable on some secondary matters.

In the same kind of ideas, I have been distressed to see one sells in the town an embroidered flag with HMS *Valiant*'s name where are written these words: Narvik, Valona, Taranto, Oran, Bardia, Sardinia, Pantelleria.

So, that awful Oran affair, which was not even a battle, and on which it seemed to me everyone in France and England would have better to make silence is considered by British sailors on the same level as their battles against Germans or Italians. Is it not sad for the great majority of us Frenchmen who still hoped to be able – if opportunity might come – to fight again with you as formerly.

Please excuse my intimacies, accept my congratulations for your victory . . .

167. *War Diary, March 1941 (concl.)*

Summary and Appreciation of Events

Strategical

The predominating feature of March was the carrying out of the operation of moving a force of about two divisions to Greece. This operation meant concentrating our forces on virtually this one object and in consequence, the work of the fleet during the month was restricted to convoys . . . The whole move was felt to be a move against time to rush our forces into Greece before the Germans opened hostilities and were able to attack the Piraeus and render the task doubly difficult. During the greater part of the move a portion of the battlefleet was kept at sea to westward of Crete to provide heavy cover for our forces.

The move to Greece so completely absorbed all resources that even the destroyers of the Inshore Squadron had to be removed and any question of considered offensive action against the enemy had to be ruled aside. The C-in-C insisted, however, that he must at some time in the month pass supplies into Malta whatever happened and some of our forces were withdrawn from Aegean duties during the period 19–25 March, whilst this operation was successfully carried out. . . .

One other form of offensive action became possible in March and that was T/B attack on shipping in the Adriatic. This was rendered possible by the aerodrome at Paramythia becoming serviceable and a series of most successful attacks on shipping in Valona and Durazzo were carried out by the FAA units.[102] . . .

March saw the break up of Italian resistance in East Africa and this resulted in an enforced breakout of the naval units in Massawa. There was some fear that an attempt would be made by the destroyers to attack the heavy concentration of shipping present in Suez due to the mining of the Canal and precautionary measures were taken by sending *Ladybird* and *Gnat* to protect the port. Further action was to dispatch all available aircraft from *Eagle* (who was

---

[102] By 815 Sqdn. See Cdr C. Lamb, *War in a Stringbag* (London, 1977), pp. 154–89.

waiting for the reopening of the Canal) to Port Sudan. These aircraft were invaluable and were responsible for breaking the back of the Italian attempt to come north to attack Port Sudan or other objectives.[103]

168. *War Diary, April 1941*

2 April

Operation LUSTRE

Convoy AS23 was attacked by 6 Ju88 dive bombers 23m S of Gavdo Island. SS *Homefield* and the Greek ship *Koulouras Xenos* were both hit and later sank. The Greek *Teti* was also damaged by a near miss but was able to make harbour in Crete. The escort, *Grimsby, Wryneck* and *Voyager*, reported shooting down one and damaging another aircraft.... Convoy ANF24 was attacked by aircraft, *Devis* being damaged.[104] ...

Submarines

3. *Rorqual* reported leaving patrol one day early, having expended all torpedoes. She sank the oiler *Laura Corrado* and a *Calva*-class U-boat and also laid three minefields in the Trapani (Sicily) area.[105] ...
4. *Utmost* and *Ursula* also returned to Malta from patrol along the Tunisian coast.... *Utmost* sank two south-bound laden ships of 12,000 tons and 6,000 tons on 28 March, and may have sunk a 5,000 ton ship on 31 March.

3 April

Operation LUSTRE

2. Convoy ANF24 was attacked by dive bombers at sunset in the Anti-Kithera Straits and the valuable ship *Northern Prince*, with ammunition and stores for Greece, was hit. She was set on fire and sank during the night. She was so urgently required in Greece that a proportion of her cargo intended for Egypt had not been unloaded.
3. In view of the recent losses the C-in-C addressed a strong signal to the AOC-in-C, Middle East, asking for more fighter protection

---

[103]There were 9 destroyers, 4 escorts, 8 s/m, auxiliaries & merchantmen at Massawa.
Gnat: 1916, 625t, 2×6in, 1×3in, 14k; t by *U-79* off Bardia, Oct. 1941; towed to Alexandria but total loss.
[104]*Grimsby*: 1933, 990t, 2×4.7in, 1×3in, 16.5k; s by a/c off Tobruk, May 1941.
[105]*Laura Corrado*: 1899, 3,645gt, SA di Nav. Corrado.
Actually *Pier Capponi* of *Mameli* cl: 1929, 824/1,009t, 1×4in, 6×21in tt; s S of Stromboli.

for LUSTRE convoys and offensive action against Dodecanese aerodromes. The fighter protection now being afforded was quite inadequate, consisting only of an occasional Blenheim.

Red Sea

4. *Janus* and *Jaguar* were dispatched to Port Said from Alexandria in case the threat of attack in the Red Sea developed. But although the enemy destroyers sailed from Massawa Northward, 2 were attacked and sunk by *Eagle*'s Swordfish. It is not clear what happened to the remainder of the force, but *Janus* and *Jaguar* were returned to Alexandria. *Greyhound* and *Griffin* continued on patrol in the Straits of Jubal.[106]

4 April

Western Desert

5. The C-in-C was asked to prevent any possibility of any enemy seaborne raid between Tolmeita and Tobruk during the next few days as this would endanger the security of the whole Cyrenaican force. The C-in-C replied that he had not sufficient cruisers and destroyers to ensure this without delaying LUSTRE and that RAF coastal reconnaissance must be relied on to safeguard against such an attack.

5 April

AA Armament

9. It was again pointed out to the Admiralty that small ships such as the 16th A/S Group and the Corvettes were arriving on the Station with an armament quite unsuitable for Mediterranean conditions. The re-arming of them was causing considerable difficulties.

169. *Middle East Commanders-in-Chiefs' Committee*

6 April 1941

110. *Immediate Policy in Cyrenaica*
... Summing up, the C-in-C, Middle East, said that the problem resolved itself into whether we were prepared to accept the risk of holding Tobruk and cover our aerodromes in that area for about two

---

[106]One destroyer and all but 4 merchant ships sunk in harbour by a/c from *Formidable* and *Hermes*; others sortied & were sunk by surface forces and *Eagle*'s a/c, or scuttled.

months with our present resources and the small scale of reinforcements that will become available in this period. From the beginning of June strong armoured forces should, however, be arriving.

The C-in-C, Mediterranean, stressed the importance of the fact that we already had considerable reserves of supplies at Tobruk, whilst we possessed none at Bardia. He considered it might take as long as two months to evacuate the supplies now held at Tobruk.

He considered that it would prove possible to evacuate personnel from Tobruk if the situation required it.

The AOC-in-C, Middle East, said that the further forward we hold the more damage we could do to the enemy, and by holding Tobruk the RAF could use the chain of aerodromes stretching back to Sollum. He stressed the need of doing all in our power to hold Tobruk, otherwise the enemy would be in a position to deliver a very heavy scale of air attack against our naval, military and air bases in Egypt, and against LUSTRE convoys. Moreover, the air reinforcement of Malta from Egypt would become more difficult.

The CIGS said that we must make certain of being able to hold the Mersa Matruh position.

After discussion it was agreed:

(a) That our forces when pressed should fall back from Derna upon Tobruk.
(b) To be prepared to hold Tobruk for at least two months.
(c) That the defence of Bardia and Sollum should be considered.
(h) That a study of the question of carrying out landing operations along the coast between Sollum and Mersa Matruh should be undertaken.
(j) That the 'Glen' ships should be sailed to Alexandria with a view to worrying the enemy as to our intentions.

170 *War Diary, April 1941 (cont.)*

7 April

Balkans-LUSTRE

The German attack on Greece and Yugoslavia began on 6 April. The Germans were advancing into Yugoslavia and down the valleys to Salonika. Belgrade and other Yugoslav cities were bombed. Our diplomatic relations were broken off with Hungary. Piraeus was heavily bombed during the night of 6/7 and mines were laid by aircraft in the entrance to the port. A number of ships unloading in the port were hit and *Clan Fraser*, with a cargo of ammunition, blew up before she could be towed clear. As a result the whole dock was set on fire. The MT ships *City of Roubaix, Clan Cumming* and *Devis* were seriously damaged by fire and *Cyprian Prince* was sunk in the roads.[107] *Calcutta* and *Ajax* were in harbour but managed to get clear through the fire and minefields. *Perth* was in Salamis Straits and all three cruisers sailed for Suda Bay p.m., 7th. There was no adequate minesweeping gear or organisation and *Hyacinth*'s LL gear was out of action. The port was closed.

2. It was decided to allow the Northbound LUSTRE convoys to continue and for the ships to be unloaded individually. . . .

8 April

3. It was decided to send a division of destroyers to Malta to operate against the Tripoli convoys. *Nubian, Hero* and *Defender* were sailed from Alexandria, *Hero* and *Defender* to relieve *Jervis* and *Janus* with convoy AN25. The latter two destroyers, together with *Mohawk* from convoy AG11 and *Nubian*, would then proceed to Malta.

171. *Middle East Commanders-in-Chiefs' Committee*

9 April 1941

112. *The Situation in Cyrenaica*

. . . The C-in-C, Mediterranean, said he would like to see some of the new long range bombers [sent] from home in order that Tripoli could be attacked without the use of Malta. The provisioning of the island was becoming a very difficult problem.

The AOC-in-C agreed to send a cable to the COS, asking for some.

The C-in-C, Middle East, said he felt there was a danger of Tobruk becoming a beleaguered garrison cut off from supplies. The C-in-C, Mediterranean, however, said he thought he would be able to run ships in when required, provided we maintained a good AA defence of the port. He went on to say that he would assist in the defence of Tobruk and would also try to deal with the small places along the coast that the enemy might use for supply purposes.

---

[107]*City of Roubaix*: 1928, 7,108gt, 13.25k, Hall Line.
Cyprian Prince: 1936, 1,988gt, 12k, Prince Line.

116. *Crete*

Discussion took place on the importance of Crete in the event of Greece being overrun. The C-in-C, Mediterranean, said from the naval point of view it was vital. The C-in-C, Middle East, drew attention to the requirements in AA guns. It would be most difficult to provide them in view of our commitments elsewhere. The AOC-in-C felt that it would be difficult to operate aircraft from Crete if Greece were overrun. After discussion it was agreed that we should hold Crete.

172. *War Diary, April 1941 (cont.)*

10 April

Greece

4. There was a further minelaying and bombing raid on Piraeus and Salamis and it was also thought possible that Khalkis had been mined. There was an urgent request for additional Sea Transport Officers at Piraeus. The enemy advance into Yugoslavia was continuing but the Greek line West of Salonika was being held.

Western Desert

5. All ports W of Tobruk were now in enemy hands. The demolition of Benghazi was reported in detail and appeared to have been thorough. It had not yet been possible to lay mines there. The Inshore Squadron now consisted of *Waterhen* and *Vendetta*, *Aphis*, *Ladybird* and *Gnat*, *Gloxinia*, whose LL sweeping gear was defective, *Bagshot*, 2 *Skudd* minesweepers, and 3 A/S trawlers.[108]

Zigzagging

8. Consequent on the circumstances of the loss of *Bonaventure*, an order was issued by the C-in-C that all HM Ships must zigzag by day and night . . .

12 April

Operation LUSTRE

4. There were more heavy raids on Piraeus during the night 11/12 and mines were laid in Phaleron Bay, Salamis Strait and Eleusis

---

[108]*Bagshot*: 1918, 800t, 1×4in, 1×3in, 16k. The *Skudds* were ex-whalers, 1929, 245–323t, adapted for minesweeping.

Bay. The oiler *Marie Maersk* was hit and set on fire. The NA, Athens, decided to risk some loss from mines and move most of the ships still seaworthy from Piraeus into deep water outside Salamis Straits. The valuable cable ship *Retriever* was sunk by bombs off Phleva Island during the night, having successfully completed her work on the Salonika cable near Lemnos.[109] There was considerable loss of life. Throughout these mining and bombing raids *Hero* was at Piraeus and operating independently between there and Suda Bay as necessary.

13 April

815 Squadron

8. 815 Sqdn in Greece laid cucumbers at Brindisi and blew up a 10,000 ton tanker by torpedo. There were more reports of an intended landing in Greece from Bari and Brindisi and the C-in-C suggested such an expedition an ideal target for 815 Sqdn.

Western Desert

6. *Stuart, Griffin* and *Gnat* bombarded enemy transport and positions in the vicinity of Sollum. This was reported to have been most effective and enabled our forces to re-occupy the village.... *Gnat* anchored at Sollum later but was engaged by an enemy mobile battery and hit several times before being able to get clear. She was able to proceed under her own power to Mersa Matruh, although considerably damaged.

7. At Tobruk enemy attacks on the perimeter were repulsed and there were several heavy dive bombing attacks. Eight enemy aircraft were shot down. *Bamora* was attacked by 9 dive bombers 7 miles off Tobruk and hit. She got into harbour with some casualties but without great damage. The hospital ship *Vita* was deliberately bombed off Tobruk and seriously damaged.[110] *Waterhen* and *Vendetta* got her back into Tobruk and *St Issey* was sent to her assistance from Mersa Matruh.

---

[109]*Retriever*: 1909, 674gt, Cable & Wireless.
[110]*Vita*: 1914, 4,691gt, 15k, Br India SN.
Bamora: 1914, 3291 gt, 12k, Br India SN.

173. *Operations in Support of the Army off the Western Desert*

(7 March 1942)

The Siege of Tobruk, 12 April–17 November 1941

2. The main naval tasks were the supply of Tobruk and the running of the ports of Tobruk and Mersa Matruh. Occasional bombardments and offensive sweeps were also carried out to keep the enemy along the coast on their toes.

3. During April the scale of air attack on Tobruk and the consequent losses of ships in harbour became so heavy that supply by merchant ship was temporarily suspended. During May and June supplies were almost entirely carried by destroyers (35–50 tons each), schooners and LCTs, but in July and subsequent months one or two merchant vessels (including a bulk petrol tanker) were run in each month during the non-moon period.

4. During August the relief of the Australian garrison in Tobruk was commenced (Operation TREACLE) and continued in September and October (Operations SUPERCHARGE and CULTIVATE). Approximately 12,000 men were brought back and 18,000 men put into the garrison.

5. By October the running in of supplies by destroyers had been reduced to a fine art. The programme was made out to take full advantage of the non-moon period whilst never becoming a routine as regards either route or time of arrival. Each serial consisted of one minelayer and two or three destroyers with either 300 tons of stores and no personnel or up to 1,000 personnel and 180 tons of stores. The ships carried out an A/S sweep as far as Mersa Matruh and then proceeded at full speed to Tobruk. They then berthed, discharged and sailed in less than an hour, returned at full speed as far as Mersa Matruh and completed the run with an A/S sweep to Alexandria.

6. To achieve these results a high standard of seamanship was required as not only had the ships to find the entrance of the Tobruk boom on a dark night (a difficult piece of navigation) but they had to berth alongside in a harbour strewn with wrecks. The naval base party had to secure the ships and lighters, discharge the stores and get the ships away, all without lights.

7. The scale of air attack on Tobruk was heavy at the commencement of the siege but the exceptionally well fought AA gun defence, assisted by the naval UP battery, first of all made daylight attacks by dive bombers unprofitable, then drove off the high level bombers

and finally kept the night bombers away from the harbour area. As far as I am aware this is the first case in this war in which AA gun defence alone, unassisted by fighters, has defeated the enemy's air effort.

8. But as the scale of air attack on Tobruk itself was reduced so it increased on the ships on passage. HM Ships *Latona, Defender, Waterhen, Auckland, Grimsby, Stoke, Fiona*, 12 small craft and three merchant ships were all sunk from the air whilst on passage, whilst 27 ships were damaged.[111] A very great deal of thought and study was given to the problem of organising fighter protection. The method eventually evolved was to route all ships close inshore when fighter protection was available and well out to sea when no fighter protection could be arranged. So close were the enemy's forward landing grounds to the sea routes it was found necessary to have not less than a squadron of fighters on patrol at a time; even then they were frequently outnumbered during attacks. Thus five or more fighter squadrons were required to pass through a convoy of one slow tanker or three LCTs. After satisfactory communications were established the co-operation with No.204 Group, RAF, was excellent.

9. The problem of providing fighter protection at dawn, dusk and in moonlight was never satisfactorily solved; night fighting naval Fulmar aircraft were trained but without fighter direction–impossible from destroyers and small ships – these were not successful.

10. The naval parties at Tobruk and Mersa Matruh with the tugs' and lighters' crews did excellent work in a role never contemplated in peacetime....

They lived and worked in the sand with little water and no fresh food side by side with the Army to whose successful resistance they largely contributed.

11. A great deal of detailed work, not made any pleasanter by the fact that it entailed sailing many ships on dangerous voyages without accompanying them to sea, was carried out by the RA, Alexandria, and his Staff to whom I delegated the day to day running of the supply programme.

12. The well organised work at the ports of the Army Movements and Transportation Staffs carried out in close liaison with the naval shore parties contributed to the smooth running of the programmes.

---

[111]*Latona*: 1940, 4,000t, 6×4in, 160 mines, 40k; s Ger a/c off Bardia, Oct. 1941.
Auckland: 1938, 1,250t, 8×4in, 19.25k; s by a/c off Bardia, June 1941.
Stoke: 1918, 800t, 1×4in, 1×3in, 16k; s by a/c Tobruk, July 1941.

13. It was, however, on the crews of the 'small ships' (including some very old merchant ships) that the chief burden fell; as always they did magnificently.

14. As the result of the combined efforts of the three services the port of Tobruk was held for seven months; thus, when the advance took place in November, the port was able to handle 2,000 tons per day and the advance could be continued to Benghazi.

174. *From the Admiralty*

0221, 4 April 1941

Enemy operations in Cyrenaica must largely depend on the maintenance of their forces through Tripoli.

In view of the situation which has arisen we are sure you are considering:

(a) The concentration of as many submarines as possible on the supply line to Tripoli.
(b) The possibility of a heavy bombardment of Tripoli.

175. *To the Admiralty*

1504, 4 April 1941

(a) This has been done for many weeks with fair results but I could use as many more submarines as can be spared for this purpose.
(b) I do not consider this a feasible operation in view of heavy scale of air attack that can be brought to bear from Sicily or Tripolitania. I should not expect to have *Formidable* at end of it.

176. *From Pound*

0154, 8 April 1941

A. If the situation in the Western Desert is as unsatisfactory as I imagine then it would appear of vital importance to prevent reinforcements reaching Tripoli.
B. If we sent *Centurion* out do you consider a blocking operation possible?[112]

---

[112]*Centurion*: battleship, 1913; target ship, 1927; 25,500t, 16k.

C. As the time element is so important she would have to risk the passage of the Narrows.
D. A possible alternative would be to use *Liverpool* and *Coventry* but it is doubtful whether anything but an armoured ship would reach the required position or last long when in position.

177. To Pound

1420, 8 April 1941

(a) If *Centurion* was already in Eastern Mediterranean I should welcome the suggestion but I cannot see how she can come through the Narrows undetected and unsubjected to heavy attack as this area is under most constant surveillance. Presumably her full speed is about 15 knots.
(b) A further difficulty is to cover the distance between Malta and Tripoli undetected which can only be done by a ship capable of 20 knots.
(c) I feel it would be wasteful to use *Liverpool* who should be, if convenient, repaired to leave Alexandria before end of April.
(d) *Coventry* in spite of her bow is doing excellent work as an AA cruiser.
(e) I still hold that use of Tripoli can be prevented by continuous and heavy air attack on a much greater scale than is possible with bomber squadrons at present available in Middle East.

178. To Pound

1430–1444, 10 April 1941
[three parts]

The situation in Western Desert appears to me to be a race against time. If Germans can get sufficient forces across in next month or so they will probably gain control up to Mersa Matruh at least and if they do this it will be questionable whether Alexandria will be usable for Fleet against fighter escorted aircraft. The German prospects of achieving above are good unless Tripoli is destroyed. As stated in my 1504/4 I do not think it feasible to do this by bombardment.

It is not only a question of risk to battlefleet but of lasting effects being sufficient to make them justifiable. The German present position is after all the same as ours at Piraeus only less advantageous.

RAF are now too far back in Western Desert to attack Tripoli and in consequence the only way is from Malta whose aerodromes are themselves so vulnerable.

I consider therefore that it is essential long range bombers should be flown out immediately to Egypt for this work and that nothing should stand in the way of this. It [may] well be a matter of days and the results will decide whether we are going to be able to hold Eastern Mediterranean. I would again emphasise time factor which is vital. Meanwhile I am doing all possible with submarines, destroyers and 830 Squadron to interfere with communications. I have discussed this matter with C-in-C, Middle East, and AOC-in-C, Middle East, and a joint telegram is being sent to COS but I consider matter of such importance that I would wish to draw your particular attention to it.

179. *From Pound*

1738, 11 April 1941

I have discussed your 1444/10 with CAS who as a result has sent a telegram to Longmore pointing out that any longer range than those he has are going through teething troubles, are not tropicalised and are not fit to be sent abroad.[113] At the same time CAS has pointed out various means by which a much lower scale of attack can be brought to bear on Tripoli with what Longmore already has.

180. *From Pound*

2151, 11 April 1941

B. I agree that everything possible should be done to render Tripoli unusable by bombing, and also by minelaying, but in view of the magnitude of the issues at stake I think we must search for every possible means by which the Navy can support the efforts of the Air Force.
C. There are two ways in which we can assist:
1. By intercepting German supply ships whilst on passage.
 . . . we are sending you 8 more submarines in addition to the *Rover* . . . and the *Olympus* . . . Also the Beaufort aircraft should reach you shortly . . . .[114]

---
[113]Probably Short Stirling 4-engined bomber, just coming into service.
[114]*Olympus*: 1929, 1,475/2,030, 1×4in, 8×21in tt, 17.5/9k; mined off Malta, May 1942.

2. Denying to the enemy a port for unloading.
It would be no good to deny the enemy the use of Tripoli unless we can also deny them the use of Benghazi and subsidiary landing places. . . .

D. The methods of dealing with Tripoli appear to be:

(i) Mining, about which I have already sent you a suggestion
(ii) Bombardment
(iii) Blocking.

E. As regards bombardment, I agree that there must be considerable risk to our ships, but if, as seems probable, German dive bombers are installed at Derna, it would appear that the danger of carrying out the bombardment of Tripoli would not be much greater than the bombardment of Benghazi . . . air reports show that there are always a considerable number of merchant ships in the harbour, and generally some cruisers and destroyers. If any of these could be sunk in the harbour it would greatly hamper the use of the port. . . .

The chief difficulty in carrying out a bombardment would, I think, be spotting the fall of shot, as it would be difficult for our spotting aircraft to maintain their position in face of German fighters. However, if protected by our own fighters they might be able to operate for a sufficient time to cover the period of bombardment. . . . it would be bound to have so much effect anyhow for a time that we should not discard it without most serious reasons.

F. As regards blocking, . . . I also realise the difficulty and lack of surprise which may be caused by bringing the *Centurion* through the Narrows, but in view of the magnitude of the stakes at issue I think we should be prepared to accept this . . .

H. We all realise what a difficult time you are having and how many commitments you have to meet.

181. *From Pound*

1949, 12 April 1941

3. We believe that considerable areas of Tripoli harbour have been dredged . . . but even if this is not so, there is a good chance that the mines would function correctly in depths under 30 feet. Even if they do not function this would not be known and a considerable sweeping effort would be imposed on the enemy.

4. . . . in view of the vital importance of doing everything we can to interfere with the enemy's supplies, it is requested that the available

stock of mines at Malta may be laid in Tripoli harbour and its approaches as early as possible.

5. Air reconnaissance will very soon show whether the mining is having the effect we anticipate. If it is, the ships which are prevented from entering the harbour should offer an admirable torpedo target. . . .

182. *To the Admiralty*

1455, 13 April 1941

Nil A Mark I mines in Malta, all having been laid or dumped .. 50 A Mark I mines ex-*Amerika* arrived Alexandria 7 April. . . . 34 now serviceable and a number will be shipped to Malta shortly.[115]

2. AM 1818/27/2 para. (d) states laying mines Tripoli (Africa) harbour is not (R) not recommended as water is too shallow.

3. Intend to lay mines between breakwaters and reefs and if practicable some in harbour as soon as they arrive from Malta.

4. Certain Wellingtons are being converted for laying Cucumbers but no (R) no parachutes are available.

183. *To the Admiralty*

2355, 13 April 1941

In the event of a heavy scale of bombing attack developing against Alexandria the situation of French Squadron will become an urgent matter [?particularly] if we are forced to withdraw the main units of the Fleet to points further east. The presence of the French ships at Haifa or Port Said would moreover be an embarrassment in what will be an overcrowded harbour.

2. The French are almost certain to ask for one of the following alternatives under guarantee:
    (a)   To return to France
    (b)   To go to North African ports
    (c)   To go to Bizerta.

They will probably not press for (a) or [?(b)] due to hazard of journey and possibility of enemy interference.

---

[115]*Amerika:* 1930, 10,218gt, 15k, E Asiatic Co, Copenhagen.

3. From our point of view alternatives are
(a) To send ships to Bitter Lake or Suez
(b) To allow them to go to Indo-China or Madagascar under some guaranteed agreement to take no part in the war against us and to scuttle rather than hand selves over to the Axis
(c) To ask them to scuttle their ships outside Alexandria, crews being sent to Syria.

4. Of these alternatives (b) would be most satisfactory to me if we could get effective guarantee. If (a) is adopted ships will only remain an embarrassment to me. I rather think French would not accept (c). If the Squadron were sent East we could control passage by rationing fuel and indicating route to be taken. This proposal might also have a bargaining value with Vichy.

5. It will be remembered under terms of agreement I cannot seize ships by force and they on their side undertake not to scuttle, attempt to break out or commit any hostile act.

6. I should be glad of a very early expression of the views of HMG in this matter as time may be short and it will take several days at least for French ships to prepare for sea after being so long immobile. . . .

184. *From the Admiralty*

0059, 15 April 1941

C. It is essential therefore to do something at Tripoli . . . and at earliest moment.

D. There are two alternatives:
(a) bombarding harbour
(b) attempting to block it.

E. Their Lordships are in agreement with you that result of bombardment is uncertain and could not be expected to drastically reduce rate of reinforcements even temporarily. In addition risk to bombarding capital ships and carrier which would have to supply fighter protection would be very considerable.

F. It has been decided therefore that an attempt must be made to carry out a combined blocking and bombardment, the latter being carried out by blocking ships at point blank range as they approach harbour.

G. After carefully considering type of ship which can be used decided *Barham* and a 'C' class cruiser should be used for this purpose. The 'C' class cruiser can be used to block that portion of entrance over which there is only 15 feet of water with a rocky bottom. *Caledon* arrives Aden about 16 April and may be selected for this duty if you wish.

H. It is realised placing of these two ships will be difficult operation but after thoroughly going into matter with an ex-navigating officer of one of *Barham* class it is considered unless navigation control arrangements are shot away ship can be placed in required position.

I. The likelihood of the 'C' class cruiser reaching required position is problematical as she will be more vulnerable to fire of shore defences, but as it is estimated capacity of port would only be reduced by 30% if a gap is left over rocky patch carrying 15 feet of water, it is essential that an attempt be made to block this part of entrance.

J. The general plan that we have in mind is that *Barham* and 'C' class cruiser escorted by destroyers should approach harbour as early as possible after daybreak, first of all engaging any batteries which are firing at them and then as soon as possible diverting their fire onto shipping or other vulnerable points inside harbour. Also their fire should continue not only whilst ships are manoeuvred into position but also after ships have been sunk.

K. It is considered that bombardment at point blank range in which turrets could work in local control would really smash up harbour facilities to a degree which it would be impossible to achieve by a bombardment from long range. For them it is also hoped any covering force which you provide would be able to keep at such a distance that they would not be subject to a heavy scale dive bombing attack.

M. ... *Queen Elizabeth* is being sent to reinforce you also additional destroyers for Malta.

N. The use of *Barham* for this purpose will no doubt fill you with deepest regret but it is considered far preferable to sacrifice one ship entirely with a chance of achieving something really worthwhile rather than to get several ships damaged in a bombardment the results of which might be most disappointing.

185.   *To the Admiralty*

2111, 15 April 1941

I fully realise the grave considerations which must have been given to the matter before Their Lordships and HMG came to the decision to make the sacrifice entailed by this operation but I would submit that such a high price is only justified if first of all the success of the operation is reasonably assured and secondly if having been successful the result will be efficaceous.

2. I do not consider either of these conditions will be fulfilled.

3. As regards success it seems to me doubtful if there is one chance in ten of getting this large ship unhandy as she will be and with probably less than 2 feet of water under her at low speed, into the right position for the following reasons.

(a) There is insufficient water to approach from the E and S of the reefs.

(b) The passage from the N through the reefs has 12 cucumbers in it as well as some more between there and the harbour entrance. If it is argued that the enemy enter the harbour I would suggest that this is done at very low speed with the assistance of tugs by ships of lighter draft. The enemy may moreover have a dredged and swept channel of which we shall be unaware.

(c) Even if higher speed is risked the chances of reaching the proper position seem to me very small however skilful the handling and I would observe in this connection that I know of no record of a completely successful blocking of a harbour done in the face of enemy opposition.

4. As regards efficacy I would observe

(a) That if the harbour were blocked it seems evident the Germans would probably use Tunisian ports if indeed they are not already doing so and there seems little likelihood of the French really trying to prevent them.

(b) They will continue to use Tripoli working inside the reefs and lightering as they are now doing. This slows work but does not prevent unloading, particularly with the good weather season ahead.

(c) Owing to the amount already landed the effect of a blocking will be unlikely to be felt for some time.

5. To sum up, even if we are successful we shall have lost a first-class fighting unit whose passing will give an inestimable fillip to the failing Italian naval morale and by this very effort we shall give the enemy this measure of how desperate we consider the Cyrenaican situation to be. If the operation fails, or is only partly successful

these aspects will be intensified. We shall furthermore have to replace the ship by taking away another unit from the battle of the Atlantic where it can doubtless very ill be spared. In return for all this at best we shall make the actual harbour unusable but unloading will still be possible and alternative French harbours are available.... Nor in these considerations have I taken into account the certain loss of nearly 1,000 officers and men from the two ships (including a larger proportion of higher gunnery ratings) who will have to be sent into this operation unaware of what they are in for and who I see no prospect of being able to bring away.

7. I hesitate to flog the air question again but when I see what the enemy is able to do to Piraeus and other Greek ports by bombers who are actually working from Sicily and when one considers the devastation we have caused to Kiel and Hamburg I find it difficult to believe that this operation is justified while this alternative exists. The *Barham* operation relies on one shot in the locker. Intensive air action over a period of a month must surely wreck this small port whilst keeping the enemy under continual strain and loss, an important factor absent in the blocking proposal.

8. For the above reasons I have seen fit to query Their Lordships' decisions and most earnestly request that reconsideration be given in the light of these remarks. Meanwhile matters will go ahead and ship will be destored and prepared under pretext of docking which is fortunately now due.

9. Rather than send in *Barham* in this way without support and with such slender chance of success I would prefer to attack with the whole Battlefleet and to accept the risks referred to in para. 4 of my 1015/13. We should at least be working in mutual support and our combined efforts would intensify the weight of bombardment and provide a more reasonable obstacle to dive bombing attacks. If in these circumstances one of the battleships were seriously damaged I should endeavour to use her as a blockship subsequently removing the ship's company by means of light craft.

186. *From Pound*

1855, 15 April 1941

Instructions have been received from HMG that navy must do everything possible to prevent supplies reaching Libya from Italy and German Forces being supplied by coastwise traffic even if this results in serious losses or damage to HM Ships.

2. As Operation MD1 does not (R) not appear to have any connection with above it would not (R) not appear to be justified at present time.

3. Also as *Barham* will presumably need certain preparations which could only be undertaken in harbour it would appear that special operation might be delayed if *Barham* takes part in MD1.

4. Every convoy that reaches Libya and any transportation of supplies along the coast will make it most difficult for Army to stabilise and improve and unless Fleet concentrates on preventing such movements to exclusion of everything that is not (R) not vital the Navy will be considered as having let side down.

187. *To Pound*

0932, 16 April 1941

... It has been usual that this type of operation is only carried out by men who have volunteered for such dangerous work.

The nature of this operation and also consideration of secrecy preclude the calling for volunteers as it is obvious that for the bombardment to be effective the complete trained turret and guns crews of *Barham* must be on board, also at least two-thirds of Engine Room ratings to enable the ship to get there at high speed. Together with the ship's company of *Caledon* it is estimated that well over 1,000 men will be involved.

I see no prospect of getting any of these men away and it is certain that casualties will be very heavy as the Castel Benito aerodrome is but a few miles away.

I am of the opinion that if these men are sent into this operation which must involve certain capture and heavy casualties without knowing what they are in for, the whole confidence of the personnel of the fleet in the higher command, not only out here but at home also, will be seriously jeopardised if not entirely lost.

188. *To Pound*

1144, 16 April 1941

I hope that I am fully conscious of the necessity for stopping supplies to Libya but this can't be considered to the exclusion of all other commitments in the Mediterranean.

2. Operation MD1 includes
   (a) Extracting three empty supply ships from Malta.
   (b) Running cucumbers into Malta.
   (c) Laying cucumbers off Benghazi.
   (d) Attack on aerodromes at Rhodes.

3. If we want the use of Malta we must keep it supplied and the extracting of the above ships is necesary before another convoy is passed in. Further in view of our heavy shipping losses they are needed here.

4. The attack on Rhodes aerodrome is much needed for the defence of our convoys running to and from Greece.

5. It is true that it may delay the preparation of *Barham* 48 hours but I am still hoping when you have received my 2111/15 [No. 185] that this operation which in my opinion has little chance of success and the preparation for which involves so many difficulties will be reconsidered. . . .

6. We are not idle with regard to the Libyan situation and nobody will say that the Navy has let them down out here. No less than four operations including two landings are in train for the next 24 hours.

7. I have postponed MD1 for a further 24 hours very much against my will.

189. *From Pound*

1719, 16 April 1941

A. If you delayed MD1 for a day or two could you carry out bombardment referred to in your 2111/15 para. 6 as part of MD1 if proposed blocking is deferred?

B. The news of D14's success is most heartening but he will presumably require reinforcements to keep it up. Six destroyers will reach Malta on 26 April as a result of WINCH. When you do MD1 could you provide D14 with reinforcements until above six arrive?

190. *From Pound*

1745, 16 April 1941

B. We have been under the impression here that the situation in the Western Desert was most critical and that only most drastic measures could rectify it. Hence our drastic [?decision] regarding

Tripoli, about which full consideration will be given to your 2111/15 and your 0932/16 [Nos 185, 187].
C. I have known how many commitments you must have but from your 1144/16 they are greater than I imagined. It looks as if evacuation of our forces from mainland Greece would be added to them.
D. When I sent my 1855/15 [No. 186] we had no knowledge of destroyer operations on Libyan coast nor of necessity for MD1 and I should have found it difficult to explain the necessity for MD1 when everyone's thoughts here were on necessity of cutting communications to Libya.
E. The more you can keep me in the picture not only as to what the Fleet has done but also what it is DOING and its future commitments the easier it will be for me to prevent interference with your plans!
F. I do realise the terrific burden you are carrying and you have not only our entire confidence but also our good wishes.

191. *To Pound*

2338, 16 April 1941

A. Hope it may be possible to arrange bombardment morning 20 or 21 April as part of MD1. Destroyer fuel is a difficulty. Malta stocks are low and [I] do not wish to encroach on them.
B. Will send two 'J' class to reinforce Captain D14 and at same time perhaps removing *Nubian*.
C. I am afraid evacuation of army from Greece may be upon us in a few days.

192. *Report of an Action against an Italian Convoy, 15–16 April 1941*

(8 June 1941)

Cunningham's Observations

2. The search for the convoy was conducted skilfully and with sound appreciation. The action itself was conducted by all concerned with determination and gallantry and was completely successful, resulting in the annihilation of the convoy and the escort.
3. These results reflect the highest credit on Captain P. J. Mack and the forces under his command. The fighting spirit and the high standard of training of the ships concerned is amply demonstrated by this incident.

4. The loss of such a fine fighting unit as *Mohawk* is much to be regretted but such losses by chance torpedoes in a melée are only to be expected, and it can be counted fortunate that Cdr J. W. Eaton and a large proportion of his ship's company were saved.[116]

Report of Captain (D), 14th Destroyer Flotilla

2. At 1800 on 15 April, *Jervis, Nubian, Mohawk* and *Janus* slipped and proceeded from Malta by the eastern searched channel to intercept the convoy reported in a signal . . .

Skirmish off Sfax – Narrative of HMS Jervis

Wind NW, Force 5.   Sea – 31.   Moon bearing 135–140°.
Course 214°.   Speed – 25 knots.   Time – Zone –2.
Single line ahead in sequence *Jervis, Janus, Nubian* and *Mohawk*.

0158. Sighted ships bearing 170° about 6 miles.
0159. Made signal 'Enemy in sight to port'.
0200. Altered course to 140°.
0201. 27 knots.
0202. Made signal 'Train torpedo tubes to starboard'.
0203. Altered course to 210° to bring enemy between me and the moon.
0205. Made signal 'Train torpedo tubes to port'.
0207. Able to count 5 ships in all.
0210. Enemy bearing 140° 4 miles.
0211. 7 ships counted. Altered course to 170°.
0212. Enemy bearing 135–150° 2½–3 miles.
0213. Altered course to 160°. Enemy now seen to consist of 5 merchant vessels, 1 large destroyer, 2 small destroyers.
0214. Altered course to 150°.
0215. Enemy bearing 128–140°.
0218. Altered course to 140°.
0220. Opened fire on enemy destroyer bearing 100°, range 2,400 yards.
0222. Enemy hit by pom-pom and 4.7-in. Enemy appeared to return fire with Breda and probably 3.9-in with flashless cordite.
0225. 1 merchant vessel on fire.
0227. Checked fire. Destroyer sinking.

[116]Cdr J. W. M. Eaton: Cdr Dec. 1937; *Venetia* Sept. 1939; *Mohawk* 1940; Capt Dec. 1941; *Eskimo* 1943; *Sheffield* 1945.

THE EFFECTS OF GERMAN INTERVENTION, 1941

From now on a general melée ensued. Fire was opened with 4.7-in, pom-pom, Breda, 0.5-in and Hotchkiss at many enemy ships at ranges varying from 50 to 2,000 yards. One merchant vessel of about 3,000 tons attempted to ram me, but I just crossed his bows in time by going full speed ahead on both engines.

Fighting lights were switched on. One large destroyer passed down the line to starboard and was heavily engaged, hit with the first salvo and set on fire amidships.

0240. Fired one torpedo at large enemy destroyer, probably obtaining a hit aft.
0244. Fired one torpedo at merchant vessel stopped and on fire, but missed.
0250. An ammunition ship blew up with an enormous explosion; smoke and flames rose to a height of 2,000 feet and *Jervis* who was 200 yards away was showered with pieces of ammunition, etc., weighing up to 20 lbs; the sea around appeared as a boiling cauldron. Inspection revealed that the ammunition was of German manufacture.
0252. Received a signal from *Nubian* that *Mohawk* had been sunk by torpedo. I ordered *Nubian* to burn masthead lights and I proceeded towards her.
0311. A torpedo track passed directly under the bridge, apparently fired from the large destroyer previously engaged, which was stopped and burning and thought to be out of action. Opened fire on the destroyer, scoring several hits, and as the bearing drew too far aft ordered *Janus* to finish her off, which she did.
0320. The situation was now as follows:

> 1 destroyer sunk; 2 destroyers and 4 merchant vessels burning fiercely; the fifth nerchant vessel (the ammunition ship) sunk; *Mohawk* sunk in about 7 fathoms lying on her side with about 50 feet of her forecastle above the water. *Nubian* picking up *Mohawk*'s survivors.

0323. Went alongside wreck of *Mohawk* and took off 2 survivors. I then picked up more survivors and ordered *Janus* to sink the remains of *Mohawk* which she did by gunfire having no torpedoes left.... whilst picking up *Mohawk*'s survivors 1 merchant vessel was seen to turn over and sink.
0403. Set course 080° 20 knots.

0418.   29 knots.
0420.   Normal night zigzag (10° either side of mean course).[117]

193.   From Churchill

1558, 16 April 1941

I was very pleased to read your report of today showing the excellent work done by your light forces along the Libyan coast, in preventing any serious landing of stores east of Benghazi and the magnificent success of the division of destroyers under Captain D14 of which we have just heard. This is certainly one of the keys to victory. It is very difficult to see how a force of any size can be kept in ammunition apart from other essentials if it is dependent upon the long road from Tripoli, and at the same time is actively engaged by our own land and air forces.

I am however a little concerned at your 2355 of 13th instant, about what is to happen to the French ships if a heavy scale of bombing attack is developed against Alexandria. Even if you thought it desirable to withdraw some of your ships to Port Said or Haifa you would no doubt leave others to operate from Alexandria, and the French ships would have to take their chance with these. Indeed they would help to dilute the risk.

3.   If the worst happened the only alternatives which should be offered to the French would be to join us or for their ships to be rendered permanently unserviceable under our supervision. There could be no question of allowing them to stay in Alexandria after we had left or to go to French or African ports or through the Canal and escape into the Indian Ocean. The United States would never forgive us if we allowed such a disturbance of the Naval balance of power. In no circumstances could these ships be allowed to fall into German hands or get loose in the world where they might be used against us by a French Government entirely under German control. I hope and believe, however, that none of these unpleasant questions will arise.

---

[117]Merchant ships sunk: *Adana*: 1922, 4,205gt, Deutsche Levant.
Aegina: 1922, 2,446gt, 9.5k, Norddeutscher Lloyd.
Arta: 1922, 2,452gt, Atlas Levant, Germany.
Iserlohn: 1922, 3,704gt, 10k, Hamburg-Amerika Line.
Sabaudia: 1911, 1,590gt, Dani & Co, Italy.
Destroyers: *Luca Tarigo:* 1929, 1,944t, 6×4.7in, 6×21in tt, 38k.
Baleno (sank next day), *Lampo* (aground, recovered Aug. 1941, recomm May 1942, s Allied a/c Apr. 1943): 1932, 1,238t, 4×4.7in, 6×21in tt, 38k.

4. It is necessary now for you among your many other cares to prepare plans for bringing off from Greece the maximum British and Imperial personnel and also as many Greeks as possible in the event of a collapse there. The more Greeks who can arrive in Crete and the more British and Imperial troops who can get back to Egypt the better. Here again however one hopes that a good battle has yet to be fought.

5. COS concur.

194. *The Chiefs of Staff to Cs-in-C, Middle East*

14.23, 16 April 1941

The Prime Minister and Minister of Defence has issued the following directive...

1. If the Germans can continue to nourish their invasion of Cyrenaica and Egypt through the port of Tripoli and along the coastal road, they can certainly bring superior armoured forces to bear upon us with consequences of the most serious character. If, on the other hand, their communications from Italy and Sicily are cut, and those along the coastal road between Tripoli and [El Agheila] constantly harassed, there is no reason why they should not themselves sustain a major defeat.

2. It becomes the prime duty of the British Mediterranean Fleet... to stop all seaborne traffic between Italy and Africa by the fullest use of surface craft, aided so far as possible by aircraft and submarines. For this all-important objective, heavy losses in battleships, cruisers and destroyers, must if necessary be accepted. The harbour at Tripoli must be rendered unusable by recurrent bombardment and/or by blocking and mining. Enemy convoys passing to and from Africa must be attacked by our own cruisers, destroyers or submarines, aided by the FAA and the RAF. Every convoy which gets through must be considered a serious Naval Failure. The reputation of the Royal Navy is engaged in stopping this traffic.

3. Admiral Cunningham's Fleet must be strengthened for the above purpose to whatever extent is necessary. The *Nelson* and *Rodney* with their heavily armoured decks, are especially suitable for resisting attacks from German dive bombers, of which undue fears must not be entertained. Other reinforcements of cruisers, minelayers and destroyers must be sent from the West as oppor-

tunity serves. The use of the *Centurion* as a blockship should be studied, but the effectual blocking of Tripoli harbour would be well worth a battleship upon the active list.

4. When Admiral Cunningham's Fleet has been reinforced, he should be able to form two bombarding squadrons, which may in turn at intervals bombard the port of Tripoli, especially when shipping or convoys are known to be in the harbour.

5. In order to control the sea communications across the Mediterranean, sufficient suitable naval forces must be based on Malta, and protection must be afforded to these Naval forces by the Air Force at Malta, which must be kept at the highest strength in fighters of the latest and best quality that the Malta aerodromes can contain. The duty of affording fighter protection to the naval forces holding Malta should have priority over the use of the aerodromes by bombers engaged in attacking Tripoli.

7. Next in importance after the port at Tripoli comes the 400-mile coastal road between Tripoli and Agheila. This road should be subject to continuous harassing attacks by forces landed from the 'Glen' ships in the special landing craft. The Commandos and other forces gathered in Egypt should be freely used for this purpose. The seizure of particular points from the sea should be studied, and the best ones chosen for prompt action. Here again, losses must be faced, but small forces may be used in this harassing warfare, being withdrawn, if possible, after a while . . .

8. In all the above paragraphs, the urgency is extreme, because the enemy will grow continually stronger in the air than he is now, and especially should his air attack on Greece and Yugoslavia be successful, as may be apprehended. Admiral Cunningham should not, therefore, await the arrival of battleship reinforcements, nor should the use of the 'Glen' ships be withheld for the sake of MANDIBLES.

9. It has been decided that Tobruk is to be defended with all possible strength. . . . It would be a great advantage should the enemy be drawn into anything like a siege of Tobruk and compelled to transport and find the heavy artillery forces for that purpose. . . .

195. *To Churchill*

1539, 17 April 1941

1. Thank you for your message. We will do all in our power to stop supplies going to Libya.

2. It is certainly not our intention to abandon Alexandria lightly and it would always have to be used as an advanced base. I am very glad of your views on the fate of French Ships in this eventuality. Most certainly they will not be left to fall into enemy hands but will be scuttled or rendered quite useless before we go.

3. Question of evacuation from Greece is now being studied and I am in hopes that we may be able to evacuate majority of Empire Troops anyway without incurring too heavy losses.

196. *To Pound*

22 April 1941

A. We are finding our present commitments rather more than we can deal with efficiently.

B. I wish to make it clear that I remain strongly opposed to this policy of bombardment of Tripoli by Mediterranean Fleet. We have got away with it once but only because the German Air Force were engaged elsewhere, thus we achieved surprise.

It has taken the whole Mediterranean Fleet five days to accomplish what a heavy flight squadron working from Egypt could probably carry out in a few hours.

The Fleet has also run considerable and in my opinion unjustifiable risks in this operation which have been at the expense of all other commitments and at a time when these commitments were at their most pressing.

Another factor is that *Barham*'s endurance only allows moderate speed for passage to [?Tripoli] and return and leaves no margin should Fleet action develop during the operation. Destroyers must fuel at Suda Bay for same reason.

As you stress in your 2007/19 every capital ship we can spare will be required in the Atlantic and I can't see how *Nelson* and *Rodney* can be spared to join Mediterranean Fleet.

C. To me it appears that the Air Ministry are trying to lay their responsibilities on Navy's shoulders and are not helping us out here on Naval side of war as they should.

I would draw your attention to latest decision not to send Beauforts to Malta. This will serve to perpetuate the present conditions where enemy can freely move his convoys by day without fear of air attack whereas, even within a few miles of our own coast, ours are only free from that danger on dark nights.

A further instance is increasing losses in LUSTRE and other Greek convoys which must be attributed, in large measure, to inadequate air support.

I have also proposed the institution of a coastal command for co-operation with Mediterranean Fleet, comparable with that at home, and equipped with aircraft to meet our urgent requirements both in defensive and offensive types.

... I am quite satisfied that AOC-in-C, Middle East, co-operates with me as far as his forces allow, but these are quite inadequate.

D.   I am sending *Gloucester* to Malta to back up Captain D14 but fuel situation there is very serious. Unless evacuation commitments forbid I shall try to run in two large tankers during operation contemplated in 2337/21 from Admiralty. This will also provide a useful diversion.

Supply of fuel to Malta will continue to be an anxiety until we get a really fast tanker.

197.   From Pound

23 April 1941

A.   Our surface forces having destroyed a convoy on the Tunisian coast at night, it looks as if the enemy intend to make this part of the passage by day under the protection of cruisers and destroyers.

C.   Whatever cruisers we base at Malta, however, the enemy can bring a superior force to bear, and if we are to make certain of stopping these convoys, which we must do if we are not to risk losing Egypt, it appears necessary to base a battleship at Malta.

E.   It has been decided that it would be worthwhile expending a battleship to prevent reinforcements getting in through Tripoli. As, however, it is unlikely that any blocking operations, however successful, would prevent the passage of lighters through the entrance, it is considered that it would be preferable to risk a battleship at Malta and fight the enemy for their line of communication.

F.   Every endeavour would be made to make full use of the limited air facilities at Malta. The following is proposed:

1. The RAF have offered to maintain at Malta six Blenheims of their specially trained anti-ship Squadron.
2. This to be contingent on your Malta Swordfish Squadron being used to lay Cucumbers at Tripoli.

3. Every endeavour would be made to send some Beaufighters to Malta to assist in the protection of the battleship against dive bombers when at sea.

G. Should the policy at E be decided on, it is assumed you would still require three capital ships in Eastern Mediterranean, in which case it would be necessary to pass *Queen Elizabeth* through with Operation TIGER and to decide whether *Queen Elizabeth, Valiant* or *Barham* should be based on Malta.
I. If we are to risk the loss of a battleship in severing the lines of communication to Tripoli, it is essential that supplies should not reach Libya through Benghazi and other subsidiary ports. It is not clear how you intend to deal with this.
J. At the moment the disposition of our submarines on the Palermo–Tripoli line appears to be based on keeping the surface force and submarine areas separate. It seems doubtful whether we can afford to do this if the enemy pass Kerkenah Bank by day. In certain areas it might be necessary to allow our submarines to attack merchant ships only, which in any case are our first objective.
K. It is realised the fuel situation at Malta is a factor which must be taken into consideration.
L. Request your early remarks.

198. *To the Admiralty*

25 April 1941
[in three parts]

I am in general agreement with the idea of putting a battleship at Malta and in fact it will be recollected that I proposed to do so in December last when [?our] battleships had obtained the measure of the Italian Air Force but whole problem rests on our ability to make Malta so thorny to attack that German Air Force will find that continued attack is too expensive. If we do not do this it appears to me that battleship will be so harassed at sea and in harbour that she will be unable to fulfil her functions. Situation seems similar to that at Brest except that weight and ease of attack is far greater at Malta.

It has always been my view that when full scale of air defence was available namely three Fighter squadrons and 112 guns Malta should be usable by a capital ship and experience might even prove this could even be increased to a formidable force. Bringing of guns up to strength cannot presumably be done in time but I consider it inadvisable to send battleship until Fighter strength is up to that mentioned or alternatively 2 Squadrons with 150% reserves ... plus [?-]. Nothing less will serve to make the idea a practical proposition.

2. Para 6. Concur in use of cruisers and *Gloucester* is already at Malta but I do not consider she can be effective by day until fighter support can be made available.

3. Para F(1). I presume ample reserves will be provided otherwise six aircraft will not suffice since it means number available to take the air will be very small. Swordfish will lay Cucumbers and in fact are doing this now but I do not want to give up entirely their use by day and night for torpedo bombing aircraft attacks particularly if Beaufighters become available to cover them.

4. It will be appreciated presence of battleship means some reduction in light forces available for offensive since a screen will be necessary but with recent reinforcements and with prospect of being relieved of commitments of Aegean convoys this point can probably be overcome.

5. Para G. I consider *Queen Elizabeth* is desirable as a reinforcement. I should use *Barham* for Malta as her lower speed and endurance will not be a hindrance and she has heavy deck armour. These points outweigh the disadvantages of her small AA power.

6. Ben[?ghazi] dealt with by cruiser action, bombardment and submarine patrol. The importance of Crete to facilitate these proposals is obvious and furnishes a further reason for its retention.

7. Para J. I am in full agreement and am going further into the matter.

8. Para K. You are already aware of my views on this and of urgent need for fast oilers to keep Malta in stock.

9. Finally I would desire to emphasise that the key to the reply to the situation here and the one which will decide the issue of our success or otherwise in holding the Mediterranean lies in air power. We can probably manage on land and on sea with forces reasonably inferior to enemy but we cannot do so if we are also inferior in the air. I consider no half measures will do. If HMG decide they must ensure we hold the Mediterranean then adequate air forces must be sent. Driblets merely get swallowed up as has been only too clearly shown in Greece and Malta.

199. *From Churchill*

26 April 1941

I am somewhat concerned at your 1436/22 [No 196]. There can be no departure from the principle that it is the primary responsibility of the Mediterranean Fleet to sever all communication between Italy and Africa.

2. I am sorry that the haze caused by the aircraft attack hampered your firing at Tripoli. We ought to have foreseen this but it is no use repining, and after all results were substantial and achieved without casualties in ships and men. Personally I was not surprised at this immunity and certainly the fact that the main batteries of the principal enemy base in Africa, although under German control, were at 20-minutes' notice, shows that the enemy cannot always be ready everywhere at the same time. I suppose there is no doubt that the blocking plan would in these circumstances have come off.

3. About your air support; you should obtain accurate information because no judgement can be formed without it. CAS tells me that the same weight of bombs as you fired of shells into Tripoli in 42 minutes, viz. 530 tons, might have been dropped,

(a) by one Wellington Squadron from Malta in 10½ weeks, or
(b) by one Stirling Squadron from Egypt in about 30 weeks.

The latter figure is theoretical since the Stirling [is not] suitable for operations under Middle East conditions . . .

4. Your remarks in para. C about our withholding Beauforts from Malta show that you do not appreciate the fact that the primary aim of the Air Force in Malta is to defend the naval base against air attack, in order that your surface craft may operate against enemy convoys with their decisive power as so successfully demonstrated. This policy may be right or wrong, it may prove too costly in ships, but we think it ought to be tried. For the purpose of TIGER, apart from what comes from DUNLOP, we are sending 15 Beaufighters to Malta, and also to supplement the efforts of the surface forces to interrupt ships between Italy and Tripoli, we are sending out today six of the specially trained Blenheim bombers which have been doing so well against coastal shipping here.

5. The first para. of your C is really not justified. The main disposition of forces between the various theatres rests with the Defence

Committee, over which I preside, and not with the Air Ministry who execute our decisions. Ever since November I have tried by every method and every route to pump aircraft into the Middle East. Great risks have been run and sacrifices made especially when two-thirds of one whole fighter squadron were drowned in trying to fly to Malta, and when *Furious* was taken off her Atlantic duties to make three voyages to Takoradi. I always try hard here to sustain you in every way and acclaim your repeated successes, and I earnestly hope you will also believe that we at the centre try to take sound and bold decisions amid our many difficulties.

6. At my request CAS will forward to you through the AOC-in-C a detailed technical note on the above points.

7. In the last para. of your B you wonder how I could have suggested that *Nelson* and *Rodney* should be spared from the Atlantic to join the Mediterranean Fleet. I thought they were specially suitable because of their deck armour and the apprehension entertained of dive bomber attack. Whether they could be spared or not depends on the situation in the Atlantic. About this, in view of your high position, I will now inform you. I have been for a long time in constant intermittent correspondence with President Roosevelt.[118] He has now begun to take over a great part of the patrolling west of the 26th meridian West. The whole American Atlantic Fleet with numerous flying boats enter into action in the first phase of this plan at midnight 24th, GMT. US warships will cruise along our convoy routes, shadow or as they call it 'Trail' all raiders or U-boats observed, and broadcast their position in plain language to the world at 4-hourly intervals or oftener if needed. It is desired that this should not be announced suddenly but become apparent as it develops. The matter is therefore confided to you in the greatest secrecy. The easement and advantage of it to the Admiralty is enormous and of course it may easily produce even more decisive events therefore you do not need at this moment to be unduly concerned about the Atlantic, and can devote your resources which we are increasing in so many ways, to the cutting-off of enemy communication with Africa whether by Tripoli or Cyrenaica. On this depends the battle of Egypt . . .

---

[118]Franklin D. Roosevelt (1882–1945): country gentleman; Democrat; NY State Senate 1911–12; Asst Sec Navy 1913–20; VPres cand 1920; polio 1921; Govr NY 1929–32; President 1933–45.

200. *To Pound*

1554, 26 April 1941

... I feel we should be blind to facts if we imagine that six destroyers or for that matter 16 can be quite sure of intercepting Libyan convoys unless they have proper air support to enable them to work by day.

2. I suggest situation is analogous to that in Channel at home where we have advantages which are absent out here and distances to go for interception are considerably less. Yet it seems enemy shipping passes freely. Therefore I feel it is wrong to expect too much of a few destroyers stationed at Malta. The fact that it is very difficult to intercept these convoys should be squarely faced.

3. I will however leave whole 5DF at Malta although this will make fuel situation there even more critical.[119] The 14DF I cannot spare from other commitments.

201. *From Pound*

28 April 1941

Your 2245/25, 1554/26.

A. The difficulty of intercepting these convoys and also your reasons against further bombarding Tripoli are very fully appreciated but if we are to defeat the German threat against Egypt every possible method must be tried against the convoys and against Tripoli and Benghazi.

B. With the Germans in Greece a much increased use of Benghazi by convoys from Italy can be expected.

C. *Submarines*: Presume you are trying out the surface night attack method with which the Germans have been very successful against us at home.

---

[119]5DF, 'J' & 'K' cl, under Capt Lord Louis Mountbatten (1900–1979), later A of F Earl M. of Burma: s of A of F Prince Louis of Battenberg, FSL in 1914; ent RN 1913; *Lion* 1916; royal tours 1920s with Pr of Wales; sig splist; snr radio appts; Cdr 1932; *Daring* 1934; Ady (FAA); Capt 1937; *Kelly* & Capt 5DF 1939; *Illustrious* June 1941; Actg VA & Chief, Comb Ops 1941–43; SAC, SE Asia 1943–45; Visct 1946; Viceroy of India 1947 & G-Gen 1947–48; RA 1CS; VA 1949; 4SL 1950; C-in-C Med 1952; Adm 1953; SACMED 1953; FSL 1954; A of F 1956; Chief of Defence Staff 1959–65. See P. Ziegler, *Mountbatten* (London, 1985); and VA Sir Ian McGeoch, *The Princely Sailor: Mountbatten of Burma* (London, 1996); and G. Till, 'Admiral Earl Mountbatten of Burma', in M. H.Murfett (ed.), *The First Sea Lords: From Fisher to Mountbatten* (London, 1995), pp. 265–82.

D. *MTBs*: You will by now have received a[n] MTB Flotilla. Every effort will be made to send you another flotilla when they are received from America.

E. *Blenheim bombers*: Six of these should have reached Malta by now. They have been very successful at home. The intention is to relieve them frequently so as to avoid overhaul difficulties at Malta.

F. *Cucumbers*: Special cucumbers [magnetic mines] for use by Wellingtons will be shipped by next WS convoy.

G. *Beaufighters*: One Flight is proceeding to Malta shortly and the balance of the Squadron will arrive in time to operate in the defence of Operation TIGER. It is important that you should realise the limitations of this aircraft. They have no rear guns and are therefore vulnerable to the German long range fighters. Their ability to support capital ships and cruisers is therefore limited.

H. *Beauforts*: Owing to the limitations of the Malta aerodromes none of these are to be sent out as it is not considered that they will be sufficiently successful. They are indifferent torpedo machines, and it is expected the Blenheims will be more effective.[120]

I. *Surface ships*: *Queen Elizabeth, Fiji* and *Naiad* (wearing Flag of FOC, 15CS) are to be sent to you with Operation TIGER. *Fiji* is instead of *Exeter* vide your 0841/23. When *Neptune* is ready would you prefer her to replace *Fiji*? There are no further modern [?-] cruisers as you will have all those fit for service.[121]

J. *Malta Defences*: Every effort has been made to send Hurricanes to Malta. Operation DUNLOP will be repeated if situation in the Atlantic permits.

By our records 104 out of 112 [heavy AA] guns have reached Malta. The balance of 8 are now in WS7 as also are the balance of 12 light AA guns.

K. *Fast Oilers*: We have none at present. Hope to get some from US.

L. *Air Forces*: Everything possible is being done to help you and Eastern Mediterranean.

---

[120]Bristol Beaufort: 1938, 4mg, 2,000lbs bombs/1 t, 265mph, range 1,035 mls. They did serve, and to good effect, in the Med. See R. C. Nesbit, *The Armed Rovers: Beauforts and Beaufighters over the Mediterranean* (Shrewsbury, 1995).

[121]*Fiji*: 1940, 8,525t, 12×6in, 8×4in, 6×21in tt, 33k; s Ger a/c off Crete, May 1941. *Naiad*: 1940, 5,450t, 10×5.25in, 6×21in tt, 33k; s *U-565*, E Med, March 1942.

FOC, 15CS was RA E. L. S. King: Capt Dec. 1926; COS to C-in-C, HF, Apr. 1938; RA Aug. 1938; 15CS, *Naiad* July 1940; VA May 1941; ACNS(T) Oct. 1941; Prin Br NLO to Allied Navies, Jan. 1943; Ret List Sept. 1944; Adm June 1945.

202. *To Churchill*

29 April 1941.

Your 1142/26 [No. 199]. I am most grateful for your message. I fully concur principal responsibility of Mediterranean Fleet at the moment is to sever all communications between Italy and Africa. There are however two other responsibilities which are of immediate importance: (A) Evacuation of Imperial Forces from Greece (B) Supply to Malta.

2. My contention is that these commitments, particularly severing of communications with Libya are not exclusively naval, and in all cases very considerable air support is required.

3. I would like to make certain points clear. (1) A high degree of air reconnaissance must be available. For instance so reduced has been our air reconnaissance that sometimes for weeks on end I have had no idea of location of enemy Battlefleet. During evacuation from Greece it was only possible to keep one flying boat at a time on patrol in Ionian Sea; this was particularly serious as Battlefleet was in Alexandria and all destroyers were actively employed in evacuation. (2) Malta must be brought up to established scale of AA defences and fighter squadrons. This has never been done and in consequence operating from Malta has always been hazardous for warships and few have emerged undamaged. With arrival of German air force in Sicily and increase in air minelaying these detached Squadrons enhance and decrease effectiveness of our operating from Malta in proportion. (3) Malta is the correct base strategically for a fleet to work from but even if this was made possible we should have to maintain proportion of fleet elsewhere to meet our various commitments all of which require air co-operation. (4) I can't agree that primary duty of air force in Malta is to defend island; surely an equally important function is to make use of this ideally placed base for offensive air action against the enemy. This second string to our bow is of highest importance to interlock with efforts of our surface craft. Indeed it is presumably for this reason that the very welcome special Blenheims are being sent out.

4. Until these facts are appreciated and made good we shall be working on unsound premises, since Navy alone can only interrupt and can't stop communications particularly in the case of Libya.

5. I have consistently put forward this view throughout the last two years and yet this very day Malta is subject to continual air attack; it is held under constant observation and movements of our warships

are dogged by shadowers from moment they put out to sea. In Greece I am endeavouring to evacuate 40–50,000 men with no air reconnaissance and against unopposed attack of German dive bombers whose strength is approximately 400. In Western Desert my convoys are consistently bombed at sea and in harbour incur heavy losses. The opposition enemy meets is meagre.

6. Everything possible will be done, of course, and when I am clear of commitment of Greek evacuation in face of unopposed air attack I hope to be in a better position to act more vigorously.

7. Arrival of German Air Force in Southern Greece is going to make our use of Suda Bay precarious, if not impossible, and will greatly complicate supplying of Malta since inlet convoy passage will be within reach of dive bombers from Greece, North Africa or Italy.

8. Air situation in Western Desert is serious. Loss in shipping increases and we are reduced to sending only one ship at a time to Tobruk owing to lack of fighter protection.

10. To turn to the broad aspect of the Egyptian situation we have to realize that the Navy alone can't save Egypt or even play its full part till air situation is squarely faced. The Army is so weak that even if nothing further entered [?-] afterwards at all except maintenance of supplies they will be hard put to it to hold [?pass] and in any case will have to do so on lines which jeopardise all our main supply bases.

11. I feel it necessary to state my view is now we shall lose Egypt in course of next few months unless every nerve is strained to increase our Air Forces here and if this is not done we stand a chance of losing as well a high proportion of our fleet in endeavour to save Port Tewfik. I know great efforts are being made as regards fighters and trust this is equally being done for bombers so that we can hit back. In effect at the moment the Libyan communications battle is between Navy and enemy Air Forces and that battle can only be won in close partnership with an adequate Air Force. We must have:

(a) Adequate naval forces – these I judge [?-] supply we can rely on obtaining as losses occur.

(b) Long range fighters; these are needed permanently and urgently. Lack of them is one of our greatest wants in all theatres.

(c) Sufficient short range fighters to give us full use of our bases Malta, Alexandria, Suda Bay and Tobruk.

(d) Adequate reconnaissance aircraft. Of these we are always desperately short.

12. I have perhaps drawn a rather gloomy picture but I am sure you would wish me to share my views quite frankly. I am not pessimistic and very much can and will be done by Navy to rectify situation but I feel if our Air Forces can't be increased in Middle East to reach some measure of parity with those of enemy we may have to face some very unpleasant alternatives.

203. *Operations MD2 and MD3: The Bombardment of Tripoli, 21 April 1941*

(16 August 1941)

Cunningham's Observations

2. It was decided to carry out this bombardment at night, using flares, rather than at first light, for the following reasons:

(i) A heavy scale of air attack was expected, and it was considered desirable for the carrier to be in close company with the battlefleet at daylight.

(ii) It was not justifiable to risk the carrier in daylight close inshore with the battlefleet where she would be in range of the shore batteries with her movements restricted.

3. The expected air attacks did not develop. This was the most remarkable feature of the operation, since the enemy was believed to have considerable air forces both near Tripoli and at Benghazi.
4. The bombarding run was designed to bring the battlefleet within 6-in secondary armament range of the harbour for as long as practicable, having regard to known mine areas.
5. The navigational approach was conducted with great accuracy and up to the time of altering course round *Truant*, proceeded exactly according to plan. . . .
9. The combined effects of the enemy's smoke screen and the dust and smoke raised by the initial salvos prevented effective air spotting and the resultant damage was less than it should have been. . . .
10. Three merchant ships and one destroyer were sunk and at least two other merchant ships damaged.[122] Besides the actual damage on shore which was considerable, there must be counted the effects on the working of the port of partial evacuation by the native population. . . .

---

[122]Only one merchant vessel sunk; some damage ashore.

11. However, in spite of our immunity on this occasion, I do not consider in general that the results to be expected justified hazarding the whole Mediterranean Battlefleet in mineable waters and exposed to potentially heavy air attacks at such a distance from their base.

204. *War Diary, April 1941 (concl.)*

24 April

The Greek Navy

7. The Greek Admiralty offered all units of the fleet to operate under the C-in-C from British bases and the C-in-C accepted this offer, welcoming it.... There had evidently, however, been a number of casualties recently, 23 merchant ships being reported sunk in the Piraeus area in the past 48 hours.

25 April

5. The following Greek ships had now arrived at Alexandria but were not yet ready for service with the fleet:

Cruiser *Averoff* flying the flag of Admiral Kavadias.
Destroyers *Queen Olga, Kondourios, Spetsai, Aetos, Ierax, Panther.*
Torpedo Boats *Niki* and *Aspis.*
S/M depot ship *Hifaistos.*
Submarines *Nereus, Triton, Glaucos* and *Katsonis.*

The submarine *Papamicolis* was on passage to Alexandria and arrived the following day. One other destroyer was reported to be at Suda Bay damaged and the remainder either sunk or too severely damaged to move.[123]

Yugoslav Navy

6. The Yugoslav submarine *Nebosja* and 2 MTBs had also arrived at Alexandria but all other Yugoslav ships were either damaged or

---

[123] Adm E. Kavadias, R Hellenic N: b 1886; ensign 1906; Balkan wars 1912–13, in destroyers; anti-Venizelos and imprisoned 1917–20; destroyer cmds 1920–22; resigned 1922; resumed N career 1925; RA & C-in-C, Fleet 1939; U Sec, N Affs May 1942; VA on Ret List Feb. 1945.
Averoff: 1910, 9,450t, 4×9.2in, 8×7.5in, 4×18in tt, 22.5k.
Queen Olga: 1938, 1,350t, 4×5in, 8×21in tt, 36k. *Kondourios, Spetsai*: 1931–32, 1,389t, 3×4.7in, 1×3in, 3×21in tt, 38k. *Aetos, Ierax, Panther*: 1911, 1,050t, 3×4in, 1×3in, 3×21in tt, 32k.
Niki, Aspis: 1905–06, 275t, 2×3.5in, 2×18in tt, 29k.
Hifaistos: repair & S/m depot ship, 1920, 4,549gt, 4×4in, 11.5k.
Nereus, Triton, Glaucos: 1927–28, 700/930t, 1×4in, 8×21in tt, 14/9.5k.
Katsonis, Papamicolis: 1926, 576/775t, 6×21in tt, 14/9.5k.

in enemy hands. A number of aircraft arrived to join the RAF or FAA.[124]

Malta

9. The Admiralty suggested that 14DF should remain at Malta after the arrival of the 5DF, for both flotillas to act against the Tripoli convoys. The C-in-C replied in his 2315/25 that this was out of the question, both on account of the air situation at Malta and the position in Greece, where it was essential for all light forces to be employed for the present. The state of affairs in the Mediterranean did not seem to be fully realised by Their Lordships.

26 April

Western Desert

7. *Ladybird* bombarded Gazala aerodrome, setting fire to at least 5 aircraft, and *Aphis* bombarded an enemy column in the Halfaya Pass. A lack of fighter protection was causing anxiety for the safety of the gunboats and also creating further difficulties at Tobruk where the scale of air attack was heavy.

Hospital Ships

8. The C-in-C asked the Admiralty for permission to capture enemy hospital ships encountered in view of the repeated and deliberate bombings of HS *Vita* and others.

27 April

Merchant Ships

11. There were now 13 merchant ships at Alexandria undergoing major repairs due to enemy action. A number of others had sailed for Port Said and beyond to complete [?repairs].

28 April

Operation SALIENT

5. *Dido, Abdiel, Kelly, Kipling, Kelvin, Kashmir, Jackal* and *Jersey* arrived successfully at Malta.[125] *Dido* and *Abdiel* fuelled and sailed again for Alexandria, accompanied by Captain (D), 14 DF with

[124]*Nebosja*: 1927, 975/1,184t, 2×4in, 8×21in tt, 15/10k.
[125]*Kelly, Kashmir* (both s Ger a/c off Crete, May 1941), *Kipling, Kelvin, Jersey* (mined Malta May 1941), *Jackal* (dmgd Ger a/c off Malta May 1942; s by own forces): 1939, 1,760t, 6×4.7in, 10×21in tt, 36k.

Jervis, Juno, Jaguar, Imperial and *Breconshire, Imperial* having completed her repairs. The 5DF were to remain at Malta with *Gloucester* to operate against the Tripoli convoys. *Janus* also remained at Malta for docking and repairs.

29 April

HMS York

6. It was decided for the present to abandon all attempts to salvage *York*.[126] She had been further damaged by near misses and several divers had been killed while working on her. Most of her crew were embarked in *Orion* for passage to Alexandria, a nucleus party being left for care and maintenance. Her HA guns were landed for local defence, as were all useful stores and equipment. Arrangements were made for demolition at short notice.

Western Desert

7. *Chakla* was hit during one of the many air raids on Tobruk and sank inside the harbour. She was alongside and sank in shallow water; it was possible later to salvage her guns and much equipment. There were only two ratings injured. A convoy of 'A' lighters which had arrived with *Chakla* carrying tanks and MT unloaded safely. There were about 30 dive bombers in each attack.

30 April

6. There were more heavy air raids at Tobruk and some casualties and damage to ships. *Aphis* and *Ladybird* bombarded the Sollum and Gazala areas respectively. The three 'A' lighters left Tobruk for Alexandria with personnel and captured tanks. The following signal was made to SNOIS:

> The difficulties of working the port of Tobruk and the danger of sailing ships to and from Tobruk without adequate fighter protection are fully realised both by myself and the AOC-in-C. Your squadron and the men at Tobruk are doing magnificent work and I trust that the present bleak period will soon be ended.

Malta

8. There were more heavy air raids, one lasting for 6 hours during the night 29/30 by about 60 bombers. *Encounter* and *Fermoy* were both badly damaged in dock and it was at first thought that

[126]*York* broken up at Bari, 1952.

Encounter could not be repaired. Later reports, however, indicated that by using parts of *Gallant*, she could be completed in some weeks. *Abingdon* was also damaged when exploding a mine, and *Trusty Star* (the only LL sweeper) was sunk in the air raid. VA, Malta, reported that it might be necessary to sail all warships in harbour each night in spite of the shortage of fuel, and that it would not be possible to have a convoy in harbour as well as warships.[127]

Summary and Appreciation of Events for Month of April 1941

General

This month was the start of an exceedingly difficult period for the Mediterranean Fleet. The opening days saw almost the whole fleet's effort concentrated in a race against time to place our troops into Greece before the threatened attack by Germany took place. This work was successfully performed without the loss of a man or of any stores at sea. On the 6th the storm broke and Greece and Yugoslavia were invaded. As had been feared problems then multiplied. The ports of entry into Greece were few and ill protected and there was a mass of valuable shipping plying the Aegean. In addition our air forces were woefully inadequate and quite unable to compete with the enemy concentrations. In consequence ports and ships in port were damaged and a big scale of minelaying developed. We were seriously short of minesweepers in Egypt but, ill though they could be spared, they had to be sent up to the Aegean.

4. April was in fact a month of disasters, only relieved by two or three satisfactory incidents. . . .
5. The end of the month thus found the Army back on the frontiers of Egypt, the Army in Greece in the course of evacuation to Crete and further south, and a very tired fleet whose light craft and cruisers in particular had been kept continuously on the move for some three weeks under the constant attacks of an infinitely superior air force working in the ideal conditions, geographically and meteorologically speaking, of a Mediterranean spring.

---

[127]*Encounter*: 1934, 1,405t, 4×4.7in, 8×21in tt, 35.5k; repaired but s Battle of Java Sea, March 1942.
  Abingdon (s Ger a/c, Malta, Apr 1942), *Fermoy* (total loss, Apr. 1941): 1918–19, 800t, 1×4in, 1×3in, 16k.
  Trusty Star: drifter, 1920, 96t; salved; mined, Malta, June 1942.

Fleet Operations

6. The successful campaign in East Africa made it necessary to send two 'J' class destroyers down into the Red Sea to protect our shipping from the Italian Naval Forces who would evidently be forced out of Massawa to avoid capture. At the same time Squadrons from *Eagle* were also sent down to Port Sudan to deal with the enemy should they break out. These aircraft operated with such success that all the enemy forces were destroyed, scuttled or interned in a very short time and a serious menace was thus removed.

7. On 7 April a force of four destroyers under Captain (D), 14DF, sailed for Malta via Suda Bay. This force was dispersed to operate against enemy convoys. The problem was not easy since our ships could be given no fighter support and it was necessary to be able to intercept convoys at a point which would allow our forces to be able to retire on Malta without being exposed to aircraft attack for too long. . . .

FAA Operations

11. A small force of Albacores was kept forward at Tobruk for work chiefly against enemy surface craft. In the absence of suitable targets, however, they were employed in co-operation with the RAF against enemy land targets. 815 Squadron of Swordfish was sent to Eleusis and thence to forward aerodromes in north western Greece. This Squadron was very well handled and was a serious menace to the enemy. A number of large ships were sunk or damaged by torpedoes and bombs at Valona, Durazzo and even Brindisi. It was unfortunate that weather conditions did not allow the use of the forward aerodromes earlier as otherwise very serious damage might have been done to enemy lines of supply.

Submarines

12. The 'U' class submarines working from Malta started to get their hand in and to be more successful and a number of enemy ships were sunk.[128] . . .

Bases

14. *Malta.* As a whole Malta had a more satisfactory month and little serious damage was done. The island was, however, fulfilling

---

[128]*Regent* was nearly lost in a brave attempt to rescue British diplomats from Kotor, Yugoslavia, then in Italian hands.

its function as a naval base in that it was harbouring our light forces which were harassing enemy convoys. This policy resulted in several successes and in consequence towards the end of the month the scale of air attack increased sensibly. Unfortunately it became necessary to withdraw light forces as every ship was needed to deal with the situation in the Eastern Mediterranean. In any case, however, damage was becoming so severe to ships in harbour that it is doubtful if it would have been wise to keep ships there.

205. *Middle East Commanders-in-Chief Committee*

28 April

120. *Crete*

C-in-C, Mediterranean, stressed the importance of Crete from the Naval point of view. If in enemy hands, the supply of Malta would be most difficult, thereby affecting the Navy's ability to interrupt enemy sea traffic to Libya.

The AOC-in-C drew attention to the difference between making full use of the island and denying it to the enemy.

In view of the recent heavy losses sustained in Hurricane aircraft, it would be impossible for some time to provide sufficient fighter protection for Crete, and therefore the use of Suda Bay by the Navy during that period would be doubtful. He hoped, however, that the fighter position would improve in about 6 weeks. The present fighter aircraft would remain there, but they could not be replaced, and if the enemy carried out heavy air attacks from the various air bases at their disposal, the usefulness of these machines would be short-lived.

In the opinion of the AOC-in-C, the danger of an airborne attack on Crete was NOT great, owing to the difficult nature of the country. There were excellent dispersal areas on the island, and provided the Greeks co-operated, we should be able to deny the island to the enemy for some time, but it would be unlikely that we could use it as a naval or air base without strong fighter protection.

... The C-in-C, Mediterranean, agreed with the AOC-in-C and said that the Navy could not guarantee to prevent a seaborne attack, but he considered it a very risky undertaking unless the enemy had previously obtained a footing on the island. He said he was looking into the possibility of making use of anchorages on the Southern or Western shores for supply purposes, and agreed that the MNBDO should proceed to Crete. He emphasised the need for air reconnaissance particularly at the present time when the Fleet is denuded of destroyers.

C-in-C, Middle East, agreed that the denial of Crete to the enemy was most important and that we must be prepared to hold it even without fighter support.

126. *Western Desert*

... The C-in-C, Mediterranean, agreed to examine the question of undertaking blocking operations in Benghazi harbour. He hoped to continue supplying Tobruk by sea. This would have to be done at night by single ships. ...

206. *Evacuation of the Army from Greece*

7 July 1941

Report on Operation DEMON
Cunningham's Observations

2. The operations were most ably conducted by the VALF, who met the needs of a confused and constantly changing military situation in a masterly manner. In this he was substantially assisted by the untiring efforts of Rear Admiral H. T. Baillie-Grohman, who was in charge of arrangements ashore in Greece.

3. The conduct of the naval forces involved including the special landing craft was, with few exceptions, beyond praise. Officers and men went for many days almost without rest under conditions of great discomfort with their ships crowded with troops under constant air attack. They were materially helped in their task by the admirable discipline and spirit among the troops they embarked.

4. A notable feature of the operation was the gallant and enterprising performance of the merchant seamen in the troopships who had to take their ships into difficult and unlighted anchorages, in many cases without charts. A high proportion of Dutch ships were included and were particularly noticeable for their efficient and seamanlike performance.

5. It was most fortunate that the 'Glen' ships with their landing craft were present in the Mediterranean. These ships, their landing craft and the tank landing craft, although playing their role in the reverse of that for which they were intended, proved invaluable and undoubtedly made it possible to embark many more troops than would otherwise have been the case.

6. This melancholy operation coming as it did on top of the prolonged operation of transporting the troops into Greece, threw a very severe strain on both men and material of the Mediterranean Fleet; a strain which was most nobly shouldered in the face of heavy air attack which usually had to be met without fighter protection of any sort.

7. The operation was throughout a most anxious one, performed, as it was, with no cover from enemy surface interference. The urgent need for destroyers for the actual evacuation precluded the provision of screens to enable the sorely needed battleship cover to be provided. Had our enemy shown more enterprise the results might have been very different.

Report of Flag Officer Attached Middle East GHQ

Cairo
13 May 1941

Remarks

Situation in Piraeus, and control of local shipping

2. On arrival in Greece, I found Piraeus failing to function as a harbour on account of the great destruction caused by the explosion of an ammunition ship, with the resultant fires in the harbour, on 7 April and continual mining or bombing since that date. Moreover, the Greek authorities, through whom the British naval authorities had been working for the control of shipping, berthing, supplies for ships and so on, had been prevented by the destruction and disorganisation caused by the explosion from attending at their posts except in one or two isolated cases. This, combined with the fact that the military and civil authorities were very properly endeavouring to send away all redundant personnel and stores as quickly and inconspicuously as possible in local ships, threw a great strain both on my staff and on the staffs of the Naval Control Service Officer and the Divisional Sea Transport Officer, whose numbers had already been greatly reduced by casualties. The language problem added to our difficulties.

The changing military situation

3. The military situation in Greece changed very quickly from day to day, and was constantly deteriorating due to three main factors. The first factor was the gradual change in the morale of the Greek

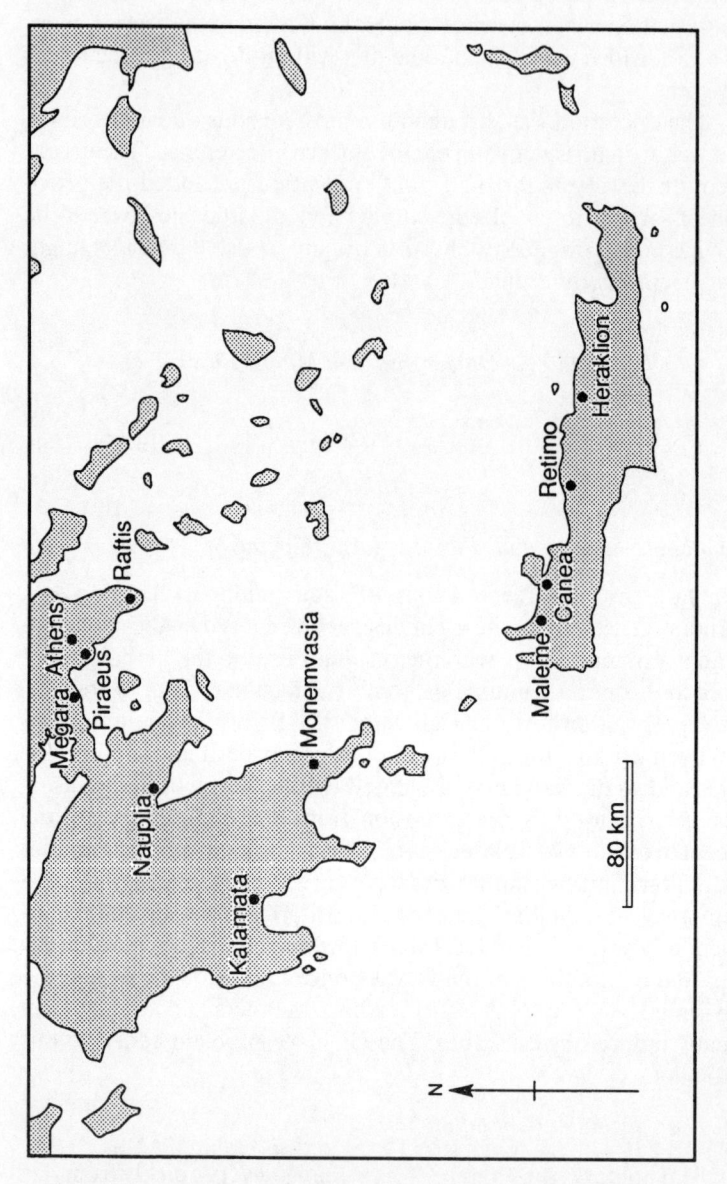

Greece and Crete, April–May 1941

fighting services, which though very mercurial was deteriorating on the whole. The second factor was the reduction of our Air Force to such small proportions that its support became completely inadequate – this chiefly due to the small numbers of our aircraft available in Greece, and to the loss of aerodromes as the Army retired. The resultant German air superiority showed itself in massed attacks on shipping in Greek waters, 23 ships being destroyed in two days, in the entire immobilisation of our armies by day, and in the severe bombing of roads in rear of our armies on which our troops depended for their supplies and for their retirement. The third factor was the sudden collapse of the Greek Army in the Epirus region which caused an immediate withdrawal from the Thermopylae line and hastened in an unexpected manner the date of final evacuation.

Decisions regarding Dates, Beaches and Numbers

4. Further, the exact military situation at the front was usually obscure to GHQ in Athens, and seldom determined until some 18 to 24 hours after the troops had moved, owing to the great unreliability of wireless in the mountain regions. This necessitated action with regard to shipping being taken in ample time, observing that 600 miles separated our bases and the coast of Greece. Even during the passage of our ships the situation could and did alter very considerably, and a selection of the right beaches under these conditions was no easy matter.

5. Owing to the very difficult nature of the military operations and the confused political situation, it was exceedingly difficult to arrive at firm figures in regard to dates and numbers. As an example of this, it was found impossible to obtain the date for D1 of the operation until approximately 48 hours before the evacuation was actually due to begin. Also estimated numbers for the total lift fluctuated between a minimum of 32,000 and a maximum of 56,000.

Failure of the Enemy to Bomb Evacuation Beaches

6. In this particular we were fortunate. The enemy made no attempt to bomb our evacuation beaches or our ships by night. This may have been partly due to our policy of not permitting ships to reach beaches till one hour after dark and so making it more difficult for the enemy to to find the exact beaches in use. Or it may have been due to lack of flares or the enemy's deliberate policy to make use of daylight only. . . .

Combined Headquarters

7. The combined HQ and Joint Planning Staff which was established at GHQ of the British Troops in Greece immediately on my arrival in Athens worked very smoothly indeed...

8. Nevertheless, as strangers in a strange town with many contacts to be established and our way to find about, the task of my staff was no easy one...; I submit, therefore, that in the future, when forces of the Army or Air Force are sent to another country by sea, it should be recognised that it is essential to appoint a Senior Naval Officer to the country of their destination. Rear Admiral Turle, the Naval Attaché in Athens, was able to carry out these duties efficiently... but as soon as a hitch occurred, his diplomatic duties increased at the same rate as did other problems. The result was that I and my staff had to be dispatched in a hurry... a properly established SNO on the spot would no doubt have functioned far more easily and with less chance of a disastrous finish.

Beach parties

9. The numbers of the beach parties... proved to be sufficient and their composition well balanced. The information brought in by beach reconnaissance parties, together with that supplied by Captain Razikostikas, Hydrographer of the Greek Navy, proved, in the event, to be accurate and was invaluable to the conduct of the operation. This officer was most helpful and the Greek Admiralty at all times most helpful.

Landing Craft

10. The operation was to a great extent rendered possible by the employment of considerable numbers of our own landing craft. Of the total approximate number of 47,000 embarked, only 14,000 were taken from recognised wharves or piers, the balance being taken from open beaches in landing craft and ships' boats.

The maximum loads which it was found practicable to lift in the various types of landing craft were:

LCT 900; LCA 60–70; LCM 150.

Although every endeavour was made to obtain as many local craft as possible, these could not be relied upon except in cases where British officers were in command, and the number of British officers available was limited.

11. It should be emphasised that the landing craft ... had neither any adequate AA armament, nor were they supplied with wireless, a very grave handicap under the circumstances.

Communications

12. The naval responsibility was the establishment of a direct W/T link to naval authorities and ships....
13. The events of the night 26/27 April ... nearly broke the all-important naval line....

Officers and Men

14. The conduct of officers and men throughout was excellent and all duties were performed with cheerfulness and efficiency....

Report on Evacuation of British troops from Greece, April 1941

17 April

I left Cairo for Greece by air at 0930 with a small staff of four specially selected officers.... I arrived at Athens at 1700 ... The point that at least four days' notice was required for the arrival of shipping in Greek waters was emphasised as strongly as possible; also that between 22 April and 2 May moonless nights would be in our favour should evacuation be decided upon....

2. It was decided to send out combined naval and military parties to reconnoitre all suitable beaches and landing places in Euboea, the Gulf of Corinth, the S and E coast between Khalkis and the Corinth Canal, and the S and E coasts of the Morea between the Corinth Canal and Kalamata.

18 April

3. I proceeded to take stock of the naval situation in the Athens-Piraeus area....

[Rear Admiral Turle] was in fact performing the duties of SBNO Greece, as well as being Naval Attaché. It soon became obvious that to control the evacuation, I would have to control the local Greek and other shipping in Greek waters ... The work of the NCSO and DSTO whose small staff had been greatly reduced by casualties and sickness, had been to a great extent carried out through the Greek harbour authorities, ... Owing to the explosion of an ammunition ship in the harbour a few nights previously, after an air raid, some 12 merchant ships in Piraeus harbour were lost. Great damage was done to the harbour facilities, tugs and small craft of all sorts were destroyed, the telephone system was put out of action, and only 5 berths of the total of 12 were available for the use of shipping. In addition, there were some 20 or more merchant ships, mostly Greek, ... who, owing to the damage done to Piraeus, could not obtain water or coal. ... 10 of these would have to sail not later than Saturday night, 19 April, otherwise they would run short of fuel.

4. About the time of my arrival the Greek harbour authorities in Piraeus showed signs of ceasing to function ... the control of shipping, loading and so on became more and more difficult. ... it was a matter of the greatest difficulty to discover what ships were in the harbour, were sailing, or expected to arrive, or even their whereabouts.

This state of affairs was further aggravated by the fact that during moonlight nights ships proceeded to sea and kept under way until daylight, with the object of avoiding bombing attacks inside the harbour or being mined in. ... some Captains refusing to bring their ships back for several days. ... I gradually took over control of Greek shipping in local waters, and eventually the conduct of all naval affairs, the DSTO and NCSO ...

5. I could appreciate at once that the bottleneck of any evacuation would be the small craft required for ferrying troops to HM Ships and transports from the beaches. It would have been a bad risk to use what quays were left available at Piraeus, and Kalamai in the SW Morea was the only other port with quays. A 'Caique and Local Craft Committee' was formed ... to charter and fit out as many caiques, motor boats and local craft as possible. As it turned out hundreds of soldiers owe their escape to caiques and small craft taken up in this manner.

6. The reconnaissance parties ... left to reconnoitre beaches and roads. ... The C-in-C was requested to send 12 officers for beaches and services with local craft and 24 Petty Officers and Leading Seamen, 72 Seamen and 6 Signalmen for beaches. These parties were considered vital as a quick turn around of craft at beaches would be essential. ...

21–22 April

18. ... there were very heavy massed air attacks on shipping and 23 vessels including two hospital ships and the Greek destroyer *Hydra* were reported sunk in local waters on these two days.[129] This

[129] *Hydra*: 1,350t, 4×4.7in, 6×21in tt, 39.5k.

did not promise well for the evacuation. After consultation with Air Vice Marshal D'Albiac, and considering both the naval and air aspects, I decided that the best time for transports to arrive at the beaches was one hour after dark, and to leave at 0300.[130] This would prevent enemy reconnaissance aircraft from spotting the exact beaches being used, and so bombing them by the light of flares, while the transports should still be able to find the beaches. The early return from the beaches would give some chance of the ships clearing the coast without being spotted, and would give them more time to reach the area within support of the fighters from Crete by daylight or as soon as possible afterwards. There would be no such support whatsoever from Greece from 24 April onwards. I decided to accept the disadvantage of reducing the time the ships were at the beaches in order to give this possible extra security, and as events turned out it appears this was justified. The only transport to leave really late, the *Slamat*, was bombed and sunk and was the only ship to become a total loss after loading.[131] . . .

23 April

19. LCT arrived at their beaches as follows:

LCT1 and 19 at Megara,
LCT6 at Nauplia,
LCT5 at Lavrion.

All except LCT6 were lost in this operation.
The fact that they had no W/T at all was a great handicap at this time, as well as decreasing their chances of survival on the Greek coast.

24 April (D1)

21. Embarkation from the area E of Athens and Nauplia on the night 24/25 was satisfactory, 10,200 personnel being embarked. Unfortunately, at Nauplia *Ulster Prince* grounded across the fairway, thus denying the use of the wharves to destroyers on succeeding nights. *Ulster Prince*'s quota of troops was taken off by *Phoebe*. This operation was greatly assisted by 10 caiques under the command of Lt-Cdr Carr, RNR, and again on the night 26/27.[132]

---

[130]AVM J. H. D'Albiac: ACdre & AOC, Palestine & Transjordan, Aug. 1939.
[131]*Slamat*: 1924, 11,636gt, 17k, Ruys & Zonen, Rotterdam.
[132]*Phoebe*: 1940, 5,450t, 8×5.25in, 6×21in tt, 33k.
Pay Cdr P. H. Carr, RNR: Pay Lt-Cdr 1928; Pay Cdr Dec. 1939; *Diomede* 1940; *Beaver* (Grimsby) Sept. 1942; *Eaglet* (Lpool) 1943.

22. HM King George and some members of the Greek Government left Athens for Crete in a flying boat.[133] ...

23. A large Greek yacht, the *Hellas*, arrived unexpectedly in Piraeus harbour, reporting that she could steam 18 knots and take 1,000 passengers. She was instructed to sail after dark, loading to take place as late as possible. About 500 of the British community (mostly Maltese and Cypriots) decided to leave in this ship and walking cases from an Australian hospital were sent on board. About 1900 the *Hellas* was dive bombed in the harbour and hit by two bombs, which set fire to the ship and jetty alongside. Col Renton, who was on board at the time, considers that four to five hundred people must have lost their lives... .[134]

25 April (D2)

28. During this day, *Ulster Prince,* on shore at Nauplia, was heavily bombed and became a total loss.

29. On this night (25/26), 5,700 troops were embarked from the Megara area (P beach) in spite of the losses of the transport SS *Pennland* on the way N, and of one of the two LCT which had arrived in this area. Seven caiques under the command of Cdr Mitchell assisted. It is believed that about 500, many of them wounded, were left on shore after waiting four days near the beach. This was due to the facts that they were to be embarked last, and that the LCT fouled her propellor with a wire on her last trip (the other engine already being out of action). It is not yet known whether the wounded were taken off from another beach, and to what extent the caiques were able to assist.[135]

26 April (D3)

34. At sunset we abandoned our HQ and the whole party proceeded to Myli pier. On arrival at the pier it was found that the flying boat had arrived, but there was no sign of the destroyer. The more important passengers were embarked in the flying boat. ... I decided to remain until the NZ Brigade under General Freyberg had been evacuated, and to proceed to their beaches at Monemvasia myself, taking with me my signal staff, W/T set, beachmasters, etc. It appeared to me at the time that if the LCT failed to

---

[133]King George II of Greece (1890–1947): attempt to return after war thwarted by civil war; forced to agree to regency.

[134]Col Renton: unidentified.

[135]*Pennland:* 1922, 16,381gt, 16k, Holland-America Line.
Probably Cdr K. Mitchell: Cdr 1931; ret; *President* 1940.

arrive, this might be a difficult operation and lengthy, and I preferred to be on the spot myself.

35. ... it was anticipated that by next morning the enemy would be in Myli and Nauplia, by which time the large embarkation, which was in the process of being carried out at the latter place, should be completed. The enemy air superiority made it necessary for us to get to Monemvasia, 56 miles distant, before daylight.... The Crown Prince of Greece's motor yacht ... had been bombed and put out of action during the course of the afternoon. The only other alternative was a caique chartered by Col Smith-Dorrien ... later the destroyer *Havock* arrived and took us off the caique, and enabled us to reach Monemvasia before daylight.[136]

27 April (near Monemvasia)

36. Off Monemvasia we unexpectedly came up with 10 LCA belonging to *Glenearn*, who had been bombed on Saturday. We landed in these and lay in a small bay 4 miles N of Monemvasia, scattering the LCA amongst the beaches about half a mile apart. It was most fortunate that these were not spotted by enemy aircraft which were constantly overhead for the next two days.

37. Heavy bombing was heard to the northward during the morning, which later proved to have been the attack on the Dutch transport *Slamat* which resulted in her loss, together with that of the destroyers *Diamond* and *Wryneck*.

38. ... After dark I sent three LCA further N to increase their dispersion.

39. ... Communication from Monemvasia was not perfect [but] all messages vital to the operation were cleared ...

Embarkations

40. On the night of 26/27 April, a total of approximately 18,000 troops were evacuated, and all areas were used except the Megara area....

41. The numbers embarked from Nauplia were greatly reduced owing to the stranding of *Ulster Prince* preventing the use of wharves by destroyers, and also to the non-arrival of *Glenearn*'s landing craft, due to the ship having been disabled by bombing attack on 26 April. The numbers actually embarked from this area were approximately 5,500 instead of the 8,000 planned.

---

[136] Col G. H. G. Smith-Dorrien: b 1904; 2Lt, KRRC, 1924; Lt 1926; Adjt 1934–36; Capt 1936; GSO2, Jan. 1941.

42. On the night of 27/28 April, approximately 4,700 embarked from the area to the E of Athens. . . .

28 April

43. Reconnaissance aircraft were over the beach on which we were established early, followed by dive bombers who made a series of heavy attacks on some craft about three-quarters of a mile distant immediately the other side of the hill behind our beach and invisible to us. It subsequently turned out that the object of their attack was LCT5 from Nauplia, which had left that beach on Sunday morning, laid up for the day and proceeded to Monemvasia on Sunday night, arriving at daylight Monday, with 600 Australians on board. The Australians had been landed at Monemvasia at dawn and took cover with the NZ Division, but the LCT was seen and bombed shortly afterwards. The LCT, though she replied vigorously at first, was soon on fire, and there was a constant series of ammunition explosions from her during the day. The fire on board prevented her being boarded to effect her complete destruction. There were no casualties.

44. The above incident left the LCA as practically the only means for embarking the NZ Division this night, and it was most fortunate they were not seen and bombed, also that the CO *Glenearn* had the foresight to send them to Monemvasia, as they could not have made Nauplia in time, after this ship had been bombed.[137]

45. After dark I proceeded with all LCA to the embarkation point at Monemvasia, where I met General Freyberg in his HQ near the beach at 2130. At this time, I had received no confirmation that ships were arriving, and also did not know whether they would be transports or HM Ships. Furthermore, it was doubtful whether my signal regarding the actual embarkation points had been received by the ships concerned; the bay is a large one. At 2230 no ships had arrived, so I dispatched Lt-Cdr Robertson in a LCA to endeavour to get in touch beyond Monemvasia Island which hid the beaches from seaward. He soon contacted the destroyers, which were actually on their way in, and I proceeded on board *Griffin* and led her close to the N jetty, leaving Lt-Cdr Robertson in the *Isis* to go to the S jetty.[138]

46. The embarkation which took place mainly from the causeway connecting the Island to the mainland, began at 2350 and was com-

---

[137]Lt-Cdr T. Hood, RNR (Ret): Lt-Cdr March 1939; Ret List Sept. 1940; *Pyramus* 1940; *Glenearn* 1940; *Parrett* 1944–45.
[138]Lt-Cdr Robertson: unidentified.

pleted by 0300/29, 3,800 men being embarked. General Freyberg and I saw the beaches cleared and went on board *Ajax* at 0300/29. Two caiques were employed on this night under the command of Lt Cumberlege RNR, and Lt-Cdr Hook, RN (Retd) and did excellent work.[139]

47. The whole embarkation was remarkably well carried out from five different points. The Army organisation in rear of the beaches and the discipline of the troops were magnificent; especially considering that they had been fighting a rearguard action for some weeks, from Salonika almost to Cape Matapan. *Ajax* and destroyers all closed well into the jetties, and the organisation for embarking the troops in the ships was excellent. The fact that we had at this time collected extra signalmen and so had good communication with the ships much accelerated the whole operation. The young officers in the LCA handled their craft very well.

48. I had arranged with the CO's of *Ajax* and *Griffin* to place charges in the LCA so as to destroy them before departure.[140] ... However, at this time fires on shore caused by burning MT lit up the ships in the bay, and the CO *Ajax* decided he could not wait to complete the destruction.... with the danger of submarines I considered he was correct to leave at once. One submarine had been depth charged on the way to the beaches. One or two LCA were destroyed by the destroyer *Hotspur*, but 4 or 5 were left afloat.

49. During the same night it had been intended to embark approximately 8,000 personnel from Kalamata. The operation was, however, frustrated, as on the arrival of the ships off the entrance to the harbour, it was reported that the harbour was in the possession of the enemy, and also the harbour had been mined. Some of our troops were collected in an area to the SE of the harbour, but in view of the close proximity of the enemy and the absence of landing craft (which had not been provided as it had been intended to use the wharves in the harbour) it was not possible to embark more than a very few of these troops. Ships withdrew at about 0230/29, leaving a total of approximately 4,000 British and 2,000 Palestinian and Cypriot troops, together with 1,500 Yugoslav refugees on shore.

---

[139]Lt C. M. B. Cumberlege, RNR: Lt July 1933; Ret List 1939; spl ops 1940–41; NID 1942; Lt-Cdr 1944.
Lt-Cdr H. Hook: Lt-Cdr 1928; Ret List 1939; Actg Cdr, STD 1943.
[140]Capt of *Ajax*: Capt E. D. B. McCarthy.
Griffin i/c: Cdr J. Lee-Barber: June 1939; Cdr June 1941; *Eskimo* 1942; *Opportune* 1943; Actg Capt, *King Alfred* (Hove) 1944–45.

50. The Germans entered the town at about 1600 ... They were counter-attacked and driven from the harbour by 2300 ... Unfortunately the naval embarkation officer, Captain Clark-Hall, and his signalman, had been captured ... and as he was the only naval officer present ashore, this doubtless had a bad effect on communication between the troops ashore and the ships. There is no evidence to show that ships were ever informed that the enemy had been driven out of the town.[141]

29 April

51. I arrived at Suda Bay in *Ajax* at 0800 ... This night destroyers were sent to Kalamata with the object of bringing off any troops that could be embarked from the beaches in the vicinity, but this only resulted in about 120 officers and men being recovered.

30 April

52. At 0430 I left for Alexandria in a flying boat. On this night destroyers were again sent to the Kalamata area, approximately 130 officers and men being recovered. Two destroyers were sent to Milos, and succeeded in evacuating 650 troops, of whom approximately 400 were Palestinians. These had reached Milos in a Greek vessel which had been bombed some days previously.

Report of Vice Admiral Pridham-Wippell

... I sailed from Alexandria in *Orion* with *Decoy, Havock* and *Hasty* in company at 1915 on 24 April, in accordance with your signal 1620/24. *Defender* joined my flag at 1000 on 25 April.

2. The situation at midnight 24/25 April was as follows:

Nauplia
  Phoebe, Stuart (Capt D10), *Voyager, Ulster Prince, Glenearn, Hyacinth* embarking troops.
Raphtis
  Calcutta, Perth, Glengyle embarking troops.
On passage
  Grimsby, Vendetta, Waterhen, SS *Themoni, Zealand, Kirkland, Araybank, Runo* : AN29 arriving in Aegean 25 April.[142]

---

[141]Capt Clark-Hall: Cdr 1928; Ret List 1929; STD 1940; Actg Capt 1941.
[142]*Themoni*: 1938, 5,719gt, Kassos SN, Greece.
Araybank: 1940, 7,258gt, Bank Line.
Runo: 1920, 1,858gt, Ellerman's Wilson Line.

THE EFFECTS OF GERMAN INTERVENTION, 1941   383

On passage
Coventry, Wryneck, Diamond, Griffin, SS *Pennland, Thurland Castle*: ANF29 arriving Aegean on 25 April.[143]

On passage
Orion, Decoy, Hasty, Havock, Defender: Arriving Suda Bay 1800/25.

On passage
Isis, Hero, Hotspur, Hereward, RFA *Brambleleaf*: Arriving Suda Bay at a.m./26.

On passage
Nubian: Arriving Suda Bay at 0400/26.

On passage
Carlisle, Kandahar, Kingston, SS *Costa Rica, City of London, Dilwara, Salween, Slamat, Khedive Ismail*: AG14 arriving Aegean at 0700/26.[144]

On passage
Flamingo: Arriving at 1700/26.[145]

On passage
Kimberley, Vampire, Auckland, SS *Ionia, Corinthia, Itria, Belray, Elenora Maersk, Comliebank*.[146]

General Considerations

3. Because of the presence in Greece of strong enemy air forces and the rapidly diminishing fighter support, it was necessary to carry out all evacuation at night and withdraw all ships to the southward during the day. The whole programme was based on this consideration. It will be noticed that nearly all losses from aircraft were sustained in the region of the parallel of 37°N, which was approximately the limit of the range of the enemy dive bombers. It was my policy to insist on all ships leaving the places of embarkation

---

[143] *Thurland Castle*: 1929, 6,372gt, J Chambers.
[144] *Costa Rica*: 1910, 8,672gt, 15.5k, R Neth SS.
City of London: 1907, 8,956gt, 14k, City Line.
Dilwara: 1936, 11,080gt, 14k, Br India SN.
Salween: 1938, 7,063gt, 14k, Br & Burmese SN, Glasgow.
Khedive Ismail:1922, 7,290gt, Khedivial Mail Line, Egypt; s *I-27*, Ind O, Feb. 1944.
[145] *Flamingo*: 1939, 1,350t, 6×4in, 19.25k.
[146] *Ionia*: either 1923, 1,936gt, 15k, Hellenic Coast Lines, *or* 1916, 5,845gt, Hellenic Tramp SS Co.
Corinthia: 1911, 3,701gt, 12.5k, Hellenic Tramp SS Co.
Itria: 1940, 6,845gt, Br India SN.
Belray: 1926, 2,888gt, 10k, C. Smith, Oslo.
Elenora Maersk: 1936, 10,694gt, Svendborg, Denmark.
Comliebank: 1924, 5,149gt, 11k, A. Weir.

in time to be S of 37°N by daylight and it will be noted that the failure of the *Slamat* to leave Nauplia at the time ordered resulted in her being within range of the dive bombers well after dawn.

Another factor to be borne in mind was the possibility of interference by surface craft from the westward.

Throughout there was no fighter support for ships at sea N of 37°N. The RAF in Crete did what they could for convoys S of this latitude, but the protection was slender, by reason of the small number of aircraft available.

Night 24/25 April

5. *Bombing of* Glenearn – At 1745 on 24 April, whilst on passage to Nauplia, *Glenearn* was attacked by two Heinkel bombers and was hit on the forecastle. The anchor and cable gear were destroyed and a fire started forward. The fire was extinguished and the ship proceeded at 1845.

6. Ulster Prince *grounding* – *Ulster Prince* in attempting to go alongside the quay ran ashore and, although every endeavour was made to get her off by towing, it was not possible to do so in the time available. The following day she was heavily bombed and gutted. Apart from the loss of the ship which was severely felt during the rest of the operation, this had an unfortunate effect in that she was a physical obstruction to destroyers and corvettes going alongside, thus slowing down the rate of embarkation at Nauplia on that and other nights. I agree with the CO of *Ulster Prince* that it was unwise to attempt to put her alongside when the information as to water, etc., was so meagre.[147]

7. *Embarkation at Nauplia* – It is estimated that the following numbers were embarked.:

Phoebe	1,131
Glenearn	5,100
Voyager	340
Stuart	1
Hyacinth	113
	6,685

8. *Embarkation at Raphtis* – Despite a slow start owing to lack of troops ready to embark, things went smoothly and about 5,000 were embarked in *Glengyle* and 700 in *Calcutta*.

---

[147]Capt, *Ulster Prince:* unidentified.

25 April

9. *Convoy to Alexandria: Diversion* – *Orion* arrived Suda at 1845. *Grimsby* and *Voyager* with certain ships from Suda were then leaving harbour for Alexandria. It was explained to the NOIC, Suda, that the contents of several of the ships which had just sailed would be urgently required at Suda, e.g. food and coal.

Grimsby was therefore ordered to return to Suda with *Themoni, Rokos, Zealand* and *Kirkland,* and *Voyager* to continue with the remainder comprising *Cherryleaf* and some Greek ships.[148]

10. *The general situation* – The military situation in Greece was obscure. The numbers to be evacuated were given . . . as:

25–26	5,000 from Megara area.
26–27	27,000.
27–28	Nil.
28–29	4,000 from Githion and Monemvasia.
29–30	4,000 from Kalamata, Githion and Monemvasia.

11. *Disposition for night's embarkation* – FOAM's programme provided for embarkation at Megara in *Pennland, Thurland Castle, Coventry, Wryneck, Diamond* and *Griffin* commencing at 2200. I also dispatched *Waterhen* and *Vendetta,* on their arrival at Suda with AN29, to assist. *Decoy, Hasty* and *Havock* were detached to Nauplia to investigate the situation there as regards troops and the *Ulster Prince* and were ordered to embark any troops available and convoy them to Suda.

12. SS *Pennland* – During the afternoon the *Pennland* was bombed and damaged. *Griffin* was ordered to stand by till dark. Later the *Pennland* was again attacked and damaged and eventually sank. *Griffin* picked up the survivors and returned to Suda. I therefore diverted *Decoy, Hasty* and *Havock* from Nauplia to Megara to embark *Pennland*'s quota as far as possible.

13. On my arrival at Suda I conferred with the NOIC and later took *Orion, Perth, Phoebe* and *Defender* to sea for the night.[149]

During the whole of this time I was in constant anxiety with regard to fuel. There was none at Suda and RFA *Brambleleaf* was not arriving until a.m./26.

---

[148]*Rokos*: 1918, 6,426gt, Ionian SS Co, Greece.
Cherryleaf: RFA, 1917, 12,370t, 14k.
[149]Capt J. A. V. Morse: Capt June 1934; *Neptune* & F Capt & COS to C-in-C Africa Sta July 1937; CSO, *Pyramus,* FO Kirkwall June 1940; MNBDO(1) May 1941; NOIC Syria & Lebanon Ports July 1941; *Hannibal* Nov. 1942; RA July 1943; FO, W Italy Sept. 1944; FO, N Area, Med, Oct. 1944.

Night of 25/26 April

14. **Embarkation** – At Megara, *Thurland Castle, Coventry, Wryneck, Diamond* and *Griffin* embarked 4,600 army personnel. *Decoy, Hasty* and *Havock* embarked 1,300. Owing to the breakdown of an LCT 250 were left ashore.

After *Glenroy* had grounded at Alexandria 6 of her LCA and a beach party were embarked in *Thurland Castle* and were of the utmost value.

26 April

15. *Disposition for embarkation 26/27 April* –

Raphina	*Glengyle, Nubian, Decoy, Hasty.*
Rapthis	*Salween, Carlisle, Kandahar, Kingston.*
Nauplia	*Slamat, Khedive Imail, Calcutta, Isis, Hotspur.*
Tolon	*Glenearn, Diamond, Griffin, Havock.*
Kalamata	*Dilwara, City of London, Costa Rica, Phoebe, Defender, Flamingo, Hero, Hereward.*

In addition *Nubian* was detailed to embark 600 men, reported at Port St Nikolo, Zea Island, and then return to escort *Glengyle*. *Havock* was detailed to embark the GOC, his Staff, and FOAM and Staff at Myli opposite Nauplia.[150]

16. Glenearn: *Damage* – *Glenearn* was bombed and hit in the engine room p.m. on 26 April. *Orion* took her in tow to Suda Bay and she was instructed to send landing craft to Monemvasia, since they could not reach Nauplia in time for that night's evacuation.

In consequence *Orion, Perth* and *Stuart* proceeded to Nauplia to assist in the evacuation.

All ships were instructed that if the weather delayed embarkation, they were to take what troops they were able and leave at 0300.

17. Scottish Prince – RFA *Brambleleaf* arrived safely at Suda a.m. The *Scottish Prince* on passage from Smyrna to Suda was bombed and damaged S of Milo at about noon. *Grimsby* was sent by the NOIC, Suda, to assist. The SO of convoy GA15 detached *Vampire* to her assistance. She was not sinking and her crew were put on board again and with the aid of some naval ratings from the *Grimsby* she eventually reached Suda.[151]

18. At 1547 information was received from the NOIC, Suda, of a Greek vessel with British troops on board, bombed and requiring

---

[150] Gen Wilson and RA Baillie-Grohman.
[151] *Scottish Prince*: 1938, 4,917gt, 10.5k, Rio Cape Line.

medical assistance off Milo. The NOIC, Suda, was instructed to send *Grimsby* if sufficient information became available.

Night of 26/27 April

19. FOAM had signalled on 25th that position C (Raphina) and T (Tolon) must each be worked by one 'Glen' ship and this had been arranged. But, during the afternoon of 28th, I received FOAM's 1103/26 asking for a 'Glen' ship to go to S (Nauplia) instead of to T. . . .

20. *Nauplia and Tolon* – I took *Orion, Perth* and *Stuart* to Nauplia to do what was possible to embark *Glenearn's* quota. On arrival I detached *Stuart* to see what was the position at Tolon while *Orion* and *Perth* went to Nauplia where *Calcutta, Slamat, Khedive Ismail* and four destroyers were already anchored.

At Nauplia there was only one motor caique transporting troops to *Slamat*. Apart from this, the warships' boats did what they could. *Khedive Ismail* received no troops at all owing to the lack of any craft to transport them to her.

Meanwhile *Stuart* reported at Tolon there was a large number of troops, and an LCT, and she (*Stuart*) was already full. I ordered *Stuart* alongside *Orion* to [dis]embark the 600 troops she had on board from Tolon and sent *Perth* and *Stuart* back to Tolon to continue the embarkation there.

In the end the ships had to sail with 4,527 troops, having left ashore a number variously reported as 2,500 and 6,000. This very unsatisfactory outcome is solely due to the bombing of *Glenearn* and the absence of her boats. All available craft and the LCT were fully employed throughout the available hours.

21. The ultimate fate of the LCT is not known. The motor caique is known to have embarked 19 military staff officers and their batmen, and beachmaster and some naval ratings and reached Monemvasia in time for the final evacuation there.

22. The following numbers were embarked during the night:

Raphina and Rapthis
Glengyle   3,500
Salween   2,000
Carlisle   1,310
Kingston   850
Kandahar   560
Nubian   3
(500 men were left at Raphina)

Nauplia

Orion	600
Slamat	500 (est.)
Calcutta	960
Isis	408
Hotspur	500
Khedive Ismail	nil
Diamond	nil

Tolon

Orion	600
Perth	850
Stuart	109

Kalamata

Dilwara	2,400
City of London	3,500
Costa Rica	2,500
Defender	250 and Yugoslav Crown jewels in cases.

23. *Zea Island – Nubian* reported that troops on Zea Island had left Port Nikolo for embarkation elsewhere.

The LCT working nightly at Rapthis is believed to have hidden off Zea each day. It is fairly certain that this party returned to Rapthis on the evening of 27 April and were embarked in *Ajax* or destroyers.

24. *Havock* embarked FOAM and the combined HQ Staff. FOAM was landed at Monemvasia.

27 April

25. *Sinking of SS* Slamat – The *Slamat* did not sail from Nauplia until 0415 although repeatedly told to do so at 0300. At 0715 she was bombed and set on fire . . . *Diamond* was ordered by *Calcutta* to go alongside to take off her troops, the convoy proceeding meanwhile. I had ordered *Wryneck, Waterhen* and *Vendetta* from Suda to join the convoy to relieve *Isis* and *Hotspur,* so they could go ahead to Suda to disembark their troops. *Wryneck, Waterhen* and *Vendetta* joined at 0910 and *Calcutta* immediately dispatched *Wryneck* to the assistance of *Diamond,* who had, at 0815, called for help in picking up survivors from the *Slamat,* reporting that she was being constantly dive bombed while doing so. At 0925 *Diamond* reported that she had picked up most of the survivors and was proceeding to Suda Bay. At 1025 *Wryneck* made a request for fighter protection.

26. I had difficulty in getting SO's of forces to say how many troops had been embarked in the large transports. On this depended the decision whether to send all ships direct to Alexandria or some to Suda. It also complicated the arrangements of escorts and fuelling before escorting. The *Khedive Ismail* had none and I thought of sending her to Suda, but there was no escort to take her there.

27. *Convoy GA14* – As there was no room in Suda and I deemed the changing situation to make further delay dangerous, Convoy GA14 was formed and proceeded, consisting of *Glengyle, Salween, Khedive Ismail, Dilwara, City of London* and *Costa Rica* escorted by *Coventry, Calcutta, Flamingo, Stuart, Vendetta, Waterhen* and *Vampire*. They were covered from the north-westward by *Perth, Phoebe, Decoy, Hasty, Nubian, Defender, Hero, Hereward* and *Wryneck* during the night 27/28 April.

It was arranged for this convoy to form up – and for escorts to be exchanged – . . . (about 20 miles N of Maleme aerodrome) and the SAFO, Crete, was asked to provide maximum fighter protection while this was in progress.

28. Glenearn – Meanwhile the *Glenearn* had been towed to Kissamo Bay by *Griffin,* and *Grimsby* was sent round from Suda to take over. *Griffin* took off 150 of *Glenearn*'s complement leaving 90 on board. The *Glenearn* had no steam and no anchors and required 12 hours to prepare for towing. She was eventually taken in tow by *Grimsby* and reached Alexandria safely although attacked by aircraft while off Gavdo on 28 April.

29. *General Movements* – *Ajax,* from Alexandria, joined my flag at 0730 and I arrived at Suda in *Orion* with *Perth* and *Ajax* in company at 1130/27 and disembarked troops. *Ajax, Kingston, Kimberley* and *Havock* sailed soon after noon for Rapthis. *Phoebe,* with *Defender, Hereward, Kandahar, Nubian, Decoy, Hasty* and *Hero* arrived at 1900, disembarked troops and fuelled. *Perth* and *Phoebe* with *Decoy* and *Hasty* left at 2030 to cover GA14. *Nubian, Hero, Hereward* and *Defender* also sailed at 2300 for the same purpose. . . .

30. *SS* Costa Rica: *Sinking* – The *Costa Rica* in GA14 was hit by a bomb at about 1500 . . . and sank 90 minutes later. *Auckland* and *Salvia* were sent out from Suda to assist, but her entire troops and crew had been taken off by *Hero, Hereward* and *Defender* and were landed at Suda.

31. *Loss of* Diamond *and* Wryneck – When it was realised that *Diamond* had not arrived with *Phoebe* and other destroyers I became anxious about her. From 1922 to 1955 *Diamond* had been called without reply. As *Diamond* had last been heard of with *Wryneck* during the

forenoon, *Phoebe* and *Calcutta* were asked whether *Wryneck* had been seen going away with GA14 since I did not wish to ask *Wryneck* herself to break W/T silence. Their replies at 2235 and 2245 gave no definite indication. I therefore dispatched *Griffin* to the position of the sinking of the *Slamat* to investigate. At 0230 *Griffin* reported that she had come upon a raft from *Wryneck* and everything pointed to the fact that *Wryneck* and *Diamond* were sunk. *Griffin* picked up about 50 survivors. *Wryneck*'s whaler was reported to have made towards Cape Malea. This eventually arrived at Suda. The total naval survivors from the two ships comprised one officer and 41 ratings. There were, in addition, about 8 soldiers. From statements of the survivors, it appears that the two ships were bombed at about 1315 both receiving hits which caused them to sink almost immediately.

Night of 27/28 April

33.   *Ajax* with *Kimberley, Kingston* and *Havock* were sent to Raphtis to arrive 2200/27, to embark the rearguard of about 3,000 and the beach party. This was the final evacuation N of the Corinth Canal.

The following were embarked:

Ajax   2,500
Kingston   640
Kimberley   700
Havock   800 from Raphena Cove.

Isis and *Hotspur* took a battalion of troops from Suda to Canea for the defence of the aerodrome at the urgent request of CRETFORCE.

28 April

34.   *Formation of convoy GA15* – I was now becoming increasingly anxious to evacuate as many troops as possible from Crete. This anxiety was also shared by the Senior Officers of the other services. There was the probability of heavy air attack at any moment and the possibility of an attempt to take Crete and interference by enemy surface forces. I therefore proposed sailing GA15 via Kaso p.m./29 or a.m./30 after the final evacuation on the night of 28/29. The route through the Kaso Strait was selected as interference from Italian forces and attack by the German air force was less likely and cover by the battleships possible. . . .

Night of 28/29 April

36.   *General* – The following arrangements were made for the final embarkation on the night 28/29 April:

THE EFFECTS OF GERMAN INTERVENTION, 1941

Kalamata
Perth, Phoebe, Nubian, Defender, Hero, Hereward, Decoy, Hasty: Direct from covering GA14 the previous night. It was estimated there were 7,000 troops remaining. The intention was that this force should sail for Alexandria on completion of embarkation.
Monemvasia
Ajax, Havock, Hotspur, Griffin, Isis.
Kithera
Auckland, Salvia, Hyacinth.

37. *Kalamata: Yugoslav Refugees* – In consequence of information received from FOAM that there were 1,500 Yugoslav refugees still at Kalamata, *Kandahar, Kingston* and *Kimberley* were sent from Suda to assist *Perth, Phoebe* and the destroyers there.

38. *Leonidion* – It was not possible to provide for the embarkation of the party at Leonidion, but the NOIC, Suda, was instructed to investigate the possibility of evacuating them by Sunderland flying boat.

39. *Kalamata* – The first report from this beach was from *Hero* at 2207 that the harbour was occupied by Germans and that British troops were to the S of the town. I sent ashore to ask General Wilson to come on board *Orion* where he could receive the latest information from Kalamata as it arrived and advise me on the military aspect of a possible further evacuation from Kalamata the following night. At 2234 a signal was received from *Hero* stating that troops were collecting on the beach SE of the town, that all firing had ceased in the town and that evacuation was considered possible from the beach. At 2240 information was received from *Hero* that the Germans appeared to have no artillery and requesting *Perth*'s position so that he could close and report the situation. At 2250 I instructed *Perth* to use his discretion but to make no promises for the following night, unless he heard from me. I impressed on him that he was to sail at the time ordered. However, at 2315/28 I received *Perth*'s 2231/28 that the town was occupied by Germans, that he had abandoned the operation and was steering 175° 29 knots with the whole of his force in company except *Hero*.

General Wilson advised me that most of the troops would probably be forced to surrender on the morning of 29 April and asked me that 2 or 3 destroyers only should be sent on the night of 29/30 to embark such small parties as might have moved down the rocky coast towards Cape Matapan.

Hero reported that he was returning at 0200 on 29th with as many as he could.

40. *Kandahar, Kingston* and *Kimberley* arrived at Kalamata at 0100, joined *Hero* off the beach; this force was able to embark the following troops in their own boats:

Kandahar	126
Hero	134
Kimberley	33
Kingston	39
	332

41. *Monemvasia and Kithera* – The embarkation at the beaches at Monemvasia and Kithera proceeded smoothly and troops were embarked as follows:

Monemvasia
Ajax	1,050
Havock	850
Hotspur	800
Griffin	720
Isis	900

Kithera
Auckland, Salvia, Hyacinth: 60 military, 700 RAF and 60 Greek soldiers.

The evacuation at Kithera was effected by an LCA ex-*Glenroy* taken in by *Ajax* and towed back to Suda Bay by *Salvia*.

42. *York* – Your 0950/28 was received at 1130/28. I decided to leave on board *York* working and maintenance parties and a nucleus salvage party. The remainder of the crew and some valuable stores were embarked in *Orion*.

29 April

43. *Convoy GA15* – Convoy GA15 sailed from Suda at 1100 on 29 April via Kaso, speed 10 knots. It was comprised as follows:

Delane (Commodore): 625 Italian officers; 700 distressed British seamen; 585 troops; 120 FAA.[152]
Thurland Castle   2,640   troops
Comliebank   1,450   "

---

[152]*Delane*: 1937, 6,054gt, 15k, Lamport & Holt Line.

Corinthia	332	troops	plus 330 Consular staff and British subjects.
Itria	237	"	and 1,775 RAF
Ionia	137	"	and 450 walking wounded and 237 nurses.
Brambleleaf	Nil.		

Escorted by

Carlisle, Auckland, Kandahar, Kingston, each with 50 troops.
Decoy, Defender, Hyacinth joined at sea.

Covered by

Orion	15	troops	and 435 naval personnel
Ajax	616	troops	and 27 naval ratings.

Perth, Phoebe, Hasty, Hereward, Nubian joined at sea.

44. The NOIC, Suda, is much to be complimented on the celerity with which this convoy was handled and sailed. The various ships bringing in over 5,000 men from Greece did not arrive at Suda till 0730 onwards and the redistribution of these troops into transports and fuelling of destroyers, as well as the embarkation of a further 5,000 men from the shore was a most complicated task in the three hours available, and fully occupied all transport available.

45. *Uncompleted evacuations –*

(a) *Kalamata –* ... I detailed *Isis, Hero* and *Kimberley* to leave Suda at 1700 and proceed to Kalamata, leaving not later than 0300/30, returning to Suda. They embarked 16 officers and 17 other ranks.

The same ships again visited the Kalamata area on the night 30 April/1 May and collected ... a total of 202. They reported that any chance of further embarkation was slender as the Germans were mopping up.

(b) *Milo and Nio (Ios) –* The NOIC, Suda, had reported 2,000 British and Greek troops in Milo, probably mostly Greeks. I later heard that there were 600 British troops at Nio and I detailed *Havock* and *Hotspur* to visit this island during the night 29/30 and, if necessary, to go on to Milo if further information was received regarding that place.

... NOIC, Suda ... stated that there were approximately 3,500 British troops on [Milo] and that those on Nio had escaped by motor caique, also that magnetic mines had probably been laid. I therefore cancelled my original instructions to *Hotspur* and

Havock and told NOIC, Suda, to endeavour to obtain more information and to use his discretion as to carrying out the operation.

Hotspur and *Havock* visited Milo on the night 30 April/1 May and evacuated 700 British and Palestinian troops, leaving none.

46.   *Passage to Alexandria* – ... I sailed from Suda at 1300/29 ... and proceeded to act as cover for the convoy with *Ajax, Perth, Phoebe, Hasty, Nubian* and *Hereward* in company. During a.m./29 *Nubian* had suffered a near miss and was damaged.

47.   During the night of 29/30 April, whilst passing through the Kaso Straits, the convoy was attacked by E-boats and possibly torpedo boats from 2315 till 0300. Some torpedoes were fired but no damage was done. Our destroyers chased off the enemy several times.

48.   At 0630/30 April, the First Battle Squadron and *Formidable* took over close escort of the convoy and I proceeded with *Ajax, Hasty* and *Hereward* in company to Alexandria in advance of the convoy, leaving *Perth, Phoebe* and *Nubian* to reinforce the Battle Squadron.

207.   *To Rear Admiral Hugh England*

1 May 1941

... we were very fortunate and things might have been very different [at the battle off Cape Matapan]. Pridham-Wippell's cruisers nearly got a doing from the *Veneto* and three 8-in cruisers in the morning but though straddled got away under smoke.

We have now fallen on rather evil times. Having landed a large army in Greece we have just finished taking it off again under direful conditions. About 400 bombers attacking troops and ships all day and not a plane of our own to defend them.

Of course and as usual the destroyers saved the day and some of the landing craft crews and beach parties were absolute heroes. Unfortunately I fear their deeds have perished with them as large numbers have not come out of it.

I lost two destroyers picking up troops from a sinking troopship. Both hit by dive bombers and went down like stones, very few saved as the Huns amused themselves for an hour or so machine gunning the men in the water. I hope I shall get my hands on a few of them.

Now we have to hold on out here. The Navy against the German Air Force and I don't doubt we shall win.

208. From the Admiralty

1111, 1 May 1941

Your 1332/30. The amount of time spent at sea by your light forces and the arduous duties during DEMON are fully appreciated but on the other hand the necessity for interrupting the communications to Benghazi is so urgent that Their Lordships trust you will review the situation and if possible provide a force to operate against the Benghazi communications between now and TIGER.

Every endeavour will be made to provide you with better air reconnaissance.

209. From Churchill

2026, 1 May 1941

We are making extreme exertions to reinforce you from the air. It has been decided to repeat as soon as possible and on a much larger scale the recent operations WINCH and DUNLOP. *Ark Royal, Argus, Furious* and *Victorious* will all be used to carry up to 140 additional Hurricanes as well as 18 Fulmars with pilots.[153] We hope that 64 Hurricanes and 9 Fulmars will arrive in Middle East by 25 May. Meanwhile 25 fighter pilots leave 23 May for Takoradi to hasten ferrying of Hurricanes and Tomahawks. Capacity of route to Egypt from Takoradi freed by above use of carriers will be employed to increase flow of Hurricanes and Tomahawks.[154] Greatest possible shipment of Blenheims will be made at the same time. I may have more to signal about bomber reinforcements later.

2. I also congratulate you on the brilliant and highly successful manner in which the Navy once again succoured the Army and brought off four-fifths of the entire force.
3. It is now necessary to fight hard for Crete, which seems soon to be attacked heavily, and for Malta as a base for flotilla action against the enemy's communications with Libya. Constantly improving attitude and their [i.e., Greek] naval co-operation justifies risks involved. Your plans for TIGER are excellent and give good chances.
4. But above all we look to you to cut off seaborne supplies from the Cyrenaican ports and to beat them up to the utmost. It is in our

---

[153]*Victorious*: 1941, 23,000t, 16×4.5in, 54 a/c, 31k.
[154]Curtiss Tomahawk: 1938, 6mg, 1,500lbs bombs, 350mph, range 750mls.

power to give you information about enemy transport movements to these ports.[155] It causes grief here when we learn of the arrival of precious aviation spirit in one ship after another. This great battle for Egypt is what the Duke of Wellington called 'A close-run thing', but if we can reinforce you and Wavell as proposed by Operations TIGER and JAGUAR and you can cut off the tap of inflow, our immense Armies in the Middle East will soon resume their ascendancy. All good wishes.

210. *To the Admiralty*

1310, 2 May 1941

Your 1111/1. No one can be more alive to implication of Benghazi situation than we are out here but I suggest I must be allowed to be judge of what can or can't be done as regards keeping units of the fleet at sea. If no action is taken to give a brief lull to man and machinery in light craft we shall find ourselves with a collection of crocks.

2. The most essential thing now is safe and timely arrival of TIGER and on that I must concentrate. For this I must be assured that as many minesweepers are available as possible and I am using these two or three days to deal with essential defects and damage due to near misses.

3. Flotillas have been running unceasingly since start of LUSTRE finishing up with Tripoli operation and DEMON and these latter meant continuous seagoing for some 17 days.

4. During and after TIGER as stated I will do all that is possible to embarass this line of supply. For the moment submarines [?-] must do what they can.

5. Reference last para. the situation now is that RAF have four Glenn Martins available now and hope in due course to increase this to eight. These aircraft will have to do all air reconnaissance needed in Aegean and Central Mediterranean (with exception of Malta reconnaissance which is so fully employed on Tripoli route that only very seldom can it search harbours for enemy battlefleet). This force is of course quite inadequate. The Sunderlands are on this [?-] assumption now of little practical use as they will merely be lost if we try to use them from Suda Bay or Malta. As you know reconnaissance

---

[155] Ultra decrypts from enemy coded signals.

has never been of greater importance and it might well be for consideration to exchange Sunderlands for land reconnaissance machines. The need is very urgent and we may meanwhile be forced to use flying boats which may result in the loss of these very valuable craft.

211. To Churchill

1812, 2 May 1941

Thank you for your 2026/1 [No. 209] with its heartening news of aircraft. I fully realise this must make great call on our resources but equally I am convinced that only by redressing the balance in the air in the Mediterranean shall we be able to defeat the enemy and bring real value of our sea power into play. The mining of Alexandria and the loss of *Jersey* at Malta are further examples of the way the air constantly checks our naval activities.

212. War Diary, May 1941

2 May

Malta

4. On the return of the 5DF, *Jersey* was mined in the entrance to the Grand Harbour. She apparently sank at once, blocking the entrance channel and could not be cleared. *Kelly, Janus, Jackal* and *Kelvin* had entered harbour ahead of her, but *Gloucester, Kipling* and *Kashmir* were outside and could not enter. They were later ordered to proceed to Gibraltar in order to join Force H for the forthcoming Operation TIGER.

4 May

2. All forces were now concentrated at Alexandria to rest and effect minor repairs after the strenuous period of Operation DEMON. Final preparations were put in hand for Operation MD4, the passage of two convoys to Malta and of TIGER convoy through the Central Mediterranean. . . . The decision to attempt the passage of this convoy through the Mediterranean in a full moon period was taken in view of the extreme urgency for MT and aircraft reinforcements in the Western Desert.

Western Desert

3. *Decoy* and *Defender* successfully bombarded troops at Tobruk during the night 3/4 May and returned to Alexandria. The hospital

ship *Karapara* was deliberately bombed at Tobruk harbour at 1900/4 by 9 aircraft and hit.[156] She was able to sail during the night on one engine. The two AA sweepers *Arthur Cavanagh* and *Milford Countess* were not able to operate efficiently in the confined waters of Tobruk by night nor in face of the day time bombing attacks. They were accordingly both relieved by LL sweepers. *Ladybird* shot down one aircraft in the raid on *Karapara*.

Submarines

5. *Upholder* returned from patrol of the East Tunisian coast and reported having boarded the wreck of *Arta* sunk by 14DF on 16 April. Her cargo was MT and many German corpses were seen. Some documents were obtained and the ship left fiercely on fire.
6. *Upholder* also sank three northbound merchant ships, one probably *Bainsizza* ... p.m., 25 April, one Fels Line of 6,000 tons ... at noon 1 May, and one *Burgland* class escort vessel previously damaged in same attack. All ships were heavily escorted.[157]

Malta

7. The position regarding 'Glen' ships was reviewed owing to the severe damage to *Glenearn*. *Glenroy* would be retained to operate in her present condition, i.e., with her outer bottom pierced and fractured over a large area. *Glenearn* would be towed to Bombay for repairs after temporary repairs and examination had been made in dock. *Glengyle* would be repaired locally and was expected to be fully fit for service in about 10 days.
8. Of the six 'A' lighters used in operation DEMON three were bombed and sunk or destroyed by their crews. One was lost and may have fallen into enemy hands and the remaining two were at Suda Bay being used for coastal work with the Army. There were also three operating at Alexandria, one having been sunk earlier at Tobruk.

213. *To Pound*

3 May 1941

A. We are not having too good a time out here and it can all be put down to lack of air support, but I won't worry you with any more

---

[156]*Karapara*: 1915, 7,117gt, 16k, Br India SN.
[157]*Bainsizza*: 1930, 7,933gt, Parodi, Italy.
Burgland cl: unidentified.
Fels Line: unidentified.

moans about that except to give you one fact. Two or three days ago the only fighters fit for action in the Western Desert were 13 in number.

Tobruk is now without fighter defence and consequently my last little ship – the *Chakla* – after a career of much gallant usefulness was sunk three days ago. Her last feat was the towing of the *Desmoulea*, a large disabled tanker, from Suda to Port Said escorted only by a trawler and she was attacked by bombers and torpedo aircraft five or six times on the way and she never broke W/T silence.

B. This mining of Alexandria is a nuisance. As usual the first time the watching organisation did not work too well though as you know it's not an easy place to watch. The mines seem to have been distributed in the entrance to the harbour and three have been swept this morning. I was not sorry to have two battleships and the carrier outside but I must get them in today to give the pilots two days' rest before TIGER.

C. I have been a little concerned and Pridham-Wippell has noted it too, in signs of strain among our officers and ratings. Particularly in the AA cruisers, but it has also appeared in the destroyers.

The former have had a gruelling time since LUSTRE started; never a sea trip without being bombed. Gilmour, Captain of the *Coventry*, has gone under and we have had to relieve some officers and ratings in the *Calcutta* . . . .[158]

One bright spot is that they all came back from DEMON in good heart and are now having a well-earned rest.

D. I am worried to death about Malta and the mining situation there. We are so short of sweepers. I have only two working here and four being fitted out the gear having only just arrived. VAM has two sets not yet fitted to ships. . . .

Of course the morale of the dockyard workmen there is going down I believe and I expect he has trouble to get divers. They are having a very bad time; never a let off from continual bombing.

Whether we shall be able to work a battleship from Malta remains to be seen. It doesn't look much like it at the moment, and until the sweeping effort grows again, I think we shall have to take *Gloucester* away. I hope to keep the destroyers there as their mere presence hampers the convoys and they may get a better chance in the moonlight.

---

[158] Capt D. Gilmour: Cdr 1932; *Sussex* 1939; Capt Dec. 1939; *Coventry* Apr. 1940; *Sultan* (Singapore base) Oct. 1941; *Lanka* i/c Mar. 1942; *Suffolk* 1944–45.

If one is to believe them the Blenheims have started well and, if the mining continues on the present scale, they may have to be the only answer from Malta except intermittently. Naturally a few more would be welcome.

E. Benghazi is a very difficult problem. I hope it's realised that it is 500 miles from Alexandria and so it's not easy to keep anything except submarines operating off it.

In two or three days I am sending destroyers to give it a close range shoot up and after TIGER it looks as if I must maintain a cruiser squadron in the Central Mediterranean and if our reconnaissance does not improve they'll have to be supported by battleships.

Of course if we are prepared to face the losses, and I understand that we are, I think it can be done, though I would wish for more adequate repair facilities.

F. That was one of the reasons I hoped *Queen Elizabeth* would be allowed to come through. I have great hopes of TIGER but if Malta is closed to destroyers I shall have to oil them all at sea from *Breconshire* and battleships.

I see one of the tank carrying ships has already broken down.

G. I don't know if you have realised the low endurance of *Abdiel*. She can't lay mines off Lampedusa from Alexandria and must refuel at Malta. So our minelaying there also depends on Malta being open.

I suggest, if it's not too late, that the question of fitting extra fuel tanks in the others be studied and, if successful, one of them be sent to replace her in due course.

H. I hope I haven't drawn too gloomy a picture. We'll hold on somehow I'm sure, but this air superiority is the devil.

Personally, though much harassed, I have never been fitter.

214. *War Diary, May 1941 (cont.)*

6 May

Operation MD4

The battle fleet left Alexandria during the forenoon for operation MD4....

Ships had to be swept out of harbour individually on account of the recent mining but the operation was completed successfully. The C-in-C was in *Warspite* with *Barham*, *Valiant* and *Formidable* in company. Light forces with the fleet were VALF in *Orion*, *Ajax*,

Perth, D14 in *Jervis, Juno, Jaguar, Kandahar, Kimberley, Kingston*, D7 in *Napier, Nizam, Imperial, Griffin, Hotspur, Havock*.[159] *Abdiel* and *Breconshire* also sailed with the fleet, the former for a minelaying operation off Lampedusa and the latter with oil and petrol for Malta, and to oil destroyers at sea.... Visibility was bad due to a dust storm and after aircraft had been flown on to *Formidable* they were kept on board. The fleet proceeded to the north-westward.

2. Convoy MW7A sailed after the fleet, consisting of the four 14-knot MT ships for Malta, *Settler, Thermopylae, Amerika* and *Talabot* escorted by *Dido, Phoebe, Calcutta*, D2 in *Ilex, Isis, Hero* and *Hereward*.[160]....

3. Force H left Gibraltar with convoy TIGER consisting of five 14½-knot ships, *New Zealand Star, Clan Lamont, Clan Chattan, Clan Campbell* and *Empire Song* with essential MT for the Middle East forces. The convoy was escorted by *Queen Elizabeth*, *Naiad* flying the flag of CS15 and *Fiji* who were to reinforce the Mediterranean Fleet. *Gloucester, Kashmir* and *Kipling* also sailed with FO (H).[161]

4. Convoy AN30 consisting of *Lossiebank, Cape Horn, City of Canterbury* and *Rawnsley* loaded with the first part of the MNBDO, sailed from Haifa and Port Said for Suda Bay.[162] *Grimsby* escorted the Haifa section and *Flamingo* the Port Said section, all to be joined N of Alexandria a.m. 7th by D10 in *Stuart, Vampire, Waterhen* and *Auckland*.

Suda Bay

7. Serious difficulties were being experienced at Suda Bay owing to the crews of the merchant ships and tugs taking to the hills in daytime to avoid the bombing. It might be necessary to provide naval crews instead.

---

[159]D7: Capt S. H. T. Arliss: Capt 1937; NA S Am (Santiago) Aug. 1938; *Napier* 1941–42; Cdre 2Cl, *Tana* (Kilindini), Jan. 1943; *Berwick* Aug. 1944.
Napier, Nizam (both RAN): 1941, 1,760t, 6×4.7in, 1×4in, 5×21in tt, 36k.
[160]*Settler*: 1939, 6,202gt, 14.5k, Harrison Line.
Thermopylae: 1930, 6,655gt, 15k, W. Wilhelmsen, Oslo.
[161]*Clan Lamont*: 1939, 7,526gt, 17k
Clan Chattan: 1937, 7,262gt, 17k
Clan Campbell: 1937, 7,255gt, 17k, all Clan Line.
[162]*Lossiebank*: 1930, 5,627gt, 14k, A. Weir.
Cape Horn: 1929, 5,643gt, 12k, Cape York MS Co.
City of Canterbury: 1923, 8,331gt, 13.5k, City Line.
Rawnsley: 1940, 5,000gt, Red 'R' SS Co.

7 May

Operation MD4

All forces continued during the day without incident. Destroyers were fuelled from *Breconshire* one at a time. *Triumph* reported 3 ships passing Burat-el-Sun at 1430/6 for Benghazi. Accordingly *Ajax* was detached at 1130 with *Hotspur, Imperial* and *Havock* to attack Benghazi during the night 7/8.

2. The VA, Malta, reported that both Marsamaxett and Grand Harbour were completely mined in and that the 5DF could not sail to meet TIGER convoy. It was decided to continue with the Malta convoys nevertheless.

Western Desert

4. The policy for supply of Tobruk was now as follows:

   (i) All supplies to be carried by small motor schooners commissioned as HM Ships. Unloading to be done at night.
   (ii) A water tanker and petrol carrier to be run in during a no-moon period as necessary.
   (iii) HM Ships to embark stores when proceeding to Tobruk and bring away personnel, but always to be well clear before dawn and at dusk.
   (iv) The average daily supply aimed at to be 70 tons a day.

8 May

Operation MD4

The visibility was still poor with patches of heavy rain. Whereas this helped greatly in preventing the fleet from being attacked by aircraft, it resulted in the loss of two Albacores. One Fulmar was lost in an engagement with enemy aircraft in which 2 Cant 1007 and 2 He111K were shot down.[163]

2. *Ajax* and 3 destroyers rejoined at 1700. Their attack on Benghazi was successful. There was little shipping in the harbour, but two supply ships were intercepted afterwards. One of 5,000 tons was carrying MT and ammunition and blew up; the other of 3,000 tons ran aground and was left on fire after several explosions.[164]

---

[163]Cant 1007: 1937, 4mg, *c.*4,000lbs bombs/2t, 288mph, range 1,370mls.
[164]*Tenace*: 1881, 1,142gt, I. Messina, Italy.
Capitano A. Cecchi: armed merchant cruiser, 1934, 2,321gt, Italian Govt.

3. The fleet remained with convoy MW7A during the day and at night moved down to the southward. *Dido, Phoebe, Calcutta, Carlisle* and *Coventry* were detached from their convoys to join convoy TIGER and the two Malta convoys made direct for Malta. *Breconshire* was also detached to Malta with *Hotspur, Havock* and *Imperial*. . . .

Malta

7. There were heavy raids on Malta during the past two nights. The damage was widespread but not extensive. The present state of the dockyard was reported in VAM's signal 0916/5. Most of the workshops were at about 50% normal efficiency but some sections were as low as 25%. Docks could only be operated by hand.

Iraq

9. The recent military coup in Iraq by Raschid Ali was being opposed by our forces and air and military engagements were taking place.[165] It was likely that the Germans would take steps to support the movement in Iraq. Mining of the Shat el Arab to cut our oil supplies and communications to Basra was probable and the two AA minesweepers *Arthur Cavanagh* and *Milford Countess* were withdrawn from the Inshore Squadron with orders to proceed there to meet this threat.

9 May

Operation MD4

Convoys MW7A and B arrived safely at Malta and were swept into harbour by *Gloxinia* who succcccded in exploding a number of mines. The 5DF were also sent out of harbour and joined the C-in-C. *Breconshire* arrived at Marsaxlokk harbour and fuelled destroyers.

2. During the night 8/9 *Empire Song* was lost in the Narrows. She blew up after being set on fire. Two mines exploded in her paravanes but she was able to steam for 4 hours before the ammunition on board exploded. Survivors were taken to Malta in *Foresight*. *New Zealand Star* was also damaged by a mine but her speed was not affected. The convoy was also attacked by T/B aircraft during the night, one torpedo passing very close to *Queen Elizabeth*.

---

[165] Raschid Ali: PM of Iraq, Mar 1940; pro-Axis; resigned Jan. 1941; PM Apr. 1941 after coup; with Vichy & German support, broke Anglo-Iraqi Treaty of 1930, menacing British interests; revolt put down spring 1941.

3. The FO, Force H, reported that Force H had been heavily attacked by enemy aircraft throughout 8th. There was no damage to any ship, however, and 7 aircraft had been shot down for certain, 2 probably and 3 more damaged. One Fulmar was lost.

4. TIGER convoy, *Naiad, Queen Elizabeth, Fiji, Dido, Phoebe* and the 3 AA cruisers were met at 1515 50 miles S of Malta. The fleet turned eastward and remained in their vicinity for the rest of the day. Owing to continued bad visibility and fog there were no air attacks though many aircraft were evidently searching in the vicinity of the fleet. During the night the battlefleet and cruisers covered the convoy from the north eastward.

10 May

2. The Battlefleet remained in company with the convoy throughout the day. Although the visibility improved conditions were still difficult for attacking and reconnaissance aircraft. One Ju88 was shot down and another damaged; one Fulmar was lost when taking off from *Formidable*. No enemy attacks developed until dark when a number of aircraft, probably T/B, endeavoured to attack the convoy and battlefleet. A very heavy blind barrage apparently kept them off and no torpedoes were seen.

3. At 1700, Captain D5 in *Kelly* with 5DF were detached to attack Benghazi and then return to Malta. This was done successfully in spite of heavy night dive bombing attacks after the bombardment....

11 May

The fleet and TIGER convoy continued eastwards, enemy aircraft were in the vicinity all day but no attacks developed. One Ju88 was shot down and another damaged, one Fulmar being lost. The cruisers were detached to Alexandria at dark and the fleet went on ahead of the convoy.

12 May

The fleet arrived back at Alexandria at 1030 and TIGER convoy at 1300.[166] ...

13 May

Fleet Ammunition

9. [Signal 1454/13] was addressed by the C-in-C to the Admiralty pointing out that in the period 20 April to 13 May, between a third

---

[166] Pridham-Wippell became VA, 1BS; King, promoted VA 28 May, CS15; Rawlings, CS7; Glennie RA(D).

and a half of the main items of Med. Fleet AA ammunition stocks had been expended. The remaining resources of 4.5-in and 5.25-in were now only three-quarters of the outfit for the fleet.

215. *Middle East Commanders-in-Chief Committee*

13 May 1941

129. Crete

... The C-in-C, Middle East, ... said we had the equivalent of 15 battalions on the island, and that General Freyberg felt reasonably confident that he could deal with the situation.

The C-in-C, Mediterranean, said he hoped to be able to interfere with a seaborne expedition against Crete, but that adequate air reconnaissance was a vital necessity to any naval operation.

A discussion then took place on defence arrangements to meet the attack from the air and by sea, and the following points emerged:

(a) The C-in-C, Mediterranean, said he had a fast ship, the *Abdiel*, which could be used to run guns and other urgent equipment into Crete.

(b) He drew attention to the desirability of establishing a port on the S coast of the island. The enemy were at present concentrating their air forces against Suda Bay.

(c) He said he would be prepared to send a ship with a battalion and a handful of vehicles direct to Heraklion. ...

216. *War Diary (cont.)*

14 May

An enemy assault on Crete with airborne and seaborne troops seemed imminent. The probable scale of air attack was such that the RAF decided that it would be necessary to evacuate the aerodromes temporarily. The Army required reinforcements to replace some of the ill-equipped troops from Greece and certain additional stores. They felt confident of withstanding any airborne attack so long as the Navy could guarantee that no seaborne landing took place.

2. Accordingly a strong force was assembled under VA1 to support operations while light forces were to be prepared to enter the Aegean from either end of Crete should an attack develop. Reinforcements were to be transported in cruisers.

16 May

Submarines

7. Owing to the German occupation of Greece, the situation was now changed for submarines. The C-in-C's signal 1734/16 to the Admiralty asked for 'O' and 'P' class submarines to reinforce the 1SF at Alexandria as soon as possible for operations in

(a) Dardanelles area
(b) Gulf of Athens area
(c) Kithera area.

217. To Pound

18 May 1941

A. We got TIGER through all right but it was mainly due to the extraordinarily thick weather experienced off Malta and the whole way to Alexandria.

Only one serious attack developed by the light of the full moon. As the battlefleet was stationed down moon from the convoy the aircraft attacked them and got rather blasted. The expenditure of ammunition in actions of this sort is however serious as it is all barrage work directed by RDF....

B. This waiting for the Crete attack and having to make dispositions for it is hampering the attack on the Libyan trade. I fear they are running a lot of stuff into Benghazi.

I was a little disappointed with the 5th Flotilla when they shelled it. They were dive bombed by moonlight and legged it to the northward. If they had gone South in accordance with their orders I think they would have picked up the four ships which arrived at Benghazi the next day. Of course they might quite easily lose a destroyer but as at the moment you get bombed daily outside 100 miles from Alexandria and sometimes nearer, it doesn't seem to matter whether you go North or South.

The interception from Malta of the Libyan convoys appears to be hanging fire. As far as I can see it is because the reconnaissance is so meagre....

I was sorry to burden you with our anxieties by signal the other day but these troubles of ours are very real to us.

We are trying to make headway against an enemy air force that outnumbers ours vastly and we are short of fleet fighters and look like being short of AA ammunition. There is also practically no reconnaissance whereas the Germans and Italians report us as soon as we put our noses out of port.

We really must get something analogous to a Coastal Command out here. I made a signal about it some six weeks ago but have so far had no reply.

C.   I don't know whether the MTBs that came out were raked up. Two, 104 and 106, have not run yet except the trip from Port Said.

Of the remaining seven, three got to Suda and four broke down on the way. All except one are at present broken down. It's no good sending us unreliable boats; we just haven't got the repair facilities to keep them running.

D.   The Canal defences did better last night and for the first time shot down one plane and probably two more. They dropped five mines in the Canal though which means another 4 or 5 days closed. However, they moved 15 ships yesterday so we must be thankful for small mercies.

E.   I have just received the Admiralty telegram about mining the Red Sea and Shatt el Arab and attacks on Red Sea shipping.

While I know we must help them as being the nearest place they can get help from, I don't see in the Admiralty message any realisation that we are still desperately short of minesweeping gear here and that if we send AA sloops away it must be at the expense of our own operations. At least there is nothing said about replacing ships or gear.

I suggest that the four 'Hunts' originally allocated there should be sent out to East Indies at once or here to replace the sloops.

F.   I am afraid you will think this letter full of moans but we are not having too good a time out here. Every one is at very high pressure and we are having some failures of personnel.... I am a little unhappy about *Gloucester*'s ship's company. They have been a long time from home and taken more bombs and mines than any other ship out here. However I am going on board as soon as they get a day in and I don't doubt I can cheer them up.

Orion is another that has been abroad a long time and if it became convenient to relieve her by *Neptune* (fitted with RDF) it might be a good move.

218. *Middle East Commanders-in-Chief Committee*

21 May 1941

138. *Syria*

... The C-in-C, Mediterranean, considered that the safeguarding of Syria was of vital importance and that he was in favour of letting the Free French in as there appeared little else available.

He understood that the French naval forces in Syria were now en route to Toulon. Provided air reconnaissance was available, he thought it would be difficult for the enemy to stage a seaborne invasion of Syria. Without this reconnaissance, however, the enemy might be able to get ships through, for his resources did not permit him to keep naval forces permanently in that area.

... The C-in-C, Mediterranean, drew attention to the danger to shipping in the Red Sea if the enemy occupied Syria.

141. *Tripoli*

The C-in-C, Middle East, drew attention to the enemy shipping which was now reaching Tripoli. DDMI (I) gave details of enemy reinforcements arriving.

The C-in-C, Mediterranean, said that he could do little to increase naval activities in that area until the Crete situation was cleared up.

219. *War Diary (cont.)*

22 May

Submarines

13. *Urge* returned from patrol and reported attacking a southbound convoy on 20 May W of Lampedusa. The convoy was escorted by 5 large destroyers and covered by a cruiser force. The attack was brilliantly executed from inside the screen and resulted in a 7,000-ton tanker and a 9,000-ton troopship being sunk. On 21st *Urge* attacked two 'Condottieri' cruisers with 3 or 4 destroyers N of Lampedusa. Two torpedoes hit and one ship was certainly sunk. It was thought to have been a destroyer as both cruisers were reported again later.[167]

---

[167] No Italian warship appears to have been sunk.

24 May

Signal to the Mediterranean Fleet

8. The following signal was made to the Mediterranean Fleet by the C-in-C:

> During the past few days the fleet has been having a hard battle against a high proportion of the German Air Force and has kept its end up by dint of determination. We have sustained some hard knocks in the process of preventing any considerable enemy seaborne landing in Crete, but we have also given some. Some thousands of enemy troops have been trapped and sunk at sea. The battle for Crete is still in progress, to win it is essential. The Army is just holding its own against constant reinforcements of airborne enemy troops, we must NOT let them down, at whatever cost to ourselves we must land reinforcements for them and keep the enemy from using the sea. There are indications that the enemy resources are stretched to the limit. We can and must outlast them. STICK IT OUT.

26 May

Operation MAQ3

Six Albacores attacked Scarpanto aerodrome with bombs at 0500 and four Fulmars half an hour later. A number of aircraft on the ground were destroyed and damaged. At 1340 between 20 and 25 dive bombers attacked Force A which had withdrawn towards Alexandria. *Formidable* was hit by two heavy bombs which put one turret out of action and opened up her starboard side forward. *Nubian* was also hit right aft and her stern blown off. She was able, however, to continue to Alexandria at 20 knots. Four enemy aircraft were shot down by *Formidable*'s fighters and two by gunfire (and *Formidable* was still able to operate aircraft).

220. To Pound

1049, 23 May 1941

The operations of the last four days have been nothing short of a trial of strength between Mediterranean Fleet and German Air Force. The immobilisation of carrier owing to fact that only five serviceable fighters could be produced coupled with inability of RAF to provide any fighters at all since no aerodromes could be used in Crete meant that we had no air assistance at all other than a relatively small scale bombing attack on the aerodrome. I am afraid that in coastal area we have to admit defeat and accept the fact that losses are too great to justify us in trying to prevent seaborne attacks on Crete. This is a melancholy conclusion but it must be faced. As I have always feared enemy command of air unchallenged by our own Air Force and in these restricted waters with Mediterranean weather is too great odds for us to take on except by seizing opportunities [for] surprise and using utmost circumspection.

I am discussing the matter today with Deputy C-in-C, Middle East, and AOC-in-C, Middle East, regarding our next moves particularly as regards Crete. In the meantime I have withdrawn all forces to re-arm and refuel.[168] It is perhaps fortunate that *Formidable* is immobilised as I doubt if she would now be afloat.

221. *From the Admiralty*

24 May 1941

A. HM Government consider successful outcome of present battle for Crete is vitally essential.
B. Unless situation in Crete is more favourable than we suppose it is essential to reinforce them.
C. It may be too late for *Glenroy* to reach Crete in time to disembark troops tonight but if it is not (R) NOT too late reinforcement should take place.
D. War Office have been consulted and consider that whatever risks to troops in *Glenroy* may be, it must be accepted if the C-in-C, Middle East, also agrees to the necessity for still [?more] reinforcements.
E. Can't Blenheims or tanked [?up] Hurricanes fighter protection be afforded during withdrawal of *Glenroy* in morning[?]

222. *To the Admiralty*

24 May 1941

I could only infer that you were in possession of information I had not received and accordingly directed *Coventry* to proceed to the northward.

---

[168]Deputy C-in-C, ME: Lt-Gen H. M. Wilson.

2. The movements of *Glenroy* and escort had been most carefully considered and her operational orders enabled her to take the maximum advantage of the dark hours.

3. Her withdrawal was ordered in consultation with C-in-C, Middle East, after a further plan for reinforcement of Crete by *Abdiel* and/or destroyers had been decided upon.

4. If *Glenroy* continues to proceed to the northward in accordance with your directions she will be in the worst possible position for dive bomber and high level bombing attacks at daylight and disembarkation of troops during daylight hours under present conditions is out of the question. In view of this I am ordering her to proceed to Alexandria forthwith.

223. *The Chiefs of Staff to the Commanders-in-Chief, Middle East*

2132, 25 May 1941

If situation is allowed to drag on the enemy will have advantage because [?unless] more drastic action is taken than is suggested in your appreciation, the enemy will be able to reinforce the island to a considerable extent with men and stores.

2. It is essential, therefore, that the Cs-in-C should concert measures for clearing up the situation without delay.

In so doing the fleet and RAF must accept risk is entailed in preventing any considerable reinforcements of men and material reaching the island by sea either by night or by day.

3. Should air reconnaissance show any movement by sea or any collection of craft at Melos it will be essential for fleet to operate north of island by day. It is probable that loss incurred in so doing will be considerable and only experience will show for how many days this situation can be maintained. This confirms that time is the dominating factor.

224. *To the Admiralty*

1834, 26 May 1941

Their Lordships may rest assured that the determining factor in operating in the Aegean is not fear of sustaining losses but the need to avoid losses which without commensurate advantage to ourselves, will cripple the fleet out here. So far as I am aware the enemy has not yet succeeded in getting any considerable reinforcement to Crete by sea if indeed he has sent any at all though I agree that this may soon be attempted.

2. ... surely we already have sufficient experience of what the losses are likely to be. In three days, two cruisers and four destroyers were sunk, one battleship is out of action for several months and two other cruisers and four destroyers sustained considerable damage. We can't afford another such experience and retain sea control in the Eastern Mediterranean.

3. In point of fact supply by sea has not yet come much into the picture as despite the losses and turning back of his convoys the enemy is so prolific in the air that for the moment he is able to reinforce and keep his forces supplied by air at will. This process is quite unchecked by air action on our part and the sight of the constant unhindered procession of Ju52s flying into Crete is amongst the factors likely to affect the morale of our forces.

4. I feel that Their Lordships should know that the effects of the recent operations on personnel is cumulative. Our light craft, officers, men and machinery alike, are nearing exhaustion. Since LUSTRE started at the end of February they have been kept running almost to the limits of endurance and now when the work is redoubled, they are facing an air concentration beside which I am assured that in Norway was child's play. It is inadvisable to drive men beyond a certain point.

5. I have been able to do rather more than was foreshadowed in our appreciation. Each night destroyers and cruisers sweep the north coast of Crete, we have bombed Maleme and this morning attacked Scarpanto. Melos is also receiving attention from a submarine. I must emphasise that air reconnaissance is the one hope of stopping seaborne reinforcements since it should allow us to keep our forces far enough away by day to avoid serious losses pending the moment when the enemy commits his convoy to the sea voyage and we go after it. I have not, however, yet received the necessary reinforcement of reconnaissance aircraft which I so earnestly requested.

6. Since writing the above I learn that *Formidable* and *Nubian* have been hit by bombs and are returning to harbour. I have no details.

225. *War Diary (cont.)*

27 May

Tedder to Cunningham

Will do all possible to provide some cover to ships. Owing to distance from our bases such cover can only be spasmodic and meagre. Anything you can do to indicate expected positions and times will help us to use to best advantage the few aircraft which can do the job. . . .

29 May

C-in-C to Admiralty

The situation regarding the evacuation of Crete is as follows:

Yesterday and today, up to noon, three cruisers and one destroyer have been damaged, the latter must be regarded as likely to be lost. The formation to which these ships belonged probably had on board some 4,000 men and with such close packing casualties must have been heavy and probably of the order of 500 men.

2. The second force which went to the South coast is being bombed but results are not yet known.

3. Tonight a 'Glen' ship in company with cruisers is due at Sphakia to take off some 6,000 men. This force is at present being shadowed on its passage north and its speed of advance is only 16 knots.

4. It is evident that tomorrow we must expect further casualties to ships accompanied with extremely [?heavy] casualties to men particularly in the case of *Glengyle* if she is hit with 3,000 men on board.

The fighter protection is very meagre.

5. The factors to be weighed are these:

   (a) Are we justified in continuing to bring out men in so closely packed ships which are being subjected to an intensive bombing for a journey of up to 24 hours and who will suffer very heavy casualties since, if a ship sinks, the others cannot embark survivors.

   (b) Are we justified in continuing to accept a scale of loss and damage to the Mediterranean Fleet which has already seriously reduced its strength and which, if continued, may make us so weak that we cannot operate.

6. The other side of the question is that to leave men deliberately in enemy hands is against all our traditions and will have a bad effect on our prestige, perhaps more particularly as so large a pro-

portion is of Empire troops. It has to be remembered, however, that in the end many men will be alive who may well be lost if they embark.
7. I am ready to continue with the evacuation as long as we have a ship with which to do so but I feel it my duty to put these considerations before Their Lordships.

226. *To Pound*

1930, 28 May 1941

Recent events make a re-appreciation out here essential. With the loss of Crete enemy air bases are moved forward and he can display heavier air attacks on Egypt and Western Desert than hitherto. In addition to this scale of attack is such that it is very clear that fleet will have to face serious loss by day whenever at sea outside range of effective fighter protection. We are thus for the moment driven back on a defensive role and our liberty of action is greatly restricted.

Immediate appreciations are threefold:

(a) [?Trade] and hence safety of Malta are jeopardised.
(b) The attack on Libyan communications is made very hazardous.
(c) Through Mediterranean route is virtually closed.

3. The answer seems clear. We have lost our Northern flank and are unlikely to regain it. We must therefore try and close Southern flank. If the army can advance sufficiently to reach, say, Derna, a good deal will have been done to mitigate the situation.

4. Any such action is, however, useless unless our air forces are adequate to make use of the situation. The whole object of thus clearing Southern flank is to provide a series of airfields from which the following can be done.

(a) Enemy airfields in Crete, Greece and Aegean continually bombed so as to make them untenable.
(b) Enemy aerodromes in Libya similarly bombed so as to force the enemy back into western aerodromes and thus relieve pressure on Egypt, and our lines of supply.
(c) To provide a chain of fighter aerodromes under cover of which Fleet can reach Central Mediterranean in reasonable protection.
(d) To provide a series of striking bases from which torpedo and bomber aircraft can operate to Seaward. This last being of

particular importance as providing protection to Egypt against seaborne attack if Fleet should be seriously reduced in strength.

5. It is understood that our air strength is increasing rapidly. If we continue to increase it and if we act as suggested we may yet prove that the enemy has made a costly blunder. To continue his present scale of attack, to go on to Cyprus and Syria as he may well intend draws his air strength increasingly into Eastern Wilderness but to take advantage of it we must have the air and immediately.

6. The lesson of [? recent events] is quite definite and repeats that of France and Norway which is that you cannot conduct military operations in modern war without air forces which will allow you at least to establish temporary air supremacy. We have now a chance from Egypt to crush a large portion of the German Air Force. If we act in time and HMG are prepared to [?regard] this theatre as of importance second only to the defence of Britain, indeed it might well be described as an integral part of the defence of Britain since it has drawn off so much scale of attack. We are on the verge of disaster here for we stand to lose fleet and thus Malta, Cyprus and Egypt unless we act at once (R) once.

7. All obstacles must be swept aside and we must have following:

(a) Coastal Command Force of torpedo bombing [and] anti-submarine bombers, and reconnaissance aircraft which can find [?convoys] and sink them and can thus take over function of carriers.

(b) Fighter and bomber forces to allow army to advance ruthlessly.

(c) Bomber forces to allow us to strike at enemy and smash his aerodromes.

8. Out here we are unlikely to have to fight more than say one-third of German Air Force. Is this not therefore supreme chance of discounting his overall supremacy? To do it all energy and best brains of three services at home and out here are needed, but it can be done. If it is not done our position in Middle and Far East will crumble completely.

227. To Pound

30 May 1941

There is no hiding the fact that in our battles with the German Air Force we have been badly battered. I always thought we might get a surprise if they really turned their attention to the fleet. No AA fire will deal with the simultaneous attacks of 10–20 aircraft.

We have brought down perhaps 30 enemy aircraft and damaged a like number but there is no question but that they have had much the best of it, and I suppose if one operates 30–40 miles off the enemy aerodromes it is to be expected.

Our losses are very heavy. *Warspite, Barham* and *Formidable* out of action for some months, *Orion* and *Dido* in a terrible mess, and I have just heard that *Perth* has been hit today. Eight destroyers lost outright and several badly damaged. All this not counting *Gloucester* and *Fiji*. I fear the casualties are over 2,000 dead.

I would not mind if we had inflicted corresponding damage on the enemy but I fear we have achieved little beyond preventing a seaborne landing in Crete and the evacuation of some of the Army there. I feel very heavy hearted about it all.

I suppose we shall learn our lesson in time that the navy and army can't make up for the lack of air forces. Three squadrons of long range fighters and a few heavy bombing squadrons would have saved Crete for us.

Some mistakes were certainly made in the conduct of our operations, the principal one being the failure of CS15 to polish off the caique convoy in the morning. It is true that he found it difficult to maintain a course towards the convoy due to dodging the heavy and persistent bombing attacks but I could cheerfully have put up with our losses had we had some thousands more Hun soldiers swimming in the Aegean.

The sending back of *Gloucester* and *Fiji* to the *Greyhound* was another grave error and cost us those two ships. They were practically out of ammunition but even had they been full up I think they would have gone.

The Commanding Officer of *Fiji* told me that the air over *Gloucester* was black with planes.[169] I doubt if anyone was saved from *Gloucester* as the Hun planes were machine gunning the boats.

---

[169] Capt P. R. B. W. William-Powlett: Capt 1938; PSD, DDPS (Manning) 1939; *Fiji* Dec. 1940; *Newcastle* Feb. 1942; *Rodney* & Capt of Fleet, HF July 1944; RA(D) 1951.

B. I have been rather anxious about the state of mind of the sailors after seven days' constant bombing attack. The only ship in which so far there has been any sign of cracking up is *Ajax*, surprisingly enough. . . . *Ajax* out of the last 60 days has spent less than 10 nights in harbour I believe. *Dido* has had one in the last 21 days and so on. The destroyers are the same – just very tired.

I had hoped that, realising the work they were doing and what they were up against the fleet might have received a message of encouragement from the Board which I feel would have done a lot of good.

C. The future out here does not look too good for the fleet. It looks as though, until we get Cyrenaica, our movements will be rather limited. The supply of Malta will be very difficult and I am already starting the two minelaying submarines running in petrol and stores. Rather a prostitution of their activities but it may just keep Malta going.

At the same time I think it would be worth considering supplying Malta from the West.

With the large air force the enemy has concentrated this end I don't think he has much left in Sicily. The mines are a difficulty but with bow protection the ships should get through.

D. I am very grateful for the reinforcements you are sending. I fear this station has been terribly expensive in cruisers and this last business has knocked out six.

E. And now about my personal position. I hear that the PM has removed Longmore (replacing a first class man with a second class in my opinion). It may be that he or the Admiralty would like a change in command of the fleet out here.

If this is so I shall not feel in any way annoyed more especially as it may be that the happenings of the last few days may have shaken the faith of the personnel of the fleet in my handling of affairs.

228. *To Pound*

1541c, 31 May 1941

... information received that *Nizam* and *Napier* are returning with further 1,700 men. *Napier* reduced to 23 knots by near miss. As reported CS15, *Abdiel* and three destroyers are carrying out final trip tonight. So far about 12,300 have been evacuated about 500 soldiers being lost as a result of air attack on passage. Number remaining most difficult to ascertain but various estimates between 4,000 and 7,000. After CS15 loads tonight there will probably be two to three thousand left behind, of those from Suda area. In addition about 1,200 from Retimo and other small parties totalling about 500 of whom trace is lost.

I have called a halt after tonight as even if CS15 suffers no damage on return trip I shall be left with only two battleships, one cruiser, two AA ships, *Abdiel* and nine destroyers fit for service (not including four destroyers of 19th Division now only fit for local duty in Western Desert). This halt has been called after consultation with Mr P. Fraser, General Freyberg and C-in-C, Middle East.[170]

229. *From Pound*

2330B, 31 May 1941

... if there is a reasonable prospect that any substantial formed body of men is capable of embarking tomorrow night, 1–2 June, HMG consider that an attempt should be made to bring them off especially in view of unexpected success last two nights.

2. It is presumed that work of aircraft has contributed largely to this success and HMG assume that this air support will also be available for further day operations.

3. Should experience tomorrow be very different from that of last two days the matter could be further considered. ...

230. *To Pound*

0445C, 1 June 1941

General Weston has just arrived back by flying boat and reports that the troops remaining, about 5,000 in all, were incapable of further resistance owing to strain and lack of food.[171] He had therefore instructed them to capitulate in accordance with General Wavell's direction sent to him previously this evening.

2. In these circumstances am sending no further ships.

---

[170]Peter Fraser (1884–1950): Labour poln, NZ; Dep PM Sept. 1939; PM Mar. 1940–49.

[171]Maj-Gen E. C. Weston, RM: Col 1937; Col 2nd Cdt, Plymouth 1939; Tempy Brig, MNBDO 1940; Actg Maj-Gen 1941; Maj-Gen Mar 1942; Lt-Gen, Ret List 1943; Col, N Ordnance Dept 1944.

231. *To Pound*

1043C, 1 June 1941

Even if capitulation had not already been advised, further evacuation efforts were not justifiable. The decision in my message timed 1541/31 was made only after most anxious consideration and had been based on the following reasons.

2. To effect embarkation on the night 1/2 June it was necessary to sail a force at 0800/1 [at] which time the only ships available were two battleships and [?eight] destroyers at Alexandria and one destroyer returning from escorting *Barham* to Port Said. The remaining ships were damaged, too slow or at 12 hours' notice for boiler cleaning. *Ajax* became available after damage repairs at 1200 and CS15's force was not due back until 1800.

3. In view of Admiralty message timed 1830B/31 the battleships and destroyers were already at one hour's notice and represent all that is available to deal with enemy action.

4. The moon now allows bombing of ships and beaches, thus considerably increasing the hazards to ships and men and though yesterday's evacuation was successful both destroyers were damaged by near misses despite fighter protection.

5. Reference para. 1 of your 2330/31, it must not be assumed that this fighter protection will remain available. It is an improvised effort which cannot possibly be sustained for more than a day or two, moreover now that our fighter aerodromes are too far back to protect Tobruk, the new long range fighters we have represent the only air support the place can be given and in the event of attack the choice will have to lie between the protection of the fleet and that of the fortress.

6. In view of the situation developing in the Western Desert and Syria, the point has been reached when to allow the possibility of further reduction of the estimated force available was out of the question. Even as it is we are in no condition to meet any serious enemy movement.

7. Since writing the above *Calcutta* has been bombed and sunk 85 miles from Alexandria.

232. *To the Admiralty*

2031, 1 June 1941

The operation of evacuating troops from Crete has now terminated with the arrival of CS15's force and 3,900 troops.

2. Figures must be regarded as approximate but consider that total evacuated to be just over 17,000 of whom some 500 were casualties.

(Note: Of these about 250 were in *Hereward*, of whom some are known to be prisoners).

3. 5,500 were left at Sphakia and had orders to capitulate and in addition must be added up to 2,000 from Retimo or in small parties who never reached the south coast. Total, therefore, left behind was about 7,000.

4. I would draw attention to the fact that owing to the inevitable confusion, figures given to me varied very greatly and up to late on 30th, I had hoped that the last trip, that of CS15, would result in almost everyone being brought off. The figures, however, suddenly increased by some 5,000 on that day.

5. Points of interest are:

(a) The evacuation had to be carried out from places which were within easy reach of enemy forces. It was not possible to cover the operation with heavy ships or cruisers and the fact that our points of embarkation might be attacked was a constant anxiety. It was only the fact that the enemy was unenterprising that justified the risk taken in this respect.

(b) The distance to point of embarkation being some 360 miles meant that each load of men had to do the whole 14 hours of daylight in face of extremely heavy scale of air attack which was increased by the fact that aircraft were freed from their duty of attacking positions in Crete.

(c) When the RAF were able to get a few improvised long range fighters in the air the effect on the enemy was noticeable and a number of attacks were beaten off and it is already known that at least 14 aircraft were destroyed for certain and a number damaged. The fighters available, however, were still very few and they were unable to prevent the heavy casualties to which must now be added *Calcutta* . . .

(d) I should like to draw particular attention to the performance of the Royal Marines of the MNBDO who in the withdrawal from Suda Bay were constituted by General Weston into a rearguard and conducted themselves in a manner worthy of the highest tradition of the corps. It is believed that a large number were left behind.

6. It is desirable to emphasise that the long range fighter effort was an improvisation of a number of types and could be worked for a few days only. Our need for long range fighters thus remains acute

and until they are available in sufficient numbers we must continue to expect losses and damage on the present scale when the fleet is at sea.

233. *War Diary, May 1941 (concl.)*

Summary and Appreciation of Events for Month

Operations

The month of May saw the hardest fighting of the war as far as the Mediterranean Fleet was concerned. It was a battle between the weight of the German Air Force and the Fleet. The latter, being virtually without air support, suffered extremely severe losses which for a period crippled our naval strength in these waters. . . .

Thereafter the tale of the Navy is one of disaster after disaster as the ships of the fleet were picked off in succession by the concentration of dive bombers. . . . Two or three enemy troop convoys were destroyed. The enemy positions in Crete were bombarded and there is no doubt that, had we only had air support available, these efforts would probably have saved Crete. . . . Thus at the close of May the Mediterranean Fleet was left in a sorry state though with the satisfaction of having achieved the almost insuperable task set to it.

234. *Cunningham's Report on the Battle of Crete*

4 August 1941

General Observations

2. The object of the operations was the prevention of enemy seaborne landings on the coast of Crete. It was known that airborne invasion of the island was impending; but it appeared almost inconceivable that airborne invasion alone could succeed against forewarned troops, that seaborne support was inevitable and that the destruction of troop convoys would win the day.

3. The Navy succeeded in its object but paid a heavy price for this achievement. The fleet was operating within easy range of enemy air bases and beyond the reach of any protection from our own air force. The fleet fighters of *Formidable* were reduced to only four as a result of casualties and unserviceability arising from the recent operation TIGER. It was, therefore, useless to send *Formidable* to assist.

So, without air support of any sort, the fleet had to be exposed to a scale of air attack which is believed to have exceeded anything of the kind yet experienced afloat.

4. The air attack on Crete started on 20 May. The sweeps of the Light Forces on the night 20/21 and during daylight 21st were uneventful except for heavy air attacks and the unlucky loss of *Juno*. As far as the Navy was concerned the real Battle of Crete began on the night of 21/22 May, with the successful encounter of Force D with an enemy convoy. This encounter was skilfully and thoroughly exploited, was a heavy blow to the Germans and an encouragement for our hard pressed troops in Crete.

5. It was on the morning of 22 May that things commenced to go awry. The enemy convoy sighted by Force C was almost certainly a large one. The RA, 15CS, was presented with a unique opportunity for effecting its destruction but unfortunately, in the face of heavy air attacks, and with HA ammunition stocks beginning to run low, he decided that he would not have been justified in pressing on to the northward and gave the order to withdraw. The situation was undoubtedly a difficult one for him, as this attack was certainly on a majestic scale but it appears that no diminuition of risk could have been achieved by retirement and that, in fact, the safest place for the squadron would have been among the enemy ships. The brief action did, however, have the effect of turning back the convoy, and the troops, if they ever did reach Crete, were not in time to influence the battle.

6. In the meantime, a further unlucky decision had been taken. *Dido*, wearing the flag of the RA (D) had expended 70% of her AA ammunition.[172] The destroyers were also running low, but *Ajax* and *Orion* had 42% and 38% respectively remaining. The RA(D) correctly decided that *Dido* must withdraw from the Aegean; but, from very natural reluctance to leave other ships of his squadron to face the music after he himself had retired, he took *Ajax* and *Orion* with him. This decision, although such results could hardly have been foreseen, deprived the hard pressed Force C of their assistance at a time when the weight of their AA fire would have been an invaluable support.

7. The junction of Forces A and C on the afternoon of the 22 May, left the RA, 15CS, after a gruelling two days, in command of the combined force. Before he really had time to grasp the situation of his force, a series of disasters occurred, the loss of *Greyhound*, *Gloucester* and finally *Fiji*.

---

[172] RA Glennie.

8. Past experience had gone to show that when under heavy scale of air attack it is essential to keep ships together for mutual support. The decision to send *Kandahar* and *Kingston* to the rescue of *Greyhound*'s people cannot be cavilled at but in the light of subsequent events it would probably have been better had the whole force closed to their support. The RA, 15CS, was however not aware of the shortage of AA ammunition in *Gloucester* and *Fiji*. As a final misfortune, when rejoining after the loss of *Gloucester*, *Fiji* steered a course diverging from that of the fleet, which she could no longer see.

9. Late on 22 May, a 'Most Immediate' message was received by the C-in-C from the RA, 7CS, from which it appeared, owing to a calligraphic error, that the battleships of Force A1 had no pom-pom ammunition left. In fact they had plenty. It was on this account that orders were given at 0408/23 for all forces to withdraw to the eastward. Had this error not occurred the battleships would not have been ordered back to Alexandria and would have been available as a support and rallying point for the 5DF on the morning of 23 May, so that the loss of *Kelly* and *Kashmir* might well have been avoided.

10. That the fleet suffered disastrously in this encounter with the unhampered German Air Force is evident but it has to be remembered on the credit side that the Navy's duty was achieved and no enemy ship whether warship or transport succeeded in reaching Crete or intervening in the battle during these critical days. Nor should the losses sustained blind one to the magnificent courage and endurance that was displayed throughout. I have never felt prouder of the Mediterranean Fleet than at the close of these particular operations, except, perhaps, at the fashion in which it faced up to the even greater strain which was so soon to be imposed upon it.

11. Where so much that was meritorious was performed it is almost invidious to particularise, but I feel that I must draw the attention of Their Lordships to two outstanding examples. These are the conduct of *Kandahar* (Cdr W.G.A. Robson) and *Kingston* (Lt-Cdr P. Somerville, DSO) during the whole period of the operation and, in particular, the rescue of the crews of *Greyhound* and *Fiji*. *Kandahar* has recorded that between 1445 and 1930 she was subjected to 22 separate air attacks and all the rescue work during daylight was carried out in the face of heavy bombing and machine gunning. The other story is that of the gallantry and devotion of Cdr

W.R. Marshall A'Deane, of *Greyhound,* whose self sacrifice stands out even amongst this record of fine deeds.[173]

After the loss of his own ship he was picked up by *Kandahar.* Whilst *Kandahar* was engaged in rescuing the crew of the *Fiji,* Cdr Marshall A'Deane dived overboard, in the darkness, to the assistance of a man some way from the ship. He was not seen again.

12. Rear Admiral H. B. Rawlings, OBE, in the *Warspite,* had a particularly anxious time. He handled a series of difficult situations in a determined and skilful manner and by his timely support undoubtedly did all possible to extricate Forces C and D from their awkward situation on the evening of the 22 May.

14. The NOIC, Suda, Captain J. A. V. Morse, DSO, followed up his excellent work in organising the port at Suda by consistently presenting a clear and concise picture of the situation by his signals during the battle. His presence at Suda was invaluable.

Narrative by the C-in-C

Phase I: Building up Suda into a Port Capable of Supplying the Needs of the Army

Operation DEMON, during which over 50,000 troops had been evacuated from Greece, was completed on 29 April. Some 25,000 of these troops, the majority of whom had no equipment other than rifles, were being re-organised in Crete. A large number was useless for defence purposes and were awaiting removal.

2. The facilities for unloading supply ships in Suda Bay were poor. The harbour was being subjected to frequent air attack which caused heavy casualties among the ships unloading. The problem of keeping up supplies was causing anxiety, but strenuous efforts on the part of the NOIC, Suda, were going some way towards solving the various local difficulties.

3. During the period from 29 April to 20 May, some 15,000 tons of Army stores were unloaded from 15 ships, whilst 8 ships were sunk or damaged in the harbour by air attack. The scale of enemy air attack was so heavy, and our fighter protection so thin, that the run-

---

[173]Cdr W. G. A. Robson: Cdr 1935; *Kandahar* Aug. 1939; Capt Dec. 1941; *Monck* Feb. 1942; CSO to Cdre, Force N (Cdre G. N. Oliver), HUSKY (Sicily), July 1943; *Iron Duke*, HQ staff, Orkney & Shetlands Sept. 1943; Capt (D), 26DF, HF Jan. 1944; *Superb* June 1945.

Lt-Cdr P. Somerville: Lt-Cdr 1937; *Kingston* 1939; Cdr Dec. 1941; lost with ship, bombed, Malta 4 Apr. 1942.

Cdr W. R. Marshall A'Deane: Cdr 1939; *Greyhound* July 1939; post. Albert Medal.

ning of convoys in and out of Crete was being carried out at considerable risk.

4. It had been intended to set up the complete MNBDO in Crete. The MNBDO AA guns had been installed at Suda but the danger of losing ships through enemy air action was considered too great to allow any further MNBDO storeships to be sent to Crete.

5. On the night of 15/16 May, *Gloucester* and *Fiji* embarked the 2nd Bn of the Leicester[shire] Regt, with their full equipment, at Alexandria, and landed them at Heraklion. During the night 18/19 May, *Glengyle*, escorted by *Coventry, Waterhen, Voyager* and *Auckland* took 700 men of the Argyll and Sutherland Highlanders from Alexandria to Tymbaki.

Phase II: Naval Dispositions to Meet the Expected Attack

6. Although intelligence suggested that an attack on Crete was very likely, the exact date of the attack could not be forecast. . . . the most probable date . . . was about the 17 May. The use of Suda Bay as an anchorage by day was limited, on account of heavy air raids. It was, therefore, necessary to operate forces from Alexandria, which is 420 miles from Suda. A force was to be held in reserve at Alexandria as an attack might start at a time when our forces at sea were getting short of fuel. Although the first airborne attack on Crete did not take place until 20 May, naval forces had to be kept ready at sea from 14 May onwards.

7. The object of the C-in-C was to prevent the enemy from landing in Crete from the sea. The most likely places for an enemy seaborne landing were thought to be Canea, Retimo and Heraklion whilst Kissamo Bay and Sitia were possibilities. On 15 May forces were at sea, to the S of Crete, ready to move to any threatened point. The C-in-C signalled his intentions as follows:

(a) Force C (RA(D) in *Dido* with *Kandahar, Nubian, Kingston, Juno* and *Coventry*) was to be available to deal with Heraklion and Sitia.
(b) Force D (*Naiad, Phoebe* and two destroyers) would deal with any landing W of Retimo.
(c) Force B (*Gloucester* and *Fiji*) would deal with enemy forces NW of Crete, or support Force D.
(d) Force A (VA, 1BS, in *Queen Elizabeth* with *Barham* and 5 destroyers) was to take up a position to the westward of Crete so as to act as cover to other forces.

(e) In reserve at Alexandria: *Warspite, Valiant, Formidable, Orion* and *Ajax* and remaining available destroyers.
(f) The general idea was for night sweeps to be carried out as follows:

   (i) Force B to sweep the W coast of Greece from Matapan;
   (ii) Force D to sweep from Anti Kithera to Piaeus;
   (iii) Force C to sweep from Kaso towards Leros.

(g) All forces were to retire from their sweeps so as to be close N of Crete by dawn. Subsequently they were to retire to the S of Crete.
(h) The submarine *Rorqual* was to operate in the vicinity of Leros.
(i) A flotilla of MTBs was based at Suda Bay.
(j) *Abdiel* was to lay a minefield between Cephalonia and Levkas, to interrupt enemy communications through the Corinth Canal.
(k) Appropriate air reconnaissance was arranged, but it was very thin.
(l) The C-in-C would control the operation from Alexandria but the SO's of the various forces were informed that they were expected to take independent action to intercept any enemy forces reported.

8. *Formidable* was reduced to only four [fighter] aircraft serviceable and was unable to provide fighter protection to our forces until 25 May. . . . There were still a few shore-based fighters in Crete but they were being rapidly reduced by enemy air action and could not be of assistance to the fleet. The fleet was thus compelled to operate close to enemy air bases without any fighter protection whatsoever.

9. . . . On the 18 May, arrangements were made to relieve forces at sea. . . .

(a) CS7 shifted his flag to *Warspite* and left Alexandria at 2000/18 with Force A1 (*Warspite, Valiant, Ajax, Napier, Kimberley, Janus, Isis, Hereward, Decoy, Hero* and *Griffin*).
(b) Force A was to return to Alexandria on relief by Force A1. . . . *Hotspur* and *Imperial* were to be transferred from Force A to Force A1.
(c) CS15 in *Naiad*, with *Perth, Kandahar, Nubian, Kingston* and *Juno* was to return to Alexandria, fuel his ships and leave again early on 19 May.

(d) RA(D) in *Dido* was to return to Alexandria and leave early on 19 May with *Orion, Greyhound* and *Hasty*. He was to be joined by *Ajax, Hero* and *Hereward* from Force A1.
(e) *Gloucester* and *Fiji*, who were getting short of fuel, were to return to Alexandria, fuel and sail again to join Force A1.

10. During the night LCT A2 escorted by KOS19 landed three 'I' tanks at Tymbaki. These tanks were to make their way to Heraklion for the defence of the aerodrome.

Phase III: The Attack on Crete

12. At 0800 on 20 May ... the Germans began their attack on Crete. This took the form of intense bombing of the vicinity of Maleme aerodrome closely followed by the landing of troops by parachute, glider and troop-carrying aircraft. The enemy's main object appeared to be Maleme but later in the day similar attacks developed at Heraklion and Retimo.

13. As regards our Air Force, the increased scale of enemy air attacks on aerodromes since 13 May had imposed a very heavy strain on the fighter force in Crete. This force by 19 May had been reduced to only 7 fighter aircraft fit for operations. No reinforcements were available in Egypt. It had, therefore, been decided to fly all serviceable aircraft back to Egypt on 19 May, until the scale of enemy air attack lessened or reinforcements became available. From 19 to 26 May naval forces operating in the vicinity of Crete were without fighter protection.

14. On learning that the attack on Crete had started, the C-in-C at once ordered forces at sea to move up towards Crete, but failing further developments they were to keep out of sight of land. During the forenoon of 20 May, the C-in-C signalled his intentions as follows:

(a) Force D consisting of RA(D) in *Dido* with *Orion, Ajax, Isis, Kimberley, Imperial* and *Janus*, was to pass the Anti Kithera Channel by 2200/20, sweep Capes Malea–Hydra–Phalconera and be off Canea at 0700/21.
(b) Force C consisting of CS15 in *Naiad* with *Perth, Kandahar, Nubian, Kingston* and *Juno* was to pass Kaso Strait at 2200/20, sweep round Stampalia and be off Heraklion at 0700/21.
(c) Force B consisting of *Gloucester* and *Fiji* was to pass close off Cape Matapan at 0400/21 and then join Force A1 about 50 miles W of Crete ... at 0700/21.

(d) *Calcutta* was to pass through the Kaso Strait after Force C which she was to join off Heraklion at 0700/21.

(e) A new Force E (D14 in *Jervis* with *Nizam* and *Ilex*) was to bombard Scarpanto aerodrome during the night 20/21 May, withdrawing to the southward before daylight.

(f) *Carlisle* who was at Alexandria would sail as soon as ready so as to join Force E 50 miles SE of Crete . . . at 0700/21 May.

15. As a result of air reconnaissance reports of caiques sighted in the Aegean, Forces C and D were ordered at 1800 to move to the N of Crete, at once. It was then thought that if our forces carried out the sweeps that had already been arranged there was a danger of their missing southbound enemy convoys in the darkness. The night sweeps for Forces C and D were accordingly cancelled. Instead Forces C and D were ordered to establish patrols N of Crete to the W and E of long. 25°E respectively. Force C was to cover the vicinity of Heraklion, whilst Force D was to guard the Maleme–Canea–Kissamo Bay area. The Retimo area was to be looked after by local craft from Suda Bay.

16. At nightfall on 20 May, the situation at Maleme and Canea was reported to be in hand, though about 1,200 of the 3,000 enemy who had landed by air were unaccounted for. In the Heraklion and Retimo area it was known that parachutists had landed, but details were lacking. Boats carrying troops had been reported off Heraklion.

17. During the night 20/21, Force C encountered about 6 MAS boats in the Kaso Strait. After being engaged by *Juno, Kandahar* and *Naiad*, the MAS boats retired, 4 of them having been damaged. Force E bombarded Scarpanto aerodrome. Results could not be observed but intelligence reports later indicated that two Do17 aircraft had been damaged.

21 May

18. At daylight on 21 May the position of our forces was:

(a) CS7 with Force A1 was 60 miles W of the Anti Kithera Strait steering to the SE to meet Force D which was returning from the Aegean patrol.

(b) RA(D) with Force D had sighted nothing . . .

(c) CS15 with Force C . . . was now withdrawing through the Kaso Strait to the southward, having been joined by *Calcutta* at 0600.

(d) D14 . . . was on his way to join Force C.

(e) Force B had sighted nothing . . . were now joining Force A1.

THE EFFECTS OF GERMAN INTERVENTION, 1941

(f) *Carlisle* was on her way from Alexandria ... to join Force C.
(g) *Abdiel* was returning to Alexandria from her minelaying operation.

It was intended that forces should remain to the S of Crete by day. After dark the night sweeps were to be repeated.

19. During daylight on 21 May our naval forces were subject to heavy air attacks. Force A1 was attacked once during the forenoon and for 2½ hours during the afternoon. Force C was bombed continuously from 0950 to 1350. At 1149 *Juno* was hit by bombs and sank in two minutes. *Carlisle* joined Force C at 1400. Force D was heavily attacked during the forenoon, *Ajax* being damaged by near misses. After 2½ hours of bombing during the afternoon, when in company with Force A1, they were again attacked in the evening. During these attacks on Force A and D at least 3 aircraft were certainly, and two more probably, shot down. The attacks on Force C were so incessant that no reliable estimate can be made of the casualties inflicted on aircraft; at least two were seen to be damaged and in difficulties, and one shot down.

20. During the day Force A1 remained to the S of Kithera where it was joined by Forces B and D.

21. The airborne attacks on Crete on 21 May continued with great intensity and Maleme was captured by the enemy.

22. No seaborne landing had yet taken place but air reconnaissance reported groups of small craft escorted by destroyers, steering towards Crete from Milo. Forces B, C and D accordingly closed in through Kithera and Kaso Straits ... If there were no developments during the night Forces C and D were to commence working northwards at 0530/22 on a wide zigzag to locate convoys.

23. At 2330/21, Force D (now consisting of RA(D) in *Dido*, with *Orion, Ajax, Janus, Kimberley, Hasty* and *Hereward* encountered an enemy troop convoy of caiques escorted by one or two torpedo boats 18 miles N of Canea. The caiques, which were crowded with German soldiers, were engaged for 2½ hours. RDF and ASV proved invaluable in leading our forces onto fresh targets. In all, one or two steamers, at least a dozen caiques, a small pleasure steamer and a steam yacht were either sunk or left burning. One of the escorting torpedo boats, after firing torpedoes at our cruisers, was damaged by gunfire from *Dido* and finally blown up by a broadside from *Ajax*. It is estimated that the vessels sunk carried about 4,000 German troops.[174]

---

[174]It is now known that only some 400 were lost. See C. MacDonald, *The Lost Battle: Crete 1941* (London, 1993), pp. 239–42.

24. After taking a further sweep to the E and N, RA(D) turned W at 0330/22 giving his force a rendezvous for 0600/22 about 30 miles W of Crete. The C-in-C's intentions had been for Forces C and D to work to the northward, commencing 0530/22, if there were no developments during the night ... The C-in-C later amplified this by ordering Forces C and D to join company and sweep to within 25 miles of Milo to locate convoys ... The latter message did not reach RA(D) until after he had withdrawn outside the Aegean. RA(D) only took the decision to withdraw after careful consideration. *Dido* had expended 70% of her AA ammunition (22% having been used up between 0600 and 0930 on 21 May). *Orion* had expended 62% and *Ajax* 58%. RA(D) felt that his force might well find itself unable to deal with the further expected scale of air attack. He reported the result of his attack on the enemy convoy to the C-in-C, adding that in view of the serious shortage of AA ammunition he was joining Force A1 ...

25. On receipt of RA(D)'s 0405/22, ... the C-in-C ordered Force D to return to Alexandria with all dispatch ...

22 May

26. At daylight on 22 May the position was as follows:

(a) Force A was about 45 miles SW of the Kithera Channel steering towards the NW.
(b) Force B was joining Force A1.
(c) Force C, having reached a position off Heraklion at 0400 was now sweeping to the north-westward in search of convoys of caiques.
(d) Force D was about 30 miles W of the Kithera Channel steering to join Force A1 but were shortly to receive orders ... to return to Alexandria with all dispatch.
(e) D5 in *Kelly* with *Kashmir, Kipling, Kelvin* and *Jackal* had left Malta at 2130/21 and had orders to join Force A1 to the W of Crete at 1000/22.
(f) D14 in *Jervis* with *Nizam* and *Ilex* had returned to Alexandria to refuel and were now steering for the Kaso Strait.
(g) D10 in *Stuart* with *Voyager* and *Vendetta* had left Alexandria on 21 May with orders to join Force A1.

27. At 0830 Force C was steering towards Milo when a single caique was sighted. This caique, which was carrying German soldiers, was sunk by *Perth* whilst *Naiad* engaged large numbers of air-

craft who were bombing. At 0909 *Calcutta* reported a small merchant vessel ahead and destroyers were ordered to sink her. At 1000 Force C was 25 miles S of the eastern corner of Milo. *Perth* had rejoined after sinking the caique but *Naiad* was still some way astern. Ten minutes later an enemy destroyer with 4 or 5 small sailing vessels was sighted to the northward. Our destroyers immediately gave chase, whilst *Perth* and *Naiad* engaged the destroyer, causing her to retire under smoke. *Kingston* engaged an enemy destroyer at 7,000 yards, claiming two hits. She also reported sighting a large number of caiques behind the smoke screen, which the enemy destroyer was now making. Although in contact with the enemy convoy, CS15 considered that he would jeopardise his whole force if he proceeded any further to the northward. HA ammunition was beginning to run low. The speed of his force, which he considered must be kept together in the face of the continuous air attacks, was limited to 20 knots, on account of *Carlisle*'s maximum speed being 21 knots. CS15, therefore, decided to withdraw and ordered the destroyers to abandon the chase. The C-in-C's ... 0941/22, which showed that this convoy was of considerable size, was not seen by CS15 until after 1100.

28. Force C was bombed practically continuously from 0945 for 3½ hours. *Naiad* was damaged by near misses which put two turrets out of action and reduced her speed to 16 knots. *Carlisle* was hit but not seriously damaged. At 1321 Force A1 was sighted coming up to the Kithera Channel from the westward, in response to an appeal for support from CS15.

29. During the night 21/22 May, Force B (*Gloucester* and *Fiji* with *Greyhound* and *Griffin*) had been patrolling off Cape Matapan. Instructions from the C-in-C to proceed to Heraklion with all despatch reached them too late to be carried out, but they entered the Aegean, and, at daylight, were about 25 miles N of Canea. Whilst withdrawing towards Force A1, Force B was attacked by dive bombers almost continuously from 0630 for 1½ hours. *Fiji* received slight damage and *Gloucester* superficial damage during these attacks. Force B joined Force A1 at 0830/22.

30. Force A1 had been 45 miles SW of the Anti Kithera Channel at daylight on 22 May and was joined by Forces D and B at 0700 and 0830 respectively. The HA ammunition situation was giving cause for anxiety, the amount remaining at 0930 being:

Gloucester 18%; *Fiji* 30%; *Dido* 25%; *Orion* 38%; *Ajax* 40%; *Warspite* 66%; *Valiant* 80%.

31. CS7 had decided that he would meet Force C in the Kithera Channel about 1530. Meanwhile he continued to patrol with Forces A, B and D between 20 and 30 miles W of the channel, apparently, to use his own words, 'serving a useful purpose by attracting enemy aircraft'.

32. At 1225, CS7 heard from CS15 that *Naiad* was badly damaged and in need of support. CS7 immediately decided to enter the Aegean and increased to 23 knots.

33. CS7 sighted AA shell bursts from Force B at 1312. Twenty minutes later *Warspite* . . . was hit by a bomb which wrecked the starboard 4.5-in and 6-in batteries.

34. At 1320 *Greyhound* was detached from Force A1 to sink a large caique between Pori and Anti Kithera Islands. She successfully accomplished this and and was returning to her position on the screen when at 1351 she was hit by two bombs and 15 minutes later sank stern first . . . CS15 (who was the SO of forces present) ordered *Kandahar* and *Kingston* to pick up survivors from *Greyhound*. At 1402 CS15 ordered *Fiji*, and 5 minutes later *Gloucester*, to give *Kandahar* and *Kingston* AA support and to stand by *Greyhound* until dark. These rescuing ships and the men swimming in the water were subjected to almost continuous bombing and machine gun attacks. CS15 did not realise at first how little AA ammunition was left in *Gloucester* and *Fiji*. At 1413 CS15 asked CS7 for close support as his force had practically no ammunition left. Force A1 closed Force C at *Warspite*'s best speed (18 knots) and CS7 who was feeling uneasy about the orders given to *Gloucester* and *Fiji*, informed CS15 about the state of their AA ammunition. At 1457 CS15 ordered *Gloucester* and *Fiji* to withdraw, with ships in company, at their discretion.

35. At 1530 *Gloucester* and *Fiji* were sighted coming up astern of Force A1 at high speed, engaging enemy aircraft. At about 1530 *Gloucester* was hit by several bombs and immobilised . . . She was badly on fire and her upper deck was a shambles. In view of the continuous air attacks, *Fiji* reluctantly decided that she must leave *Gloucester. Fiji* reported the situation to CS15. After consulting CS7, CS15 decided that to take the battlefleet back in support of *Gloucester* would only be risking more ships.

36. Air attacks on Force A1 had continued intermittently from 1320 until 1510. At 1645 further high level attacks were made and *Valiant* was hit aft by two medium bombs but no serious damage was done.

37. By this time Force C was nearly out of HA ammunition and both forces were withdrawing to the south westward. Course was

altered to the southward at 1830 and to the eastward at 2100. At 1700 *Fiji*, who had *Kandahar* and *Kingston* in company, reported her position... 30 miles due E from Forces A1 and C...

38. At 1845 *Fiji* who had survived some 20 bombing attacks by aircraft formations during the past 4 hours, fell victim to a single Me109.[175] This machine flew out of the clouds in a shallow dive and dropped its bomb very close to the port side, amidships. The ship took up a 25° list and soon came to a stop with her engines crippled. Half an hour later another single machine dropped 3 bombs which landed over 'A' boiler room. The list soon increased to 30° and at 2015 the ship rolled right over. *Kandahar* and *Kingston* lowered boats and rafts and withdrew to avoid almost certain damage from air attack. They returned after dark to pick up more men and finally succeeded in rescuing a total of 523. They had been subjected to no less than 22 air attacks between 1445 and 1920 and were now getting short of fuel. At 2245 they proceeded at 15 knots to join CS15.

39. At 1928 CS7 learned from *Kandahar* that *Fiji* was sinking. CS7 immediately ordered D10 [in *Stuart*], who was to join him on the following day, to proceed with *Voyager* and *Vendetta* to *Fiji*'s position. At 2030, in accordance with instructions received from the C-in-C, he detached *Decoy* and *Hero* to the S coast of Crete to embark the King of Greece.

41. Captain D5, in *Kelly*, with *Kashmir, Kipling, Kelvin* and *Jackal* ... joined CS7 at 1600/22. At 2030 *Kelly, Kashmir* and *Kipling* were detached to look for survivors from *Fiji* and half an hour later, *Kelvin* and *Jackal* were sent to try and pick up any of *Gloucester*'s crew who could be found. CS7, however, subsequently ordered the search to be abandoned and sent the 5th DF to patrol inside Kissamo and Canea Bays. On arrival at the Anti Kithera Channel, *Kipling* developed a steering defect and D5 ordered her to join CS7. Continuing into Canea Bay, *Kelly* and *Kashmir* encountered a troop-carrying caique, which they damaged badly by gunfire. These two ships then carried out a short bombardment of Maleme. Whilst withdrawing they encountered another caique which they engaged and set on fire....

42. Force E patrolled off Heraklion during the night 21/22 May without incident and then withdrew to Alexandria. During the afternoon the C-in-C gave orders for *Ajax* and *Orion*, who were returning with RA(D) to Alexandria, to join D14 about 80 miles SW of Kaso. The intention was for this force to cover Heraklion during the night

---

[175]Messerschmitt Me109: 1935, 2 cannon, 2mg, 500lbs bombs, 380mph, range 350mls.

22/23 May. . . . In the meantime, the C-in-C had ordered D14 to pass the Kaso Strait at 2100/22 . . . *Ajax*, realising that she could not possibly join D14 in time, decided to rejoin RA(D) and informed the C-in-C accordingly.

43. At Alexandria, *Glenroy* embarked 900 men of the Queen's Royal Regt, the HQ of the 16th Infantry Bde and 18 vehicles. She sailed for Tymbaki p.m. 22 May escorted by *Coventry, Auckland* and *Flamingo*. *Jaguar* and *Defender*, after embarking ammunition urgently required by the Army, left Alexandria to join Force A1 and then proceed so as to arrive Suda during the night 23/24 May.

44. Minefields were successfully laid by *Abdiel* between Cephalonia and Lekas and by *Rorqual* in the Gulf of Salonika.

45. Meanwhile, in Crete, the enemy was concentrating on the Maleme area, where his troop carriers continued to arrive and depart on 22 May at the rate of more than 20 per hour. A plan to counter-attack Maleme had to be abandoned and our troops commenced to withdraw to a new line.

46. At 2230/22 a 'Most Immediate' message was received from CS7 . . . It appeared from this message that the battleships had run right out of pom-pom ammunition. The C-in-C accordingly decided to withdraw all forces to Alexandria . . .

23 May

48. Captain D5 with his flotilla had been retiring at full speed from Canea since dawn. After surviving two air attacks without being damaged they were attacked at 0755 by 24 Ju87 dive bombers. *Kashmir* was hit and sank in two minutes. *Kelly* was doing 30 knots, under full starboard rudder, when she was hit by a large bomb. The ship took up an ever-increasing list to port, finally turning over with considerable way on. After floating upside down for half an hour she finally sank. The dive bombers, before leaving, machine gunned the men in the water, killing and wounding several.

49. *Kipling* immediately closed to pick up survivors from *Kelly* and *Kashmir*. For three hours *Kipling* continued with her rescue work, in which she was considerably hampered by 6 high level bombing attacks. After picking up 279 officers and men from the water *Kipling* left the scene, at 1100, for Alexandria. She estimated that between 0820 and 1300 no less than 40 aircraft attacked her, dropping 83 bombs, but she emerged from this ordeal unscathed. CS15 reluctantly decided that he could send her no help from Force C or Force A1. It was necessary to send *Protector* to meet her at 0800 the next day, 50 miles from Alexandria, as she had run right out of fuel.

In these engagements, the 5th DF shot down at least two, and damaged at least four, enemy aircraft.

50. In view of the intense scale of air attack off Crete, the C-in-C, after consulting the C-in-C, Middle East, ordered *Glenroy* and escort, at 1127, to return to Alexandria. The C-in-C then made a further plan for the reinforcement of Crete, using *Abdiel* and/or destroyers. The Admiralty, at 1559, ordered *Glenroy* to turn northwards, pending instructions. At 1651 the Admiralty urged the C-in-C to land the reinforcements from *Glenroy* in Crete, if it could be done that night. At 1837 the C-in-C informed the Admiralty that it was much too late for *Glenroy* to reach Tymbaki that night (23/24 May). At 2237 the Admiralty was informed that the *Glenroy*, had she continued northward, would have been in the worst possible position for enemy air attacks at daylight. Disembarkation of troops by day was out of the question. She had, therefore, been ordered to Alexandria.

51. In Crete the Army formed a new line in the Maleme–Canea sector. Very heavy air attacks were being made on our troops, who were without fighter cover, and the enemy kept up a steady flow of reinforcements with his troop carriers. The 5 MTBs of the 10th Flotilla in Suda Bay were singled out for attack by aircraft and all were sunk. During their operations off the Cretan coast and while in harbour, the MTBs accounted for 2 aircraft for certain and 2 probably shot down. The NOIC, Suda Bay, decided that the time had come to consider plans for evacuation. . . .

52. During the night 23/24 May, *Jaguar* and *Defender* disembarked ammunition in Suda Bay and returned to Alexandria via Kaso Strait.

27 May

73. The naval situation at daylight on 27 May was:

(a) Force A, now consisting of *Queen Elizabeth, Barham, Jervis, Janus, Kelvin, Napier, Kandahar* and *Hasty*, were about 250 miles SE of Kaso. (*Ajax* and *Dido* were detached at 0600 to Alexandria.)

(b) *Abdiel, Hero* and *Nizam* had disembarked troops at Suda and were on their way back to Alexandria via the Kaso Strait, carrying 930 personnel not wanted in Crete.

(d) *Auckland* with Convoy AN31 was about 150 miles N of Alexandria, making for Crete.

74. . . . the enemy had broken through our line defending Suda with great suddenness. Four days earlier, the NOIC, Suda, had fore-

seen that this might happen and had taken a number of precautionary measures which would facilitate arrangements for evacuation.

75. Early in the forenoon, Convoy AN31 ... was ordered to turn back as it was realised that it had no chance of reaching Crete under present conditions of air attacks.

76. VA, 1BS, with Force A ... at daylight on 27 May were steering towards Kaso Strait to cover the return of *Abdiel, Hero* and *Nizam*. ... At 0858 this force was attacked by 15 Ju88s and He111s who appeared from the direction of the sun. *Barham* was hit on 'Y' turret and two of her bulges were flooded by near misses. A fire was started in *Barham* and this necessitated the force steering downwind to the S until the fire was extinguished two hours later. Two aircraft were shot down and one was seen to be damaged by gunfire. At 1230, on receipt of instructions from the C-in-C, VA, 1BS, shaped course for Alexandria, arriving there at 1900.

77. In a message timed 0824/27 ... General Wavell informed the Prime Minister that he feared we must recognise that Crete was no longer tenable and that troops must be withdrawn as far [fast] as possible. The Chiefs of Staff replied that Crete was to be evacuated forthwith. ...

78. The Navy could claim to have prevented any seaborne invasion of Crete and to have kept the Army supplied with essential reinforcements of men and stores. The RAF, owing to circumstances beyond their control, had so far been unable to give any direct help to the Navy. The fleet had inflicted considerable losses on the German troop-carrying convoys ... Twenty enemy aircraft had been shot down for certain, with 11 probables. At least 15 aircraft appeared to have been damaged. But the losses and damage sustained by the fleet had been severe. Officers and men had been subject to prolonged strain from the constant bombing. Little rest could be given, as a formidable task lay before the Fleet – the evacuation of some 22,000 men from Crete to Egypt.

235 *Cunningham's Dispatch on the Evacuation of Crete*

14 September 1941

Phase IV: The evacuation of British and Imperial troops from the island

Cunningham's Observations

2. The evacuation followed without intermission on the Battle of Crete ... and threw a final and almost intolerable strain on the light

forces, most of whom had been operating at sea almost continuously since the beginning of operation LUSTRE on 4 March.

3. Only one of the evacuations, that from Heraklion, could be made from a port with any facilities at all. All the remainder had to be taken from the small open beach at Sphakia to which access from the land was difficult and slow. This, together with the disorganisation resulting from the events previously described, led to a constant fluctuation in the forecast of numbers to be embarked and made both the organisation and performance of the evacuation most difficult.

4. ... Major General J. F. Evetts was sent from the GHQ, Middle East, to act as Military Liaison Officer on my staff. His judgement and co-operation were invaluable.[176]

At the same time an organisation was set up in the C-in-C's offices for the co-ordination of fighter protection at sea. Group Captain C. R. B. Pelly was sent from the HQ, RAF, Middle East, to undertake this organisation which, under his able management, pulled rapidly into shape and undoubtedly saved us many casualties.[177]

5. The first day of the evacuation was not encouraging. In the evacuation of Heraklion, Rear Admiral H. B. Rawlings, CS7, was faced with many difficult decisions. It was unfortunate that *Ajax* was not retained with Force B and much overcrowding thereby avoided, but the slight nature of her damage was not apparent to CS7 ...

6. The actual embarkation from Heraklion was most expeditiously carried out and reflected credit on all concerned both ashore and afloat.

7. The breakdown of *Imperial*'s steering gear was a bitter misfortune which carried disaster in its train. The handling of *Hotspur* in embarking and carrying a total of 900 men must have been admirable.[178]

8. As a direct result of this delay, Force B and the RAF fighters failed to make contact at daylight. The force was consequently exposed, starting only a few miles from the enemy's air base in Scarpanto, to the full weight of enemy air attack without any air support, until the first of our fighters eventually gained contact at 1200.

---

[176]Evetts left shortly after for India.

[177]Gr Capt (later ACM Sir Claude) C. R. B. Pelly (1902–72): IDC 1952–53; C-in-C, MEAF 1953–56; Controller of A/c, M. Supply, 1956–59; ret 1959.

[178]*Hotspur*'s 1st Lt, Lt (later Cdr) H. Hodgkinson, in *Before the Tide Turned: The Mediterranean Experiences of a British Destroyer Officer in 1941* (London, 1944), pp. 142–54, describes this incident graphically. The Capt was Lt-Cdr C. P. F. Brown: Lt-Cdr 1934; *Gallant* July 1938; temp i/c *Hotspur* 1941; Cdr June 1942; *Swiftsure* Nov. 1943; *Pickle* & SO, 7th M/S Flo. Feb. 1945.

The consequence of this unhampered onslaught of aircraft was the loss of *Hereward* and the damage to *Orion* and *Dido*. The difficult decision to leave *Hereward* to her fate was undoubtedly correct and it is at least some consolation that a large proportion of those on board survived.

9. This disastrous voyage left the C-in-C in a most unpleasant quandary. Of the 4,000 troops embarked in Force B no less than 800 had been killed, wounded or captured, after leaving Crete. If this was to be the scale of casualties, it appeared that, quite apart from our own prospective losses of ships and men, who could ill be spared, our efforts to rescue the Army from capture might only lead to the destruction of a large proportion of the troops. It was only after long and anxious consideration that the decision to continue the evacuation could be taken.

10. The decision to continue, once taken, was amply justified, for the remainder of the evacuation proceeded almost without casualty to personnel. Fighter protection became steadily more effective and the enemy less enterprising; his failure to interfere with the nightly embarkation at Sphakia was most surprising, and reminiscent of the Greek evacuation.

11. Vice Admiral E. L. S. King, CS15, carried out two successful evacuations, embarking large numbers of troops each time on the nights of 29/30 May and the final night 31 May/1 June. On the first occasion we were fortunate that, although *Perth* was hit and damaged, *Glengyle* escaped unscathed with her load of some 3,000 men. The landing craft she carried to Crete on this occasion were invaluable at this and subsequent embarkations.

12. The achievement of Captain S. H. T. Arliss, Captain (D), 7DF, in *Napier* in embarking 700 men each in *Napier* and *Nizam* on the night 30/31 May was noteworthy. He had been deprived, by defects and damage, of two of his force, but accomplished his tasks without any reduction in the numbers to be embarked.

13. The loss of *Calcutta* on 1 June, only 100 miles from Alexandria, came as a final blow. This fine little ship had a record of arduous service and gallant endeavour in the face of air attack which must be almost unsurpassed in the Royal Navy. She fell, it may almost be said, to 'a bow drawn at a venture' and the Mediterranean Fleet is the poorer by her loss.

Captain W. P. Carne, in *Coventry*, had an anxious time recovering her survivors and did well to save so many.[179]

[179] Capt W. P. Carne: fmly FTO; Actg Capt *Coventry* May 1941.

14. The decision to attempt no further evacuation on the night 1/2 June was made with the greatest reluctance, but with dwindling forces and men and machinery at the point of exhaustion, a further attempt when the forces had already been ordered to surrender could not be justified. It was particularly galling that a large proportion of the men left to surrender consisted of the Royal Marines, who fought so gallant a rearguard action.

15. Where so much fine service was performed it is difficult, as ever, to pick out individual acts of merit. Reference must be made however to the fearless judgement and gallant bearing of Rear Admiral Rawlings... in extricating his shattered squadron on 29 May and in bringing it safely to harbour....

16. The bearing and discipline of officers and men of all services in this ordeal was a source of inspiration. In particular the behaviour of men in the crowded ships of Force B on 29 May was most notable in face of the hammering they endured.

17. ... It is not easy to convey how heavy was the strain that men and ships sustained. Apart from the cumulative effect of prolonged seagoing over extended periods it has to be remembered that in this last instance ships' companies had none of the inspiration of battle with the enemy to bear them up. Instead they had the unceasing anxiety of the task of trying to bring away in safety, thousands of their own countrymen, many of whom were in an exhausted and dispirited condition, in ships necessarily so overcrowded that even where there was opportunity to relax conditions made this impossible. They had started the evacuation already over-tired and they had to carry it through under conditions of savage air attack such as had only recently caused grievous losses in the fleet.

There is rightly little credit or glory to be expected in these operations of retreat but I feel that the spirit of tenacity shown by those who took part should not go unrecorded.

More than once I felt the stage had been reached where no more could be asked of officers and men, physically and mentally exhausted by their efforts and by the events of these fateful weeks. It is perhaps even now not realised how nearly the breaking point was reached, but that these men struggled through is the measure of their achievement and I trust that it will not lightly be forgotten.

Narrative

... the Mediterranean Fleet had already lost two cruisers and four destroyers besides having the aircraft carrier, two battleships, one cruiser and one destroyer virtually out of action. Another five cruisers and four destroyers had suffered minor damage, which did not, however, greatly affect their steaming powers or fighting efficiency. The fleet was now given the task of attempting to evacuate some 22,000 men, mostly from an open beach on the S coast of Crete, 360 miles from the fleet base at Alexandria.

2. Up to date the fleet had been required to operate without fighter protection (except for the brief period on 26 May, when *Formidable*'s fighters were available).... the RAF would do all possible to provide some fighter cover for ships but owing to the distance from our bases, the cover would be only meagre and spasmodic....

28/29 May

6. At 0600 on 28 May, Force B, consisting of CS7 in *Orion* with *Ajax, Dido, Decoy, Jackal, Imperial, Hotspur, Kimberley* and *Hereward*, left Alexandria to evacuate the Heraklion garrison. Force B was about 90 miles from Scarpanto at 1700 and from then until dark was subjected to a series of air attacks, consisting of high level bombing, dive bombing and torpedo attack. At 1920 *Imperial* was near-missed but at the time appeared to be undamaged. At 2100 *Ajax* had a close miss which started a small fire, seriously wounded 20 men and caused slight damage to the ship's side. In view of the need for ships to be fully efficient to carry out the night evacuation and to cope with the almost certain air attacks on the following day, CS7, after receiving a report of damage from *Ajax*, decided that she should return to Alexandria....

7. After passing through the Kaso Strait and turning to the westward, Force B was attacked by a torpedo plane, without result. The force arrived off Heraklion at 2330. The destroyers immediately entered harbour to embark troops from the jetties and ferry them to the cruisers outside. By 0245 the ferrying was complete and by 0300 *Kimberley* and *Imperial* had embarked the rearguard. At 0320 the force proceeded at 20 knots, having embarked the whole of the Heraklion garrison, amounting to some 4,000 troops. Twenty-five minutes later *Imperial*'s steering gear failed and she narrowly missed colliding with both cruisers. This could scarcely have happened at a more inopportune time since it was essential to be as far from enemy air bases as possible by daylight. CS7 was faced with the difficult decision whether to wait in the hope that the steering gear could be repaired or to sink the *Imperial* and carry on.

8. On hearing that *Imperial* was quite unable to steer, CS7 reduced the speed of his force to 15 knots and gave *Hotspur* orders to take off all *Imperial*'s troops and crew and then sink her. This was successfully accomplished at 0445 and *Hotspur*, who now had a total of 900 men on board, rejoined the squadron just after daylight.

9. The delay over *Imperial* had caused Force B to be an hour and a half late on their time table and it was not until sunrise that they turned to the southward through the Kaso Strait. Air attacks began at 0600 and continued at intervals until 1500 when Force B was within 100 miles of Alexandria.

10. At 0625 *Hereward* was hit by a bomb which caused her to reduce speed and fall away from her position on the screen. The force was now in the middle of the Kaso Strait and CS7 had to make the difficult decision whether to wait, in order to assist *Hereward*, or to leave her behind. He decided that to wait would be to invite further casualties. As *Hereward* could then be seen making for Crete, which was only 5 miles away, CS7 proceeded on his way. *Hereward* was last seen making slowly towards the island, with her guns engaging enemy aircraft.

11. Arrangements had been made for fighter protection to be provided at 0530 in the Kaso Strait and CS7 had corrected, by signal, his time of arrival in the Strait to 0630. It is believed that the fighters did reach the Strait at the corrected time but they were unable to make contact with the ships.

12. At 0645 *Decoy* reported fractured turbine feet and circulator damage, as the result of a near miss. This caused the speed of the squadron to be reduced to 25 knots. At 0700 a very close miss on *Orion* caused a further reduction to 21 knots.

13. The C-in-C realised from CS7's signals that our fighters had not yet appeared and every endeavour was made to put this right. It is probable, however, that the aircraft had navigational difficulties as they were unable to make contact with the ships until 1200. By this time the force had suffered severely. At 0735 the Flag Captain in the *Orion* (Captain G. R. B. Back) had been severely wounded by an explosive bullet from a Ju87 and he died two hours later.[180] At 0815 *Dido* was hit on 'B' turret and 45 minutes later *Orion* was hit on 'A' turret, both by bombs from Ju87s. In each case the turrets were put out of action. At 1045 *Orion* was again attacked by 11 Ju87s and a bomb passed through her bridge putting the lower conning tower

---

[180]Capt G. R. B. Back: Capt 1936; Capt (D) 21DF, *Duncan,* China, July 1939; *Orion* Jan. 1940.

out of action. The force was then about 100 miles from Kaso and this was the last attack to be made by Ju87s.

14. The *Orion* had nearly 1,100 troops on board and the casualties on the crowded mess decks were very heavy. Three of the Engineer Officers were killed, all normal communication between bridge and engine room was destroyed, the steering gear was put out of action and three boiler rooms were damaged. It is believed a total of 260 were killed and 280 wounded.

15. *Orion* was out of control until the after steering wheel could be connected and a chain of men arranged to pass orders from the Emergency Conning Position to the wheel. Owing to contamination of the oil fuel with salt water, *Orion*'s speed varied from 12 [to] 25 knots but she was able to average about 21 knots.

16. There was a lull in the air attacks until about 1300 when there was a high level attack followed by another at 1330 and a final one at 1500. The first and only friendly fighters to be seen were two Naval Fulmars which appeared at noon. RAF squadrons had made several attempts to find our ships and in the course of a number of engagements had shot down two Ju88s for the loss of one Hurricane. One Ju87 was shot down by ships' gunfire.

17. The force arrived at Alexandria at 2000 on 29 May, *Orion* having only 10 tons of fuel and two rounds of 6-in HE ammunition remaining.

18. While the troops were being taken off at Heraklion, destroyers were withdrawing a smaller party from Sphakia on the S coast of Crete.

19. Sphakia is a small fishing village with one shingle beach, of which a stretch less than a cable in extent could be used for embarking in boats. The road over the mountains from Suda to Sphakia finished up with a series of acute hairpin bends and came to an abrupt termination at the top of a 500-foot escarpment. From this point a precipitous goat track led down to the village. It was necessary for the troops to remain hidden from air observation until actually called forward to embark. Touch between the beach area and the top of the escarpment had to be maintained on foot as there was no signal communication. The climb required at least two hours to complete.

20. The HQ of the GOC, Troops in Crete, and the NOIC, Suda, had been shifted to a cave near Sphakia.... The RAF W/T set at the Sphakia HQ was used for outside naval communications.

21. Force C consisting of D7 in *Napier* with *Nizam, Kelvin* and *Kandahar,* had left Alexandria at 0800 on 28 May after embarking

additional whalers and some provisions and small arms for the troops ashore. After an uneventful passage, the force arrived off Sphakia and started the evacuation at 0300/29.

22. The embarkation was completed by 0300 by which time the four destroyers had embarked nearly 700 troops and had landed badly needed rations for 15,000. Soon after 0900 on 29 May, Force C was attacked by 4 Ju88s and *Nizam* suffered minor damage from a near miss. Fighter protection for Force C had been arranged from 0545/29 and at 0940 a crashed enemy aircraft was sighted, probably shot down by fighters. The remainder of the passage was uneventful, Force C arriving Alexandria at 1700/29.

23. At 2100/28, Force D, consisting of CS15 in *Phoebe*, with *Perth*, *Glengyle*, *Calcutta*, *Coventry*, *Jervis*, *Janus* and *Hasty* left Alexandria for Sphakia, where they were to embark troops during the night 29/30 May.

24. ... It was deduced ... that the situation in Crete was very bad but that 10,000 troops remained to be evacuated. Of these, only 2,000 would be in organised bodies. The night 29/30 May would have to be the last night for evacuation.

29/30 May

29. Captain D10 in *Stuart*, with *Jaguar* and *Defender* left Alexandria p.m. on 29 May to join Force D. These destroyers had no troops and the intention was that in addition to providing extra protection to Force D they would be available to take troops off any ship which might be damaged by air attack.

30. ... it became clear that the situation in Crete was not so desperate as had been thought. The C-in-C therefore decided to send four destroyers to embark men on the night of 30/31 May.

31. Meanwhile Force D under CS15 were proceeding to Sphakia. At 1003 on 29 May, a single Ju88 dropped a stick of bombs close to *Perth* without result. *Glengyle* and the cruisers of Force D were anchored off Sphakia by 2330/29 whilst the AA cruisers and destroyers patrolled to seaward. The AA cruisers were not required to embark any troops but the destroyers closed in one at a time to embark their quota. The troops were ferried from the beach to the ships in *Glengyle*'s landing craft, assisted by two LCAs which had been carried in *Perth*. The beach was too small for ships' boats to be used in addition. By 0320/30 a total of about 6,000 men had been embarked and Force D proceeded towards Alexandria. Three motor landing craft were left behind for use on subsequent nights.

30/31 May

32. At 0645/30, *Stuart, Jaguar* and *Defender* joined Force D... There were three air attacks on the force during the passage to Alexandria. In the first of these at 0930, *Perth* was hit and her foremost boiler room put out of action. In the second and third attacks there was no result although bombs fell very close to *Perth* and *Jaguar*. Some of our fighter patrols failed to make contact with Force D but the force was covered by two or three RAF fighters during most of the day. These fighters, on one occasion, drove off 20 Ju87s and Ju88s, and in various engagements shot down two He111s and damaged a number of other aircraft. In addition one Ju88 was seen to be damaged by ships' gunfire.

33. At 0915/30, Force C consisting of D7 in *Napier*, with *Nizam, Kelvin* and *Kandahar*, left Alexandria for Sphakia, where they were to embark troops during the night 30/31 May. At 1245, *Kandahar* developed a mechanical defect and was ordered to return to Alexandria. At 1530 three Ju88s carried out an unseen dive from astern of Force C, causing damage to *Kelvin* from a near miss, reducing her speed to 20 knots. Captain D7, therefore, ordered *Kelvin* back to Alexandria. Half an hour later Force D was sighted returning to Alexandria. CS15 was prepared to augment D7's reduced force by detaching *Jaguar* but found that she was too short of fuel.

34. Force C arrived off Sphakia at 0030/31 and commenced the embarkation of troops using the three motor landing craft..., supplemented by ships' boats. By 0300/31, *Napier* and *Nizam* had embarked about 700 troops each and started on their return journey to Alexandria.

35. The usual fighter protection had been arranged and D7 reports sighting friendly fighters at 0625. These RAF fighters claim to have shot down three Ju88s and one Cant 1007 during the day. One Ju88 was shot down by gunfire and three were damaged. From 0850 to 0915 Force C was attacked by about 12 Ju88s which were not seen before they dived in to the attack. As a result of the air attack, *Napier* sustained damage in the engine and boiler rooms from near misses, reducing her speed to 23 knots.

The force arrived at Alexandria at 1900/31.

38. A number of small naval craft had been employed on local defence duties in Crete. When the evacuation commenced all small craft fit to move were sailed to Alexandria. Those which had to be destroyed or beached in Suda Bay were KOS23, *Widnes* and LCT

A16. Craft sunk by air attack on passage to Alexandria were ML1011, KOS22 and *Syvern*. Nothing is known of the fate of ML1030 and LCT A6 and A20, and it is presumed that they were sunk by enemy air action on passage. The only vessels of the original local defence flotilla to reach Alexandria were KOS21, *Lanner*.[181]

31 May/1 June

39. At 0600/31, CS15 in *Phoebe*, with *Abdiel, Kimberley, Hotspur* and *Jackal* left Alexandria to carry out the final evacuation from Sphakia.

40. During the forenoon of 31 May, the C-in-C received a message from Captain D7, which indicated that there were roughly 6,500 more men to come off from Crete. The C-in-C accordingly authorised CS15 to increase the maximum number to be brought off to 3,500.

43. At about 2030 on 31 May, the C-in-C received a message from General Blamey, who was perturbed at the small number of Australians so far taken out of Crete and asking for a ship to be sent to Plaka where he believed a number of our troops had assembled.[182] The C-in-C replied that at this late hour it was not possible to alter the destination of the ships.

44. During the passage to Sphakia, CS15's force was attacked by aircraft on three occasions between 1825 and 1905/31. None of the bombs fell very close and it was believed that one Ju88 was damaged. Many bombs were seen to be jettisoned on the horizon, indicating successful combats by our fighter aircraft.

45. CS15 arrived at Sphakia at 2320/31. Three fully-loaded LCMs ... immediately went alongside the ships, thus saving a valuable 40 minutes. The embarkation proceeded so quickly that for a time the beach was empty of troops. This was unfortunate, as it caused a last minute rush of troops, some of whom had necessarily to be left behind.

46. Some medical stores were landed by the ships and finally the three LCMs were sunk or disabled. The force sailed at 0300 on 1 June, having embarked nearly 4,000 troops.

---

[181]KOS 21, KOS 22: ex-whalers, Norway, 1921; A/S vessels, 350t; KOS21 s, bombs, Oct. 1941.
Widnes: 1918, 800t, 1×4in, 1×3in, 16k; salved by Germans, recom *Uj-2109;* s by Allied ships, Aegean, Oct. 1943.
Syvern: whaler, 1937, 307t.
LCT *A16:* 1940, 226t.
[182]Gen Sir Thomas Blamey (1884–1951): WW1 staff officer, Aust Imp Forces; police chief between wars; cmdg Aust Corps Feb. 1940; C-in-C Aust Mil Forces Mar. 1942; Allied army cdr, SW Pacific Area; FM 1950.

48. ... Included in the rearguard, who were left behind, were a large number of the Special Service troops landed as a final reinforcement at Suda and many Royal Marines of the MNBDO. Of the 2,000 Royal Marines employed in Crete, only 1,000 got back to Egypt.

49. In order to provide additional protection to CS15's force, the AA cruisers *Calcutta* and *Coventry* were sailed from Alexandria early on 1 June to rendezvous with the returning ships. At 0900 aircraft were detected by RDF approaching from the N, and at 0917 the ships hoisted the red warning. It was unfortunate that an 'up sun' barrage was not then fired as five minutes later two Ju88s dived on the cruisers from the direction of the sun. A stick of bombs from the first machine just missed *Coventry* but two bombs from the second machine hit *Calcutta,* who settled fast and sank within a few minutes. *Coventry* was able to pick up 23 officers and 232 men with whom she at once returned to Alexandria.

50. The force with CS15 had an uneventful passage to Alexandria where they arrived at 1700 on 1 June.

PART IV

THE FIGHT AT ODDS,
JUNE 1941 TO MARCH 1942

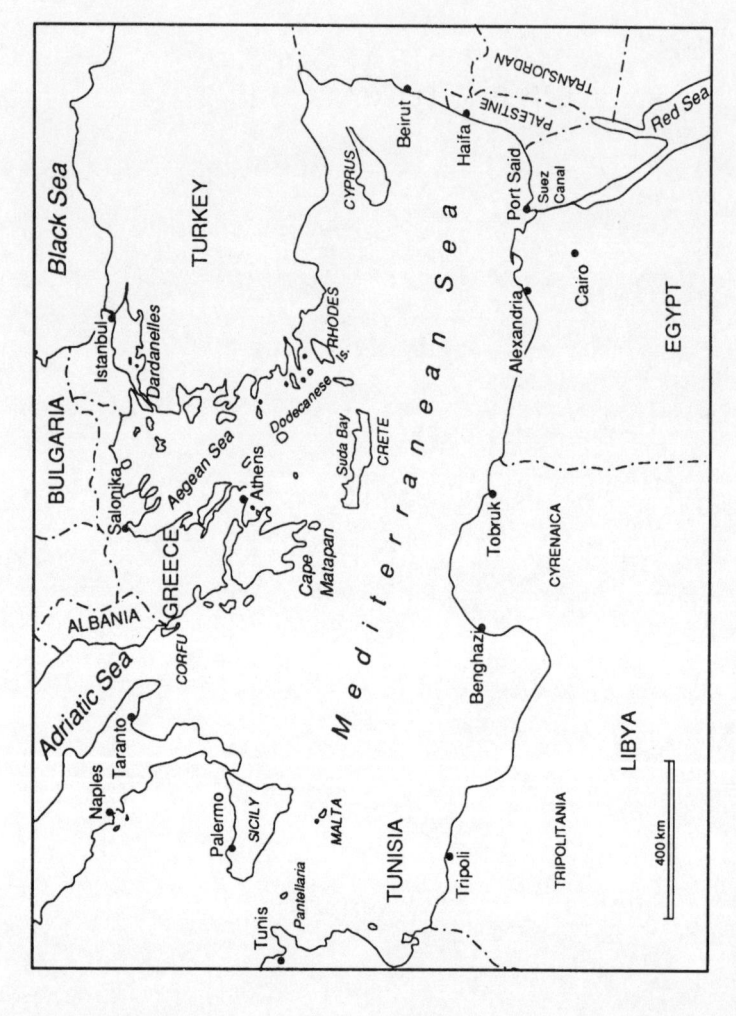

The Eastern Mediterranean, 1941–42

This phase was a galling one for the offensively minded Cunningham, for he was compelled, by his fleet's general weakness, the lack of a carrier and the loss of Libyan airfields, to adopt a specifically defensive strategy [236]. He told Admiral Kelly in Ankara, 'I hate this being cooped up in the Eastern Mediterranean and very nearly go into a frenzy when I hear of Italian surface ships being at sea in the Central Mediterranean'.[1] Only local initiatives were possible, such as the stationing of Force K at Malta. Otherwise, the fleet was unable to move without peril beyond shore-based air cover, or because destroyers could not be spared to screen the battleships [260].

Even before the end of the Cretan débacle, Cunningham had to turn his attention to the Levant. The Vichy regime in Syria and Lebanon, always hostile and pro-Axis, had begun to afford the Germans airfield and other facilities, thus assisting the Nazi scheme to foment an anti-British revolt in Iraq [214]. Cunningham was perturbed by the increased threat to the fleet's oil supplies and to shipping and bases right down to the Red Sea should the Luftwaffe use Syrian airfields [218, 236]. It was decided to mount a joint British and Free French assault on the colonies from Palestine. The Navy was to provide a squadron to deal with French naval units at Beirut, coastal patrols, flank protection, bombardment and naval fighter and strike aircraft. Godfroy eased Cunningham's mind by assuring him that operations against Syria, which began on 7 June, would not affect the situation in Alexandria [244]. Cunningham, hoping for a speedy end to the operation, sought to limit the conflict while affording effective support to the Army's advance [238–9]. Fighters and torpedo bombers performed valiantly in the face of fierce resistance, though in general air cover for the ships was inadequate, despite other areas being denuded to supply it. Little in the way of Vichy reinforcements reached Syria. The principal opposition came from Vichy submarines and several well-handled, powerful and exceptionally fast *contre-torpilleurs*, which conducted brief, high-speed, long-range engagements and were difficult to counter.[2]

[1]Cunningham to Kelly, 4 Aug. 1941, KEL 43, *Kelly Papers*, NMM.
On the new situation, see Jt Planning Ctee, appreciations, 15 May 1941, CAB79/11, & 22 & 24 July 1941, CAB79/13.
[2]*Valmy* (1930), *Vauquelin* (1934), *Guépard* (1929): 2,450t, 5×5.5in, 6–7×21.7in tt, 39k.

Several British destroyers were damaged in the five-week campaign but the net result was to give Cunningham control of the Syrian and Lebanese ports [244, 246–7, 250–1, 255].

A consequence of British reverses and weaknesses on land, in the air and at sea was to intensify the interdependence of the three services and to focus the minds of the Commanders-in-Chief on the establishment of firm control of the Middle East and eastern basin, the rebuilding of their strength, and concentration on a single offensive – clearing the enemy from North Africa. Thus, when the Chiefs of Staff, prodded by Churchill, sought to commit them to an early invasion of Sicily, they dissented diplomatically but firmly, for good reasons. London, anxious to capitalise on presumed Italian demoralisation following a renewed British desert offensive, and the new preoccupation of the Germans with a winter campaign in the Soviet Union, ordered plans to be made for a descent on Sicily. Its conquest would safeguard the trans-Mediterranean route, relieve Malta and give Britain a handy foothold for an eventual invasion of mainland Europe. The Middle East commanders, in the light of local conditions, responded with caution. The planned British offensive had not yet begun and it was still possible that Britain would have to counter a German advance into the Middle East from southern Russia. Cunningham, with the Greek and Cretan experiences etched vividly in his mind, feared a premature invasion, the likely aerial toll on ships, the diversion of forces from other vital operations, and the launching of an assault inadequately prepared and equipped. Like his fellow Commanders-in-Chief, he was sceptical about the rosy picture painted by Churchill and the Chiefs of Staff. Opposed landings on an unfamiliar coast in midwinter would be hazardous. The adventure was likely to turn into another Greece, as the enemy could bring superior strength to bear. Moreover, maintenance of the island would entail a fresh major burden on the scarcest of all resources – merchant shipping. Furthermore, Tripoli, relatively easier to seize, hold and maintain, would serve just as well as Sicily to control the sea lanes and as an air base from which to attack Italy. Another alternative, the capture of Bizerta, while strategically appealing, was unacceptable politically as it would probably throw Vichy fully into Axis arms. In the face of all the objections raised by the Mediterranean high command, the operation was cancelled. One senses that the Chiefs of Staff were grateful to their Middle Eastern subordinates for enabling them to wriggle free from yet another bizarre exercise in armchair strategy. When one considers the extensive planning and enormous forces required for the invasion of Sicily in 1943, one marvels at the serious attention given to WHIPCORD in London in 1941, especially as events in the Far East were moving Asia rapidly towards war [265–73].[3]

The Army's desert offensive of November 1941 was a limited but temporary success, for early in 1942 British forces were driven back relentlessly by Rommel, halting only at El Alamein in Egypt in the summer. Cunningham assisted the offensive by bombardments, though causing little damage. The Inshore Squadron again performed heroically, chiefly on the Tobruk run, suffering numerous casualties. Fleet destroyers also shouldered much of the burden and equally hazardous service was performed by numerous auxiliaries and schooners. This commitment, which should have been ended by Wavell's BATTLEAXE offensive of June 1941, extended into the autumn as a consequence of that operation's failure. Since fighter cover was at best patchy, as much of the voyage as possible was made at night. Admiral Sir Walter Cowan, serving with the commandos at Tobruk, recalled 'the destroyers creeping in unfailingly, night after night, never a light, hardly a whisper, shooting out all the 40 tons of cargo and soldiers, bundling in the wounded and more soldiers and out again in under the hour'.[4] An added burden (unneccessary in Cunningham's view) was the replacement of Australian by Polish troops. CRUSADER required more supplies and the clearance of captured ports and led to more loss and damage. However, it did raise the siege of Tobruk, which, thanks to the maritime effort, was able to play a role in the offensive. By that time, Cunningham seems to have been rueing his springtime promise to succour Tobruk; it was hardly a cost-effective operation [244, 247, 250, 253, 255–6, 259–61, 263–4, 268, 275, 281–2, 289, 291, 296–7, 301, 319]. Enormous sacrifices had been made in support of the Army and it was vital to hold the enemy as far to the west as possible in order to defend the convoys to Malta. Thus early in 1942 Cunningham was alarmed, understandably, by the Army's gloomy forecast that the retreat would continue and that a counter-attack was not possible before August 1942 [313, 317, 322].

Following Greece and Crete, Cunningham reassessed the general air situation and his own specific problems [226]. The key to the Navy's ability to sustain both Malta and Tobruk, indeed to all of its operations, was air power. In the absence of a carrier, this involved greater dependence on the RAF and the necessity for closer co-

---

[3]See S. W. C. Pack, *Operation 'Husky': The Allied Invasion of Sicily* (Newton Abbot, 1977).
[4]Cowan to Cunningham, 16 Jan 1942, BM Add Mss 52562, *Cunningham Papers,* BL.

operation. However, relations with the RAF were much less happy following Longmore's departure in the spring. Tedder, though undoubtedly able and a man of wide vision, seemed rather less sympathetic to naval requests.[5] The RAF had been unable to afford cover during the Greek and Crete operations but there was now an imperative necessity to have effective land-based fighter protection for convoys, harbours and fleet operations. The absence of a carrier meant that shore-based air reconnaissance would have to be much more comprehensive and reliable. There was a need also to keep enemy ports, convoys and airfields under constant attack.

Cunningham believed that the Government failed to understand the crucial role of air power in the theatre. Recognising that Tedder's forces were fully stretched, he maintained the pressure for more substantial reinforcements [226, 289]. He complained that RAF aircrew were untrained for operations over the sea and that they snubbed the Navy's offer to train them. Not only was their navigation poor but reconnaissance was patchy and they were reluctant to attack shipping by day and often unable to score hits when they did so. He made damaging comparisons on their respective efficiency between the RAF and the Axis air forces [244, 246–7, 255, 259–60, 263, 287, 289, 292, 301, 305, 307–8, 312].

Cunningham concluded that the solution lay in a Naval Co-operation Group under his operational control, analogous to the Admiralty's relationship with Coastal Command at home . His campaign turned into 'a fierce battle with Tedder' [241, 248, 255, 274]. Cunningham wanted squadrons to be assigned permanently to maritime tasks, for which they would be specially trained [251]. Tedder felt that between the Army's demands for ground support and the Navy's call for a Coastal Command, the junior service was in danger of losing its rationale and independence [240, 248, 312]. He refused also to allocate any of his scant forces solely to maritime duties which might be intermittent, thus leaving valuable aircraft idle [238–9]. As there was deadlock in Cairo, Cunningham sought Pound's assistance and in October after 'a pretty stiff fight', the Chiefs of Staff agreed to the setting up of No.201 Naval Co-operation Group. Though it would remain under RAF command and its aircraft could be seconded to other duties when they had priority

---

[5]Longmore seems to have been the scapegoat for the RAF's inability to provide adequate air cover in the Greek and Cretan campaigns. C. MacDonald, *The Lost Battle: Crete 1941* (London, 1993), pp. 127, 234. See esp. *The Papers of Marshal of the RAF Lord Portal*, File 12, 'RAF Middle East', folder 1; Files 1 & 2 'Prime Minister's Minutes', 1941; & Box 9, letters by or about Longmore and Tedder (Library, Christ Church College, Oxford).

(such as the Army's forthcoming CRUSADER offensive), the group headquarters were to be alongside Cunningham's, aircrew were to be trained in maritime operations, which was to be their principal function, and Cunningham was to wield operational control [262-3]. A 'first class' man, Air Commodore Slatter, was appointed to command the group and by November Cunningham reported that 'matters are much improved' [282, 293, 301].[6] Co-operation was much more effective, aircraft more efficient and, with common headquarters, problems could be resolved at once. A definite programme of building up the group was undertaken. It was intended to raise its strength to about 20 squadrons of reconnaissance planes, bombers, torpedo bombers, and long-range and short-range fighters [290, 299, 311].

Cunningham had largely won his 'fierce battle' but shortcomings in performance remained [286, 301, 307, 308]. When the Far Eastern war broke out on 7 December, followed shortly by the loss of *Prince of Wales* and *Repulse,* Pound raised with Cunningham the issue of withdrawing the heavy ships and some other vessels from the Mediterranean to furnish the new Eastern Fleet [294].[7] Cunningham, while understandably reluctant to contemplate such a drastic step, was prepared to do so provided that 201 Group was greatly strengthened and dedicated solely to maritime functions. As a convinced Mediterraneanist, he warned that efforts to shore up the Far East should not be at the expense of Britain's hard-won and strategically vital and promising Mediterranean position [295, 300]. More importantly, lamentable performances by the RAF quickly caused him to withdraw his cautious and grudging acknowledgment that air power might take the place of capital ships [301, 305]. The crippling of his last two battleships by Italian human torpedoes on 19 December made the question academic.

A number of FAA squadrons remained in the Middle East after *Formidable* went for repair in the United States. Some operated already from shore stations, notably 830 (Swordfish) at Malta, soon joined by 828 (Albacores, ex-*Formidable*), achieving significant successes against enemy convoys and mining harbours. A fighter wing supported land operations in the Western Desert and in Syria, while

---

[6]Air Cdre (later AM Sir) Leonard H. Slatter (1894–1961): b Durban; H Spd Flt 1926–27; CO ftr sqdns 1929–31; Snr RAF Ofcr *Courageous* 1932–35; Admin, Br Forces in Iraq Feb 1940; AOC Abyssinia 1940–41; 201 N Co-op Grp 1941–42; 15 Grp, Coastal Cmd 1943; C-in-C, Coastal Cmd 1945–48.

[7]*Prince of Wales*: 1941, 35,000t, 10×14in, 16×5.25in, 28k; s 10 Dec. 1941.
Repulse: 1916, 32,000t, 6×15in, 15×4in, 8×21in tt, 29k; s 10 Dec. 1941.

the TSR squadrons proved to be extremely accurate bombers over land [244, 246, 250, 257, 260, 263–4, 310].

The loss in November of *Barham* and in December of *Queen Elizabeth* and *Valiant*, together with the continued absence of a carrier, meant that 'there is now no fleet to go to sea in', though fleet operations had been few and far between since Matapan [322]. The demands for light craft made by the Greek and Cretan situations and by the many local convoys and Tobruk meant that often there were insufficient destroyers to form a screen. Casualties sustained in the spring of 1941 further reduced the flotillas. The departure of *Formidable* meant that the fleet was tied to night operations or to movements within reach of shore-based fighters, few of which were long-range machines. When the HALBERD and SUBSTANCE convoys were run from Gibraltar to Malta by Force H in July and September respectively, Cunningham could do little but feint briefly with the fleet and transmit misleading signals [251, 260, 282, 298]. A sortie by the fleet in November in support of light striking forces from Malta, which put to sea to attack Italian convoys resulted in the sinking of *Barham* by one of the newly arrived German U-boats, which actually aimed at *Queen Elizabeth* but missed her because the fleet was turning away. Lack of asdic practice, the failure to respond to a contact and the absence of carrier-borne anti-submarine patrols, as well as extreme skill on the part of the U-boat, led to her loss with heavy casualties [291, 293].[8]

If the fleet was relatively inactive, the period from the spring of 1941 to the spring of 1942 was probably the most productive one of the war for British submarines. During this period, the 1st Flotilla (Alexandria) and the 10th Flotilla (Malta) sank 69 ships totalling 292,000 tons, for the loss of 12 boats, four of which were destroyed by bombing at Malta. The focus was squarely on the Libyan convoys though they also operated in the Adriatic and Aegean, penetrating harbours, landing agents and demolition parties, and attacking small craft by gunfire. They performed also important reconnaissance roles. Some of the large, old boats and minelayers were employed in running vital supplies to Malta when surface convoys could not be sailed. High standards of initiative, boldness, persistence and marksmanship were achieved. Cunningham was fully alive to their splendid work and priceless value and sensitive to the stresses and dangers faced by their crews. He took personal charge

---

[8]Cdr H. Hodgkinson, *Before the Tide Turned: The Mediterranean Experiences of a British Destroyer Officer in 1941* (London, 1944), pp. 224–30.

THE FIGHT AT ODDS, 1941–1942 455

of their disposition, deploying the 'U' class in the Ionian Sea and the Straits of Messina and the larger boats in the Adriatic and Aegean and off Benghazi and calling for additional boats. The enemy responded by laying more minefields and by equipping Italian escorts with German sonar; Axis anti-submarine work became increasingly effective.[9] However, the German Naval High Command noted in September 1941 that 'the most dangerous British weapon in the Mediterranean is the submarine.... A very serious supply crisis must occur relatively soon', reiterating this concern in November: 'Enemy submarines definitely have the upper hand'.[10] Together with Malta-based aircraft and surface striking forces, they began to have an alarming impact on Rommel's supplies and reinforcements [243, 251, 256–61, 264, 268, 274, 281, 286, 289, 291, 293, 297, 302, 305–7, 313, 315, 318–21, 325].

One or two submarine minelayers were generally on the station and occasionally one or two of the new fast minelayers but the submarines were frequently engaged in ferrying aviation spirit and other goods to Malta and the minelayers exploited their 40-knot speed on the Tobruk run [245, 247, 255, 264, 281, 289, 291, 313]. Enemy mining continued to be much more extensive and a serious menace everywhere. Aerial, submarine and surface minelayers laid mines of several types off harbours, in deep water channels and, most persistently, in the Suez Canal. Cunningham's minesweeping force was probably the most overworked component of his fleet. Often only one minesweeper was available for an important harbour, specialised vessels having to move quickly about the station and they were frequently under air attack and without fighter cover. Enemy mines accounted for submarines and occasionally other vessels but the most destructive field was an unknown one off Tripoli which, early on 19 December, crippled the hitherto all-conquering Force K, sinking a cruiser and a destroyer and seriously damaging two other cruisers [259, 263–4, 297, 301–2, 323–4].

The Axis air forces continued to be potent, enjoying successes against small craft on the Tobruk run, in the creeks of Grand Harbour and against the Malta convoys [245, 255–6, 262–3, 310, 315, 317, 319, 323]. Moreover, 'The Italians and Germans quarter the whole Mediterranean daily' with reconnaissance flights; naval movements could not long remain hidden [251]. Long-range

---

[9]VA Sir A. Hezlet, *The Submarine and Sea Power* (London, 1967), pp. 141–8; Naval Staff History, *Submarines*, vol 2, *Operations in the Mediterranean, passim*, ADM234/381.
[10]Naval Staff History, *Submarines*, vol 2, flyleaf, p. 61.

bombers were able to range down to the Red Sea, bombing and mining; such defence as there was came from Cunningham's precious AA cruisers and naval fighters. Ironically, President Roosevelt, helpfully but optimistically, had just declared the Red Sea safe for American shipping and the great monster liners began to discharge thousands of troops at Suez from July 1941 [250–1, 256, 259–61, 276, 291]. Naval and shore AA fire was still inadequate in quality and quantity. Cunningham made strenuous efforts to fit radar and really good light AA weapons but both were in short supply [257]. Enemy air power was so ubiquitous, overwhelming and lethal that it came to determine the nature and timing of almost all naval activities, in harbour as much as at sea. The fleet used moonless nights for docking, evasive routeing, night passages and the fastest ships to minimise attacks [244, 247, 275, 277, 286].

During the autumn of 1941, German U-boats began to appear in the Mediterranean; there were half-a-dozen by the year's end and the number was growing [282]. They were a very different proposition from the Italian submarines, which found few targets and suffered heavy losses. The U-boats, most of whom had gained experience in the Battle of the Atlantic, made themselves felt quickly, sinking *Ark Royal*, *Barham*, *Galatea* and *Naiad* and they were 'taking a steady toll of ships on the Tobruk run' [291, 293, 296, 301, 319, 322, 323].[11] Cunningham was short of A/S craft to meet this grave menace and his destroyers rarely had time to practice their asdic work [292–3, 297]. Convoy escorts were thin and often consisted of auxiliaries [259, 281–2, 291, 315, 323]. There were few aircraft in the Mediterranean suitable for, or trained in, A/S operations. To meet this new threat, attempts were made, with some success, to deny U-boats passage through the Straits of Gibraltar [290, 292].[12] Additional Coastal Command aircraft and a handful of A/S vessels were assigned to the eastern basin. Efforts were made to improve the efficiency of A/S craft [293]. Cunningham also persisted with anti-submarine sweeps, despite all the evidence that this was a redundant exercise. While it may have given asdic operators some much needed practice, its chief results were to increase wear and tear on already overworked ships and to expose them to torpedo attack, since they proceeded at a slow pace. One destroyer was

---

[11]*Galatea*: 1935, 5,220t, 6×6in, 4×4in, 6×21in tt, 32.25k; s *U-557*, off Alexandria, 15 Dec. 1941.

[12]Hezlet, *The Submarine and Sea Power*, p. 145; M. Simpson, *The Somerville Papers* (Aldershot: Scolar Press for Navy Records Society, 1995), pp. 79–80; documents 199–200, 204–5, 207.

sunk by a U-boat (which remained undetected) while engaged on a hunt, surely the supreme irony [243, 261, 263–4, 297, 315, 318, 323]. Like many senior officers, Cunningham failed to digest fully the lesson of the First World War – that convoys, acting as bait, offer the best opportunities for sinking submarines.

The increased weight of mining and submarine attacks and the widespread escort commitments, together with the emphasis on submarine, light forces and air attacks on enemy communications helped to shift the balance of the fleet away from heavy ships and fleet operations, a process aided, of course, by damage to or loss of *Formidable, Warspite, Barham, Queen Elizabeth* and *Valiant*, for whom there were no replacements, especially after the Far Eastern situation deteriorated in the autumn of 1941. Cunningham's strength at the end of his term in command, March 1942, was the lowest it had been since the days of the 'Phoney War' – a handful of the Navy's lightest cruisers (essentially AA ships), a dozen or so battered destroyers, two flotillas of submarines, assorted escort destroyers ('Hunts'), sloops, corvettes, minesweepers, trawlers and other auxiliaries, supported by two dozen FAA torpedo bombers and 24 fighters. Australian, New Zealand, South African, Free French, Dutch, Greek and Yugoslav warships also played major roles in the fighting. Even when he still had battleships, they were often unable to put to sea because the destroyers were scattered on escort work, the Tobruk run, or in dockyard hands; reinforcements barely made up for losses and departures [244–5, 250, 255–6, 258–60, 262–4, 268, 281, 288, 290–1, 318, 323].

For a traditional battle fleet admiral, intent on bringing the enemy fleet to decisive battle and ruling the waves Nelson-fashion, the steady decline of the battle squadron in the second half of 1941 was a mortifying experience yet events since June 1940 had led him to value even more carrier air power. It can be argued that *Formidable* (and perhaps *Illustrious*) were needlessly exposed when unable effectively to defend themselves. After *Formidable* was put out of action, Pound, who was always sceptical of the value and survival of carriers in the Mediterranean, was unable – and unwilling – to find a replacement. The crippling of two of the new armoured carriers in five months was an unacceptable rate of attrition. When *Illustrious* and *Formidable* returned to active service early in 1942, they joined the new Eastern Fleet, together with the newer *Indomitable,* though they never saw action.[13] Cunningham must have felt aggrieved at this situation, since

---

[13]*Indomitable*: 1941, 23,000t, 16×4.5in, 36 (later 54) a/c, 31k. Simpson, *Somerville Papers,* pp. 353–63; documents 211–285.

a carrier would have eased considerably the increasing problem of fighting convoys through to Malta and, when he still had a battle squadron, a carrier would have enabled him to contest control of the central Mediterranean. He pleaded with Pound but in vain [277, 282]. He appeared to have learned the lesson, expensively taught, that the Luftwaffe could be combated only by a strong fighter force (at least two squadrons, with 100 per cent reserves). If he had only one carrier, he would vary the air component according to the mission. Two carriers would enable one to provide air defence while the other concentrated on reconnaissance, A/S patrols and strikes. A major lesson of Matapan was that a greater weight of attack was necessary to ensure the slowing down of enemy capital ships; a second carrier would allow at least two strike squadrons to be embarked. These arguments proved academic and while it might be said that Cunningham did not deserve to be given a third new carrier force, there was no denying his point that without one, more ships were likely to be lost or damaged.

It was ironic that the battleships sunk or put out of action after Crete fell to underwater rather than aerial weapons. Lack of anti-submarine practice and experience and probably the absence of carrier A/S patrols led to the loss of *Barham,* though the attack was a skilful one. The crippling of *Queen Elizabeth* and *Valiant* in Alexandria harbour was a stupendous feat by the Italian human torpedo crews but it led to a top-level court of inquiry and responsibility for the disaster is still a matter of debate.[14] Advance warning of an attack of some kind was given by signal decrypts and Cunningham issued a general order instructing everyone to be vigilant. However, early on 19 December, three Italian two-man human torpedoes, launched from a submarine off the harbour entrance, passed through the open boom, following returning British warships. They were not spotted until after they had planted their warheads. The two British battleships were put out of action for longer than the Italian ships at Taranto. Because of the Far Eastern situation, no replacements were available; even the promised *Warspite* went to the Indian Ocean as Somerville's flagship [290, 292–3, 297, 299, 301, 311].

Following the incident, Pridham-Wippell, assisted by Baillie-Grohman and Glennie, RA(D), conducted an inquiry.[15] Their con-

[14]See VAdm V Spigai, Italian N, 'Italian Naval Assault Craft in Two World Wars', *US N Inst Proceedings,* March 1965, pp. 50–9, and Cdr L. Durand de la Penne and Capt V Spigai, 'The Italian Attack on the Alexandria Naval Base', *US N Inst Proceedings,* Feb. 1956, pp. 125–35; P. Kemp, *Underwater Warriors* (London, 1996), pp. 26–33.

[15]Report of Board of Inquiry: Attack on Alexandria Harbour, Dec 1941, PWL3, *Pridham-Wippell Papers,* NMM.

clusions identified a failure of the look-out system, a lack of supervising officers, the absence of radar, the inability of submarine detector loops and asdic to range far enough to locate the parent submarine (*Sciré*), a shortage of patrol vessels, lack of illumination, the failure of the dusk air patrol to detect the submarine, the inability of anti-submarine nets to prevent the attackers reaching their targets, and the lack of safeguards when the boom was opened. The Rear Admiral in charge of Alexandria offered his head on the block, to be told by the C-in-C that it was not his fault. It was difficult to defend a foreign harbour which had an awkward entrance and shallow water. Booms and nets were clearly defective. However, the principal reason for the calamity appears to have been the lack of clear responsibility for local defence; a sea defence officer was appointed only a day before disaster struck. Cunningham kept all appointments on the station in his own hands and, mindful of the general shortage of officers, refused repeated requests from the port Rear Admiral for sea defence officers. He was much less interested in shore administration than seagoing operations and perhaps over-frugal in matters of expenditure. Nevertheless, while he undoubtedly bears a share of the blame, full credit must be given to Italian skill and courage, and recognition to the almost impossible task of ensuring a watertight defence against such attacks. Such steps as could be taken to rectify the situation were put in hand at once [297, 301].[16]

Most of the senior officers from the previous phase remained throughout this period. Pridham-Wippell, who had encouraged *Barham's* survivors while they were in the water, was somewhat shaken by his ordeal but recovered and became Acting C-in-C when Cunningham left in the spring of 1942. Rawlings and Baillie-Grohman continued to grow in the C-in-C's esteem and Rear Admiral Glennie, who had arrived in the spring of 1941, became RA (D) but Vice Admiral King, in command of the 15th Cruiser Squadron, left in the autumn to take up an Admiralty appointment. Cunningham felt that he was a fine staff officer but probably unsuited to command at sea.[17] Rear Admiral Vian, who took over

---

[16]A radar set suitable for the detection of this form of attack should have been installed but the order, made on 24 Oct. 1941, had not yet been fulfilled. See also Baillie-Grohman, 'Flashlights on the Past', vol 2, pp. 193–9, *Baillie-Grohman Papers*, NMM.

Sciré: 1938, 698/866t, 6×21in tt, 14/8.4k; s off Haifa, *Islay,* 10 Aug. 1942.

RA Alexandria: Actg RA G. H. Cresswell. See also R. L. Ollard, *Fisher and Cunningham: A Study of the Personalities of the Churchill Era* (London, 1991), p. 123.

[17]Cunningham to Baillie-Grohman, 4 May 1961, XGRO 2, *Baillie-Grohman Papers*, NMM. Hodgkinson, *Before the Tide Turned,* pp. 224–30.

15th Cruiser Squadron, was well known to Cunningham as a bold leader with a distinguished war record, to which he added with his conduct of the two engagements in the Gulf of Sirte.[18] Cunningham also felt that Vice Admiral Ford had been the perfect Vice Admiral Malta – resolute, cheerful, energetic, astute – and was sorry to see him leave after five years, particularly since he was not convinced of Leatham's ability to sustain Ford's outstanding record [244–5, 262–3, 274, 282, 293, 301, 322].[19]

Cunningham had been greatly worried by the depressed state of morale in the fleet in the aftermath of Crete. He gave ships' companies what respite he could and sought to calm and encourage them [245]. The C-in-C continued to visit ships, hospitals, shore establishments, explaining, exhorting and encouraging as he went. He found time to write to wounded ratings and to chastise the Admiralty over the tardy mail service and London's lack of appreciation for the herculean services rendered by the fleet [252, 254, 261, 291, 298, 301, 304, 322, 323]. Vessels leaving the station and other ships which had performed well continued to receive warm messages of thanks and congratulation [244, 250, 256, 259, 291, 293, 319, 325]. He was not slow, however, to censure poor conduct and inefficiency [251]. Cunningham was reluctant to accept Wrens on the station, feeling, as did most men of his generation, that women were incapable of performing traditional male tasks and that Egypt was no place for them. However, he was persuaded to accept them by his old friend Admiral Sir Jock Whitworth, then Second Sea Lord, who was concerned at the alarming shortage of manpower. Having agreed to receive a draft, he accepted them with good grace and came to appreciate their fine service [279].[20] In March 1942, Cunningham was about to offer himself for relief when Pound nominated him as Head of the British Admiralty Delegation in Washington [322]. At the end of his tenure of com-

---

[18]RA (later A of F Sir) Philip Vian (1894–1968): Lt 1916; Jutland; gunnery splist; Cdr 1929; Capt 1934; Res F DF; 1DF, Spain 1936; *Arethusa* 1937; convoy DF 1939–40; 4DF 1940; in *Cossack*, rescued Br POWs from *Altmark* Feb. 1940; *Bismarck* action May 1941; RA July 1941; Force K, Spitzbergen Aug. 1941; actions off Norway; 15CS, Med F Oct. 1941; Sicily landings 1943; Eastern TF, D-Day 1944; cmd Fleet carriers, BPF Nov. 1944; VA 1945; 5SL 1946–48; C-in-C Home F 1950–52; Adm & A of F 1952. See his *Action this Day: A War Memoir* (London, 1960). S. Howarth, 'Admiral of the Fleet Sir Philip Vian', in Howarth (ed.), *Men of War: Great Naval Leaders of World War II* (London, 1992), pp. 491–505.

[19]VA (later Adm) Sir Wilbraham Ford: Capt 1922; RA 1932; VA & FOIC Malta 1937–41; Adm Dec. 1941; C-in-C Rosyth April 1942-Jan 1944; ret June 1944.

[20]VA (later Adm) Sir William 'Jock' Whitworth: Capt 1925; Capt of F, Med F, *Resolution* 1935; RA 1936; BCS, Home F 1939; VA 1940; 2nd Battle of Narvik April 1940; 2SL 1941–44; Adm Dec. 1943; C-in-C Rosyth Feb. 1944.

mand, he paid warm tributes to the fleet, base personnel and those at Malta then experiencing their worst ordeal [325]. The Admiralty made him a signal of gratitude for his outstanding term in command in the Mediterranean [326].

Much the most persistent, intractable and considerable of Cunningham's problems was that of Malta which towards the end of this period underwent its gravest siege since 1565. There were three aspects to the problem – sustenance, defence and offensive capability. Though Malta's supply situation did not become as desperate in Cunningham's time as it did in the spring after he left, it was a constant headache for him. A quarter of a million civilians and 50,000 servicemen had to be sustained Two major convoys, SUBSTANCE in July and HALBERD in September, sailed from Gibraltar, escorted by an augmented Force H in view of the likelihood of a fleet action.[21] Both convoys, though suffering damage and loss, reached Malta with most of their cargoes, relieving the general supply situation for several months. In support of these convoys, Cunningham's battered and carrier-less fleet could undertake only brief diversionary sorties and transmit false messages [244, 251, 258–9, 260, 262]. Thereafter, though Force H continued to fly fighters into Malta from *Ark Royal*, it did not conduct any more convoys; indeed, following the loss of *Ark Royal* in November 1941, it could not do so [290]. The burden therefore shifted to Cunningham. He was coping already with Malta's chronic shortage of fuels of various kinds, notably aviation spirit and fuel oil for ships. The expedients adopted were to run aircraft fuel in the larger submarines and three boats were generally engaged on this exercise [251, 257, 306]. As there was no fast tanker, the auxiliary *Breconshire*, which had a speed of 18 knots. was adapted to carry fuel and, alternately with the 15-knot *Glengyle,* she was run to Malta on several occasions, under heavy escort.[22] Cunningham had to await favourable opportunities – moonless nights, the availability of destroyers and a low level of enemy air and naval activity. Nevertheless, fuel for the surface craft was always scarce, inhibiting the stationing at Malta of a strong cruiser and destroyer striking force [282, 293, 295, 296, 313].

One such dash resulted in the first battle of Sirte. Vian, with two cruisers, an AA cruiser and seven destroyers, left Alexandria after dark on 15 December, shepherding *Breconshire* to a rendezvous

---

[21]Simpson, *Somerville Papers,* pp. 59–64; documents 168, 171–3, 177, 184–6, 188.
[22]*Breconshire*: 1939, 9,000gt, 18k, Glen Line.
D. Alves, 'The Resupply of Malta in World War II', *Naval War College Review,* Sept. 1980, pp. 63–72.

with two cruisers and six destroyers from Malta, who would escort her there while Vian returned to Alexandria. False radio signals suggesting that the battlefleet was at sea were made by three ships which then returned to Alexandria. When late on 16 December an enemy squadron including battleships was reported to be at sea, Cunningham ordered Vian to ensure *Breconshire*'s safety until she could be detached to Malta and told Ford to sail all other cruisers and destroyers to join him. Four destroyers reached him early on 17 December, when the force was subjected to heavy air attack. More seriously, owing to a lack of air reconnaissance, in the early evening and unexpectedly, he encountered the Italian force while still fighting off an air attack. The Italians opened fire but made off when Vian, following Cunningham's orders, turned to attack with torpedoes. *Breconshire*, with two destroyers, had been detached to the south but was safely met and conducted to Malta by the cruisers and destroyers dispatched by Ford. The Italian force was covering a convoy and, after the skirmish, Vian turned eastward to find it but it had turned back, and he returned to Alexandria. *Breconshire*, with 5,000 tons of fuel, arrived safely at Malta [297]. Cunningham considered that the misleading radio messages had made the Italians apprehensive and applauded Vian's conduct [301]. Historians of the Italian Navy, however, claim that 'First Sirte' 'ended in the Italians' favour' and that it represented 'an Italian tactical and strategic success'.[23] On Boxing Day, two cruisers and four destroyers convoyed four fast merchantmen from Malta to Alexandria, joining up with a small force from the latter port, two destroyers going on to Malta. Despite several air attacks, the convoy reached Egypt unharmed [297].

Early in 1942, Admiral Ford implored Cunningham to send a five-ship convoy and on 25 January, forces escorting merchant ships and *Breconshire* set out from Malta and Alexandria respectively, weathering the inevitable air attacks and delivering their charges, most importantly *Breconshire's* fuel, in safety [310]. Some short-range and long-range fighter cover had been available for convoys thus far but the British defeat in Libya in February 1942 and the subsequent headlong retreat spelt danger for the Malta passage. Cunningham observed that the loss of forward airfields,

---

[23]Vian, *Action This Day*, p. 78; M. A. Bragadin, *The Italian Navy in World War II* (Annapolis, Md, 1957), pp. 146–51; J. J. Sadkovitch, 'The Italian Navy in World War II', in Sadkovitch (ed.), *Reevaluating the Major Combatants of World War II* (Westport, Conn., 1990), p. 146.

together with the crippling of his battle squadron, would have 'a serious effect on the Malta situation' and London 'must prepare for serious losses which might well be almost the whole convoy' since there was little to counter either air or surface attacks [313–14]. Submarines continued to keep Malta's planes flying but could not effectively sustain the fortress. Oil fuel was running very short and a convoy would have to be risked. Elaborate measures were taken for the defence of the February convoys – three vessels from Alexandria and three plus *Breconshire* from Malta, with escorting groups. Unfortunately, Cunningham's fears were justified; all three of the Malta-bound ships were sunk or disabled by bombing [315]. Despite Malta's continuing oil crisis, Cunningham despaired of getting a convoy through until air cover improved [316–17, 320]. A further force from Malta survived heavy air attacks but lost Cunningham's favourite cruiser, *Naiad*, to a submarine [319, 322].

Despite the deteriorating air and land situation, Malta's plight being even more desperate, Cunningham, with even more misgivings, was forced to organise another convoy [322]. Once again, the most thorough measures were taken to clear the passage and three cargo ships and the faithful *Breconshire* left Alexandria on 20 March with a close escort of an AA cruiser and five destroyers. Vian, with three cruisers and four destroyers, provided cover, six 'Hunts' joining the convoy on the following day. A cruiser and a destroyer left Malta on 21 March, meeting Vian the next day. Heavy air attacks were experienced but long-range fighters assisted in driving them off. Attacks by the Army and the RAF in the Western Desert also provided effective diversions. It was known that Italian forces, including a battleship, were at sea and at 1430 on 22 March they made contact with Vian, the *Littorio* coming up at 1640. There had been brief exchanges of fire earlier but between 1700 and 1900, in heavy seas, a real battle ('Second Sirte') took place. The enemy's intention was to stand between the convoy and Malta, Vian's to fight the convoy through at all costs. He had discussed with Cunningham what he should do. As so often, the C-in-C refused to give him precise orders, remarking merely that he 'must act as judgement dictated'. Vian ordered the convoy, in charge of *Carlisle* and the 'Hunts', to turn south, away from the enemy. Vian disposed his cruisers and destroyers, 15 ships, in five groups. They would have tactical freedom to lay smoke and threaten torpedo attack, Cunningham having advised him that 'if he made enough smoke, the Italian Fleet would not come through it'.[24] Gunfire was exchanged when visibility and range permitted and torpedoes were fired on several occasions. Only one shell struck the Italians, who scored several hits on the British force, seriously damaging two destroyers. Despite this, Vian's force prevented the enemy coming within range of the convoy. As one of Vian's captains wrote, 'The Italian Admiral could easily have wiped us out, but he could not bring himself to enter the smokescreen knowing that we were waiting for him on the other side'.[25] At nightfall, the Italians withdrew to the northward and the convoy proceeded towards Malta, Vian returning to Alexandria. Unfortunately, the convoy had been driven southward, within range of enemy bombers. In severe air attacks on 23 March, *Clan Campbell* was sunk and *Breconshire* disabled on Malta's doorstep, while *Pampas* and *Talabot* were seriously damaged after arrival; only 5,000 tons of the convoy's 26,000 tons of supplies were saved. In addition, two of the escorting destroyers were lost [322–4].[26]

Cunningham remained in the operations room at Alexandria throughout the action, fretting at his helplessness. Reading all the signals, he fully approved all of Vian's actions and forbore to interfere. In fact, Vian anticipated everything that Cunningham himself would have done. In his autobiography, Cunningham wrote, 'I shall always consider the Battle of Sirte on March 22nd, 1942 as one of the most brilliant naval actions of the war, if not the most brilliant'.[27] Vian returned to a hero's welcome, a warm message from the Prime Minister and a knighthood. The Italian historian Bragadin, however, charged that the British ships 'manoeuvred in a disorganised fashion and with unusual timidity' and it was claimed that the Italian shooting was far more accurate than that of the British. Moreover, the Italian force drove the convoy into the arms of the bombers and brought about its decimation by other means.[28] There is no doubt that Vian saved the convoy from a superior force – a modern 15-in battleship, two 8-in and one 6-in cruisers and eight destroyers. His plans for such an eventuality were well worked out and he had established a Nelsonian understanding with his division leaders. His

---

[24]Vian, *Action This Day*, p. 87; Cunningham, note, n.d., p. 36, BM Add Mss 52581B, Cunningham Papers, BL.
[25]Capt E. W. Bush, *Bless Our Ship* (London, 1958), p. 229.
[26]*Pampas*: 1940, 5,580gt, 15k, R Mail Lines.
Talabot: Norway, 1936, 6,798t, W. Wilhelmsen.
[27]Cunningham, *A Sailor's Odyssey* (London, 1951), p. 454.
[28]Bragadin, *The Italian Navy*, pp. 159–66; Sadkovitch, 'The Italian Navy', p. 145; E. J. Grove, *Sea Battles in Close Up*, vol. 2 (Shepperton, 1993), pp. 101–15.

puny force exhibited great courage and superb seamanship in closing a more powerful enemy and driving him off. Cunningham had been unwilling to penetrate a smokescreen at Calabria and acknowledged the danger of doing so. However, while Vian might well have disabled or sunk some enemy units, his own force would have been savaged had the Italians pressed on through the smoke; he would have been in no condition to save the convoy following a close range encounter. In the end, Vian achieved his object at small cost and the Italians, while pushing the convoy further into the path of the bombers, did not. The discipline, training, morale, confidence, seamanship, initiative, teamwork and tactical acumen of the British force were of the highest order.

This final convoy brought just enough to keep Malta going but at considerable cost. The more famous PEDESTAL convoy of August 1942, which came from the west, was an enormous fleet operation and yet suffered heavy losses in the face of 700 enemy aircraft. In Cunningham's mind there was no question that Malta must be sustained; therefore, the effort and costs were justified. However, he informed the Admiralty that very much greater fighter cover and a stronger destroyer force were essential in future convoys, as well as deception measures [325]. There was little that could be done to minimise losses, for the enemy had overwhelming air strength and sea power, aided by effective reconnaissance, whereas the Mediterranean Fleet was at its weakest, reconnaissance was negligible and fighter cover sporadic. With each passing month the balance appeared to move further in the enemy's favour.

At the opening of this phase Malta was experiencing a reduced scale of air attack, the result of the diversion of German squadrons to the campaign in Russia, which began on 22 June [244]. With repeated flights of Hurricanes and successful convoys from the west during the summer, Malta's defences were strong enough to ward off serious damage, comprehensively defeating a seaborne attack on 26 July [250]. Nevertheless, deficiencies in the organisation and strength of the defences remained and enemy bombing was still disruptive and damaging to oil and other stocks [274]. However, Malta used the relative easing of the bombing to increase its offensive activity. As in the winter of 1940–41, this invited retaliation, especially as the Malta striking forces were strangling Rommel's supply line. In December 1941 the Axis high command decided to finish off Malta by cutting off supplies and bombing the islands to destruction, demoralisation and starvation. Fliegerkorps II, with 335 aircraft, was transferred from Russia and, with the Italian Air Force, unloaded up to 6,700 tons of bombs per month on the island.[29] By the New Year, Ford was recording round-the-clock raids; the tone and content of his message of 3 January 1942 clearly indicate that a crisis had been reached. Malta's fighters (Hurricane I's) were obsolescent, outnumbered and tactically defeated before they got airborne. Many planes were burnt out on the ground, ships were mined into the harbour and the dockyard's work was seriously disrupted. [302, 306]. Cunningham reported that Malta was being 'neutralised' and endorsed Ford's call for the latest aircraft [305, 307]. Shortly thereafter, Ford was relieved by Vice Admiral Leatham, who, though reporting that Malta's morale remained high, had been forced underground, as had workshops, offices, barracks and civilians [309]. Within a fortnight, however, the defences were on the point of being overwhelmed as the enemy steadily increased the weight, frequency and variety of his bombing, the planes concentrating on airfields and ships. Submarines were forced to submerge by day but four were destroyed and they were shortly to be withdrawn [314, 316, 318, 320]. As Leatham intimated, Malta's survival was now in the balance.

On leaving the station, Cunningham acknowledged 'That the defence of Malta has been an epic', recognising the direct link between the island's offensive against enemy ports and convoys and the current determination of the Axis to eliminate it [322–3]. Malta's ordeal was inevitable in any war with Italy but such a conflict was not considered likely before 1935 and it was feverishly avoided thereafter. Thus the island was left virtually defenceless; only when a fear of war with Italy began to creep in from 1937 were limited efforts made to build up its defences. It was largely Cunningham himself, conscious of Malta's great strategic potential and the immense disadvantages of operating from Alexandria, who pressed for their speedy enhancement. By the summer of 1940, it was impossible to do so in time to defeat the enemy bombardment. The garrison was quickly raised to a strength adequate to repulse an invasion but the Navy was unable to provide sufficient minesweepers and the RAF could not keep pace with the high rate of fighter attrition. Much could have been done before the war to place workshops, headquarters, accommodation and even submarines and flying boats underground, for on Malta there was nowhere to run or hide.

---

[29]E. Bradford, *Siege: Malta, 1940–1943* (London, 1985), pp. 125–72; P. Elliott, *The Cross and the Ensign: A Naval History of Malta, 1798–1979* (London, 1982), pp. 143–64; VA Sir A. Hezlet, *Aircraft and Sea Power* (London, 1970), pp. 226–31.

Hawker Hurricane I: 1935, 8mg, 330mph, range 470 mls.

Churchill's government, which otherwise did as much as it could for Malta under the conditions of 1940–42, was slow to send to the island (and to the Mediterranean in general) high-performance fighters. This delay very nearly lost Malta. As they proved over Malta in the summer of 1942, Spitfires could gain daytime mastery of the skies as they had in the Battle of Britain.[30]

Cunningham believed that Malta must become first the lynchpin of Axis defeat in North Africa and then the springboard for the invasion of Italy. When Malta was well supplied and had strong defences, it was possible to station there surface forces, submarines and bombers. This offensive power was increasingly crucial to the winning of the desert war, as Malta was in a unique position to seriously disrupt Axis communications with Libya. The offensive, effectively begun in December 1940, was to reach its peak about a year later. It benefited from Ultra decrypts and ASV reconnaissance, though air patrols were still below the level required to protect convoys and give early warning of enemy forces at sea. In May 1941, Air Vice Marshal Lloyd was appointed AOC Mediterranean to galvanise the anti-shipping offensive.[31] RAF Wellingtons, Beauforts and Blenheims flew bombing and torpedo missions; an increasing number of aircrews were trained in anti-shipping strikes.[32] The FAA, represented by 830 (Swordfish) Squadron from early in the war and 828 (Albacore) Squadron from October 1941, was chiefly engaged on torpedo attacks but also undertook ASV reconnaissance, flare dropping, minelaying and the bombing of Tripoli. All aircraft which attacked shipping necessarily did so from a low altitude and had to brave a wall of flak, which made attacks costly and difficult [244, 256–60, 264, 274, 289, 291–2, 297, 301, 305–7, 309–10, 319–20, 323].[33]

Submarine attacks against enemy convoys were shared by the Alexandria and Malta flotillas and there were many enterprising

---

[30]Supermarine Spitfire: 1936, (Mk V) 2×20mm cannon, 4mg, 374mph, range 1,135 mls.
On Malta's situation, see Chiefs of Staff to Cs-in-C, Mediterranean and Governor of Malta, 27 Feb. 1942, and memoranda, 24 Feb. and 20 March 1942, CAB79/18.

[31]Actg AVM (later ACM Sir) Hugh Lloyd (1894–1981): RE 1915; RFC 1917; India 1920–24; RAF Staff Coll; Sqdn Ldr 1932; Instr, Quetta 1931–32; 1 Indian Grp staff 1932–35; Staff Coll Camberley 1936–38; W Cdr 1936; 9 Sqdn; G Capt, Marham; Snr Air SO, 2 Grp, for strikes on Ger shipping; Actg AVM & AOC, Med, Malta, May 1941; Snr Air SO, ME July 1942; AOC, NW Af Coastal AF Mar 1943; Actg AM, Tiger Force 1945; IDC 1945–47; FEAF 1947–49; Bom Cmd 1949; ACM 1951; ret 1953. See his *Briefed to Attack* (1949).

[32]Bristol Blenheim: 1936, 5mg, 1,000lbs bombs, 266mph, range 1,460 mls.

[33]K. Poolman, *Night Strike from Malta: 830 Squadron Royal Navy and Rommel's Convoys* (London, 1980).

and fruitful patrols, though several losses were incurred, including the four bombed at Malta. Though never engaging in 'wolf pack' tactics, the 10th Flotilla did develop effective 'team work' [244, 256–61, 264, 281, 291, 297, 315, 318–19, 325]. The new dimension was the introduction of surface striking forces. Small groups of destroyers had enjoyed a brief harvest in the spring before the demands of Greece and Crete called them back to Alexandria. However, with the approach of the British offensive, timed for November 1941, London began to emphasise the necessity of denying the enemy army mobility by destroying the convoys to Libya. Additional submarines and aircraft were made available but, while they sank ships regularly, it was rare for them to dispatch more than two at a time. The firepower of a force of cruisers and destroyers, on the other hand, could annihilate a whole convoy and its escort, thereby virtually doubling the pressure on Rommel's supply line. Malta was experiencing a reduced scale of air attack in the second half of 1941, so surface ships would be relatively safe. However, neither Pound nor Cunningham favoured it. Even if a force could be scraped together from a Navy stretched further than at any other point in the war, it was unlikely to match the strength of Italian covering forces. If at sea during the day, it could not expect fighter protection but it could be certain of devastating enemy air attacks. It would have to be well served by comprehensive air reconnaissance, a perennial weakness in the Mediterranean, while the Axis air patrols were sure to give early warning of the force's approach [258–9]. The admirals' scepticism was tempered by their realisation that the Army was counting on the Navy to reduce drastically the enemy's ability to halt the CRUSADER offensive [262, 268].

In the event, Force K (two light cruisers and two destroyers) demonstrated the unique ability of a surface squadron to inflict crippling losses in a single action. Ably directed by Ford, with the help of Ultra and effective air reconnaissance, the force surprised and totally destroyed a convoy of ten merchant ships and sank three of the escorts [278, 282, 293]. Cunningham recalled, 'I thought they were wasted as I did not think the Italians would be so foolish as to give them a chance'.[34] The chance having been offered and seized, and on learning of Rommel's critical supply situation, it was decided to send a second, similar squadron, Force B, and to support it with the battle fleet [283–7, 289–90]. Unfortunately, this sortie led to the loss of *Barham*, though two more supply ships were sunk [291]. The

[34] Cunningham to Kelly, 11 Nov. 1941, KEL 43, *Kelly Papers*, NMM.

Italians, after suspending convoys briefly, responded as Cunningham expected, by despatching strong covering forces; any future sallies by the Malta groups would need good air reconnaissance to avoid destruction by superior forces [292, 296]. However, the use of warships in place of merchantmen saved the Italians nothing. Ultra and ASV enabled a group of destroyers, reinforcements for the fleet, to surprise and sink two light cruisers, carrying cased petrol, and an escort vessel, off the African coast. Sadly, this run of success ended in calamity on the morning of 19 December, when one cruiser and a destroyer were sunk by mines and two other cruisers badly damaged, while a fourth cruiser had to leave the station with defective engines [296–7, 301, 303, 319]. The shortage of fuel at Malta and the renewed German air attacks in December made the continued presence of the force uncertain. Moreover, the overwhelming covering forces now deployed by the Italians would probably rule out future attacks [310, 317–18]. Furthermore, the ships at Malta were increasingly engaged in the desperate convoy battles to supply the island. By the end of Cunningham's term, it was becoming impossible to berth safely even tugs. The remaining ships of Force K, most of which needed further repairs, left in the spring of 1942, together with the submarines [322–4].

Malta's striking forces had enjoyed dramatic success in the second half of 1941, when the enemy's monthly losses of supplies ran from 40 to 80% of those dispatched.[35] This was achieved by less than 100 strike aircraft, a flotilla of submarines and Force K, with an average of two cruisers and two destroyers. At that rate, Malta would bring Rommel to a standstill. Were that to happen, the monthly 'club runs' would be cost effective. However, in the first half of 1942, Malta's offensive wilted under Axis air attack, less than 20% of enemy cargoes being lost. The greater their supplies, the nearer Axis forces drove towards the Suez Canal. There was a direct relationship between the strength of Malta's fighter defences, Axis air raids, the island's offensive capability and success, the fluctuations in enemy supplies, and the location of the opposing armies in the Western Desert, with about a month's time lag between the effect of one factor on another. Was the expensive investment in Malta between June 1940 and November 1942 justified in terms of the island's impact on the Mediterranean war? Cunningham and many of his contemporaries were in no doubt that it was; recent

---

[35]'The Effect of Malta Upon the Land Campaigns in Libya', in Cunningham, *A Sailor's Odyssey*, p. 670.

writers, while never arguing that Malta should have been abandoned, disagree.[36] It is well-nigh impossible to draw up a balance sheet but both sides were convinced of Malta's crucial role in the Mediterranean campaign; both exerted immense efforts on it and it is difficult to see how any British government could have abandoned Malta. In 1940, Malta survived Italian air attacks without heavy damage and was supplied from both east and west without undue difficulty, but had no striking power. In 1941, it weathered the first onslaught of the Luftwaffe and achieved spectacular successes with small forces and its re-supply, though occasioning at least two major fleet operations from the west, was accomplished without heavy losses. From the Luftwaffe's return in December 1941 until August 1942, a direct response to the effect Malta was having on Rommel's supplies, the cost of keeping Malta going far outweighed its contribution to operations in North Africa.

When Cunningham departed the Mediterranean on 3 April, he left behind little more than light forces. Greece, Crete, German U-boats and Italian human torpedoes had destroyed the fleet and its remnants clung on to a shrinking portion of the eastern basin. It was a force which enjoyed little scope for initiative and, with Malta's desperate hour at hand, even less in the months to come. The Far East had reasserted its strategic primacy and the Mediterranean could expect no more capital ships. The Italian Fleet was at sea more often but Cunningham was unable to strike at it, while the problems posed by the Luftwaffe ashore and at sea were still unsolved.

Also unresolved was the issue of overall command and Cunningham ventured a contribution to the discussion. He always felt that the trio of Wavell, Longmore and himself had worked smoothly, as it had, largely because of their personal compatibility. He found it much harder to co-operate with the sharper, more detached Tedder and the less communicative and more narrowly focused Auchinleck [227, 239, 282, 301, 322]. Cunningham's insistence on remaining with his fleet instead of basing himself in Cairo with the other two caused some friction. He felt he had answered this complaint by installing there an additional Chief of Staff and meeting his two colleagues on a weekly basis. He argued for a gen-

---

[36]See C. Barnett, *Engage the Enemy More Closely* (London, 1991), pp. 491–526; C. Giorgerini, 'The Role of Malta in Italian Naval Operations, 1940–1943', in Dept of History, US Naval Academy (ed.), *New Aspects of Naval History* (Baltimore, 1985), pp. 189–92.

eral coincidence of areas of command and, after his departure, for the Naval C-in-C to be based in Cairo with the fleet commander subordinate to him. He felt, rightly, that his presence with the fleet was vital and that only he could supply the invincible determination and the confidence in the fleet's command which were essential to maintain morale and engender efficiency and maximum effort. As the crisis deepened from the spring of 1941, his presence with his ships and men became even more crucial to morale and to extracting full value from diminished resources. He hinted also at his rooted opposition to the idea of a Supreme Commander but insisted that if there had to be one for the Middle East, it should be the Naval C-in-C. Quite apart from the difficulty of executing both a specific role and a supervisory one, his assumption that the Mediterranean conflict was essentially maritime in character is debatable. It is arguable that it was primarily a land campaign, to which the other services were handmaidens; this was certainly the case after El Alamein and TORCH [327].

The desperate situation at his departure was scant reward for Cunningham's vigorous, bold, courageous and resolute leadership. His reputation for brusqueness, acerbity, toughness and impatience was seemingly well deserved yet he was ever mindful of the welfare of those under him, which they appreciated, and ever ready to speak to the humblest of them.[37] One can argue that the losses of or damage to some of his big ships might have been avoided. However, he had maintained the highest traditions of the service in the Mediterranean, standards set by Nelson in the 1790s. His example inspired his subordinates, who profited from his minimalist approach to orders and exercised their initiative to the great discomfort of the opposition. He carried the fight to the enemy, recognising the importance of establishing at once a moral ascendancy, and he outclassed the Italian admirals in tactical acumen and fleet-handling. Furthermore, he understood the interdependence of the three services and the necessity of integrating their strategies and efforts. He appreciated that 'In modern war sea power is compounded of surface force and its essential component in the form of air support' [327]. He was in truth the very model of a modern admiral.

The principles underlying command of the sea, however, are timeless and in his single-minded pursuit of the enemy to destruc-

---

[37]G. G. Connell, *Mediterranean Maelstrom: HMS Jervis and the 14th Flotilla* (London, 1987), p. 164.

tion, he exhibited many of the characteristics and espoused many of the objects associated with Nelson. The instilling in his captains of a simple, well-understood doctrine and a corresponding expertise in carrying it out, together with the latitude to exercise one's judgement, was a policy he shared with Nelson. He had similarly an instinctive grasp of what to do at crucial moments and his orders were deft, to the point and rapid. Like Nelson, he took risks but only if the object justified them. He made optimum use of the limited forces at his disposal. He shared the dangers and discomforts of the sea with his men and fretted when he could not do so. In the manner of all great leaders, he never asked anyone to undertake what he would not suffer himself. Ruthless in battle, he was as solicitous as Nelson for the safety of enemy survivors. His steely spirit he communicated to his command and he was unmatched in stamina, purpose and determination. Though not a student of history in the vein of Mahan or Richmond, he had a sense of the past, its traditions and continuities, and the inspiration and perspective one gained from it.[38] It was Nelson who, by the taking of Malta and the defeat of the French fleet at Aboukir Bay, had given Britain mastery of the Mediterranean; it fell to Cunningham to defend that legacy. He did so in the full knowledge that he was Nelson's heir. Moreover, in his relations with his men, his handling of the fleet, his firm grasp of Mediterranean strategy, and his constant urge to close with the enemy, he had the Nelson touch.

---

[38]Capt A. T. Mahan, US Navy (1840–1914), instructor at US Naval War College and author of *The Influence of Sea Power Upon History* (Boston: 1890), etc. Admiral Sir Herbert Richmond (1871–1946), a founder of *The Naval Review* and later Professor of Imperial and Naval History, Cambridge; author of *Statesmen and Sea Power* (Oxford: 1946).

236. *To the Admiralty*

2348, 2 June 1941

Further to my 1931/27. I have been considering the immediate policy to be adopted by the Fleet. My forces as Their Lordships will be aware have been weakened but I hope 10 June to have available 2 battleships, 5 cruisers, 2 AA ships and 14 destroyers which will be rested and patched up ready for action. This force in itself is sufficient to deal with enemy surface force likely to break into Eastern Mediterranean though it is questionable whether it is really strong enough to work in the Central Mediterranean owing to its low speed and absence of aircraft carriers which has undoubtedly been the major factor in keeping Italian Fleet in harbour.

2. The whole policy however has to be considered in terms of the air. If I could put above force in contact with the enemy I should be satisfied of result provided it came into action fresh and undamaged. But if that contact has to be made after 48 hours' continuous bombing and torpedo attacks and with consequent damage to expect judging from our recent experience then position will be rather a different one. These facts have to be borne in mind therefore in considering our immediate line of action.

3. I have received no specific reply to my 1931/27 but I earnestly trust that some of its proposals are being put into effect and would be glad to know Their Lordships' view of that appreciation and what is considered possible in the way of implementing it.

4. My immediate tasks out here are

(a) *Attack on Libyan communications.* This attack I feel at present must be dealt with by aircraft based on Malta and in Western Desert and by submarines. It is not at present sound to move fleet out onto line of communications.

(b) *Supply to Malta.* As stated in 1122/2 it is probable that this can be undertaken from the West.

(c) *Support in Western Desert.* This duty is one more for submarines and light craft and the extent to which it can be maintained will depend solely on efficiency of fighter cover. At present Western Desert supply is nearly at a standstill W of

Mersa Matruh owing to the enemy aircraft who sweep daily down the coast unhindered and bomb our small coasting ships on their way to Tobruk. The sinking of *Grimsby* and *Helka* was an example of [enemy] mobility.[39] Should enemy move up a heavy surface force to bombard, say, Tobruk, I shall hope to deal with it by shore-based torpedo bombing attacks.

(d) *Support [?given by] Syria.* In this area so long as we hold Cyprus we can operate in reasonable comfort but how long we shall retain that is rather a matter for enemy than of selves.

5. The policy enunciated is eminently unsatisfactory since it is almost entirely defensive. The problem is how to turn it into an offensive one. In my 1931/27 I have pressed with all my strength for air forces that alone can rectify the matter.

Meanwhile we are pushing ahead. We have achieved some degree of success in working long range fighters [?over] Fleet and as soon as a reasonable number of proper aircraft intended for their purpose arrive we shall as a first step be able to cover our Western desert supply which is at the moment the one urgent need. If we can then get sufficient bombers to blow the enemy off Cretan and Libyan landing grounds we shall begin to free ourselves of the restraint put on us by enemy air forces and shall I trust be able then to resume attack on Libyan route plus supplies to Malta and redress present situation. But we must have the fighters, the bombers and reconnaissance or remain pinned in this corner of the Mediterranean.

237. *War Diary, June 1941*

1 June

Submarines

9. The following signal was made to the SO (S), Malta:

> I wish to congratulate you and your command on the excellent results which have been obtained against the Tripoli convoys in the last few weeks. Your work is invaluable to the Empire's effort and more than ever important in the present difficult times. Keep it up.[40]

---

[39]*Helka*: 3,471gt, Euxine Shipping.
[40]Capt G. W. G. Simpson: Mid 1917; GF 1917–18; *Whitley*, Baltic 1919; *Benbow*, Black Sea; S-Lt, s/m 1921; *L15, L7*, China 1923; *L18,* MF 1926–27; *H49* i/c, Dec. 1927; *Nelson* 1929; 1sr Lt, *Thames* 1932; *L27*, Aden 1935; Cdr Dec. 1935; OD; *Porpoise* Aug. 1938; 2i/c, 3SF, Harwich 1939–40; 10SF, Malta, Jan. 1941–Feb. 1943; Capt June 1941; *Talbot* Sept. 1941; Cdre (D), W Apps, Londonderry 1943–44; RA. Known as 'Shrimp'. See his *Periscope View* (London, 1972).

2 June

State of the Fleet

3. As a result of the recent operations both during the Battle for Crete and the evacuation, the Mediterranean Fleet had suffered the following losses:

Sunk: *Gloucester, Fiji, Calcutta, Juno, Greyhound, Imperial, Hereward, Kelly, Kashmir.*

Damaged beyond repair in Egypt: *Warspite, Barham, Formidable, Orion, Dido, Kelvin, Nubian.*

Of these *Formidable, Warspite* and *Nubian* would each be three or four weeks before they could be made fit for an ocean passage and *Orion* would require to be docked.

Of the remainder, *Perth, Naiad* and *Carlisle* would be under repair for some weeks. *Valiant* and *Ajax* were fit for service in their present condition. *Napier, Kipling* and *Decoy* would take three–four weeks for repair and *Havock, Kingston* and *Nizam* about a fortnight. The following battleships, cruisers and destroyers were fit for service:

Queen Elizabeth	Jervis	Ilex	Stuart
Valiant	Kandahar	Hero	Voyager
Ajax	Kimberley	Hasty	Waterhen
Phoebe	Janus	Isis	Vendetta
Coventry (with temporary bow)	Jaguar	Hotspur	Defender
	Jackal	Griffin[41]	

238. *Middle East Commanders-in-Chief Committee*

4 June

151. *Syria*

The C-in-C, Mediterranean, gave certain details regarding his plans for support of operations against Syria. He had signalled the Admiralty with a view to clarifying the policy to be adopted against the French Fleet, etc., in Syria. He had also suggested to the Admiralty that a further friendly agreement with the French Navy at Alexandria would be desirable, as he did not want a battle in Alexandria harbour as a result of our action against Syria. At the

---

[41]*Leander* (RNZN): 1933, 7,270t, 8×6in, 8×4in, 8×21in tt, 32.5k; and *Paramatta* (RAN): c.1939, 1,060t, 3×4in, 16.5k; s by U-boat, Nov. 1941, off Tobruk; see P. and F. M. McGuire, *The Price of Admiralty* (Melbourne, 1944). These ships joined about this time.

worst, however, the French Fleet in Alexandria was only a nuisance value.

The C-in-C, Mediterranean, felt it would be wise to avoid clashes with the French Navy in Syrian waters in the early stages as retaliation by those anti-British elements might encourage resistance by the Army.

He agreed that the Navy would support the Army in their advance along the coast road....

152. *Tobruk*

... The C-in-C, Mediterranean, drew attention to the difficulty of supplying Tobruk. Ships were continually being sunk. Without fighter protection the slow small ships now being used had little chance of accomplishing their journey in safety.

The AOC-in-C explained the difficulty of providing air protection on these occasions. It was a costly commitment and to provide increased protection to shipping would involve a reduction in the aircraft available for direct support of the Army in the Western Desert.

It was accepted that with the present air bases available to the RAF little fighter support could be given to Tobruk.

It was agreed that nothing much could be done to improve the position at present, but that CGS should inquire whether it was in fact necessary to send ships to Tobruk every night.[42]

The C-in-C, Mediterranean, said he now felt it had become necessary to organise a special group to supply naval needs on the parallel of Coastal Command at home. He considered the present system was unsatisfactory. He pressed for the allotment of air forces specifically for naval co-operation and asked that the Beaufort aircraft now being sent out from Coastal Command at home be devoted specifically to naval needs.

The AOC-in-C was unable to agree to the suggestions that air forces should be locked up for this purpose. Our resources were still relatively limited and such a policy would be uneconomical. The Fleet was not always at sea, and we had to use our resources to the best advantage in each changing situation. It was of course a different thing when there was a definite commitment involving the full time employment of air units.

He suggested the Navy should now examine future possible operations in the Mediterranean, from which could be seen what air

---

[42]CGS, ME: Lt-Gen Sir Arthur Smith: Ft Gds; Col 1932; Maj-Gen July 1938; Actg Lt-Gen Apr. 1941; Lt-Gen Feb. 1944.

commitments were involved and to what extent our resources were adequate or should be strengthened.

He was fully sympathetic to the suggestion that the present organisation for controlling air forces allotted for co-operation with the Navy should be improved and extended as necessary.

239. *To Pound*

11 June 1941

A. Firstly may I bring Lees to your especial notice. He has done splendidly out here. His ship was most efficient and he kept the morale of his ship's company very high throughout a very gruelling time and even in the water after they were sunk.

Calcutta is a sad loss to us. Lees is a born leader and I strongly recommend him for a more important command after a few weeks' rest.

B. Though GHQ state they are satisfied I fear the Syria business is not moving so fast as we had hoped. Perhaps the tempo will improve as they move forward but matters are very slow at the moment.

The destroyers are doing good work on the flank and I think the Army are very glad to have their assistance. They are getting moderately bombed. . . .

While they are in harbour I have kept my hands off the French destroyers that attacked ours but I mean to sink them should they emerge. They shouldn't have got away last time but a submarine frightened our cruisers into Haifa. This, I hope, will not occur again.

May I offer one criticism of the ships when they come out from home and that is that they don't realise that out here they have to accept risks. An impossible frame of mind.

C. I had an interview with Godfroy yesterday. I am so glad that the Admiralty take the same view that I do, i.e., that it is better to avoid a scrap as long as possible. Godfroy, I think, realises that he is on a bad wicket and is fairly amenable. We have had five or six further deserters and they tell us that all is prepared for instant scuttling. . . .

Actually if they do scuttle themselves in their present berths little harm will be done except that we lose the ships, and I have my eye on *Lorraine* to help *Anson* block Tripoli!![43]

D. I am not aware what your intentions are as regards battleships out here. At the moment we have only two, *Valiant* and *Queen Elizabeth*, serviceable.

---

[43]*Anson* was the latest British battleship: 1942, 35,000t, 10×14in, 16×5.25in, 28k.

... if it is understood that we stand on the defensive say East of 25°E, these should be sufficient but without any margin in case of damage. But should we be expected to proceed into the Central Mediterranean, say if Malta is attacked by a seaborne squadron, it would be most risky to do so without something behind us.

Further, if BATTLEAXE meets with success and I can get proper fighter support, it should, I think, be possible to operate in the Central Mediterranean again and do something towards supplying Malta's needs.

I am rather diffident about putting this before you as I know how much the heavy ships are wanted in the Atlantic but while *Warspite* and *Barham*, to say nothing of *Formidable*, are away, probably for some months, I should feel happier if I had a reinforcement handy.

E. Another point is submarines. If any more can be spared I can use any number profitably. The Athens, Salonika and Dardanelles areas would be most profitable and I can only spare one at a time to go there.

We have already bagged about four or five ships in the Aegean. I may be wrong but I hold that if we can sink enough enemy shipping in the Mediterranean we shall impose severe limitations on the enemy operations. They have only 300 [merchant vessels] left. We have sunk or seized somewhere in the neighbourhood of 150; if we can put another 150 out of action I am sure we shall have them in difficulties out here.

F. I am not very happy about our relations with the Air out here. Since Crete, about which they came in for much criticism and odium, largely undeserved, they have been very touchy and difficult. Wavell, I think, has found the same.

I am now trying to get Tedder to produce an organisation, analogous to the Coastal Command at home, with its HQ down here.

The Beaufighters and the reconnaissance Blenheims to be the nucleus of the force.

Although Tedder has accepted the principle he is being most dilatory in setting up the organisation and he positively refuses to allot aircraft for the sole duty of Naval Co-operation. I have now addressed a letter to him and if he refuses I shall have to ask for your assistance.

G. You will have seen that we have had a couple of air raids on Alexandria. ...

The direct military and naval damage was small but the whole port came to a standstill next day and hasn't restarted yet. ...

H. I haven't yet answered your signal about the C-in-C being in Cairo.

... though it might be a convenience to the other two at times, it is quite unnecessary. There wouldn't be a full day's work for him at any time and he would become totally divorced from the operations of the fleet ...

As far as strategy is concerned the co-operation at the present moment is quite good. In other words in the higher ranks I don't think anything further is necessary. It is on the operational side on the rather lower plane that we are not close enough to each other ...

I. I am much concerned about Cyprus. I know that the Chiefs of Staff have decided that it must be just let go and I also know that no troops are available to defend it but the consequences of its occupation by the Germans are very serious. We shall, I expect, lose the use of Haifa oil and Port Said and Suez are so much nearer to air attack.

Of course, if we do take Syria my forebodings will be falsified.

240. *From Vice Admiral Sir James Somerville*

Gibraltar
12 June 1941

... it makes my blood boil. To think that you of all people should have your action questioned in withdrawing the Fleet to Alexandria [from Crete]. We were amazed that you were able to keep the ships there as long as you did. It must have been agony for you not being on the spot yourself but you can't be in part of the fight and at the same time conduct the major operation. I'm glad you've sent Dickie Mount B[atten] home to report matters. He's forceful and has the gift for putting a case.

I'm not surprised that the sailors were shaken. I watched carefully what happened at Dunkirk and saw the results of continuous bombing at sea. On shore you don't feel that *you* are the target. At sea it is just too bloody obvious and has its effect accordingly.

But I do trust Andrew old boy that TL's won't be quite such *bloody* fools as to try to find someone to relieve you, at least not until the situation in the Eastern Med is a little more stabilised. After that has been achieved I'm sure the whole Navy would welcome your relief so that you can return home and become CNS. We might then hope for *someone* who is not a yes man and who will see that important decisions are not usually relegated to the mid watch amidst the aroma of very old brandy and expensive cigars. I speak with some acidity because I've seen it all happening.[44]

What you say about the Air Force is also true. There is no place for an independent Air Force . . .

In view of what your letter told me I feel rather guilty about not having taken a chance and perhaps saved 24 hours in delivering this batch of Hurris. But I hope we shall continue to deliver . . . we proceed to sea on *Friday 13th*. . . .

241. *To Rear Admiral Willis*

12 June 1941

. . . Just as you and I thought so the Greek expedition turned out. Dunkirk was nothing to it except the scale. Our wretched soldiers never saw a British plane for 12 days before they evacuated and of course our ships and shipping had no fighter protection. I had only five Fulmars left after TIGER (tanks to Egypt) and so kept *Formidable* and battleships in harbour to release destroyers to take off the soldiers.

Then came Crete – much worse proposition. Again I did not dare to go to sea myself so as to keep my finger on matters here. Oh! that I had. I am sure two good cruisers and two destroyers would now be afloat had I been there.

Gloucester and *Fiji* were dispatched to stand by *Greyhound* 30 miles off the enemy aerodrome. Neither had more than 15% AA amm. on board so the expected happened. . . .

It was not all gloom though. On the days that mattered no German soldier came to Crete by sea and we drowned about 4–5,000 one night. It should have been double but one cruiser squadron allowed themselves to be driven off a convoy of over 30 caiques stiff with soldiers by dive bombers. The *Calcutta* and *Carlisle* were right in among them and were recalled. . . .

. . . The Air Force did not take a hand till too late. Actually there was little they could do but they have incurred considerable odium among the troops and there have been scraps ashore . . . .[45]

---

[44]Churchill, a creature of the night, had scant regard for his military colleagues, who had already put in a hard day, and many suspected that he called midnight meetings because he knew their resistance to his hare-brained schemes would then be low. Somerville had been home twice in the past year.

[45]Cdr Somerville recalled that local RAF-inspired publicity tended to magnify the RAF's contribution to the evacuations from Greece and Crete, much to the annoyance of sailors and soldiers. He remarked also that a sailor, on blowing up his lifejacket, observed 'That's the only bloody air support we'll get today!' Cdr Somerville to editor, 6 Oct. 1997.

I am now engaged in a pitched battle with the RAF and I'm in no mood for compromise. It's about Coastal Command and I'm just going to hammer the thing through.

242. *Middle East Commanders-in-Chief Committee*

18 June 1941

163. *Western Desert*

... The C-in-C, Mediterranean, said he hoped to carry on operating four destroyers for the supply of Tobruk, but his present resources ruled out the question of being able to send convoys to Malta.

... The general opinion was that for the present the policy should be to hold on to Tobruk and to hammer away by all means available at the enemy's supply. In this connection, the AOC-in-C said he would continue for the present to attack the enemy's L of C with the maximum forces, and the C-in-C, Mediterranean, said he had already asked for some more submarines. ...

243. *From Pound*

19 June 1941

... I know what a difficult time you have been having with the German dive bombers. Your experience has only confirmed our previous opinion that nothing but fighters can deal with a determined attack in large numbers. ...

At the moment there is no armoured carrier available. *Victorious* is to receive her complement of aircraft and will no longer be used for ferrying fighters. I do not feel, however, that it would be any good sending you a carrier whilst the present conditions in the Eastern Mediterranean continue, as I think it would be a sheer waste because the carrier would be bound to be knocked out in a very short time.

The U-boats are working very far afield in the Newfoundland and Freetown areas, ...

We have also had to send destroyers and corvettes to Freetown. Had it not been for the above I should have endeavoured to have sent you some more destroyers, but I do not see how I possibly can, in spite of knowing how short you are. If, however, at any time you feel you must have reinforcements, then please do not hesitate to say so, though I can't guaranteee that it will be possible to spare them. . . .

. . . I have not the slightest fear that what has happened will have shaken the faith of the personnel of the Fleet in your handling of affairs.

244. *War Diary, June 1941 (cont.)*

7 June

Operations – Syria

CS15 sailed from Alexandria in *Phoebe* with Force B consisting of *Ajax, Kandahar, Kimberley, Jackal* and *Janus*. This force had to be off the Syrian coast at daylight 8 June when CS15 would take control of all forces in the area and operate in support of the Army.

2. Force C, *Glengyle, Coventry, Ilex, Hotspur, Isis* sailed from Port Said to effect a landing with S[pecial] S[ervice] troops from *Glengyle* at the mouth of the Litani river during the night 7/8. Troops were then to hold the bridge at Kann for the advance of the Army. *Hero* reported that a fairly heavy swell which might hold up the landing was decreasing.

3. Fighter protection for the ships at sea was to be provided by Fulmars based at Lydda. 815 Squadron at Nicosia was reinforced with more Swordfish aircraft and was to operate under the orders of CS15.

4. The following general directions of policy had been given by the Admiralty:

- (a) No action is to be taken against French warships unless they attempt to interfere with our operations.
- (b) HM Ships to be in readiness and to act as developments indicate.
- (c) Any French shipping encountered to be sent into Haifa.

Western Desert

5. *Vendetta* and *Voyager* arrived at and left Tobruk during the night 6/7 returning to Mersa Matruh. In view of the recent losses and scale of air attack being experienced the C-in-C ordered the suspension of all shipping other than destroyers running supplies to Tobruk. This decision was reached after consultation with the AOC-in-C and the C-in-C, Middle East. Normal service would be resumed as soon as adequate fighter protection was available.

9 June

Operations – Syria

2. There was an action off Sidon with two French flotilla leaders from Beirut in which *Janus* was severely damaged. The French destroyers were bombarding our advanced forces and were intercepted by *Janus, Jackal* and *Hotspur*. The French opened an accurate fire at long range and *Janus*, who was ahead of the other two, was hit by five or six shells, one of which exploded in the boiler room and disabled her. *Jackal* and later *Hotspur* drew the fire from her until *Isis* came to their support whereupon the French destroyers retired at high speed apparently undamaged. They were chased into Beirut harbour. *Janus* was later towed to Haifa by *Kimberley*.

3. CS15 was operating off the coast with the remainder of his force. *Phoebe* was missed by a torpedo thought to have been fired from a French submarine. The Fulmars protecting this force were attacked by French fighters and badly cut about, three were shot down and two seriously damaged.

4. Captain (D), 10DF, in *Stuart*, was sailed from Alexandria p.m. with *Jaguar, Griffin* and *Defender* to reinforce CS15 and to act as an A/S striking force.

Alexandria

6. The effects of the air raids of the night 7/8 were being severely felt in the Dockyard. Only one contract firm had as much as 40% of the labour at work and others were down to 10% and 20%. Night work was out of the question and there were no native crews for the armament tugs and lighters and other harbour services.

10 June

Operations – Syria

Force B continued to operate off the Syrian coast . . . As a result of the action of the previous day in which the French opened fire first on our destroyers, the C-in-C gave instructions that all French surface ships and submarines should be treated as hostile. . . .

Swordfish bombers should be ready to attack ships in harbour at Beirut but were not to do so without authority from the C-in-C. . . .

11 June

MTBs

8. A signal was sent to the Admiralty with reference to a proposal to send out more MTBs. The 10th MTB Flotilla had been practically

useless due to their continual breakdowns and low endurance. Another flotilla would be welcome, but it must be of a more robust type.

Malta

9. VAM suggested the running of ME8 Malta convoy & of an increase in the Malta bomber strength in order to take advantage of the reported withdrawal from the Mediterranean of large numbers of the German Air Force. VAM also suggested that it would now be possible to refit one or more destroyers at Malta.

12 June

Air Reconnaissance

9. Owing to the scale of enemy air attack it was not practicable to maintain surface patrols or covering forces at sea within dive-bomber range ... The importance of accurate and extensive air reconnaissance was therefore much greater and difficulties were being experienced in achieving the necessary close co-operation with the RAF. The following signal was made by the C-in-C to HQRAFME:

> Following received from 201 Group. Begins: A159 12/5. Regret unable carry out ME1 patrol today due unserviceability and communication commitments 1150/12. Ends.
> Suggest it is essential the reconnaissance requirements take precedence over communication. It is quite unacceptable that important reconnaissance should be unexpectedly withdrawn without warning during the progress of operations.

13 June

Operations – Syria

Destroyers successfully bombarded a large battery of French 75s near Saida and continued to act in close support of the Army. Force B was attacked at 1530 on 13th by nine Ju88s without damage. Fighters came to the assistance of Force B and shot down three Ju88s and seriously damaged two more.

14 June

Alexandria – French Squadron

9. The leave of the personnel of the French Squadron had been stopped since the advance into Syria in order to avoid the possibility

of a difficult situation arising. Admiral Godfroy now assured the C-in-C that in spite of events in Syria nothing altered the situation as laid down in the agreement of July 1940. Leave was accordingly recommenced the following day. The attitude of the Vichy Government was still uncertain but there seemed to be a wish to localise hostilities in Syria.

15 June

Operations – BATTLEAXE

The advance in the Western Desert was timed to commence a.m. 15th. There was to be no naval bombardment in order that the maximum fighter effort might be concentrated in support of the Army. The naval objective was:

(a) to establish an advanced supply base at Sollum.
(b) to increase the supply rate to Tobruk, unloading by day.

Both these requirements depended on fighter protection being available over the ports before they could be commenced. Accordingly the Sollum Naval Base party was embarked in *Parramatta* and *Southern Sea* and sailed to Mersa Matruh with *St Issey* (who was to tow water barges to Sollum) to await developments. Loading of *Glenroy* and *Protector* was commenced, five 'D' lighters, some stores, petrol and military personnel being embarked in *Glenroy* and a full load of cased petrol in *Protector*. Both ships remained at Alexandria for the present.[46]

16 June

Operations – Syria

3. C-in-C's message 1004/16 gave CS15 further instructions as to the conduct of the operation. It was pointed out that we could not afford to have destroyers knocked out at the present rate and that Force B must retire into Haifa during daylight unless adequate fighter protection was available. The Army GOC must choose between naval support for his left flank and fighter protection for his troops.[47]

---

[46]*Southern Sea*: S Af A/S whaler: 1936, 344gt, 14k, S Whaling & Sealing Co.

BATTLEAXE failed and Wavell was replaced by Gen (later FM) Sir Claude Auchinleck (1884–1981): most of career in India; Maj-Gen 1939; IV Corps; Norway Spring 1940; V Corps; S Cmd; Lt-Gen July 1940; Gen & C-in-C India Nov. 1940; C-in-C ME, July 1941–Aug. 1942; C-in-C India 1943–47; FM 1946.

[47]Army GOC was Gen Wilson. *Ilex* & *Isis* were badly damaged by Fr & Ger bombers but Swordfish of 815 Sqdn sank a Fr reinforcement, *Chevalier Paul*: 1934, 2,441t, 5×5.5in, 6×21.7in tt, 36k.

17 June

Submarines

5. *Torbay* returned to Alexandria from patrol of the northern Aegean and reported the following sinkings:

(a) by gunfire: 1 June – German caique with personnel and stores for Mitylene.
3 June – A caique with oil drums for Mitylene.
12 June – Italian schooner with troops, ammunition and stores for Lemnos.
(b) by torpedo: 6 June – French tanker *Alberta*.
10 June – Italian tanker *Giuseppina Ghirhardi*.[48]
(c) by ramming: 11 June – A caique proceeding to Mitylene.

Torbay torpedoed *Alberta* S of the Dardanelles on 5 June when she grounded and was abandoned. She was then boarded and set on fire, her papers having been examined. The following day a Turkish tug proceeded to tow her away when *Torbay* torpedoed her again and she was abandoned in a sinking condition.

18 June

Western Desert – BATTLEAXE

3. *Stuart* and 19th Division continued to run supplies to Tobruk. Destroyers were now working in pairs and unloading on two nights out of three. . . . schooners would continue to run to maximum capacity; one small steamer would be escorted in at irregular intervals and also a petrol carrier to unload at night only.

19 June

Operations – Syria

The Staff Officer to CS15 . . . came to Alexandria and a clearer picture of the situation in Syria was available to the C-in-C.[49] Owing to the requirements of the Army continuous fighter protection was not available for ships at sea; with good reconnaissance and the short distance to Syrian air bases the enemy could choose their

---

[48]*Alberta*: 1938, 3,357gt, French Shell.
Giuseppina Ghirhardi: 1892, 3,319gt, L. Ghirardi, Genoa.
[49]SO, CS15: VA King.

opportunity for air attack. Similarly French destroyers could always slip out from Beirut with air cover, bombard our advanced forces and return before our patrols could reach them. These sorties generally coincided with an advance by tanks in order to draw naval support away from the Army. The Army advance had been checked in order to allow of re-organising and forming a Corps HQ.

23 June

At 0148/23 *Naiad, Leander, Jaguar, Kingston* and *Nizam* encountered two French destroyers . . . 10 miles N of Beirut. An engagement ensued lasting 11 minutes in which both French destroyers were reported to be hit. They then retired under a smokescreen under the guns of Nahr-el-Kelb.[50] . . .

HMS Orion

3. . . . The following signal was made to *Orion* by the C-in-C:

I much regret that *Orion* has to leave the station where she has played such a distinguished part since the outbreak of war with Italy.
2. She has a record of good service in the Mediterranean which all on board may be proud of culminating in the very difficult operation of evacuating troops from Crete – an operation most gallantly achieved though most regrettably at the cost of many lives and serious damage to the ship.
3. I hope you will all have a very happy homecoming and enjoy some leave you have earned so well.

24 June

Western Desert – Loss of HMS Auckland

5. *Parramatta* and *Auckland* escorting SS *Pass of Balmaha* to Tobruk were heavily attacked by enemy aircraft. An unsuccessful T/B attack in the forenoon was followed at 1430 by divebombing attacks estimated at 16 Ju87 each. The majority concentrated on *Auckland*, who was hit aft and disabled, and sank at 1530 . . . after being hit several times again. There were further high level attacks and a second wave of divebombing attacks at 1900, again by three formations of about 16 aircraft each. *Parramatta* shot down 2 aircraft and possibly another and returned undamaged to Alexandria

---

[50]*Guépard* was hit by a 6in shell.

with *Auckland*'s survivors; SS *Pass of Balmaha* was slightly damaged by a near miss but got into Tobruk during the night. She was towed in by *Waterhen* who was running in supplies but was therefore unable to unload them. There was no fighter protection due partly to a failure in communication, and partly to aircraft being grounded by enemy action and largely to the slow speed (6 knots) of SS *Pass of Balmaha* putting her outside fighter range. Later intelligence showed that the enemy probably knew of these movements. . . .

25 June

Malta

5. ... The Constructive Department was now working at about 50%, the Engineering at about 70% and Electrical at 80%. Three docks were in action without electric power being available. Excavation for the underground workshop was proceeding satisfactorily. The scale of air raids had evidently been reduced recently.

30 June

3. *Flamingo, Cricket* and convoy were heavily bombed from 1340/30 onwards by a total of at least 60 Ju87 and Ju88 escorted by Me110s while approaching Tobruk. *Antiklia* and *Miranda* got into Tobruk safely but *Flamingo*'s machinery was damaged by a near miss and *Cricket* had one boiler room flooded and several other leaks caused by near misses. *Flamingo* took *Cricket* in tow at dark for Alexandria. *St Issey* was sent to assist. *Flamingo* reported shooting two aircraft down and damaging four more and fighters claimed another three while patrolling over the convoy. *Southern Isles* also reported 2 aircraft shot down. The C-in-C congratulated all concerned on this determined action.[51]

Submarines

6. The special dispositions of submarines from Malta ordered the previous day necessitated their normal rest periods being again broken into. The following signal was addressed to the Malta submarines from the C-in-C:

---

[51]*Cricket*: 1915, 625t, 2×6in, 1×3in, 14k; tot loss foll bombing off Libya June 1941.
*Southern Isle*s: 1936, 344gt, 14k, S Whaling & Sealing.
Antiklia: 1892, 951gt, Dwaris & Tzanetatos, Piraeus.
Miranda: 1920, 1,328gt, AS Miranda, Bergen.
Escort of 4 ftr sqdns.

I fully appreciate the heavy call which is being made on you all but I am confident you will realise the necessity and meet it with that ready efficiency you have always displayed.[52]

Summary and Appreciation of Events for Month of June 1941

Strategical

The German occupation of Greece and Crete had materially altered the whole strategical position. Not only could the through-Mediterranean supply line now be controlled by the enemy should he decide to concentrate powerful air forces in Crete and Cyrenaica, but the security of our position in Egypt itself was threatened. German infiltration into Syria had increased recently and Germany was giving direct help via Syria to the revolutionary and pro-Nazi Government established in Teheran. It seemed quite possible that an airborne attack might be expected both upon Syria and upon Cyprus. Consequently it was felt to be essential to forestall the enemy and secure our northern flank in Syria before the enemy was sufficiently well established in Crete to launch a further attack in either direction.

3. The Syrian operation cost us three valuable destroyers put out of action at a time when they could ill be spared. But our command of the sea, both in giving direct support to the Army and in preventing reinforcements from reaching Syria, proved a decisive factor in the campaign.

5. Before the end of the month it became clear that the immediate German objective was not to the south-eastward, if indeed it ever had been, for on 22 June the German Army advanced into Russia. . . .

245. *To Rear Admiral Burrough*[53]

30 June 1941

Things went well for us out here up to a point, in fact as long as we pursued one object. When we started pursuing two or more at the same time catastrophe resulted not very surprisingly. Do not read into this

---

[52]A possible sortie by Italian fleet.
[53]RA (later Adm Sir) Harold M. Burrough Mid 1904; Capt 1928; gunnery splist; Capt *Excellent* 1937; RA & ACNS(T) 1939–40; 10CS Sept 1940; Vaagso raid; Malta convoys 1941–42; VA Oct. 1942; FO Gibraltar & Med Approaches Sept. 1943; Actg Adm & ANCXF, NW Eur Jan. 1945; SBNO, Germany 1945–46; C-in-C Nore 1946.

that I was against sending help to the Greeks. I was sure it was the right policy but I knew and said in no uncertain terms that our resources were unequal to it. It may be that the merit we acquired in the USA was a set off worth our defeat in Libya & our evacuation of Greece.

The latter was an expensive amusement but reflected nothing but credit, though I says it as shouldn't, on the RN & merchant vessels which took part. Some of the doings of the little ships, landing craft and such like which are only coming to light now are just fine and you may be sure the destroyers were in the thick of it.

Crete was just saddening. I must say I was quite sure that, if the soldiers were given two or three days to deal with the airborne troops without interference by seaborne forces, Crete could be held. And at great cost to ourselves we gave them their three days & fairly sickened the Hun of the sea but in vain. Our badly equipped troops handicapped by a want of preparation for which as one of the three Cs-in-C I must accept a share of the responsibility (chiefly for not being rude enough to the other two) just couldn't hold the well-equipped Hun though there was a slaughter 'grim and great' of parachutists.

I had several cruisers and destroyers knocked out during the evacuation which was a dire business. A fact, which you can keep to yourself, & a sad one was that in some ships the sailors began to crack a bit. It gave you a line on the officers and some surprises too. Thank God they have all recovered now. Rawlings who had his ship knocked to hell & the Lord only knows how many casualties among his sailors and 1,000 troops was absolutely grand. So cheery though he had a bit of bomb through his thigh. A great leader.

I am pretty well skinned of ships & destroyers & losing more every day. I must say when they set their mind to it the Hun Air Force is very efficient & they take a nasty toll of my little ships running supplies to Tobruk. The *Auckland* two days ago & last night the old *Waterhen*. Why is it that the morale of the small ship sailors stands up so much more than that of the larger ships? I mustn't malign my old *Warspite* though who had 90 casualties from a bomb but whose tail was more erect than ever after it.

This Syrian business saddens me. Everyone says we should have had the place days ago if only we had been without the Free French. The mainstay of the resistance is I think the French Admiral and his ships. I am not sure Admiral Gouton is quite so happy now though as we have mauled his forces pretty effectively.[54]

---

[54] VA Pierre V. G. Gouton (1890–1956): ent N 1908; cruisers & destroyers 1914–18; Lt de V 1918; Cdt *Vauban* 1931–33; Capt de V 1935; *Colbert* 1936–38; Contre-Amiral Oct 1939; Cdt, Levant Div., July 1940–Aug. 1941; VA Aug. 1941; admin posts 1941–43; ret 1944.

246. *Cunningham's Report on the Syrian Campaign*

2 September 1941

Cunningham's Observations

2. This campaign had three main features of naval interest:

(i) Our naval forces provided vital assistance to the Army in their advance along the coast road. These operations were generally very satisfactory.
(ii) The encounters between the opposing surface forces were defintely not satisfactory and it must be conceded that the honours rest with the Vichy destroyers.
(iii) There was a very considerable drain on our slender air resources both for reconnaissance and fighter protection throughout the campaign.

Fighter Protection and Reconnaissance

3. Although a minor campaign, some troublesome problems were presented from a naval point of view. The scale of the air attack, though not by any means heavy, was enough to be tiresome and caused considerable hull damage to two destroyers which could ill be spared.

4. This resulted in the movements of naval forces being largely limited to darkness unless fighter protection could be continuously given. The number of fighters available was insufficient to meet the needs of both land and sea operations; in consequence a balance had constantly to be struck between the need for naval guns to support and guard the flank of the Army, and the need of direct air support and defence for the troops in the field.

5. The situation was further complicated by the presence of two and later three Vichy French destroyer leaders at Beirut. These fast well armed ships were admirably placed to seize on any momentary absence or weakness of our forces to make 'tip and run' raids or bombardments and scuttle back into Beirut before harm could overtake them.

6. The reconnaissance and striking forces of naval co-operation squadrons (201 Group) and of the FAA had to be concentrated in Cyprus for reconnaissance to the N and W against the arrival of reinforcements. The reconnaissance on the Syrian coast had perforce to be left to aircraft of the Palestine and Trans-Jordan command which had no sea experience whatever. Their reconnaissance

left much to be desired and was frequently misleading. In the extreme instance this inexperience led to the bombing of our own ships by our own aircraft. ...

7. Even the reconnaissance from Cyprus was not wholly satisfactory. No 203 Sqdn (Blenheims), which had recently joined 201 Group as a GR Sqdn, proved to be very ill trained, and it was solely due to this lack of training that the Flotilla Leader *Vauquelin* was allowed to reach Beirut in spite of ample warning and after having been sighted by our air reconnaissance.

8. In contrast to these failures the work of 230 Sqdn, RAF, and of 815, 826 and 829 Sqdns, FAA, conformed to their usual high standard. The activities of 230 Sqdn were considerably cramped by the need to keep out of enemy fighter range both from Rhodes and Syria. The FAA squadrons carried out a great deal of flying, under difficult maintenance conditions, from Nicosia aerodrome which was virtually unprotected and subject to intermittent air raids. In the course of these operations they sank the *Chevalier Paul* in addition to several night raids on Beirut harbour. They also sank the Vichy ship *St Didier* in Adalia Roads.[55]

Surface Actions

9. The engagements which took place between our naval forces and the French destroyers were disappointing. The first, on 9 June, when *Janus* was damaged, was an example of the ease with which the French could seize a temporarily favourable situation and retire unhurt. The remarks of the VA, 15CS, are concurred in. It is considered that more satisfactory results would have ensued had *Janus* kept his force concentrated. This action is an example of the importance of immediately organising a force of ships, however small, to enable them to act cohesively as a unit. HMS *Jackal*'s successful screening and defence of *Janus* in face of superior force reflects credit on her CO (Lt Cdr R. McC. P. Jonas, RN).[56]

10. The action was fought at what is considered long range by our destroyer standards (18,000 to 10,000 yards), against an enemy superior in speed and gunpower. Both sides made large alterations of course and presented targets at fine inclinations. In these circumstances the gunnery of one Vichy destroyer (green splashes) was

---

[55]*St Didier*: 1920, 2,778gt, Soc Navale de l'Ouest.
[56]Lt-Cdr R. McC. P. Jonas: Lt-Cdr 1934; *Triad* 1939; *Fernie* 1940; *Jackal* Mar. 1941; Cdr Dec. 1941; OD 1942.

very good particularly as regards range accuracy. *Janus*, not yet fitted with cross-levelling gear, had much difficulty with line keeping. *Jackal* fired more accurately and straddled continuously but did not hit. Although at 10,000 yards there was a considerable element of luck in obtaining three simultaneous hits including a 'stopping' hit on *Janus* at fine inclination, there is no doubt that the good Vichy destroyer produced long range gunnery of an accuracy considerably above our destroyer standard.

11. The second contact of surface forces on 14 June was merely irritating. The Vichy destroyers kept out of range and retired within their shore defences.

12. The third contact at 0148/23 was unsatisfactory. The destroyers were engaged by *Naiad, Leander* and three destroyers for 11 minutes at ranges too long for effective night work (5,000 yards and upwards) while they were retiring at high speed making smoke.... One destroyer only was hit by a six inch [shell] from *Leander* which is alleged to have been blind.

13. Taking all in all it must be stated that the Vichy destroyers were well and boldly handled and took good advantage of their situation.

Coastal Operations and Bombardments

15. At the outset of the campaign both the C-in-C, Middle East Forces, and the GOC, Palestine and Trans-Jordan, were not a little sceptical of the value of having naval forces operating on the flank, in spite of experience in the Cyrenaican campaign.

It was actually suggested that owing to their need for fighter defence they should be withdrawn from the flank of the Army so that fighters could be released for Army support. This produced a categorical statement from the Brigadier on the left that he would prefer to be without the fighters rather than lose his naval support on the left flank.

In the event our naval forces became a vital factor in enabling the Army to advance along the coast road and they undoubtedly saved our troops much loss of life.

16. The country, with a restricted coastal corridor, and the vital coastal road in full view from the sea over long stretches, was ideal for naval co-operation. Apart from pre-arranged bombardments of Vichy areas and batteries, and the ability to bring enfilade fire to bear on defended positions, there were some glorious opportunities for direct fire on Vichy tanks and MT on the road.

General

19. In conclusion it is of interest to note that this comparatively petty campaign absorbed the entire effort of all reconnaissance aircraft available for naval co-operation in the Eastern Mediterranean, with the exception of those based on Malta. To achieve the requisite number of aircraft for the Syrian campaign, all reconnaissance to the W of Alexandria had to be stopped and Tobruk left wide open to surprise. Even so the available aircraft were insufficient and reliance for coastal reconnaissance had to be placed on the untrained aircraft of the Palestine and Trans-Jordan command.

247. *War Diary, July 1941*

1 July

Western Desert

4. The RAF reported shooting down 9 enemy aircraft the previous day; *Flamingo* and *Southern Isles* each claimed two also. But the RAF would not be able to continue fighter protection for such slow convoys. Over 70 aircraft had been employed using up 212 engine hours and the patrols of about 12 had usually met 30–40 enemy fighters. The inevitable losses and unserviceability of our aircraft was unacceptable. Accordingly it was decided to employ 'A' lighters on the Western Desert Supply service instead of the small supply steamers who were evidently too slow and vulnerable. Eight 'A' lighters, capable of about 10 knots, were to be used, running in pairs unescorted.

2 July

Aircraft minelaying

3. The C-in-C suggested to HQRAFME that cucumbers might be laid during the coming full moon period off Benghazi, in the Corinth Canal or off Salonika.

Russian Mission

6. A British Liaison Mission had been sent to Russia, The naval section was instructed that the only direct action possible to prevent enemy naval forces entering the Black Sea from the Mediterranean was by maintenance of submarine patrols off the Dardanelles and in the Aegean.

3 July

Operations – Syria

CS7 sailed from Alexandria at 0100/3 in *Ajax* with *Phoebe, Nizam* and *Kimberley* to reinforce CS15. The C-in-C suggested that CS15 should now form two forces, one under CS7 of *Ajax, Perth* and destroyers for bombarding, and the other of *Naiad, Phoebe* and destroyers for intercepting Vichy reinforcements. The extra two cruisers and two destroyers would be withdrawn when the situation regarding Vichy reinforcements was cleared up.

Fast Supply Ships

9. In view of recent experience which showed that Army supplies could only be satisfactorily run in fast ships in face of enemy air opposition, the C-in-C asked the Admiralty if two or more 1,500–2,000 ton cargo ships capable of 15 knots could be provided by conversion or from another station.

11 July

Operations – Syria

4. The C-in-C instructed CS15 ... that the following rules with regard to Vichy ships were to be observed:

(a) Ships moving on Syrian coast are to be captured if possible, otherwise to be sunk.
(b) Westbound ships in Turkish territorial waters are not to be molested.
(c) Westbound ships outside territorial waters to be ordered to Famagusta or Haifa on pain of sinking. Force may be used.
(d) Eastbound ships to be sunk. If in Turkish territorial waters may be sunk if definitely identified as enemy.

CS15 is requested to send MTBs to Famagusta to assist in bringing ships in under headings (a) and (c). Yugoslav MTBs to be included if the CO is agreeable.

248. *To Willis*

6 July 1941

... I wrote to DP five weeks ago after the Crete affair and told him if the Naval Staff (with whom I had some fierce passages at the time) or the PM would like a change I was quite willing. I had a reply that there had never been any idea of making a change ... But I don't feel the PM will let me stay long. .....

I am having a fierce battle with Tedder over the Coastal Command. Things are worse than when you were here. .....

Of course the real truth is that there is no function for an independent air force out here and Tedder is fighting hard to maintain it.

249. *Middle East Commanders-in-Chief Committee*

17 July 1941

200. *Corinth Canal*

The C-in-C, Mediterranean, said it was most important that the Corinth Canal should be blocked as soon as possible. He considered that about 80% of the traffic from the Aegean passed through the Canal. By closing the Canal, therefore, shipping would be forced out into the Mediterranean. Blocking could be achieved either by mining from aircraft or by sinking a ship in the Canal by submarine.

The C-in-C, Mediterranean, said that in his opinion attacks on enemy shipping were all-important and would do more to bring about the downfall of the enemy in the Middle East than any other method. He felt that the Italian seamen must be already feeling the strain of these continued submarine and air attacks.

250. *War Diary, July 1941 (cont.)*

22 July

Aircraft

11. HQ, RAF Middle East were asked to initiate attacks on Suda Bay where the damaged merchant ships were reported as being salvaged. Heavy bombs in daylight while the divers were working would probably prove most effective.

23 July

Loss of Defender

9. The following signal was made by the C-in-C:

> In reading the account of the loss of HMS *Defender* I noticed with interest and pleasure the seamanlike and determined efforts made by all concerned to save the ship.

I wish to congratulate the officers and ships' companies of *Defender* and *Vendetta* on this good work.

25 July

Canal Area

5. *Queen Mary*, the first of the monster liners with troops from Australia arrived at Suez and unloaded successfully. She was sailed again at dark, the intention being for ships to unload singly in two day periods, each waiting meanwhile in other anchorages further South. The ships were to proceed to sea at night to avoid risk of bombing.[57]

26 July

Malta – Abortive Attack on the Grand Harbour

The Grand Harbour was heavily attacked by about 20 E-boats and one-man torpedo boats at dawn 26 July. The attack was repulsed most successfully. The E-boats scored hits on the viaduct of St Elmo breakwater but the harbour defence guns prevented any E-boat or torpedo craft from following through, and in about three minutes the attack was entirely frustrated. It was believed that all 20 were destroyed, those that escaped the harbour defence guns being sunk by fighters. *Diana*, the torpedo craft carrier, was apparently taking part but escaped.[58]

Syria

2. The Naval Attaché, Ankara, reported that the Turks intended moving the interned Vichy French warships from Ayas Bay to Erdek.[59] The C-in-C gave instructions that everything should be done to prevent this as the ships would then be much more liable to seizure by the Axis.

Summary and Appreciation of Events for Month of July 1941

Strategical

Our whole position in the Middle East was greatly strengthened by the successful completion of the Syrian campaign in the middle of the month, and the unexpectedly stout resistance of the Russian armies. . . .

---

[57]*Queen Mary*: 1936, 80,774gt, 29.5k, Cunard White Star.
[58]*Diana*: 1940, 1,764t, 2×4in, 32k (s *Thrasher*, 29 June 1942).
[59]Capt O'Donnell.

Fleet Operations

4. The fleet was still too weak for any major offensive action. An increased force of four cruisers and eight destroyers was maintained on the Syrian coast until the signing of the armistice when it was reduced to a sub-division of destroyers. A number of bombardments were carried out in support of the army's final offensive and the FAA in Cyprus were successful in preventing reinforcements from getting through to Syria from the Aegean either in warships or in merchant ships. Although the blockade was effective it was disappointing that the French destroyers were able to escape without interception. The remaining French warships interned themselves at Iskanderun.

251. To Pound

Navy House
Alexandria
25 July 1941

B. I haven't got any details yet but SUBSTANCE appears to have been a success. At least the supply ships got into Malta, not without some damage, I understand. Our small contribution this end kept the Germans guessing and they had their reconnaissance out at 0600 over the position West of Crete where our two submarines had made manoeuvring signals during the night. One rather annoying fact is that the *Leinster* which went ashore off Gibraltar had all the RAF personnel on board which were to maintain the Beaufighters.[60]

Although Malta should be fairly well off for supplies now I will continue running aviation spirit in the minelaying submarines, but it's only a flea bite – 3 days' flying each load I believe.

C. I am not very happy about the *Georgic* affair at Suez. There seems to have been considerable stupidity. . . .

I have sent King down there to conduct a full enquiry. I think I shall have to fling out a few of the Navy element there. The trouble is we want a first class man there and I haven't got one.[61] . . .

D. I don't know if anything is moving at home about a Coastal Command or some such organisation out here. There is a slight stirring of dry bones out here but nothing very much doing.

[60]*Leinster*: 1937, 4,302gt, 17k, Br & Irish SP Co.
[61]*Georgic*: 1931, 27,759gt, 17.5k, Cunard White Star; dive bombed off Suez & burnt out.

Tedder is on the whole sympathetic but he can't handle his staff.
... Drummond, now Deputy AOC-in-C, obstructs on principle and is a thorough non-co-operator.[62]

What we want is more aircraft devoted to fleet co-operation and personnel that is trained in work over the sea and we shan't get those without considerable re-organisation and a special organisation running them in close touch with us. ...

The Italians and Germans quarter the whole Mediterranean daily and look into our ports but we don't touch the fringe of it. I haven't had a report about the Piraeus or Suda for over a week.

E. ... We have been having a lot of trouble with de Gaulle over Syria. He became almost unbalanced and wanted to denounce the Armistice terms and threatened all sorts of trouble. Lyttelton succeeded in quietening him down but he is a bad man, I'm afraid.

I don't know what you think about it but I consider it essential that the major Syrian ports should be under our control. I have Morse there now in charge, doing very well, and Catroux agreed to him being in charge at Beirut but I am expecting trouble as I see de Gaulle has appointed his own NOIC to Beirut.[63]

G. ... If the American yards are any good they ought to complete *Warspite*'s repairs in under six weeks. I feel we could have done it here except we were so pressed.

Formidable, looking absolutely 100%, has just left. Such a pity she had to go but she has no capstan gear at all and her Starboard A bracket is badly cracked.

252. *From Able Seaman L. Atkinson*

63 General Hospital
Middle East Forces
29 July 1941

Please allow me to thank you for your most heartening letter of the 23rd instant, and your kind condolements.

Your remarks have greatly cheered me, and will undoubtedly help me in the future.

---

[62]ACdre (later AM Sir) P. R. M. Drummond (1894–1945): b Australia; Gallipoli 1915; RFC Palestine 1916–18; FLt, RAF 1919; Dep Chief, RAAF 1925–29; Snr Air SO, MEAF Nov. 1937; AVM & DAOC 1941; Actg AM Nov. 1941; Air Mem Trng 1943–45; d in air crash.

[63]Rt Hon Oliver Lyttelton (later Visct Chandos; 1893–1972): Gren Gds, W Frt 1914–18; businessman; Con MP; Pres BOT 1940; MP Aldershot 1940–54; Minr State ME & War Cab 1941; Minr Prodn 1942–45; Col Sec 1951–54; Visct 1954.

It is now six years since I was accepted for service in the Royal Navy, and I have enjoyed every moment of that time. It has taught me, among other things, the true meaning of comradeship, and you can probably realise how great is the blow, to leave under such circumstances.

We did our job up to the best of our abilities, and am sure, did not 'let the side down'.

I have conveyed your kind wishes to my shipmates who are in hospital with me, and they thank you most earnestly, and join with me in wishing you every success in the future.

There is no doubt as to the eventual result of this war, and I only regret that I shall not be sailing with you when the 'Cease Fire' is sounded.

Thanking you again for your letter, which I shall always treasure.

253. *War Diary, August 1941*

3 August

Russia

5. The C-in-C expressed concern that after six weeks of the Russian War, there was still no liaison with Russian Naval command ... Conversations with the Turks were about to begin and the future activities of the Russian Black Sea Fleet were of great importance to them as well as to ourselves.

4 August

AA armament

8. The C-in-C signalled to the Admiralty urgently requesting a further supply of Oerlikon guns. These had proved very effective but there were still not nearly enough; such ships as SS *Lesbos* and *Pass of Balmaha* were in urgent need of them for service on the Tobruk supply run.[64]

---

[64]Oerlikon ('Ooligan'): Swiss 20mm AA gun.
Lesbos: 1893, 1,009gt, Hellenic Coast Lines, Piraeus.

9 August

Malta – Aircraft

5. The C-in-C suggested that Taranto might again be given the attention of the RAF and FAA as it was evidently being used more extensively than at any time since the big FAA attack. Large concentrations of warships and of merchant ships had been reported there.

254. *From Mrs F. Palmer*

Taupo
New Zealand
10 August 1941

Will you accept the grateful thanks of a humble mother of three sons on active service, two of whom were in the Greek and Crete Campaign.

I feel so strongly that it was owing to your wonderful bravery, that my boys were safely evacuated, from Crete, as we read accounts in our newspapers, of how, at great risk to yourself and your brave men, you returned and took many hundreds of New Zealanders to safety. You have my undying gratitude, and also that of thousands of New Zealand mothers, . . .

255. *To Pound*

15 August 1941

I send you as ammunition a further letter I have addressed to the AOC-in-C on the subject of Air Co-operation.

This last operation of trying to intercept the small ship making for Bardia was a lamentable exhibition of disorganisation and inefficiency. . . .

It is most disheartening the lack of progress we make in this matter just through sheer obstinacy and refusal to face facts. We have a few weeks left in which to try and get the Naval Co-operation aircraft trained, but nothing is being done. They refused to accept our help in training their completely ignorant pilots and observers, and it looks as if our time of activity, which I hope is not too far away now, will come with us still hampered by inadequate and inefficient air co-operation.

I should have thought that it was self-evident that if it has been necessary to associate the Admiralty closely with air operations over the sea at home it was even more necessary in these narrow waters.

B. Many thanks for your most valuable help over the fast ships for the supply of Tobruk. Our destroyers get bombed going there and coming back all night when there is enough light and I fear we shall have more casualties but it can't be helped. Tobruk is causing the enemy a lot of trouble and I hope will help in his final defeat when the moment comes.

C. If you are badly in need of *Abdiel* or *Latona* or both I can do without them. They are most useful running troops but I have at the moment no use for them as minelayers.

D. The question of our control of the Syrian ports appears to be settling itself well. Morse is evidently handling the Free French with great tact and will I am sure retain the real control though they may have the facade.

256. *War Diary, August 1941 (concl.)*

19 August

Operations – TREACLE

Operation TREACLE was commenced to relieve the 18th Australian Infantry Brigade at Tobruk by the Polish Brigade. This entailed the transport by sea of some 7,000 troops in HM Ships. It was intended to run convoys nightly into Tobruk, consisting of 2 destroyers and generally one minelayer with personnel, and one destroyer with stores; when a minelayer was employed, cruisers would cover the force to give AA protection by the use of RDF. Maximum fighter protection would be given, but by day only. It was intended to complete the operation during the 'no moon' period.

20 August

Yugoslav Navy

6. ... The two MTBs with 4 officers and 30 men were efficient and being employed operationally. The submarine *Nebojsca* was unfit for further service and her crew of 4 officers and 39 men were partly trained. The SO, Yugoslav Navy, hoped to collect sufficient personnel from these and other sources to man a small submarine and a small destroyer in addition to the 2 MTB.

22 August

HMAS Stuart

6. *Stuart* was sailed from Alexandria to undergo repairs in Australia. One engine was out of action altogether and she was seriously in need of a refit. On her departure, the 10DF ceased to exist, *Vendetta* being attached to the 7DF and *Decoy* to the 2DF.

The following signal was made to the Australian Commonwealth Naval Board:

> It is with great regret that we part with HMAS *Stuart* ... Under the distinguished command of Captain Waller she has an unsurpassed record of gallant achievement. She has taken a leading part in all the principal operations of the Mediterranean Fleet, and has never been called upon in vain for any difficult job. The work of her engine room department in keeping this old ship efficient and in good running order has been beyond all praise.

The Mediterranean Fleet is the poorer by the departure of this fine little ship, and her gallant ship's company.

27 August

Submarines

7. *Upholder* returned from patrol off Marittimo and reported:
  (a) Sinking a 2,000-ton eastbound merchant ship ... at 0920/20.
  (b) At 1633/22 scored two hits on a [depot ship *Lussino*] in a westbound convoy[65] ...
  (c) At 1034/24 attacked the force already reported of 3 cruisers and destroyers ... One torpedo hit and ... one of the escort had been torpedoed.

The C-in-C made the following signal to *Upholder*:

> Congratulations on a further successful patrol. Your work is excellent.

Summary and Appreciation of Events

3. August recorded a heartening series of successes both by submarine and aircraft attack ... The effect on the enemy was very seri-

---

[65]*Lussino*: 1912, 222gt, Soc Fiumana di Nav, Fiume.

ous and laid the seeds of acute shortage of the sinews of war which so greatly assisted our advance in December into Libya.

Western Desert

8. Activities were confined to supplying Tobruk. Apart from the major move of the Australian division and replacement by the Poles an average of 150 tons/day was disembarked. This had to be done in the face of heavy air attack both at sea and in the harbour. AA defence was restricted to the gun as our fighters could neither operate at Tobruk or cover the convoys in the latter stages of the approach. A good deal of minelaying had also to be contended with. Thirty-seven high level and 11 dive bombing attacks took place on Tobruk as well as 31 night raids but little damage was done. AA shot down about 13 aircraft. There was also a large number of raids on Mersa Matruh. During the month Tobruk harbour was shelled intermittently but without serious damage. *Skudd III* was sunk and *Lesbos* slightly damaged.[66]

Canal Area

9. The enemy made sustained attacks on the Canal Area and Gulf of Suez, apparently concentrating on US ships. There were 10 raids during the month including minelaying and attacks on Port Said, Ismailia, Suez and Port Tewfik and attacks on shipping in the Gulf of Suez. On the whole little was achieved. Our AA defences already fully extended had to cover a large new area. . . . but as an attempt to disorganise our supplies it was really a failure.

257. *War Diary, September 1941*

1 September

Submarines

12. During the month of August, submarines inflicted the following damage on the enemy:

Sunk – 9 ships totalling 17,252 tons for certain and one schooner probably also.
Damaged – one 8-in cruiser, one 6-in cruiser and one destroyer probably damaged. Four ships totalling 18,957 tons.

---

[66]*Skudd III*: A/S whaler, 1929, *c.*300t.

... In addition 68 passengers and 120,000 gallons of white oils, 12½ tons of stores, 359 bags of mail and certain other items were transported from Alexandria to Malta by the three submarines working on transport duty.

2 September

Close range weapons

6. The C-in-C's signal timed 1206/2 to the Admiralty giving requirements of Oerlikons for ships in the Eastern Mediterranean gave a total requirement of 254 for HM Ships and 15 for Greek, irrespective of those required for DEMS.

Malta Aircraft

5. Nine Swordfish attacked a southbound 14-knot convoy of 7 destroyers and 5 merchant ships sighted at midnight 2/3 E of Cape Spartivento. The convoy was taken completely by surprise and put into wild disorder, the destroyers firing on their own ships. Four merchant ships were certainly hit by torpedoes and two of 9,000 tons each blew up. . . .

258. *From Pound*

3 September 1941

... Dreyer has done most admirable work here in teaching the Merchant Navy how to shoot, . . . I am sure he will be of assistance to you in organising the provision of guns and training of crews which have to proceed up and down the Red Sea and Gulf of Suez.[67]

Fleet Destroyers

The situation in these is most unsatisfactory. At the beginning of the war we had 103 Fleet destroyers of which 100 were serviceable. At the present moment we have 88 . . . of which only 49 are serviceable and in which are included the 13 which we believe you have serviceable. The other remaining 36 we have to provide for Home Fleet, North West Approaches, Force H and Freetown and I am not

---

[67]Adm Sir Frederic Dreyer (1878–1956): ent RN 1891; gun splist; Lt 1898; GO, *Exmouth, Dreadnought* 1903–07;Cdr 1907; F Cdr to Jellicoe, Atl F 1913; Capt 1913; *Amphion, Orion*; F Capt *Iron Duke*, GF 1915–16; Jutland; DNO 1916–19; Cdre & COS to Jellicoe's Empire mission; Dir Gun Div 1920–22; *Repulse* 1922–23; RA 1923; ACNS 1924; BCS 1927; VA 1929; DCNS 1930; Adm 1932; C-in-C China 1933–36; Ret List 1939; convoy cdre 1939–40; Inspr merchant ship gunnery 1941; 5SL 1942; DCN Air Eqpt 1943.

at all sure, taking it all round, you are not better off than any of the other places.

Interruption of Enemy Communications with Libya

I know that you realise the vital importance of this as much as we do. I am sending you every available submarine; in fact, except for the 'S' class, which are not considered to be very suitable for the Mediterranean, and two 'P' class, which are operating from Murmansk, you either have or will have every available submarine. I only hope your Captain S1 will not treat them too rough.[68]

Surface Forces at Malta

Having reviewed the destroyer situation in the light of all our commitments, I do not think there is any chance of our being able to send you any specially for this purpose. Personally, I am extremely doubtful whether a weak force of two 6-in cruisers and four destroyers would be able to achieve anything commensurate with their loss in the face of air and surface force attack. I do not think the latter can be ruled out as the Italians must be more miserable people than we think if they could allow such a weak force to dominate the Central Mediterranean without any support nearer than Alexandria.

My own view is that as we are sending you additional submarines and as the Air Ministry are endeavouring to send two more Blenheim Squadrons to Malta we should see how these additions affect the situation before putting a surface force at Malta.

In any case, I am afraid the force would have to be provided by you and I can't really hold out any hope that we should be able to replace any of these ships which were lost.

Cruisers

The situation as regards cruisers is not as bad as that of destroyers, but all the same it is pretty bad. During the next month our commitments for the Malta convoy, other convoys and North Russia will be such that C-in-C Home Fleet will only be left with one cruiser and sometimes none.

Malta Convoy

It looks as if the the Italians were at last toying with the idea of using their surface forces to try and prevent us putting convoys into

---

[68]'S' cl: 1930s, 670/960t, 1×3in, 6×21in tt, 13.75/10k; imp vsn: 715/1000t, 1×4in, 7×21in tt, 14.5/10k, WW2. From 1942 they served effectively in Med. Capt S1 was Capt S. M. Raw.

Malta, so we shall have to be prepared to give battle on the next occasion. I only hope we have good luck as we did last time....

259. *To Pound*

18 September 1941

... I have had long talks with Dreyer and certainly some of the ideas he has brought seem very sound not only for the the merchant ship gunners but also for those in all small ships.

Our chief trouble, of course, is lack of the necessary guns but some are on the way.

B. The Red Sea position is unsatisfactory. Actually the enemy aircraft have done us little damage up to date; about 5 or 6 ships attacked, one sunk, the American, and two damaged. Quite bad enough and if the attack is increased next moon period it may be very serious.[69]

We are getting very little help from the RAF in meeting the threat. They have no RDF so *Coventry* and *Carlisle* have had to take on this job and also the AA fire protection.

They did send down four Beaufighters but I have had to replace them by Fulmars as the Beaufighters must go to Malta for HALBERD.

The trouble is the RAF are desperately short of aircraft and technical equipment like RDF and are too frightened to press the Air Ministry to hasten their programme of supply which is obviously much too leisurely.

The imminent arrival at Suez of the monster liners is giving me much anxiety. They are crammed with men and we can't afford to have them hit up so I have sent *Naiad* and *Galatea* to escort them through the danger area. I can do this at present while there is a lull but there may come a time when I shall want all the cruisers I can get in the Mediterranean.

The Beaufighter question is quite hopeless. There are 20 or rather less in the Middle East of which 10 are serviceable and there are calls on them for Malta, for the Red Sea and for the battle fleet when it goes out to provide a diversion for HALBERD.

Of course they go to Malta.

[69] *Steel Seafarer*: *c.*1920, *c.*6,000gt, 11k, Isthmian SS Co, NY.

C. ... It seems evident that again the Red Sea must be run under one command, and have its own forces for escort and air protection of shipping.

I assure you I have no wish to assume responsibility for the Red Sea but things seem to be shaping that way. ...

D. The situation as regards fleet destroyers doesn't seem too good. ... I nearly always have four out of action. Actually, unless we have more losses, which is always possible on the Tobruk run, I think we can manage with the number of *fleet* destroyers we have at present including those on passage, but we could do with some more 'Hunts' for escort and multifarious duties. I don't know what their endurance is but they seem ideal for the battlefleet screen.

I don't want to ask for too much but if there is a spare AA cruiser we could do with one. *Coventry* will be off to Bombay in a week or two for repairs which will leave us with *Carlisle* only.

E. I know we are being treated very generously as regards submarines. Every one is worth its weight in gold and they are doing fine work.

I hear, however, that the Malta ones are feeling the strain a bit. Two have been heavily depth charged and damaged and, of course, they have lost five out of 12. I can't help thinking *P32* and *P33* blundered into a minefield. Perhaps lately laid.[70]

The time of flat calms and clear skies round Malta is drawing to a close so they may have an easier time.

F. ... I do not think surface forces from Malta would achieve anything in an attempt to stop supplies coming from Italy down the Greek coast to Benghazi. In fact, far as they would be from fighter support, I think they might have heavy losses by air attack even if the Italians didn't send a large force to cut them off.

You see retreat to the Eastward would be highly risky.

In any case with this Gulf of Suez commitment I now can't spare any cruisers, let alone destroyers.

Malta has done well and touched up a couple of convoys well over towards Greece but I can't get the RAF here to try much. We don't seem to have aircraft with the necessary range for reconnaissance and the bombers' range is shorter still.

The whole air situation out here fills me with anxiety. We should be getting superiority or at least equality and we never seem to

---

[70]*P32* (mined), *P33* (s by escorts): 'U' cl, 1941; M/L S/M *Cachalot* (1938, 1,520/2,117t, 1×4in, 6×21in tt, 50 mines, 15.75/8.75k) rammed by It T/B *Papa,* also off Libya, 30 July 1941.

achieve it. I don't know if home experience is the same but the German reconnaissance and bombing performances are infinitely better than ours out here, neither does our reconnaissance approach the Italian in efficiency.

K. This relief of the Australians from Tobruk comes at a bad time and may have serious repercussions. It may mean that the Western Desert offensive may have to be postponed 2–4 weeks. . . .

It may interfere with the diversion I was hoping to make to assist HALBERD through lack of destroyers to take the battlefleet to sea.

260. *War Diary, September 1941 (concl.)*

20 September

Submarines

6. *Thunderbolt* returned from patrol off Benghazi, where considerable destroyer and other A/S activity was experienced. *Thunderbolt* reported:

(a)	7 September	– Torpedoed a 974-ton merchant ship 50 miles W of Benghazi. The ship was believed to have sunk.
(b)	9 September	– Bombarded Fortina Beroli, Sirte.
(c)	10 September	– Attacked and repeatedly hit with gunfire a large schooner at El Auegia. Shore batteries forced *Thunderbolt* to retire before the schooner was finally seen to sink.
(d)	11 September	– Torpedoed a camouflaged merchan ship off Benghazi. The ship was seen later heavily on fire.
(e)	13 September	– Attacked and probably sank a *Crotone* class minelayer laying a minefield off Benghazi.[71]
(f)	14 September	– Attacked a 5,000-ton escorted ship 30 miles N of Benghazi but the result could not be observed.

7. *Unbeaten, Upholder, Ursula* and *Upright* were disposed on 17 September NE of Tripoli to intercept a convoy of liners reported by

[71]*Crotone* cl: probably *Curtatone* cl: T/B, 1923–24, 876t, 4×4in, 6×17.7in tt, 32k.

reconnaissance. *Unbeaten* sighted the convoy at 0317/18 and reported it. *Upholder* and *Upright* closed the convoy and *Upholder* attacked scoring one hit on each of two liners, which were both then seen to be damaged and one stopped. *Upholder* later closed and sank the damaged liner. *Ursula* then attacked the convoy and hit another liner, identified as *Vulcania* which continued into Tripoli at reduced speed and appeared to have been damaged. It was later established that the two liners *Oceania* and *Neptunia* were both sunk in this attack and *Vulcania* avoided *Ursula*'s torpedoes.[72]

8. The C-in-C congratulated the 10SF on such a fine piece of team work.

Aircraft

9. Tripoli harbour was again bombed heavily by the RAF. The RAF's effort against Benghazi was considerably hampered by the inability of Wellington aircraft to lay mines. The C-in-C again asked the Admiralty to arrange for the necessary equipment to be sent out.

27 September

Aircraft

6. The state of the FAA aircraft in the Eastern Mediterranean was as follows:

Squadron	Aircraft	Station
815	6 Swordfish	Cyprus
	6 Albacores	
826	12 Albacores	Western Desert
803	8 Hurricanes	" "
805	10 Martlets	" "
	6 Hurricanes	" "
Fulmar Flight	6 Fulmar II	Hurghada, G of Suez
700 & Sea Rescue	5 Walrus	Dispersed
	2 Swordfish	
Training, etc.	8 Swordfish	Dekheila
	4 Roc	
	5 Gladiators	
	2 Albacores	
	4 Fulmar I	

[72]*Unbeaten*: 'U' cl, 1940 (s Biscay, Br a/c Nov. 1942).
Vulcania: 1928, 24,469gt, 22.43k.
Oceania: 1933, 19,507gt, 22.16k.
Neptunia: 1932, 19,475gt, 21.3k. All SA di Nav Italia.

26 September

Operations – HALBERD

The C-in-C sailed from Alexandria in *Queen Elizabeth* with *Barham* (VA1), *Valiant, Ajax* (CS7), *Neptune, Hobart, Jervis* (D14), *Jupiter, Kingston, Kipling, Hero, Hotspur, Decoy* and *Vendetta* at 0900/26.[73] *Napier* was delayed sailing in order to complete with oil and joined the fleet at 1430/26. The C-in-C's intention was to give the impression that the convoy was being passed right through the Mediterranean and to draw the enemy air effort away from Force H. No fighter protection was available, all long range fighters having been moved to Malta. The Battlefleet set course to the NW at 18 knots and continued throughout the day without incident. An enemy air reconnaissance plane was reported over Alexandria shortly after the fleet sailed.

Summary and Appreciation

General

4. The Mediterranean heavy forces were not able to take much active part against the enemy as several heavy commitments used up all the available light craft. There were first the landing of 6,000 men in Tobruk and removal of a similar number, apart from the ordinary maintenance of the fortress, secondly a series of A/S sweeps to deal with the increasing submarine menace and thirdly the need to send ships into the Red Sea to deal with enemy air attack there.

5. The enemy started a new line of attack by means of these air incursions to the Red Sea using Focke Wulf and similar aircraft. At the time large and important convoys, including the giant liners, were in the Red Sea, and the canal ports were necessarily packed with shipping. The C-in-C thus had considerable anxiety in the matter. The Canal defences were strengthened, such fighters as could be spared were sent to the area and two AA cruisers and some sloops and destroyers were sent down to assist. During September these measures were efficacious at least as regards the ships, only one being lost and two slightly damaged. Our resources as usual were far too weak for their engagements and there was some difficulty with US ships owing to their complaint of insufficient AA protection at Ataka.

---

[73]*Hobart*: 1934, 7,105t, 8×6in, 8×4in, 8×21in tt, 32.5k.

6. The outstanding features of the month, however, were the magnificent efforts of the submarines and FAA and RAF aircraft. Hardly a day passed without some heavy loss to the enemy and it is doubtful if 50% of his shipping reached Libya.

... submarines and aircraft sank 20 ships and possibly another 9 totalling 132,000 tons and damaged a further 188,000 tons. Apart from this one [submarine chaser, *Albatros*,] was sunk and a cruiser and two destroyers damaged. The strain on the enemy must therefore have been very serious.[74]

Alexandria, Canal Area and Suez

7. ... these areas were subjected to systematic attack evidently to interfere with the Middle East supply. The result achieved was very small but it had an important effect in making it necessary to send quite a large force south of the canal to convoy ships. This was always a matter of anxiety since if the Canal were blocked it would have seriously weakened the Mediterranean Fleet and it naturally curtailed forces available for offensive operations.

The Canal was attacked 12 times and Alexandria five times. ...

261. War Diary, October 1941

3 October

Red Sea

3. The anchorages in the Straits of Jubal were still very crowded and operations continued to protect the shipping at anchor and on passage through the Gulf. The Suez Escort Force consisted of *Naiad, Galatea, Coventry, Carlisle, Napier, Jackal, Avon Vale, Eridge, Flamingo* and *Parramatta*. There was still no air opposition.[75]

4 October

Submarines

5. *Triumph* returned to Alexandria from patrol in the Adriatic. At 0800/18 she torpedoed and hit the escorted Italian tanker *Liria*, which was able, however, to get into Crotone harbour. *Triumph* closed the harbour but was unable to attack again. Off Split at 0800/23 *Triumph* sank a 3,000-ton merchant ship. On 24th off

---

[74]*Albatros*: 1934, 339t, 2×4in, 24.5k; s *Upright*.
[75]*Avon Vale, Eridge* (irrep dmgd, E-b, Aug. 1942): 'Hunt' cl; 1940, 1,050t, 6×4in, 27k.

Ortona she torpedoed a tanker, reducing its speed, and then attacked and hit it again. The tanker was then abandoned and when tugs came to her assistance, *Triumph* surfaced and set her on fire by gunfire, also sinking a pilot cutter. *Triumph* was forced to withdraw when a shore battery opened fire.[76]

7 October

Air Transport

5. The provision of regular air transport to Malta and the Middle East from the UK was again urged as being of the first importance. The existing lack of transport for personnel as well as of mail was seriously affecting the efficiency of the fortress of Malta.

9 October

Levant

4. The C-in-C ordered an intensive A/S search to be made of the area between Syria and the east coast of Cyprus. All available corvettes were ordered to concentrate in the area and an air search was arranged by 815 Sqdn in moonlight during the nights 10/11 and 11/12.

10 October

Operations

2. Three 'A' lighters (nos 2, 7 and 18) on passage from Mersa Matruh to Tobruk encountered a U-boat at 0520... (off Ishailia Rocks). A spirited action ensued in which the 'A' lighters reported hits with their pom-poms on the U-boat. The U-boat then submerged and *A2* and *A7* continued to Tobruk. *A18* became detached and returned to Mersa Matruh having one or two wounded and slight damage.

262. *From Pound*

11 October 1941

I had a pretty stiff fight to get the agreement about the Naval Co-operation Group, and I very much doubt whether we should have achieved this had you not sent Boyd home....

---

[76]*Liria*: 1922, 1,133gt, Anglo-Saxon Petm, London.

It was a great relief to have got such a large part of the convoy through to Malta, as they are now well fitted up for some months.

Leatham has been offered and has accepted VA, Malta, in place of Ford, who I understand thinks that five years at Malta is long enough. Ford will go to Rosyth. Leatham will, I think, fill the appointment very well.... he now realises the importance that everyone attaches to Malta and that at the present time it is the one and only fighting job for a shore Admiral....

It is with great reluctance that we are sending *Aurora* and *Penelope* to Malta, but I can see that it is quite impossible with the Gulf of Suez situation as it is for you to provide any cruisers. I have no exaggerated hopes as to what these two ships will be able to achieve, and I think it quite likely that at the least we shall get both ships badly damaged but, should CRUSADER fail, ... then I think there would have been lasting criticism because we had not made any attempt to cut the communications to Africa by surface forces.[77]

263. To Pound

14 October 1941

First let me thank you most sincerely for your fight on our behalf over the air co-operation question....

B. I had a long talk with the Minister of State over the liaison question. He told me he fully realised how quite impossible it was for the C-in-C, Mediterranean, to run the fleet from Cairo – so you did him a lot of good in that direction.[78] ...

C. We had a visitation last moon period to the Red Sea by enemy long range bombers. Unfortunately they got two good ships in the so-called safe anchorages. They did not, however, get away unscathed as out of six they lost three. One flew into the masts of a ship and I think *Carlisle* damaged the other two. We have put it down to night fighters for propaganda purposes and we are passing round that some of the crew were taken by sharks!! I wish to make the Hun airmen a bit nervous and anxious to keep out of trouble....

---

[77]*Aurora, Penelope* (s *U-410,* Anzio, Feb. 1944): 1936–37, 5,270t, 6×6in, 8×4in, 6×21in tt, 32.25k.

[78]Lyttelton.

It will be a good thing when Hallifax takes up his residence at Suez and takes hold of this shipping protection question but I fear it means asking for some AA ships.[79]

If we could get Jibouti off our hands it would release seven sloops, I believe, which, by changing them round with some with good AA armaments would probably fill the bill. . . .

D.   There seems to be a considerable concentration of submarines in these parts. I can't think why. . . .

As soon as I can spare a destroyer or two I'll get after them. I'm not at all sure that *Peony* didn't get one off Haifa a week ago. . . .[80]

E.   May I ask you to put in a word for us about minesweepers? At present they seem to get as far as Mombasa and then get diverted to the Persian Gulf.

I am frightfully short now for all our commitments and if CRUSADER brings any more, as I hope it will, we just can't meet them as at present placed.

The sweepers at Tobruk are liable to be sunk or damaged at any moment and the Canal has nothing like enough yet.

The ships running to Tobruk are having a poor time. These Hun aircraft are most efficient at night – I wish ours were 50% as efficient. You will have seen about the epic battle . . . between our three tank lighters (full of tanks) and a submarine . . .

Unfortunately, returning from Tobruk the day before yesterday, two of them just disappeared. Bombed and sunk, I fear.

I *shall* be glad when Tobruk is relieved.

F.   The fleet has been at sea the last two days – at least two battleships. *Valiant* is practically out of action until docked which we hope to undertake in a day or two.

I have had them out in connection with this mysterious enemy operation 'B' which, myself, I think is minelaying off Benghazi.

They were attacked by torpedo bombers yesterday afternoon and another attack is at present in progress. No hits yesterday but I fear they also failed to bring any aircraft down. Our close range fire is most disappointing; of course they may be damaged and come down later.

G.   I am very anxious about the aircraft situation for CRUSADER. The more so since I discovered that the total figure is only 520 and includes the Naval Co-operation Squadrons, i.e., Beaufighters and

---

[79] VA R. H. C. Hallifax: Capt 1927; RA 1938; RA(D), HF May 1939; FO Red Sea Force, Aden Apr. 1941; SNO Suez Canal Nov. 1941; VA Feb. 1942; d 1943.

[80] *Peony* was unsuccessful but *Hyacinth* s *Fisalia* (1932, 650/810, 1×4in, 6×21in tt, 15/7.6k.) off Jaffa. 28 Sept.

Beauforts and reconnaissance Blenheims. The total number of fighters is 192 and this includes 24 FAA fighters!!! Naturally I am throwing in every machine we have got and we are having a squadron and a half of Albacores in the desert. But we are still woefully weak.

The RAF have at last discovered that the much despised Swordfish and Albacores are the most accurate bombers we have got because they dive bomb and also they go so slowly they invariably find their targets. I believe the Germans are said to have reported that the British have some high capacity bombers in the Western Desert which are very accurate. This, of course, is the Swordfish going up wind!!

H. You speak of finding a command for Baillie-Grohman. I think he would be excellent. He is, as you know, a bit of an individualist and does not fit in with everybody but his work out here has been consistently good and he is a strong character and not afraid to speak his mind to anyone. If you take him I should like a relief if one can be found. Having a spare Flag Officer has proved most valuable time and again.

264. *War Diary, October 1941 (concl.)*

11 October

Submarines

5. *Talisman* returned from a successful patrol in the Aegean. She sank three ships totalling 15,000 tons. The first was already aground off San Giorgio Island on 2 October and was probably the same ship which *Talisman* attacked off the Dardanelles the previous day; the result then was uncertain. The second was the French ship *Théophile Gautier* heavily escorted and making for the Zea Channel on 3 October. The third was a ship in convoy northbound off Suda Bay on 6 October.[81]

Aircraft

6. FAA aircraft from Malta twice attacked a southbound convoy during the night 10/11. Two merchant ships of 5,000 and 6,000 tons were sunk and one damaged in the first attack and another damaged by torpedo in the second attack.

---

[81]*Talisman*: 1940, 1,090/1,575t, 1×4in, 10×21in tt, 15.25/9k; s off Malta Sept. 1942.
Théophile Gautier: 1926, 8,194gt, 13.5k, Messageries Maritimes.

12 October

Operations – CULTIVATE

Operation CULTIVATE was commenced to relieve the remainder of the Australian troops in Tobruk by a further part of the 6th Division from Syria. The operation was to be similar to SUPERCHARGE; troops would be transported in both directions in a minelayer and three destroyers and running nearly every night. The minelayer would carry 150 tons of stores and 25 men westward, and 450 men eastward. Destroyers would carry 325 men and 15 tons of stores or 75 men and 50 tons of stores; in the moonlit period numbers returning eastward were to be reduced to 100. Ships were instructed to reduce speed to carry out A/S sweeps between Alexandria and Mersa Matruh.

2. *Abdiel, Hero, Kipling* and *Nizam* sailed from Alexandria at 0700/12 for Tobruk for Serial One of CULTIVATE.

14 October

Minesweepers

8. The C-in-C's message 1857/13 requested the Admiralty to hasten the progress of fitted LL minesweepers joining the Mediterranean Station; two had recently been diverted to the Persian Gulf. There were at present 26 LL M/S craft, including 7 corvettes and 4 converted Greek schooners, to meet all the extensive commitments in the Mediterranean. For several days recently the main fleet base at Alexandria had been left with one LL whaler and 4 schooners (speed 3–5 knots) for the protection of the fleet.

18 October

Levant

4. Corvettes had to be withdrawn from A/S searches in order to provide A/S escorts for the large amount of valuable shipping now moving in the Levant.

20 October

RDF

8. The C-in-C asked the Admiralty that all possible steps might be taken, both in research and in dispatching equipment to the fleet, to overcome our present inability to detect with certainty low flying aircraft. The Admiralty replied that every opportunity was being

taken to fit Type 281 in ships refitting. These sets should be available to the Mediterranean by the spring 1942.

25 October

Western Desert 'A' Lighters

4. The 'A' lighters on the Western Desert supply service were withdrawn to Port Said to refit. The C-in-C congratulated them on their good work in running so many valuable cargoes successfully into Tobruk. Since 11 July 10 lighters in all had carried 2,900 tons of stores, 48 heavy and 7 light tanks and a number of guns and MT into Tobruk. Five of the 10 were sunk.

29 October

Aircraft

4. The C-in-C suggested to the VA, Malta, that, with the recent reinforcement of TSR aircraft, consideration might be given to attacking destroyer escorts with bombs as well as torpedoing the ships in convoy.

Submarines

5. The C-in-C ordered a redisposition of submarines to intercept the traffic, which was now considered of vital importance, between Italy and Benghazi. Two submarines of the 1SF would be maintained on patrol off Benghazi and E of 18°W; two submarines of the 10SF were to maintain patrol between 14°E and 18°E. This would employ a total of six submarines; the remaining six of the 10SF should be disposed NE of Malta to intercept any convoys that might be reported at sea on the Benghazi route.

265. *From the Chiefs of Staff*

2047A, 17 October 1941

On assumption that operation CRUSADER results in a decisisve victory HMG are considering possibility of exploiting situation by attacking and capturing Sicily.

266. *From the Chiefs of Staff*

1300A, 18 October 1941

Defence Committee, yesterday evening, considered rough outline for operation and ordered preparations to proceed with utmost speed. They regard it as of first importance that we should be in a position to exploit CRUSADER by all means in our power not only as an end in itself but also in view of long period of apparent quiescence which has coincided with great struggle in Russia. Operation is therefore to have absolute priority over all else except of course CRUSADER.

2. In order that you may lose no time in considering the part you will have to play, you should know we are aiming at an assault to take place about 9 December or earlier if preparations can by any means be accelerated.

3. The assumption is that Italian morale will have collapsed as a result of a heavy defeat and that, in consequence, there may be a psychological moment for striking at Sicily simultaneously with an advance on Tripoli (Africa). . . .

267. *The Cs-in-C, Middle East, to the Chiefs of Staff*

2301B, 21 October 1941

1. We appreciate the great advantages which would accrue if WHIPCORD is successful and the tonic effect which would be produced on the British Army and on public opinion in Russia and the Empire. . . . the attractions of such an operation . . . clearly are first a great blow to Italian morale, secondly the possibility of reopening the Mediterranean route and increasing productivity of our shipping and thirdly best way of carrying war into Europe.

2. We suggest that there should be no (R) no fixed date on which the expedition should sail from England.

3. There should be in our opinion three prerequisites in addition to those set out in JP(41) 860 [not reproduced] before the expedition is committed,

    a. That we have already captured Benghazi
    b. That there are only beaten troops in front of us and that either capture of Tripoli is stated by the Cs-in-C to be reasonably certain in a short time or alternatively that enemy is

considered unable to operate any considerable air force from Tripolitania.

c. That the Russian front is stabilised north of the Caucasus without aid from us.

4. These are the minimum prerequisites but we feel that it would be preferable to secure Tripolitania firmly before committing WHIPCORD beyond Gibraltar.

5. If we have to provide help on any scale to Russia and Turkey offensive operations in the west would have to cease. . . .

268. *To Pound*

23 October 1941

C. I can't say I like WHIPCORD. It seems to me that up to date we have failed through not sticking to one object at a time and I feel that before embarking on another operation we should hold North Africa up to the Tunisian border firmly. I agree that, if we can spare the shipping and the forces, the expedition should be in readiness in case of a complete collapse of Italian morale but it will be very difficult to assess when that has happened.

I doubt if the morale of the Air Force, mostly officers, will collapse and heavy air attacks on our convoys from Sardinia, Italy and Sicily – on troopships not merely storeships – might wreck the expedition before it arrives.

Another smaller point is that I haven't enough A/S forces to protect the battlefleet, two convoys and keep open the very vulnerable supply route to Tobruk and Benghazi. I think I should have a carrier and I gather from Boyd that there is no hope of one before January. . . .

E. The four or five Hun submarines have been giving us a shake up. There is no question about their efficiency. We lost two good little ships on the Tobruk run although they were escorted and I think the torpedoing of *Gnat* drawing only 3ft 6in was a clever bit of work. . . .

G. I fully agree with you about Force K. They may not achieve much but their presence should result in the Italians having to put up a much greater escort effort and it may be that they will put an end to this running of Hun soldiers in destroyers from Augusta to Benghazi.

Regent, off Benghazi, fired six torpedoes at the last lot but unfortunately missed.

I. Two more trips will finish the relief of the Australians at Tobruk. How pleased we shall all be. It has been at the expense of the reserves of stores and ammunition in the fortress...

I have had small forces bombarding the enemy camps and concentrations between Sollum and Tobruk the last few nights and they have done some good I hope and also put our people on their toes.

269. *The Cs-in-C, Middle East, to the Chiefs of Staff*

1912B, 24 October 1941

1. We repeat our opinion that the conception of this operation seems to us sound. Our principal preoccupation concerns not the operation itself but the timing.

3. (a) It is probable in our opinion that the landing will be opposed and coastal guns in action, and that Italian morale will not have entirely collapsed by the capture of Cyrenaica alone.

(b) We consider that there are enough Germans in Augusta and Southern Italy to make it certain that the landing will be opposed by them if not by the Italians.

(c) ... We should have thought that some more definite evidence of unrest among the Italian population such as an insurrection was necessary before the operation was likely to succeed this winter. ...

(d) Exact meteorological data is being collected but in meantime C-in-C Med considers it probable that in the winter there are not likely to be many days in each month on which landings are possible simultaneously on both sides of the island.

(e) We do not think we can afford to interrupt supplies by cancelling convoys to Middle East until Turkish atttitude and Russian position much clearer, especially in Caucasus, and think that assumption that Germany will continue to be inextricably involved in Russia during winter too uncertain to be counted on.

4. We are most anxious to be given chance of finishing one job before taking on another. Moreover while operation WHIPCORD is greatly facilitated especially from Naval point of view if we can base it on Tripoli C-in-C Med considers that capture of Tripoli by itself opens passage through Mediterranean for strongly escorted convoys.

5. We think that our first strategical aim must be to secure firmly our bases in the Delta and at Basra. This object will not have been achieved until we are firmly established in North Africa and the position in Turkey and the Caucasus is stabilised. We consider this

object vital to the future successful prosecution of the war and that any diversion of effort from it would be most unsound.

6. Until enemy further weakened strain involved by maintenance of troops after WHIPCORD will be great. It appears to us that enemy's communications after occupation are certainly not worse and possibly better than ours, and the potential forces which he can bring to bear if he chooses are much greater.

7. We feel that failure now would more than counteract any success in Libya. We can't afford failure or evacuation and the chances are against success this winter. We think that the odds will be shortened greatly and wide results may be expected if we wait for a more favourable moment. We are now in sight of having air and land forces of a quantity and quality which should enable us to strike further blows when the time is ripe.

8. To sum up we are agreed that the operation is attractive but consider it premature.

9. Notwithstanding the above we are pushing on with all preparations. We would, however, press for a decision as to date because these preparations are already causing the diversion of craft and resources from CRUSADER which we all realise should be our primary preoccupation.

270. *The Cs-in-C, Middle East, to the Chiefs of Staff*

2108B, 24 October 1941

1. ... Moon conditions on 9 December not favourable for landing on east coast. We prefer to have either no moon at all or for moon to rise about one hour after first flight lands. Supposing Z hour to be 0200 this brings date to 15 December, which has advantage of giving almost maximum cover of darkness to Forces B and D while on passage.

2. *Landing craft.* Maximum of 20 MLCs likely to be available. Can only assemble these by withdrawing craft from Tobruk which may increase difficulties of maintenance for CRUSADER. Additional 8 MLCs arrive with *Derwentdale* but arrival in time for D1 doubtful.[82] We reckon 36 MLCs required to land one Brigade and consider 20 definitely inadequate for Force B. We are considering possibility making up deficiency by use TLCs but their lack of speed, even if fast TLCs ready in time, is serious objection to putting them into convoy from Egypt. ...

---

[82]*Derwentdale*: 1941, LS, 17,000t, 1×4in, 15 LCM, 11.5k.

12. *Defence against air attack.* The only fighter cover available during the first two or three days will be the Beaufighter Squadron from Malta and the aircraft from Force A carriers who may be needed for dealing with enemy surface forces. AA defences unlikely to be in action ashore in less than a minimum of 24 hours after first landing. If the assumption that the Italian air resistance will only be negligible is falsified or if German air forces in Greece are unexpectedly reinforced the prospect of serious air attack on the ships lying inshore will have to be faced.

13. *Maintenance.* We think very urgent and clear consideration should be given to problem of maintenance after capture of WHIPCORD. In particular 5 Indian Division will have to be maintained from Mideast.

271. *Churchill to Minister of State, Cs-in-C Committee, Middle East*

0206A, 26 October 1941

2. No one must suppose therefore that things will be better for us next year or in spring. On contrary for WHIPCORD it is probably a case of 'now or never'. In my view by end of December these prospects will be indefinitely closed.

3. Hitler's weakness is in air. . . .

4. It is therefore of importance to us to seek situations which enable us to engage enemy's air force under favourable conditions in various theatres at same time.

Such an opportunity is presented in a high degree by WHIPCORD.

5. If we can before January secure combination of air fields – Tripoli, Malta, Sicily and Sardinia – and can establish ourselves upon them, a heavy and possibly decisive attack can be made upon Italy, the weaker partner in the Axis, by bombers from home based on above system of airfields. . . .

6. [?Other] advantages would be gained from British air predominance in Mediterranean. . . . the sea route from Mediterranean would be opened to strongly escorted convoys with all saving in shipping accruing therefrom, as well as stronger support of eastern operations.

7. The reaction upon France and French North Africa following such achievements, including arrival in area of forces on Tunisian border, might bring Weygand into action, with all the benefit that would come from that.

8. The foundation of above is of course a victorious CRUSADER. You ought to welcome very powerful diversion of enemy strengths, which WHIPCORD would bring provided it runs concurrently with ACROBAT. Nothing gives us greater safety or baffles enemy more than sudden simultaneous uprising of a great variety of targets.

272. Cs-in-C, Middle East, to Churchill

2137B, 27 October 1941

1. We understand the great desirability of not confining our action to CRUSADER and ACROBAT. It appears to us however that when faced by numerous superior forces we must fix our eyes on what is strategically essential. We regard these strategic essentials as defence of Delta and Canal, Basra and Caucasus, and add to these bastion of Taurus Range as [?-] if the Turkish attitude permits, the immediate object being to secure our bases so as to permit of our passage to the offensive at the earliest possible date which must remain our ultimate aim.

Our feelings are that WHIPCORD cannot be regarded as essential especially in view of C-in-C Mediterranean's view that capture of Tripoli by itself goes a long way to securing the through Mediterranean route.

2. Your telegram foresees substantial reinforcement German air forces in Southern Europe as soon as some stabilisation Russian front achieved.

This appears to give some weight to para. 6 of our telegram 0/18988 [No.269] which points out drain which may be caused by maintenance of WHIPCORD

5. ... We should say which alternative appears to us the better. We regard this as sending help to Russian left flank in the actual Caucasus Range to cover Baku, Batum and the passes through Caucasus.

6. We suggest there is a third course open to us namely the occupation of Bizerta.

7. On the information available here we should sum up as follows:

(a) WHIPCORD not (R) NOT essential.
(b) Help to Russia would be direct action towards securing strategical essentials though the extent of our help would be limited by the fact that air forces committed there could not be retrieved if required for defence of UK, and by supply difficulties.

(c) Best action for new forces from UK would appear to be occupation of Bizerta. Is it beyond possibilities to provoke invitation from French? Shortage of hostages and general hostility to Germans in France makes us feel on limited information available that we should bend all efforts to this end. Without invitation from French or against opposition we regard capture of Bizerta as impracticable. Bizerta gives essentially same opportunity as WHIPCORD to bomb Italy thus fulfilling your para. 3 and 4 and in addition is excellent naval base. We consider that possession of Bizerta will secure passage of Mediterranean for convoys.
(d) Meanwhile diversion of convoys for Middle East is weakening our ability to secure strategical essentials set out in para. 1 above.

273. *Chiefs of Staff to Cs-in-C, Middle East*

2023A   28 October 1941

In view of your 0/19301 of 27 October [no. 272] and of very heavy Naval commitments required and its effect on our convoys, COS no longer recommend WHIPCORD. The PM has accepted this conclusion and operation is therefore abandoned.

274. *From Vice Admiral Ford*

Malta
26 October 1941

... I also am very sorry to be leaving Malta and your command – I wrote to the First Sea Lord some time ago to say not only was I prepared to stay but that I should like to do so and see Malta through its troubles.... I think Leatham will do very well and he is a good choice. We were most unfortunate in Saturday's strafe to lose so much kerosene – a bad blow, but I hope replenishments may arrive in the two [?ships] coming along alone. Out of all our fighters all they got up in the air was 11 [against] 25–30 [enemy] fighters above covering the bombers.

Our barrage can only be described as b–y. The bombers came over at 20,000 [feet], enormous fellahs in serried array apparently steaming dead slow. Bursts kept a steady 10,000 feet below and behind and they did not waver. Just before they dropped their eggs, two or three bursts got near them and they slowly turned off away from their intended objective, the cruisers and big M/Vs littering the harbour. The gunners patted themselves on the back. I [disabused] them harshly of any idea they had of good shooting and told them the Navy gunners were in fits of laughter and perhaps next time they will do better. The answer is lack of practice as the Air prevents them shooting. There is always a controversy at night as to whether we should put up a barrage or no guns and use Night Fighters. AOC is not keen on Night Fighters but as I keep telling him I don't care a damn about the 'bag' he may claim but the fact remains that the blighters have dropped their eggs and done the damage before they are attacked and it's 20:1 against bringing a bandit down and then they blame searchlights. A barrage upsets their aim, puts the wind up Italians anyway and inclines them to drop the stuff any old place – fields, sea, etc. I endeavour to persuade them that a happy co-ordinated combination of barrage and Night Fighters is the best. Stopping barrage when they are (say) a mile off the Grand Harbour and letting the fighters who should be off Halfar get in. . . . I am not very happy about it and the Italians are getting cheekier every day. Even machine gun aerodromes and ships in broad daylight. Rotten!

. . . These airmen know nothing about ships, organisation, etc. and I have to put 3 NOs in their operations room to do the job *faute de mieux*. I should be ashamed to ask the RAF for officers to do watchkeeping in a cruiser. Their hides are abnormally thick. I can't help thinking their claims of great destruction are grossly exaggerated. Give me the Swordfish and S/M's for choice. The Albacores that we got are meanwhile quite useless. Not one lad had ever flown at night and not one had ever dropped a torpedo. Am endeavouring to train them but it's very difficult to do so from here. Why send such stuff to a place like Malta? . . . I can't help thinking that in the Mediterranean we should have a proper Coastal Command and a C-in-C quite separate from RAF. . . . I consider Force K is rather wasted chasing and trying to intercept enemy destroyers – much faster and extremely difficult to intercept. I reckon I should employ them solely against fairly big convoys (escorted) and so bag M/Vs and destroyers if I am lucky. I should be glad of a decision from you. N[o] B[looming] G[ood] enemy landing troops if they can't get in their stores and fighting equipment. . . .

. . . I reckon we have practically stopped West-about convoys of any tonnage and that shipping for North Africa is passing across to West Coast of Greece and thence to Benghazi and possibly on to Tripoli – all outside our range. . . .

275. *Bombardment Operations, 18–26 October 1941*

28 January 1942

Be pleased to lay before Their Lordships the attached reports of Operation ME4 – bombardment of enemy positions on the North African Coast... immediately preceding the Army advance into Libya.

2. No target was as attractive as those available in the previous advance, because the enemy has now learnt the value of dispersal. In consequence the material damage was small, though it is possible the moral effect was satisfactory.
3. These bombardments were carried out by night as fighter protection in sufficient strength could not be provided W of Ishailia Rocks.
4. One feature of these operations which is noteworthy is that the pilots and observers of the aircraft in every case were able to discuss each operation before and after it took place with the officers of the ships taking part. This resulted in very good team work and a considerable advance in the technique of night bombardment....

276. *War Diary, November 1941*

2 November

Red Sea

4. The FO Red Sea sailed from Aden in SS *Tarifa* with his staff to proceed to Suez. His flag was flown on shore at Suez.[83]
5. The following ships were formed into the Aden Force under the operational control of the NOIC Aden: *Indus, Hindustan, Savorgnan de Brazza, Ratnagiri, Netravati, Bathurst* and *Lismore*.[84]
6. The Suez Escort Force now consisted of *Carlisle, Avon Vale, Eridge, Flamingo, Parramatta, Falmouth, Shoreham* and *Sutlej*. *Yarra* was on passage to relieve *Falmouth*.[85] A full escorting programme

---

[83]RA Hallifax.
Tarifa: 1936, 7,229gt, 16.25k, W Wilhelmsen, Oslo.
[84]*Indus*: RIN, 1934, 1,190t, 2×4.7in, 16.5k.
Hindustan: RIN, 1930, 1,190t, 2×4in, 16.5k.
Savorgnan de Brazza: Fr N, 1931, 1,969t, 3×5.5in, 15.5k.
Ratnagiri: 1935, 606gt, Ratnagar SN, Bombay.
Netravati: 1909, 1,540gt, Bombay SN.
Bathurst, Lismore: RAN, 1940, 700t, 1×3in, 15k.
[85]*Falmouth*: 1932, 1,060t, 2×4in, 16k.
Shoreham: 1931, 1,105t, 2×4in, 16k.
Sutlej: RIN, 1940, 1,300t, 6×4in, 18k.
Yarra: RAN, 1940, 1,060t, 3×4in, 16.5k; later lost.

was to commence on 4 November with *Carlisle* and one of the sloops or destroyers at Anchorage 'B'. All ships slower than 10 knots, and therefore unable to pass through the danger zone in daylight, were required to anchor at Abu Zemina (B) at night.

7. Shipping in the Gulf of Suez was atacked unsuccessfully during the night of 1/2 by one or two aircraft. *Carlisle* drove off 3 attacks by gunfire.

277. *To the Admiralty*

2 November 1941

A. It is most disappointing to learn that neither *Illustrious* nor *Formidable* will be available before 15 March [1942] though this date would be considerably advanced were they to come through Mediterranean.

C. If CRUSADER succeeds it will be necessary for the Battlefleet to operate in the Central Mediterranean

    (a) To secure our supply lines to Benghazi.
    (b) To ensure severance of enemy's supply lines to Tripoli and thus to assist further land operations.
    (c) To ensure supplies to Malta and to enable us again to use the sorely needed repair facilities there.

D & E. I cannot agree with this argument that no bread is better than half a loaf. One carrier is better than none at all. She may indeed become a casualty, though the situation in which she would be required to operate would be much better than when we last had a carrier here.

It is certain, carrier or no carrier, Battlefleet must go into Central Mediterranean and equally certain lacking a carrier it will be subject to air attack without fighter protection. It is a question of weighing *possible* damage to a carrier and almost certain damage to battleships, which are equally necessary to conserve. The enemy Battlefleet of five battleships may come out. This need cause no undue alarm but, lacking a carrier, we should have nothing to fix them with and without fighters with the fleet, combined action of enemy air and surface forces might lead to an awkward situation.

Illustrious and *Formidable* were damaged in first case by tactical and material surprise and in latter case when serviceability of fighters was down almost to none.

One good carrier filled with fighters should be well able to look after herself, particularly if fighter effort is conserved by making use of shore-based fighters during passages along African coast. *Ark Royal* has succeeded notably as a single carrier and the case in the Central Mediterranean is not so different. Should German Air Force return in force to Greece and Sicily the situation would need reconsideration. . . .

F & G. When *Eagle* is available I should be glad to have her provided *Warspite* has by then returned. Two carriers with only three battleships would be a most unbalanced force. *Eagle* would serve to house the strong reserve of fighters required to meet a massed attack, leaving *Indomitable* to maintain standing patrols and reconnaissance. Disparities of capacities and speeds would not be unduly awkward with this arrangement.

Surely *Ark Royal* can stick it a little longer until *Illustrious* and *Formidable* are back in service.

H. It is not proposed to operate carrier by day within reach of strong enemy fighter forces. Fulmar IIs seem adequate to deal with Ju88s. I trusted *Indomitable*'s outfit of fighters would be increased before leaving UK. She would be further reinforced from local resources here.

In short my conclusions are that, if a success in CRUSADER

(a) Maintenance of momentum depends on ability of Mediterranean Fleet to operate in Central Mediterranean.
(b) Ability of Mediterranean Fleet to operate in Central Mediterranean with reasonable success depends on having a carrier stuffed with fighters.
(c) Two carriers are better and safer than one, but one is essential.

The alternative is to have sufficient long range fighter aircraft based in Malta and Cyprus to maintain a strong fighter patrol consistently over the Fleet.

278. *War Diary, November 1941 (cont.)*

9 November

Central Mediterranean

Force K intercepted the convoy reported the previous day at 0040/9 . . . It was apparently making for the Libyan coast and consisted of four destroyers and eight merchant ships, and another convoy of two destroyers and two merchant ships was joining from the NE. Force K worked round and attacked the convoy with great success. Two large destroyers were sunk and another damaged. Seven merchant ships were sunk or left in a sinking condition. Force K ... suffered no casualties or damage and returned safely to Malta during the forenoon. An enemy T/B attack when Force K was approaching Malta was unsuccessful.[86]

279. *From Vice Admiral Whitworth*

11 November 1941

... I was glad to see that you have agreed to accept Wrens, and a large number of them. We shall have to send them out gradually as they become available. I do hope that they will prove to be a success. I am very much impressed with their work and their keenness. They take their service very seriously and join up to play their part in the war, rather than to have a good time; although they don't mind having a good time in non-working hours, which is as it should be. ...

Mountbatten has arrived back from America and taken over the PM's private army from RK[eyes], and I anticipate his staging some side shows in the near future. He is as usual full of enthusiasm, and goes full out at anything new. It will be interesting to see what sort of a fist he makes of it.

280. *Middle East Cs-in-C Committee*

12 November

300. *Heavy Bomber Programme*

The C-in-C, Mediterranean, said that he would like again to draw attention to the Piraeus. There was a good deal of activity going on there and he thought that it was being used for ships sailing to North Africa. German submarines which might be a greater danger to the movement of shipping along the N African coast than enemy air forces were also based at Piraeus.

The AOC-in-C said that both Piraeus and Crete were tempting targets and he would like to go for both of them. He thought, how-

---

[86] Force K arrived Malta 21 Oct. *Fulmine*: 1932, 1,238t, 4×4.7in, 6×21in tt, 38k. *Libeccio*: 1934, 1,640t, 4×4.7in, 6×21in tt, 38k; actually s by *Upholder*. 7 merchant Ships (39,000t) s. Close escort 6 destroyers; support force 2 heavy cruisers, 4 destroyers.

ever, that at the present time he should continue to concentrate on immediate tasks in Cyrenaica.

281. War Diary, November 1941 (cont.)

13 November

Levant

5. Ships continued to escort many small convoys and were employed at present as follows:

> *Erica* and Greek TBD *Niki* with convoy from Port Said to Alexandria.
> *Snapdragon* with convoy from Alexandria to Port Said.
> *Peony* with convoy from Haifa to Port Said.
> *Hyacinth* with convoy from Haifa to Famagusta.
> *Primula* at Haifa waiting to escort a merchant ship to Mersin.
> *Delphinium* with convoy from Port Said to Haifa and Beirut.
> *Fareham* was sweeping and escorting between Tripoli [Levant] and Beirut.[87]

14 November

Middle East Merchant Seaman Pool

6. The C-in-C pointed out to the Admiralty that *Toneline* and *Pass of Balmaha* had been commissioned solely because no British crew could be obtained locally to go to Tobruk.[88] The usual crews on these runs were mixtures of many nationalities other than British. It was hoped that active steps were being taken to make the Middle East Merchant Seaman Pool a reality.

15 November

MNBDO

8. The C-in-C pointed out to the Admiralty that the highly trained personnel of the MNBDO was still without sufficient guns and equipment for employment on other than guard and suchlike duties.

---

[87]*Erica* (mined, Libya, Feb. 1943), *Snapdragon* (s Ger a/c, E Med, Dec. 1942), *Primula*, *Delphinium*: 'Flower' cl corvettes, 1940, 925t, 1×4in, 16k.
[88]*Toneline*: 1928, 811gt, Toneline Tpt, London.

18 November

Operation *AGGRESSION*

2. The Army offensive was estimated to need the following supplies by sea:

Mersa Matruh	–	600 tons per day fresh water for the first 14 days; then 80 tons per day.
Tobruk	–	1,100 tons per day of stores and petrol.
Derna	–	200 tons/day of stores.
Benghazi	–	600 tons/day petrol and stores.

Orders were issued for Operation AGGRESSION, to clear the ports and provide these supplies as well as for the evacuation of wounded and prisoners of war.

3. Initially the Inshore Squadron was to consist of *Aphis, Moy,* 4 MLs, 2 LL minesweepers and 3 small tugs. The Western Desert Escort Force for the convoys was to consist of *Flamingo, Parramatta* and *Yarra* and the 22nd and 25th South African A/S Groups. HM Ships *Chakdina, Chantala* and *Woolborough* were to carry stores and personnel, and *Toneline* petrol, in addition to merchant ships.[89]

Submarines

7. The C-in-C ordered a new disposition of submarines consequent upon altered conditions. The 1st S/M Flotilla was to maintain one submarine off Benghazi and one off Misurata, two in the Aegean, one in the Adriatic and one minelaying. The 10th S/M Flotilla was to maintain a patrol line in the Ionian Sea to intercept convoys to Benghazi, and one submarine off the Straits of Messina.

282. *To Willis*

20 November 1941

Things have been fairly dull here from a fleet point of view the last few months. Not that there hasn't been plenty going on, but fleet operations have been conspicuously few, mostly as diversions for the operations of Force H.

---

[89]*Chakdina*: 1914, 3,033gt, 14k.
Chantala: 1920, 3,129gt, 14k. Both Br India SN.
Woolborough: A/S trawler, 1937, 459t.

The running of those two convoys into Malta from the West was a good show. I doubt if it would have been possible had they had opposition from the German AF but the Germans have abandoned Sicily and are now in Crete and Greece and keep a very close watch on us.

Tobruk has been very expensive both in small merchant ships and destroyers, sweepers, etc. Eventually practically all supply except petrol was done by destroyers. We lost the poor little *Pass of Balmaha* which set us back in the petrol line. A Hun S/M – we have I think six of them operating in the E Med at the moment.

The sinking of the convoy in the Central Med was nice work by that small force. Nothing whatever to do with me. A good appreciation by old Ford put them right on the spot. I personally thought they were wasted at Malta and that the Iteys would not be BF enough to give them a chance but they did and Agnew leaped at it.[90] . . .

Of course when they ran the convoys into Malta they quite forgot about oil fuel and so they are very short. In fact Force K may have to depart. . . .

I would have liked to use the preoccupation of the Hun by running convoys into and out of Malta but I am so short of destroyers that I can only do so one thing at a time. The supply line will be heavily attacked from Crete and by the Hun S/M, so I shall have to keep the D[estroyer]s busy on it and not running round with the fleet. For the time being anyway.

I haven't got a carrier either, the sinking of the *Ark Royal* has put that luxury a long way away as *Formidable* and *Illustrious* cannot be here till March at the earliest.[91] In fact we are back to the old business – we can't strafe the shadower.

We won, to a great extent, our battle for a Coastal Command. 201 is now 201, Naval Co-operation Group. The Air Ministry fought like tigers not to have anything naval in the name but DP and I stood firm. A very good fellow Slatter who has done a lot of carrier work is now the AOC and matters are much improved.

I cannot say I am as happy with the present lot in Cairo as I was with Wavell and Longmore. . . . Auchinleck is undoubtedly a fine man but narrow viewed in comparison with his predecessor. Having served in India all his life he views himself as heaven-born and does not lightly tolerate other heaven-borns such as the C-in-C Med. . . .

---

[90]Capt (later VA Sir) William G. Agnew (1898–1960): M/sman 1914; gun splist; Cdr 1932; Capt 1937; AMC *Corfu* 1939; *Aurora* 1940; SO, Force K 1941; Cdre, 12CS 1943; *Excellent* 1943; *Vanguard* 1946; RA & DPS 1947–49; VA on ret list 1950.

[91]*Ark Royal* s W Med, 13–14 Nov., by *U-81*.

... They look on me I'm afraid as a porcupine all prickles but as you know I am anything but. At the same time I feel that last February Longmore and I were not outspoken enough about the Greek adventure and apparently I never got over to the other two the dire consequences of the loss of Crete so I have made up my mind that I will speak my mind although I may be wrong. I think this will probably result in my early relief but I don't really mind. ...

283. *From Pound*

23 November 1941

I have just been discussing with the Prime Minister the situation in the Western Desert and three things were apparent:

(a) the enemy's shortage of petrol
(b) the extreme efforts the enemy are making to put supplies of petrol into Benghazi. ...
(c) the enemy's air situation is such that it is more than doubtful whether he can spare any aircraft for work over the sea in the vicinity of the African coast.

The effect of keeping the enemy short of petrol will have such far-reaching results that we are sure you are considering whether in view of (c) above it will not be possible to use surface forces for the interruption of traffic to Benghazi during the coming very critical period.

284. *To Pound*

24 November 1941

I have long had this matter under consideration and orders are in force ready for immediate execution for combined action with Force K.

Enemy recce. is still active and every westward movement is seen. Consequently enemy convoys play cat and mouse and can always take full advantage of our fuelling periods.

Only feasible method is by cruiser raid of which westward movement from Alexandria simulates a night bombardment of Bardia. Force can then pass S of Crete at high speed by night and meet Force K at dawn in vicinity of convoy.

Operation entails cruiser force spending daylight of one day unprotected in Central Mediterranean. I have not sufficient destroyers to send adequate force with cruisers and screen battlefleet reasonably. In any case Battlefleet spoils the game – see para. 2 above.

It is a chancy enterprise; cruisers must rely on air recce. to keep them clear of superior force and it is none too good.

Cruisers and destroyers are sailing at 0400 today to intercept MK16, 18 and 106.

It must be accepted that this operation is a one-shot affair. If it misses fire on one day the enemy convoys have a clear run for the two succeeding ones. The movements forecast in MK information are all too frequently postponed and communication lags delay appropriate action this end. Air recce. is too thin to be certain of obtaining confirmation.

All these considerations are I am sure well known to you and I hope you will be able to explain to the Prime Minister the problem presented in organising interception by a force based 550 miles from the scene of operations and constantly under observation by the enemy reconnaissance.

285. *From Churchill*

23 November 1941

I asked the First Sea Lord to wireless you today about the vital importance of intercepting surface ships bringing reinforcements, supplies and above all fuel to Benghazi.

Our information here was a number of vessels now approaching or starting. Request has been made by enemy for air protection but this can't be given owing to the absorption in battle of his African Air Force....

I shall be glad to hear from the Admiralty what action you propose to take. Stopping of these ships may save thousands of lives apart from aiding a victory of cardinal importance.

286. *To Churchill*

24 November 1941

I am naturally very much alive to the vital importance of the Benghazi supply route and the First Sea Lord will by now have told you of the dispositions which were already in hand to deal with the situation. Our first move was to hold up enemy convoys by means of threats from the forces at either end of the Mediterranean. This has had considerable success. Now that convoys are resuming sailings they will be attacked by surface, air and submarine forces. Unfortunately the reported absorption of the German Air Force in the land battle to which you refer has not been borne out in practice and a very lively interest is being taken by the enemy in our movements. Conversely our own weakness in reconnaissance forces is adding a heavy hazard to the work of our light forces who have of necessity to operate without close support if use is to be made of their speed.

287. *From Pound*

25 November 1941

A. The difficulty of interception from Alexandria is realised owing to (1) its distance from Navarin–Benghazi supply line, (2) location of your forces by enemy air recce.

B. These difficulties will be increased when method described in MK[?-] is in force but amount of fuel [?-] transported in this way will be limited and some slow merchant vessels will probably be used.

C. The interception of ships on passage to Benghazi is easier from Malta due to distance but as lag in receipt of information may preclude action unless a force is actually at sea it would appear necessary to have a cruiser and destroyer force at Malta in addition to Force K during these very critical days when the whole success of CRUSADER may depend on interruption of the supply line. Such additional force would have to come from your command.

D. Attack on departure points such as Argostoli and Navarin and arrival points such as Benghazi and Derna is most necessary by every practicable means and I am sure you have considered naval bombardment, air attack and laying of both moored and magnetic mines.

E. It is realised that policy to date has been to put every available aircraft into the land battle but if denial of fuel to African ports is of importance we attach to it here, then it would seem that air force should give you greater assistance.

288. *From Pound*

25 November 1941

... There is nothing I should like better than to send you a present of 20 or 30 destroyers and a dozen cruisers with an intimation that, if necessary, they might be considered expendable. You know, however, how terribly hard pushed we are in every direction and this will account for the smallness of our presents. ... It was only after most thorough consideration that I stole two destroyers from you to give to the Far East, but I could see no other alternative. ...

289. *To Pound*

26 November 1941

1. I am in entire agreement. I have hesitated to send further forces to Malta owing to the fuel situation but in view of the overriding necessity to stop enemy supply I am sending two cruisers and two destroyers tomorrow to operate in Central Mediterranean and thence to Malta. My calculation however is that we can't hope for more than three sorties each by Force K and this new force.
2. *Porpoise* is already under orders to mine Navarin. *Abdiel* is just completing essential docking.
3. Bombardments have been carried out in accordance with Army priorities and when the more important requirement of intercepting supplies allows. *Aphis* is continuously at Army disposal for this purpose.
4. I will discuss the air effort with AOC-in-C, but I know how completely extended his forces are. You will recollect my anxieties on this score. Yet again we are learning the lesson of the lack of shore-based T/B aircraft and of their enormous value to the enemy. I am continually pressing AOC-in-C to have magnetic mines laid since suitable objectives are outside naval aircraft range but I have not been successful recently partly due to aircraft shortage and partly to lack of suitable mines.

290. *From Pound*

27 November 1941

A. We thoroughly appreciate the altered conditions in the Eastern Mediterranean due to the arrival of U-boats there, and the fact that there is every indication that they will be reinforced.

B. At first sight it might appear that the situation in the Atlantic has been drastically altered due to the diversion of these U-boats to the Eastern Mediterranean, but with our knowledge of the number of U-boats available for service and the number coming into service from new construction, we estimate by 15 December the enemy will be able to operate 36 U-boats in the North Atlantic, apart from those in the Gibraltar, Freetown and Cape areas.

C. It is not possible, therefore, to denude our troop and trade convoys in the Atlantic of their escorts to reinforce the Eastern Mediterranean to the extent that we would like.

D. We do appreciate, however, the commitments which face you both in interrupting the enemy's supplies to North Africa and in maintaining our own to the advanced bases of the Army.

E. We also appreciate the added risks to the Battlefleet when at sea, and the risk to unsupported light forces operating in the Central Mediterranean, unless the latter have adequate warning of the approach of superior enemy surface forces.

F. We note your intention of stationing a force of cruisers and destroyers at Malta in addition to Force K, and we feel convinced that these forces will for a time be able to threaten or interrupt the enemy's lines of communication to North Africa to a great extent.

G. The steps we are taking to deal with this submarine situation as far as is practicable with the means at our disposal are as follows:

(1) To provide temporarily as heavy a concentration of A/S vessels in the Straits of Gibraltar as possible in order to prevent the ingress of the U-boats into the Mediterranean. To assist this we have held up convoy HG76, in order that its escorts may help.

(2) Arrangements are being made for the dispatch of six Coastal Command Hudsons to Gibraltar during the next few days.[92]

(3) Arrangements are being made for the dispatch of 20 Wellingtons, whose crews are well trained in A/S work, to the Eastern Mediterranean to join 201 Naval Co-operation Group for A/S work. They should arrive in the first week in December.

H. We hope that with the air reinforcements outlined in AM1640A/20, this will materially improve the situation in the Eastern Mediterranean.

---

[92] Lockheed Hudson: 1938, 5–7mg, 1,400lbs bombs, 253mph, range 2,800 mls.

I. It does not seem possible to put *Malaya* through the Eastern Mediterranean and in any case this would mean leaving Force H without a capital ship.

We know you hold the same views as we do regarding unsuitability of 'R' class [battleships] for Mediterranean.

Warspite on completion on 1 January will of course join you as soon as possible.

J. As you will have seen from AM1835A/26 we are endeavouring to stop the entry of the U-boats into the Mediterranean. As soon as this phase is past reinforcements of Fleet destroyers from Force H will be available to you these being replaced at Gibraltar by one of the [?true] escort groups.

We estimate that *Legion, Isaac Sweers, Maori, Zulu* and *Sikh* will be ready to leave Gibraltar for the Eastern Mediterranean about 6 December. We are accelerating *Norman* and *Nestor* and they should be ready to leave Gibraltar about 15 December. *Gurkha* will also be sent as soon as rough weather damage has been repaired. *Lance* and *Lively* will join Mediterranean Fleet in place of the two 'Tribals' mentioned in AM2338/10, when Force K is no longer required.[93]

K. It is not practicable at present to replenish oil fuel supplies at Malta from the West as Force H is not strong enough to operate in support. It will therefore be necessary to send an oiler from Eastern Mediterranean as soon as you consider the situation allows her a reasonable chance of getting through...

291. *War Diary, November 1941 (concl.)*

22 November

Red Sea

6. SS *Queen Mary* arrived at Suez being the first of the 17 monster liners and other big personnel ships due to arrive during the next fortnight. The C-in-C was unable to spare any reinforcements for

---

[93]*Legion* (bombed Malta Mar. 1942), *Gurkha* (s *U-133*, off Libya, Jan. 1942), *Lance* (bombed Malta 1942), *Lively* (s Ger a/c E Med May 1942): 1940–41, 1,920t, 8×4in, 8×21in tt, 36.5k.

Isaac Sweers: R Neth N, compl 1940 in UK, 1,628t, 5×4.7in, 8×21in tt, 36k; s off N Africa Nov. 1942.

Maori (bombed Ger a/c, Malta Feb. 1942), *Zulu* (s It a/c, off Tobruk, Sept. 1942), *Sikh* (s shore batts, Tobruk, Sept. 1942): 'Tribal' cl.

Norman (RAN), *Nestor* (s Ger a/c, C Med June 1942): 1941, 1,760t, 6×4.7in, 1×4in, 5×21in tt, 36k.

the Suez escort force which consisted of *Shoreham, Sutlej* and *Jumna*.[94]

23 November

6. The C-in-C pointed out to the Admiralty that in the event of war with Japan enemy submarines operating in the Red Sea would threaten our Middle East communications very seriously. It was requested that consideration be given to the laying of indicator loops across the Perim Straits.

24 November

Operation ME5

2. Two convoys were reported at sea making for Benghazi and Force B consisting of *Ajax* (CS7), *Neptune, Naiad, Euryalus, Galatea, Kandahar, Kingston, Kimberley* and *Hotspur* sailed from Alexandria at 0400/24. Force K returned to Malta to fuel. A dividing line of 33° 30'N was appointed with Force K ordered to operate to the N of it and Force B to the S.[95]

3. The C-in-C sailed from Alexandria at 1500/24 in *Queen Elizabeth* with *Barham* (VA1), *Valiant, Jervis, Griffin, Decoy, Napier, Nizam, Kipling, Jackal* and *Hasty*, to support Force B if necessary. . . .

25 November

Operation ME5 – Loss of Barham

At 1629 *Barham* was torpedoed by a U-boat . . . She was hit probably by three torpedoes on the port side and three minutes later she listed to port on her beam ends with bow and stern under water. A magazine amidships blew up and she sank at 1634. *Jervis* and *Jackal* were ordered to hunt the U-boat, and *Nizam* and *Hotspur* to rescue survivors. *Queen Elizabeth* and *Valiant* continued to the westward with *Napier, Griffin, Kipling, Hasty* and *Decoy* escorting. The U-boat broke surface between *Barham* and *Valiant* but no further contact was made in the subsequent hunt. About 450 survivors were taken on board the destroyers including Vice Admiral Pridham-Wippell. Captain G. C. Cooke was lost.[96] . . . No contact was reported though it later appeared that *Jervis* had made an unreliable A/S contact as the U-boat passed through the screen.

[94]*Jumna:* RIN, 1940, 1,300t, 6×4in, 18k.
[95]*Euryalus:* 1940, 5,450t, 10×5.25in, 6×21in tt, 33k. Capt E. W. Bush, i/c: see his *Bless Our Ship* (London, 1958).
[96]Capt G. C. Cooke: Capt 1933; NID 1939; *Barham* 1940.

2. *Penelope* and *Lively* of Force K intercepted one convoy of two merchant ships and two destroyers at 1610/24. After a short engagement the two destroyers made off and both merchant ships were destroyed. They blew up and sank, probably without survivors; both were apparently carrying war material to Libya. The two destroyers escaped. . . .

26 November

22nd A/S Group

9. The one year period of loan of the 22nd South African A/S Group to the Mediterranean was due to expire in December. The C-in-C asked for its extension and signalled to the Admiralty:

> I should view the departure of these fine little ships and their outstandingly efficient ships' companies with the greatest regret. I trust therefore that the Union Government may be asked to allow them to continue on their present valuable work which is a fitting counterpart to the fine showing of the South African troops in the field.

27 November

Operation ME5

Force B consisting of *Ajax* (CS7), *Neptune*, *Kimberley* and *Kingston*, and Force C consisting of *Naiad* (CS15), *Euryalus*, *Griffin* and *Hotspur*, sailed westward from Alexandria at 0800/27. Force B was to proceed to Malta to reinforce Force K after attempting to intercept enemy supplies to Benghazi. Force C was to return to Alexandria a.m. 28th after operating off the Cyrenaican coast. Additional ammunition and submarine torpedoes were embarked in ships of Force B.

30 November

Mails

6. The C-in-C again protested strongly to the Admiralty at the disgraceful state of affairs regarding mails which still showed no signs of improvement. The last all sea route mail received by the fleet was that for 28 August . . .

Summary of Events during November

General

All efforts were concentrated in support of the 8th Army advance in Libya, which was commenced on 18 November. A heavy supply programme was completed during the dark period leading up to it by destroyers running to Tobruk. The actual advance was supported by three fleet operations with the object of diverting the enemy air strength and of threatening a possible landing in his rear. It was during the last of these that *Barham* was torpedoed by a U-boat and sunk. By the end of the month the Tobruk garrison had been relieved and the first large convoy was sailed from Alexandria, but the position of the relieving forces was by no means secure.

2. In the Central Mediterranean Force K's brilliant interception and annihilation of a large convoy during the night 8/9 had a profound and lasting effect upon the all important Libyan supply problem. The enemy was then forced to provide cruiser escort for subsequent convoys; ...

Western Desert

5. Consequent upon the employment of destroyers during the October dark period to relieve the Australian division from Tobruk, supplies had run low, and a heavy supply programme (APPROACH) was run by 3 destroyers nightly, *Abdiel* and a few small store carriers from 11 to 18 November. After the commencement of the Army advance, naval movements and operations were reduced to the minimum, in order to release fighters for the desert battle. A number of trips were run to Tobruk, however, to meet especially urgent requirements. In one of these the Australian sloop *Parramatta* was torpedoed and sunk by a U-boat. Operation AGGRESSION, the opening of Tobruk as a main supply port, was commenced in spite of the lack of fighter protection at Tobruk. *Glenroy* was torpedoed while taking the harbour clearance party and lighters to Tobruk. She was ultimately towed back to Alexandria.

Malta

7. The successful operations of Force K was the outstanding feature of the month. A total of 12 merchant ships and 2 destroyers were sunk and a heavy requirement placed upon the enemy for escorting future convoys.... The 10SF, the Blenheims and T/B aircraft continued their excellent work. The Blenheims are particularly successful.

292. *To Pound*

1 December 1941

Your 2008/27/11 [No. 290]. I am in general agreement with your views. My first need is adequate reconnaissance for protection force operating from Malta and this is doubly necessary now that enemy is using important force to cover his convoys. I am sure that you are doing everything possible to implement your 1640/20/11 in this respect as soon as possible in view of the vital importance of proper reconnaissance.

2. From past experience I do not feel we can place any great hope in stopping passage of U-boats into Mediterranean but am glad to note the measures being taken to attempt to do so.

3. It is evident therefore that we must set out to harry this submarine force by every means in our power and proposed additions to my destroyer strength will be more than welcome as will the 20 Wellingtons. Constant calls for transport and army work on Mediterranean light forces have led to a falling off in A/S efficiency but every effort is being made to give opportunity for exercise to work up A/S standard. . . .

4. I agree *Malaya* can't be passed through Mediterranean and that Force H must retain at least one capital ship. There appears therefore no alternative but to await *Warspite* providing situation will allow detachment of a capital ship from Force G. It is evident of course that a fast ship such as *Repulse* or even an 8-in cruiser would be invaluable in present circumstances to back up our small cruisers. I trust all possible will be done to expedite *Warspite*. . . .

293. *To Pound*

4 December 1941

A. I very much appreciated your signal about the *Barham*. She is indeed a heavy loss. We blundered straight on to the submarine . . . At first we thought that the submarine had not been pinged but on investigation it was found that she actually came in under the screen and was actually pinged by one of the destroyers, who unfortunately discarded it as a non-sub echo. It was a most daring and brilliant performance on the part of the submarine, who fired from a position about 200 yards ahead of *Valiant*. If there is anything to be learnt from it, it is that our A/S vessels are sadly out of practice and

I am withdrawing *Otus* from operational duty to run her as a clockwork mouse. She is of little value anyway, as she is constantly breaking down.[97]

Pridham-Wippell had a bit of a shake up but I hope he will be all right in a few days.

I did not think there would be a battleship to replace *Barham*. With luck the *Warspite* will be here nearly as soon as anything could come from the Atlantic.

We must just do with two for the time being but you will realise that I must keep them rather in cotton wool as it won't do to get another put out of action. It is all right so long as the *Littorios* can be kept facing West though to me that looks as if Force H will have to be made powerful enough to form a real threat.

B. Force K is doing splendidly and I think a great deal of it is due to Ford, who seems to have a flair for putting them in the right place. Are you sure that he ought to be relieved? It seems a pity seeing that he is doing such good work and I am not confident that his successor will do as well. I doubt if Ford himself wishes to leave.

C. The question of getting oil into Malta is giving us cause for much thought. As an interim measure, as soon as the moon is more suitable, I am getting *Breconshire* here and will run her in with 5,000 tons, but that is only a flea-bite and we must face running a convoy. The difficulty is that we can get nothing faster than 10 knots. It also means the Battlefleet going to sea covering the operation and what with the Tobruk supply, the convoy escort and the battleship screen, I just do not know where the destroyers are coming from. It would probably be best to combine this operation with a move by Force H and bring in from the West the destroyers you have allocated to us.

D. I am very grateful to you for your assistance in getting PO Sephton the VC. He was a very fine man and undoubtedly deserved it and I feel that the effect on the personnel of the Fleet will be very marked.[98]

E. ... I do not wish to appear grasping but I wonder if you realise that I have only a total of 26 A/S vessels exclusive of destroyers and MLs. This has to cover the A/S protection of Malta, Alexandria, Port Said and all the Palestine and Syrian coast as well as supply escorts for the slow convoys.

---

[97]*Jervis*, though unfortunately Capt Mack was not on the bridge.
Otus: 1929, 1,475/2,030t, 1×4in, 8×21in tt, 17.5/9k.
[98]PO A. E. Sephton, VC: gunnery direction, *Coventry;* mortally wounded by a/c fire but continued to direct fire, despite immense pain.

The lack of small A/S craft is rather grim. I don't know if you can spare another four corvettes and a group of trawlers but they are badly wanted.

F. We had another bit of bad luck in *Jackal* being torpedoed. She was attacked by five T/B aircraft and hit by a shallow running torpedo about five feet from right aft. She is all right except her steering compartment and steering gear are wrecked.

We may be able to patch her to go to Malta where, if they can get a steering engine, they should repair her fairly quickly.

H. The agreement you made with the Air Ministry on Naval Cooperation is working well. Air Cdre Slatter is a first class man and out to do all he can to help. Of course practically everything is thrown into the battle [in the Western Desert].

The Albacores are recognised as the best bombers there are – within their limitations of course. I sent you a signal about their squadron leader, Corbett.[99]

294. *From Pound*

0012A, 10 December 1941

What do you condsider the consequences would be of:

(a) Withdrawing from Eastern Mediterranean all capital ships and carriers but not remaining ships now under your command.
(b) Withdrawing capital ship and carrier force from Force H.
(c) Withdrawing ships as at (a) and (b).

Very early reply is requested.

295. *To Pound*

2022B, 10 December 1941

Your 0012/10/12. Para. A.

The consequences of this proposal must vary with degrees of success of Army in Africa.

2. Under present circumstances it can't be doubted that capital ships are the essential factor on which the stopping of enemy supply

---

[99]Lt-Cdr J. W. S. Corbett: Lt Feb. 1932; *Cardiff* 1939; FAA July 1939; Lt-Cdr, *Merlin* (Donibristle) Feb. 1940; CO 826 Sqdn, *Grebe* (Dekheila) Jan. 1941–Jan. 1942; MIA.

and any hope of supply to Malta rests, and their immediate removal would be most unfortunate.

3. Should we however attain a firm hold on whole of Cyrenaica, and provided that really adequate Air Forces are based there and at Malta under my operational control it appears that the supply of Army and maintenance of Malta by fast ships will be possible albeit rather precariously in the absence of capital ships.

4. The gravest disadvantages would be

(a) The Italian fleet would get a great fillip to morale and might well become aggressive. At present their tails are down.

(b) The political effect of withdrawal of Battlefleet in Egypt and Turkey is incalculable.

(c) The ability to continue pressure on enemy supply to Africa would be seriously compromised.

(d) There would be no absolute guarantee against the enemy operating in the Eastern Mediterranean particularly by sortie from Aegean.

5. I realise the urgency of present situation in the East and am most anxious to assist.

There seems to be considerable political unrest with you and it looks to me as though the public are right this time. The outcry to get Winston to do his Prime Minister's job and not be Minister of Defence is absolutely right. He's a bad strategist but doesn't know it and no one has the courage to stand up to him. . . .

6. Reference your para. (b) the [?withdrawal] of heavier [?units] of Force H would simply lead to concentration of Italian Fleet Eastwards and render our task more difficult. This withdrawal would also be known to enemy immediately and certainly the existence of Force H is a potent factor in operations of Eastern Mediterranean Fleet – quite apart from its value as an Atlantic Force, it is also a standing threat to any seaborne expedition to North Africa.

7. (c) The conclusion is that the maintenance of a heavy ship force at Gibraltar is of great importance from all aspects: but that given conditions outlined in para. 3 the withdrawal of further ships from the Eastern Mediterranean could be reluctantly accepted as a gambler's stake.

8. In conclusion I have not entered an absolute caveat in proposal (a) as I am not fully aware of situation but you will understand I regard it with most serious misgivings. If we are driven to such a course our salvation will be in the air and I urge with all the energy

at my command that every step is taken to ensure that not only needful Air Forces for reconnaissance and striking [?] over whole Central and Eastern Mediterranean are available but that they are [?placed in] Naval co-operation [?group] and working in close conjunction with me and untrammelled by outside commitments otherwise they will fail in their function and air effort which will be provided obviously at greatest sacrifice will fail in its object. I would reiterate that unless these conditions can be fulfilled I do not consider that removal of capital ships from Eastern Mediterranean should be countenanced.

296. *To Pound*

15 December 1941

The following is my view of present situation.

Enemy have temporarily stopped sailings of merchant ships to Africa and are relying on destroyers, submarines and aircraft. Unless enemy are prepared to abandon North Africa, which I do not believe, I consider that sailing of merchant ships must start within next few days. These will probably be supported by heavy ships.

2. The enemy's immediate plan may however have been upset by the sinking of two cruisers off Cape Bon and the torpedoing of a battleship South of Messina.[100] . . .

3. In view of this I am taking opportunity to sail *Breconshire* to Malta so that she can arrive there before enemy sailings are restarted.

4. There appear to be three U-boats operating between Alexandria and Tobruk and it is obvious the enemy will make every effort to cut this vital supply line. I am naturally most anxious to meet the Army's request for supply of their troops in Western Desert. These requirements have greatly and unexpectedly [?increased] having now reached [?1,500] tons a day at Tobruk.

5. The arrival of *Sikh, Maori, Legion* and *Isaac Sweers* will undoubtedly help and will enable me to strengthen the escorts of

---

[100]Cdr G. H. Stokes: b 1902; s/m; *Wolverine*; *Keppel*, China; *Tempest* i/c; pilot; *Griffin*, MF; OD 1939; *Mackay* 1940; Dunkirk; *Sikh* Oct. 1940; Force H & *Bismarck* action 1941; Capt & CO RN Air Sta 1943; SO of a force of 4 destroyers, reinforcing MF, sank *Alberico da Barbiano* & *Alberto di Giussano*: 1931, 5,200t, 8×6in, 6×3.9in, 4×21in tt, 37k. E-boat also sunk. *Vittorio Veneto* hit by 2 t from *Urge*.

the Tobruk convoy. These will, however, not be sufficient and I consider the early arrival of the 20 Wellingtons ... to be a matter of highest urgency. Request every step possible to expedite them none having yet arrived so far as I am aware.

297. *War Diary, December 1941*

13 December

Central Mediterranean – Action off Pantelleria

1. Group 1 destroyer force consisting of *Sikh, Legion, Maori* and *Isaac Sweers* made contact with an enemy force of two 6-in cruisers and two small destroyers or E-boats at 0230/13 ... Our force engaged at close range and sank both cruisers, and one of the two torpedo boats. The other was thought to have been badly damaged. An ASV Wellington had reported the enemy force earlier which caused it to turn back northward enabling Group 1 to intercept. A T/B striking force was despatched from Malta but did not make contact until after the action. Group 1 arrived safely at Malta with no damage or casualties in any ships. The enemy cruisers sunk were later identified as *Alberto di Giussano* and *Alberico da Barbiano*.[101]

Operation ME9

2. Operation ME9 was ordered to intercept enemy units reported to be operating in the Ionian Sea, covering convoys to Libya. CS15 sailed westward from Alexandria after dark 13th with *Naiad, Galatea, Euryalus, Jervis, Kimberley, Kingston, Napier, Nizam, Kipling, Griffin, Havock* and *Hotspur*. W/T silence was ordered at Alexandria and *Abdiel* sailed for Haifa to create a W/T diversion giving the impression of the battlefleet being at sea. Forces B and K were to sail from Malta to co-operate with CS15 during the night 14/15. All available submarines were sailed from Malta to patrol positions in the Ionian Sea.

14 December

Submarines

2. Heavy submarine concentrations had been placed to intercept the enemy S of Messina, in the Gulf of Taranto or on the convoy route W of Cephalonia. *Urge* reported two and possibly three hits

---

[101]Force K had also sunk a M/V, *Adriatico*: 1931, 1,976gt, Adriatica SA di Nav, Bari.

on the second of two *Cavour* class battleships steering southward through the Straits of Messina at 0858/14 ... It was not certain what damage had been inflicted, but about an hour later only one undamaged battleship was sighted by *Urge* and by *Unique*, steaming eastward at 15 knots. A prisoner later stated that the torpedoed battleship reached harbour.

3. *Upright* reported four hits on two large unidentified ships escorted by destroyers ... at 0210/13. Other explosions followed and both ships were considered to have sunk.

15 December

Operations – Loss of HMS Galatea

1. *Galatea* was torpedoed by a U-boat and sunk ... at 2359/14. *Galatea*, in company with CS15, was about to enter the Alexandria searched channel. The destroyer screen had been released shortly before the torpedoing. At least two torpedoes hit her amidships and she sank almost immediately. *Naiad* and *Euryalus* continued to Alexandria. The destroyers rescued 13 officers and 141 men. Captain E. W. B. Sim was missing.[102] The subsequent A/S hunt was unsuccessful as was that by D7.

2. CS15 sailed again at 2200/15 in *Naiad* with *Euryalus, Carlisle, Jervis, Kimberley, Kingston, Kipling, Nizam, Havock* and *Decoy* escorting *Breconshire* with oil fuel to Malta.[103] It was thought that *Breconshire* could be got through to Malta before the enemy had reorganised sufficiently to intercept with surface forces or sail the Libyan convoys again. *Decoy* was proceeding to Malta for repairs....

16 December

Operations

Group 1 destroyers ... sailed from Malta at 1100/16 and Force K consisting of *Aurora, Penelope, Lance* and *Lively* at 1800/16. Both forces were to join CS15 on the 17th, Force K returning to Malta with *Breconshire* and Group 1 to Alexandria with CS15. *Carlisle, Hasty* and *Kingston* were detached by CS15 at dark 16th to make a W/T diversion to the eastward at midnight 16/17 and thence to Alexandria. Enemy heavy forces were reported at sea 2230/16, by *Unbeaten* and by *Utmost* in the Gulf of Taranto area; *Unbeaten* was kept down by the escort and *Utmost* was unable to attack having expended all torpedoes. CS15 was instructed by the C-in-C that

---
[102]Capt E. W. B. Sim: Cdr 1933; *Arethusa* 1939; Capt June 1940; *Galatea* 1941.
[103]CS15: RA Vian.

should an encounter with the enemy become probable, his object was the security of *Breconshire* until dark 17th (when she was to be detached to Malta) and thereafter to attack the enemy with torpedoes. He should be E of 21° by 0800/18 if possible. The VA, Malta, was instructed to sail all available forces to join CS15.

17 December

1. CS15 made contact with Group 1 destroyers at daylight 17th and continued westward with *Breconshire,* two cruisers and 10 destroyers. His force was shadowed and attacked by enemy high level and T/B aircraft throughout the day. Two S79s were shot down. Enemy heavy forces were reported by aircraft at 0825 to the northward and again with a convoy at 1525 about 60 miles N of CS15. Very few aircraft were available for reconnaissance and shadowing was not carried out. At 1745 CS15 most unexpectedly encountered an enemy force of two battleships and numerous light forces to the westward of him. The encounter coincided with a heavy air attack. The battleships opened fire but drew off to the northward when our forces closed to attack and contact was lost at dark. *Aurora* and Force K made contact with *Breconshire* who was detached southward with *Havock* and *Decoy* and were enabled to steer round the enemy force by reports from an ASV Wellington. *Neptune, Jaguar* and *Kandahar* sailed from Malta p.m. and gave additional cover to *Breconshire*. CS15 withdrew eastward to patrol N of Benghazi to intercept the enemy convoy.[104]

Submarines

9. *Talisman* returned to Alexandria from a most successful patrol in the Aegean and off Cephalonia. After several unsuccessful encounters with enemy destroyers and a U-boat, *Talisman* attacked a ship thought to be a U-boat at 2154/8 . . ., torpedoes ran under and *Talisman* engaged with gunfire scoring four hits near the bridge when it was seen that the enemy was a destroyer attempting to ram. *Talisman* dived and was undamaged in the subsequent attack.

10. At 1615/11 *Talisman* torpedoed with four hits and sank a large enemy transport eastbound... At 1952/14 while returning to Alexandria, *Talisman* encountered a U-boat... opened fire and scored a direct hit at the base of the conning tower. The U-boat submerged with the conning tower open and was considered to have sunk as an underwater explosion followed.[105]

[104]Known as 1st Battle of Sirte.
[105]No Ger or It s/m sunk.

18 December

Central Mediterranean

1. The enemy convoys were apparently turned back after dark 17th and CS15 did not make contact again during the night. His force proceeded at high speed to the eastward and arrived at Alexandria during the night 18/19. . . .

2. *Breconshire* and the Malta force arrived safely at Malta, largely due to the good work of the ASV Wellington during the night 17/18. The Malta force now consisted of *Ajax*, with machinery defects and speed thereby reduced to 20 knots, *Aurora, Penelope, Neptune, Lance, Lively, Kandahar, Jaguar* and *Havock. Decoy* was taken in hand for repair.

3. Air reconnaissance reported the enemy battlefleet remaining in an area halfway betwen Malta and Benghazi throughout the day, and it became apparent that the convoys had been turned once again to make Benghazi and Tripoli during the night 18/19. *Neptune, Aurora, Penelope, Kandahar, Lance, Lively* and *Havock* sailed again after fuelling to intercept the enemy near Tripoli. A T/B striking force was also despatched at dark. Two enemy destroyers apparently damaged in collison were sighted in the vicinity of the enemy battlefleet making north eastward at slow speed, but daylight air attacks on these and other enemy forces at sea could not be carried out.

Alexandria

5. The C-in-C made the following general signal:

> Attacks on Alexandria by air, boat or human torpedo may be expected when calm weather conditions prevail. Look-outs and patrols should be warned accordingly.

19 December

Attack on Alexandria Harbour

1. *Queen Elizabeth* and *Valiant* were both seriously damaged in an attack on Alexandria harbour by human torpedoes and the oiler *Sagona* and *Jervis* were also damaged.[106]

2. The sequence of events was as follows:

---

[106] *Sagona*: 1929, 7,554gt, A/S Sagona, Norway.

0325/19	Two Italians picked up on *Valiant*'s bow buoy. The general warning passed and ship's patrol boats sent away. Interrogation produced no result.
0547	Explosion under the stern of *Sagona* which also damaged *Jervis*'s bow.
0606	Explosion under 'A' turret of *Valiant*.
0610	Explosion under boiler room of *Queen Elizabeth*.

3. *Valiant* was flooded forward and heavily down by the bow. *Queen Elizabeth* had three boiler rooms flooded and a considerable list to starboard. She was unable to raise steam and two submarines were moved alongside to provide power.

Queen Elizabeth's list was corrected by counter flooding, but neither ship could be docked in their present condition owing to draught.

4. Interrogation of the six prisoners afterwards captured established that three human torpedoes were launched from a U-boat, probably *Sciré*, near the eastern harbour and made their way to the main harbour entrance. The boom gate was opened several times during the night for HM ships and it was not, therefore, certain whether or not the boom itself had been lifted.

Central Mediterranean – Loss of HMS Neptune

7. The Malta force ran into a minefield about 20 miles E of Tripoli at 0530/19 in attempting to intercept the enemy. *Neptune* was mined twice and disabled . . . *Aurora* was also mined but was able to steam at 20 knots to Malta and arrived there safely escorted by *Lance* and *Havock*. *Penelope* was slightly damaged by a mine exploded in her paravanes. She was about to close *Neptune* to tow her when *Kandahar* who was also closing to take off personnel, was also mined aft and disabled. *Penelope* was then forced to abandon both ships and returned to Malta with *Lively*, arriving there at noon.

8. *Neptune* later drifted onto a third mine and sank, all her crew being either lost or taken prisoner. *Kandahar* remained afloat all day without interference by the enemy; *Jaguar* was sailed from Malta to make contact with her at midnight 19/20 when she should have drifted clear of the minefield.

20 December

Alexandria

1. Work proceeded as fast as possible to lighten *Valiant* sufficiently to be docked and to ascertain the underwater damage in *Queen*

Elizabeth. Jervis was docked and would take about a month to repair. The oiler *Sagona* was lightened sufficiently to get the main damage above water. She was badly holed aft and her shafts and rudder were damaged.

2. Steps were taken to strengthen the harbour patrols and increase the number and size of charges to be exploded at intervals in fine weather. The boom was not to be opened at night except in emergency.

Central Mediterranean

3. *Jaguar*, assisted by an ASV Wellington, made contact with *Kandahar* during the night 19/20 and rescued the Captain, 7 officers and about 150 other ratings. *Kandahar* was then scuttled. It was necessary for *Jaguar* to be clear of the area by daylight and some of *Kandahar's* crew may have been left.

21 December

Alexandria

1. *Valiant* was docked but further lightening was necessary before she could be made dry. The damage was evidently extensive.

Western Desert

3. To meet the increasing U-boat threat, RA(D) was instructed to detail an A/S striking force of 2 destroyers to reinforce the escort of all AT convoys. The striking force would normally proceed to hunt any U-boat reported within 25 miles of the convoy.

Submarines – RDF

7. As a result of experience with *Proteus*, the C-in-C recommended that RDF should continue to be fitted to submarines and increased in power if possible. . . .

Aircraft

8. Experiments were continuing to fit Wellington aircraft with torpedoes and so enormously increase the range of torpedo carrying aircraft. Initial experiments with torpedo dropping had been successful.

23 December

Damaged Battleships

2. . . . *Queen Elizabeth* had two large underwater holes, A, B and X boiler rooms being flooded. Her draught was 41 feet. Attempts were

being made to patch her temporarily and experienced salvage divers were asked for.

3. *Valiant*'s damage was worse than expected and extended over about 80 feet including the keel. . . .

26 December

Central Mediterranean

1. Operation MF1 was ordered to commence. CS7 sailed after dark for Alexandria with the four 14-knot MT ships, *Clan Ferguson, Sydney Star, Ajax* and *City of Calcutta. Breconshire* remained for docking. CS7 was in HMS *Ajax* whose speed was only 22 knots, in company with *Dido, Arrow, Foxhound, Gurkha* and *Nestor*.[107]

2. D7 sailed from Alexandria p.m. 26th in *Napier* with Force B consisting of *Carlisle, Nizam, Kingston* and *Isaac Sweers* to join CS7 before dark 27th.

28 December

1. D7's force joined CS7 and the convoy at 0700/28 . . ., when *Lance* and *Lively* were detached to Malta. The convoy was attacked several times during the day by Ju88s and once by T/B aircraft. The torpedo attack was broken up most gallantly by the solitary Martlet escort who shot down one of the T/Bs before being shot down himself.[108] The relief escort of two Fulmars broke up an attack by 10 to 20 Ju88s. One other S79 was shot down by gunfire.

One Fulmar forced landed, the crew being saved. *Maori* had some minor damage from near misses. Several A/S contacts were reported and attacked by the screen.[109]

Summary of Events for December

. . . Our strategical position was vastly improved by the capture of the whole Cyrenaican coastline and the resultant use of the Barce airfields: but this was largely offset by the damage to *Queen Elizabeth* and *Valiant* and by that which virtually immobilised the whole Malta force on 19 December. The striking power of the fleet was thus seriously reduced just at the time when we had at last reached a position to operate offensively in the Central Mediterranean.

[107]*Ajax*: 1931, 7,539gt, 16k, A. Holt.
Sydney Star: 1936, 11,095gt, Blue Star Line.
Foxhound: 1935, 1,405t, 4×4.7in, 8×21in tt, 35.5k; RCN 1943.
Arrow: 1930, 1,350t, 4×4.7in, 8×21in tt, 35k; tot loss, Algiers, Aug. 1943.
[108]Grumman Martlet (Wildcat): 1937, 4mg, 328mph, range 1,150mls.
[109]*U-79* s by *Hasty, Hotspur*, 23 Dec.; *U-75* s by *Kipling* 28 Dec.

298. *From Somerville*

Gibraltar
21 December 1941

What a shocking run of bad luck you have had lately.... I'm so damned sorry that this should have happened at a time when I can do nothing to create a diversion.

I *quite* agree with your remarks about Tobruk. When I was at home the PM blathered to me about the number of times Force H had been engaged on operations. I told him that whereas we have had an occasional run your ships were *always* in action and that there was no comparison between the strain on the two parties. It looks to me as if the work of your ships has been entirely overlooked. One doesn't care for oneself but it's very bad on the officers and men who have done so well....

299. *From the Admiralty*

1655A, 24 December 1941

Your 1147B/19/12. Events have now forced us to accept the position discussed in your 2022B/10/12 [No.295] and even after the repair of the ships concerned it is almost certain that they will have to proceed East.

2. For the same reasons it will be necessary to divert *Illustrious, Formidable* and *Indomitable* to the Far East. The question of what Air Forces will be required in substitution is therefore urgent.

3. *TSR.* You now have sufficient reserves of Albacore and Swordfish aircraft and crews in Middle East to maintain existing Squadrons and to form an additional Squadron...

4. As far as can be foreseen at present, it will not be necessary to withdraw any TSR flying personnel from the Middle East for the Carriers but request you will report after survey of your commitments whether any could be spared for this purpose.

5. As regards replacements, it is anticipated that we can send you 14 Albacores and 8 Swordfish in January, but it will only be possible to send 8 Albacores in February. Subsequently it is hoped to send sufficient TSRs to replace wastage.

6. *Fulmars.* It is anticipated it will be necessary to withdraw most of your reserve Fulmars and Naval fighter crews to be based in Ceylon for the defence of the Naval base and as a reserve for the

Carriers. These would be replaced in Middle East by RAF fighter squadrons.

7. The COS have approved the following units to proceed to Middle East:

> Three torpedo bomber squadrons when new construction is available to replace squadrons now operating at home to go out.
> Half a GR squadron.
> Two Heavy Bomber squadrons.
> One Beaufighter squadron.

The total number of Beaufort squadrons to be maintained in the Middle East is four.

8. Some of the items in 7 are long term but Tedder will be able to give you details.

9. Against this certain Blenheim and fighter squadrons are probably being transferred from the Middle East to Far East.

300. *To the Admiralty*

1338B, 26 December 1941

Your 1655/24 [No. 299]. I suggest that the criterion in deciding on movement of Air Forces in so far as Sea Operations are concerned is that we should have sufficient aircraft to enable us to control the Central Mediterranean despite absence of battleships. The presence of these aircraft moreover is of immediate urgency lest our weakness should allow the enemy control long enough to establish himself in his object in a manner which would not allow us subsequently to rectify the situation.

2. It seems to [me] highly important that in their [HMG's] endeavour to right the situation in the Far East we do not lose our position in Mediterranean as well and the telegram under reply gives one some anxiety on that score. If we can't achieve success against the enemy's heavy ships in the next months he will control Mediterranean which will enable him to reinforce Tripolitania at will, to make an attack on Malta and to jeopardize our forces in Cyrenaica. I most strongly urge therefore that our reinforcements of the Far East should be based on a foundation of security in the Mediterranean.

3. This foundation must be laid on adequate and suitable Air Striking Force strength. The details of components still necesary will

follow shortly as I wish to confine this message to undecided questions of broad principles.

4. The remaining factor which reinforces the above consideration is that of our offensive against the enemy. The offensive from the Mediterranean and/or from North Africa provides our chief card of re-entry into Europe where Germany must be defeated. The need to retain our control in this theatre is thus paramount.

301. *To Pound*

28 December 1941

A. We are having shock after shock out here. The damage to the battleships at this time is a disaster and my chief concern is that it has added so much to your burdens and anxieties.

The worst feature is that we do not know how they penetrated the boom defences.

The prisoners state they came in through the gate when it was opened for the destroyers to come in. This is certainly quite possible but they must have been prepared to come under, through or over the net. Charges were being dropped but do not seem to have deterred them which lends colour to the suggestion that they came through when the gate was opened.

We are now getting concrete blocks right across the entrance with a *chevaux de fuse* top up to a 40ft depth and close to the foot of the gate. It is costing a lot but we must get this harbour really secure – the last few days everyone has had the jitters seeing objects swimming about at night and hearing movements on the ships' bottoms. That must stop.

We have got all of the enemy operators we think – six in number and I am having them segregated; no communication with the outside world by letter or other means. In fact they will just die for six months and I hope to give the Italians the impression that they perished in the attempt. Furthermore although the photo reconnaissance showed two submarines alongside *Queen Elizabeth* they do not seem to have made any claims of damage to battleships yet. If the RAF will only do their job we may bluff them that only one has been damaged as in a few days I hope to get *Queen Elizabeth* looking like a seagoing ship again and on an even keel.

Valiant is in dock and will be there for two months and perhaps another month to complete after that. We are working every second of the day on her and I have told Malta they must send some more shipwrights.

Queen Elizabeth will have to go home or to a big yard I fear. Two boiler rooms arc wrecked.

B.   We are getting badly reduced in cruisers. *Neptune* and party running into that minefield off Tripoli was sheer bad luck. We had no knowledge of it but it was what I thought might well happen to the battleships when we went to bombard. . . .

We can't yet work the *Didos* from Malta as there is no spare 5.25-in ammunition – I am getting some there as soon as possible. *Ajax* has died on us due to turbine trouble and it will be some months before she can steam more than 22 knots.

Her pinions, or rather some of them, are on the way to Alexandria but perhaps if a relief could be sent she might be more useful on the trade routes.

C.   The German submarines are being a nuisance and taking a steady toll of ships on the Tobruk run. They are not getting it all their own way, however. We have bagged two certain, two very probable and given another a very bad headache. When the ASV Wellingtons arrive we will get busier and perhaps increase our bag.

D.   I have made a strong case about the late operation of running the *Breconshire* through to Malta. When Vian was surprised by the Italian battleships, Vian handled the situation with great skill and not only got his convoy to Malta but spent the night hunting the enemy one.

He lost touch with the enemy battleships after dark but even if he had not I told him not to go for them as his destroyer force was not adequate for the task.

I can't get the RAF to see that it is all wrong for our ships to be bombed all day and that the enemy ships go completely unattacked for the three days they were in the Central Mediterranean. The truth is that they will not bomb warships by day, they are afraid of the AA fire and unless we get a change of major policy issued by the Air Ministry I doubt if they will ever go for the enemy warships in daylight.

It is all nonsense to talk of them securing the sea communications, under the present orders they can't do it and I fear I do not look forward to the next few months with much pleasure.

E.   I got no support from the General on this point and the Minister was neutral. The General in fact supports Tedder. He is I think an excellent fighting soldier but his ignorance on naval matters is colossal. He shows no appreciation of what the Navy is doing for him and you know we are at the moment the Army's handmaiden and only keeping them supplied with great difficulty and considerable loss.

Part of the trouble is that we are given no credit at home. I fear that the PM's speech on the supplies at Tobruk made everyone out here in the Service very angry.

I sent a signal to the Admiralty showing the losses in keeping Tobruk supplied during the siege. Shortly, 27 of HM ships were sunk and 27 damaged without counting the merchant vessels.

Do you think that even at this late hour the Admiralty might make a signal recognising the work of these small ships[?] It would I think be very well received. The men I hear are a bit sore hearted at receiving no official recognition of what has been as gallant work as has ever been done.

I issued a message to the little ships myself but it is not the same thing.

F. Tennant has passed through.[110] I didn't gather there was much to learn; it just confirmed our experiences out here. It was most interesting that the Japs did not synchronise their high level attacks with their torpedo attacks. The Italians have learnt that, and when the other day the battleships opened fire on Vian they put in a torpedo bomber attack at the same time. They also put a balloon over him presumably for ranging on.

G. My tale this time is I fear a gloomy one but we are not a bit downhearted and all are going strong enough though I am a bit doubtful about Pridham-Wippell.

... If you can spare me the old *Warspite* out here or even something faster as a stiffener for the cruisers I can make good use of her. I fear I do not trust the Air Force control of sea security after this last affair, at least until a definite change of heart has taken place. Much will be promised but little fulfilled. Also they are quite untrained for sea work.

... we have an excellent man in Slatter who I think realises only too well the deficiencies of the RAF for operations over the sea.

---

[110]Capt (later Adm Sir) William G. Tennant (1890–1963): ent RN 1905; Navigator 1912; N Sea & Med 1914–18; Nav O, *Renown;* Nav Sch; Nav O *Repulse;* Cdr *Sussex;* Staff Coll; Capt 1932; IDC 1939; *Arethusa;* CSO to FSL; SNO, Dunkirk May–June 1940; Capt *Repulse* May–Dec. 1941; RA, 4CS, EF, Feb. 1942; RA i/c Mulberry harbours 1944; Actg VA & FO Levant & E Med Oct. 1944; FO Egypt; C-in-C NA & WI 1946–49.

302. *From Ford*

Malta
3 January 1942

... As for the war things here are extremely brisk – I've given up counting the number of air raids we're getting. For instance at the time of writing, 4.0 p.m., we've had exactly seven bombing raids since 9.0 quite apart from over a month of night attacks. The enemy is definitely trying to neutralise Malta's effort and I hate to say so but gradually doing so. They've bust a sad number of our bombers, fighters, etc., and must continue to do so. We brought three down this morning of theirs for a change – two Ju88s and one Me[?109 or 110], very welcome... I consider Malta must be made stiff with *modern* fighters – Mosquitos which can fly out from UK on their own and Spitfires via Takoradi if a carrier can't buzz them off.[111] Guns and stores must come in a S/M beforehand... Bombing to be done from North Africa leaving Malta with more reconnaissance machines and plenty of proper T/Bs. Our ancient Hurrys can't get height and certainly can't get speed and chase the bandits – naturally the pilot boys feel sadly depressed. I don't blame them.

To sum up the powers at Home must give up safety first and send out the very latest if they want to hold Malta and use it as a base. Invasion of UK to my mind is off the cards for many months if ever and Russia will not ease up. Minesweeping is now difficult and they appear to be laying them everywhere. Poor *Abingdon* the only sweeper and in daylight they get machine gunned. Eight casualties in *Abingdon* alone. I am trying to sweep during the dark hours and [?hasten it] by putting temporary lights on the coast and exposing them for fixing at certain intervals. So we carry on. I much regret being unable to help you with shipwrights and have done everything possible to get them without result. ... work in the yard is naturally very much slowed up at present as the result of constant raids and there is a very great amount to do keeping the yard fully occupied. Until we get more net defences I shall continue to be worried especially for Marsaluesitto [Marsaxlokk] and the S/Ms. Nothing really to stop them. Why oh why did DP not press for my Manderaggio scheme of underground shelters. They would have been completed long ago. As I write another bombing raid just over and at least two

[111]De Havilland Mosquito: 1938, 4 cannon, up to 4,000lbs bombs, *c.*400mph, range *c.*1,500mls; extremely versatile.

more of ours burnt out. Damnable ack-ack *quite* useless. Something must be done at once. How I can unload convoys I can't think or who with as the Maltese will run like rabbits and not return and soldiers are useless at such jobs. These new rocket bombs 500–600lbs [?-] – that are the devil. Some [?-] as after the burst the noise – terrific – seems to carry on ahead. I thought they were power diving and alongside one, as I usually stand on the roof to see the happenings – but actually they appear to glide in and not come below 6–8,000 feet. I must say they are quite alarming.... If they [8th Army] delay much longer reinforcements must arrive in Tripoli and though we will do our best I do not see how we can stop them. Very depressing indeed. Sorry – we can and will stick it ... *Breconshire* luckily only got superficial damage. Compass and fire control on other ships near misses....

303. *From Godfroy*

3 January 1942

Since the loss of HMS *Neptune* has been officially announced, I may tell you our deep regret about her fate which has been specially felt on board the *Duquesne* who spent many months in the first part of the war, with HMS *Neptune* at Dakar and at sea around West Africa....

304. *From General Freyberg*

New Zealand Expeditionary Force
7 January 1942

You have given me the greatest pleasure by your letter which is by far the nicest I have ever received. The Royal Navy to New Zealanders have always been a service apart. After the battle of the Mediterranean and our close association during Greece and Crete we feel it more than ever. Thank you again.

305. *To Vice Admiral Moore*[112]

9 January 1942

... I am fully in agreement with the view that the situation in the Far East must be restored and stabilised but I must point out that the war will only be won by beating Germany. The defeat of Japan will not necessarily win the war while the defeat of Germany will mean the defeat of Japan.

We have built up a position out here to the effect that the enemy fleet will not face us even if in great superiority. In fact before emerging from his base he usually assures himself by reconnaissance over Alexandria that we are not at sea.

This has not been achieved without very heavy losses and it should be noted that all our losses are from air attack or infernal machines such as the two-man submarines.

Not one loss have we had from the clash of surface forces.

To me it appears that if the purport of your 0136A/7 is carried out all this is thrown away. In my 2022B/10 December [No. 295] ... I rather grudgingly admitted that it might be possible to control the Central Mediterranean waters with air forces instead of surface forces.

Our late experiences have caused me to modify my then expressed opinion.

I fear from the last two convoy operations the enemy have learnt the utter futility of our air forces over the sea and I fear that he will now run convoys to Tripoli without worrying himself about our air.

I fear we are courting disaster out here if we remove the heavy ships from the Mediterranean without first providing air units to take their place. These air units must be trained over the sea and under my control (if necessary through the Naval Co-operation Group) and they must not be liable to be removed for other duties.

Further to ensure proper reconnaissance Malta must be in a condition to operate aircraft. At the moment Malta is being neutralised and it may be that with the growing enemy air strength Malta will be unable to assist and I may be forced to withdraw the surface forces at present based there. I have already had two destroyers and submarines damaged.

---

[112]VA Sir Henry Moore: VCNS 1941–42.

306. *From Ford*

Malta
10 January 1942

... I agree absolutely about the lack of ... reconnaissance planes – though God knows we've screamed hard enough for them. They are all-important to us having to cover such a large area. Re your question about fighters here – we have a sufficiency in number but they are outspeeded by Macchis and Me's and every enemy plane.[113] The bandits do not leave Sicily until they have sufficient height and our chaps can't get high enough in the time. Consequently they go for the Ju's and get pounced upon by the fighters above. What we want and *must have* are Spitfires and Mosquitos – the very latest fighters obtainable and safety first must be given up in UK for say three months. Otherwise the protection of aerodromes and harbour will be most difficult. We've already lost far too many bombers here on the ground. AOC has pushed hard for all this. To sum up our requirements, etc., ... Malta to be used as a fuelling base for delivering planes though I gather delivering bombers can now or will soon fly direct from Gibraltar or UK to Benghazi or nearby. Here we require 100–200 fast fighters – latest torpedo bombers – Beaufighters for strafing Sicilian dromes and Blenheims. Due to the efforts of AOC our dispersal of planes is pretty good but not sufficient to prevent serious losses.... I conclude you want me to sail *Rowallan Castle* with *Glengyle* – the former received a large bunch of splinters from the stick that got *P31*.[114] *Zulu* had a narrow escape when a charge in her magazine ignited possibly through a bomb splinter which penetrated her magazine. Convoys must if possible arrive off the breakwater by 0500 at the latest. Can it be arranged[?] *Glengyle* was lucky as the bandits did their best to find her but visibility suddenly decreased. She was several hours late of her expected TA.... *Que voulez-vous Glengyle* bar her oil fuel [?capacity] is not half so good as *Breconshire*. Small bad holds therefore difficult to work quickly. I could manage five ships at a pinch in next convoy – four ships just keep us level, five would be a small reserve. Shuttle service extremely useful. Air liaison going much better now after difficulties.

---

[113]Me109s; & Macchis: C200: 1937, 2mg, *c.*400lbs bombs, 312mph, range 354mls; C202: 1940, 4mg, 369mph, range 475mls.
[114]*Rowallan Castle*: 1939, 7,798gt, 16.5k, Union Castle Line; bombed 13 Feb. 1942. *P31*: Not this no.

307. *To the Admiralty*

10 January 1942

The following is a review of events in Central Mediterranean on 4 and 5 January during the passage of an Italian convoy from Italy to Tripoli.

2. One battleship, three cruisers, 8 destroyers sighted by aircraft at 1040/4 in position 3[?-]° 00′N, 20° 00′E steering 200°. Blenheim striking force and relief shadowers failed to find. Force was sighted again at 1730/4 in position 35° 00′N 18° 30′E still steering SW. 826 Squadron and heavy bombers sent out to attack night of 4/5 failed to locate. Malta had only one Maryland serviceable for reconnaissance.

3. One battleship, three cruisers, four destroyers sighted by aircraft at 1000/5 in position 32° 57′N, 14° 20′E steering 70°. A convoy of nine merchant vessels and three destroyers sighted entering Tripoli at 1135/5. No further air reports were received.

4. One battleship, cruiser and 5 destroyers sighted by *Unique* at 1530/5 in position 40° 07′N, 17° 07′E [?approaching] Taranto, a possible hit was obtained on battleship.

5. It was observed that convoy was not sighted until it was entering Tripoli and that force sighted by *Unique* was not sighted by aircraft. As a result of this inadequate reconnaissance not a single air attack was made on Italian fleet. Flying conditions at Malta were very bad during this period.

6. The seriousness of the situation now developing must be [?accepted]. Enemy has experienced freedom of movement and must enjoy the taste. His anxiety must diminish and he will become more venturesome.

7. In face of enemy's strength existing surface forces are powerless to intervene. Air forces trained for operation over sea are inadequate even to maintain sufficient reconnaissance, let alone provide an adequate striking force.

8. Unless some naval and strong air reinforcements are shortly forthcoming I can't see how Malta can be maintained far less the enemy's supplies to Tripoli stopped. Nor can a seaborne attack on Malta be ruled out, particularly observing the increased scale [of] air attack to which they are now being exposed and appear unable to defeat.

308. *To the Admiralty*

15 January 1942

I wish to make it clear that I have no desire to criticise the cooperation afforded by the RAF either here or in Malta on this or the previous occasion on 17 December. To the contrary. The point which needs emphasis is the lack of suitable air forces. Air forces available for reconnaissance from Malta were on both occasions placed at the disposal of the Vice Admiral Malta and reconnaissance was flown as required by him within the limits of forces available. Some errors were made in the positioning of [?forces] in the existing situations and were made by the Naval Staff concerned but they were presented with an almost impossible problem owing to lack of aircraft. A further trouble was that neither the fleet nor myself were informed of this lack.

I am very anxious at the moment about the situation out here. I see nothing to prevent the enemy running sufficient supplies into Tripoli in the next few weeks as to completely prejudice the success of ACROBAT which would be a tragedy....

I ask you to read my 2022B/10[/12/41] [No.295] and my 1338B/26[/12/41] [No .300] again and should you require any further information Captain Dick of my staff is at present at the Admiralty.[115]

309. *From Vice Admiral Leatham*

Office of Vice Admiral, Malta
24 January 1942

If I may say so, I am very happy to have come under your Command in such a lively place as this – that is, provided you are able to continue to keep me fed.

... What struck me at once was the cheeriness of everyone and their confidence. The three Services seem to be pulling in the same direction on the same rope – helped and guided by the Navy. I hope to continue this happy state of affairs. The AOC appears an all out man bent on hitting the enemy wherever he can – and the new general is a real live wire with the latest ideas from home, which he is

---

[115]Capt Royer M. Dick.

rapidly and forcibly driving into his Command, which he says has hitherto been working on pre-war notions.[116] . . .

Ford felt his going very deeply, and one is not surprised that he should after so long and doing so much here. . . . The naval side seems to be a thoroughgoing concern with reasonably efficient fellows to help me – and the job as a whole promises to be most interesting. This underground life (especially sleeping in a stone tomb) is all very strange at first but I shall get used to it. . . .

I don't think the bombing worries ships' companies very much – that is my first impression. The majority now sleep under cover at night and the fug they work up and the feeling of security keeps them happy! But I will watch it and let you know. . . .

310. *War Diary, January 1942*

23 January

Central Mediterranean

Reconnaissance aircraft reported two enemy forces in the Ionian Sea making southward. One contained a *Cavour* class battleship and a large liner and the other three large merchant ships and three cruisers (probably six [?] *Condottieri* 'C' and 'D' class), each with destroyer screens. It was also possible that another battleship force was at sea covering the two forces. RAF and naval aircraft from Malta, Libya and Egypt carried out a series of bombing attacks from noon onwards; further bombing and torpedo attacks were ordered at dusk and during the night 23/24 Force K was at short notice, but the enemy was in too great strength to make interception practicable.

24 January

The enemy convoys were heavily attacked by aircraft throughout the night 23/24 in bad weather conditions. Results could not be accurately assessed. After one unsuccessful attack, 830 Squadron returned to Malta, attacked again and reported two torpedo hits on the liner; 826 (Libya) Squadron reported one certain torpedo hit on the liner and another on a destroyer. Wellingtons also scored two hits on the liner and on other merchant ships and a cruiser. The merchant ships were sighted entering Tripoli harbour, but the liner

---

[116] AVM H. P. Lloyd.
GOC: unidentified.

was considered to have sunk. The battleships were not sighted again ... The leader of 826 Squadron, Lt-Cdr J. W. Corbett, who had done excellent work in this and other recent operations, was missing. The VA, Malta, reported on the exceptional work of Lt-Cdr F. H. E. Hopkins, leader of 830 Squadron, who carried out two attacks himself and organised the operation.[117]

25 January

Operation MF4

Force K consisting of *Penelope, Zulu, Lance, Legion, Lively* and *Maori* sailed p.m. 25th from Malta, escorting *Glengyle* and *Rowallan Castle* to Alexandria. Force B [from Alexandria] was shadowed by enemy aircraft, and was attacked by 8 Ju88s between 1445 and 1520. Ships were undamaged. Two Ju88s were considered to have been shot down, and three damaged, by gunfire and fighters. One Hurricane was lost.

26 January

Forces B and K made contact at 1200/26, when Force B turned back with *Glengyle* and *Rowallan Castle*, while *Breconshire* continued to Malta with Force K. *Lance* joined Force B and *Kingston* joined Force K. It was intended to arrange a short period away from Malta for each of the Force K destroyers in turn.

2. Force K was bombed during the forenoon and both Forces B and K were attacked by T/B aircraft during the afternoon without damage to any ship. . . .

27 January

Force K and *Breconshire* arrived safely at Malta in spite of some bombing. Force B and convoy ME9 continued towards Alexandria. On account of the military situation, no fighter protection was available from the forward aerodromes, but although the force was shadowed, no attacks developed.

---

[117]Lt-Cdr F. H. E.. Hopkins: Lt 1933; *Peregrine* 1939–40; *Grebe* 1941; Lt-Cdr Dec. 1941; *Saker II* (BAD) Sept. 1942; Actg Cdr 1944; *Golden Hind* (RN base, Sydney) Jan. 1945; Cdr June 1945.
Victoria: troopship, 1931, 13,098gt, Lloyd Triestino, Genoa.

Summary and Appreciation of Events for January 1942

General

4. The outstanding features of the month were the magnificent efforts of our submarines, FAA and RAF aircraft. Hardly a day passed without some loss to the enemy which must have complicated his problem of supplying North Africa. . . .

311. *From Pound*

29 January 1942

A. I had an interview with Drummond and finished with the impression that everything in the garden was rosy. . . . This means that No.201 Group will have three GR squadrons, one ASV squadron, 4 TB squadrons, 2 TSR squadrons, three long range Fighter squadrons and six short range Fighter squadrons. He also said that it was the C-in-C's intention to allocate temporarily, say two Heavy Bomber squadrons and four Light Bomber squadrons to No.201 Group, so that they could be trained over the sea by Slatter. These squadrons might have to go one day over the sea and the next day over the land but I thought it a great advance that they should have received the same training for working over the sea.

B. . . . If the HQ of 201 Group [?were at Cairo] they would apparently find themselves alongside of Bomber and Fighter HQ so that co-operation should be easy. I said that this was a matter which he must discuss with you because it would divorce you from close contact with Slatter and I did not know whether you were prepared to accept it.

C. . . . Portal . . . said that he considered:[118]

(i) that when there were any naval forces taking part in an operation in which air forces were also engaged you would direct the whole with Slatter.

(ii) that when there were no naval forces at sea operating against enemy surface forces which the Air Force were attacking, then all the aircraft, including 201 Group, should come under the AOC.

---

[118]ACM (later M of RAF Visct) Sir Charles Portal (1893–1971): RFC 1914–18; RAF 1918; AVM, Air Mem Pers 1939; Actg AM Sept. 1939; C-in-C Bomber Cmd Apr. 1940; ACM & CAS Oct. 1940; M of RAF Jan. 1944; ret 1945.

D. There are three ways of dealing with this question of control:
- (i) Not to take any action at the present time and wait for the RAF to make a mess of it.
- (ii) To raise the question for discussion with the Minister of State in the Chair.
- (iii) To thrash the matter out here as a matter of principle.

E. I can't see how AOC controlling air forces against moving targets at sea is ever likely to be a success. He will not know the position of minefields, of our submarines or what the weather conditions are, and therefore it will be impossible for him to forecast the enemy's movements. If you decide that the best course is to thrash the matter out at home I am quite prepared to take it on, but I should like you to give me as many reasons as possible ... why this system of AOC taking over when there are none of our naval forces at sea must produce poor results.

F. ... Portal [said] that if you would only shift your HQ to Cairo so that you could sit in the pockets of the other two Cs-in-C everything would be splendid.

K. As you know we are sending you two cruisers and will bear in mind that you want two *Fiji*s. We told [Captain R. M.] Dick to look round the maps in the War Room and see how he could produce two for you at the present time, but I gather that he failed to produce any!

L. I will also bear in mind that you would like one capital ship. At the present time there is no chance of giving you one unless the situation changes in some way. I think it will be much better not to make any suggestions at the present time as regards the return of either capital ships or carriers to the Mediterranean, because if we did it might interfere with the provision of adequate air forces over the sea. ...

312. *From Willis*

2 February 1942

... I'm so sorry that Cairo Air team are still so trying – but they just don't understand strategy much less the sea aspect – and their extravagant claims are fooling the public and themselves. ...

... and it's astonishing that the Cairo pundits won't attack the Italian Fleet – I suppose it's because they don't know how to hit it. Drummond admitted to me in an unguarded moment that they can't hit ships and it's only too true. ...

313. *To Pound*

1630B, 6 February 1942

You will have appreciated the serious effect on the Malta situation following the recent military reverses in Libya. These reverses have been a bitter disappointment after efforts and sacrifices made in supporting Tobruk and in moving army supplies forward. It is not yet possible to say how far the retirement will continue. Auchinleck realises need to hold as far to Westward as possible and is making every effort to do so, but the line is already too far to the East from the Naval and Air viewpoint and we may yet find ourselves back on the frontier. It has always been my view that if we can hold the line at Derna it would just be possible to run Malta convoys with a reasonable degree of safety. That line is now gone and the Army does not forecast a limit to offensive until 1 April at earliest or even as late as 1 May.

2. We are thus faced with a period of some enemy action during which the passage of convoys from the East will be a very great hazard since there will be a long stretch where no air cover can be provided. Unfortunately we can provide no serious surface deterrent to the Italian heavy ships at least by day and scale of air attack such as was put down on the Italian battleships on 24 January is no longer possible from our present forward aerodromes. In view of these facts I feel my revised views on Malta prospects may be of assistance to you.

3. Broadly it appears that Malta has aviation fuel up to 1 August but other supplies only up to 1 June. There is about [?5] thousand tons of oil fuel remaining.

4. In these new circumstances it appears to me necessary to accept a considerable degree of risk at once in order to build up Malta supplies and that as the risk will certainly increase the sooner we can run a convoy the better while the enemy Air Forces are still not reorganised and the enemy remains preoccupied with his offensive. I am actively studying available information with other two Services in order to gauge these hazards and unless they appear prohibitive I intend to sail a convoy which is now loading as fast as possible and should be ready within a week. It has to be realised however that we must prepare for serious losses which might well be almost whole convoy if we are unlucky. On other hand we might get good proportion through and thus cover immediate anxiety Malta supply.

THE FIGHT AT ODDS, 1941–1942   571

5. I shall hope to use *Cleopatra* and *Fortune* to bring out ships of MW8 now in Malta.[119]

6. Other action which I am taking is to direct *Porpoise* to carry vital stores and in this connection I should be glad if the question of using *Surcouf* could be reinvestigated to see if it really is impossible to use her for similar duty. We shall need every available device if we are to keep Malta going.[120]

7. In view of fuel shortage I am considering reducing Force K to 2 cruisers and 2 destroyers.

8. I have made no mention of running convoys from Westward. At present this would have fair chance of success but I am sure that chances of providing necessary forces for Force H are at present negligible. . . .

314. *To Pound*

10 February 1942

Further to my 1630/6 [No. 313] I am now informed that the fighter situation has deteriorated at Malta to such an extent that it is doubtful if any effective fighter protection can be afforded to incoming convoys. I am nevertheless intending to run the convoy for reasons already given in my signal quoted above. This state of affairs is due partly to the very large proportion of fighters now working from Sicily and partly because Hurricane performance is insufficient to enable them to gain height in time and to be able to deal with the present German fighters. We had a similar situation before when Malta was nearly neutralised by better equipped air forces in Sicily and it is evidently of utmost urgency to build up our fighter strength in Malta. This unfortunately can't be done from here without the Western Cyrenaican aerodromes. The Spitfires now on their way will be a palliative but I feel we should urge a further increase and that pressure should be maintained on RAF to ensure that a continuous watch is kept on the Malta fighter situation to see that in future they reinforce in time and do not wait until the situation has reached so serious a stage as at present. It appears to argue failure to look ahead.

[119]*Cleopatra*: 1941, 5,450t, 10×5.25in, 6×21in tt, 33k.
Fortune: 1935, 1,405t, 4×4.7in, 8×21in tt, 35.5k; RCN 1943.
[120]*Surcouf*: Fr N; 1929, 2,880/4,300t, 2×8in, 10×21in, 18/10k; lost in collision, N Atl, 1942; largest s/m in world.

315. War Diary, February 1942

4 February

Operation MBD 4

D14 sailed from Alexandria at 1700/4 with a destroyer force consisting of *Jervis, Jaguar, Kelvin, Lance, Griffin, Hero, Arrow* and *Havock*. This force carried out an A/S sweep to the westward in conjunction with ASV Swordfish and Wellington aircraft maintaining an A/S patrol 5 miles ahead. *Heythrop* and *Hurworth* sailed in company with D14 and were detached off Tobruk to escort a convoy to Alexandria.[121] . . .

10 February

Levant

4. On account of reports of U-boats operating in the Levant, the C-in-C gave instructions that all ships over 2,000 tons and all cased petrol ships were to be escorted. Previously only tankers and especially valuable ships had been escorted. The 2nd Trawler Group was to be used for escorting in addition to the 10th Corvette Group and the 25th A/S Group. A new traffic route close inshore was established between Port Said and Tripoli (Syria). 201 Naval Co-operation Group would provide an ASV aircraft reconnaissance of the area.

Submarines

6. *Thorn* returned from a successful patrol in the Adriatic. Two operations of landing political agents on the coast of Yugoslavia were completed successfully. At 1030/28 off Mulo Island, *Thorn* attacked a 4,500-ton laden merchant ship northbound. Having missed with torpedoes, *Thorn* engaged with gunfire, firing 71 rounds most of which hit, before a shore battery forced her to dive. *Thorn* then sank the disabled ship by torpedo. At 1400/30 . . . *Thorn* attacked a *Sirena* class U-boat and sank it with one torpedo. There were no survivors.[122]

11 February

4. Submarines in the Central Mediterranean were placed under the operational control of S10 and redisposed to cover the

---

[121]*Heythrop* (s *U-652*, off Libya, Mar. 1942), *Hurworth* (mined, Aegean, Oct. 1943): 1941, 1,050t, 6×4in, 27k.

[122]*Medusa*: 1932, 650/810, 1×4in, 6×21in tt, 14/8k. *Thorn*: 1941, 1090/1575 t, 1×4 in, 11×21in tt, 15.25/9k; (s It escort, off Tobruk, Aug 1942).

approaches to the Gulf of Taranto and South Messina, and give warning of the movement of enemy heavy forces.[123] The C-in-C intended to run a convoy into and out of Malta shortly, and it was essential to have warning of possible enemy movements.

5. *Thunderbolt* reported the following successes on patrol off Cephalonia:

(a) at 0920/30 ... attacked a 5,000-ton merchant ship (*Gaeta* class) southeast bound, and escorted by two destroyers. Result uncertain due to heavy counter attack.

(b) at 1030/1 ... torpedoed and sank one of two 5,000-ton merchant ships in convoy northeast bound.

(c) at 1105/3 off the entrance to Argostoli harbour engaged an armed trawler with gunfire. After about 15 hits, the trawler's crew abandoned ship but the trawler remained afloat, *Thunderbolt* being forced to dive by shore batteries.

(d) at 1811/6 ... attacked a 750-ton U-boat probably German. Two hits were heard, but the U-boat remained afloat. *Thunderbolt* engaged with gunfire, when the U-boat began to sink and disappeared 9 minutes after the torpedoes hit. It was considered probably sunk.[124]

12 February

Operation MF5

Operation MF5 was commenced to run convoy MW9 into Malta and ME10 from Malta to Alexandria. MW9 sailed from Alexandria in two sections.

MW9A: *Clan Chattan* and *Clan Campbell* at 1600/12 escorted by *Carlisle, Heythrop, Lance, Avon Vale* and *Eridge*.

MW9B: *Rowallan Castle* at 1700/12 escorted by *Southwold, Beaufort, Dulverton* and *Hurworth*.[125]

CS15 was to sail with Force B, all other available cruisers and destroyers, during the night 12/13. Convoy ME10 was to sail from Malta after dark. The maximum possible air reconnaissance and fighter protection was to be provided by 201 Naval Co-operation Group. Fighter protection was necessarily weak W of Sidi Barrani and from Malta, where heavy enemy air attacks were being experienced.

---

[123]Capt G. W. G. Simpson.
[124]No U-boat sunk.
[125]*Southwold* (mined, Malta, 24 Mar. 1942), *Beaufort, Dulverton* (s Ger a/c, Aegean, Nov. 1943): 1941, 1,050t, 6×4in, *Southwold* 2×21in tt, 27k.

13 February

CS15 sailed from Alexandria at 0200/13 in *Naiad* with Force B, consisting of *Dido, Euryalus, Jervis, Kipling, Kelvin, Jaguar, Griffin, Arrow, Hasty* and *Havock*.

2.   At 1730/13 *Clan Campbell* was bombed and damaged. . . . She was hit in the coal bunker, and also damaged by a near miss. *Avon Vale* and *Eridge* were detached with her from convoy MW9A and escorted her to Tobruk, rejoining the convoy on her arrival there. Both sections of the convoy were attacked by aircraft during the day. Force B was also attacked unsuccessfully at dusk by about 9 Ju88s.
3.   Convoy ME10 consisting of the MT ships *Clan Ferguson, City of Calcutta* and *Ajax* and HMS *Breconshire* sailed from Malta after dark 13th, escorted by *Penelope, Sikh, Zulu, Legion, Lively, Fortune* and *Decoy*.

14 February

Force B and convoys MW9A and B joined at 0700/14, and were shadowed throughout the day. High level and divebombing attacks started at 1345, and continued until 1600, bombers coming apparently from Greece, Crete and Sicily. *Clan Chattan* was hit in the after hold and caught fire . . . She was disabled and was later sunk by our own forces, all personnel having been taken off.

2.   Force K and ME10 were met at 1440 and escorts were exchanged while in action against bombers, Force K turning back with *Rowallan Castle*, and Force B with [ships from Malta]. Both forces continued to be attacked by bombers and T/Bs, and *Rowallan Castle* was near missed at 1515 . . . Her engines were disabled and she was taken in tow by *Zulu*, but could not make sufficient speed to have any chance of reaching Malta safely. The C-in-C accordingly ordered her to be sunk which was done at 1956, all personnel having been removed. *Zulu, Sikh* and *Legion* were then ordered to join CS15 leaving only *Penelope, Lively* and *Lance* to return to Malta.
3.   *Carlisle* and *Eridge* received minor damage from near misses while escorting ME10, but no serious damage was inflicted on this force.

15 February

Penelope, Lance and *Lively* returned to Malta. Two enemy forces were at sea, evidently attempting to intercept disabled ships from the convoy. *P36* reported two cruisers steering S from Messina at

THE FIGHT AT ODDS, 1941–1942 575

0121/15 and another force of three cruisers was sighted by aircraft 80 miles SE of Malta at 1245/15. Unfortunately the aircraft was shot down, and the report was received after the crew were rescued, too late for aircraft to attack.[126]

Force B and convoy ME10 continued to be bombed throughout the day by single Ju88s and T/Bs. No damage was done.

Southwold, Dulverton, Beaufort and *Hurworth* were detached to Tobruk and left there at 1830 for Alexandria with *Clan Campbell.*

16 February

3. During the operation fighters shot down 4 enemy aircraft and probably 4 more; and and probably 2 more were shot down by gunfire. Two others were damaged. The expenditure by 15CS of 3,700 rounds of 5.25-in ammunition was a serious strain on the reserves available in Egypt.

316. *From Leatham*

Malta
12 February 1942

Yesterday was very tiresome. First, *Cleopatra* and *Fortune.* Accurate bombing on the former and the latter nearly capsizing – overloaded with a topweight of stores, I fancy, most of which and all her boats went over the side. They were badly enough caught as it is but it might have been very much worse.

The *Maori* – a sad sight – at no. 3 buoy with her bow (still buoyant) pointing up in the air. We are salving what we can. The fire spread terribly quickly and I have seldom seen such a Brock's benefit from aft – ending in a terrific explosion after an hour or so's burning. But the greatest danger was the burning oil fuel with the wind (luckily light) blowing it towards French Creek full of ships. But with the help of the Lord and foamite we kept it at bay until it went out – and saved the floating crane. Lucky there were so few casualties. . . . Perhaps we should be thankful it has not happened more often in the last two years.

All or most of our troubles here at the present time are from the weakness of our fighter strength. Reconnaissance is dreadfully weak too and our striking power is none too grand either.

I'm not very much in love with CRACK – a somewhat hazardous high speed approach and not much time when you get there.

[126]*P36*: 1941, 545/730t, 1×3in, 4×21in tt, 11/9k; s It a/c, Malta, 31 Mar. 1942.

Shorter nights make it more difficult and in any case it would be best done in the first moon, I feel. However, I realise its great importance, provided we bag something.

Destroyer defects are maddening and fuel is scarce and has to be carefully watched.

I am in the closest touch and on the best of terms with AOC who is doing his damnedest to help us.

Good luck to MF5 and thank you for *Lance*.

317. *To Pound*

14 February 1942

I fear our attempt to run a convoy into Malta has failed and has cost us two valuable merchant ships. I am withdrawing all surface craft from Malta except the two damaged cruisers, *Penelope, Lance* and *Legion*. It appears useless to try further to pass in a convoy until the air situation in Malta and military situation in Cyrenaica have been restored.

318. *War Diary, February 1942 (concl.)*

16 February

Russian Ships
[Message from Cunningham]:

The operation of bringing down these ships has been very well conducted by all concerned and shows what careful organisation combined with good relations with local authorities can achieve.

The excellent handling of the Russian ships and the seamanlike conduct of their crews has impressed all the British conducting officers.

18 February

Operation MF6
Griffin, Arrow, Hasty, Hero, Heythrop and *Avon Vale* sailed at 1800/18 from Alexandria to Haifa for an A/S sweep under the orders of D2.[127] U-boats had been reported in the Levant and D2 was instructed to operate off the Levant ports by day and along the

---

[127] D2: Capt H. StL. Nicolson.

coastal shipping routes by night. A squadron of ASV Swordfish was sent to Haifa to co-operate.

20 February

2nd Destroyer Flotilla

2. The C-in-C proposed to the Admiralty to sail 6 destroyers from the 2DF to meet the requirements of the C-in-C, Eastern Fleet. *Janus, Javelin* and *Nubian* would rejoin the Mediterranean Fleet on completion of repairs. *Griffin* (D2), *Decoy* and *Fortune* were sailed from Alexandria at 1800/20 for Port Said and Aden. *Arrow, Foxhound* and *Hotspur* would follow shortly.

21 February

Destroyers

3. Consequent upon the departure of ships of the 2DF, the destroyer command was reorganised as follows:

14DF	22DF
Jervis (Capt D)	*Sikh* (Capt D)
Kelvin	*Zulu*
Kimberley	*Legion*
Kipling	*Lance*
Kingston	*Lively*
Jaguar	*Havock*
Jackal	*Hasty*
Queen Olga (Greek)	*Hero*

5DF
all 'Hunts', under direct administration of RA(D).

Captain StJ. A. Micklethwaite assumed command of 22DF. It was intended to attach each of the Greek destroyers to the 14DF on return from refit and fitting of Asdics.[128]

22 February

Central Mediterranean

Reconnaissance aircraft reported two enemy convoys apparently of three and six merchant ships with battleship cover in the Central Ionian Sea making for Tripoli. Malta aerodromes were heavily

---

[128]Capt StJ. A. Micklethwaite: Cdr 1935; *Eskimo* 1939–40; Capt Dec. 1940; *Cardiff* 1941; *Sikh* Feb. 1942.
RA(D): RA Glennie.

attacked throughout the day, and the weather was bad. T/B striking forces were unable to attack during the day owing to their limited range.

Upholder, Unbeaten, P35 and *P36* were concentrated E of Tripoli.[129]

2. Another T/B striking force from Malta attacked a 4,000-ton tanker off the Tripoli coast during the night 21/22, and reported one definite torpedo hit.

25 February

Submarines

4. Captain (S) 1 resumed operational control of his submarines E of 22°E.[130] The C-in-C gave instructions for the 10SF to operate against the Naples–Tripoli traffic. The 1SF were to operate against the Patras–Brindisi traffic with occasional patrols in the Adriatic and Aegean. Greek submarines were to operate against the Piraeus–Suda Bay–Candia traffic.

319. War Diary, March 1942

2 March

Western Desert

The fighter protection available at Tobruk was insufficient to compete with the scale of attack. The C-in-C decided to withdraw MTBs 259 and 260 to Alexandria and to defer sending *Vulcan* to Tobruk for the present.[131]

4. A conference was held at Alexandria to consider whether the strain on fighter protection could be reduced by sending larger convoys less frequently. It was decided that this was unacceptable owing to the number of ships that would be berthed in Tobruk for long periods. The army agreed to increase the supply by land in order to reduce the frequency of convoys.

HMS Ajax

6. *Ajax* sailed for Suez to proceed to the UK via the Cape for repairs. Due to engine defects her speed was reduced to 20 knots. The C-in-C made the following signal to *Ajax*:

---

[129]*P35* (later *Umbra*): 1941, 545/730t, 1×3in, 4×21in tt, 11/9k..
[130]Capt S. M. Raw. *Tempest* & *P38* were lost to It escorts.
[131]*Vulcan*: MTB depot ship, 1933, 623t, 11.5k.

I much regret that you are leaving the Mediterranean where you have achieved so much.

You should all be proud of the part *Ajax* has played in the last 18 months. You thoroughly deserve a rest and I hope you will have a good passage and a very happy homecoming.

5 March

Submarines

5. *Thrasher* returned to Alexandria from patrol off Crete and SW Greece. At 1155/16 . . . *Thrasher* attacked a well escorted 3,000-ton merchant ship entering Suda Bay. Two torpedoes hit and the ship sank. *Thrasher* was then heavily counter-attacked by three A/S vessels who were apparently using Asdics and by two aircraft. Depth charging was exceedingly accurate and the hunting more efficient than usual; but *Thrasher* escaped without serious damage. On surfacing after dark two unexploded 100lb bombs were found in the fore casing; these were successfully lifted overboard, after much difficulty and with great personal gallantry on the part of the disposal squad.[132]

11 March

Central Mediterranean

Cleopatra and *Kingston* met CS15 at 0800/11 and the whole force set course at high speed for Alexandria in the absence of any further report of the damaged enemy cruiser. The force was shadowed and attacked by a total of about 80 aircraft throughout the day but without damage. Beaufighters did excellent work providing fighter protection at very long range from their base, but were unable to drive off all the shadowers. Three enemy aircraft were shot down and probably three more damaged by the Beaufighters, two of which were lost while returning to their base. One Ju88 and one T/B were damaged by AA fire.

Loss of HMS Naiad

2. At 2005/11 . . . *Naiad* was hit amidships by one torpedo from a U-boat. She took up a heavy list immediately and sank after 20 minutes. Two officers and 75 ratings were lost; Rear Admiral Vian and

---

[132]*Thrasher*: 1941, 1,090/1,575t, 1×4in, 11×21in tt, 15.25/9k. Lt P. S. W. Roberts: S-Lt 1938; *Saltburn* 1939; Lt Nov. 1939; *Ambrose* May 1940; *Thrasher* 1941; *Beagle* 1942; trng course 1943; Instr, *Vernon* 1944–45. Together with PO T. W. Gould, he was awarded the VC.

the remainder were rescued by *Kipling, Jervis* and *Lively. Zulu* sighted the U-boat after it had fired torpedoes, and attacked it, but apparently without result.[133]

320. From Leatham

Malta
12 March 1942

... It was nice to see the Spitfires in the sky yesterday – they gave much heart to the Maltese who pin the most extravagant hopes on them. The raids yesterday and so far today have been much less heavy, but I think it is not only the Spitfires who have brought this respite. The enemy attacked the aerodromes very heavily while the convoy was passing and it is a wonder to me how AOC keeps operating *something* while the raids are on.... I have some 50 sailors from *Aurora* lending a hand out there – it is hardening their hands and giving them a welcome change! Lazaretto had a warm time for a few days and their nice mess and establishment is a bit of a shambles ... I don't very much like this lying on the bottom by day but for the time it must be accepted. It slows up repair work and it must eventually tell on the crews. The aiming mark is no longer there but I am not sure that the damage from a lucky near miss on a submerged boat will not be worse than on a boat on the surface. It is all a gamble but the fact remains that the base has not been attacked so far since we took this measure. Perhaps the enemy thinks he has sunk the lot. Simpson is first class and imbues everyone with the best of spirits. I hope his services will be recognised soon and I intend recommending him in due course.

You ask whether I think Dockyard Creek would be better than French Creek for berthing destroyers and possibly cruisers. From the point of view of ease of attack I don't think there is much in it – the airmen whom I've asked confirm this. I should say that if anything more bombs have fallen recently in Dockyard Creek. In the other the attacks seem to have been directed more at ships in dock than alongside. Facilities for repair work, sheltering, recreation, etc., are of course much better up French Creek and I already have quite a number of small craft (*Abingdon*, trawlers, etc.) in the other. When Force K was larger at least one destroyer was berthed in Dockyard Creek. SS *Essex* has been at the outer (Grand Harbour)

---

[133] *U-565*, which escaped.

end of the creek and I am looking for somewhere better to put her, for if she were sunk it would make entry difficult.

The battle will be half won if only the Army can push into Cyrenaica and get us back into Benghazi. I wish we could put a more effective stop to the traffic to Tripoli – things (and alas! sizeable convoys) keep slipping through because either our small air striking force is made useless at the eleventh hour or information reaches me too late to send out the surface ships even if the fuel can be spared. When we get a bit more command of the air, perhaps it will be possible to keep surface craft out for a whole day which will be a surer way of catching the ships and not necessarily more expensive in fuel, as the speed can be less.

I believe a few MTBs – good fast ones and burning the right sort of fuel (100 octane, or DTD224 or Diesel) – might prove useful on occasion. We would manage to berth and maintain them somehow ... I hope FOCNA's MLs will get through safely – risky journey it is true but they are a small target.[134]

The enemy has not given the Dockyard the attention I would have expected. I think the intense barrage frightens them away, especially when there are a lot of ships to augment it. The boat shed got a direct hit with a very big bomb on 3 March and some 15 power boats (including my high speed barge!) and 18 pulling boats went west. I am looking into the question of greater dispersal for what remains. Repairs etc. go steadily on – estimates are very uncertain because they depend on the number of raids threatening the area – and I am afraid we are finding things more seriously wrong with destroyers than was first expected. I hope *Legion* can be ready p.m. 19th which may now be early enough for you. . . .

321. *War Diary, March 1942 (cont.)*

14 March

Operation MF8 – Bombardment of Rhodes

A Force consisting of *Dido, Euryalus, Sikh, Zulu, Lively, Hero, Havock, Hasty* under the command of *Dido* sailed from Alexandria at 0100/14 and proceeded northeastwards to pass through a position close SW of Cyprus at dusk. Fighter protection was provided from Cyprus. The force was apparently not sighted on passage.

---

[134]VA Sir G. Frederick B. Edward-Collins: Capt 1923; RA 1935; RA 2CS Apr. 1938; VA 1939; FOCNA Jan. 1941; Adm on Ret List Jan. 1943; FOIC, Falmouth, Feb. 1944.

15 March

The bombardment of military targets in Rhodes was carried out successfully from 0130 to 0145. Cruisers fired 150 rounds each and destroyers 100 rounds. The RAF provided a diversion by bombing and also provided good illumination for the main target. Aircraft observation was ineffective however due to low cloud and bad communication. *Dido* and *Euryalus* with *Hero, Havock* and *Hasty* providing minesweeping protection, engaged the Alliotti Flour Mills, hangar and workshops in the vicinity. Fires were started and direct hits were seen on the flour mills. *Sikh, Zulu* and *Lively* engaged the harbour installation and shipping but results could not be assessed. No surface craft were encountered and opposition from shore batteries was negligible.

2. The force withdrew eastward at 0145, and returned to Alexandria at high speed routed again close W of Cyprus. No air attacks developed; Beaufighters drove off one shadower.

18 March

Submarines

6. *Torbay* returned to Alexandria from a most remarkable 26 day patrol in the Corfu-Taranto and Messina areas. At 1437/27 30 miles N of Cape Dukato, *Torbay* attacked a small convoy with the gun. A 1,000-ton merchant ship was sunk but a trawler and another ship escaped when *Torbay* was forced by a shore battery to dive. At 0930/4 when about 25 miles NW of Cape Dukato *Torbay* sighted four large troopships heavily escorted. Being unable to get in an attack she followed them right into Corfu harbour but found they had gone on. However, two supply ships of 5,000 and 8,000 tons were lying in Corfu harbour and *Torbay* torpedoed them both. Torpedoes were also fired at a destroyer but missed. *Torbay* then withdrew having spent 17 hours inside an enemy harbour.[135]

322 To Pound

15 March 1942

A. Your signal re Washington came rather as a surprise, although it had been my intention to write to you at the end of this month

---

[135] Following this exploit, Miers was awarded the VC.

(two months short of my 3 years out here) and tell you that, though I was perfectly fit and ready to go on if desired, if you felt that a change was desirable to make it without considering me. I was perfectly ready to go.

As you say, there is now no fleet to go to sea in, but counting heads this is still the largest command, The personnel numbers over 25,000!!!

For the last nine months politico-strategic problems have occupied much of the C-in-C's time, but as I see it, one of his most difficult jobs is keeping up the morale of the sailors – the seagoing ones – in present circumstances. It is not easy to sit in an armchair and send ships out while knowing the time they are going to have until they return to harbour. If one went oneself it would make all the difference.

In the circumstances I should feel happier if someone more experienced and better known to the personnel was to relieve me.[136]

Pridham-Wippell will certainly be able to carry on for the time. With my strong staff team behind him he won't go far wrong.

B.   Many thanks for consenting to Baillie-Grohman staying. He really is doing useful work and is not afraid to speak his mind to the soldiers. We have put up a proposal that he should command all personnel, craft and training centres for Combined Operations. This, I gather, is in line with Home organisation.

For some queer reason the soldiers are hotly opposing it. I believe they strongly object to putting any soldiers under the command of a sailor. . . .

As things are shaping it looks as though Alexandria is going to be the centre of training activities of every description for the Far and Middle East.

We already have schools for Gunnery, AA, Signals and what not, and are preparing to train torpedomen, stokers, the CW [Commissioned or Warrant] candidates, paymasters, etc. . . . I feel we shall shortly want a Commodore in charge of training establishments – a retired officer with some experience of this work would do.

C.   The *Cleopatra* arrived here in a poor state. She apparently was prevented by weather from doing any working up at home, and after her lively reception at Malta, Slattery had some trouble with her ship's company. . . . She is, in fact, in a state of gross inefficiency. . . .

[136]VA Sir Henry Harwood, then ACNS(F), had been selected.

I have put Grantham in command and Vian has hoisted his flag there, and I addressed the ship's company this morning and I am quite sure she will be all right, especially as the *Naiad*'s staff officers are working up the gunnery, etc.; . . .[137]

D. Such a loss that little *Naiad* !! A highly efficient weapon with a ship's company with a grand spirit. The four cruisers were bombed from 9.30 a.m. to 6.30 p.m. coming between Crete and Cyrenaica without damage and then to stumble on a submarine was just too sickening.

The American liaison commander who was on board and sustained a badly smashed ankle told me that the behaviour of the ship's company was wonderful when she sank.

Incidentally there is some mystery why she sank as a result of one torpedo hit. I am having this closely examined. She may, however, have been hit by two torpedoes.

E. I can't conceal from you that I look on this next Malta convoy operation which starts tomorrow with some apprehension. If we are lucky with the weather all may be well, but if not, we may easily lose the convoy, and a ship or two as well. The cruisers' AA ammunition is a cause for anxiety; they used roughly 50% bringing the *Cleopatra* from Malta, and this time they will have at least three different periods at sea. If the Italians in strength make contact with him [Vian, CS15] in the middle is another risk. Our reconnaissance is so sketchy and one never knows from day to day what Malta will be able to put out.

However, it is a good gamble and I am full of optimism.

F. I do not find the attitude of the soldiers to this Malta problem much to my liking. The latest idea is that an advance in Cyrenaica can't be undertaken before 1 June, and it may not be possible until August. I have pointed out that we can't gamble on the convoys getting through and that we may well lose Malta, and even if we don't lose it, Malta's power to interrupt the Libyan supply [line] will fade out and so the date will recede, as the enemy will be able to reinforce at will; but I am met with the reply that it is better to lose Malta than Egypt. However, the general is re-examining it, and I hope for a more favourable date.

---

[137]Capt M. S. Slattery: Capt Dec. 1938; Dir, Air Matl, Oct. 1940; *Cleopatra* June 1941.
Capt (later Adm Sir) Guy Grantham: b 1900; Capt 1937; *President* June 1939; *Phoebe* June 1940; *Cleopatra* Mar. 1942; *Cormorant* (Gibraltar base) Aug. 1943; DPD Dec. 1943–45; COS, MF 1946–48; FO(S/M) 1948–50; 2i/c MF 1950–51; VCNS 1951–54; C-in-C Med & Allied Forces Med 1954–57; C-in-C Portsmouth, Channel & Southern N Sea 1957–59; Ret List 1959; Govr & C-in-C Malta 1959–62.

At the moment I am having examined how much we can put into Malta by taking the large submarines off operations and putting them onto supply.

323. *War Diary, March 1942 (cont.)*

19 March

Operation MG1

The passage of convoy MW10 to Malta was to commence on 20th. *Southwold, Dulverton, Beaufort, Hurworth, Heythrop* and *Eridge* were sailed from Alexandria for an A/S sweep of the convoy route ... Submarines were disposed off Taranto and Messina to attack and give warning of enemy surface forces during the operation.

20 March

Convoy MW10 sailed from Alexandria at 0700/20 escorted by *Carlisle, Sikh* (D22), *Zulu, Lively, Hero, Havock* and *Hasty*. MW10 consisted of HMS *Breconshire* and SS *Clan Campbell, Pampas* and *Talabot*. Naval liaison officers and signalmen were embarked in ships of the convoy.

2. CS15 left Alexandria at 1800/20 in *Cleopatra* with *Dido, Euryalus, Jervis* (D14), *Kipling, Kelvin* and *Kingston* in company.

Loss of HMS Heythrop

3. At 1100/20 ... while the 5DF were carrying out their A/S sweeps, *Heythrop* was torpedoed by a U-boat. She was taken in tow by *Eridge* towards Tobruk but sank at 1600 ... There were 15 ratings killed and missing. The remaining destroyers hunted the U-boat without success.[138]

4. The 5DF proceeded to Tobruk after dark, refuelled and sailed again to join the convoy at daylight. The rate of fuelling was only 20 tons per hour per ship and some ships could not complete to full stowage. *Beaufort* was delayed by a foul propellor.

Army Offensive

5. The Army commenced an offensive to threaten enemy forward aerodromes and thereby divert aircraft from the convoy.

[138] *U-562*, which also sank *Jaguar* 26 Mar.

21 March

Southwold, Dulverton, Hurworth, Eridge and *Avon Vale* joined the escort of MW10 at daylight and CS15 with Force B made contact soon after. *Beaufort* sailed from Tobruk at 0945 to join the convoy. The convoy was apparently not sighted by aircraft on 20th or 21st. The successful action by the army in shelling Martuba landing ground and threatening Tmimi probably contributed largely to this immunity.

22 March

At 0130/22 *P36* reported heavy ships leaving Taranto. Continued large scale bombing of Malta prevented the intended reconnaissance being flown from Malta. *Penelope* and *Legion* sailed from Malta after dark 21st and joined CS15 a.m. 22nd. Light enemy air attacks commenced during the forenoon and developed into a heavy attack during the afternoon and evening. A total of about 150 T/B, dive and high level bombers were employed and concentrated on the convoy which was escorted by *Carlisle* and the 5DF. No ships were hit. Five aircraft were shot down and at least four more damaged. Two more aircraft were shot down by *Euryalus* during the surface action. Beaufighters did good work in escorting the convoy until 0900/22.

2. At 1430 in position 33° 05'N, 17° 47'E CS15 sighted four cruisers to the northeastward which were successfully driven off.

3. At 1640 one *Littorio* battleship, four 6-in cruisers and a few destroyers were sighted to the northward. A strong southeasterly wind was blowing. A brilliant delaying action was fought by the cruisers and destroyers, making full use of smoke while the convoy continued westward. Destroyers pressed home a torpedo attack to 6,000 yards and reported one hit on the battleship. The battleship was also hit by gunfire and seen to be on fire aft. One cruiser was seriously damaged by gunfire and another hit. *Cleopatra* was hit on the bridge with only minor damage. *Kingston* was hit in the engine room and *Havock* in the boiler room, both being reduced to 15 knots. *Lively* was hit forward but not seriously damaged.

4. At dusk (1900) the enemy, who had never got within range of the convoy, withdrew to the northward and the convoy was dispersed to Malta with *Carlisle* and the 'Hunts' escorting individual ships. *Penelope, Legion, Kingston* and *Havock* were also detached to Malta. CS15 set course for Alexandria with the remainder of the force.

6. A Beaufort striking force from Libya and Albacores from Malta were unable to make contact with the enemy before dark and [were] recalled after dark by order of the C-in-C.

23 March

Ships of the convoy MW10 were again subjected to a very heavy scale of bombing from daylight 23rd as they approached Malta. *Clan Campbell* was hit and sunk at 1040 ... *Eridge* rescued 112 officers and men. *Breconshire* was hit in the engine room at 1030, when about 8 miles from the Grand Harbour. She was disabled and attempts by *Penelope* to tow her were unsuccessful. She drifted towards the shore and came to an anchor off Zonkor Point. Owing to the gale and very heavy swell attempts to tow her had to be abandoned. *Pampas* and *Talabot* arrived in harbour safely. *Legion* was hit but reached Marsaxlokk harbour and anchored in shallow water. Fighters did excellent work but were greatly handicapped by the weather and by enemy action. Three bombers were shot down, probably two more, and 6 to 8 damaged. One Ju88 was shot down by gunfire and six damaged. *Carlisle* and the 'Hunts' remained at Malta to give *Breconshire* AA protection. *Avon Vale* was damaged in collision with *Breconshire* and by a near miss, and was unseaworthy. Two officers and six ratings in *Havock* and 13 ratings in *Kingston* were killed during the recent action.

2. CS15's force was delayed by an easterly gale, some of the destroyers being damaged by weather. The force was bombed during the day but on a comparatively light scale and without damage. Beaufighters again did good work providing protection at very long range from their base.
3. An aircraft search of the Ionian Sea for the damaged enemy battleship was unsuccessful and nothing further was seen of her.

A/S Craft

5. The C-in-C ordered a redisposition of A/S craft as follows:

Escort Forces
Western Desert   5DF, 11 Corvette Group, 25 A/S Group.
Levant   10 Corvette Group, 22 A/S Group.
Local A/S Patrols
Alexandria   28 A/S Group, 3HDMLs
Port Said   4 A/S Group (2 ships)
Haifa   2 Trawler Group
Levant Ports   5 HDMLs

W. Desert Force   4 HDMLs
Malta   4 A/S Group (2 ships)
Aden   5 A/S Group.

24 March

Operation MG1

CS15 arrived at Alexandria with *Cleopatra, Dido, Euryalus, Sikh, Zulu, Hero, Hasty, Jervis, Kelvin* and *Kipling*. Merchant ships sounded their sirens and ships' companies cheered as the force entered harbour. The C-in-C made a general signal:

> Well done 15 Cruiser Squadron and Destroyers.

Lively was delayed owing to flooding forward and arrived later. All ships were damaged by weather. *Cleopatra* had minor damage as a result of a hit on the bridge which killed one officer and 15 ratings.

Loss of HMS Southwold

2. At Malta the heavy weather persisted and it was still impossible to move *Breconshire* into harbour. *Southwold* was mined while operating near her and later sank while on tow to the Grand Harbour.

Mediterranean Fleet Destroyers

5. As a result of weather and action damage the shortage of destroyers was serious. The situation was as follows:

Damaged at Alexandria
Zulu and *Lively* each extensive structural repairs to foc'sle likely to take six to eight weeks.
Jackal repairs completing middle or end of April.
Sikh serviceable but reduced in efficiency for 14 days.
Jervis, Kelvin and *Kipling* out of action until 31 [March].
Hero and *Hasty* ready in four or five days.

Damaged at Malta
Kingston seaworthy about 25 April but complete repairs estimated two months.
Havock seaworthy early April but considerable further damage.
Legion and *Gallant* seriously damaged, time uncertain.
Avon Vale seaworthy about 28 March, complete repairs about one month.

THE FIGHT AT ODDS, 1941–1942

Serviceable
Jaguar and *Queen Olga* at Alexandria, *Eridge, Dulverton, Beaufort* and *Hurworth* at Malta.
Janus was expected to complete repairs at the Cape very shortly and *Nubian* at the end of the month.
Airedale was leaving the UK round the Cape to replace *Farndale*.[139]

25 March

Malta
Breconshire was moved by tugs to Marsaxlokk harbour where she was berthed at 1045/25.

2. *Carlisle* sailed from Malta for Alexandria at 2100/25 with *Hurworth, Dulverton, Beaufort* and *Eridge*. The force made a feint to the westward and turned to Alexandria after moonset, keeping well to the southward in order to make the passage between Crete and Cyrenaica during the following night. Air reconnaissance was very weak.
3. Among the many signals of congratulation on the recent engagement, the following was received by the C-in-C from the Prime Minister:

> I shall be glad if you will convey to Admiral Vian and all who sailed with him the admiration which I feel at this resolute and brilliant action by which the Malta convoy was saved. That one of the most powerful modern battleships afloat attended by two heavy and four light cruisers and a flotilla should have been routed and put to flight with severe torpedo and gunfire injury in broad daylight by a force of five British light cruisers and destroyers constitutes a naval episode of highest distinction and entitles all ranks and ratings concerned, and above all their commander, to the compliments of the British Nation.

Merchant Shipping

7. The C-in-C made a general signal stressing the vital need for economy in shipping and for every effort to be made to speed up the turn round of ships in harbour. Developments in the Far East had placed a greatly increased strain upon merchant shipping.

---

[139]*Airedale* (s Ger a/c, C Med June 1942): 1942, 1,050t, 4×4in, 2×21in tt, 27k. *Farndale*: same but 1941, 6×4in, no tt.

324. From Leatham

Malta
25 March 1942

... We are having a hectic time. It was good to see the convoy come in but sad the one should be sunk and the other damaged on the doorstep. The 'Hunts' have had to work very hard but have come up to scratch very well indeed. Jellicoe seems A1 – should be with that name; the loss of his ship was a blow.[140]

Since a.m. there have been the heaviest raids I have yet experienced and I hope to get the ships away tonight without further damage. Yesterday when HQ was demolished one bomb fell in the middle of the courtyard and another on a newly decorated office and sitting room for me which is now a heap of ruins under which are my few cases of clothes not yet unpacked. They are probably well pressed now! Brigadier Clinch, the GOC's GSI was smothered and killed in his office and Major Ellis his assistant hurt.[141] The only casualties, as luckily and for once, all the others (including myself) were in our rock shelters. All of our offices have now gone west, also feeding arrangements – so we are living a rather crowded picnic existence in holes and corners.

I am anxious about *Breconshire* – they made a big attack (Ju87) this afternoon but all missed. There will be many more I am afraid and I don't know when I can get her here – perhaps tomorrow night but I doubt it as I must have a flat calm for entering. In swell and wind she tows at angles at times – no rudder and tugs not strong enough to steady. Nichol and Master Murphy were splendid and Hutchison too of course.[142] All I *can* say is that she is better protected overhead than where she was and she isn't now lying in a minefield! *Southwold* was close to her stern trying to take off passengers when she was mined. The RAF and Army have been splendid in their help – former always out to a clinch – score today *may* be as much as 15 enemy definitely down and as many damaged. It makes them quite shy at times. ...

---

[140]Cdr C. T. Jellicoe: Cdr June 1939; *Winchelsea* Sept. 1939; *Southwold* 1940; *King George V* 1942; *Duke of York* 1943; Capt Dec. 1943; *Colombo* 1944; OD 1945.
[141]Brig A. D. Clinch: b 1902; 2Lt KOYLI 1922; Lt 1924; KAR 1927–32; Adjt 1933–36; Capt 1934; Maj Aug. 1939; GSO, Snr Officers' Sch, Quetta, Dec. 1940.
Maj Ellis: unidentified.
[142]Nichol & Murphy unidentified.
Capt C. A. G. Hutchison: Cdr 1924; Capt (Ret List) 1935; *Breconshire* Aug. 1940.

... Without being gloomy, a very difficult time ahead for us here. I think it was splendid you taking a chance of getting stuff through and I thought Vian's handling of the battle masterly – but I was left very in dark at end! 'White 80' was the last signal I got from him!

[PS]   A bad letter but I am rather stressed in a room with everyone working, telephoning and interrupting. No bed last night.

325. *War Diary, March 1942 (concl.)*

26 March

Malta

Three very heavy dive bombing attacks were concentrated on the ships unloading in the harbour. *Talabot* was hit twice and was on fire. She was scuttled to avoid her ammunition exploding. *Pampas* was also hit and was grounded on an even keel with decks awash. It was hoped to save a good portion of both cargoes.

2. *Breconshire* was hit and set on fire. *Penelope* was near-missed and holed but was not in danger. Her officers and men did great work both in fighting the ship and in dealing with fire and explosions in the merchant ships and elsewhere. *P39* was near-missed and badly damaged, being split amidships, and was later beached. *Legion* was got round to Grand Harbour but was hit again and sank alongside. RFA *Plumleaf* was also hit and aground at Parlatorio wharf, where tug *Ancient* was near-missed and beached.[143] Six enemy aircraft were shot down and probably four more. Twelve others were damaged.

27 March

Breconshire sank at No 1 buoy Marsaxlokk at 1103/27 with part of her side above water. It had not been possible to get the fire entirely under control. It seemed that her cargo of fuel oil was now reasonably safe from enemy action, and it was hoped to save most of it. The work of saving the cargoes of *Pampas* and *Talabot* was proceeding.

2. *Penelope* had been holed both forward and aft by near misses and though flooded forward was in no danger. In view of the continued scale of air attack and also of the oil fuel situation which

---

[143]*P39*: 1942, 545/730t, 1×3in, 4×21in tt, 11/9k.
Ancient: paddle tug, 1915, 690t.

would limit the operations of surface forces seriously, the VA, Malta, proposed to sail *Penelope, Aurora* and *Avon Vale* to Gibraltar as soon as seaworthy. Repairs to *Aurora* were sufficiently advanced to make this possible though she would have to be redocked. The C-in-C instructed VA, Malta, to sail *Aurora* and *Avon Vale* as soon as ready, but decided to await a report on docking of *Penelope* before sailing her.

28 March

The C-in-C represented to the Admiralty in his 1248/28 the serious situation concerning future convoys to Malta. Before any further attempt could be made it was necessary

(a)   for destroyers to be reinforced
(b)   to strengthen Malta fighters very substantially
(c)   to plan some form of diversion to disperse the enemy's air and surface forces.

Central Mediterranean

2.   *Carlisle, Beaufort* and *Hurworth* arrived at Alexandria on completion of a successful passage from Malta. The C-in-C signalled to them: 'Well done indeed. I am pleased to see you back.' *Eridge* and *Dulverton* were detached p.m. 27th for escort duty from Tobruk.

29 March

W/T Equipment

4.   The C-in-C represented to the Admiralty that the efficiency of fighter protection during recent operations in the Central Mediterranean had been greatly impaired by poor communication between ships and aircraft. The early provision of VHF equipment was a matter of great importance.

30 March

Aircraft Torpedoes

7.   The C-in-C again pointed out to the Admiralty the present serious position regarding the supply of aircraft torpedoes in the Mediterranean. With our reduced surface forces the control of the Mediterranean now rested largely on the effective use of T/B aircraft.

31 March

Malta

Havock was now ready for sea though further repairs would be necessary. The C-in-C decided that she should remain at Malta as a possible escort for *Penelope* until a further report was received concerning the latter.

Enemy Losses

7. During the month of March the enemy shipping losses were estimated to be 19 ships sunk totalling 45,000 tons, 5 ships totalling 18,000 tons probably sunk and 5 ships totalling 37,000 tons damaged.

1 April

Copy of Signal Sent by C-in-C to VA, Malta

On my departure, I particularly wish to send a special message to the officers and men of your command. That the defence of Malta has been an epic is well known, and has been stressed from many sources, but I would draw attention more to the other aspect, namely, that of the enormous damage done to the enemy for which the submarine, air and surface forces in your command have been so largely responsible. The record has been magnificent and I heartily thank every officer and man who has taken part, not forgetting those who have had the less spectacular, but nonetheless exacting, task of maintaining and bringing back into action our ships and aircraft to the discomfiture of the enemy.

The very extent of the success of the forces based on Malta has led to the ceaseless battering of the fortress, but one has only to think of the air effort the enemy is diverting to this purpose to realise that this is but another of the services that Malta is rendering to the Empire.

Copy of Signal Sent by C-in-C to Mediterranean Shore Station Authorities

There is probably no theatre of war in which more tenacity and courage has been required of the Merchant Navies than in the Mediterranean. During my tenure of command I have seen innumerable instances of the unobtrusive yet sterling work of the Masters, officers and crews under conditions often of great difficulty and danger. It has been possible to keep an Army and Malta supplied only because the Merchant Navies have surmounted these difficulties.

I thank you for your good work which we in the Royal Navy fully appreciate and which we greatly admire.

Copy of Signal Sent by C-in-C to Mediterranean Station

You will understand, one and all, the deep regret with which I lay down command of the Mediterranean Station. It has been my greatest pride that throughout the war the Mediterranean Fleet has consistently shown itself the master of the enemy in every branch of naval warfare, whether in the air, in submarine warfare or surface fighting. It is this factor which has enabled us during the last two years to impose our will on the enemy to a very high degree, despite his superiority in every class of ship and his almost overwhelming strength in the air. This achievement of the officers and men of the Mediterranean Fleet in some two years of the most strenuous naval fighting on record, is one which I greatly treasure, as greatly as I do the privilege of having led the Fleet during that period.

The enemy knows we are his master on the sea, and we must strain every nerve to keep our standard of fighting so high that that lesson never fails to be borne in on him.

Our worldwide commitments at present mean that we have not, at times, as large forces as we would like to carry the war to the enemy's front door. This will not always be so, and I look forward to the day when the Mediterranean Fleet will sweep the sea clear and re-establish our age old control of this waterway so vital to the British Empire. I am confident that day is not far distant and meanwhile I wish you all good fortune and Godspeed.

326. *From the Admiralty*

31 March 1942

On the hauling down of your flag the Board of Admiralty wish to express their high appreciation of the most able manner in which you have commanded the Mediterranean Fleet since the outbreak of war. Your many successes, often against superior enemy forces, have been a constant source of inspiration. Through your leadership and courage the Mediterranean Fleet has upheld the highest traditions of the Navy.[144]

---

[144]Captain Lee has remarked that, on his arrival at Paddington, Cunningham was greeted by the full Board of Admiralty, surely the ultimate tribute. Captain Lee to editor, 20 Oct. 1997.

327. Cunningham's Memorandum on Command in the Middle East

10 June 1942

The question of the inter-service co-ordination of command in the Middle East has been the subject of some controversy during the last two years. Various solutions have been tried, one of these was the establishment of an additional Chief of Staff to C-in-C, Mediterranean. This does not however appear to have satisfied the other two services though in my view it worked efficiently and perhaps had the arrangement been more heartily accepted it would have been still more efficient. The latest solution is the maintenance of an establishment in Cairo by the C-in-C, Mediterranean. The effect and intention of this arrangement is that the C-in-C, Mediterranean, should spend a large proportion of his time in Cairo. I view this arrangement with concern. We are at present going through a most critical time in the Mediterranean and I regard it as of cardinal importance that the Admiral should be in the closest touch with his Fleet, with his small craft and with the Merchant Navy. It is illusory to suppose that this can be effectively done if the Admiral is 100 miles from the sea for half the week. When hard fighting and difficult conditions have to be met the leader should not be 100 miles away from his forces. . . .

3. (a) *Arrangements for co-ordination*
The C-in-C, Middle East Forces, and AOC-in-C, have their GHQ in Cairo in the same building which allows not only of close co-ordination but permits them to conduct their operations from that GHQ.

The C-in-C, Mediterranean, has an additional Chief of Staff plus a small planning and intelligence staff and a combined operations staff in Cairo. He himself attends in Cairo as necessary but since he is also charged with the administration and the *direct operation* of naval forces his 'headquarters' are necessarily at the main Fleet base. . . . There is thus a complete operations, intelligence and communications organisation at Alexandria. To this organisation are attached Army and RAF liaison Officers and the staff of the Naval Co-operation Group work in close touch.

(b) *Areas of command*
The three Cs-in-C do not command the same areas, the notable differences are:

C-in-C, Mediterranean, and AOC-in-C, cover the whole Red Sea but C-in-C, Middle East Forces, does not deal with Eritrea or Somaliland.

C-in-C, Middle East Forces, and AOC-in-C, cover Iraq, Persia (and hence Persian Gulf) which are outside C-in-C, Mediterranean's command.

AOC-in-C takes in virtually all East Africa and Madagascar which are not covered by either of the other Cs-in-C.

4. It will be noted

(a) That the active command and administration of the Fleet (the former including as it does taking the Fleet to sea) make the presence of the C-in-C, Mediterranean, in Alexandria essential for much of the time . . .

(b) The different areas of command involve different responsibilities and while the AOC-in-C's Command covers his lines of supply this does not apply to the other two Cs-in-C.

5. It is my view that the situation described in paragraphs 4(a) and (b) is unsatisfactory and the remedy I propose will solve both difficulties; it is that a Flag Officer of high standing and experience should be appointed to command the Middle East Area. He should have his HQ in Cairo in GHQ. He should have under his orders one Flag Officer in command of the Mediterranean Fleet and one Flag Officer in command of the Red Sea, the Arabian Littoral and the Persian Gulf. It is furthermore of importance that the commands, of the C-in-C, Middle East Forces, and the AOC-in-C, Middle East, should be altered as far as practicable to that proposed above in order to allow the three Cs-in-C to be able to speak with one voice on the problems of the Middle East theatre of war.

6. There is one further aspect however that needs careful consideration. There have been of late signs of a desire to institute unified commands covering large portions of the globe and there may well be such a project put forward for the Middle East. It is my strong conviction that if such an appointment is necessary the proper person to exercise it is the Naval Officer discharging the functions of C-in-C in that area.

7. . . . This is a war of sea power, our greatness has been built up on our aptitude for sea warfare and we should be chary in turning the use of this weapon over to those who have not been trained primarily to that end.

8. The strategic reason for our presence in Gibraltar, Malta and the Middle East is in order that we may have control of the Mediterranean Sea. At the moment that control has lapsed to an alarming extent owing to our weakened sea power which is due in

part to war losses and weakness in the air and in part to the enemy success on land in capturing the important air and sea bases which we need.

9. The course of this war has demonstrated more clearly than ever how vital a factor is sea power. Our reverses in Libya, Crete, Greece and the Far East are due to our inability to provide sufficient strength at sea to enable our forces and their supplies to pass unhindered whilst denying the vital routes to the enemy. In modern war sea power is compounded of surface force and its essential component in the form of air support. The lack of the latter has had far reaching effect and has led to an idea that sea power is no longer the vital factor and can be replaced by aircraft alone.

10. Until our strategical direction is fully alive to the implications of sea power we shall fail to achieve our objects. Within the Mediterranean the problem is principally that of the application of sea power and our fighting ashore should be directed to assist in that application. Outside the Mediterranean the whole structure of the Middle East War effort is dependent on the use of our sea routes of supply. The logical outcome of these statements is surely that the controlling voice should lie with those trained to the exercise of sea power.

11. It is my view that the above proposals would achieve three things

(a) They would ensure that the strategic conduct of the war in the Middle East was conducted with proper weight given to the determining factor of sea power.

(b) They would allow greater opportunity of inter-service co-ordination since the Flag Officer would be permanently at GHQ and this would be practicable as he would not be involved in the routine of Fleet work. The greatly extended sphere of influence would justify the presence of so senior an officer permanently in Cairo which is not the case in present conditions.

(c) A Flag Officer based at Alexandria could perform the present duties of C-in-C, Mediterranean, and would not be torn as now between his paramount duty to the Fleet and the need to ensure that proper weight is being given in Cairo to the Sea aspects of our Middle East operations and strategy.

DOCUMENTS AND SOURCES

The British Library

The Papers of Admiral of the Fleet Viscount Cunningham of Hyndhope (BL Add Mss 52560–52570). [Listed here as BLAM.]

Churchill Archives Centre, Churchill College, Cambridge

The Papers of Admiral of the Fleet Viscount Cunningham of Hyndhope (4 boxes). [Listed here as CUNN.]

The Public Record Office, Kew, Richmond, Surrey

Admiralty papers [ADM]
Cabinet papers [CAB]

NOTE: Other collections were consulted at *The National Maritime Museum, Greenwich, London*, and *The Imperial War Museum, Lambeth, London*.

NUMBERED DOCUMENT SOURCES

Part I

1.	From Admiral Sir Dudley Pound	24 July 1939	BLAM 52560
2.	To Pound	26 July 1939	BLAM 52560
3.	To Pound	1 August 1939	BLAM 52560
4.	To Pound	5 August 1939	BLAM 52560
5.	From Pound	18 August 1939	BLAM 52560
6.	From Pound	24 October 1939	BLAM 52560
7.	To Pound	31 October 1939	BLAM 52560
8.	To Pound	18 December 1939	BLAM 52560
9.	To Pound	30 December 1939	BLAM 52560
10.	From Pound	1 January 1940	BLAM 52560
11.	From Pound	7 January 1940	BLAM 52560

12.	To Air Chief Marshal Sir W. Mitchell	9 January 1940	BLAM 52569
13.	From Mitchell	17 January 1940	BLAM 52569
14.	From Captain B.A.W. Warburton-Lee	22 January 1940	BLAM 52569
15.	To Pound	11 February 1940	BLAM 52560
16.	To Pound	2 March 1940	BLAM 52560
17.	To Pound	26 March 1940	BLAM 52560
18.	From Admiral Esteva	29 March 1940	BLAM 52569
19.	From Pound	30 March 1940	BLAM 52560
20.	To Pound	17 April 1940	BLAM 52560
21.	From Pound	29 April 1940	BLAM 52560
22.	To Pound	2 May 1940	BLAM 52560
23.	To Admiral Darlan	7 May 1940	BLAM 52569
24.	From Pound	20 May 1940	BLAM 52560
25.	From Vice Admiral Sir Geoffrey Blake	21 May 1940	BLAM 52569
26.	To Pound	29 May 1940	BLAM 52560
27.	From Pound	6 June 1940	BLAM 52560
28.	To Pound	9 June 1940	BLAM 52560
29.	To Pound	7 June 1940	BLAM 52566
30.	To Pound	7 June 1940	BLAM 52566
31.	To the Admiralty	10 June 1940	ADM 199/386

Part II

32.	Mediterranean Fleet War Diary	10–14 June 1940	ADM 199/386
33.	War Diary	14–15 June 1940	ADM 199/386
34.	To Pound	15 June 1940	BLAM 52560
35.	From Pound	16 June 1940	BLAM 52566
36.	To Pound	17 June 1940	BLAM 52566
37.	To Pound	18 June 1940	BLAM 52566
38.	War Diary	16–27 June 1940	ADM 199/386
39.	To Pound	27 June 1940	BLAM 52560
40.	War Diary	28–30 June 1940	ADM 199/386
41.	To the Admiralty	25 June 1940	BLAM 52569
42.	To the Admiralty	27 June 1940	BLAM 52569
43.	From the Admiralty	27 June 1940	BLAM 52569
44.	From Pound	28 June 1940	BLAM 52560
45.	To the Admiralty	28 June 1940	BLAM 52569
46.	To the Admiralty	29 June 1940	BLAM 52569
47.	From the Admiralty	30 June 1940	BLAM 52566
48.	To the Admiralty	30 June 1940	BLAM 52566
49.	From the Admiralty	2 July 1940	BLAM 52566

50.	From the Admiralty	3 July 1940	BLAM 52566
51.	Interview between the C-in-C and Admiral Godfroy	3 July 1940	BLAM 52569
52.	To the Admiralty	3 July 1940	BLAM 52566
53.	To the Admiralty	3 July 1940	BLAM 52567
54.	From the Admiralty	3 July 1940	BLAM 52567
55.	From Godfroy	3 July 1940	BLAM 52569
56.	To the Admiralty	4 July 1940	BLAM 52567
57.	From the Admiralty	4 July 1940	BLAM 52566
58.	To the Admiralty	4 July 1940	BLAM 52567
59.	To the Admiralty	4 July 1940	BLAM 52567
60.	To the Admiralty	4 July 1940	BLAM 52567
61.	To the Admiralty	5 July 1940	BLAM 52566
62.	To the Admiralty	6 July 1940	BLAM 52566
63.	From Godfroy	30 July 1940	BLAM 52569
64.	War Diary	1–5 July 1940	ADM 199/386
65.	Report of Action off Calabria	9 July 1940	CAB 106/338
66.	To Pound	13 July 1940	BLAM 52560
67.	War Diary	13–18 July 1940	ADM 199/386
68.	To the Admiralty	16 July 1940	ADM 186/800
69.	From the Admiralty	19 July 1940	ADM 186/800
70.	To the Admiralty	21 July 1940	ADM 186/800
71.	To the Admiralty (*Sydney* & Italian cruisers)	21 September 1940	ADM 199/1048
72.	Rescue of enemy survivors	22 July 1940	ADM 199/1048
73.	From Pound	24 July 1940	BLAM 52560
74.	War Diary	25–26 July 1940	ADM 199/386
75.	War Diary	2–3 August 1940	ADM 199/386
76.	To Pound	3 August 1940	BLAM 52561
77.	War Diary	4–12 August 1940	ADM 199/386
78.	From Pound	14 August 1940	BLAM 52561
79.	From Pound	14 August 1940	BLAM 52561
80.	To Pound	19 August 1940	BLAM 52561
81.	Attack on Bardia, 15–17 August 1940	10 December 1940	ADM 199/446
82.	From Blake	17 August 1940	BLAM 52569
83.	To Blake	29 August 1940	BLAM 52569
84.	War Diary	14–24 August 1940	ADM 199/386
85.	Account of Torpedo Attack at El Gazala, 22 August 1940	13 September 1940	ADM 199/798
86.	To the Admiralty	22 August 1940	ADM 186/800
87.	From the Admiralty	25 August 1940	BLAM 52567

88.	To the Admiralty	26 August 1940	BLAM 52566
89.	War Diary	29 August–5 September 1940	ADM 199/386
90.	Operation HATS, 29 August–5 September 1940	14 January 1941	ADM 199/1049
91.	War Diary	3–5 September 1940	ADM 199/386
92.	From Churchill	9 September 1940	BLAM 52566
93.	To Pound	10 September 1940	BLAM 52566
94.	War Diary	9 September 1940	ADM 199/387
95.	Middle East Cs-in-C Cttee	11 September 1940	CAB 106/722
96.	War Diary	13–21 Sept 1940	ADM 199/387
97.	From Pound	20 September 1940	BLAM 52561
98.	To Pound	22 September 1940	BLAM 52561
99.	War Diary	25 September 1940	ADM 199/387
100.	From Blake	25 September 1940	BLAM 52569
101.	Operation MB5, 28 September–3 October 1940	24 January 1941	ADM 199/1049
102.	War Diary	3–4 October 1940	ADM 199/387
103.	From the Admiralty	2 October 1940	ADM 186/800
104.	To the Admiralty	5 October 1940	ADM 186/800
105.	Report on Operation MB6	9–15 October 1940	ADM 199/446
106.	Cunningham's Observations on *Ajax*'s Action with Italian Destroyers, 12 October 1940	7 April 1941	ADM 199/797
107.	To Pound	16 October 1940	BLAM 52561
108.	From A.V. Alexander	16 October 1940	BLAM 52566
109.	From Vice Admiral Tovey	17 October 1940	BLAM 52569
110.	War Diary	25–29 October 1940	ADM 199/387
111.	To Naval Attaché, Athens	31 October 1940	ADM 199/810
112.	War Diary	1–6 November 1940	ADM 199/387
113.	Report on Operation MB8, 6–14 November 1940	3 March 1941	ADM 199/797
114.	Fleet Air Arm Operations against Taranto, 11 November 1940	16 January 1941	CAB 106/616
115.	From Godfroy	15 November 1940	BLAM 52569
116.	To Pound	21 November 1940	BLAM 52561
117.	To Rear Admiral Hugh England	23 November 1940	CUNN 5/3
118.	War Diary	14–23 November 1940	ADM 199/387
119.	Report on Operation COLLAR, 23–30 November 1940	20 July 1941	ADM 199/797
120.	War Diary	25–30 November 1940	ADM 199/387

DOCUMENTS AND SOURCES

121.	From Pound	1 December 1940	BLAM 52561
122.	From Admiral of the Fleet Sir Roger Keyes	3 December 1940	BLAM 52569
123.	From Churchill	11 December 1940	BLAM 52567
124.	To Churchill	12 December 1940	BLAM 52567
125.	From Pound	12 December 1940	BLAM 52561
126.	From Pound	15 December 1940	BLAM 52567
127.	War Diary	3–16 December 1940	ADM 199/387
128.	Report on Operations MC2 & MC3, 16–24 December 1940	5 February 1941	ADM 199/797
129.	War Diary	17–31 December 1941	ADM 199/387
130.	Operations in Support of Army, 7 December 1940–31 May 1941	1 January 1942	ADM 199/446
131.	War Diary	2 January 1941	ADM 199/414
132.	Operation MC5: Bombardment of Bardia, 3 January 1941	6 March 1941	ADM 199/798
133.	War Diary	5 January 1941	ADM 199/414
134.	To Pound	5 January 1941	BLAM 52561

Part III

135.	Report on Operation EXCESS, 7–11 January 1941	19 March 1941	CAB 106/346
136.	War Diary	15–19 January 1941	ADM 199/414
137.	To Pound	18 January 1941	BLAM 52561
138.	War Diary	19–22 January 1941	ADM 199/414
139.	Middle East Cs-in-C Cttee	22 January 1941	CAB 106/722
140.	War Diary	23–25 January 1941	ADM 199/414
141.	Passage of *Illustrious*, Malta–Alexandria	19 March 1941	ADM 199/446
142.	War Diary	25–31 January 1941	ADM 199/414
143.	From Pound	27 January 1941	BLAM 52561
144.	War Diary	1–8 February 1941	ADM 199/414
145.	From Pound	8 February 1941	BLAM 52561
146.	War Diary	9–10 February 1941	ADM 199/414
147.	To Pound	10 February 1941	BLAM 52561
148.	War Diary	13–20 February 1941	ADM 199/414
149.	Eden to Churchill	20 February 1941	BLAM 52569
150.	Operations in Support of Army	19–27 February 1941	ADM 199/446

151.	Operation MC8, 21 February 1941	16 July 1941	ADM 199/797
152.	War Diary	23–27 February 1941	ADM 199/414
153.	War Diary	4–8 March 1941	ADM 199/414
154.	To the Admiralty	4 March 1941	BLAM 52567
155.	Report on Operation LUSTRE	11 December 1941	CAB 106/639
156.	To Pound	11 March 1941	BLAM 52561
157.	War Diary	11–16 March 1941	ADM 199/414
158.	To Pound	16 March 1941	BLAM 52567
159.	From Pound	16 March 1941	BLAM 52567
160.	To Pound	17 March 1941	BLAM 52567
161.	War Diary	19 March 1941	ADM 199/810
162.	Report on Malta Convoy, 20–24 March 1941	30 April 1941	ADM 199/445
163.	War Diary	26–31 March 1941	ADM 199/414
164.	From Pound	28 March 1941	BLAM 52561
165.	Despatch on Battle of Matapan, 27–30 March 1941	11 November 1941	CAB 106/628
166.	From Godfroy	31 March 1941	BLAM 52569
167.	War Diary	March 1941	ADM 199/414
168.	War Diary	2–5 April 1941	ADM 199/414
169.	Middle East Cs-in-C Cttee	6 April 1941	CAB 106/722
170.	War Diary	7–8 April 1941	ADM 199/414
171.	Middle East Cs-in-C Cttee	9 April 1941	CAB 106/722
172.	War Diary	10–13 April 1941	ADM 199/414
173.	Operations in Support of Army: Siege of Tobruk, April–Nov 1941	7 March 1942	ADM 199/799
174.	From the Admiralty	4 April 1941	BLAM 52567
175.	To the Admiralty	4 April 1941	BLAM 52567
176.	From Pound	8 April 1941	BLAM 52567
177.	To Pound	8 April 1941	BLAM 52567
178.	To Pound	10 April 1941	BLAM 52567
179.	From Pound	11 April 1941	BLAM 52567
180.	From Pound	11 April 1941	BLAM 52567
181.	From Pound	12 April 1941	BLAM 52567
182.	To the Admiralty	13 April 1941	BLAM 52567
183.	To the Admiralty	13 April 1941	BLAM 52567
184.	From the Admiralty	15 April 1941	BLAM 52567
185.	To the Admiralty	15 April 1941	BLAM 52567
186.	From Pound	15 April 1941	BLAM 52567
187.	To Pound	16 April 1941	BLAM 52567
188.	To Pound	16 April 1941	BLAM 52567
189.	From Pound	16 April 1941	BLAM 52567

190.	From Pound	16 April 1941	BLAM 52567
191.	To Pound	16 April 1941	BLAM 52567
192.	Report of an Action against an Italian convoy, 15–16 April 1941	8 June 1941	CAB 106/339
193.	From Churchill	16 April 1941	BLAM 52567
194.	Chiefs of Staff to Cs-in-C, Middle East	16 April 1941	BLAM 52567
195.	To Churchill	17 April 1941	BLAM 52567
196.	To Pound	22 April 1941	BLAM 52567
197.	From Pound	23 April 1941	BLAM 52567
198.	To the Admiralty	25 April 1941	BLAM 52567
199.	From Churchill	26 April 1941	BLAM 52567
200.	To Pound	26 April 1941	BLAM 52567
201.	From Pound	28 April 1941	BLAM 52567
202.	To Churchill	29 April 1941	BLAM 52567
203.	Operations MD2 & MD3: Bombardment of Tripoli, 21 April 1941	16 August 1941	ADM 199/798
204.	War Diary	24–30 April 1941	ADM 199/414
205.	Middle East Cs-in-C Cttee	28 April 1941	CAB 106/722
206.	Evacuation of Army from Greece	7 July 1941	CAB 106/639
207.	To Rear Admiral England	1 May 1941	CUNN 5/3
208.	From the Admiralty	1 May 1941	BLAM 52567
209.	From Churchill	1 May 1941	BLAM 52567
210.	To the Admiralty	2 May 1941	BLAM 52567
211.	To Churchill	2 May 1941	BLAM 52567
212.	War Diary	2–4 May 1941	ADM 199/414
213.	To Pound	3 May 1941	BLAM 52561
214.	War Diary	6–13 May 1941	ADM 199/414
215.	Middle East Cs-in-C Cttee	13 May 1941	CAB 106/722
216.	War Diary	14–19 May 1941	ADM 199/414
217.	To Pound	18 May 1941	BLAM 52561
218.	Middle East Cs-inC Cttee	21 May 1941	CAB 106/722
219.	War Diary	22–26 May 1941	ADM 199/414
220.	To Pound	23 May 1941	BLAM 52567
221.	From the Admiralty	24 May 1941	BLAM 52566
222.	To the Admiralty	24 May 1941	BLAM 52566
223.	Chiefs of Staff to Cs-in-C, Middle East	25 May 1941	BLAM 52567
224.	To the Admiralty	26 May 1941	BLAM 52567
225.	War Diary	27 May 1941	ADM 199/810
226.	To Pound	28 May 1941	BLAM 52567
227.	To Pound	30 May 1941	BLAM 52561
228.	To Pound	31 May 1941	BLAM 52567

229.	From Pound	31 May 1941	BLAM 52567
230.	To Pound	1 June 1941	ADM 199/810
231.	To Pound	1 June 1941	ADM 199/810
232.	To the Admiralty	1 June 1941	ADM 199/810
233.	War Diary	May 1941	ADM 199/414
234.	Cunningham's Report on Battle of Crete	4 August 1941	CAB 106/640
235.	Cunningham's Dispatch on the Evacuation of Crete	14 September 1941	CAB 106/640

Part IV

236.	To the Admiralty	2 June 1941	BLAM 52567
237.	War Diary	1–2 June 1941	ADM 199/415
238.	Middle East Cs-in-C Cttee	4 June 1941	CAB 106/722
239.	To Pound	11 June 1941	BLAM 52561
240.	From Vice Admiral Sir James Somerville	12 June 1941	BLAM 52563
241.	To Rear Admiral A.U. Willis	12 June 1941	CUNN 5/9
242.	Middle East Cs-in-C Cttee	18 June 1941	CAB 106/722
243.	From Pound	19 June 1941	BLAM 52561
244.	War Diary	7–30 June 1941	ADM 199/415
245.	To Rear Admiral H.M. Burrough	30 June 1941	CUNN 5/2
246.	Cunningham's Report on Syrian Campaign	2 September 1941	ADM 199/679
247.	War Diary	1–11 July 1941	ADM 199/415
248.	To Willis	6 July 1941	CUNN 5/9
249.	Middle East Cs-in-C Cttee	17 July 1941	CAB 106/722
250.	War Diary	22–26 July 1941	ADM 199/415
251.	To Pound	25 July 1941	BLAM 52561
252.	From AB L. Atkinson	29 July 1941	BLAM 52569
253.	War Diary	2–9 August 1941	ADM 199/415
254.	From Mrs F. Palmer	10 August 1941	BLAM 52569
255.	To Pound	15 August 1941	BLAM 52561
256.	War Diary	19–31 August 1941	ADM 199/415
257.	War Diary	1–2 September 1941	ADM 199/415
258.	From Pound	3 September 1941	BLAM 52561
259.	To Pound	18 September	BLAM 52561
260.	War Diary	20–30 Sept 1941	ADM 199/415
261.	War Diary	3–10 October 1941	ADM 199/415
262.	From Pound	11 October 1941	BLAM 52561
263.	To Pound	14 October 1941	BLAM 52561

DOCUMENTS AND SOURCES

264.	War Diary	11–29 October 1941	ADM 199/415
265.	From the Chiefs of Staff	17 October 1941	BLAM 52567
266.	From theChiefs of Staff	18 October 1941	BLAM 52567
267.	Cs-in-C, Middle East to Chiefs of Staff	21 October 1941	BLAM 52567
268.	To Pound	23 October 1941	BLAM 52561
269.	Cs-in-C, Middle East to Chiefs of Staff	24 October 1941	BLAM 52567
270.	Cs-in-C, Middle East to Chiefs of Staff	24 October 1941	BLAM 52567
271.	Churchill to Minister of State, Middle East	26 October 1941	BLAM 52567
272.	Cs-in-C, Middle East to Churchill	27 October 1941	BLAM 52567
273.	Chiefs of Staff to Cs-in-C, Middle East	28 October 1941	BLAM 52567
274.	From Vice Admiral Sir W. Ford	26 October 1941	BLAM 52569
275.	Bombardment Operations, 18–26 October 1941	28 January 1942	ADM 199/681
276.	War Diary	2 November 1941	ADM 199/415
277.	To the Admiralty	2 November 1941	BLAM 52567
278.	War Diary	9 November 1941	ADM 199/415
279.	From Vice Admiral Sir Jock Whitworth	11 November 1941	BLAM 52569
280.	Middle East Cs-in-C Cttee	12 November 1941	CAB 106/722
281.	War Diary	13–18 November 1941	ADM 199/415
282.	To Willis	20 November 1941	CUNN 5/9
283.	From Pound	23 November 1941	BLAM 52566
284.	To Pound	24 November 1941	BLAM 52566
285.	From Churchill	23 November 1941	BLAM 52566
286.	To Churchill	24 November 1941	BLAM 52566
287.	From Pound	25 November 1941	BLAM 52566
288.	From Pound	25 November 1941	BLAM 52561
289.	To Pound	26 November 1941	BLAM 52566
290.	From Pound	27 November 1941	BLAM 52567
291.	War Diary	22–30 November 1941	ADM 199/415
292.	To Pound	1 December 1941	BLAM 52567
293.	To Pound	4 December 1941	BLAM 52561
294.	From Pound	10 December 1941	BLAM 52567
295.	To Pound	10 December 1941	BLAM 52567
296.	To Pound	15 December 1941	BLAM 52561
297.	War Diary	13–31 December 1941	ADM 199/415
298.	From Somerville	21 December 1941	BLAM 52563
299.	From the Admiralty	24 December 1941	BLAM 52561

300.	To the Admiralty	26 December 1941	BLAM 52561
301.	To Pound	28 December 1941	BLAM 52561
302.	From Ford	3 January 1942	BLAM 52570
303.	From Godfroy	3 January 1942	BLAM 52570
304.	From General Sir Bernard Freyberg	7 January 1942	BLAM 52570
305.	To Vice Admiral Sir Henry Moore	9 January 1942	BLAM 52561
306.	From Ford	10 January 1942	BLAM 52570
307.	To the Admiralty	10 January 1942	BLAM 52561
308.	To the Admiralty	15 January 1942	BLAM 52561
309.	From Vice Admiral Sir Ralph Leatham	24 January 1942	BLAM 52570
310.	War Diary	23–31 January 1942	ADM 199/650
311.	From Pound	29 January 1942	BLAM 52561
312.	From Willis	2 February 1942	BLAM 52570
313.	To Pound	6 February 1942	BLAM 52561
314.	To Pound	10 February 1942	BLAM 52561
315.	War Diary	4–16 February 1942	ADM 199/650
316.	From Leatham	12 February 1942	BLAM 52570
317.	To Pound	14 February 1942	BLAM 52567
318.	War Diary	16–25 February 1942	ADM 199/650
319.	War Diary	2–11 March 1942	ADM 199/650
320.	From Leatham	12 March 1942	BLAM 52570
321.	War Diary	14–18 March 1942	ADM 199/650
322.	To Pound	15 March 1942	BLAM 52561
323.	War Diary	19–25 March 1942	ADM 199/650
324.	From Leatham	25 March 1942	BLAM 52570
325.	War Diary	26–31 March 1942	ADM 199/650
326.	From the Admiralty	31 March 1942	BLAM 52567
327.	Memorandum on Command in the Middle East	10 June 1942	BLAM 52561

INDEX

Aboukir, 149, 472
Aboyneau, Captain (French Navy), 57, 95
Abu Zemina, 528
Abyssinia, 6, 26, 61, 64
Adalia Roads, 492
Addis Ababa, 128
Aden, 37, 79, 102, 527, 577
Admiralty, 7, 23, 24, 32, 41, 43, 64, 69, 78, 80–3, 85–97, 98, 111–14, 122, 131, 134, 138–41, 147, 149, 153–4, 158–62, 174, 227, 251, 261, 264, 270, 280, 297, 301, 302, 336, 340–4, 354, 365, 395, 396–7, 404–5, 407, 410–14, 417, 419–21, 435, 452, 459, 460, 461, 473–4, 475, 477, 479–80, 482, 483–4, 495, 500, 502, 510, 517, 527, 528–9, 535, 540, 541, 555–7, 559, 562, 564–5, 592, 594
Adriatic, 192, 193, 201, 203, 212, 214, 219, 221, 272, 274, 277, 302, 327, 454, 455, 512, 532, 572, 578
Aegean, 17, 28, 34, 46, 49, 50, 51, 77, 81, 97, 115, 125, 133, 142, 157, 167, 193, 195, 200, 236, 242, 249, 254, 267, 270–2, 275, 279, 280, 285, 293, 305, 308, 313, 314, 315, 324, 327, 356, 367, 383, 396, 405, 411, 414, 416, 428, 430, 431, 454, 455, 478, 486, 494, 496, 498, 516, 532, 546, 550, 578
Africa, North, 51, 55, 69, 71, 73, 74, 85, 171, 273, 293, 362, 450, 467, 469, 470, 514, 520, 521, 526–7, 530, 534, 538, 545, 546, 547, 557, 560, 568
Agnew, V-Adm Sir W., 533
Air Defence of Great Britain, 24, 26, 30, 47
Air Ministry, 82, 84, 121, 353, 358, 506, 507, 533, 545, 558
Aircraft, British: Albacore, 249, 368, 402, 453, 467, 510, 516, 526, 540, 545, 555, 587; Beaufighter, 355, 356, 357, 360, 478, 498, 507, 515, 523, 556, 563, 579, 582, 586, 587; Beaufort, 160–1, 338, 353, 360, 467, 476, 516, 587; Blenheim, 109, 121, 310, 323, 329, 354, 357, 360, 361, 395, 400, 410, 467, 478, 492, 506, 516, 542, 556, 563; Fulmar, 60, 63, 120, 141, 143–6, 155–7, 176–7, 198, 226, 231, 233, 249, 254–7, 262, 266, 275, 289, 291, 324, 335, 395, 402, 404, 409, 440, 442, 480, 482, 483, 507, 510, 529, 554, 555–6; Gladiator, 60, 63, 84, 109, 111, 124, 131, 141, 142, 148–9, 176, 193, 218, 266, 275, 295, 510; Hudson, 538; Hurricane, 64, 72, 73, 111, 116–17, 121, 125, 233, 262, 266, 291, 295, 300, 302–04, 360, 369, 395, 410, 465, 466, 510, 560, 567, 571; Lysander, 121; Martlet, 510, 554; Maryland, 61, 153, 159, 160, 178–81, 202, 220, 291, 396, 564; Mosquito, 560, 563; Roc, 510; Skua, 74, 141; Spitfire, 467, 560, 563, 571, 580; Stirling, 338, 357; Swordfish, 58, 60, 62–3, 67, 82, 85, 100, 122–3, 137–8, 143–5, 152, 153, 156, 160, 177–89, 192, 213, 223, 232–3, 255, 257, 261, 266, 269, 281, 283, 284, 285, 301, 319, 329, 354, 356, 368, 453, 467, 482, 483, 510, 516, 526, 542, 555, 564, 572, 577; Sunderland, 97, 102, 103, 121, 123, 152, 153, 161, 164, 165, 172, 178, 192, 202, 220, 237, 255, 271, 285, 296, 301, 310, 318–20, 325, 361, 378, 382, 391, 396–7, 418; Tomahawk, 395; Walrus, 510; Wellington, 64, 67, 211, 217–20, 227, 291, 294, 340, 357, 360, 467, 510, 538, 543, 548, 550, 551, 553, 558, 566, 572
Aircraft, German: Do17, 428; Do215, 291; Fw200, 511; He111, 264–5, 282, 291, 298, 384, 402, 444; Ju52, 412; Ju87, 144, 146, 150, 152, 198, 231–32, 257, 291, 305, 321, 434, 441, 442, 444, 488; Ju88, 249, 257, 281, 291, 298, 306, 312, 318, 324, 328, 404, 442–4, 484, 488, 529, 554, 560, 567, 574, 579, 587; Me109, 433, 563, 571; Me110, 488

INDEX

Aircraft, Italian: Cant 506B, 176; Cant S507, 155; Cant Z501, 143, 152, 164, 165, 177, 178; Z510, 142; Cant 1007, 402, 444; Fiat CR42, 198; Macchi C200, 563; Macchi C202, 563; Savoia-Marchetti SM79, 143–5, 155–6, 164–5, 176, 177, 209, 231, 256, 324, 550, 554, 567, 574, 579
Albania, 21, 29, 192
Aleppo, 39
Alexander, A.V. (Visct Alexander of Hillsborough), 168
Alexandria, naval base, 16, 17, 27–8, 31, 35, 42, 43–5, 48, 50–1, 55, 57, 58–60, 64, 76, 79–81, 87–90, 92, 95, 96, 101, 108–11, 117, 123–4, 127–9, 131–5, 140, 142, 145–7, 151–2, 155, 157–62, 165–6, 171–4, 176, 178, 180, 194–202, 210–11, 213, 216, 217, 223–5, 232, 237, 245, 248, 250, 254, 255, 259, 261, 264, 265, 267, 270, 276–9, 281, 283, 291–93, 298, 299, 304, 305, 307, 308, 313, 315, 323, 324, 329–31, 334, 335, 337, 350, 353, 361, 364–6, 382, 385, 386, 389, 391, 394, 399–400, 404, 406, 409, 419, 423, 425–30, 433–6, 438, 440, 442–6, 449, 454, 458, 462–4, 466–8, 475–8, 479, 482–5, 487, 488, 494, 495, 505, 506, 511, 517, 531, 536, 540, 542, 544, 547–54, 557–8, 567, 572–6, 578, 579, 581–3, 585–9, 592, 595; defences, 24, 26, 27, 42, 46, 47, 63, 65, 73, 124–5, 134–5, 140, 191–4, 218, 220–1, 235, 241, 274, 544; air attacks on, 128, 129, 132–3, 140, 166, 191–4, 201, 244, 397, 478, 483, 512
Algeria, 129, 326
Anatolia, 36
Ancona, 277
Ankara, 25, 34, 77, 449
Anti-Aircraft measures, 17, 24, 26, 27–9, 30, 33, 45, 46, 59, 61, 64, 65, 67, 72, 97, 107–13, 115, 117, 121, 124, 130, 133–4, 136–7, 140, 146, 148, 157–9, 165–6, 168, 173, 192–4, 201–2, 206, 207, 209, 218, 221, 222, 232, 234, 235, 241, 242–50, 252, 253, 262–3, 265, 267, 268–9, 274, 275, 278–80, 282, 284, 287–8, 291, 294, 296, 299, 300, 301, 329, 331, 332, 334–5, 337, 355–6, 375, 404–7, 416, 418, 422–3, 430, 431, 434–6, 438, 441, 442, 444–6, 456, 480, 488, 500, 502, 504, 505, 507, 511, 515, 523, 526, 558, 560, 575, 579, 583, 584
Anti-Kithera Strait, 118, 255, 261, 280, 328, 426, 427, 431, 432, 433

Anti-Submarine measures, 21, 43, 60, 64, 67, 69, 71–4, 79, 81, 82, 85, 102, 125, 129, 140, 142, 145, 149, 154–7, 162, 173, 203, 210–11, 217, 218, 250, 256, 279, 283, 301, 306, 307, 324, 329, 332, 334, 454, 456–7, 458, 483, 511, 513, 520, 532, 538–9, 540, 543–5, 549, 553, 554, 558, 572, 576–7, 579–80, 585, 587–8
Arbuthnot, R-Adm Sir R., 4
Argostoli, 172, 313, 536, 573
Argyll & Sutherland Highlanders, 425
Arliss, Capt S.H.T., 401, 438, 444, 445, 549
Army, British, strength, 47, 125–7, 140, 146, 200–1, 204–6, 362, 396, 405, 517; operations, 63, 67, 75, 210, 240–8, 277–9, 282, 367, 368, 370, 373, 381, 391, 449, 451–3, 462–3, 475–8, 480–87, 490, 493, 509, 514, 532, 536, 545, 561, 570, 581; naval relations, 18, 25, 33, 129–31, 134, 147–8, 152, 169–70, 175, 193–4, 200–1, 206–11, 217–26, 232, 233, 240–8, 251–2, 261, 263, 264, 271, 272, 274, 278–9, 281–4, 286–8, 293–300, 329–38, 345, 365–6, 369–99, 402, 405, 408–46, 449, 468, 476, 477, 482, 484, 485, 487, 489, 491–5, 502, 504, 509, 511, 517, 527, 532, 537, 541–2, 543, 546, 547, 558–9, 578, 585, 593, 595–7
Ataka, 511
Athens, 98, 125, 136, 171, 173, 209, 242, 261, 266, 323, 324, 373, 374, 375, 377, 378, 380; Gulf of, 118, 156, 164, 406, 478
Atkinson, A/B L., 499–500
Atlantic, Battle of, 24, 38, 55, 75, 76, 77, 114, 303, 344, 353, 358, 456, 478, 538
Auchinleck, F-M Sir C., 470, 485, 533, 558, 570, 584
Augusta, 31, 50, 51, 70, 74, 78, 80, 83, 85, 100, 108, 114, 153, 520–1
Australia, 32–3, 83, 226, 334, 378, 380, 445, 451, 497, 502, 502, 503, 509, 517
Axis, 15, 25, 27, 209, 239, 244, 455, 465, 466, 467, 469, 497, 523
Ayas Bay, 497

Back, Capt G.R.B., 441
Backhouse, Adm of F Sir R., 7, 8, 301
Bailey, Sub-Lt J.S., 183, 189
Baillie-Grohman, V-Adm H.T., 244, 300, 370–94, 458–9, 516, 583
Baker-Cresswell, Capt A.J., 34
Baku, 524

INDEX

Balkans, 15, 32, 33, 34, 37, 229, 280, 330
Baltic, 5, 8
Barce, 554
Bardia, 79, 84, 129–31, 211, 217, 220, 222–6, 264, 271, 274, 279, 294, 330, 501, 534
Bari, 153, 157, 173, 192, 333
Barnard, V-Adm Sir G., 14
Basra, 403, 521, 524
Batum, 524
Bayly, Lt G.W.L.A., 186, 191
Beatty, Adm of F Earl, 7
Beirut, 34, 42, 47, 50, 51, 79, 86, 98, 135, 449, 487, 491, 492, 499, 531
Belgrade, 330
Benghazi, 103, 122, 126, 157, 160, 170, 201, 202, 222, 226, 235, 236, 255, 265, 273, 274, 277, 279, 282, 283, 284, 286, 287–8, 293, 294, 299, 332, 336, 339, 346, 350, 355, 359, 363, 370, 395, 396, 400, 402, 404, 406, 455, 494, 508–10, 515, 518–20, 526, 528, 532, 534–6, 540, 541, 550, 551, 563, 581
Bitter Lakes, 24, 341
Bizerta, 42, 44, 70, 74, 135, 450, 524–5
Black Sea, 34, 36, 38, 39–40, 74, 115, 242, 494, 500
Blake, V-Adm Sir G., 7, 19, 46, 48, 131–4, 153–4
Blamey, F-M Sir T., 445
Bolt, Lt-Cdr A.S., 311
Bombay, 508
Bordeaux, 98
Bosphorus, 29, 125
Bowker, Actg Sub-Lt(A) J.A., 185, 190
Boyd, Adm Sir D., 62, 180–89, 231–2, 283, 315, 513, 520
Brest, 303, 355
Bridge, Capt A.R.M., 100, 124, 137, 239
Brindisi, 78, 153, 173, 213, 271, 333, 368, 578
Britain, Battle of, 55, 467
British Admiralty Delegation (Washington, DC), 460
British Pacific Fleet, 248
Brooke, Capt B.C.B., 262
Brown, Cdr C.P.F., 437
Brownrigg, Capt T.M., 14
Bruce, Visct, 32–3
Bulgaria, 39,
Bull, Sub-Lt(A) W.A., 184, 191
Burat-el-Sun, 402
Burrough, Adm Sir H., 487–8
Buscall, Temp Sub-Lt J., 183–4, 189
Byatt, Nona (Lady Cunningham), 6

Cagliari, 255
Cairo, 17, 45, 48, 75, 128, 134, 300, 375, 452, 470–1, 514, 568–9, 595–7
Calabria, 274, 277; action off, 58–9, 60, 99–111
Callato, 144–5
Candia, 156, 193, 194, 578
Canea, 173, 390, 425, 427, 428, 429, 431, 433, 434, 435
Cankale, 77
Cape Bon, 129, 141, 160, 547
Cape Colonne, 217
Cape Dukato, 582
Cape of Good Hope, 18, 72, 75, 77, 116, 117, 121, 126–7, 200, 538, 578
Cape Malea, 390, 427
Cape Mari di Lenca, 50
Cape Passero, 81
Cape Spartivento (Sicily), 19, 193, 217, 505
Carline, Lt G.A., 186, 190
Carne, Capt W.P., 14, 438
Carr, Pay-Cdr P.H., RNR, 377
Casablanca, 55, 57
Castel Benito, 218, 345
Catania, 266, 273, 285
Catroux, Gen (French), 499
Caucasus, 39, 518–19, 524
Cephalonia, 70, 180, 426, 434, 548, 550, 573
Ceylon (now Sri Lanka), 555–6
Chakmak, Marshal F., 25, 28, 29, 39
Chatfield, Adm of F Lord, 7, 323
Chatham, 6
Cheeseman, Lt(A) N.A.F., 138
Chiefs of Staff, 15, 19, 28, 56, 139–40, 147, 204, 208, 247, 263, 274, 300, 331, 338, 351–2, 411, 436, 450–1, 452, 479, 518–25, 556
China, 40, 124
Churchill, Rt Hon Sir Winston, career, 15; as First Lord, 41; as Premier, 15, 19, 204, 479–80, 530, 546; and Pound, 19–20, 41, 47, 126–8, 150, 151, 204, 208, 239–40, 417, 534, 535; and Mediterranean, 55, 59, 63, 126–8, 139–40, 146–7, 204–9, 239–42, 245, 342–5, 436, 467, 523–5, 555, 559, 589; and Cunningham, 18, 19, 47, 57–8, 59, 132, 146–7, 168–9, 205–7, 233, 239–43, 344–6, 350–3, 357–8, 395–7, 417, 450, 496, 518–25, 535–6, 546, 555, 559, 589
Clark-Hall, Capt, 382
Clifford, Lt E.W., 181, 187, 191
Clinch, Brig A.D., 590

Collins, V-Adm Sir J., 118–19
Collishaw, Air Cdre, 269
Combined Operations, 46, 148, 191, 196–7, 204–9, 221–2, 242, 263, 274, 289–93, 352, 450–1, 482, 518–25, 530, 583
Comiso, 285
Committee of Imperial Defence, 30
Contraband Control, 29, 35
Convoys, 58, 59–60, 62, 63, 73, 77, 97, 108, 109, 123, 141–4, 148, 150, 153, 162–8, 170–8, 194–200, 204, 206, 209, 211–17, 219, 225, 226, 234, 236, 237, 241–3, 250, 269–72, 277–8, 281, 283, 286, 291, 296, 297–303, 305–7, 313–14, 324, 328–9, 331, 346, 382–90, 395–7, 401, 404, 406, 414, 417, 435, 450, 454, 456, 461–67, 484, 506, 507, 511, 523, 525, 531, 533, 542–4, 549–50, 553, 563, 570–1, 572–5, 584–92
Cooke, Capt G.C., 540
Corbett, Lt-Cdr J.W.S., 545, 567
Corfu, 171, 582
Corinth, Canal, 85, 313, 323, 375, 426, 494, 496; Gulf of, 193, 373
Cowan, Adm Sir W., 5, 8, 300, 451
Cresswell, Actg R-Adm G.H., 276, 335, 459
Crete, 46, 47, 50–1, 60, 65, 81, 99, 118, 129, 131, 144, 156, 157, 165, 170–74, 190–1, 205, 207, 221, 233, 236, 237, 239, 261, 263, 265, 273, 289, 297, 314, 315, 319, 327, 328, 377, 378, 384, 389, 474, 489, 490, 498, 501, 530, 533, 534, 561, 574, 579, 584, 589, 597;
campaign in, 244–50, 313, 332, 351, 356, 367, 369–70, 390, 395, 405, 406, 408–46, 449–51, 454, 458, 460, 468, 470, 475, 478–80, 487
Crotone, 512
Cumberlege, Lt C.M.B., RNR, 381
Cunningham, Gen Sir Alan, 63, 300
Cunningham, Adm of F Visct (Andrew Browne), childhood, 3; character, 3, 4, 6, 8–9, 471–2; naval training, 3–4; early naval service, 4–9; First World War, 5; Baltic service, 5, 8; inter-wars career, 5–7, 15; marriage, 6; and Churchill, 18, 19, 20, 47, 131, 145–6, 168–9, 205–7, 233, 239–42, 344–5, 350–3, 357–8, 395–6, 397, 450, 495–6, 518–25, 535–6, 546, 555, 559, 589; and Pound, 7, 8, 18, 19–20, 22–36, 38–43, 45–51, 55, 66, 73–7, 82–4, 87, 109–11, 120–21, 123–5, 126–9, 150–52, 167–8, 190–92, 204, 208–9, 225–7, 233, 234, 239–43, 247, 249, 250, 251, 262–4, 274–5, 280–1, 282–3, 299–301, 302–04, 307–8, 336–40, 344–7, 353–6, 359–60, 398–400, 406–7, 409–11, 414–19, 452, 453, 457–8, 460, 468, 477–9, 481–2, 501–2, 505–9, 513–16, 520–1, 528–9, 534–9, 543–8, 557–9, 568–71, 576, 582–5; and Somerville, 3, 6, 8, 9, 19, 67, 85, 111, 132, 142, 226–7, 401–4, 47–80, 555, 577; and staff, 13–14, 66, 237, 583; and other naval personnel, 4, 5, 8, 13, 65–6, 85–6, 124, 126, 240, 245, 248–9, 251, 276–7, 344, 345, 366, 370–1, 399, 407, 409, 416–17, 423–4, 439, 454–5, 460, 474, 482, 487, 488–9, 490, 496–7, 503, 510, 513, 518, 541, 544, 559, 566, 578–9, 583, 588, 592, 593–4; as C-in-C, Mediterranean, strategy, 17, 18, 26, 27, 48–51, 55, 56, 59, 61–4, 76–7, 83–4, 85, 111, 114–16, 132, 138–9, 140, 159–62, 190–2, 200–203, 221–2, 242–5, 252, 271, 327–8, 332, 361–3, 411–14, 449, 452–3, 454, 471–5, 489, 491, 524–5, 545–8, 556–7, 562, 583; action off Calabria, 58–9, 99–111; raid on Taranto, 60–2, 174–90, 192; battle of Matapan, 235, 236–9, 251, 308–27, 394, 454, 458; and French Navy, 14, 16, 18, 25–7, 32, 33–4, 38, 39–40, 42–5, 50–1, 56, 57–8, 71, 74, 78, 79–83, 86–97, 135–6, 190, 477; as fleet commander, 8–9, 13, 17, 19, 58–62, 68, 69–72, 73, 99–111, 128–31, 134–5, 140–6, 154–8, 162–8, 171–2, 174–89, 195–200, 210–16, 223–5, 231–2, 236–9, 241, 245–52, 253–9, 269–70, 282, 283–4, 290–2, 296–9, 305–7, 308–27, 347–8, 363–4, 365, 370–1, 394, 396–7, 400–4, 417, 422–46, 459–61, 462, 463–6, 471–2, 473, 480, 483, 484, 485, 491–5, 497, 500–1, 510, 511, 513, 517–18, 527, 531, 540, 541, 549–50, 551, 553, 564, 572–3, 574, 576, 577, 578, 587, 589, 592, 593–4
Cunningham, Prof Daniel, 3
Cunningham, Mrs Elizabeth, 3
Cunningham, Lady (née Byatt, Nona), 6
Cunningham, Adm of F Sir John, 14
Cyprus, 18, 59, 65, 76, 82, 122, 147, 151, 266, 289, 290, 378, 381, 415, 474, 479, 489, 491–2, 510, 529, 581–2
Cyrenaica, 28, 63–4, 110, 241, 243, 260, 266, 271, 281, 288, 296, 299, 314, 315, 329, 336, 343, 351, 358, 395, 417, 489, 493, 521, 531, 541, 546, 554, 556, 571, 576, 581, 584, 589

INDEX

Dakar, 55, 57
D'Albiac, Air V-M J.H., 377
Danube, 39, 125, 191
Danzig, 22
Dardanelles, 5, 39, 78, 81, 125, 406, 478, 486, 494, 516
Darlan, Adm J.-F. (French Navy), 16, 22, 31, 43–5, 46, 56, 82, 87, 88
Defensively Equipped Merchant Ships, 302
De Gaulle, Gen Charles, 82, 88, 499
Dekheila, 73, 98, 149, 510
Derna, 162, 265, 271, 275, 276, 278, 279, 294, 330, 339, 414, 532, 570
De Robeck, Adm of F Sir J., 8
Dick, R-Adm R.M., 14, 565, 569
Dickens, Adm Sir G., 29, 39
Dill, F-M Sir J., 242–3, 286, 300, 304, 330
Dodecanese, 21, 23, 49, 50, 51, 55, 61, 65, 66, 74, 110, 122, 133–4, 171, 191, 201, 202, 206–7, 212, 242, 244, 261, 263, 265, 274, 279, 285, 289, 296, 297, 313, 329
Donovan, Col W.J., U.S.A., 264
Doro Channel, 78, 157, 170, 210
Dover, 5
Dreyer, Adm Sir F., 505, 507
Drummond, Air M. Sir P.R.M., 499, 568
Dundas, R-Adm J.G.L., 27–8
Dunkirk, 48, 57, 251, 415, 479, 480
Durazzo, 157, 193, 285, 327, 368
Durban, 168

East Indies, 24, 49, 65, 99, 116, 134, 148, 281, 350, 407
Eastern Fleet, 22, 24, 25–6, 30, 453, 458, 577
Eaton, Capt J.W.M., 348
Edelsten, Adm Sir J., 288, 301
Eden, Rt Hon R.A. (Earl of Avon), 242–3, 286, 300, 302, 304
Edward-Collins, Adm Sir G.F.B., 581
Egypt, 15, 23–4, 25, 27, 35, 38–9, 48, 63, 72, 73, 75, 76, 82, 121, 122, 125, 127–8, 140, 146–8, 158, 192, 201, 203, 217, 231, 239, 274, 281, 297, 328, 330, 351, 352, 354, 358, 362, 367, 395, 396, 414–15, 427, 446, 451, 460, 462, 489, 522, 524, 546, 584
El Agheila, 351–2
El Alamein, 451, 471
El Auegia, 509
El Gazala, 137–8, 366
Elaphonisos, 272

Eleusis, 310, 332, 368
Elliott, R-Adm F., 135, 172
England, R-Adm H., 394
English Channel, 359
Epirus, 373
Erdek, 497
Eritrea, 64, 595
Esteva, Adm J.-P. (French Navy), 38, 40, 42–3, 78
Euboea, 375
Evetts, Maj-Gen J.F., 300, 437

Famagusta, 147, 290, 291, 495, 531
Far East, 22–3, 24, 26, 30, 280, 415, 451, 453, 457, 458, 470, 555–6, 562, 589, 597
Fisher, Adm of F. Lord., 4
Fisher, Adm Sir W.W., 6, 7, 8, 323
Fleet Air Arm, strength, 222–3, 245, 250, 267, 271, 280, 406–7; carriers, 31, 33, 48, 49, 51, 58–62, 66, 67, 70, 80, 99–100, 103, 106, 108–12, 115, 128–9, 137, 141–5, 151–2, 155–7, 162–5, 170, 172, 174–89, 192, 193, 195–200, 202, 204, 210–14, 223–4, 227, 231–3, 236–9, 249–50, 252–7, 271, 273, 289, 303, 308–26, 402, 404, 440, 457–8, 481, 528–9, 555, 569; shore-based, 82, 84, 85, 98, 123, 131, 137–8, 149, 201, 211, 218, 241, 242, 261, 266, 269, 273, 277, 279, 281, 283, 284, 285, 301, 314, 327–8, 333, 338, 351, 356, 365, 368, 449, 453–4, 456, 457, 467, 482, 491–2, 498, 501, 505, 510, 512, 513, 516, 518, 526, 545, 554–6, 566–8, 572, 577, 578
Forbes, Adm of F Sir C., 22, 30
Force H, 57, 59, 67, 77, 85, 111, 114, 132, 142, 153, 192, 195–200, 204, 213–16, 226–7, 233, 254, 280, 303, 397, 401–4, 461, 511, 532, 533, 539, 543–6, 555, 571
Force K, 449, 454, 455, 461, 467–9, 506, 508, 514, 520, 526, 529–30, 533, 534, 536–8, 540, 541, 542–4, 548, 549, 550, 566–7, 571, 574
Ford, Adm Sir W., 73, 78, 81, 85, 102, 111, 122, 123, 128, 129, 138, 154, 164, 173, 175, 188, 258, 259, 260, 262, 291, 296, 367, 402, 460, 462, 466, 468, 484, 514, 525, 533, 544, 550, 560–1, 565, 566
Forde, Actg Sub-Lt (A) A.J.B., 185, 190
Fort Capuzzo, 130, 134, 211
Fort Ramla, 130
Fortina Benoli, 509

France, Air Force, 25, 40; Army, 16, 25, 32, 33–4, 47, 55; Navy, 14, 16, 18, 25, 26–7, 30, 34, 38, 40, 42–5, 47, 50–1, 56, 71, 74–5, 78, 98, 113, 221; squadron at Alexandria, 16, 50–1, 55, 57–8, 71, 79–80, 82–3, 86–97, 120, 169, 190, 203, 326–7, 340–1, 350, 353, 449, 475–6, 477, 484–5; Anglo-French co-operation, 15, 16, 23, 25, 29, 33–4, 38, 39–40, 42–5, 46, 50–1, 56, 78–80; Free French, 221, 408, 449, 457, 490, 499, 502; Vichy France, 55–7, 82, 98, 113, 122, 135–6, 203, 280, 326, 340–1, 343, 350, 408, 449–50, 475–7, 482–7, 490, 491–3, 495, 497, 498, 523, 525
Franco, Gen Francisco, 55
Fraser, Rt Hon P., 418
Freetown, 38, 191, 192, 303, 481, 505, 538
Freyberg, Gen Sir B., 378, 380, 381, 405, 418, 442, 561

Gabes, Gulf of, 78
Galita Island, 78
Gallipoli, 134
Garside, Capt F.R., 102
Gavdo Island, 165, 285, 298, 306, 306, 314, 315, 318, 325, 328, 389
Genoa, 213; Gulf of, 27, 42
Gensoul, Adm M.-B. (French Navy), 88
George II, King of Greece, 378, 433
Germany, policy and strategy, 14, 15, 17, 22, 32, 39–40, 55, 56, 88, 146, 158, 209, 220, 236, 243, 296, 327, 403, 415, 450, 465, 489, 557, 562; intervention in the Mediterranean, 231, 293, 338, 343, 350, 352, 367, 406, 449, 479; Air Force, 59, 63, 162, 196, 231–37, 239–41, 243, 245–52, 253–8, 260–1, 264–5, 267, 273, 276, 281, 283–4, 286, 287–8, 289, 293, 296, 303, 306, 312, 313, 321, 324, 328, 330–1, 333, 334–5, 339, 351, 353, 355, 360–2, 366, 371, 373, 377, 378, 380, 383–6, 388–90, 394, 399, 401, 404, 406–7, 409–17, 421–5, 427–9, 431–46, 449, 452, 455–6, 458, 464–6, 469, 470, 480, 481, 484, 487–90, 494, 498, 499, 502, 504, 509, 514–15, 523, 524, 533, 535–6, 554, 563, 567, 570, 574, 579, 586–7, 590–1; Army, 63, 140, 206, 243, 245–6, 381–2, 391, 409, 422, 427, 428, 434, 435, 480, 489, 490, 521; Afrika Korps, 229, 239, 291, 335, 349, 355, 357, 468–9, 516, 520; Navy, 132, 455; U-boats, 24, 40, 63, 232, 356, 454, 456–7, 470, 481, 513, 520, 530, 533, 537–40, 542, 543, 547, 549, 550, 558, 572, 573, 573, 576, 579–80, 585
Gibraltar, 28, 30, 42, 43–4, 55, 59, 72, 75, 77, 111, 114, 116, 127, 128, 142, 146, 195, 197, 199, 213, 254, 259, 272, 397, 401, 454, 456, 461, 498, 520, 538, 539, 546, 563, 592, 596
Gilmour, Capt D., 399
Githion, 385
Glennie, V-Adm Sir I., 301, 404, 422, 428, 429–30, 433, 434, 458–9, 553, 577
Godfroy, V-Adm R.E. (French Navy), 16, 57–8, 82–3, 86–97, 135–6, 169, 190, 203, 326–7, 449, 477, 485, 561
Going, Lt G.R.M., 181, 187, 191
Goodwin, Lt P.G., 184, 191
Gordon, Dr G. A. D., 18
Gould, P/O T.W., VC, 579
Gouton, Adm P.V.G. (French Navy), 490
Grand Fleet, 26
Greece, 15, 29, 32, 33, 36, 55, 59–60, 65, 70, 81, 98, 131, 136, 171–4, 179, 193, 194, 200, 203, 206, 207, 226, 231, 233, 236, 239, 261, 263, 274, 284, 285, 328, 489, 508, 517, 523, 526, 529, 530, 574, 579; expedition to, 241, 242–4, 245, 247, 266, 272, 286, 296–9, 308, 310, 313–14, 327, 330–3, 347, 351, 352–3, 354, 356, 359, 361–2, 365, 367, 370–96, 406, 414, 424, 448, 450, 451, 452, 454, 466, 470, 480, 490, 501, 534, 561, 597; Navy, 209, 218, 220–1, 226, 244, 272, 313, 315, 323, 324, 364, 374, 395, 457, 577, 578
Green, Sub-Lt(A) R.A., 186, 191
Grieve, Lt K.C., 184, 190

Haifa, 24, 65, 81, 98, 113, 122, 125, 147, 148, 151, 152, 340, 401, 477, 479, 482, 483, 485, 495, 515, 531, 548, 576–7, 587
Hale, Lt-Cdr J.W., 186, 190
Hal Far, 295
Hallifax, V-Adm R.H.C., 515, 527
Hamburg, 344
Hamilton, Lt R.W.V., 187, 190
Harwich, 5
Harwood, Adm Sir H., 169, 208, 583
Henderson, Adm Sir R., 7
Heraklion, 196, 261, 405, 425, 427, 428, 430, 431, 433, 437, 440, 442
Hickling, R-Adm H., 225, 261, 268
Hine, Lt-Cdr J.F.W., 253
Hitler, Adolf, 51, 63, 280, 523

INDEX

Hodgkinson, Cdr H., 437
Holland, V-Adm L.E., 198
Home Fleet, 44, 116, 150, 208, 303, 505, 506
Hong Kong, 27, 43
Hood, Lt-Cdr T., RNR, 380
Hook, Lt-Cdr H., 381
Hopkins, Cdr F.H.E., 567
Horton, Adm Sir M., 131
Humphreys, Lt P.N., 186–7, 191
Hungary, 330
Hurd Bank, 167, 198, 305
Hutchison, Capt C.A.G., 590
Hydra, 136, 427

Iachino, Adm A. (Italian Navy), 238, 239, 302
Imperial Defence College, 5–6, 134
India, 33, 83, 523, 533
Indo-China, 341
Intelligence, 74, 85, 234, 236, 260, 264–5, 269, 396, 408, 467, 468–9, 544
Invergordon Mutiny, 6
Ionian Sea, 148, 153, 170–2, 306, 315, 361, 455, 532, 548, 566–7, 577, 587
Ios, 393
Iran, 33, 596
Iraq, 403, 449, 596
Ishailia Rocks, 513, 527
Iskanderun, 498
Ismailia, 278, 282, 504
Ismet Inonu, 29
Istanbul, 22
Italian East Africa, 20, 23, 26, 63, 111, 201, 327–8, 368, 596
Italy, Policy and Strategy, 6, 14–17, 20–1, 34, 37, 40–2, 44, 45, 47, 48, 55, 56, 65, 76, 80–1, 88, 114–15, 146, 160–1, 171, 195–6, 231, 519–20; Air Force, 18, 20–1, 27–9, 31, 33, 55, 59, 60, 63, 67, 69, 73, 81, 84, 98, 99, 102, 108–13, 122–5, 128–33, 136, 140–6, 148, 164–6, 173, 176–8, 191–2, 194, 201–03, 218, 231, 236, 238, 254, 256, 267, 289, 299, 301, 302, 303, 306, 313, 315, 318, 355, 403, 404, 407, 452, 455, 462, 465–6, 470, 487, 499, 509, 511, 515, 520, 523, 530, 534–7, 545, 550, 554, 559, 563, 567, 570, 574, 579, 586; Army, 20, 23, 26, 63, 126–31, 139–40, 147–8, 152, 201, 205, 206, 209, 223–6, 242, 243, 271, 285, 288, 299, 450, 519, 521; Navy; 17–21, 23, 27–31, 45, 49, 51, 55, 58, 60–2, 66–7, 69, 70, 71, 77, 83–5, 88, 98–111, 114–15, 118–24, 126–8, 132–3, 135–8, 145–6, 152, 154–6, 159, 160–5, 174–89, 200, 203, 215, 217, 219, 220, 233, 234, 235, 236–9, 245–6, 250, 251, 252, 255, 264, 271, 290, 292–3, 296–9, 302, 307–28, 344–5, 347–50, 351, 353, 357, 358, 359, 361–2, 365, 368, 390, 394–6, 406, 408, 429, 449, 453, 454, 456, 458–9, 461–5, 468–71, 473, 474, 478, 481, 486, 497, 503, 505, 506, 508–10, 512, 514–16, 518, 520, 526, 528, 529–30, 533–8, 541, 542–4, 546–54, 556–9, 562, 564, 566, 569, 570, 572–5, 577–8, 582, 584, 584–9, 591, 592, 594

Janvrin, Lt H.R.B., 184, 190
Japan, 14, 15, 540, 559, 562
Jellicoe, Capt C.T., 590
Jibouti, 48, 89, 515
Joint Planning Staff, 147, 154, 266
Jonas, Cdr R. McC. P., 492
Jones, Sub-Lt(A) P.D., 186, 190
Jubal, Straits of, 329, 512
Jutland, Battle of, 6

Kabbo Point, 180
Kalamai, 376
Kalamata, 244, 375, 381, 382, 385, 386, 388, 390, 392, 393
Kann, 482
Kavadias, Adm E. (Greek Navy), 364
Keighly-Peach, Cdr C.L., 124
Kemp, Lt N. McI., 183, 189
Khalkis, 332
Kiel, 344
Kiggell, Lt(A) L.J., 184, 190
King, Adm E.L.S., 246, 360, 401, 404, 416–20, 422, 423, 428, 430–5, 431, 438, 443–6, 459, 482–3, 485, 486, 492, 495, 498
Kissamo Bay, 389, 425, 428
Kithera, 391, 392, 406; Channel, 259, 261, 272, 277, 279, 280, 285, 296, 306, 319, 429, 430

Lamb, Cdr C.B., 184, 190, 231
Lampedusa, 236, 401, 408
Lampson, Sir M., 75, 128
Layton, Adm Sir G., 13, 30
Lazaretto Creek, 47
Lea, Lt C.S.E., 186, 190
Leatham, Adm Sir R., 460, 466, 514, 525, 544, 565, 575–6, 580–1, 590–1, 592, 593
Lee, Capt E.H., 237–8, 251, 309
Lee-Barber, Cdr J., 381
Leicestershire Regiment, 425

Lemnos, 333, 486
Lend-Lease Bill (U.S.), 243
Leonidion, 391
Lepida Cove, 165
Leros, 28, 78, 165, 195, 242, 301, 426
Levant, 16, 18, 59, 449, 513, 517, 531, 572, 576–7, 587
Libya, 17, 18, 20, 21, 23, 26, 28, 42, 51, 58, 64, 65, 66, 69, 81, 111, 112, 114, 115, 120, 122–3, 126, 131, 143, 145, 146, 148, 157–62, 170–1, 175, 202–3, 206, 211, 217, 232, 234, 235, 239, 242, 251, 269, 271, 278, 293, 344, 345, 346, 350, 361, 369, 395, 406, 414, 454, 467, 468–9, 474, 490, 506, 512, 522, 527, 529, 541, 548, 566, 570, 584, 587, 597
Linosa Island, 256
Linton, Cdr J.W., VC, 236
Lissmoss, 298
Litani River, 482
Little, Adm Sir C., 3
Lloyd, Air C. M. Sir H.P., 469, 563, 565, 576, 580
Longmore, Air C.M. Sir A., 16, 63, 73, 111, 113, 121, 148, 153, 218, 226, 233, 240, 243, 260, 262, 287, 303–4, 328–9, 330, 331, 332, 338, 354, 358, 369, 417, 452, 470, 533–4
Loraine, Sir P., 34
Luqa, 291
Lydda, 482
Lyddeker, Capt G.O., 199
Lyster, Adm Sir A. L., 62, 128, 165, 172, 174–89, 196, 199, 210, 212, 214, 216, 231, 283
Lyttleton, Rt Hon O., 82, 120, 499, 514, 523, 558, 569

McCarthy, R-Adm E.D.B., 166–7
Macdonald, Sub-Lt(A) J.M., 183, 189
McKendrick, Mrs H., 13
Maarten Bagush, 137
Mack, R-Adm P.J., 80, 210, 212, 215, 216, 218–19, 279, 311, 312, 315, 321, 322, 323, 346–50, 354–5, 365, 368, 401, 428, 434, 511, 572, 577, 585
Madagascar, 341, 596
Mahan, Capt A.T., U.S.N., 472
Makryalo, 144–5
Maleme, 261, 273, 285, 310, 319, 323, 389, 412, 427, 428, 429, 433, 434, 435
Malta, naval base, 6, 16, 17, 30, 31, 35, 39, 42, 43, 47, 65, 67, 73, 78, 108, 111–12, 128, 129, 131, 133, 138–41, 144, 146, 148, 149, 151, 152, 154–5, 156, 158–62, 167, 170, 175, 176, 197–8, 200, 202, 209, 214–16, 231–32, 234, 248, 253, 255, 257, 259, 265, 267, 276, 301, 328, 337, 340, 359, 368–9, 397, 399, 403, 404, 430, 461–70, 472, 484, 488, 514, 545, 552, 557, 560–1, 565–6, 580–1, 583, 588–93, 596;
military defence, 51, 55, 76, 138, 155, 296, 314, 466, 478, 497, 556, 564; air defence, 17, 23–4, 26, 27–8, 30, 47, 59, 64–5, 67, 73, 74, 84, 97, 111–12, 116–17, 121, 133, 138–9, 146, 148, 159–62, 202, 221, 232–4, 262, 266, 271, 280, 291, 294, 296, 300, 302–04, 330, 352, 355–7, 360, 361, 414–5, 466, 507, 511, 526, 560–1, 562–4, 571, 580–1, 590–1, 593; Italian air attacks, 72, 73, 81, 97, 108, 194, 202, 234, 470, 525–6; German air attacks, 259–60, 261–2, 265, 271, 273, 281, 283, 294, 295, 296, 300, 301, 303, 361–2, 366–7, 397, 403, 465–6, 470, 488, 525–6, 560–1, 565–6, 573, 575, 577–8, 580–1, 590–1; supply of, 18, 50, 63, 67, 77, 81–2, 101, 114, 123, 143, 150, 151, 161–8, 174–8, 195–200, 213, 215, 226, 236, 242, 244, 250, 251, 253, 254, 256–7, 259, 282, 289, 294, 296, 297, 300, 302, 305–7, 327, 345–7, 354, 355–6, 359–60, 361, 369, 397, 401–4, 417, 450, 451, 454, 458, 461–6, 469–70, 473, 478, 481, 484, 498, 505–7, 513, 514, 528, 533, 537, 539, 544, 546, 547, 549–50, 554, 558, 560, 563, 567, 570–1, 573–6, 584–93; air reconnaissance, 61, 70, 74, 116, 122–3, 128, 129, 133, 153, 159–62, 178–81, 188, 192, 202–3, 212, 217–20, 234, 259, 296, 306, 308, 362, 370, 396, 400, 426, 428, 508, 535, 543, 550, 551, 560, 563–6, 575–6, 577, 587; naval offensive operations from, 17, 85, 158–62, 206, 234, 251, 293, 331, 346–50, 352, 354, 356, 357, 359, 361, 365–6, 368, 369, 395, 397, 399, 406, 449, 454, 455, 463, 467–70, 473, 506, 508, 514, 526, 529–30, 533–44, 548, 550, 551, 554, 558, 562, 565, 567, 571, 580–1, 586; air offensive operations from, 64, 67–8, 82, 122–3, 138, 148, 154, 173–4, 201, 202, 211, 212, 218–19, 233, 234, 251, 266, 269, 273, 277, 284, 285, 294, 301, 331, 338, 352–7, 361, 400, 455, 463, 467–70, 473, 484, 501, 505, 506, 507, 516, 518, 523, 526, 529, 542, 548, 560, 566, 573, 587

INDEX

Mardel-Ferreira, Probny Sub-Lt(A) A.F.X., 185, 190
Marittimo, 503
Maritza, 144
Marsa-el-Ramla, 130
Marsaxlokk, 215, 403, 560, 587, 589, 591
Marsh P/O(A), 137–8
Marshall A'Deane, Cdr W.R., AM, 423–4
Martuba, 586
Massawa, 24, 28, 45, 327–8, 329, 368
Matapan, Cape, 43, 51, 84, 196, 381, 391, 426, 427, 431; Battle of, 235, 236–9, 251, 308–27, 394, 454, 458
Maund, Lt M.R., 184, 191
Maynard, Air V-M F.H., 111, 123, 154, 170–4, 181, 217–18
Medina Bank, 176, 198, 255, 259
Mediterranean Chiefs of Staff, 16–17, 25–31, 48–9, 63, 67, 120, 134, 139–40, 147–9, 152, 243, 245, 265–6, 329–30, 331–2, 338, 351–2, 369–70, 405, 408, 411, 450–1, 470–1, 475–7, 479, 481, 482, 490, 496, 514, 518–25, 530–1, 533–4, 558, 565, 569, 570, 595–7
Mediterranean Fleet, pre-war, 6, 13, 19; staff, 13–14; strength, 21, 30, 31, 32, 35, 36, 40–1, 42, 44, 45, 48, 59, 66, 100, 114–17, 131–3, 149–54, 174–8, 195–200, 207, 248–58, 270, 278, 280–1, 300–03, 346, 351–2, 353, 360, 365–6, 401, 412, 414, 416, 418, 419, 421, 439–40, 454, 457, 469, 470, 473, 477–8, 481–2, 485, 489, 490, 505–6, 508, 509, 520, 528–9, 533, 537–48, 540–8, 551–9, 564, 569, 577, 583, 588–9; strategic role, 18, 23, 26, 31, 48–51, 200–203, 219–21, 291, 552–3; fleet operations, 51, 58–9, 60–2, 67, 69–74, 75–7, 78–85, 97–113, 118–19, 124–5, 128–31, 141–6, 154–8, 162–8, 170–89, 192–203, 209–25, 231–2, 236–9, 242–52, 263, 265, 266–7, 275, 279–80, 289–93, 296–301, 305–7, 308–27, 336–50, 353, 363–4, 367–8, 395–8, 400–4, 409–46, 454, 482–7, 492–5, 498, 511, 512, 515, 527, 532, 534–5, 540–2, 544, 548, 554, 555, 581–2, 585–92; Inshore Squadron, 222, 224–5, 233, 240–1, 261, 264, 268, 279, 281, 283, 287–8, 327, 332, 366, 370, 397–8, 403, 451, 474, 482, 483, 486, 487–8, 494, 532, 542, 587–8;
Minelaying, 78, 235, 236, 274, 277, 295, 301, 333, 339–40, 343, 346, 351, 354, 356, 360, 400, 401, 426, 453, 455, 494, 502, 510, 536–7; Minesweeping, 125, 129, 217, 235, 241, 269, 276, 277, 278, 282, 285–6, 294–7, 305, 331, 332, 367, 396, 397, 399, 400, 402, 403, 407, 417, 455, 466, 504, 515, 517, 532, 560; Submarines, 64, 72, 73, 78, 83, 102, 114, 122–4, 126, 131, 143, 157–8, 170, 173, 203, 210, 217, 221, 234, 235–6, 237, 259, 274, 276, 277, 295, 328, 336, 338, 355, 359, 368, 396, 406, 408, 426, 454–5, 463, 466, 467–8, 469, 473, 474, 478, 481, 486, 488–9, 498, 503, 504–6, 508, 509–10, 512, 516, 518, 526, 532, 542, 548–50, 560, 572–3, 578, 580, 582, 585, 586
Megara, 378, 370, 385, 386
Melos, 411, 412
Merchant Navy, 7, 241, 244, 249, 490, 505, 531, 593–4
Merchant Ships, British and Commonwealth: *Ajax*, 554, 574; *Antenor*, 35; *Araybank*, 382; *Bamora*, 333; *Bantria*, 200; *Breconshire*, 254, 262, 265, 289, 366, 400–04, 461–4, 544, 549–51, 554, 558, 561, 567, 574, 585–93; *Brisbane Star*, 174; *British Lord*, 299; *British Science*, 299; *British Sergeant*, 174; *British Union*, 98; *Cape Horn*, 401; *Chakdina*, 532; *Chakla*, 172–3, 200, 217, 218, 281, 366, 399; *Chantala*, 532; *City of Calcutta*, 554, 574; *City of Canterbury*, 401; *City of Lincoln*, 305; *City of London*, 383, 386, 388, 389; *City of Manchester*, 305; *City of Roubaix*, 331; *Clan Campbell*, 401, 464, 573–5, 585, 587; *Clan Chattan*, 401, 573–4; *Clan Cumming*, 254, 261, 331; *Clan Ferguson*, 162, 554, 574; *Clan Forbes*, 198, 213; *Clan Fraser*, 198, 213, 330–1; *Clan Lamont*, 401; *Clan Macaulay*, 162, 254, 262, 265, 289; *Clan MacDonald*, 254; *Comliebank*, 383, 392; *Cornwall*, 141–3, 199–200; *Cyprian Prince*, 331; *Delane*, 392; *Derwenthall*, 276; *Desmoulea*, 270, 275, 283–4, 399; *Devis*, 174, 199, 211, 298, 328, 331; *Dilwara*, 383, 386, 388, 389; *Dorsetshire*, 275; *Empire Song*, 254, 401, 403; *Essex*, 254, 257, 260, 273, 580; *Ethiopia*, 270; *Fiona*, 171–3, 200, 335; *Georgic*, 496; *Glenearn*, 263, 274, 300, 330, 352, 370, 379, 380, 382, 384, 386, 387, 389, 398; *Glengyle*, 263, 274, 300, 330, 352, 370, 382, 384, 386,

Merchant Ships, British and Commonwealth: *cont.*
389, 398, 413, 425, 438, 443, 461, 482, 563, 567; *Glenorchy*, 111; *Glenroy*, 263, 274, 300, 330, 352, 370, 386, 392, 398, 410, 411, 434, 435, 485, 542; *Helka*, 474; *Homefield*, 298, 328; *Itria*, 383, 393; *Karapara*, 397–8; *Kirkland*, 101, 382, 385; *Knight of Malta*, 101, 217; *Lanarkshire*, 162, 211; *Leinster*, 498; *Levernbank*, 270; *Masirah*, 101; *Memnon*, 162; *Myriel*, 217; *Netravati*, 527; *New Zealand Star*, 198, 401, 403; *Northern Prince*, 272, 298, 328; *Pampas*, 464, 585–7, 591; *Pass of Balmaha*, 174, 487–8, 500, 531, 533; *Perthshire*, 305; *Queen Mary*, 497, 539; *Ranee*, 278; *Ranpura*, 35; *Ratnagiri*, 527; *Rawnsley*, 401; *Retriever*, 333; *Rosaura*, 290; *Rowallan Castle*, 563, 573–4; *Runo*, 382; *Salween*, 383, 389; *Scottish Prince*, 386; *Settler*, 401; *Sydney Star*, 554; *Thurland Castle*, 383, 385, 386, 392; *Toneline*, 531, 532; *Ulster Prince*, 196, 200, 281, 377–9, 382, 384, 385; *Vita*, 333, 365; *Volo*, 142, 163, 165, 174, 199; *Waiwera*, 174, 199, 211; *Zeeland*, 101, 382, 385; Other nations: *Adana*, 347–50; *Adinda*, 174, 279; *Adriatico*, 548; *Aegina*, 347–50; *Aghios Georgios*, 277–8; *Alberta*, 486; *Amerika*, 340; *Antiklia*, 488; *Arta*, 347–50, 398; *Atid*, 217; *Athos II*, 135; *Bainsizza*, 398; *Belray*, 383; *Capitano A. Cecchi*, 402; *Citta di Messina*, 259; *Corinthia*, 383, 393; *Costa Rica*, 383, 386, 388, 389; *Coulouris Xenos*, 298, 328; *El Nil*, 101; *Elenora Maersk*, 383; *Farouk*, 217; *Fawzia*, 217; *Giuseppina Ghirhardi*, 486; *Hellas*, 378; *Hoegh Hood*, 211, 215; *Ionia*, 383, 393; *Iserlohn*, 347–50; *Juventus*, 284; *Khedive Ismail*, 383, 386–9; *Laura Corrado*, 328; *Lesbos*, 500, 504; *Liguria*, 98; *Liria*, 512; *Lussino*, 503; *Manzoni*, 98; *Marie Maersk*, 298, 306, 333; *Miranda*, 488; *Neptunia*, 510; *Nicholas Embiricos*, 298; *Novasli*, 101; *Oceania*, 510; *Organkar*, 78; *Patria*, 199; *Pennland*, 378, 385; *Pericles*, 307; *Providence*, 135; *Rodi*, 101, 174, 199, 279; *Rokos*, 385; *St Didier*, 492; *Sabaudia*, 347–50; *Sagona*, 551–3; *Slamat*, 377, 379, 383, 384, 386–8, 390; *Solheim*, 298;
Sollum, 272; *Steel Seafarer*, 507; *Talabot*, 464, 585, 587, 591; *Tarifa*, 527; *Tenace*, 402; *Teti*, 298, 328; *Themoni*, 382, 385; *Theophile Gautier*, 516; *Thermopylae*, 401; *Victoria*, 567; *Vulcania*, 510; *Zamzan*, 201
Mers-el-Kebir, 42, 55, 57
Mersa Matruh, 133, 140, 152, 210, 217, 275, 330, 333, 334, 337, 474, 482, 485, 504, 513, 517, 532
Mersin, 531
Messina, 78, 108, 114, 153, 156, 213, 255, 547, 548, 574, 582, 585; Straits of, 80, 108, 122, 157, 171, 455, 532, 549, 573
Metaxas, Gen I., 171
Micklethwaite, Capt StJ. A., 577, 585
Middle East, 15, 18, 19, 33–4, 36, 39, 55, 89, 111, 116, 120, 131, 150, 169, 222, 233, 274, 295, 304, 337, 358, 395, 396, 401, 415, 450, 471, 497, 507, 512, 513, 521, 523, 525, 555–6, 595–7
Miers, V-Adm A.C.C., VC, 236, 582
Milo, 47, 315, 386, 387, 393, 429, 430, 431
Milos, 382
Misurata, 259, 277, 532
Mitchell, Cdr, 378
Mitchell, Air C.M. Sir W., 16–17, 25, 28–9, 31, 36–7
Mitylene, 486
Mobile Naval Base Defence Organisation, 27, 295, 369–70, 401, 420, 425, 446, 531
Mombasa, 515
Monemvasia, 378–80, 385–8, 391, 392
Moore, Adm Sir H., 14, 562
Morea, The, 375, 376
Morford, Lt(A) W.D., 186, 191
Morse, R-Adm J.A.V., 279, 385, 386, 387, 391, 393, 394, 424, 435, 442, 499, 502
Mountbatten, Adm of F Earl, 249, 301, 359, 404, 406, 430, 433, 434, 479
Mulo Island, 572
Murray, Lt(A) J.B., 185, 191
Mussolini, Benito, 16, 21, 45, 55, 57, 63, 231
Myli, 378, 379

Nahr-el-Kelb, 487
Naples, 62, 173, 211, 213, 217–20, 255, 259 302, 578
Narrows, The (Sicily), 60, 197–8, 206, 213, 215, 225, 226, 235, 264, 270, 337, 339, 403
Narvik, 43, 46

INDEX

Nauplia, 377–80, 382, 384–8
Naval Review, The, 9
Navarin, 536, 537
Neale, Sub-Lt(A) J.W., 182–3, 189
Nelson, Adm Lord, 13, 18, 58, 234, 457, 471–2
Netherlands, The, 370, 379, 457
New Zealand, 83, 378, 380, 418, 457, 501, 561
Newall, M of RAF Sir C., 24
Newfoundland, 303, 481
Nicholls, Lt-Cdr O.E., 29
Nicolson, Capt H.StL., 79, 118–19, 128, 176, 181, 211, 315, 318, 321, 401, 576–7
Nicosia, 482, 492
Nile, River, 236, 521
Nio, 393
Noble, Adm Sir P., 22
Norman, Capt H.G., 154
North America & West Indies Station, 5
North Sea, 35, 36, 121
Norway, 43, 231, 251, 412, 415
Nyon Convention, 113

O'Connor, Gen Sir R., 63–4, 218, 224
O'Donnell, Capt G.E.M., 77, 497
Odend'hal, Adm J.E. (French Navy), 44
Oerlikon Gun, 500, 505
Ollive, Adm E.L.H. (French Navy), 25, 26–7
Operations, ABSTENTION, 289–93, 299–300; ACROBAT, 554, 565; AGGRESSION, 532, 542; APPROACH, 542; BARBARITY, 193; BATTLEAXE, 451, 485, 486; BONNET, 128–9, 132, 150; CHURCH, 171; COAT-JUDGMENT, 60–2, 174–89; COLLAR, 195–200, 213; CRACK, 575; CRUSADER, 451, 453, 468, 514, 515, 518, 519, 522, 524, 528–9, 536; CULTIVATE, 334, 517; DEMON, 243–4, 370–96, 397, 399, 424; DUNLOP, 357, 360, 395; EXCESS, 209, 213, 231–2, 236, 253–9, 263, 272; HALBERD, 454, 461, 507, 509, 511; HATS, 59, 126, 128, 132, 133, 141–6, 150; JAGUAR, 396; LUSTRE, 236, 242–3, 296–301, 302, 305, 308, 327, 328–33, 354, 396, 399, 412; MANDIBLES, 206–7, 242, 283, 296, 300, 352; PEDESTAL, 465; SALIENT, 365–6; SHELFORD, 283; SUBSTANCE, 454, 461, 498; SUPERCHARGE, 334, 517; TIGER, 236, 245, 355, 357, 360, 395, 396, 397, 399, 400–04, 406, 421, 480; TORCH, 471; TREACLE, 334, 502; WHIPCORD, 450–1, 518–25; WINCH, 346, 395; WORKSHOP, 204–9, 242, 263, 274
Opie, Lt-Cdr, U.S.N., 141
Oran, 88, 89, 90, 94, 97, 169, 326
Ortona, 513
Ostend Raid, 5
Otranto, Straits of, 50, 60, 78, 158, 175, 191–2, 197, 214

Pact of Steel, 15
Paine, Actg Sub-Lt S.M., 185, 191
Palermo, 27, 355
Palestine, 76, 82, 381, 382, 394, 449, 491, 494, 544
Palliser, Adm Sir A., 213
Pantelleria, 160, 204–09, 216, 242, 256, 264, 548
Paramythia, 327
Patch, Maj O., RM, 137, 184–5, 191
Patras, 578
Pearl Harbor, 62
Pegadia Bay, 144
Pelly, Air C.M. Sir C., 437
Peloponnese, 244
Perkins, Temp Sub-Lt(A) E.A., 187, 190
Persian Gulf, 515, 517, 596
Petain, Marshal H.P., 56, 82
Phalconera, 193, 427
Phaleron Bay, 332
Phleva Island, 333
Pipon, V-Adm Sir J., 267–8, 282, 295
Piraeus, 60, 174, 193, 194, 196, 200, 210, 216, 221, 225, 236, 244, 254, 255, 258, 259, 261, 270, 272, 297, 314, 315, 324, 327, 330–1, 332, 337, 344, 364, 371, 375–6, 378, 426, 499, 530, 578
Plate, River, Battle of, 208
Plymouth, 307
Poland, 451, 502, 504
Poland, Capt A.L., 275, 281, 283, 366
Pori Island, 432
Port Laki, 195–6, 199
Port Maltezana, 157, 170, 172
Port St Nikolo, 386
Port Said, 24, 27, 46, 50, 76, 81, 98, 102, 128, 132, 147, 149, 151, 152, 170, 171, 174, 193, 200, 225, 272, 278, 329, 340, 365, 399, 401, 407, 419, 479, 482, 504, 518, 531, 544, 572, 577, 587
Port Sudan, 328, 368
Port Tewfik, 362, 504
Portal, M of RAF Visct, 226, 338, 357, 358, 568–9

619

INDEX

Porto Lago, 165
Portsmouth, 6
Pound, Adm of F Sir Dudley, career, 7, 18, 19; C-in-C, Mediterranean, 7, 19; First Sea Lord, 8, 17–18, 23–36, 154, 477–8, 523, 533, 558; and Churchill, 19–20, 41, 47, 126–8, 150, 204, 208, 239–40, 417, 532, 533; and Cunningham, 7, 8, 18–19, 20, 22–36, 38–43, 45–51, 55, 66, 73–7, 82–4, 87, 109–11, 120–1, 123–9, 150–2, 167–8, 190–2, 204, 208–9, 225–7, 233, 234, 239–40, 241, 243, 247, 249, 250, 262–4, 274–5, 280–1, 282–3, 299–301, 302–4, 307–8, 336–47, 353–6, 359–60, 398–400, 406–7, 409–10, 414–19, 450, 451, 455–6, 458, 466, 475–7, 479–80, 499–500, 503–7, 511–14, 518–19, 526–7, 531–7, 541–6, 555–7, 566–9, 574, 580–1
Power, V-Adm Sir M.L., 14, 237
Pretty, Capt F.C., MN, 141
Pridham-Wippell, Adm Sir H., 66, 102, 108, 109, 144–6, 157, 165–6, 168, 172, 174, 175–6, 177, 193, 196–7, 214, 216, 236–9, 244, 249, 255, 258, 259, 265, 266–7, 282, 306, 308–26, 370–94, 400, 404, 405, 458–9, 510, 540, 559, 583

Quarnero, Gulf of, 277
Queen's Royal Regt, 434

Radar (RDF, inc. ASV), 7, 17, 21, 59, 61, 62, 66, 115, 125, 141, 158, 165, 167, 168, 178, 194, 200, 201, 238, 253, 255, 262, 263, 269, 280, 306, 311, 321, 406, 407, 429, 446, 467, 469, 502, 507, 517–18, 550, 551, 553, 558, 572, 577
Ramsay, Adm Sir B., 8
Raphena Cove, 390
Raphina, 386, 387
Raphtis, 382, 384, 386, 388, 389
Ras Amer, 158
Ras-el-Tin, 201
Raschid Ali, 403
Raw, Capt S.M., 506, 578
Rawlings, Adm Sir B., 172, 178, 193, 210, 211, 217, 220, 221, 247–8, 259, 265, 266, 315, 404, 423, 424, 432–4, 437, 439–41, 459, 490, 495, 511, 540, 554
Raz Azzaz, 217
Razikostikas, Capt (Greek Navy), 374
Red Cross, 291
Red Sea, 18, 48–9, 65, 73, 75, 79, 81, 111, 115, 117, 127, 132, 148–50, 252, 329, 368, 407, 408, 449, 456, 505, 507, 508, 511, 512, 514, 539–40, 595–6
Renouf, V-Adm E. de F., 46, 84, 109, 125, 181, 209–10, 216, 256, 258, 263, 289, 290, 291, 292, 299, 301
Renton, Col, 378
Reserve Fleet, 22, 24, 28, 31
Retimo, 418, 420, 425, 427, 428
Rhodes, 28, 78, 129, 145, 213, 242, 249, 264, 273, 274, 275, 279, 280, 292–3, 346, 492, 581–2
Richmond, Adm Sir H., 472
Rio de Janeiro, 38
Roberts, Lt P.S.W., VC, 579
Robertson, Lt-Cdr, 380
Robson, Cdr W.G.A., 423–4
Rome, 81, 302
Rommel, F-M E., 231, 234, 239, 451, 455, 468, 469, 470
Roosevelt, President F.D., 358, 456
Rosyth, 514
Roumania, 15, 39
Royal Air Force, strength, 17, 37, 60, 65, 116–17, 120, 121, 122, 125, 221, 240, 242–3, 245, 360, 362–3, 365, 395–7, 414–16, 537–8, 547, 560, 568–9; naval co-operation, 17, 19, 25, 33, 37, 47, 55, 58–61, 69, 79, 81, 98, 102–3, 108, 109, 120, 128–31, 133, 137, 147–9, 152, 153–4, 159–62, 169–75, 178–9, 181, 188, 193, 201, 202–3, 210–13, 217–19, 225–7, 233, 236–9, 240, 241, 243, 255, 259, 261, 265, 266, 268, 271, 276, 283, 285, 287–8, 296, 300, 306, 310, 314, 315, 318–19, 323, 324, 325, 328–9, 330, 332, 335, 338, 351, 353, 354, 357–8, 365, 367, 368, 369, 373, 374, 377, 383, 384, 389, 395, 396, 398–9, 405, 407, 409–16, 418–21, 426, 427, 436, 437, 440, 441–44, 451–3, 454, 455, 456, 465, 467, 474, 476–7, 478, 480–1, 482, 484, 485, 488, 491–4, 496, 498–9, 501, 504, 506–116, 523, 526, 527, 533, 536, 538, 542, 545–7, 550, 551, 553, 556–7, 558–9, 562, 563–5, 566, 567, 568–9, 570–3, 575, 577, 578, 579, 581–2, 586–7, 589, 592, 595–7
Royal Australian Navy, 32–3, 41, 75, 76, 118–19, 132, 457, 503
Royal Marines, 27, 289, 290, 420, 439, 446
Royal Naval Air Service, 16
Royal Navy, 3–4, 17, 18, 61, 90, 241, 244, 345–6, 351, 490, 561

Saida, 484
Salamis, 332; Straits of, 331, 332, 333

INDEX

Salonika, 32, 33, 46, 286, 330, 333, 381; Gulf of, 434, 478, 494
San Giorgio Island, 165, 261, 516
Sansego Island, 277
Sapienza, 81
Sardinia, 114, 204, 259, 520, 523
Sarra, Sub-Lt(A) W.C., 185, 190
Saseno Island, 214
Savona, 27
Scapa Flow, 150, 307
Scarlett, Lt(O) N.J., 182, 189
Scarpanto, 144, 213, 249–50, 263, 280, 409, 412, 428, 437, 440
Sea Transport Dept, 222
Sephton, P/O A.E., VC, 544
Sfax, 88, 89
Shatt-el-Arab, 403, 407
Shaw, Pay-Capt A.P., 14
Shipping, 81–2, 98, 112, 125–8, 209, 220, 241, 267, 269–70, 286, 298–9, 362, 364, 365, 373, 376, 407, 450, 495, 511, 589
Sicily, 26, 27, 28, 31, 71, 81, 84, 114, 126, 141, 160, 170, 173, 195, 201, 212, 216, 232, 253, 262, 264, 295, 336, 344, 351, 361, 417, 450, 518–25, 529, 533, 563, 571, 574
Sidi Barrani, 152, 169, 201, 210, 573
Sidon, 483
Sidra, Gulf of, 274
Sim, Capt E.W.B., 549
Simpson, R-Adm G.W.G., 474, 572, 580
Singapore, 15, 22, 27, 32, 43, 121
Sirte, 1st Battle of, 250, 460, 461–2, 549–51, 558; 2nd Battle of, 250, 460, 463–5, 585–92
Sitia, 156, 425
Slatter, Air M Sir L., 453, 533, 545, 559, 568
Slattery, Capt M.S., 583–4
Skelton, Lt(A) R.G., 187, 190
Slaughter, Lt H.J., 186, 191
Smith, Lt-Gen Sir A., 476
Smith-Dorrien, Col G.H.G., 379
Smuts, F-M J.C., 300
Smyrna, 386
Sollum, 65, 129, 210, 211, 217, 218, 222, 235, 264, 266, 269, 274, 275, 276, 279, 294, 330, 333, 366, 485
Somaliland, 127, 595
Somerville, Adm of F. Sir James, 3, 6, 8, 9, 19, 41, 57, 85, 132, 192, 195–200, 250, 401, 458, 479–80, 555, 577
Somerville, Cdr John, 13, 480
Somerville, Lt-Cdr P., 423–4

South Africa, 457, 532, 541
Soviet Union, 15, 32–3, 39–40, 56, 450, 465, 489, 494, 497, 500, 506, 519, 520, 521, 524, 560, 576
Spain, 55, 75, 84, 113, 114, 280
Sparke, Sub-Lt(A) P.D.J., 182, 189
Spezia, 62, 157, 213
Sphakia, 413, 420, 437, 442, 443
Stampalia, 155, 157, 170, 213, 280, 427
Stevens-Guille, Capt G.F., 146
Stokes, Capt G.H., 547–8
Suda Bay, 47, 50, 55, 60, 65, 70, 172–8, 190–1, 193–4, 196–200, 206, 209–11, 213, 216, 221, 235, 236, 244–5, 255, 258, 259, 261, 270, 273, 275, 279, 285, 290, 292, 295, 296, 298, 299, 304, 307, 315, 324, 325, 331, 333, 353, 362, 364, 366, 368, 369, 382, 383, 385, 386, 388–94, 396, 398, 399, 401, 405 407, 418, 420, 424, 425, 434, 435, 442, 444, 446, 496, 516, 578, 579
Sudan, 266
Suez, 18, 127, 132, 168, 278, 294, 327, 341, 479, 497, 498, 504, 505, 507, 508, 510, 512, 515, 527–8, 539, 578
Suez Canal, 18, 45, 48, 50, 65, 75, 76, 89, 173, 232, 235, 242, 244, 260–1, 267–8, 274, 276, 278–80, 282, 285–6, 294–7, 300, 327–8, 407, 455, 469, 497, 504, 511, 512, 515, 524
Sutton, Lt(A) W.F., 186, 190
Swayne, Lt(A) H.L.A., 183–4, 189
Syria and Lebanon, 34, 81, 89, 98, 122, 203, 252, 341, 408, 415, 419, 449–50, 453, 474, 475–6, 477, 479, 482–7, 489, 490, 491–5, 498, 499, 502, 517, 544

Takoradi, 233, 280, 358, 395, 560
Taranto, 28, 31, 50, 58, 78, 103, 104, 114, 126, 153, 156, 162, 170–2, 174, 213, 219, 501, 548, 549, 564, 573, 582, 585; Fleet Air Arm raid on, 60–2, 174, 174–90, 200, 202, 220, 458
Taurus Mountains, 524
Tedder, M of RAF Lord, 233, 240, 410, 413, 452–3, 470, 476–7, 478, 481, 482, 496, 499, 499, 530–1, 537, 556, 558, 568, 569
Teheran, 489
Tenedos, 157
Teppeleni, 285
Thermopylae, 373
Thrace, 32, 33, 36
Tinos, 136
Tmimi, 586

Tobruk, 31, 50, 69, 79, 98, 162, 202, 210, 222, 226, 231, 232, 235, 241, 251, 259, 261, 263, 264, 266, 268, 269, 271, 272, 275, 277–9, 281–4, 287–9, 293, 294, 299, 329–36, 352, 362, 365, 366, 368, 370, 397–9, 402, 419, 451, 454, 456, 457, 474, 476, 481, 482, 485–8, 490, 494, 502, 504, 508, 509, 511, 515, 518, 520–2, 531–3, 542, 544, 547, 548, 555, 558–9, 572, 574, 575, 578, 585, 586
Tolmeita, 329
Tolon, 386–8
Torrens-Spence, Lt F.M.A., 186, 190, 310
Toulon, 42, 135, 408
Tovey, Adm of F Lord, 14, 35, 36, 41, 79, 84, 100, 102, 106, 110, 122, 145, 168, 169
Tower, R-Adm I.B.B., 168
Trans-Jordan, 491
Trapani, 255, 328
Trieste, 85, 152
Tripoli (Africa), 19, 153, 162, 195, 197, 199, 201, 202, 211, 215, 218, 233, 239–40, 255, 273, 276, 277, 281, 294, 295, 331, 336–55, 358, 359, 363–4, 365, 366, 396, 408, 450, 455, 467, 477, 509, 519–21, 523, 524, 526, 551, 552, 556, 558, 564, 565, 566, 577–8, 581
Tripoli (Levant), 531, 572
Troubridge, R-Adm E.C.T., 208
Tunisia, 51, 153, 171, 221, 268, 276, 277, 285, 293, 328, 343, 354, 520, 523
Turkey, 14, 15, 29, 32–4, 36–43, 51, 65, 76, 77, 125, 147, 168, 194, 203, 206, 207, 242, 263, 274, 486, 495, 497, 500, 520, 521, 524, 546
Turle, R-Adm C.E., 98, 173, 209, 285, 323, 333, 374, 375
Tymbaki, 425, 427, 434, 435
Tyrwhitt, Adm of F Sir R., 4, 5, 8

United Kingdom, resources, 14, 116, 296, 298, 513–14, 560; strategy, 14–16, 18, 20, 25, 34, 40, 48, 55–7, 75, 233, 239, 242, 341, 344, 356, 410, 415, 418, 518–25, 536, 562
United States, 43, 56, 89, 153, 232, 243, 249, 250, 264, 302, 350, 358, 360, 456, 490, 499, 504, 507, 511, 530, 584
UP Rockets, 146

Valletta, 235
Valona, 177, 212, 214, 327, 368
Van Ryneveld, Gen P. (South Africa), 300
Vian, Adm of F Sir P., 459–60, 461–4, 482–3, 548, 549–51, 558, 573–5, 584, 585–92

Waller, Capt H.M.L., RAN, 217, 260, 315, 321, 401, 433, 443, 483, 503
Wanklyn, Lt-Cdr M.D., VC, 236
War Office, 139, 147, 204, 410
Warburton-Lee, Capt B.A., VC, 37–8
Warships: British: BATTLESHIPS: *Anson*, 477; *Barham*, 22, 30, 115, 116, 128, 133, 150, 153, 174–7, 190, 193, 209, 210, 223–4, 239–40, 250, 305, 315, 317, 318, 322, 342, 344–6, 353, 355–6, 400, 416, 419, 425, 435, 454, 456–8, 468, 475, 478, 511, 540, 542–4; *Malaya*, 22, 30, 43, 44, 49, 51, 75, 77, 80, 99, 102, 106–10, 115, 124, 128–30, 132, 142, 144, 150, 157, 162, 162, 168, 170, 172, 175, 176, 196, 197, 209, 211–15, 225, 254, 539, 543; *Nelson*, 22, 351, 353; *Queen Elizabeth*, 22, 61, 280–1, 342, 355, 356, 360, 400, 403, 404, 425, 435, 454, 457, 458, 475, 477, 540, 551–9; *Prince of Wales*, 453; 'R' class, 77, 115, 539; *Ramillies*, 22, 23, 30, 42, 46, 49, 101, 109, 116, 128, 129, 130–1, 133, 152, 157, 162, 163, 168, 172, 175–8, 195–7; *Resolution*, 22; *Revenge*, 22; *Rodney*, 6, 18, 22, 351, 353; *Royal Oak*, 22, 30; *Royal Sovereign*, 22, 43, 44, 99, 101–2, 106–10, 116, 128, 133; *Valiant*, 22, 59, 115–17, 124, 128, 141, 143, 144, 146, 151, 155–6, 162, 165–6, 172, 176, 193, 196, 209–11, 214, 223–5, 236, 254, 256–8, 305, 309, 315, 317, 318, 321, 355, 400, 426, 431, 432, 454, 457, 458, 475, 477, 511, 515, 540, 543, 551–9; *Warspite*, 22, 31, 42–4, 51, 75, 77, 90, 99, 100–10, 112, 115, 124, 128–31, 142, 145, 155–6, 162, 165–6, 172, 176, 196, 211, 213–16, 223–4, 232, 250, 254, 257, 258, 260, 261, 267, 305, 310–11, 312, 315, 317, 318, 320–2, 394, 400, 416, 424, 426, 431, 432, 457, 458, 475, 478, 490, 499, 529, 543–4, 559; BATTLECRUISERS: *Renown*, 199, 254; *Repulse*, 453, 543; AIRCRAFT CARRIERS: *Argus*, 117, 121, 395; *Ark Royal*, 59, 197, 199, 250, 254, 280, 303, 395, 456, 461, 529, 533; *Eagle*, 49, 51, 58, 61, 62, 72, 74, 76, 81, 82, 99, 100–11, 114, 115, 117, 124, 136, 142–5, 148, 152, 157, 162, 165, 170, 172, 176, 179, 181, 191, 193, 196, 197, 199, 218, 223, 232, 261, 267, 273, 275, 277, 282, 300, 327–8, 329, 368, 529; *Formidable*, 232, 236–9, 249–50, 275, 282, 296, 300, 302, 305, 309, 310,

INDEX

312, 315, 317–19, 321–6, 394, 400, 404, 409, 410, 412, 416, 421, 426, 440, 453, 454, 457, 475, 478, 480, 499, 528–9, 533, 555; *Furious*, 280, 358, 395; *Glorious*, 31, 33; *Hermes*, 329; *Illustrious*, 48, 49, 59, 61. 62, 66, 74, 111, 115–17, 120, 132, 141, 144–6, 151, 152, 155–6, 162, 165, 166, 172, 176–89, 196, 196, 199, 202, 210–15, 224, 225, 231–2, 250, 253–7, 259–62, 265–9, 271, 273, 274, 282, 283, 300, 303, 457, 528–9, 533, 555; *Indomitable*, 457, 529, 555; *Victorious*, 395; CRUISERS: *Ajax*, 60, 153, 157, 162, 163–7, 172–74, 176, 178, 193, 200, 216, 255, 270, 292, 315, 324, 331, 381, 382, 388–94, 400, 402, 417, 419, 422, 426, 427, 429–31, 433–5, 440, 475, 482, 495, 511, 551, 554, 558, 578–9; *Aurora*, 514, 549–52, 580, 592; *Berwick*, 174–8, 181, 190, 193, 195–7; *Birmingham*, 38; *Bonaventure*, 254, 256, 259, 291, 292, 298, 306, 323, 324, 332; 'C' class, 33, 75, 76; *Calcutta*, 5, 144, 157, 162, 163, 170, 172–4, 196, 197, 199, 215, 254, 256, 331, 382, 384, 387–8, 399, 401, 403, 404, 419, 420, 428, 431, 438, 443, 446, 475, 480; *Caledon*, 69, 109, 342, 345; *Calypso*, 69, 71, 73; *Capetown*, 109; *Carlisle*, 111, 115, 301, 315, 383, 386, 393, 403, 404, 428, 429, 431, 463, 475, 480, 507–8, 512, 514, 527–8, 549, 554, 573, 585–7, 589, 592; *Cleopatra*, 571, 575, 579, 583–6, 588; *Coventry*, 157, 162–3, 165, 167, 170, 172–4, 177, 193, 196, 197, 210, 219, 301, 383, 385, 386, 389, 399, 403, 404, 410, 425, 434, 438, 443, 446, 475, 482, 507–8, 512; 'D' class, 33; *Despatch*, 5, 199; *Dido*, 248, 250, 365, 401, 403, 404, 416, 417, 422, 425, 427, 429–31, 435, 438, 440, 441, 475, 554, 558, 574, 581–2, 585, 588; *Euryalus*, 540, 549, 574, 581–2, 585, 586, 588; *Exeter*, 110, 115, 263, 307, 360; *Fiji*, 360, 401, 404, 416, 422–5, 427, 431–3, 475, 480, 569; *Fox*, 4; *Galatea*, 456, 507, 512, 540, 549; *Glasgow*, 65, 174–7, 181, 193, 196–9, 209, 220, 225, 260, 305; *Gloucester*, 49, 69, 73, 102, 104, 111, 124, 125, 142, 155–7, 161–2, 165, 172, 176, 181, 193, 196, 199, 209, 211, 216, 232, 254, 256, 258, 261, 264, 269, 289, 291, 309, 315, 317, 324–6, 354, 356, 366, 397, 399, 401, 407, 416, 422–3, 425, 427,

431, 432, 475, 480; *Kent*, 130, 133, 142, 149, 153; *Liverpool*, 46, 49, 73, 84, 102, 106, 124, 125, 142, 155–7, 162, 164–8, 194, 304, 337; *Manchester*, 195, 197–9; *Naiad*, 360, 401, 404, 425, 426, 428, 430–2, 456, 463, 475, 487, 493, 495, 507, 512, 540, 549, 574; 579–80, 584; *Neptune*, 79, 104, 106, 109, 127, 360, 407, 511, 540, 550, 551–2, 558, 561; *Newcastle*, 195, 196; *Orion*, 79, 106, 109, 141, 144–5, 155, 157, 162, 164, 166, 168, 170, 172, 174, 177, 193, 197, 213, 216, 248, 255, 258, 315, 324, 326, 366, 382, 383, 385–9, 391–3, 400, 407, 416, 422, 426, 427, 429–33, 438, 440, 441, 475, 487; *Penelope*, 514, 541, 549, 551–2, 567, 574, 576, 586–7, 591–3; *Phoebe*, 377, 382, 384–6, 389–91, 393, 394, 403, 404, 425, 443, 445, 475, 482, 495; *Sheffield*, 199, 254; *Southampton*, 195, 197–9, 232, 253, 256, 258, 262–4, 271; *York*, 110, 115, 125, 153, 155–6, 162, 164–5, 172, 176, 177–8, 180, 193, 196, 210, 211, 216, 255, 258, 263, 269, 279, 280, 307, 366, 392; DESTROYERS: *Airedale*, 589; *Arrow*, 554, 572, 574, 576, 577; *Avon Vale*, 512, 527, 573, 574, 576, 586–8, 592; *Beaufort*, 573, 575, 585–6, 589, 592; 'D' class, 35, 131, 145; *Dainty*, 69, 79, 85, 102, 142, 149, 157, 162, 193, 197, 210, 211, 216, 216, 254, 270, 275, 289, 299; *Decoy*, 69, 73, 79, 101, 144, 145, 157, 162, 163, 166, 171, 176–7, 198, 201, 273, 289–93, 382, 383, 385–7, 391, 397, 426, 433, 440, 441, 475, 503, 511, 540, 549–51, 574, 577; *Defender*, 102, 149, 157, 162, 162–3, 165, 171, 173, 176–7, 198, 211, 254, 258, 306, 315, 323, 324, 331, 335, 382, 383, 385, 386, 388, 389, 391, 393, 397, 434, 435, 443; *Diamond*, 85, 101, 104, 142, 149, 157, 174, 193, 200, 211, 254, 256, 258, 289, 379, 383, 385, 386, 388–90; *Dulverton*, 573, 575, 585–6, 589, 592; *Encounter*, 366–7; *Eridge*, 512, 527, 573, 574, 585–7, 589, 592; *Farndale*, 589; *Faulknor*, 177; *Foresight*, 403; *Fortune*, 177, 571, 574, 575, 577; *Foxhound*, 554, 577; *Fury*, 177; *Gallant*, 146, 193, 210, 211, 254, 256–8, 263, 264, 367, 588; *Grenville*, 38; *Greyhound*, 146, 193, 211, 216, 218, 254, 258, 301, 315, 321–3, 329, 416, 422–4, 427, 431, 432, 475, 480;

Warships: British: *cont.*
Griffin, 146, 193, 198, 218, 254, 256, 258, 315, 322–4, 329, 333, 380, 381, 383, 385, 386, 389–92, 401, 426, 431, 475, 483, 540, 572, 574, 576, 577; *Gurkha*, 539, 554; 'H' class, 128; *Hardy*, 37; *Hasty*, 37, 79, 102, 118–20, 155, 157, 162, 163, 181, 210, 211, 257, 292, 306, 307, 324–6, 382, 383, 385, 386, 389, 391, 391, 394, 427, 429, 435, 443, 475, 540, 549, 574, 576, 577, 581–2, 585, 588; *Havock*, 79, 109, 118–20, 149, 154, 157, 162, 164–5, 170, 176, 181, 215, 216, 289, 305, 306, 312, 315, 322–4, 379, 382, 383, 385, 386, 388–94, 401–3, 475, 549–52, 572, 574, 577, 581–2, 585–8, 593; *Hereward*, 79, 101, 125, 145, 155, 162, 163, 164, 166, 198, 210, 211, 256, 258, 289, 290, 306, 315, 324, 383, 386, 389, 391, 393, 394, 401, 420, 426, 427, 429, 438, 440–1, 475; *Hero*, 37, 79, 101, 118–20, 125, 129, 155, 163, 165, 170, 177, 210, 211, 257, 258, 289, 291, 292, 331, 333, 383, 386, 389, 391–3, 401, 426, 427, 433, 435, 475, 482, 511, 517, 572, 576, 577, 581–2, 585, 588; *Heythrop*, 572, 573, 576, 585; *Hostile*, 37, 79, 85, 102, 132; *Hotspur*, 146, 198, 289, 305, 315, 381, 383, 386, 388, 390, 391, 392–4, 401, 402, 403, 426, 437, 440–1, 443, 475, 482, 483, 511, 540, 577; 'Hunt' class, 7, 43, 405, 457, 463, 508, 577, 590; *Hurworth*, 572, 575, 585–6, 589, 592; *Hyperion*, 79, 102, 118–20, 129, 155, 162, 163, 170, 176, 181, 193, 211, 212, 215–16, 225; *Ilex*, 79–80, 102, 118–20, 129, 129, 144, 145, 149, 155, 162, 163, 171, 176, 181, 210, 211, 212, 215–16, 225–6, 254, 307, 315, 325, 401, 428, 430, 475, 482; *Imperial*, 79–80, 102, 109, 125, 145–6, 149, 155, 162, 167, 366, 401–3, 426, 427, 437, 440–1, 475; *Isis*, 380, 386, 388, 390–3, 401, 426, 427, 475, 482, 483; 'J' class, 97, 347, 368; *Jackal*, 365, 397, 430, 433, 440, 445, 475, 482, 483, 492, 493, 512, 540, 577, 588; *Jaguar*, 253, 256, 259, 279, 292, 315, 323, 329, 366, 401, 434, 435, 443, 444, 475, 483, 487, 550–3, 572, 577, 589; *Janus*, 102, 144, 146, 155, 162, 165, 170, 199, 210, 211, 215–16, 254–8, 279, 315, 329, 331, 347–50, 366, 426, 427, 429, 435, 443, 475, 482, 483, 492–3, 577, 589; *Javelin*, 577; *Jersey*, 365, 397; *Jervis*, 77, 101, 125, 142, 142, 155, 162, 165, 170, 193, 210, 211, 215, 218, 254, 258, 279, 315, 331, 347–50, 366, 401, 428, 430, 435, 443, 475, 511, 540, 549, 551–3, 572, 574, 577, 580, 585, 588; *Juno*, 102, 129, 142, 155, 162, 165, 170, 199, 210, 211, 215, 218, 247, 258, 315, 319, 323, 366, 401, 422, 425–9, 475; *Jupiter*, 511; 'K' class, 131; *Kandahar*, 383, 386, 389, 391–3, 401, 423–8, 432–3, 435, 442–3, 444, 475, 482, 540, 550–3; *Kashmir*, 247, 365, 397, 401, 423, 430, 433, 434, 475; *Kelly*, 365, 397, 404, 423, 430, 433, 434, 475; *Kelvin*, 365, 397, 430, 433, 435, 442, 444, 475, 572, 574, 577, 585, 588; *Khartoum*, 83; *Kimberley*, 383, 389–93, 401, 426, 427, 429, 445, 475, 482, 483, 495, 540, 549, 577; *Kingston*, 383, 386, 389–93, 401, 421, 423–7, 431–3, 475, 487, 511, 540, 549, 554, 577, 579, 585–8; *Kipling*, 365, 397, 401, 430, 433, 434, 475, 511, 517, 540, 549, 574, 577, 580, 585, 588; *Lance*, 539, 549, 551–2, 554, 567, 572, 573, 576, 577; *Legion*, 539, 548, 567, 574, 576, 577, 581, 586–8, 591; *Lively*, 539, 541, 549, 551–2, 554, 567, 574, 577, 580–2, 585–6, 588; *Maori*, 539, 547–8, 554, 567, 575; *Mohawk*, 101–2, 125, 144, 145, 149, 149, 155–6, 170, 175, 177, 193, 199, 211, 218, 254, 256, 258, 279, 315, 317, 319, 331, 347–50; *Nubian*, 79–80, 101, 107, 144, 145, 149, 149, 155, 162, 163, 165, 165, 175, 193, 199, 210, 218, 254, 258, 292, 315, 317, 319, 347–50, 383, 386, 388, 389, 391, 393, 394, 409, 412, 425–7, 475, 589; 'S' class, 27, 43; *Scorpion*, 5; *Seafire*, 5; *Sikh*, 539, 547–8, 574, 577, 581–2, 585, 588; *Southwold*, 573, 575, 585–6, 588; *Termagant*, 5; 'Tribal' class, 97, 128, 135, 160–1, 539; 'V' & 'W' classes, 75, 131; *Wallace*, 5; *Wryneck*, 149, 162–3, 165, 170, 172, 210, 328, 379, 383, 385, 386, 388, 389–90; *Zulu*, 539, 563, 567, 574, 577, 580, 581–2, 585, 588;
SUBMARINES: *Cachalot*, 56; *Grampus*, 24, 78; 'O', 'P' & 'R' classes, 64, 124, 210, 406, 506; *Odin*, 78, 85; *Olympus*, 338; *Orpheus*, 78, 85; *Osiris*, 158; *Oswald*, 78, 122–3; *Otus*, 544; P31, 563; P32, 508; P33, 508; P36, 574–5, 578; P38, 578; P39, 591; *Pandora*, 78, 126, 158, 259; *Parthian*, 143, 211, 289; *Phoenix*, 78, 102; *Porpoise*, 537, 571; *Proteus*, 78, 157, 553; *Rainbow*, 143,

INDEX

157, 170; *Regent*, 157, 259, 368, 520; *Regulus*, 221; *Rorqual*, 24, 78, 157, 210, 235, 274, 277, 328, 426, 434; *Rover*, 157, 259, 276, 277, 315, 338; 'S' class, 506; 'T' class, 66, 170, 210, 235–6; *Talisman*, 516, 550; *Tempest*, 578; *Tetrarch*, 157–8, 276, 277; *Thorn*, 572; *Thrasher*, 579; *Thunderbolt*, 509, 573; *Torbay*, 236, 486, 582; *Triad*, 158, 170; *Triton*, 157–8, 221; *Triumph*, 277, 315, 402, 512–13; *Truant*, 158, 217, 277; *Turbulent*, 236; 'U' class, 66, 170, 210, 234, 235, 368, 455; *Unbeaten*, 509–10, 549–50, 578; *Unique*, 277, 549, 564; *Upholder*, 236, 276, 398, 503, 509–10, 530, 578; *Upright*, 277, 509–10, 549; *Urge*, 408, 548–9; *Ursula*, 277, 328, 509–10; *Usk*, 277; *Utmost*, 277, 328, 549–50; ESCORT VESSELS & MINESWEEPERS: *Abingdon*, 174, 367, 560, 580; *Auckland*, 299, 335, 383, 389, 391–3, 401, 425, 434, 435, 487–8, 490; *Bagshot*, 332; *Delphinium*, 531; *Enchantress*, 22; *Erica*, 531; *Falmouth*, 527; *Fareham*, 172, 287–8, 531; *Flamingo*, 383, 386, 389, 401, 434, 488, 494, 512, 527, 532; *Gloxinia*, 195, 198, 277, 332, 403; *Grimsby*, 328, 335, 382, 385–7, 389, 401, 474; *Huntley*, 217, 272, 275, 278, 282; *Hyacinth*, 195, 256, 277, 331, 382, 384, 391–3, 515, 531; *Peony*, 195, 254, 256, 277, 515, 531; *Primula*, 531; *Salvia*, 195, 256, 277, 287–8, 389, 391, 392; *Shoreham*, 527, 540; *Snapdragon*, 531; *Stoke*, 335; *Widnes*, 444–5; MINELAYERS: *Abdiel*, 400, 401, 405, 417, 418, 426, 429, 434, 445, 502, 517, 537, 542; *Latona*, 335, 502; OTHER WARSHIPS: *Aphis*, 163, 169–70, 210, 217, 222, 225–6, 332, 365, 366, 532, 537; *Cricket*, 488; *Derwentdale*, 522; *Gnat*, 327–8, 332, 333, 520; *Ladybird*, 152, 210, 217, 222, 225–6, 289–90, 299, 327, 332, 365, 366, 398; *Medway*, 76, 135; *Protector*, 172–4, 200, 217, 434, 485; *Resource*, 43; *TB14*, 4; *Terror*, 47, 175, 177, 200, 210, 211, 217–18, 222, 223, 225–6, 269, 287–8; *Woolwich*, 131–2, 150, 199; *Vulcan*, 578; AUXILIARIES: *Arthur Cavanagh*, 275, 276, 398, 403; *Brambleleaf*, 172, 174, 254, 255, 383, 385, 386, 393; *Centurion*, 336, 337, 339, 352; *Cherryleaf*, 385; *Fellowship*, 197–200; *Kingston Chrystal*, 174; *Kingston Cyanite*, 174; *KOS 19*, 427;

KOS 21, 445; *KOS* 22, 445; *KOS* 23, 444; *Lanner*, 197–200, 443; *Milford Countess*, 275, 276, 398, 403; *Moonstone*, 79; *Moy*, 125, 217, 276, 532; *Olna*, 172, 216; *Ouse*, 125; *Plumleaf*, 114, 141, 163, 174, 591; *St Issey*, 166, 217, 333, 485, 488; *Skudds*, 332, 504; *Syvern*, 445; *Trusty Star*, 367; *Woolborough*, 532; MOTOR LAUNCHES, ETC.: 66, 130, 153, 190, 360, 407, 426, 435, 445, 483–4, 495, 502, 532, 578, 581; LANDING CRAFT: 66, 244, 334, 335, 366, 370, 374–5, 377–81, 386–8, 392, 398, 427, 438, 443–5, 485, 494, 513, 518, 522, 542 Commonwealth: Australian: *Bathurst*, 527; *Hobart*, 511; *Lismore*, 527; *Napier*, 401, 417, 426, 435, 442, 444, 475, 511, 512, 540, 554; *Nestor*, 539, 554; *Nizam*, 401, 417, 428, 430, 435, 442–4, 475, 487, 495, 517, 540, 549, 554; *Norman*, 539; *Parramatta*, 475, 485, 512, 532, 542; *Perth*, 219, 255, 259–60, 267, 270, 273, 291, 292, 315, 324, 331, 382, 385–9, 391, 393–4, 401, 416, 426, 427, 430–1, 438, 443, 444, 475, 495; *Stuart*, 33, 38, 79, 85, 101, 103, 107, 149, 155, 157, 162, 255, 281, 306, 315, 322, 324, 333, 382, 384, 386–9, 401, 430, 433, 443, 444, 475, 483, 486, 503; *Sydney*, 49, 60, 79, 106, 118–20, 142, 144–5, 155, 157, 162–4, 170, 172, 174, 176, 192, 216, 255; *Vampire*, 33, 102, 104, 149, 157, 162, 162, 165, 169, 173, 193, 199, 209, 217, 260, 383, 386, 389, 401; *Vendetta*, 33, 109, 157, 162, 165, 177, 193, 199, 200, 209, 217, 260, 315, 317, 324, 325, 332, 333, 382, 385, 388, 389, 430, 433, 475, 482, 503, 511; *Voyager*, 33, 85, 102, 104, 149, 156, 157, 162, 170, 173, 199, 209, 217, 258, 260, 281, 328, 382, 384, 385, 425, 430, 433, 475, 482; *Waterhen*, 33, 157, 162, 163, 165, 173, 193, 200, 217, 298, 332, 333, 335, 382, 385, 388, 389, 401, 425, 475, 488, 490; *Yarra*, 527, 532. Indian: *Hindustan*, 527; *Indus*, 527; *Jumna*, 540; *Sutlej*, 527, 540. New Zealand: *Leander*, 475, 487, 493. South African: *Southern Isles*, 488, 494; *Southern Sea*, 485. Dutch: *Isaac Sweers*, 539, 547–8, 554.

Warships: French: BATTLESHIPS: *Lorraine*, 79, 80, 83; BATTLECRUISERS: *Dunkerque*, 42; *Strasbourg*, 42; CRUISERS: *Colbert*, 34; *Dougay-Trouin*, 79–80; *Duquesne*, 93–4, 559; *Suffren*, 79–80; *Tourville*, 34; DESTROYERS: *Chevalier Paul*, 485, 492; *Guépard*, 449, 485; *Valmy*, 449; *Vauquelin*, 449, 492; SUBMARINES: *Espadon*, 78; *Narval*, 221; *Phoque*, 78; *Protée*, 78; *Surcouf*, 571; ESCORT VESSELS: *D'Iberville*, 34; *Savorgnan de Brazza*, 527.
German: *Goeben*, 208; *Graf Spee*, 38; *Hipper*, 303; *Admiral Scheer*, 303.
Greek: *Aetos*, 364; *Aspis*, 364; *Averoff*, 364; *Glaucos*, 364; *Helle*, 136; *Hifaistos*, 364; *Hydra*, 376; *Ierax*, 364; *Katsonis*, 364; *Kondourios*, 364; *Nereus*, 364; *Niki*, 364, 531; *Panther*, 364; *Papanicolos*, 364; *Queen Olga*, 364, 577; *Spetsai*, 364; *Triton*, 364.
Italian: BATTLESHIPS: *Andrea Doria*, 21; *Caio Duilio*, 21, 177, 179–88; *Cavour class*, 106, 156, 192, 219, 255, 318–29, 566; *Conte di Cavour*, 21, 106, 127, 177, 179–88; *Giuilio Cesare*, 21, 58, 106, 127, 156, 217; *Impero*, 21; *Littorio*, 21, 61, 152, 156, 162, 177, 179–88, 253, 544; *Roma*, 21; *Vittorio Veneto*, 21, 61, 152, 156, 217, 219, 236–9, 309, 310, 312, 313, 318–20, 323, 324, 394, 544, 547; CRUISERS: *Alberico di Giussano*, 547–8; *Alberto da Barbiano*, 547–8; *Armando Diaz*, 320; *Bartolomeo Colleoni*, 60, 118–20, 164; *Bolzano*, 106; 'Condottieri' classes, 566; *Eugenio di Savoia*, 320; *Fiume*, 164, 238, 324; *Giovanni delle Bande Nere*, 302; *Giuseppe Garibaldi*, 70, 74; *Pola*, 238, 310, 312, 318, 323, 324; *Zara*, 106, 238, 313, 318, 320, 321, 323–5; DESTROYERS: *Alfieri*, 238; *Airone*, 164; *Ariel*, 164; *Artigliere*, 164; *Baleno*, 347–50; *Carducci*, 238; *Espero*, 84; *Euro*, 98; *Fulmine*, 530; *Lampo*, 347–50; *Leon Pancaldo*, 108; *Libeccio*, 530; *Lince*, 290; *Lupo*, 245–6, 290; *Navigatore*, 108, 320; *Sagittario*, 246; *Spica*, 256; *Vega*, 256; *Zeffiro*, 98; SUBMARINES: *Anfitrite*, 85, 301; *Argonauta*, 85; *Berillo*, 157; *Dagabur*, 324; *Gondar*, 156; *Iride*, 137–8; *Liuzzi*, 85; *Macalle*, 73; *Medusa*, 572; *Naiade*, 211; *Ondina*, 84–5; *Pier Capponi*, 328; *Rubino*, 85; *Salpa*, 85; *Scire*, 552; *Uebi Scebeli*, 85; OTHER VESSELS: *Albatros*, 512; *Burgland class*, 398; *Curtatone class*, 509; *Diana*, 497; *Giuseppe Miraglia*, 45.
Polish: *Garland*, 146.
Yugoslav: *Nebosjca*, 364, 502.
Washington, DC, 458, 580
Wavell, F-M Earl, 9, 16–17, 25, 31, 32, 33–4, 63, 76, 83, 126–8, 147, 191, 193–4, 205, 243, 261, 286, 287, 331–2, 338, 370, 396, 405, 408, 410, 411, 418, 435, 451, 470, 481, 493, 533
Weekes, Mid(A) J.R.B., 187, 190
Welham, Lt(A) J.W.G., 137–8, 186–7, 191
Wellington, Duke of, 396
Wester-Wemyss, Adm of F Lord, 4
Western Approaches, 505
Western Desert, 18, 63, 130, 131, 207, 209, 210, 220, 224–6, 231, 233, 243, 261, 263, 264, 274, 275, 279, 281, 287–8, 293–4, 329, 332, 333, 336, 337–8, 346, 362, 365, 366, 370, 397–8, 402, 418, 419, 450–1, 453, 463, 469, 474, 476, 482, 485, 486, 487, 494, 509, 516, 518, 528, 534, 545, 547, 578, 587–8
Weston, Lt-Gen E.C., RM, 418, 420
Weygand, F-M M., 32, 33–4, 82, 264, 523
Whitworth, Adm Sir W., 460
William-Powlett, Capt P.R.B.W., 416
Williamson, Lt-Cdr K., 182, 189
Willis, Adm of F Sir A., 14, 36, 39, 66, 97, 269, 282, 301, 480–1, 495–6, 532–4, 569
Wilson, F-M Sir H.M., 284, 386, 391, 410, 485, 493
Women's Royal Naval Service, 460
World War, First, 5, 20, 457
Wray, Sub-Lt A.L.O., 182, 189

Yemen, 48

Zea Channel, 516; Island, 386, 388
Zeebrugge raid, 5, 205

Navy Records Society
(Founded 1893)

The Navy Records Society was established for the purpose of printing unpublished manuscripts and rare works of naval interest. Membership of the Society is open to all who are interested in naval history, and any person wishing to become a member should apply to the Hon. Secretary, Dr A. D. Lambert, Department of War Studies, King's College London, Strand, London WC2R 2LS, United Kingdom. The annual subscription is £30, which entitles the member to receive one free copy of each work issued by the Society in that year, and to buy earlier issues at reduced prices.

A list of works, available to members only, is shown below; very few copies are left of those marked with an asterisk. Volumes out of print are indicated by **OP**. Prices for works in print are available on application to Mrs Annette Gould, 5 Goodwood Close, Midhurst, West Sussex GU29 9JG, United Kingdom, to whom all enquiries concerning works in print should be sent. Those marked 'TS', 'SP' and 'A' are published for the Society by Temple Smith, Scolar Press and Ashgate, and are available to non-members from the Ashgate Publishing Group, Gower House, Croft Road, Aldershot, Hampshire GU11 3HR. Those marked 'A & U' are published by George Allen & Unwin, and are available to non-members only through bookshops.

Vol. 1. *State papers relating to the Defeat of the Spanish Armada, Anno 1588,* Vol. I, ed. Professor J. K. Laughton. TS.

Vol. 2. *State papers relating to the Defeat of the Spanish Armada, Anno 1588,* Vol. II, ed. Professor J. K. Laughton. TS.

Vol. 3. *Letters of Lord Hood, 1781–1782,* ed. D. Hannay. **OP**.

Vol. 4. *Index to James's Naval History,* by C. G. Toogood, ed. by the Hon. T. A. Brassey. **OP**.

Vol. 5. *Life of Captain Stephen Martin, 1666–1740,* ed. Sir Clements R. Markham. **OP**.

Vol. 6. *Journal of Rear Admiral Bartholomew James, 1725–1728,* ed. Professor J. K. Laughton & Cdr. J. Y. F. Sullivan. **OP**.

Vol. 7. *Holland's Discourse of the Navy, 1638 and 1658*, ed. J. R. Tanner. **OP**.

Vol. 8. *Naval Accounts and Inventories in the Reign of Henry VII*, ed. M. Oppenheim. **OP**.

Vol. 9. *Journal of Sir George Rooke*, ed. O. Browning. **OP**.

Vol. 10. *Letters and Papers relating to the War with France, 1512–1513*, ed. M. Alfred Spont. **OP**.

Vol. 11. *Papers relating to the Spanish War, 1585–1587*, ed. Julian S. Corbett. **TS**.

Vol. 12. *Journals and Letters of Admiral of the Fleet Sir Thomas Byam Martin, 1773–1854*, Vol. II (see No. 24), ed. Admiral Sir R. Vesey Hamilton. **OP**.

Vol. 13. *Papers relating to the First Dutch War, 1652–1654*, Vol. I, ed. Dr S. R. Gardiner. **OP**.

Vol. 14. *Papers relating to the Blockade of Brest, 1803–1805*, Vol. I, ed. J. Leyland. **OP**.

Vol. 15. *History of the Russian Fleet during the Reign of Peter the Great, by a Contemporary Englishman*, ed. Admiral Sir Cyprian Bridge. **OP**.

*Vol. 16. *Logs of the Great Sea Fights, 1794–1805*, Vol. I, ed. Vice Admiral Sir T. Sturges Jackson.

Vol. 17. *Papers relating to the First Dutch War, 1652–1654*, ed. Dr S. R. Gardiner. **OP**.

*Vol. 18. *Logs of the Great Sea Fights*, Vol. II, ed. Vice Admiral Sir T. Sturges Jackson.

Vol. 19. *Journals and Letters of Admiral of the Fleet Sir Thomas Byam Martin*, Vol. II (see No. 24), ed. Admiral Sir R. Vesey Hamilton. **OP**.

Vol. 20. *The Naval Miscellany*, Vol. I, ed. Professor J. K. Laughton.

Vol. 21. *Papers relating to the Blockade of Brest, 1803–1805*, Vol. II, ed. J. Leyland. **OP**.

Vol. 22. *The Naval Tracts of Sir William Monson*, Vol. I, ed. M. Oppenheim. **OP**.

Vol. 23. *The Naval Tracts of Sir William Monson*, Vol. II, ed. M. Oppenheim. **OP**.

Vol. 24. *The Journals and Letters of Admiral of the Fleet Sir Thomas Byam Martin*, Vol. I, ed. Admiral Sir R. Vesey Hamilton. **OP**.

Vol. 25. *Nelson and the Neapolitan Jacobins*, ed. H. C. Gutteridge. **OP**.

Vol. 26. *A Descriptive Catalogue of the Naval Mss in the Pepysian Library*, Vol. I, ed. J. R. Tanner. **OP**.

Vol. 27. *A Descriptive Catalogue of the Naval Mss in the Pepysian Library*, Vol. II, ed. J. R. Tanner. **OP**.

Vol. 28. *The Correspondence of Admiral John Markham, 1801–1807*, ed. Sir Clements R. Markham. **OP**.

Vol. 29. *Fighting Instructions, 1530–1816*, ed. Julian S. Corbett. **OP**.

Vol. 30. *Papers relating to the First Dutch War, 1652–1654*, Vol. III, ed. Dr S. R. Gardiner & Mr C. T. Atkinson. **OP**.

Vol. 31. *The Recollections of Commander James Anthony Gardner, 1775–1814*, ed. Admiral Sir R. Vesey Hamilton & Professor J. K. Laughton.

Vol. 32. *Letters and Papers of Charles, Lord Barham, 1758–1813*, ed. Professor Sir John Laughton.

Vol. 33. *Naval Songs and Ballads*, ed. Professor C. H. Firth. **OP**.

Vol. 34. *Views of the Battles of the Third Dutch War*, ed. by Julian S. Corbett. **OP**.

Vol. 35. *Signals and Instructions, 1776–1794*, ed. Julian S. Corbett. **OP**.

Vol. 36. *A Descriptive Catalogue of the Naval Mss in the Pepysian Library*, Vol. III, ed. J. R. Tanner. **OP**.

Vol. 37. *Papers relating to the First Dutch War, 1652–1654*, Vol. IV, ed. C. T. Atkinson. **OP**.

Vol. 38. *Letters and Papers of Charles, Lord Barham, 1758–1813*, Vol. II, ed. Professor Sir John Laughton.

Vol. 39. *Letters and Papers of Charles, Lord Barham, 1758–1813*, Vol. III, ed. Professor Sir John Laughton.

Vol. 40. *The Naval Miscellany*, Vol. II, ed. Professor Sir John Laughton.

*Vol. 41. *Papers relating to the First Dutch War, 1652–1654*, Vol. V, ed. C. T. Atkinson.

*Vol. 42. *Papers relating to the Loss of Minorca in 1756*, ed. Captain H. W. Richmond, R.N.

*Vol. 43. *The Naval Tracts of Sir William Monson*, Vol. III, ed. M. Oppenheim.

Vol. 44. *The Old Scots Navy, 1689–1710*, ed. James Grant. **OP**.

Vol. 45. *The Naval Tracts of Sir William Monson*, Vol. IV, ed. M. Oppenheim.

*Vol. 46. *The Private Papers of George, 2nd Earl Spencer*, Vol. I, ed. Julian S. Corbett.

Vol. 47. *The Naval Tracts of Sir William Monson*, Vol. V, ed. M. Oppenheim.

Vol. 48. *The Private Papers of George, 2nd Earl Spencer*, Vol. II, ed. Julian S. Corbett. **OP**.

*Vol. 49. *Documents relating to Law and Custom of the Sea*, Vol. II, ed. R. G. Marsden.

*Vol. 50. *Documents relating to Law and Custom of the Sea*, Vol. II, ed. R. G. Marsden.

Vol. 51. *Autobiography of Phineas Pett*, ed. W. G. Perrin. OP.

Vol. 52. *The Life of Admiral Sir John Leake*, Vol. I, ed. Geoffrey Callender.

Vol. 53. *The Life of Admiral Sir John Leake*, Vol. II, ed. Geoffrey Callender.

Vol. 54. *The Life and Works of Sir Henry Mainwaring*, Vol. I, ed. G. E. Manwaring.

Vol. 55. *The Letters of Lord St Vincent, 1801–1804*, Vol. I, ed. D. B. Smith. OP.

Vol. 56. *The Life and Works of Sir Henry Mainwaring*, Vol. II, ed. G. E. Manwaring & W. G. Perrin. OP.

Vol. 57. *A Descriptive Catalogue of the Naval Mss in the Pepysian Library*, Vol. IV, ed. Dr J. R. Tanner. OP.

Vol. 58. *The Private Papers of George, 2nd Earl Spencer*, Vol. III, ed. Rear Admiral H. W. Richmond. OP.

Vol. 59. *The Private Papers of George, 2nd Earl Spencer*, Vol. IV, ed. Rear Admiral H. W. Richmond. OP.

Vol. 60. *Samuel Pepys's Naval Minutes*, ed. Dr J. R. Tanner.

Vol. 61. *The Letters of Lord St Vincent, 1801–1804*, Vol. II, ed. D. B. Smith. OP.

Vol. 62. *Letters and Papers of Admiral Viscount Keith*, Vol. I, ed. W. G. Perrin. OP.

Vol. 63. *The Naval Miscellany*, Vol. III, ed. W. G. Perrin. OP.

Vol. 64. *The Journal of the 1st Earl of Sandwich*, ed. R. C. Anderson. OP.

*Vol. 65. *Boteler's Dialogues*, ed. W. G. Perrin.

Vol. 66. *Papers relating to the First Dutch War, 1652–1654*, Vol. VI (with index), ed. C. T. Atkinson.

*Vol. 67. *The Byng Papers*, Vol. I, ed. W. C. B. Tunstall.

*Vol. 68. *The Byng Papers*, Vol. II, ed. W. C. B. Tunstall.

Vol. 69. *The Private Papers of John, Earl of Sandwich*, Vol. I, ed. G. R. Barnes & Lt. Cdr. J. H. Owen, R.N. OP.

Corrigenda to *Papers relating to the First Dutch War, 1652–1654, Vols I–VI*, ed. Captain A. C. Dewar, R.N.

Vol. 70. *The Byng Papers*, Vol. III, ed. W. C. B. Tunstall.

Vol. 71. *The Private Papers of John, Earl of Sandwich*, Vol. II, ed. G. R. Barnes & Lt. Cdr. J. H. Owen, R.N. OP.

Vol. 72. *Piracy in the Levant, 1827–1828*, ed. Lt. Cdr. C. G. Pitcairn Jones, R.N. OP.

Vol. 73. *The Tangier Papers of Samuel Pepys,* ed. Edwin Chappell.

Vol. 74. *The Tomlinson Papers,* ed. J. G. Bullocke.

Vol. 75. *The Private Papers of John, Earl of Sandwich,* Vol. III, ed. G. R. Barnes & Lt. Cdr. J. H. Owen, R.N. **OP**.

Vol. 76. *The Letters of Robert Blake,* ed. the Rev. J. R. Powell. **OP**.

*Vol. 77. *Letters and Papers of Admiral the Hon. Samuel Barrington,* Vol. I, ed. D. Bonner-Smith.

Vol. 78. *The Private Papers of John, Earl of Sandwich,* Vol. IV, ed. G. R. Barnes & Lt. Cdr. J. H. Owen, R.N. **OP**.

*Vol. 79. *The Journals of Sir Thomas Allin, 1660–1678,* Vol. I (1660–1666), ed. R. C. Anderson.

Vol. 80. *The Journals of Sir Thomas Allin, 1660–1678,* Vol. II (1667–1678), ed. R. C. Anderson.

Vol. 81. *Letters and Papers of Admiral the Hon. Samuel Barrington,* Vol. II, ed. D. Bonner-Smith. **OP**.

Vol. 82. *Captain Boteler's Recollections, 1808–1830,* ed. D. Bonner-Smith. **OP**.

Vol. 83. *Russian War, 1854. Baltic and Black Sea: Official Correspondence,* ed. D. Bonner-Smith & Captain A. C. Dewar, R.N. **OP**.

Vol. 84. *Russian War, 1855. Baltic: Official Correspondence,* ed. D. Bonner-Smith. **OP**.

Vol. 85. *Russian War, 1855. Black Sea: Official Correspondence,* ed. Captain A. C. Dewar, R.N. **OP**.

Vol. 86. *Journals and Narratives of the Third Dutch War,* ed. R. C. Anderson. **OP**.

Vol. 87. *The Naval Brigades in the Indian Mutiny, 1857–1858,* ed. Cdr. W. B. Rowbotham, R.N. **OP**.

Vol. 88. *Patee Byng's Journal,* ed. J. L. Cranmer-Byng. **OP**.

*Vol. 89. *The Sergison Papers, 1688–1702,* ed. Cdr. R. D. Merriman, R.I.N.

Vol. 90. *The Keith Papers,* Vol. II, ed. Christopher Lloyd. **OP**.

Vol. 91. *Five Naval Journals, 1789–1817,* ed. Rear Admiral H. G. Thursfield. **OP**.

Vol. 92. *The Naval Miscellany,* Vol. IV, ed. Christopher Lloyd. **OP**.

Vol. 93. *Sir William Dillon's Narrative of Professional Adventures, 1790–1839,* Vol. I (1790–1802), ed. Professor Michael Lewis. **OP**.

Vol. 94. *The Walker Expedition to Quebec, 1711,* ed. Professor Gerald S. Graham. **OP**.

Vol. 95. *The Second China War, 1856–1860,* ed. D. Bonner-Smith & E. W. R. Lumby. **OP**.

Vol. 96. *The Keith Papers, 1803–1815,* Vol. III, ed. Professor Christopher Lloyd.

Vol. 97. *Sir William Dillon's Narrative of Professional Adventures, 1790–1839*, Vol. II (1802–1839), ed. Professor Michael Lewis. **OP**.

Vol. 98. *The Private Correspondence of Admiral Lord Collingwood*, ed. Professor Edward Hughes. **OP**.

Vol. 99. *The Vernon Papers, 1739–1745*, ed. B. McL. Ranft. **OP**.

Vol. 100. *Nelson's Letters to his Wife and Other Documents*, ed. Lt. Cdr. G. P. B. Naish, R.N.V.R. **OP**.

Vol. 101. *A Memoir of James Trevenen, 1760–1790*, ed. Professor Christopher Lloyd & R. C. Anderson. **OP**.

Vol. 102. *The Papers of Admiral Sir John Fisher*, Vol. I, ed. Lt. Cdr. P. K. Kemp, R.N. **OP**.

Vol. 103. *Queen Anne's Navy*, ed. Cdr. R. D. Merriman, R.I.N. **OP**.

Vol. 104. *The Navy and South America, 1807–1823*, ed. Professor Gerald S. Graham & Professor R. A. Humphreys.

Vol. 105. *Documents relating to the Civil War, 1642–1648*, ed. The Rev. J. R. Powell & E. K. Timings. **OP**.

Vol. 106. *The Papers of Admiral Sir John Fisher*, Vol. II, ed. Lt. Cdr. P. K. Kemp, R.N. **OP**.

Vol. 107. *The Health of Seamen*, ed. Professor Christopher Lloyd.

Vol. 108. *The Jellicoe Papers*, Vol. I (1893–1916), ed. A. Temple Patterson.

Vol. 109. *Documents relating to Anson's Voyage round the World, 1740–1744*, ed. Dr Glyndwr Williams. **OP**.

Vol. 110. *The Saumarez Papers: The Baltic, 1808–1812*, ed. A. N. Ryan. **OP**.

Vol. 111. *The Jellicoe Papers*, Vol. II (1916–1935), ed. Professor A. Temple Patterson.

Vol. 112. *The Rupert and Monck Letterbook, 1666*, ed. The Rev. J. R. Powell & E. K. Timings.

Vol. 113. *Documents relating to the Royal Naval Air Service*, Vol. I (1908–1918), ed. Captain S. W. Roskill, R.N.

*Vol. 114. *The Siege and Capture of Havana, 1762*, ed. Professor David Syrett.

Vol. 115. *Policy and Operations in the Mediterranean, 1912–1914*, ed. E. W. R. Lumby. **OP**.

Vol. 116. *The Jacobean Commissions of Enquiry, 1608 and 1618*, ed. Dr A. P. McGowan.

Vol. 117. *The Keyes Papers*, Vol. I (1914–1918), ed. Professor Paul Halpern.

Vol. 118. *The Royal Navy and North America: The Warren Papers, 1736–1752*, ed. Dr Julian Gwyn. **OP**.

Vol. 119. *The Manning of the Royal Navy: Selected Public Pamphlets, 1693–1873*, ed. Professor John Bromley.
Vol. 120. *Naval Administration, 1715–1750*, ed. Professor D. A. Baugh.
Vol. 121. *The Keyes Papers*, Vol. II (1919–1938), ed. Professor Paul Halpern.
Vol. 122. *The Keyes Papers*, Vol. III (1939–1945), ed. Professor Paul Halpern.
Vol. 123. *The Navy of the Lancastrian Kings: Accounts and Inventories of William Soper, Keeper of the King's Ships, 1422–1427*, ed. Dr Susan Rose.
Vol. 124. *The Pollen Papers*: *The Privately Circulated Printed Works of Arthur Hungerford Pollen, 1901–1916*, ed. Professor Jon T. Sumida. A & U.
Vol. 125. *The Naval Miscellany*, Vol. V, ed. N. A. M. Rodger. A & U.
Vol. 126. *The Royal Navy in the Mediterranean, 1915–1918*, ed. Professor Paul Halpern. TS.
Vol. 127. *The Expedition of Sir John Norris and Sir Francis Drake to Spain and Portugal, 1589*, ed. Professor R. B. Wertham. TS.
Vol. 128. *The Beatty Papers*, Vol. I (1902–1918), ed. Professor B. McL. Ranft. SP.
Vol. 129. *The Hawke Papers: A Selection, 1743–1771*, ed. Dr R. F. Mackay. SP.
Vol. 130. *Anglo-American Naval Relations, 1917–1919*, ed. Michael Simpson. SP.
Vol. 131. *British Naval Documents, 1204–1960*, ed. Professor John B. Hattendorf, Dr Roger Knight, Alan Pearsall, Dr Nicholas Rodger & Professor Geoffrey Till. SP.
Vol. 132. *The Beatty Papers*, Vol. II (1916–1927), ed. Professor B. McL. Ranft. SP.
Vol. 133. *Samuel Pepys and the Second Dutch War,* transcribed by William Matthews & Charles Knighton; ed. Robert Latham. SP.
Vol. 134. *The Somerville Papers*, ed. Michael Simpson, with the assistance of John Somerville. SP.
Vol. 135. *The Royal Navy in the River Plate, 1806–1807*, ed. John D. Grainger. SP.
Vol. 136. *The Collective Naval Defence of the Empire, 1900–1940*, ed. Nicholas Tracy. A.
Vol. 137. *The Defeat of the Enemy Attack on Shipping, 1939–1945*, ed. Eric Grove. A.
Vol. 138. *Shipboard Life and Organisation, 1731–1815*, ed. Brian Lavery. A.

Vol. 139. *The Battle of the Atlantic and Signals Intelligence: U-boat Situations and Trends, 1941–1945,* ed. Professor David Syrett. A.

OCCASIONAL PUBLICATIONS

Vol. 1. *The Commissioned Sea Officers of the Royal Navy, 1660–1815,* ed. Professor David Syrett & Professor R. L. DiNardo. SP.